DIGITAL CIRCUITS
AND MICROPROCESSORS

Computer Engineering and Switching Theory

Consulting Editor
Stephen W. Director, Carnegie-Mellon University

Bartee: *Digital Computer Fundamentals*
Bell and Newell: *Computer Structures: Readings and Examples*
Clare: *Designing Logic Systems Using State Machines*
Garland: *Introduction to Microprocessor System Design*
Givone: *Introduction to Switching Circuit Theory*
Givone and Roesser: *Microprocessors/Microcomputers: An Introduction*
Hamacher, Vranesic, and Zaky: *Computer Organization*
Hayes: *Computer Organization and Architecture*
Kohavi: *Switching and Finite Automata Theory*
McCluskey: *Introduction to the Theory of Switching Circuits*
Peatman: *Design of Digital Systems*
Peatman: *Digital Hardware Design*
Peatman: *Microcomputer Based Design*
Sandige: *Digital Concepts Using Standard Integrated Circuits*
Scott: *Electronic Computer Technology*
Taub: *Digital Circuits and Microprocessors*
Wiatrowski and House: *Logic Circuits and Microcomputer Systems*

DIGITAL CIRCUITS
AND MICROPROCESSORS

Herbert Taub

Professor of Electrical Engineering
The City College of the
City University of New York

McGraw-Hill Book Company

New York   St. Louis   San Francisco   Auckland   Bogotá   Hamburg
Johannesburg   London   Madrid   Mexico   Montreal   New Delhi
Panama   Paris   São Paulo   Singapore   Sydney   Tokyo   Toronto

This book was set in Times Roman by A Graphic Method Inc.
The editors were Frank J. Cerra and Madelaine Eichberg;
the production supervisor was Leroy A. Young.
The drawings were done by J & R Services, Inc.
The cover was designed by Nicholas Krenitsky.

DIGITAL CIRCUITS AND MICROPROCESSORS

4567890 HDHD 8976543

Library of Congress Cataloging in Publication Data

Taub, Herbert, date
    Digital circuits and microprocessors.

    (McGraw-Hill series in electrical engineering.
Computer engineering and switching theory)
    Includes index.
    1. Digital electronics.   2.   Microprocessors.
I. Title. II. Series.
TK7868.D5T36   621.3815'3   81-3729
ISBN 0-07-062945-5   AACR2

To
Esther

CONTENTS

Appendixes

Problems

Index

PREFACE

This book is an introductory text suitable for a one-semester course. It covers all the basic principles of digital systems and logic design and provides as well an introductory presentation to microprocessor and microprocessor-based systems. The present and growing importance of microprocessors makes it important that these versatile components be introduced into an engineering or computer science curriculum at the earliest opportunity.

The subject of logical variables and boolean algebra is covered in Chapter 1. Logic gates and logical connectives are described and analyzed. The binary number system is introduced here principally to allow some systemization of truth tables. Chapter 2 deals with the standard forms of logic functions and with Karnaugh maps. Chapter 3 considers basic combinational circuits including decoders, encoders, code converters, multiplexers and demultiplexers. It is emphasized that all these components are available as integrated-circuit chips, and a brief discussion is provided of *families* of integrated circuits. Conventions dealing with the characterization of control terminals on chips are explained, and this discussion leads to a consideration of the convention of *mixed logic* which, in certain applications, is gaining popularity. Examples are given of the newer logic symbols which are presently being introduced for combinational and other components. The basic storage element, the flip-flop, is examined in some detail in Chapter 4. A careful distinction is drawn between a latch and a flip-flop. The characteristics required of a flip-flop in order that it be able to function properly in a synchronous system are examined. Assemblages of flip-flops into storage registers, shift registers, and counters are also considered. Again, in this chapter it is emphasized that the components described are available as integrated-circuit packages and examples of such devices are described. Chapter 5 deals with the subject of arithmetic operations, principally addition. The look-ahead carry principle is explained and analyzed. Memory is the subject of Chapter 6. This chapter covers the RAM, both static and dynamic, the ROM, the PLA, serial memories, and memories for bulk storage. Also described are timing considerations in reading from and writing into memories. Chapter 7 introduces the subject of the analysis and design of sequential systems, both synchronous and fundamental mode. The concepts of flow diagrams, state diagrams, and tables are presented, and also described are procedures for eliminating redundant states. While there is some discussion of sequential circuits in Chapter 4 in connection with shift registers and counters, the formal organized and systematized presentation is given in Chapter 7.

The material on controllers in Chapter 8 is written with a view toward microprocessors. A microprocessor consists of a number of storage and working registers, and ALU, and a controller. The controller appears to be endowed with uncanny abilities. It does exactly the right thing at the right time in precisely the right sequence and, having completed one task, proceeds unerringly to the next. Truly enough, the controller is nothing more than a special-purpose sequential circuit involving no difficult concepts. Still, to the beginning student, the vagueness associated with the controller is inevitably a source of uneasiness. It is very difficult to accept the generalizations with which controllers are described when there is no concrete and specific example that can serve as a model. Chapter 8 is written in a manner which will, hopefully, provide some reassurance to the uninitiated. It makes clear at the outset that all of the digital operations which are possible are relatively few and fundamentally simple, and that all are executed in response to the enabling of a gate or set of gates. Next there is presented the architecture of a very simple system which then requires a controller to be effective. A controller is designed in detail, first by using the procedures of Chapter 7 which yield a sequential system with a minimum number of states. Next this initial controller is replaced by a shift-register controller. The shift-register controller uses more hardware but has the great merit that the details of its operation are easily apparent and that required modifications for the purpose of elaboration can be added almost by inspection. Finally a controller is designed in detail to serve a very simple minded (4-instruction) "computer." The design makes clear in an entirely unambiguous manner how a controller can be made to modify its behavior in response to an *instruction*. Also in this chapter the student encounters the concepts of the *program counter*, the *memory address register*, and the *instruction register*. The reader sees, in simple form, the overall architecture which characterizes a microprocessor as well as the typical content of a memory which holds instruction and data for a stored program computation.

Chapter 9 is also written with an eye toward microprocessors. Here there is presented the architecture of a simple (16-instruction) computer. The structure provides a preview of the type of instructions to be encountered in more sophisticated systems. The *jump* and *subroutine call* instructions are presented and some simple programs are written in an assembly language. Also in this chapter the subject of control by *microprogramming* is presented and simple examples given.

Some authors invent a hypothetical microprocessor to have an example through which to introduce the subject. This procedure has the unfortunate feature that the student misses the exposure to a real device while the hypothetical microprocessor eventually turns out to be very nearly as complicated as a real component. Other authors undertake to include a number of real microprocessors in their descriptions and explanations. This approach, all too often, leads to vague generalizations. A third widely used approach, also used in this text, is to concentrate on a single real device. This method allows the analysis to be pointed and specific and, furthermore, a good familiarity with one device provides a background that allows an easy understanding of other devices. In this text, the microprocessor selected for study is the 8080 which is widely known and used and is highly regarded. Even though the 8080 has been updated by the 8085, we have stayed with the 8080 precisely because it is somewhat less sophisticated and, therefore, better suited to an introductory presentation. The 8080, its architecture, instructions, and programming is the subject of Chapter 10. Chapter 11 is devoted entirely to input-output operation of the 8080.

There is some more material in the text than can be covered conveniently in one semester. From the author's prejudicial point of view an effective way of employing the book is to use it for one full semester and for about one fifth of a second semester. Thereafter, for the remainder of the second semester, a new text should be adopted that covers microprocessors and microcomputers generally and in greater depth. On the other hand, it is entirely feasible to cover the book in one semester by omitting some material which is not essential in a first approach. Candidates for omission include the following sections: 1.17, 1.25, 1.26, 2.12, 5.10 through 5.12, 6.10 through 6.17, 7.6 through 7.9, 7.11 through 7.19, 8.12 and 8.13.

A large number of homework problems have been provided. A solutions manual is available that instructors can obtain from the publisher.

I am grateful to Professor Mansour Javid, chairman of the Department of Electrical Engineering at the City College of New York, who read a large part of the manuscript and made many valuable suggestions. Mr. Lewis Jay Taub provided a great deal of very effective assistance in the preparation of the manuscript and I am pleased to express to him my most sincere thanks. Mrs. Joyce Rubin's skillful typing of the manuscript is appreciated.

Herbert Taub

ONE

ALGEBRA OF LOGICAL VARIABLES

1.1 VARIABLES AND FUNCTIONS

We are familiar with the concept of a *variable* and with the concept of a *function* of a variable. The *field* of a variable, i.e., the range of values which can be assumed by a variable x, can by specified in a limitless number of ways. For example, x may range over all the real numbers from minus to plus infinity; or x may be restricted to the range from -17 to -4; or x may be restricted to the positive integers from 1 to 10; and so on.

A *function* is a *rule* by which we determine the value of a second (dependent) variable y from the (independent) variable x, the dependency of y on x being written $y = f(x)$. Thus, for example, suppose we intend that y is to be determined from x through the rule that x is to be multiplied by itself, that this product is to be multiplied by 5, and that thereafter 3 is to be added. We would then express the functional relationship between x and y by the equation $y = 5x^2 + 3$. In this simple example we determined y by applying the mathematical processes of multiplication and addition. However, when the number of allowable values of x is finite, it is possible to specify a function simply by making a *table* in which y is given for each value of x. When the number of possible values for x is small, it may well be feasible and most convenient to use such a table. Consider that in the example referred to above ($y = 5x^2 + 3$) we restrict x to the integral values $x = 0, 1, 2,$ and 3. Then, as is indicated in Fig. 1.1-1, the functional relationship between y and x can be specified in tabular form.

By an easy extension of these elemental ideas, it is clear that the variables, dependent and independent, need not be numerical. For example, let the independent variable x have as its field the colors of the traffic light at an intersection, and let the dependent variable y represent the expected behavior of a mo-

1

x	$y = f(x)$
0	3
1	8
2	23
3	48

x	$y = f(x)$
Green	Continue
Amber	Slow down
Red	Stop

Figure 1.1-1 A numerical function.   **Figure 1.1-2** A functional relationship.

torist approaching the intersection. Then the functional relationship between x and y is as given in Fig. 1.1-2. The values which can be assumed by x are expressed by the declarative statements "the light is green" or "the light is amber" or "the light is red." Similarly the values which can be assumed by y are "the motorist should continue," etc.

1.2 LOGICAL VARIABLES

A *logical* variable is a variable which has three distinctive properties:

1. The logical variable may assume one or the other of only *two* possible values.
2. The values are expressed by declarative statements, as in the traffic-light example given above.
3. The two possible values expressed by the declarative statements must be such that, on the basis of human reason, i.e., on the basis of logic, they are *mutually exclusive*.

Although, as noted, the variable need not have numerical significance, there is no reason to preclude situations in which the variable does. Thus the variable x may have the two and only two, alternative, mutually exclusive values expressed by the statements "the value of x is 7" and "the value of x is 13." Other properties of the logical variable will appear in the following discussion, in which we return to the example of the traffic light.

Suppose that we postulate that the traffic light can be only green or red. We exclude the possibility that the light may be amber and exclude as well the possibility of an interval when the light is changing and neither green nor red is showing. Then in this case the variable x in the table of Fig. 1.1-2 is a logical variable. Either we shall have that "the light is green," which we can represent as $x =$ green, or we shall have that $x =$ red. Note especially that because of the mutual exclusivity, if we want to indicate that $x =$ red we can indicate it either in that way or by writing $x = not$ green. In a simpler notation, the "not" is represented by placing a bar over the value. Thus $x =$ not green can be written $x = \overline{green}$. Finally we have that $x = \overline{green} =$ red.

1.3 VALUES FOR A LOGICAL VARIABLE

In the general case of an arbitrary type of variable, say the type of variable which assumes numerical values, the variables may represent anything. Thus x and y may represent temperature or pressure or distance or velocity or time, etc. In considering the functional relationship between variables from a mathematical point of view we have no interest in what is represented by the variables. Thus from the equation $y = 5x^2 + 3$ we have the result that $y = 8$ when $x = 1$ quite independently of what x and y may stand for. The values which can be assumed by the variables are the same in the sense that in both cases the values are numbers.

In the same way, let us assign to the two possible values of our logical variable two names, so that we can consider a variable independently of what it may represent. Any two readily distinguishable names would be suitable, but it would also be useful to have names which convey the notion of mutual exclusivity. For this reason such names suggest themselves as "hot and cold," "in and out," "high and low," etc. Another possible set of names, which we shall comment on further at a later point, uses the values "true" and "false." Thus a logical variable, say A, will either have the value $A = $ true (abbreviated $A = $ T) or the value $A = $ false (abbreviated $A = $ F). If, indeed the fact is that $A = $ true ($A = $ T) we can equally well write that $A = \overline{\text{false}}$ ($A = \overline{\text{F}}$).

Now let us return to our traffic-light example. (Since we are dealing with logical variables, we shall follow the more usual custom of using A and Z for the independent and dependent variables, respectively, rather than x and y.) The functional relationship between the color of the light and the motorist's proper response is given in Fig. 1.3-1a. Suppose that in the matter of the variable A we *arbitrarily* assign the value $A = $ T to the statement "the light is red." Then automatically $A = $ F represents the statement "the light is green." Similarly let us *arbitrarily* associate the value $Z = $ T with the statement "the motorist continues." Then the functional relationship between the color of the light and the behavior of the motorist is equally well given by Fig. 1.3-1b. If the assignment of A and Z with color and motorist behavior were differently made, the pattern of entries T and F in Fig. 1.3-1b would appear different, but of course the functional relationship between color and behavior would not be altered.

A table like that in Fig. 1.3-1b with entries T and F is called a *truth table*.

A	$Z = f(A)$
Green	Continue
Red	Stop

(a)

A	$Z = f(A)$
F	T
T	F

(b)

Figure 1.3-1 A functional relationship in (a) becomes a truth table in (b).

A	Z = f(A)
F	F
T	T

A	Z
F	T
T	F

A	Z
F	F
T	F

A	Z
F	T
T	T

    (a)   (b)   (c)   (d)

Figure 1.4-1 The four functions of a single variable.

1.4 FUNCTIONS OF A SINGLE LOGICAL VARIABLE

All the possible functions $Z = f(A)$ of a single logical variable are given in the four truth tables of Fig. 1.4-1. To assure ourselves that we have missed none of the possible functions we proceed in the following way. In the A column we simply list its two possible values F and T. We now have *two* places in the Z column where we must make entries. In each of the places there are *two* possible entries. Hence the number of distinct possible columns Z is $2 \times 2 = 4$. These four are given, and we can be confident that there are no more. In Fig. 1.4-1a, since in each row the entry under Z is the same as under A, we write $Z = A$. In Fig. 1.4-1b $Z = \overline{A}$. In Fig. 1.1-4c $Z = F$, and in Fig. 1.4-1d $Z = T$. The reader may well decide to take the attitude that Fig. 1.4-1c and d really do not express functions at all. For in one case Z is false and in the other case Z is true quite independently of the logic value of A.

1.5 FUNCTIONS OF TWO LOGICAL VARIABLES

We consider now the functions $Z = f(A, B)$ of two logical variables A and B. To form such functions we would start out with a truth table as in Fig. 1.5-1. Here we have provided a row for each possible combination of logic values for A and B. There being two variables and two values for each, four combinations are possible. Now, to generate a function we need only make entries in the column for Z. There are four entries to be made, and for each entry there are two possibilities. Hence the total number of distinct columns possible under Z is $2 \times 2 \times 2 \times 2 = 16$, and correspondingly there are 16 possible functions of two variables. As we shall see, and as was the case with the functions of a simple variable, we may want to take the attitude that some of these "functions" are

A	B	Z = f(A, B)
F	F	
F	T	
T	F	
T	T	

Figure 1.5-1 An incompleted truth table for two variables.

really not functions at all. We shall eventually consider all the possible functions. For the present we consider some of the functions which are of special
interest.

The AND Function

As we have already noted, a logical function is defined by a truth table. The
function $Z = f(A, B)$, which is defined by the truth table in Fig. 1.5-2, is called
the AND *function*. We express the dependence of Z on A and B by writing

$$Z = A \text{ AND } B \tag{1.5-1}$$

The motivation for this terminology lies in the consideration, which can be
verified from the truth table, that $Z = $ T only when A *and* B are both true. An
alternate symbolism for the AND function is

$$Z = A \cdot B \tag{1.5-2}$$

or even more simply

$$Z = AB \tag{1.5-3}$$

Equations (1.5-2) and (1.5-3) suggest that Z is the result of a "multiplication" in
which A and B are factors. Of course A and B are not numbers, and multiplication in the usual arithmetic sense is not intended. Nonetheless, as we shall see,
the suggestion of multiplication conveyed by the symbolism is deliberate, and
the function A AND B is often referred to as the *logical product* of A and B.

A first property of the AND function is that it is *commutative*; i.e., if the
order of A and B is interchanged (A and B are commuted), the function Z is unaltered, so that

$$Z = AB = BA \tag{1.5-4}$$

That such is the case is immediately apparent from the truth table of Fig. 1.5-1.
If we had arranged the table so that the B column was the leftmost rather than
the A column, the entries in the Z column would not change.

A second property of the AND function is that it is *associative*. Suppose
that we have three variables A, B, and C and that we first form the logical product AB. Since this product is itself a logical variable, we can form its logical
product with C, giving $(AB)C$. On the other hand, suppose we form first BC

A	B	$Z = A$ AND B
F	F	F
F	T	F
T	F	F
T	T	T

Figure 1.5-2 Truth table which defines the AND function.

and then finally form $A(BC)$. As we shall verify, how the variables are associated does not make any difference, so that

$$Z = (AB)C = A(BC) \qquad (1.5\text{-}5)$$

The fact that the AND function is associative is very nearly obvious. Nonetheless we shall go through the formality of a proof in order to have the opportunity to point out a basic procedure for proving any theorem concerning logical variables. The procedure consists of generating a truth table and thereafter simply recognizing that any functions which yield identical columns, i.e., identical T and F entries in each row, are identical functions.

Example 1.5-1 Verify that the AND function is associative; i.e., prove that Eq. (1.5-5) is valid.

SOLUTION We are dealing now with three variables A, B, and C. Since each variable allows two values, there are $2 \times 2 \times 2 = 8$ possible combination of values of the three variables. Accordingly, the truth table for three variables must have eight rows, as indicated in Fig. 1.5-3. In this table in columns A, B, and C we have listed all the possible different combinations of values for the three variables. (At a later point we shall indicate how to make such a listing easily with the assurance that no combination is duplicated and none missing.)

In the fourth column we generate one logical product AB, row by row, using the definition of the logical product given by the truth table of Fig. 1.5-2. In the fifth column we generate $(AB)C$ using the entries in column 3 and column 4. In a similar way $A(BC)$ is calculated and yields the entries in column 7. We note, finally, that the entries in column 5, $(AB)C$, are in *every instance* the same as the entries in column 7, $A(BC)$, so that the truth table proves that $A(BC) = (AB)C$.

1	2	3	4	5	6	7
A	B	C	AB	$(AB)C$	BC	$A(BC)$
F	F	F	F	F	F	F
F	F	T	F	F	F	F
F	T	F	F	F	F	F
F	T	T	F	F	T	F
T	F	F	F	F	F	F
T	F	T	F	F	F	F
T	T	F	T	F	F	F
T	T	T	T	T	T	T

Columns 5 and 7 are Identical

Figure 1.5-3 Verification of associativity of AND function.

A	B	$Z = A$ or B
F	F	F
F	T	T
T	F	T
T	T	T

Fig. 1.6-1 Truth table which defines the OR function.

1.6 THE OR FUNCTION

The function Z, which is defined by the truth table of Fig. 1.6-1, is called the OR function. We express the dependence of Z on A and B by writing

$$Z = A \text{ or } B \tag{1.6-1}$$

The motivation for this terminology lies in the fact, which can be verified from the truth table, that $Z = T$ if $A = T$ *or* if $B = T$, *or* if *both* A and B are true. An alternate symbolism for the OR function is

$$Z = A + B \tag{1.6-2}$$

Of course, the plus sign in Eq. (1.6-2) is not intended to indicate addition in the usual arithmetic sense. Nonetheless, as we shall see, the suggestion of addition conveyed by the symbolism is deliberate and the function $A + B$ is often called the *logical sum* of A and B.

It is easily verified that, like the AND function, the OR function is both commutative and associative. Thus

$$A + B = B + A \tag{1.6-3}$$

and
$$A + (B + C) = (A + B) + C \tag{1.6-4}$$

1.7 AN IMPLEMENTATION OF A LOGICAL SYSTEM

The concept of a logical variable was introduced in about 1850 by the mathematician George Boole in connection with his studies of thought processes. The algebra of logical variables, which we shall consider below, is called *boolean algebra*. The adaptation of boolean algebra to digital systems, our present interest, was introduced in 1938 by Claude Shannon of The Bell Laboratories.

To give somewhat more concrete significance to the concept of a logical function and to see the relevance of the term "logic" let us consider the following simple example related to the AND function. We consider that we are passengers in the cabin of an airplane being piloted by two pilots. If we should see one pilot leave the cockpit *and* then also see the second pilot leave before the

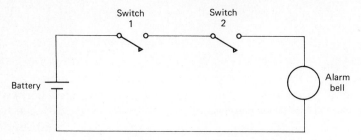

Figure 1.7-1 A switch arrangement causes the bell to sound when switch 1 AND switch 2 are closed.

first returns, then as a matter of logic, we would *deduce* that the plane was pilotless. (Depending on circumstances, we might also deduce that the plane was in danger and that emergency corrective measures were in order.)

We can construct a simple machine which will perform the logical operation of deducing when the plane is pilotless. Such a machine is indicated in Fig. 1.7-1. We place switches 1 and 2 in the cockpit seats of the pilots, P_A and P_B, respectively. The switches are arranged to close when a pilot leaves his seat. Now let A represent the logical variable which is *true* when P_A is not in his seat and is *false* when P_A is in his seat. Let B represent the corresponding variable for pilot P_B, and let Z be a variable which is *true* when the plane is pilotless. When Z is indeed *true*, the machine of Fig. 1.7-1 will so indicate by ringing the alarm. The logical variables Z, A, and B are connected by the functional relationship $Z = AB$; that is, when it is true that pilot P_A has left the cockpit and also simultaneously true that P_B has left his seat, it is true that the plane is pilotless (and possibly in danger). Further, in any situation other than circumstances where $A = B = T$, we shall have $Z = F$.

Suppose that we judge that the plane requires the simultaneous services of both pilots for safety. Then we would arrange that $Z = T$ if either A is *true* or B is *true*; i.e., we want to perform the logic $Z = A + B$. A simple machine, again employing switches, which performs this logic is shown in Fig. 1.7-2.

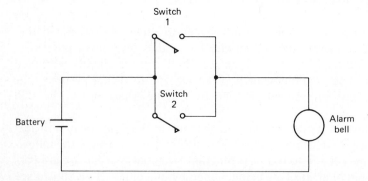

Figure 1.7-2 A switch arrangement causes the bell to sound when either switch 1 OR switch 2 OR both are closed.

1.8 ELECTRIC VOLTAGE REPRESENTATION OF LOGICAL VARIABLES

In the preceding section we saw how the value of a logical variable can be indicated by the position of a switch. There we found it convenient to arrange for a closed switch to represent the value "true" and an open switch the value "false." In other circumstances, it might well be found more convenient to reverse the representation of values provided by a switch, i.e., closed and open positions representing "false" and "true" values respectively.

More generally at present, in fast digital systems, logical values of a variable are represented by the electric voltages maintained between a pair of wires. For example, we might arrange that when a logical variable A is represented by a voltage V, the variable is $A = F$ when $V = 3$ V and $A = T$ when $V = 7$ V. More realistically, since precise voltages are maintained only with difficulty, we would adopt the representation that $A = F$ when $V = 3$ V or *less* and $A = T$ when $V = 7$ V or *more*. If, in some physical situation using this representation, we should encounter a voltage in the range between 3 and 7 V we would judge that the system was malfunctioning and call the repairman.

In the example just cited, both voltage levels were positive. Such need not be the case. We may allow both to be negative or one to be positive while the other is negative, or one or the other to be at 0 V. Again, in our example, we selected the more positive voltage and the more negative voltage to represent the logical values T and F, respectively. Such a representation is characterized by the designation *positive logic*. If we reverse matters, so that the value *true* is represented by the more negative voltage, we have *negative logic*. In principle, there is no relative merit of one system over the other, although positive logic is generally employed. This preference for positive logic is of historical and psychological origin, however, and has no essential significance.

We shall see that there are circumstances in which it is useful to use both positive and negative logic in the same discussion. This matter of the use of *mixed logic* is discussed in Chap. 3.

The symbol for a device which forms the logical product $Z = AB$ of the two variables A and B is shown in Fig. 1.8 1a. In view of the commutativity and associativity of the AND function, a device which forms the logical product of many variables can reasonably be represented as in Fig. 1.8-1b. The symbol for a device which forms the logical sum $Z = A + B$ is shown in Fig. 1.8-1c for two inputs and in Fig. 1.8-1d for many inputs. In general, a structure which generates a logic function Z is referred to as a *logic gate*. Thus in Fig. 1.8-1a and b we have AND gates, and in Fig. 1.8-1c and d we have OR gates. The variables A, B, etc., are the gate inputs, and Z is the gate output. The nature of the electronic devices by which AND gates and OR gates are realized is such that additional input can be provided with relatively little complication. Hence multi-input AND and OR gates are readily available.

The logical function which a particular physical device generates depends on whether the convention of positive logic or negative logic is adopted. An OR

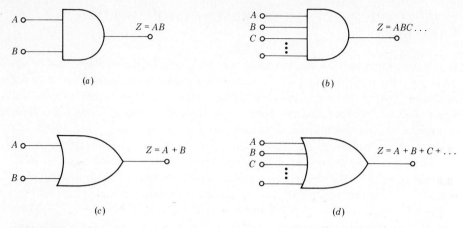

Figure 1.8-1 (*a*) A two-input AND gate; (*b*) a multi-input AND gate; (*c*) a two-input OR gate; and (*d*) a multi-input OR gate.

gate for positive logic is an AND gate for negative logic and vice versa (see Prob. 1.8-1). At the present time, quite uniformly, manufacturers specify the logic of their gate devices on the basis of the positive logic convention.

1.9 INVERSION

An *inverter* is a logical gate which has a single input and a single output and whose output is the logical *complement* of the input. When the input is *true*, the output is *false* and vice versa; i.e., when the input is A, the output is $Z = \bar{A}$. Alternatively, when the input is at $V(T)$, the output is at $V(F)$ and vice versa.

The logical symbol for an inverter is shown in Fig. 1.9-1a. The essential part of the symbol is the small circle at the apex of the triangular form. When the inversion is to be indicated on a logical diagram which has other logical gates or symbols to which the circle can be affixed, the triangular form is omitted. Thus, suppose that we have an AND gate which generates the logical product AB and we want to complement this product to generate $\overline{AB}$. The logical symbol for the combined product formation and inversion would appear as in Fig. 1.9-1b. Inversion circles can also be used at gate inputs, as shown in Fig. 1.9-1c.

1.10 THE 0, 1 NOTATION

Up to the present we have indicated the two possible values of a logical variable A by the notation $A = T$ (true) or $A = F$ (false). We now introduce an alternative notation, which, as we shall see, has many useful features. We shall use the notation $A = 0$ as an alternative to $A = F$ and $A = 1$ as an alternative to

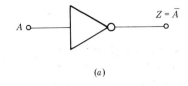

(a)

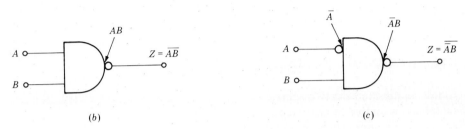

(b)　　　　　　　　　　　　　　　　(c)

Figure 1.9-1 (*a*) The symbol for logical inversion. (*b*), (*c*) When used in conjunction with other gates, the inversion symbol is reduced to an appended open circle.

$A = T$. It must be emphasized that the 0 and the 1 used here are not numbers but are instead logical-variable values. In some texts, the logical values 0 and 1 are set in boldface type to distinguish them from numbers. We shall not do so in the present text because it will always be clear from the context whether the symbols represent logic values or numerical values.

Let us now rewrite the truth tables for the AND and OR functions (Figs. 1.5-2 and 1.6-1) using the 0, 1 notation. In so doing we shall see not only the merit of the notation but also a motivation for the use of "multiplication" to represent the AND operation and "addition" to represent the OR operation. The truth tables appear in Fig. 1.10-1*a* and *b*. The individual rows of the truth tables are written out in the form of equations in Fig. 1.10-1*c* and *d*. Our notations ·,

A	B	$Z = A$ AND B
0	0	0
0	1	0
1	0	0
1	1	1

(a)

A	B	$Z = A$ OR B
0	0	0
0	1	1
1	0	1
1	1	1

(b)

AND

$A \cdot B = Z$
$0 \cdot 0 = 0$
$0 \cdot 1 = 0$
$1 \cdot 0 = 0$
$1 \cdot 1 = 1$

(c)

OR

$A + B = Z$
$0 + 0 = 0$
$0 + 1 = 1$
$1 + 0 = 1$
$1 + 1 = 1$

(d)

Figure 1.10-1 AND and OR truth tables and equations using 0, 1 notation.

+, 0, and 1 constitute a very effective mnemonic device. For if we pretend that the 0 and 1 are numbers and pretend further that multiplication and addition are really intended, then, with the single exception of the equation $1 + 1 = 1$, the equations conform to ordinary arithmetic. We may actually judge that the fact that the correspondence is not complete is an advantage. For the equation $1 + 1 = 1$ serves to remind us that we are actually dealing with logic and not arithmetic.

1.11 THE BINARY NUMBER SYSTEM

In this and in the next two sections we digress briefly from the subject of logic to discuss a matter of arithmetic.

In the number system of everyday life, the *decimal* system, we employ the ten digits $0, 1, \ldots, 9$. A number larger than 9 is represented through a convention which assigns a significance to the *place* or *position* occupied by a digit. For example, by virtue of the positions occupied by the individual digits in the number 6903, this number has a numerical significance calculated as

$$6903 = 6 \times 10^3 + 9 \times 10^2 + 0 \times 10^1 + 3 \times 10^0 \qquad (1.11\text{-}1)$$

We note, as in Eq. (1.11-1) that a number is expressed as the sum of *powers of 10* multiplied by appropriate coefficients. In the decimal system, 10 is called the *radix* or *base* of the system. There are ten digits, the largest being 9. In a numerical system with base n, there are n digits and the largest digit is $n - 1$.

In connection with systems described in terms of logical variables it turns out to be very convenient to use the numerical system with the base 2. Such a system is termed a *binary* system and uses only the numerical digits 0 and 1. The advantage of using the binary system is that we can arrange a one-to-one correspondence between the two digits (numbers) 0 and 1 and the logic values (not numbers) 0 and 1. As a matter of fact, the association becomes, on occasion, so intimate and so convenient that it is sometimes useful to lose sight of the distinction.

When a number is written out in the binary system, the individual digits represent the coefficients of powers of 2 rather than powers of 10 as in the decimal. For example, the *decimal* number 19 is written in the *binary* representation as 10011 since this array of binary digits has the significance

$$1\,0\,0\,1\,1 = 1 \times 2^4 + 0 \times 2^3 + 0 \times 2^2 + 1 \times 2^1 + 1 \times 2^0 \qquad (1.11\text{-}2a)$$

$$= 16 + 0 + 0 + 2 + 1 = 19 \qquad (1.11\text{-}2b)$$

A short list of equivalent numbers in decimal and binary arithmetic is given in Table 1.11-1. Since we have allowed five binary digits there, accordingly, the largest number we can represent is $11111 = 31$.

A number which is not an integer can be expressed using *decimal-point* notation. For example the number 1.8125 has the numerical significance

Table 1.11-1 Equivalent numbers with decimal and binary base

Decimal	Binary	Decimal	Binary	Decimal	Binary	Decimal	Binary
0	00000	8	01000	16	10000	24	11000
1	00001	9	01001	17	10001	25	11001
2	00010	10	01010	18	10010	26	11010
3	00011	11	01011	19	10011	27	11011
4	00100	12	01100	20	10100	28	11100
5	00101	13	01101	21	10101	29	11101
6	00110	14	01110	22	10110	30	11110
7	00111	15	01111	23	10111	31	11111

$$1.8125 = 1 \times 10^0 + 8 \times 10^{-1} + 1 \times 10^{-2} + 2 \times 10^{-3} + 5 \times 10^{-4} \quad (1.11\text{-}3)$$

Similarly, we can express a noninteger binary number using *binary-point* notation. For example,

$$1.1101 = 1 \times 2^0 + 1 \times 2^{-1} + 1 \times 2^{-2} + 0 \times 2^{-3} + 1 \times 2^{-4} \quad (1.11\text{-}4)$$

Thus bits to the right of the binary point are coefficients of 2^{-n} when n is the distance of the bit to the right of the binary point. In decimal arithmetic, moving the decimal point k places to the left or right divides or multiplies the number by 10^k. In binary arithmetic such a left or right displacement divides or multiplies by 2^k.

1.12 CONVERSIONS BETWEEN DECIMAL AND BINARY NUMBERS

The conversion from a binary to a decimal number is readily accomplished by the simple arithmetic illustrated in Eqs. (1.11-2) and (1.11-4).

Converting a number N from a decimal representation into a binary representation is easy with the following rules. Let us assume, as a first case, that N is integral so that, in decimal form, all digits to the right of the *decimal* point are 0s. Correspondingly, as a binary number, all the digits to the right of the binary point will be 0s, and N will have the form $N = \cdots x_8 x_4 x_2 x_1.000 \cdots$ Here, the x's are 0s or 1s, and the subscripts indicate the numerical significance to be assigned each binary digit in accordance with its position.

Now let us divide N by 2, keeping the result in integral form. Then, since each division moves the binary point one place to the left, we have

$$\frac{N}{2} = \frac{\cdots x_8 x_4 x_2 x_1.}{2} = \cdots x_8 x_4 x_2. + \text{remainder } x_1$$

Thus, the least significant digit x_1 is the *remainder*, and the result of the division gives us a new number $N' = \cdots x_8 x_4 x_2.$, in which x_2 has become the least significant digit. Altogether, then, a sequence of divisions by 2 will yield the binary form of N through the remainders. As an example, let us find the binary representation of the decimal number 19. We have

$$
\begin{array}{r|l}
2 & 19 \\
\hline
2 & 9 \\
\hline
2 & 4 \\
\hline
2 & 2 \\
\hline
2 & 1 \\
\hline
 & 0
\end{array}
\qquad
\begin{array}{ll}
\textit{Remainders} & \\
1 & \text{least significant digit} \\
1 & \\
0 & \\
0 & \\
1 & \text{most significant digit}
\end{array}
$$

and $19_{\text{decimal}} = 1\,0\,0\,1\,1_{\text{binary}}$

Suppose now, as the second case, that the number N is less than unity so that, as a decimal number, all digits to the left of the *decimal* point are 0s. Correspondingly, as a binary number, all digits to the left of the *binary* point will also be 0s. We shall then have $N = \cdots 000.x_{1/2}x_{1/4}x_{1/8}\cdots$ We can test whether $x_{1/2}$ is 0 or 1 by multiplying N by 2. For if $x_{1/2}$ is 1, the product $2N$ will be larger than unity but will remain less than unity if $x_{1/2}$ is 0. Further, the multiplication by 2 moves the binary point one place to the right, thereby moving the digit $x_{1/4}$ into the position previously occupied by $x_{1/2}$. Hence, the binary representation can be found by a series of multiplications by 2. As an example, let us find the binary form of the decimal number 0.69. We have

$$
\begin{array}{lll}
0.69 \times 2 = 1.38 & 1 & \text{most significant digit} \\[4pt]
0.38 \times 2 = 0.76 & 0 & \\[4pt]
0.76 \times 2 = 1.52 & 1 & \\[4pt]
0.52 \times 2 = 1.04 & 1 & \\[4pt]
0.04 \times 2 = 0.08 & 0 & \\[4pt]
0.08 \times 2 = 0.16 & 0 & \text{least significant digit} \\
\cdots\cdots\cdots\cdots\cdots\cdots
\end{array}
$$

So that $0.69_{\text{decimal}} = .1\,0\,1\,1\,0\,0\cdots_{\text{binary}}$.

Finally, of course, if the decimal number has both an integral and a decimal part, the two parts are dealt with separately in the manner indicated and the results are then combined.

1.13 THE OCTAL AND HEXADECIMAL NUMBER SYSTEMS

The *octal* and *hexadecimal* number systems are of interest to us because they have a special relationship to the binary system. In the octal system, the base is eight (8), and the digits employed are 0, 1 ..., 7. In the hexadecimal system the base is sixteen (16), and the usual ten decimal digits 0, 1 ..., 9 provide ten of the required digits and the other six are generally represented by the letters A, B, C, D, E, F. Table 1.13-1 lists the octal and hexadecimal representations of the numbers in Table 1.11-1.

The special relationships of the octal and hexadecimal systems to the binary system result from the fact that three binary digits can represent exactly

Table 1.13-1 Equivalent numbers with decimal, octal, and hexadecimal bases

Decimal	Octal	Hexa-decimal	Decimal	Octal	Hexa-decimal	Decimal	Octal	Hexa-decimal	Decimal	Octal	Hexa-decimal
0	00	00	8	10	08	16	20	10	24	30	18
1	01	01	9	11	09	17	21	11	25	31	19
2	02	02	10	12	0A	18	22	12	26	32	1A
3	03	03	11	13	0B	19	23	13	27	33	1B
4	04	04	12	14	0C	20	24	14	28	34	1C
5	05	05	13	15	0D	21	25	15	29	35	1D
6	06	06	14	16	0E	22	26	16	30	36	1E
7	07	07	15	17	0F	23	27	17	31	37	1F

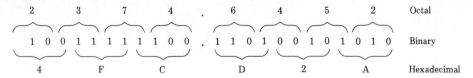

Figure 1.13-1 Conversions between octal, binary, and hexadecimal number systems.

eight (2^3) different numbers and four binary numbers can represent exactly sixteen (2^4) different numbers. Hence, as indicated in Fig. 1.13-1, the conversion from binary to octal or hexadecimal or vice versa is easily effected. To go from binary to octal, we group the binary digits in threes, working in both directions from the binary point. We then replace each such group by its octal equivalent. To go to the hexadecimal, we group the binary digits in fours. In Fig. 1.13-1 we assume that the leftmost 1 in the binary number is the most significant bit. Hence, on the left, the digits required to complete groups of three and four are presumed to be 0s. To go from octal (or hexadecimal) to binary we simply replace each octal (or hexadecimal) digit by its 3-bit (or 4-bit) binary equivalent.

1.14 BINARY NUMBERS AND LOGICAL VARIABLES

As one may well imagine, the special usefulness of the binary number system in connection with the algebra of logical variables stems from the fact that logical variables have just two values and the binary system has just two digits. This usefulness is enhanced, as we shall now see, by the 0, 1 notation introduced in Sec. 1.10 to represent truth values of a logical variable.

By way of example, consider that we want to define a function Z of three variables $Z = f(A, B, C)$ by its truth table. We would start by forming the *structure* of the truth table; i.e., we would draw a truth-table structure of four columns. Three columns, say the leftmost three, would be labeled A, B, and C, respectively, while the fourth column would be labeled Z. In columns A, B, and C we would list, as in Fig. 1.5-3, all the possible combinations of truth values of three variables. We would have to be quite certain to miss no possible combination and, of course, to avoid redundancy we would not want to duplicate any combination. In principle, the order in which the combinations are listed is of no consequence. In any event, having formed the structure of the three-variable truth, we would use this structure to define Z simply by entering T's and F's in appropriate positions in the Z column.

Such a three-variable truth table used to define a function Z appears in Fig. 1.14-1*a*. (The student may verify that the function here, expressed algebraically, is $Z = A + BC$, although the particular function represented is not relevant to the present discussion.) In Fig. 1.14-1*b* we have repeated the table except that we have used the 0, 1 notation and have decimally numbered the ($2^3 = 8$) rows from 0 to 7. We acknowledge, of course, that the entries in the

A	B	C	Z
F	F	F	F
F	F	T	F
F	T	F	F
F	T	T	T
T	F	F	T
T	F	T	T
T	T	F	T
T	T	T	T

(a)

Row no.	A	B	C	Z
0	0	0	0	0
1	0	0	1	0
2	0	1	0	0
3	0	1	1	1
4	1	0	0	1
5	1	0	1	1
6	1	1	0	1
7	1	1	1	1

(b)

Fig. 1.14-1 A three-variable truth table.

table are not numbers. Nonetheless, let us benignly ignore this fact and *pretend* that the entries are numbers. Then we observe that each row of entries in the independent-variable columns, A, B, and C, precisely represent, in binary arithmetic, the number of that row. Of course, this outcome is the result of the forethought we gave to the matter in arranging the order of the rows in Fig. 1.14-1a for, as noted, interchanging rows in a truth table does not change the truth table.

As a generalization of these observations we can now establish the following as a useful procedure for preparing the structure of an n-variable truth. We make an $(n + 1)$-column table, the first n columns being reserved for the n independent variables and the last for the function Z. To ensure that we have listed all possible combinations of the independent variables without duplication, we simply write down in order and in binary arithmetic the numbers from 0 to $2^n - 1$. Of course. in the table so prepared, the 0s and 1s are interpreted as logical truth values and not as numbers.

No matter in what order we list the combinations of possible values of the independent variables, we have a unique method of assigning a *number* to each combination or row. We simply pretend that the truth values are binary digits and read the number. This feature allows us an additional alternative method of defining a function. For example, we can say (1) that $Z = A + BC$ or (2) that the function is defined by the truth table of Fig. 1.14-1a or b or (3) that the function is defined as having entries 1 in the Z column of a three-variable truth table in rows 3, 4, 5, 6, and 7 (alternatively 0s in rows 0, 1, 2, and 3). Note that in the third alternative we have a way of defining the function without explicitly displaying the truth table.

1.15 BOOLEAN ALGEBRAIC THEOREMS

We now develop a number of theorems involving the OR, the AND, and the NOT operation which are useful for simplifying expressions of logical variables. We shall employ the symbols for addition and multiplication to represent these operations and the 0, 1 notation to represent that a logical variable is false or true, respectively.

We note at the outset that there is a special principle, described by the term *duality*, which applies between theorems involving the AND and OR operations. (see Prob. 1.15-1). This principle has already been suggested in the truth tables of Fig. 1.10-1. Consider any row of either of these tables. We find that if, in that row we (1) interchange $+$ and $\cdot$ signs and (2) interchange 0s and 1s, we shall have replaced the original equation by an equally valid equation. For example, consider the equation $0 \cdot 0 = 0$, which appears as the first row of the AND truth table. Making the two interchanges, this equation becomes $1 + 1 = 1$, which is also a valid equation, appearing in the fourth row of the OR truth table. In the same way it can be verified that applying the interchanges to all the equations in the AND truth tables leads, in a one-to-one correspondence, to the equations in the OR truth table and vice versa.

On the basis of this principle of duality we have the following useful result. If we have a *theorem* relating logical variables, we can immediately write down a second theorem by interchanging $+$ and $\cdot$ signs and interchanging 0s and 1s. The two theorems so related are referred to as *dual theorems*, and the expressions derived by the two interchanges are called duals of each other.

A word of caution is in order. Suppose that we have some function f of logical variables and a second function g of the same variable, and suppose that even though f and g appear different we are able to establish that $f = g$ no matter what the values of the variables. That is, we are able to establish the theorem that $f = g$. Then the principle of duality tells us that if we form the duals f_D and g_D of the functions f and g, respectively, we shall have an alternate valid theorem, namely $f_D = g_D$. The principle of duality does *not* say that $f_D = f$ or that $g_D = g$.

Turning now to the listing of theorems, we note initially a very important albeit rather self-evident theorem. From the fact that a variable has only two possible values we have the result that the complement of the complement of a variable A is the variable A itself; i.e.,

$$\bar{\bar{A}} = A \qquad (1.15\text{-}1)$$

Correspondingly, Eq. (1.15-1) leads to the dual equations $\bar{0} = 1$ and $\bar{1} = 0$. Continuing, we have

$A + 0 = A$	(1.15-2a)	$A \cdot 1 = A$	(1.15-2b)
$A + 1 = 1$	(1.15-3a)	$A \cdot 0 = 0$	(1.15-3b)
$A + A = A$	(1.15-4a)	$A \cdot A = A$	(1.15-4b)
$A + \bar{A} = 1$	(1.15-5a)	$A \cdot \bar{A} = 0$	(1.15-5b)

These eight theorems involve a single variable and have been listed as dual pairs. Thus applying the principle of duality to Eq. (1.15-2a) yields Eq. (1.15-2b), etc. The proof of the validity of any one of the theorems is readily established by considering the theorem for every possible value of the variable and showing that the theorem holds in each case. Since the variable has only two possible values, this manner of establishing the validity of a theorem is entirely feasible. Consider, for example, Eq. (1.15-5a). If $A = 0$, the equation says that $0 + \overline{0} = 0 + 1 = 1$, which is correct. If $A = 1$, the equation says that $1 + \overline{1} = 1 + 0 = 1$, which is also correct.

Next we tabulate some theorems involving two and three variables. Again, we present the theorems in sets of dual pairs.

$$A + AB = A \qquad\qquad (1.15\text{-}6a)$$

$$A(A + B) = A \qquad\qquad (1.15\text{-}6b)$$

$$AB + A\overline{B} = A \qquad\qquad (1.15\text{-}7a)$$

$$(A + B)(A + \overline{B}) = A \qquad\qquad (1.15\text{-}7b)$$

$$A + \overline{A}B = A + B \qquad\qquad (1.15\text{-}8a)$$

$$A(\overline{A} + B) = AB \qquad\qquad (1.15\text{-}8b)$$

$$A + BC = (A + B)(A + C) \qquad\qquad (1.15\text{-}9a)$$

$$A(B + C) = AB + AC \qquad\qquad (1.15\text{-}9b)$$

$$AB + \overline{A}C = (A + C)(\overline{A} + B) \qquad\qquad (1.15\text{-}10a)$$

$$(A + B)(\overline{A} + C) = AC + \overline{A}B \qquad\qquad (1.15\text{-}10b)$$

$$AB + \overline{A}C + BC = AB + \overline{A}C \qquad\qquad (1.15\text{-}11a)$$

$$(A + B)(\overline{A} + C)(B + C) = (A + B)(\overline{A} + C) \qquad\qquad (1.15\text{-}11b)$$

Equation (1.15-9b) is of special interest since it indicates that the *distributive* law applies to our algebra of logical variables; i.e., given an expression involving a parenthesis like $A(B + C)$, we can remove the parenthesis by "multiplying" through as in ordinary algebra and get $A(B + C) = AB + AC$. Alternatively, the theorem indicates that a common "factor" can be "factored" out. Thus in $AB + AC$, the A is a common factor to the two terms and it can be factored out to yield $A(B + C)$. This theorem is rather intuitively acceptable because of its correspondence with ordinary algebra. The dual theorem, Eq. (1.15-9a), looks a little strange and needs getting used to.

Any of the theorems tabulated above can be verified by substituting all possible combinations of the variables in the equation. Where two variables are involved, there are four combinations. Where three variables are involved, there are eight combinations.

Example 1.15-1 Prove that Eq. (1.15-8a) is correct.

SOLUTION The verification of Eq. (1.15-8a) follows directly from a comparison of the truth tables for $A + \overline{A}B$ and for $A + B$:

A	B	$Z_1 = A + \bar{A}B$	$Z_2 = A + B$
0	0	$0 + 1 \cdot 0 = 0$	$0 + 0 = 0$
0	1	$0 + 1 \cdot 1 = 1$	$0 + 1 = 1$
1	0	$1 + 0 \cdot 0 = 1$	$1 + 0 = 1$
1	1	$1 + 0 \cdot 1 = 1$	$1 + 1 = 1$

The entries in the column for Z_1 are in every instance the same as the entries in the column for Z_2, and hence $Z_1 = Z_2$ and Eq. (1.15-8a) is thereby verified.

Example 1.15-2 Prove that Eq. (1.15-11b) is correct.

SOLUTION The verification of Eq. (1.15-11b) follows directly from a comparison of the truth table for $(A + B)$ $(\bar{A} + C)$ $(B + C)$ and $(A + B)$ $(\bar{A} + C)$. A truth table for three variables is required and is shown below. Note that in preparing the structure of the truth table we have followed the procedure described in Sec. 1.14.

A	B	C	$Z_1 = (A + B)(\bar{A} + C)(B + C)$	$Z_2 = (A + B)(\bar{A} + C)$
0	0	0	$(0 + 0)(1 + 0)(0 + 0) = 0$	$(0 + 0)(1 + 0) = 0$
0	0	1	$(0 + 0)(1 + 1)(0 + 1) = 0$	$(0 + 0)(1 + 1) = 0$
0	1	0	$(0 + 1)(1 + 0)(1 + 0) = 1$	$(0 + 1)(1 + 0) = 1$
0	1	1	$(0 + 1)(1 + 1)(1 + 1) = 1$	$(0 + 1)(1 + 1) = 1$
1	0	0	$(1 + 0)(0 + 0)(0 + 0) = 0$	$(1 + 0)(0 + 0) = 0$
1	0	1	$(1 + 0)(0 + 1)(0 + 1) = 1$	$(1 + 0)(0 + 1) = 1$
1	1	0	$(1 + 1)(0 + 0)(1 + 0) = 0$	$(1 + 1)(0 + 0) = 0$
1	1	1	$(1 + 1)(0 + 1)(1 + 1) = 1$	$(1 + 1)(0 + 1) = 1$

Since $Z_1 = Z_2$ for each of the possible combinations of A, B, and C, the theorem is verified.

If we write boolean algebraic expressions in terms of the AND, OR, and NOT operations, then the basic theorems are the theorems which involve just a single variable, Eqs. (1.15-2) through (1.15-5) and the two distributive theorems A $(B + C) = AB + AC$ and $A + BC = (A + B)$ $(A + C)$, Eqs. (1.15-9a) and (b). All of the other theorems and, in particular all the other theorems given in this section can be proved by algebraic manipulation using these basic theorems. For example the theorems of Eq. (1.15-6a) and (b) are proved as follows:

Eq. (1.15-6a)	Eq. (1.15-6b)
$A + AB = A.1 + AB$	$A (A + B) = (A + 0)(A + B)$
$\quad = A(1 + B)$	$\quad = A + 0.B$
$\quad = A.1$	$\quad = A + 0$
$\quad = A$	$\quad = A$

Note particularly that corresponding to each of the basic theorems we used to prove Eq. (1.15-6a), we used the dual theorem to prove Eq. (1.15-6b). Thus when on the one side we use $A = A.1$ on the other side we use the dual $A = A + 0$. When on the one side we use the distributive theorem in the form of Eq. (1.15-9a), on the other side we use its dual, Eq. (1.15-9b), etc. Hence, generalizing, we have established the principle of duality. For, if we are able to prove a proposed theorem by following a sequence of steps, we can also prove its dual, since all we need to do is to replace each step by its dual.

1.16 DE MORGAN'S THEOREM

One last theorem is of sufficient importance to deserve being singled out. Known as *De Morgan's theorem*, it applies to an arbitrary number of variables and in its dual forms is given by

$$\overline{A \cdot B \cdot C \cdots} = \bar{A} + \bar{B} + \bar{C} + \cdots \qquad (1.16\text{-}1)$$

$$\overline{A + B + C + \cdots} = \bar{A} \cdot \bar{B} \cdot \bar{C} \cdots \qquad (1.16\text{-}2)$$

In words, these equations say that (1) the complement of a product of variables is equal to the sum of the complements of the individual variables and (2) the complement of a sum of variables is equal to the product of the complements of the individual variables.

The theorem is readily proved for two variables by simply resorting to a two-variable truth table to test each of the four possibilities. Having thus proved that, say, $\overline{AB} = \bar{A} + \bar{B}$, let us examine the three-variable case $\overline{ABC}$. We let $Z = AB$ so that $\overline{ABC} = \overline{ZC}$. We then have a two-variable case so that we can write $\overline{ZC} = \bar{Z} + \bar{C}$. Now applying the two-variable theorem to $\bar{Z} = \overline{AB}$, we have $\overline{ABC} = \overline{ZC} = \bar{Z} + \bar{C} = \bar{A} + \bar{B} + \bar{C}$. Having proved the theorem for $2 + 1 = 3$ variables, we can by the same procedure prove the theorem for $3 + 1 = 4$ variables, and so on for an arbitrary number of variables. The dual theorem $\overline{A + B + C \cdots} = \bar{A} \cdot \bar{B} \cdot \bar{C} \cdots$ is similarly established.

1.17 VENN DIAGRAMS

There is an interesting geometrical patterning which can be put in a one-to-one correspondence with the concepts of logical variables. These patterns, known as *Venn diagrams*, are also useful in allowing a geometrical visualization of the theorems of boolean algebra.

In Fig. 1.17-1 the space inside the rectangle is our universe of interest. We have divided this universe into two mutually exclusive regions, the region inside the circle and the region outside the circle. Since there are just two regions and they are mutually exclusive, we can associate with them a logical variable A. We associate the logical variable A with the space inside the circle and the variable $\bar{A}$ with the space outside the circle. The boolean theorem that

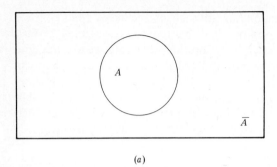

(a)

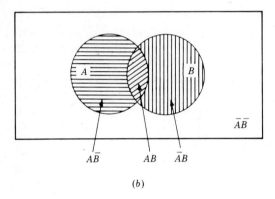

(b)

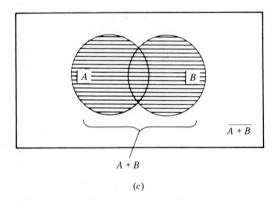

(c)

Figure 1.17-1 (a) A single-variable Venn diagram. (b), (c) Two variable diagrams. Some of the areas are identified in terms of their boolean representation.

$A + \bar{A} = 1$ can now be given the geometric interpretation that it is always true (logic 1) that a point is either inside the circle OR that it is outside the circle. Logically, the 1 in $A + \bar{A} = 1$ represents the inevitable truth that a point is either inside or outside the circle. Geometrically the 1 represents the universe of our interest, i.e., the totality of points in the rectangle.

A Venn diagram for two variables is shown in Fig. 1.17-1b. For the sake of generality we have arranged an overlap in the circles representing the variables.

The universe is now divided into four regions. There is a region inside the A circle but simultaneously outside the B circle, i.e., in the A circle and *not* in the B circle. This region is identified with the logical function $A\bar{B}$. The other regions are, then correspondingly AB (inside A and B), $\bar{A}B$ (not in A but in B), and finally $\bar{A}\bar{B}$ (not in A and also not in B). From the geometry, since any point must be in one of those four regions we find that

$$A\bar{B} + AB + \bar{A}B + \bar{A}\bar{B} = 1 \qquad (1.17\text{-}1)$$

That Eq. (1.17-1) is valid algebraically is readily verified by the application of the theorems of Sec. 1.15.

As appears in Fig. 1.17-1c, the total region encompassed by the two circles can also be represented by $A + B$; that is, any point in the shaded region is either in A OR B. Correspondingly the area not shaded is $\overline{A + B}$. Comparing Figure 1.17-1b and c, we then have that $A + B = A\bar{B} + AB + \bar{A}B$ and also that $\overline{A}\overline{B} = \overline{A + B}$. The first result is readily verified by the theorems. The latter result is of course recognized as De Morgan's theorem.

In Fig. 1.17-1b the region AB is the region of overlap between A and B. In the area AB the A and B circles cut through each other; i.e., they intersect. This consideration provides the motivation for referring to AB as the *intersection* of A and B, often represented by $A \cap B$. In the same way $A + B$ is the *total* region encompassed by A and B and is therefore often referred to as the *union* of A and B, represented by $A \cup B$.

A three-variable Venn diagram is shown in Fig. 1.17-2. Some of the areas are identified in terms of their boolean representations. Note that, as appears in Fig. 1.17-1 and 1.17-2, the Venn diagrams divide the universe (the rectangle) into 2^n distinct identifiable areas, n being the number of variables involved. Thus the number of such areas is equal to the number of rows in the truth table for the corresponding number of variables.

Venn diagrams are useful to allow geometrical visualization of boolean functions and can also be used, as in the following example, to establish or verify boolean algebraic theorems.

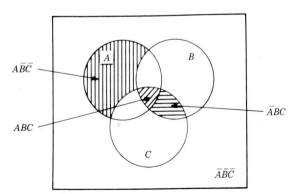

$A\bar{B}\bar{C}$

ABC

$\bar{A}BC$

$\bar{A}\bar{B}\bar{C}$

Figure 1.17-2 A three-variable Venn diagram. Some of the areas are identified in terms of their boolean representation.

Example 1.17-1 (*a*) Use a Venn diagram to verify the theorem of Eq. (1.15-10*b*), that is, $(A + B)(\bar{A} + C) = AC + \bar{A}B$. (*b*) Use a Venn diagram to verify the validity of the theorem of Eq. (1.15-11*a*), that is, $AB + \bar{A}C + BC = AB + \bar{A}C$.

SOLUTION (*a*) In Fig. 1.17-3*a* the horizontal shading covers the region $A + B$; that is, it covers all the area which is either in A OR in B. The vertical shading encompasses the area $\bar{A} + C$, that is, the area which is either outside A OR inside C. The doubly shaded area is *both* in the region $A + B$ AND *also* in the region $\bar{A} + C$. Hence it represents $(A + B)(\bar{A} + C)$. In Fig. 1.17-3*b* the horizontal shading is AC, and the vertical shading is

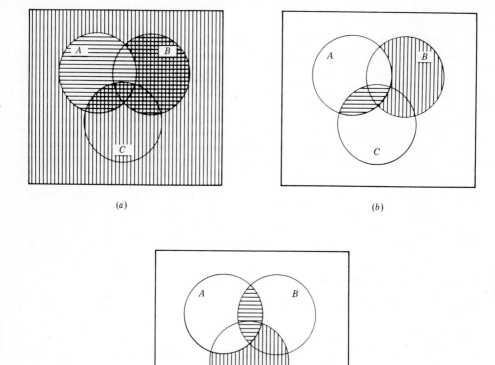

(*a*)   (*b*)

(*c*)

Figure 1.17-3 (*a*) Horizontal shading is $A + B$. Vertical shading is $\bar{A} + C$. Double shading is $(A + B)(\bar{A} + C)$. (*b*) Horizontal shading is AC. Vertical shading is $\bar{A}B$. Total shaded area is $AC + \bar{A}B$. (*c*) Horizontal shading AB, vertical shading $\bar{A}C$. Total shading $AB + \bar{A}C$ encompasses BC.

$\bar{A}B$. The total shaded area is $AC + \bar{A}B$. Finally since the shaded area in Fig. 1.17-3b is the same as the double-shaded area in Fig. 1.17-3a, we have established that $(A + B)(\bar{A} + C) = AC + \bar{A}B$.

(b) In Fig. 1.17-3c the horizontally shaded area is AB, and the vertically shaded area is $\bar{A}C$. The total shaded area is $AB + \bar{A}C$. We note that this total area encompasses the region BC even though we did not explicitly shade this BC region. Hence $AB + \bar{A}C$ automatically includes BC, so that we have the result $AB + \bar{A}C = AB + \bar{A}C + BC$.

Venn diagrams for more than three variables are not widely used because they are rather difficult to draw and confusing in appearance (see Prob. 1.17-1).

1.18 THE FUNCTIONS OF TWO VARIABLES

In Sec. 1.5 we pointed out that, at least in principle, there are 16 possible functions of two variables. In that section we considered the AND function and the OR function. In the present section we consider the remaining functions.

A two-variable truth table has four rows, and in such a table a function is defined by specifying the four entries T or F (0 or 1) in the column for $Z = f(A, B)$. Since each entry allows two values and there are four entries, the total number of functions is $2 \times 2 \times 2 \times 2 = 16$. The 16 functions are shown in Table 1.18-1, where we have used the 0, 1 notation. As a matter of convenience, here we have arranged the table so that entries that generally appear in columns are here listed in rows and vice versa. To avoid an entirely random ordering of the functions we have pretended that the logical en-

Table 1.18-1 The 16 logical functions of two variables

| A | 0 | 0 | 1 | 1 | |
B	0	1	0	1	Function
f_0	0	0	0	0	$f = 0$
f_1	0	0	0	1	$f = AB$ (AND)
f_2	0	0	1	0	$f = \overline{A \supset B}$
f_3	0	0	1	1	$f = A$
f_4	0	1	0	0	$f = \overline{B \supset A}$
f_5	0	1	0	1	$f = B$
f_6	0	1	1	0	$f = A \oplus B$ (EXCLUSIVE-OR)
f_7	0	1	1	1	$f = A + B$ (OR)
f_8	1	0	0	0	$f = \overline{A + B}$ (NOR) $= A \downarrow B$
f_9	1	0	0	1	$f = \overline{A \oplus B}$ (EXCLUSIVE-NOR)
f_{10}	1	0	1	0	$f = \bar{B}$
f_{11}	1	0	1	1	$f = B \supset A$ (B implies A)
f_{12}	1	1	0	0	$f = \bar{A}$
f_{13}	1	1	0	1	$f = A \supset B$ (A implies B)
f_{14}	1	1	1	0	$f = \overline{AB}$ (NAND) $= A \uparrow B$
f_{15}	1	1	1	1	$f = 1$

tries 0 and 1 are numerical digits and we have arranged the function in order of increasing number. We arbitrarily consider that the first-column entry is the least significant. Thus the sixth function f_5 is the function for which the digits appear in the order 0101.

We find that $f_0 = 0$ and $f_{15} = 1$, so that these are not really functions of A and B. Also we have $f_3 = A, f_{12} = \bar{A}, f_5 = B$, and $f_{10} = \bar{B}$. Thus these functions are functions of only a single variable rather than of both.

The function f_1 is the AND function $f = A \cdot B$, and f_7 is the OR function $f = A + B$, both of which we have already considered. The function f_{14} is the complement of the AND function $\overline{AB}$; that is, having formed A AND B, we then form NOT (A AND B). This NOT-AND operation is abbreviated NAND. Similarly $f_8 = \overline{A + B}$ is the NOT-OR function, abbreviated NOR. We shall comment further on the NAND and NOR functions.

1.19 THE EXCLUSIVE-OR

The function f_6 is called the EXCLUSIVE-OR function, represented by the symbol $\oplus$; thus

$$f_6 = f(A, B) = A \oplus B \qquad (1.19\text{-}1)$$

This function takes its name from the consideration that when $Z = A \oplus B$, $Z = 1$ if one of the variables A or B, to the *exclusion* of the other, has the logic value 1. That is, $Z = 1$ if $A = 1$ or if $B = 1$ but not if both A and B are 1. For the sake of precision in language we might then refer to the OR function considered earlier (f_7 in Table 1.18-1) as the INCLUSIVE-OR. Generally, however, when the INCLUSIVE-OR is intended the simple designation OR is used.

The EXCLUSIVE-OR operation is commutative ($A \oplus B = B \oplus A$) and associative [$(A \oplus B) \oplus C = A \oplus (B \oplus C)$]. That such is the case is readily verified (Prob. 1.19-1) by resort to the truth table.

The symbol for a gate which forms the EXCLUSIVE-OR function of the two input variables is shown in Fig. 1.19-1a. Since the EXCLUSIVE-OR operation is both commutative and associative, we would imagine that if three variables were presented and we wanted a symbol to represent a gate which forms $A \oplus B \oplus C$, we might simply use the symbol in Fig. 1.19-1a except with three inputs. Such was the symbolism used in a previous section (Fig. 1.8-1) in connection with the AND and OR operation. However, in the present instance, such generally is not the case, and a gate structure to accommodate three inputs is represented as in Fig. 1.19-1b. The reason for this complication is that the hardware implementation of the AND and OR gates allows easy accommodation of additional inputs. In comparison, the EXCLUSIVE-OR gate is a more complicated gate to realize in hardware, i.e., to fabricate physically. There is no simple way of modifying a two-input EXCLUSIVE-OR gate to allow additional inputs. Hence physically fabricated EXCLUSIVE-OR gates accommodate two inputs, and to handle n inputs $n - 1$ gates are used. Inputs can be interchanged arbitrarily without effect on the output.

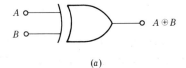

(a)

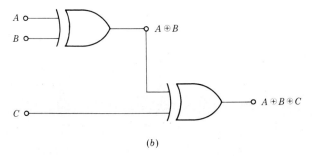

(b)

Figure 1.19-1 (*a*) The symbol for an EXCLUSIVE-OR gate. (*b*) Two such gates are used to generate $A \oplus B \oplus C$.

The function f_9 in Table 1.18-1 is the complement of the EXCLUSIVE-OR; that is, f_9 is the EXCLUSIVE-NOR

$$f_9 = \overline{A \oplus B} \qquad (1.19\text{-}2)$$

This gate is also called the EQUIVALENCE gate since it yields a logic 1 output when and only when $A = B$.

1.20 THE NAND AND NOR FUNCTIONS

The function f_{14} when represented by its own distinctive symbol is written

$$f_{14} = A \uparrow B \qquad (1.20\text{-}1)$$

As can be verified by comparing f_{14} with f_1 in Table 1.18-1

$$f_{14} = A \uparrow B = \overline{AB} \qquad (1.20\text{-}2)$$

That is, $f_{14} = $ NOT (A AND B), which is abbreviated A NAND B. Accordingly, also we can represent a NAND gate or an AND gate with an inversion circle appended to the gate-output side, as in Fig. 1.20-1a.

Similarly we note that the function f_8 has 0 and 1 entries which are in every case the complement of the entries in $f_7 = A$ OR B. When represented by its own distinctive symbol, f_8 is written

$$f_8 = A \downarrow B \qquad (1.20\text{-}3)$$

so that $\qquad f_8 = A \downarrow B = \overline{A + B} \qquad (1.20\text{-}4)$

Since $f_8 = $ NOT (A OR B), we find the function abbreviated A NOR B. A symbol for a NOR gate is shown in Fig. 1.20-1b.

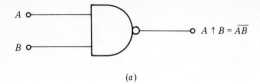

(a)

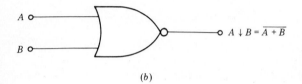

(b)

Figure 1.20-1 (*a*) The symbol for a NAND gate. (*b*) The symbol for a NOR gate.

Both the NAND operation and the NOR operation are commutative; i.e., as appears immediately by inspection of the truth table,

$$A \uparrow B = \overline{AB} = B \uparrow A = \overline{BA} \qquad (1.20\text{-}5)$$

and

$$A \downarrow B = \overline{A} + \overline{B} = B \downarrow A = \overline{B} + \overline{A} \qquad (1.20\text{-}6)$$

On the other hand, neither the NAND nor the NOR operation is associative, i.e. (Prob. 1.20-1),

$$(A \uparrow B) \uparrow C \neq A \uparrow (B \uparrow C) \qquad (1.20\text{-}7)$$

or in the alternative symbolism

$$\overline{\overline{AB}\,C} \neq \overline{A\,\overline{BC}} \qquad (1.20\text{-}8)$$

Similarly

$$(A \downarrow B) \downarrow C \neq A \downarrow (B \downarrow C) \qquad (1.20\text{-}9)$$

or

$$\overline{\overline{A+B}+C} \neq \overline{A+\overline{B+C}} \qquad (1.20\text{-}10)$$

The NAND operation, like all the other operations, involves just two variables. If we intend to generate a function involving only the NAND operation and more than two variables are involved, we need to specify the order in which the variables are operated on by the NAND operation. Thus, $(A \uparrow B) \uparrow C$ is not the same as $A \uparrow (B \uparrow C)$, which is not the same as $B \uparrow (A \uparrow C)$, etc. There is, however, another sense in which the term NAND is used in connection with more than two variables. In this second sense, the term NAND applied to say, three variables, means simply $\overline{ABC}$. That is, the variables are initially combined through the AND operation. Thereafter, the single variable ABC is complemented. Since the AND operation is commutative, when the NAND operation is used in this sense, the total operation is commutative and we need not specify an order of combination of variables. A multiple-input NAND gate, according to the second sense, is shown in Fig. 1.20-2*a*. Of course, when only two variables are involved, the two senses in which the term NAND is used

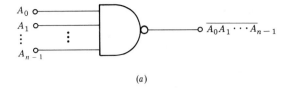

(a)

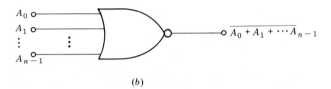

(b)

Figure 1.20-2 (a) A multiple-input NAND gate. (b) A multiple-input NOR gate.

become the same. Correspondingly, a gate which generates $\overline{A + B + C}$ is called a NOR gate. A multiple-input NOR gate appears in Fig. 1.20-2b.

1.21 THE IMPLICATION FUNCTIONS

The function defined as f_{13} in the truth table of Fig. 1.18-1 is called the *implication function* and is written $f_{13} = A$ implies B or, in symbols, $A \supset B$. A word is in order concerning the term *implication*. Consider the following elementary example. Let us use the variable A to represent the statement "It is raining"; i.e., when it is raining, $A = \text{T}$ and when it is not raining, $A = \text{F}$. Also let B represent the statement "People are using umbrellas." Suppose that we want to write a logical equation that says A implies B; that is, the occurrence of rain implies that people use umbrellas. If we introduce a variable $Z = A \supset B$, Z is related to A and B in the manner prescribed by f_{13} in Table 1.18-1. For, now, if the situation with respect to A and B is consistent with the concept that A implies B, we find that $Z = \text{true}$. The one possibility which is not consistent with A implying B is that A be true and B be false. In this case we find from the truth table that $Z = \text{false}$.

As is intuitively obvious or can readily be verified from a truth table, the implication operation is neither commutative nor associative. Since the operation is not commutative, we anticipate and indeed find in Table 1.18-1 the commuted relationship $f_{11} = B \supset A$. Finally, the remaining two functions in Table 1.18-1 are now noted as simply $f_2 = \overline{A \supset B}$ and $f_4 = \overline{B \supset A}$.

1.22 RELATIONSHIP BETWEEN OPERATIONS

The logical operations defined by the truth table of Table 1.18-1 are not independent of each other. To see that such is the case, we shall now display that any of the functions we have defined can be expressed using only the AND the OR functions and using, as well, the NOT operation. We have

$$f_0 = A\bar{A} = B\bar{B} = 0 \qquad\qquad f_1 = AB \qquad\qquad f_2 = A\bar{B}$$

$$f_3 = A \qquad\qquad f_4 = \bar{A}B \qquad\qquad f_5 = B$$

$$f_6 = A\bar{B} + \bar{A}B \qquad\qquad f_7 = A + B \qquad f_8 = \overline{A + B} = \bar{A}\bar{B} \qquad (1.22\text{-}1)$$

$$f_9 = \bar{A}\bar{B} + AB \qquad\qquad f_{10} = \bar{B} \qquad\qquad f_{11} = A + \bar{B}$$

$$f_{12} = \bar{A} \qquad\qquad f_{13} = \bar{A} + B \qquad f_{14} = \overline{AB} = \bar{A} + \bar{B}$$

$$f_{15} = A + \bar{A} = B + \bar{B} = 1$$

That each of the expressions given in Eq. (1.22-1) is indeed correct is again readily verified by resorting to a truth table. By way of example, consider $f_6 = A\bar{B} + \bar{A}B$, which it is here claimed is the same function as $A \oplus B$. We have

A	B	$\bar{A}$	$\bar{B}$	$A\bar{B}$	$\bar{A}B$	$A\bar{B} + \bar{A}B$
0	0	1	1	0	0	0
0	1	1	0	0	1	1
1	0	0	1	1	0	1
1	1	0	0	0	0	0

Comparing the column here for $A\bar{B} + \bar{A}B$ with the column $f_6 = A \oplus B$ in Table 1.18-1, we do indeed find that $A\bar{B} + \bar{A}B = A \oplus B$. In the same way all the other equivalences indicated in Eq. (1.22-1) can readily be verified. In the tabulation of equivalences we have used De Morgan's theorem to write f_8 and f_{14} in two ways.

Note then that any logical function of variables can be expressed in terms of the AND and OR operations (which connect two variables) and the NOT operation (which is applied to one variable). This situation applies whether there are just two variables or more than two variables are involved. For in the case of many variables, functions are generated by the repeated application of the operations which connect two variables. Further, we may note that the AND and OR functions are especially convenient to work with because they are both commutative and associative. Altogether, then, we are not suprised to find, as will indeed turn out to be the case, that we shall generally express logical functions in terms of the AND, OR, and NOT operations.

1.23 SUFFICIENCY OF OPERATIONS

We have seen in the preceding section that the AND, OR, and NOT operations are sufficient to express any logical function. We can now go one step further and note that actually the NOT operation together with *either* the AND or the OR operation is sufficient. For as we can readily verify, the AND operation itself is expressible in terms of OR and NOT, and, alternatively, the OR operation is expressible in terms of AND and NOT.

We have

$$AB = \overline{\bar{A} + \bar{B}} \tag{1.23-2}$$

On the left side we have used the AND operation, and on the right side we have used OR and NOT. Similarly we have

$$A + B = \overline{\bar{A}\bar{B}} \tag{1.23-3}$$

in which we have replaced an OR operation with an AND operation and a NOT operation. Equations (1.23-2) and (1.23-3) are recognized as simply applications of De Morgan's theorem.

In spite of the fact that we can dispense with either the AND or the OR operations, for the sake of simplicity, we generally shall not do so.

1.24 SUFFICIENCY OF NAND; SUFFICIENCY OF NOR

Having noted above the sufficiency of the combination NOT and AND and of the combination NOT and OR, we now note further that the NAND operation by itself is sufficient and that, similarly, the NOR operation by itself is also sufficient. That such is indeed the case is readily established. Consider, say, the NAND function. We have

$$A \uparrow A = \overline{AA} = \bar{A} \tag{1.24-1}$$

and
$$(A \uparrow A) \uparrow (B \uparrow B) = \overline{\overline{AA}\,\overline{BB}} = \overline{\bar{A}\bar{B}} = A + B \tag{1.24-2}$$

we thus observe from Eq. (1.24-1) that if we apply the variable A to both inputs of a two-input NAND gate, the gate will yield $\bar{A}$; that is, the NAND operation can be used to perform the NOT operation on a single variable A. Again, we observe from Eq. (1.24-2) that the repeated application of the NAND operation will allow us to form the function $A + B$. [The rightmost equality in Eq. (1.24-2) is an application of De Morgan's theorem.]

Altogether, then, we note that the NAND operation can replace both the NOT and the OR operation. We also noted earlier that the combination of NOT and OR is sufficient to generate all functions. Hence, it follows that the NAND operation by *itself* is sufficient. In a similar way, we can establish as well the sufficiency of the NOR operation.

It is often a practical convenience to be able to design a logic circuit using only a single type of gate. NOR and NAND gates are suitable for this purpose because, as we have seen, NAND and NOR gates have the property of sufficiency, so that any required logical operation can be realized with an array of identical gates. However, logical design with NAND or with NOR gates is inconvenient at best. This inconvenience results from the fact, noted above, that neither the NAND nor the NOR operation is associative. Accordingly, in designing gate structures, the usual procedure is to design using the AND, OR, and NOT operations. Thereafter the completed gate structure is transformed into an equivalent structure using only NAND or only NOR gates as required. The procedure for effecting this transformation is quite simple and is presented in Sec. 2.7.

1.25 EXAMPLES OF APPLICATION OF BOOLEAN ALGEBRAIC THEOREMS

We have introduced the concept of a logical variable and the concept of a function of one variable and of two variables. A logical functional operation joining two variables, such as the AND, the OR function, etc., is often referred to as *connectives*. Functions of more than two variables are formed by repeated application of these two-variable connectives.

We shall often encounter a boolean algebraic expression which is susceptible to simplification by the application of the boolean theorems [Eqs. (1.15-2) to (1.15-11)] by virtue of the fact, noted in Sec. 1.22, that the various logical operations can be expressed in terms of each other and that certain of the operations are commutative or associative or both.

In this section we present an array of examples of such simplifications. The example will be worked out on the left side while the theorem, the principle, or other justification for the procedure will be stated on the right. We need to avoid confusion between the symbols used in the example and the symbols used to express a theorem, etc. For this reason we shall use capital letters at the beginning of the alphabet (A, B, C, etc.) to express the theorems, etc., and in the examples we shall use lowercase letters at the end of the alphabet ($\ldots, x, y, z$).

Example 1.25-1 Simplify $w = xy + \overline{yx}\,z$.

$w = xy + \overline{xy}\,z$ $AB = BA$ (commutativity of AND)

Let $v = xy$;   The function of logical variables is itself a variable

then $\bar{v} = \bar{x}\bar{y}$

and $w = v + \bar{v}z$

$\qquad = v + z = xy + z$ $A + \bar{A}B = A + B$ [Eq. (1.15-8a)]

Observe incidentally that while $\overline{xy}$ is the complement of xy, as noted above, $\bar{x}\bar{y}$ is *not* the complement of xy.

Example 1.25-2 Simplify $w = x(\bar{x} + y)$.

$w = x(\bar{x} + y) = xy$ $A(\bar{A} + B) = AB$ [Eq. (1.15-8b)]

or alternatively

$$w = x(\bar{x} + y) = x\bar{x} + xy \qquad A(B + C) = AB + AC \quad [\text{Eq. } (1.15\text{-}9b)]$$
$$= 0 + xy \qquad A\bar{A} = 0$$
$$= xy \qquad A + 0 = A$$

Example 1.25-3 Simplify $w = \bar{x}(x + y) + \bar{z} + zy$.

$\bar{x}(x + y) + \bar{z} + zy = \bar{x}(x + y) + \bar{z} + y \quad A + \bar{A}B = A + B \quad [\text{Eq. } (1.15\text{-}8a)]$;
$\qquad\qquad A$ is identified here with $\bar{z}$,
$\qquad\qquad$ so that $\bar{A} = z$

$= \bar{x}x + \bar{x}y + \bar{z} + y = \bar{x}y + \bar{z} + y \quad A(B + C) = AB + AC \ (1.15\text{-}9b)$
$\qquad\qquad$ and $\ \bar{\bar{A}}A = A\bar{A} = 0$

$= y + \bar{x}y + \bar{z} = y + y\bar{x} + z \quad A + B = B + A ; AB = BA$
$\qquad\qquad$ (commutativity of OR and AND)

$= y + \bar{z} \qquad\qquad A + AB = A \ (1.15\text{-}6a)$

The following examples illustrate the use of De Morgan's theorem.

Example 1.25-4 Simplify $v = \overline{w + w\bar{x} + yz}$.

$\overline{w + w\bar{x} + yz} = \bar{w} \cdot \overline{w\bar{x}} \cdot \overline{yz} \quad$ De Morgan's theorem $\quad [\text{Eq. } (1.16\text{-}2)]$

$= \bar{w}(\bar{w} + \bar{\bar{x}})(\bar{y} + \bar{z}) \qquad$ De Morgan's theorem again

$= \bar{w}(\bar{w} + x)(\bar{y} + \bar{z}) \qquad \bar{\bar{A}} = A \ [\text{Eq. } (1.15\text{-}1)]$

$= \bar{w}(\bar{y} + \bar{z}) \qquad A(A + B) = A \ [\text{Eq. } (1.15\text{-}6b)]; A = \bar{w}, \bar{A} = w$

Alternatively, some simplification may be effected before the application of De Morgan's theorem. In such case we have

$\overline{w + w\bar{x} + yz} = \overline{w + yz} \qquad A + AB = A \ [\text{Eq. } (1.15\text{-}6b)]$

$\overline{w + yz} = \bar{w} \cdot \overline{yz} \qquad$ De Morgan's theorem $[\text{Eq. } (1.16\text{-}2)]$

$\qquad = \bar{w}(\bar{y} + \bar{z}) \qquad$ De Morgan's theorem again

Example 1.25-5 Simplify $v = \overline{w[(x + y(z + \bar{w})]}$.

$\overline{w[(x + y(z + \bar{w})]} = \bar{w} + \overline{x + y(z + \bar{w})}$ De Morgan's theorem $[\text{Eq. } (1.16\text{-}1)]$

$= \bar{w} + \bar{x} \cdot \overline{y(z + \bar{w})} \qquad$ De Morgan's theorem again
$\qquad\qquad\qquad [\text{Eq. } (1.16\text{-}2)]$

$= \bar{w} + \bar{x}(\bar{y} + \overline{z + \bar{w}}) \qquad$ Again

$= \bar{w} + \bar{x}(\bar{y} + \bar{z}w) \qquad$ Again and $\bar{\bar{A}} = A$

$= \bar{w} + \bar{x}\bar{y} + \bar{x}\bar{z}w \qquad A(B + C) = AB + AC$
$\qquad\qquad\qquad [\text{Eq. } (1.15\text{-}9b)]$

$= \bar{w} + \bar{x}\bar{y} + \bar{x}\bar{z} \qquad A + \bar{A}B = A + B$
$\qquad\qquad\qquad [\text{Eq. } (1.15\text{-}8a)]; A = \bar{w}, \bar{A} = w$

We can factor $\bar{x}$ from the last two terms, leading to an alternative if not simpler expression

$$\bar{w} + \bar{x}\bar{y} + \bar{x}\bar{z} = \bar{w} + \bar{x}(\bar{y} + \bar{z}) \quad AB + AC = A(B + C) \quad [\text{Eq. } (1.15\text{-}9b)]$$

The following example illustrates the use of the theorem of Eq. (1.15-11). Note in Eq. (1.15-11a) that the terms on the two sides of the equation are identical except that the BC term (which is the product of the coefficients of A and $\bar{A}$) may be added or deleted as we please. A corresponding comment applies to the factor $B + C$ in Eq. (1.15-11b).

Example 1.25-6 Simplify $v = wx + x\bar{y} + yz + x\bar{z}$.

$v = wx + x\bar{y} + yz + x\bar{z} + xy$ From Eq. (1.15-11a); since we have the terms xy and $x\bar{z}$, we can add the term xy

$= wx + x(\bar{y} + y) + yz + x\bar{z}$ Factoring x from the second and fifth terms as allowed by $AB + AC = A(B + C)$ [Eq. (1.15-9b)]

$= wx + x + yz + x\bar{z}$ $\bar{A} + A = 1$ [Eq. (1.15-5a)]   and $A \cdot 1 = A$ [Eq. (1.15-2b)]

$= x + yz + x\bar{z}$ $A + AB = A$ [Eq. (1.15-6a)]

$= x + yz$ $A + AB = A$

Example 1.25-7 Simplify $v = (w + x + y)(w + \bar{x} + y)(\bar{y} + z)(w + z)$.

$v = (w + y)(\bar{y} + z)(w + z)$ From Eq. (1.15-7b) applied to first two factors in v; $A = w + y$, $B = x$

$= (w + y)(\bar{y} + z)$ From Eq. (1.15-11b)

1.26 ADDITIONAL EXAMPLES

This section gives some additional examples showing how relatively involved statements and conditions can be expressed as boolean algebraic expressions. We then use the theorems of boolean algebra to find equivalent simpler statements, thereby illustrating how the concept of the logical variable and its associated algebra is used, in effect, to perform a process of logical reasoning.

Example 1.26-1 A student consults the university bulletin and finds that she may enroll in a particular course in electronics only if she satisfies the following conditions:

1. She has completed at least 60 credits and is an engineering student in good standing.
2. Or she has completed at least 60 credits and is an engineering student and has departmental approval.
3. Or she has completed fewer than 60 credits and is an engineering student on probation.
4. Or she is in good standing and has departmental approval.
5. Or she is an engineering student and does not have departmental approval.

Find a simpler equivalent statement which will spell out the student's eligibility to take the course.

SOLUTION We introduce logical variables w, x, y, z, and v to represent the statements as follows:

w = student has completed at least 60 credits
x = student is an engineering student
y = student is in good standing
z = student has departmental approval
v = student is eligible to take the course

Thus, by way of example, $y = $ T (true) or $y = 1$ represents the proposition that it is true that the student is in good standing. Correspondingly, $\bar{y} = 1$ or $y = 0$ represent the proposition that the student is on probation, etc. When the variables w, x, y, and z assume such values that $v = $ true, the student is eligible to take the course. Then we can write the entire specification in the logical algebraic equation

$$v = wxy + wxz + \bar{w}x\bar{y} + yz + x\bar{z} \qquad (1.26\text{-}1)$$

If, say, condition 1 is satisfied, that is, $w = 1$ and $x = 1$ and $y = 1$ simultaneously, then the first term wxy in Eq. (1.26-1) is $wxy = 1$, and consequently $v = 1$ independently of the logical values of the remaining terms in Eq. (1.26-1). The terms in Eq. (1.26-1) are joined by the OR operation corresponding to the word "or" in the original specification of the conditions.

Simplification proceeds as follows:

$v = wxy + \bar{w}x\bar{y} + yz + x(\bar{z} + zw)$ Factor x from second and fifth terms
$\quad = wxy + \bar{w}x\bar{y} + yz + x(\bar{z} + w)$ From Eq. (1.15-8a)
$\quad = wxy + \bar{w}x\bar{y} + yz + x\bar{z} + wx$ From Eq. (1.15-6b)
$\quad = wx(y + 1) + \bar{w}x\bar{y} + yz + x\bar{z}$ Factor wx from first and last term
$\quad = wx + \bar{w}x\bar{y} + yz + x\bar{z}$ $A + 1 = 1$, $A \cdot 1 = A$
$\quad = x(w + \bar{w}\bar{y}) + yz + x\bar{z}$ Factor x from first and second terms
$\quad = x(w + \bar{y}) + yz + x\bar{z}$ From Eq. (1.15-8a)
$\quad = xw + x\bar{y} + yz + x\bar{z}$ From Eq. (1.15-6b)

The resultant expression is now identical to the expression in Example 1.25-6, so that we have finally

$$v = x + yz \qquad (1.26\text{-}2)$$

That is, the student is eligible ($v = 1$) if she is an engineering student ($x = 1$) or if she is simultaneously in good standing and has department approval ($y = z = 1$).

Example 1.26-2 There are five books on a shelf v, w, x, y, and z. You are instructed to select from among them in such manner that your selection satisfies all the following conditions:

1. Select v or w or both.
2. Select x or z but not both.
3. Select either v and z together or make a selection which includes neither of these.
4. If you select y, you must select z as well.
5. If you select w, you must select both v and y.

We let the variables v, w, x, y, and z (which we have used to name the books) represent, as well, the propositions "the book v is selected," "the book w is selected," etc. Also allow u to represent the proposition that the selection made meets all requirements. Then, as we shall verify, the logical relationship between the variables is

$$u = (v + w)(x \oplus z)\overline{(v \oplus z)}(y \supset z)(w \supset vy) \qquad (1.26\text{-}3)$$

Each of the expressions in the individual parenthesis refers to one of the above conditions. Since the problem requires that all the conditions be satisfied simultaneously, these expressions are ANDed together. The first parenthesis involves the INCLUSIVE-OR as specified by condition 1, while the second parenthesis involves the EXCLUSIVE-OR, as specified in 2. The EXCLUSIVE-OR connection between two variables requires selection of one or the other but not both and also not neither. Correspondingly, the complement of the EXCLUSIVE-OR requires the selection of both or neither of the two. This connection is precisely what is specified in condition 3 for books v and z. Hence the third parenthesis in Eq. (1.26-3) is $\overline{v \oplus z}$. Condition 4 specifies that the selection of y *implies* that z must be selected, that is, $y \supset z$, and finally condition 5 requires that w implies both v and y, that is, $w \supset vy$.

To allow us to manipulate Eq. (1.26-3) conveniently we rewrite the equation using only the operations AND, OR, and NOT. From Table 1.18-1 and Eq. 1.22-1 we find that

$$u = (v + w)(x\bar{z} + \bar{x}z)(vz + \bar{v}\bar{z})(\bar{y} + z)(\bar{w} + vy) \qquad (1.26\text{-}4)$$

We then have

$$u = (vz + \bar{v}w\bar{z})(x\bar{z} + \bar{x}z)(\bar{y} + z)(\bar{w} + vy)$$

Multiplying first and third parenthesis and using $AA = A$, $A\bar{A} = 0$, and $A + AB = A$

$$= (v\bar{w}z + vyz)(x\bar{y}\bar{z} + \bar{x}\bar{y}z + \bar{x}z)$$

Multiplying first and fourth parenthesis immediately above and also by multiplying the second and third parenthesis; using again $AA = A$, $A\bar{A} = 0$

$$= v\bar{w}\bar{x}\bar{y}z + v\bar{w}\bar{x}z + v\bar{x}yz$$

Multiplying parenthesis and using again $AA = A$, $A\bar{A} = 0$

$$= v\bar{x}z(\bar{w}\bar{y} + \bar{w} + y)$$

Factoring the common factor as allowed by $AB + AC = A(B + C)$ [Eq. (1.15-9b)]

$$= v\bar{x}z(\bar{w} + y)$$

$A + AB = A$ [Eq. (1.15-6a)]

We would read the result $u = v\bar{x}z(\bar{w} + y)$ as follows: you must select v and z and reject x and, at the same time, if you select $\bar{w}$, you must select y. (If you reject w, you may select or reject y as you please.) Alternatively, we can write the result as $u = v\bar{x}z\bar{w} + v\bar{x}zy$. In words, you can select v and z, rejecting x and w (y optional), or else you can select v, z, and y, rejecting x(w optional).

1.27 LOGIC DIAGRAMS

There is an easy correspondence between a logical expression and a diagram of logical gates. By way of example, consider the expression for u given in Eq. (1.26-4). A structure of gates which generates the logical function u from the variables v, w, x, y, and z is shown in Fig. 1.27-1. Here we have used AND gates, OR gates, and logical inversion represented by the open circles affixed to gates. In each case the functions or variables input to a gate or output from a gate are specified. The three gates marked 2, 3, and 4 together generate $x \oplus z$ ($= x\bar{z} + \bar{x}z$). Hence these three gates could have been replaced by a single

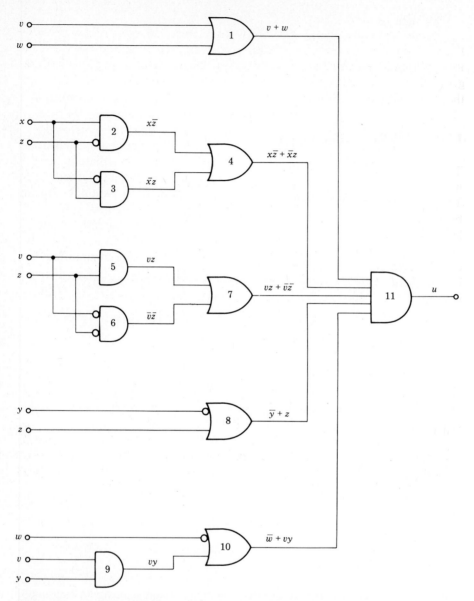

Figure 1.27-1 The logic diagram of a gate structure which generates the function $u = (v + w)$ $(x\bar{z} + \bar{x}z)$ $(vz + \bar{v}\,\bar{z})$ $(\bar{y} + z)$ $(\bar{w} + vy)$

EXCLUSIVE-OR gate whose symbol is given in Fig. 1.19-1. The output $vz + \bar{v}\bar{z}$ of gate 7 is, as noted in the previous section, $vz + \bar{v}\bar{z} = \overline{v \oplus z}$. Hence gates 5, 6, and 7 could have been replaced by an EXCLUSIVE-NOR gate, the symbol for which is an EXCLUSIVE-OR gate with an appended inversion circle at the output. Gates 8 and 10 perform the implication function, for which there is no special symbol.

Rather generally, logical functions of variables are expressed in terms of the AND, the OR, and the NOT operations with an occasional appearance of the EXCLUSIVE-OR or EXCLUSIVE-NOR operation. In the same way, gate structures generally use AND and OR gates and inverters, with an occasional appearance of the EXCLUSIVE-OR or NOR.

1.28 NUMERICAL CODES

The binary number system, i.e., the binary numerical code, has the merit that its digits fall into an exact correspondence with the values of a logical variable. The binary code has the disadvantage that a numerical magnitude written out in binary code generally requires more than 3 times as many digits as the equivalent decimal number. This inconvenience can be circumvented, as required, by employing the octal or hexadecimal code. A second disadvantage of the binary code is apparent when we contemplate conversions, back and forth, between binary and decimal code. The conversions are relatively complicated because, in general, *every* binary digit may have an effect on *each* decimal digit and vice versa. When it is important to remedy this matter, the binary-coded decimal (BCD) system of number representation may be used.

Binary-Coded Decimal

In the BCD system four binary digits A, B, C, D are used to represent the decimal digits 0 to 9 in the manner indicated in Table 1.28-1. These binary representations for single-decimal digits are observed to be the same as those we have already encountered. When we have a multidigit decimal number, there is a one-to-one correspondence between the *individual* decimal digits and the binary group $ABCD$. Thus, for example, the decimal number 9603 compared with its BCD equivalent appears as

$$
\begin{array}{cccc}
9 & 6 & 0 & 3 \\
\underbrace{1001} & \underbrace{0110} & \underbrace{0000} & \underbrace{0011}
\end{array}
$$

Table 1.28-1 BCD representations of the decimal digits

Decimal digit	BCD				Decimal digit	BCD			
	A	B	C	D		A	B	C	D
0	0	0	0	0	5	0	1	0	1
1	0	0	0	1	6	0	1	1	0
2	0	0	1	0	7	0	1	1	1
3	0	0	1	1	8	1	0	0	0
4	0	1	0	0	9	1	0	0	1

Hence in converting from decimal to binary we need look at only one decimal digit at a time, and in converting the other way we need only examine four binary digits at a time. One disadvantage of the BCD code is that, of the sixteen combinations possible with four digits, only ten are used. As a consequence, a BCD number uses more digits than the equivalent number written out in straight binary. A second disadvantage appears when we try to do arithmetic with BCD numbers (see Sec. 5.14).

Reflected Code

A second code we shall have occasion to use is called a *reflected code*. Its development is shown in Fig. 1.28-2. In Fig. 1.28-2*a* we have set down the first two binary numbers. In Fig. 1.28-2*b* we have located a "mirror" under these two numbers and set down, as well, the "reflection" of these numbers in the mirror. In Fig. 1.28-2*c*, to make four individual numbers we have prefixed a 0 to the numbers above the mirror and a 1 to the reflections. In Fig. 1.28-2*d* we have used the mirror again, and finally in Fig. 1.28-2*e* we have made eight different numbers by prefixing a 0 or a 1 as before. Repeating the development once more would yield 16 numbers, etc.

This reflected code has two distinctive features: (1) each number representation differs in only *one* digit from the next smaller and from the next larger number, and (2) at each point in the development of the code the first number and the last number again differ in only a single digit. One application of this reflected code is considered in Prob 1.27-1. We shall also have occasion to refer to this code in the next chapter.

				Decimal equivalent	
0	0	00	00	000	0
1	1 Mirror	01	01	001	1
	1	11	11	011	2
	0	10	10 Mirror	010	3
(*a*)	(*b*)	(*c*)	10	110	4
			11	111	5
			01	101	6
			00	100	7
			(*d*)	(*e*)	

Figure 1.28-2 The development of the reflected code.

1.29 NOMENCLATURE

The possible values of a logical variable, which may or may not stand for the numerical digits of the binary system, are called *binary digits*, abbreviated *bits*. An array or group of such bits which together convey an item of information is called a *word*. For reasons that will become abundantly clear there is an advantage in arranging for words to consist of a number of bits which is a power of 2, and quite generally this practice is applied in digital systems.

A group of 4 bits is called a *nybble*, and a group of 8 bits is called a *byte*. If it happens that the nybble or the byte conveys a complete item of information, then that nybble or byte is also a word. A 32-bit word or a 16-bit word may be referred to as a 4-byte word or 2-byte word, respectively.

1.30 DATA CODES

Strings of bits, i.e., words, may be used to stand for data and information generally, not only to represent numbers. All that is required is that there be an understanding, i.e., a code known to the data generator and the data receiver. A code widely used for the transmission of decimal digits, letters of the alphabet, punctuation marks, and instructions to a teletypewriter is the ASCII code (American Standard Code for Information Interchange). The code uses 7 bits, so that $2^7 = 128$ different items of information can be transmitted. The code is given in Appendix A.

Parity Bit

Frequently, an eighth bit is added to the 7-bit ASCII code, thereby rounding out the code word to a full byte. In many cases, if this bit were not added, its place would be wasted since most digital systems handle data in units of full bytes. This extra bit can be used effectively to assign to the byte a *parity*. A byte has odd or even parity depending on whether the number of 1s in the byte is odd or even. Thus, the byte 10000011 has odd parity and 10000001 has even parity. In the 8-bit ASCII code, the extra bit, taken to be the leftmost (the bit which would be of most numerical significance if the word represented a number) is selected to provide odd parity. Thus, the letter S in the 8-bit odd parity code becomes 1101 0011, and in the 7-bit code is 101 0011.

The establishment of a parity is of advantage whenever words have to be transmitted from one point to another and there is a possibility that random and unpredictable disturbance may cause an error in transmission, so that a transmitted 0 is received as a 1 or a 1 received as a 0. However, if a single received bit is in error, we shall find the parity in error and we shall be alerted to take some corrective action. If 2 bits or any even number of bits are in error, we shall not detect an error at all, and if a parity change occurs, we cannot really be sure whether the number of bit errors is one or any other odd number. A practical fact, however, is that any respectable transmission facility will have a very low probability of error in the first place. Thus, suppose that the probability of a bit error is 1 part in 10^4. Then the probability of two bit errors is 1 in 10^8. A system which detects the 1 in 10^4 error, even if it misses or misinterprets the 1 in 10^8 errors and errors of substantially lower likelihood, is well worthwhile.

LOGICAL FUNCTIONS

In Chap. 1 we introduced the concepts of a logical variable and functions of a logical variable. We also developed some theorems of boolean algebra which we were then able to use to simplify boolean algebraic expressions. The process by which we achieved such simplification was less than completely satisfactory since it depended on our ability to recognize what theorems might be used effectively and then to recognize how best to use them. More generally systematic and effective procedures for effecting simplifications are the subject of this chapter. Especially useful in this connection is the Karnaugh map.

2.1 STANDARD FORMS FOR LOGICAL FUNCTIONS: THE STANDARD SUM OF PRODUCTS

With a view toward developing a procedure for simplifying functions, we introduce two *standard forms* in which logical functions can be expressed. The first is the *standard sum-of-products* form, illustrated in the following examples. The second is the *standard product of sums*, which will be discussed beginning in Sec. 2.2.

First, as we shall now see, by example, any logical function can be written as a *sum of products*.

Example 2.1-1 Given the logical function of four variables

$$f(A,B,C,D) = (\bar{A} + BC)(B + \bar{C}D) \qquad (2.1\text{-}1)$$

express the function as a sum of products.

SOLUTION We use the distributive law [Eq. (1.15-9b)], which allows us to remove a parenthesis by multiplying through as in ordinary algebra, and we find

$$f(A,B,C,D) = \bar{A}(B + \bar{C}D) + BC(B + \bar{C}D) \qquad (2.1\text{-}2)$$

$$= \bar{A}B + \bar{A}\bar{C}D + BBC + BC\bar{C}D \qquad (2.1\text{-}3)$$

$$= \bar{A}B + \bar{A}\bar{C}D + BC \qquad (2.1\text{-}4)$$

Since, as given by the theorem in Eq. (1.15-4b), $BB = B$, and since $C\bar{C} = 0$, as given by the theorem in Eq. (1.15-5b), we note in Eq. (2.1-4) that f is expressed as a sum of terms and each of the terms is a product of the individual logical variables, which appear complemented in some cases and not complemented in others.

Example 2.1-2 Given the logical function of five variables

$$f(A,B,C,D,E) = (A + \overline{BC})(\overline{D + BE}) \qquad (2.1\text{-}5)$$

express the function as a sum of products.

SOLUTION We use De Morgan's theorem [Eqs. (1.16-1) and (1.16-2)] and the distributive law to find

$$f(A,B,C,D,E) = (A + \overline{BC})(\overline{D + BE}) \qquad (2.1\text{-}6)$$

$$= (A + \bar{B} + \bar{C})[\bar{D}(\overline{BE})] \qquad (2.1\text{-}7)$$

$$= (A + \bar{B} + \bar{C})[\bar{D}(\bar{B} + \bar{E})] \qquad (2.1\text{-}8)$$

$$= (A + \bar{B} + \bar{C})(\bar{B}\bar{D} + \bar{D}\bar{E}) \qquad (2.1\text{-}9)$$

$$= A\bar{B}\bar{D} + A\bar{D}\bar{E} + \bar{B}\bar{D} + \bar{B}\bar{D}\bar{E}$$
$$+ \bar{B}\bar{C}\bar{D} + \bar{C}\bar{D}\bar{E} \qquad (2.1\text{-}10)$$

Again, as in the previous example, the function appears as a sum of products.

These examples indicate how an arbitrary logical expression can be written as a sum of products. If only individual variables appear complemented, as in the first example, we need only use the distributive law. If a complement sign appears over a combination of variables, as in the second example, we shall need to use De Morgan's theorem as often as is necessary until the complement sign appears only over single variables. In any event, it is always possible to write a logical expression as a simple sum of terms where each term is a product of some combination of variables, some complemented, some not. The same variable need never appear twice in a product. For if such a repetition of a variable or complemented variable should develop in the course of multiplying out, we can eliminate the repetition through the use of the theorem $AA = A$ or $\bar{A}\bar{A} = \bar{A}$. If, on the other hand, we find the term $A\bar{A}$ in a product, the entire term can be discarded since $A\bar{A} = 0$.

We notice that in the sum-of-products expressions of Eqs. (2.1-4) and (2.1-10) the individual terms do not all involve the same number of variables and, as happens in these particular examples, no term involves all the variables. A further standardization can be effected which leads to an expression in which *all* terms do involve *all* the variables (complemented or uncomplemented). Such a further standardization is illustrated in the following example.

Example 2.1-3 Consider the logical function of three variables

$$f(A,B,C) = A + BC \qquad (2.1\text{-}11)$$

This function is already in the form of a sum-of-products although the first product term A is a term of just a single factor. Rewrite Eq. (2.1-11) so that it becomes an expression in which all three variables appear in each product term.

SOLUTION In the first term of Eq. (2.1-11) neither the variable B nor C appears. We therefore multiply this term by $(B + \bar{B})(C + \bar{C})$. This operation does not change the logical value of the function since $B + \bar{B} = C + \bar{C} = 1$, as noted in Eq. (1.15-5a). Similarly, since the second term does not include the variable A, we multiply this term by $A + \bar{A}$. We then have

$$f(A,B,C) = A(B + \bar{B})(C + \bar{C}) + (A + \bar{A})BC \qquad (2.1\text{-}12)$$

Multiplying through, i.e., using the distributive law, we have

$$f(A,B,C) = ABC + AB\bar{C} + A\bar{B}C + A\bar{B}\bar{C} + ABC + \bar{A}BC \quad (2.1\text{-}13)$$

We note that the term ABC appears twice in Eq. (2.1-13). Since $ABC + ABC = ABC$, we drop one of these terms and find finally that

$$f(A,B,C) = ABC + AB\bar{C} + A\bar{B}C + A\bar{B}\bar{C} + \bar{A}BC \qquad (2.1\text{-}14)$$

The function $f(A,B,C)$ is now in the standard sum-of-products form, "standard" indicating that *each* of the variables A, B, and C appears (sometimes complemented, sometimes not) in each of the product terms. Each such product is called a *minterm*. To be sure, the expression in Eq. (2.1-14) appears rather more complicated than the original expression in Eq. (2.1-11), but, as we shall see, the development we are pursuing will eventually lead to a very useful procedure for simplifying and minimizing logical functions.

2.2 THE STANDARD PRODUCT OF SUMS

From the principle of duality we might well imagine that a logical expression can also be written out as a *standard product of sums*. Such is indeed the case, as we shall now see. Let us consider again the functions of the preceding examples. First we shall see how to write these functions in the form of a product of sums.

Example 2.2-1 Given the logical function of four variables

$$f(A,B,C,D) = (\bar{A} + BC)(B + \bar{C}D) \qquad (2.2\text{-}1)$$

express the function as a product of sums.

SOLUTION Previously, to generate a sum of products we used the distributive law in the form given by Eq. (1.15-9b). Now we use the distributive law in its dual form of Eq. (1.15-9a), and we find

$$f(A,B,C,D) = (\bar{A} + B)(\bar{A} + C)(B + \bar{C})(B + D) \qquad (2.2\text{-}2)$$

We note in Eq. (2.2-2) that f is expressed as a product of terms, each term being a *sum* of the individual logical variables, a variable appearing sometimes complemented and sometimes not.

Example 2.2-2 Given the logical function of five variables

$$f(A,B.C,D,E) = (A + \overline{BC})(\overline{D + BE}) \qquad (2.2\text{-}3)$$

express the function as a *product of sums*.

SOLUTION As in Example 2.1-2, we must first use De Morgan's theorem to arrange that the complement sign appear only over single variables. This application of De Morgan's theorem was already carried out in the earlier example, and we therefore start with Eq. (2.1-8) of that example, which reads

$$f(A,B,C,D,E) = (A + \bar{B} + \bar{C})[\bar{D}(\bar{B} + \bar{E})] \qquad (2.2\text{-}4)$$

We want to arrange a result in which f appears as a product of sums of terms in parentheses. We now use the distributive law in the form of Eq. (1.15-9b) to find

$$f(A,B,C,D,E) = (A + \bar{B} + \bar{C})(\bar{B}\bar{D} + \bar{D}\bar{E}) \qquad (2.2\text{-}5)$$

By repeated application of the distributive law in the form of Eq. (1.15-9a) we now find

$$f(A,B,C,D,E) = (A + \bar{B} + \bar{C})(\bar{B}\bar{D} + \bar{D})(\bar{B}\bar{D} + \bar{E}) \qquad (2.2\text{-}6)$$

$$= (A + \bar{B} + \bar{C})(\bar{B} + \bar{D})(\bar{D} + \bar{D})$$
$$(\bar{B} + \bar{E})(\bar{D} + \bar{E}) \qquad (2.2\text{-}7)$$

$$= (A + \bar{B} + \bar{C})(\bar{B} + \bar{D})(\bar{D})$$
$$(\bar{B} + \bar{E})(\bar{D} + \bar{E}) \qquad (2.2\text{-}8)$$

We could have simplified Eq. (2.2-6) by recognizing that $\bar{B}\bar{D} + \bar{D} = \bar{D}$, but we have chosen not to do so because at present we are concerned with displaying simply how a particular form of logical expression is generated and are not now looking for the simplest form. In any event, we observe that in Eq. (2.2-8) we have arrived at a form in which f is expressed as a product of terms, each term being a sum of the individual variables, sometimes complemented sometimes not. In one case, to be sure, in this example, the "sum" consists of just a single variable.

In each sum a variable will appear just once, either complemented or uncomplemented. For if such a repetition of a variable should develop in the course of applying the distributive law, we can readily eliminate it since again $A + A = A$, etc. Suppose we should find in a parenthesis a variable and its complement, say $A + \bar{A}$. Then since $A + \bar{A} = 1$ and 1 added to anything else is still 1, such a parenthesis can be altogether replaced by 1 and need not be written explicitly.

As in the case of the standard sum of products, so also in the present case, the *standard* form for the product of sums is one in which *each* parenthesis contains all the variables (complemented or uncomplemented). The procedure for generating such standardization is illustrated in the following example.

Example 2.2-3 Consider the logical function of three variables

$$f(A,B,C) = A(\bar{B} + C) \tag{2.2-9}$$

This function is already in the form of a product of sums. Rewrite Eq. (2.2-9) so that it becomes an expression in which all three variables appear in each of the product terms.

SOLUTION In the sum term $(\bar{B} + C)$ the variable A (or $\bar{A}$) does not appear, while in the "sum" term A neither variable B nor C appears. Accordingly, to A we add $B\bar{B} + C\bar{C}$ while to $(\bar{B} + C)$ we add $A\bar{A}$. We can do so since $A\bar{A} = B\bar{B} = C\bar{C} = 0$. We have accordingly

$$f(A,B,C) = (A + B\bar{B} + C\bar{C})(A\bar{A} + \bar{B} + C) \tag{2.2-10}$$

We now make repeated application of the distributive law in the form of Eq. (1.15-9a) and have

$$f = (A + B\bar{B} + C)(A + B\bar{B} + \bar{C})(A + \bar{B} + C)(A + \bar{B} + C) \tag{2.2-11}$$

$$= (A + B + C)(A + \bar{B} + C)(A + B + \bar{C})(A + \bar{B} + \bar{C})$$
$$(A + \bar{B} + C)(\bar{A} + \bar{B} + C) \tag{2.2-12}$$

We observe that the term $(A + \bar{B} + C)$ is duplicated. Eliminating this duplication, as we can since $XX = X$, we have finally

$$f = (A + B + C)(A + \bar{B} + C)(A + B + \bar{C})$$
$$(A + \bar{B} + \bar{C})(\bar{A} + \bar{B} + C) \tag{2.2-13}$$

Equation (2.2-13) presents the function in the *standard* product-of-sums form in which every variable (complemented or not) appears in each parenthesis. Each such complete sum term is called a *maxterm*.

2.3 NUMBERING OF MINTERMS AND MAXTERMS

Having introduced such organization and systemization into expressions for logical functions, we shall now find it useful to introduce a scheme for assigning numbers to minterms (complete products) and maxterms (complete sums).

Consider, first, the numbering of minterms. By way of example, and to be specific, let us deal with a logical function involving three variables, A, B and C. A minterm will then involve each variable just once (complemented or uncomplemented). We now assign the binary *number* 0 to each complemented variable and the binary *number* 1 to each uncomplemented variable in the minterm. Thus suppose the minterm involves A, B, and $\bar{C}$. Then the binary numbers assigned are respectively 1, 1, and 0. Next we form the three digits into a three-digit number. This three-digit binary number is the *minterm number*. The numerical value of this three-digit number will depend, of course, on which digit is placed in the most significant numerical position, which in the position of least significant numerical position, etc. Suppose, for example, that we agree that the digit assigned to the A variable is to occupy the most significant numerical position, the B digit next, and the C variable the least significant position. Then the three-digit number would read $110 = 6$, and the minterm would be called minterm 6, represented as m_6. On the other hand, if we had arbitrarily decided to reverse the order of numerical significance, we would read $011 = 3$ and would have m_3.

We see then that we need to adopt a consistent (although it may be arbitrary) scheme for assigning numerical significances. Note, however, that the generally accepted scheme of assigning minterms is simply to agree at the outset on the order in which the variables are to be written in the minterm and to assign numerical significances in the same order. Thus suppose that our minterm involving A, B, and $\bar{C}$ is written $AB\bar{C}$ (and never $A\bar{C}B$ or $BA\bar{C}$, etc.); then the minterm is 110 and $AB\bar{C} = m_6$. If we agree to write $\bar{C}BA$ we would have $\bar{C}BA = 011 = m_3$. Other orders would yield still other minterm numbers for the same minterm.

When we deal with maxterms, the rule for assigning digits 0 and 1 is *reversed*. A complemented variable is assigned the numerical digit 1 and an uncomplemented variable is assigned the numerical digit 0. Thus the maxterm $\bar{A} + B + C$ is assigned the number $100 = 4$ and the maxterm is represented as M_4. Similarly $\bar{A} + \bar{B} + \bar{C}$ becomes M_7, etc. Of course, the comments made earlier in connection with minterms concerning an agreement about the order of the variables applies equally in the case of maxterms.

2.4 SPECIFICATION OF FUNCTIONS IN TERMS OF MINTERMS AND MAXTERMS

A logical function can be expressed most conveniently using the convention we have adopted for numbering minterms and maxterms. For example, consider the function $f(A,B,C)$ given in Eq. (2.1-14). Here the function is expressed in the standard sum-of-products form, i.e., as a sum of minterms. We rewrite Eq. (2.1-14) with a view toward putting the minterms in increasing order of minterm number and have

$$f(A,B,C) = \bar{A}BC + A\bar{B}\bar{C} + A\bar{B}C + AB\bar{C} + ABC \qquad (2.4\text{-}1)$$

$$\begin{array}{ccccc} 011 & 100 & 101 & 110 & 111 \\[4pt] 3 & 4 & 5 & 6 & 7 \end{array}$$

Under each variable we have written 0s and 1s as required, thus generating the binary representation of the minterm number, and in the third row we have replaced the binary numbers by their decimal equivalents. We can now write

$$f(A,B,C) = m_3 + m_4 + m_5 + m_6 + m_7 \qquad (2.4\text{-}2)$$

which is written more compactly as

$$f(A,B,C) = \Sigma m(3, 4, 5, 6, 7) \qquad (2.4\text{-}3)$$

or even $\qquad\qquad f(A,B,C) = \Sigma(3, 4, 5, 6, 7) \qquad\qquad (2.4\text{-}4)$

Consider next the function of Eq. (2.2-11), in which a logical function is expressed as a standard product of sums i.e., as a product of maxterms. We have

$$\begin{aligned} f(A,\,B,\,C) \\ = (A + B + C)(A + B + \bar{C})(A + \bar{B} + C)(A + \bar{B} + \bar{C})(\bar{A} + \bar{B} + C) \end{aligned} \quad (2.4\text{-}5)$$

$$\begin{array}{ccccc} 000 & 001 & 010 & 011 & 110 \\[4pt] 0 & 1 & 2 & 3 & 6 \end{array}$$

so that $\qquad\qquad f(A,B,C) = M_0 \cdot M_1 \cdot M_2 \cdot M_3 \cdot M_6 \qquad\qquad (2.4\text{-}6)$

or $\qquad\qquad f(A,B,C) = \Pi M(0, 1, 2, 3, 6) \qquad\qquad (2.4\text{-}7)$

or finally $\qquad\qquad f(A,B,C) = \Pi(0, 1, 2, 3, 6) \qquad\qquad (2.4\text{-}8)$

2.5 RELATIONSHIP BETWEEN MINTERMS, MAXTERMS, AND THE TRUTH TABLE

A logical function can be expressed in a truth table, as a sum of minterms, or as a product of maxterms. The relationships between these modes of representation are shown in Fig. 2.5-1 for an arbitrarily selected function. In the truth table each row has been assigned the number which would result if the logical entries under A, B, and C were read as binary digits.

We note that the truth table specifies in the first row (row 0) that $f = 1$ when $A = 0$, $B = 0$, and $C = 0$. If we propose to write the function as a sum of minterms, it is apparent that we can assure that $f = 1$ for $A = B = C = 0$ by including the minterm $\bar{A}\bar{B}\bar{C}$, for having included such a minterm, we are assured that $f = 1$ for $A = B = C = 0$ no matter what other terms are later added since $1 + \text{anything} = 1$. This first row, we note, bears a row number which is the

Row no.	A	B	C	$f(A, B, C)$
0	0	0	0	1
1	0	0	1	0
2	0	1	0	1
3	0	1	1	1
4	1	0	0	0
5	1	0	1	0
6	1	1	0	1
7	1	1	1	1

$$f = \bar{A}\bar{B}\bar{C} + \bar{A}B\bar{C} + \bar{A}BC + AB\bar{C} + ABC$$
$$= \Sigma(0, 2, 3, 6, 7)$$
$$= (A + B + \bar{C})(\bar{A} + B + C)(\bar{A} + B + \bar{C})$$
$$= \Pi(1, 4, 5)$$

Figure 2.5-1 A three-variable truth table. The rows have been assigned the number which would be read in each row if the logical entries were read as binary digits in the order A, B, C. The function defined by the table is expressed as a sum of minterms and as a product of maxterms.

same as the minterm number of the minterm which we must include to satisfy the specification of this first row. In the same way, we see that to satisfy the specification in the truth table that $f = 1$ in row 2 requires that we include m_2 in the standard sum of products. Altogether, it now appears that a function expressed as a sum of minterms includes precisely the minterms whose numbers are the same as the numbers of the rows in the truth table for which $f = 1$.

In the same way, it can be established that when a function is expressed as a product of maxterms, the maxterm numbers which appear are precisely the row numbers for which $f = 0$. Consider, by way of example, row 1 in the truth table of Fig. 2.5-1. To assure, as required, that $f = 0$ when $A = 0$, $B = 0$, and $C = 1$ we shall have to include the maxterm $(A + B + \bar{C})$. For, having such a maxterm, we shall be assured that $f = 0$ for $A = 0$, $B = 0$, $C = 1$ no matter what other maxterms are appended later (0 multiplied by anything $= 0$). Note that, as in the columns for the variables A and B where 0s occur in the truth table, it is necessary in the maxterm to use the variables A and B *uncomplemented*. The C variable appears complemented in the maxterm since there is a 1 in the column for the variable C.

In a truth table, rows which do not have $f = 1$ have $f = 0$ and vice versa. Each $f = 1$ generates a minterm, and each $f = 0$ generates a maxterm. Suppose that we have a function which is expressed as a sum of minterms and we want to express it instead as a product of maxterms. Then we need only include in the maxterm listing precisely those maxterms whose numbers do *not* appear in the minterm listing. For example, suppose we have a three-variable function with numbers from 0 to 7. Say we have $f = \Sigma(0, 3, 6, 7)$. Then the *same* function can also be written $f = \Pi(1, 2, 4, 5)$. Or, again, given $g = \Pi(0, 2, 6)$, we can also write $g = \Sigma(1, 3, 4, 5, 7)$.

On the other hand, suppose we want to write the *complement* of a function. In a truth table we would interchange each $f = 0$ with each $f = 1$. Correspondingly we need only replace minterms by equally numbered maxterms or vice versa. Thus given $f = \Sigma(0, 3, 6, 7)$, we have $\bar{f} = \Pi(0, 3, 6, 7)$.

In summary, then, an arbitary logical function can be written as a sum of minterms, the minterm numbers being the truth-table row numbers in which the function has the value 1. Or the function can be written as a product of maxterms, the maxterm numbers being the truth-table row numbers in which the function has the value 0.

2.6 TWO-LEVEL GATE STRUCTURES

Consider a logical function which is expressed either in the form of a sum of products or a product of sums. Since the forms need not be standard forms, the individual terms are not necessarily minterms or maxterms. When such logical forms are physically implemented with gates, the pattern of gates which results is a two-level gate structure. For example, consider the function

$$f(A,B,C) = A\bar{B}C + \bar{A}\bar{C} + \bar{A}B \qquad (2.6\text{-}1)$$

which is realized through the gate structure of Fig. 2.6-1. Each product term is generated with an AND gate, and the outputs of the AND gates are logically added by an OR gate. More generally, if a function appears as the sum of n product terms, the physical gate structure would have n AND gates and a single OR gate.

Correspondingly, a function which is expressed as a product of sums can be realized as an array of OR gates followed by a single AND gate. For example, if a function $g(A,B,C)$ were given as

$$g(A,B,C) = (\bar{A} + B + \bar{C})(\bar{A} + \bar{B})(\bar{B} + C) \qquad (2.6\text{-}2)$$

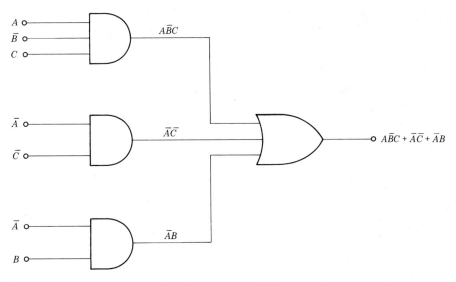

Figure 2.6-1 A gate structure which generates the function $A\bar{B}C + \bar{A}\bar{C} + \bar{A}B$.

the corresponding gate structure would appear as in Fig. 2.6-2. If the function had n sum terms, the gate structure would have n OR gates followed by a single AND gate.

Gate structures like those in Figs. 2.6-1 and 2.6-2 are called *two-level* gate structures since the influence of an input logical variable must pass through two gates before the variable can make itself felt at the output. As noted earlier, the truth values of logical variables are generally represented by electric voltages. A change in value of a variable is evidenced by a change in voltage. When such a voltage change takes place at a gate input, the effect of the change will not immediately be noted at the gate output. Instead there is a delay, called the gate *propagation delay*, between the input change and the corresponding output change if any. (Of course, not every input change will produce an output change. In a two-input AND gate, if one input is held at logic 0, the gate output will not respond to changes in the other input.) In the gate structures of Figs. 2.6-1 and 2.6-2 the delay between input-variable changes and corresponding change in the output function is the delay of *two gates*, and hence the characterization as a two-level gate structure.

Any function can be written as a sum of products or as a product of sums and can therefore be realized in the AND-OR structure (Fig. 2.6-1) or in the OR-AND structure (Fig. 2.6-2). On the other hand, if we choose to do so, we can equally well realize functions with gate structures which use more than two levels. For example, if we rewrite Eq. (2.6-1), we have

$$f(A,B,C) = A\bar{B}C + \bar{A}\bar{C} + \bar{A}B = A\bar{B}C + \bar{A}(\bar{C} + B) \qquad (2.6\text{-}3)$$

which leads directly to the realization of Fig. 2.6-3. Here we have a three-level

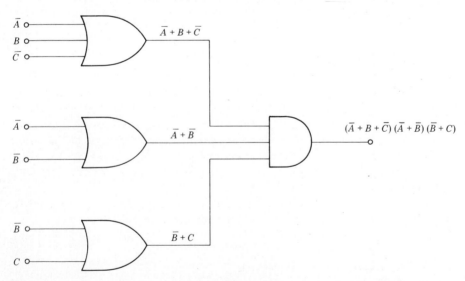

Figure 2.6-2 A gate structure which generates the function $(A + B + \bar{C})\,(\bar{A} + \bar{B})\,(\bar{B} + C)$.

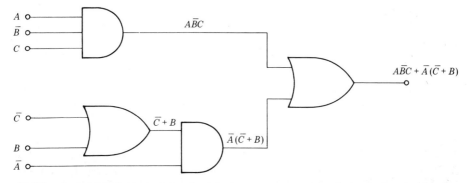

Figure 2.6-3 An alternative structure involving more than two levels which will generate the same function as that in Fig. 2.6-1.

gate structure since some of the logic variables will have to propagate through three gates. Given an involved logical function, we can, if we choose, realize it in a form which involves many levels of gates. However, as we shall see, the overall propagation delays encountered in a gate structure limit the speed with which digital operations can be performed. Therefore, rather generally, there is an interest in minimizing such delays, and except in special situations the two-level gate structure is the structure of choice.

The two-level structures of Figs. 2.6-1 and 2.6-2 can indeed generate any arbitrary function of the input variable but require, in general, that in the case of some inputs both complemented and uncomplemented variables be available. Quite frequently, but not always, as a matter of practice it turns out that when a variable is available, so is its complement. If not, inverters must be used and the propagation delay is thereby increased.

2.7 STRUCTURES USING ONE GATE TYPE

As we shall see in the next chapter, because of the way gates are made available commercially, it is often a convenience to be able to generate an arbitrary logic function using only a single type of gate. The structures of Figs. 2.6-1 and 2.6-2 do not measure up to this requirement since they require three gate types, AND, OR, and NOT. As we shall now see, there is a simple procedure for converting the structures of Figs. 2.6-1 and 2.6-2 into structures involving only NAND gates or only NOR gates.

Consider the sum-of-products expression in Eq. (2.6-1). Let us comple- ment the function twice, leaving the function unaltered. We have

$$f(A,B,C) = \overline{\overline{A\bar{B}C + \bar{A}\bar{C} + \bar{A}B}} \qquad (2.7\text{-}1)$$

Using De Morgan's theorem, we find

$$f(A,B,C) = \overline{(\overline{A\bar{B}C})(\overline{\bar{A}\bar{C}})(\overline{\bar{A}B})} \qquad (2.7\text{-}2)$$

The function $\overline{A\bar{B}C}$ can be generated by applying A, $\bar{B}$, and C to the inputs of a NAND gate, and a similar comment applies to the terms $\overline{\bar{A}\bar{C}}$ and $\overline{\bar{A}B}$. Finally the function $f(A, B, C)$ can be produced by applying the terms $\overline{A\bar{B}C}$, $\overline{\bar{A}\bar{C}}$, and $\overline{\bar{A}B}$ to still another NAND gate. Altogether the function can be generated by the two-level NAND-gate structure of Fig. 2.7-1. Observe that as a formalized matter the conversion from the two-level AND-OR structure (Fig. 2.6-1) to the NAND-NAND structure (Fig. 2.7-1) requires no change other than a replacement of *all* the gates by NAND gates.

In a similar way, we can establish that an OR-AND two-level structure can be converted into a two-level NOR-NOR structure simply by replacing *all* the gates by NOR gates. By way of example, consider the OR-NOR structure of Fig. 2.6-2. This structure is shown converted into a NOR-NOR structure in Fig. 2.7-2.

Altogether, then, if we are required to generate a function using only NAND gates, we first express the function as a sum of products. We next draw the corresponding AND-OR two-level gate structure, and finally replace all the gates by NAND gates. If we want to use only NOR gates, we start by writing the function as a product of sums, draw the corresponding OR-AND structure, and then replace all the gates by NOR gates.

A precaution must be observed when a sum of products involves a product term in which only one variable appears or when a product of sums involves a sum term in which only one variable appears. Consider, for example, that

$$f(A, B, C) = A + BC \qquad (2.7\text{-}3)$$

The AND-OR structure to generate this function is shown in Fig. 2.7-3a. If, in this case, we simply replace all the gates with NAND gates, we arrive at the gate

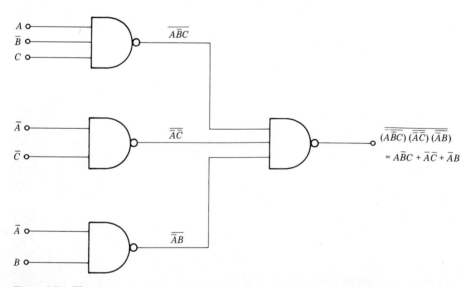

Figure 2.7-1 The NAND-NAND gate structure which generates the same function as the AND-OR structure of Fig. 2.6-1.

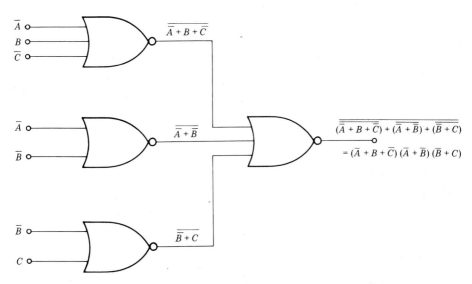

Fig. 2.7-2 The OR-NOR gate structure of Fig. 2.6-2 converted into a structure using only NOR gates.

structure in Fig. 2.7-3b, which clearly gives the wrong result. To get the correct result we must be sure that the initial AND-OR structure is in standard form; i.e., *every* input variable must be applied to an AND gate, and *all* the OR-gate inputs must come from the outputs of the AND gates. In Fig. 2.7-3c we have added an AND gate to put the structure in standard two-level form. (This added gate, of

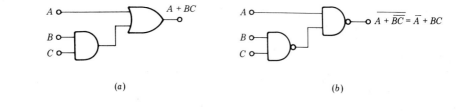

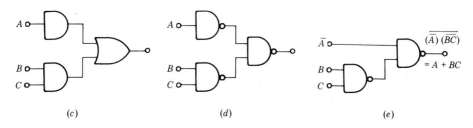

Figure 2.7-3 (*a*) An AND-OR structure which generates $A + BC$. (*b*) The structure [not equivalent to (*a*)] which results when all gates explicitly shown in (*a*) are replaced by NAND gates. (*c*) The AND-OR structure for $A + BC$ which explicitly shows two levels for every logical variable. (*d*) The correct NAND-NAND replacement for (*a*). (*e*) The one-input NAND gate deleted, and the variable A replaced by $\bar{A}$.

course, in this configuration actually does nothing.) In Fig. 2.7-3d we have replaced every gate in Fig. 2.7-3c by a NAND gate. Finally, as in Fig. 2.7-3e, we may, if we choose, delete the one-input NAND gate and compensate for this omission by replacing A by $\bar{A}$.

If we should need to provide the complement of an input variable, then again the NAND or the NOR gate can be used for this purpose. It can readily be verified that a NAND gate or a NOR gate used in the manner of Fig. 2.7-4 will provide logic inversion.

AND-OR-INVERT (AOI) Gate

Another type of gate (actually a gate structure) also available commercially which can be used exclusively to generate any logic function is the AND-OR-INVERT (AOI) gate. It consists of a number of input AND gates all of whose outputs are inputs to a single NOR gate. The NOR-gate output is the output of the AOI gate. Thus it has precisely the structure of Fig. 2.6-1 except that it has an inversion circle added at the output.

First, we can readily establish that, like the two-level AND-OR or OR-AND configurations, an AOI gate can realize any logical function provided input variables in uncomplemented and complemented form are available. We would start by writing the required function as a product of sums. Thus suppose the function were

$$f = (A + \bar{B} + C)(D + \bar{E})(\bar{F} + G) \tag{2.7-4}$$

Then we can write, using De Morgan's theorem,

$$f = \bar{\bar{f}} = \overline{\overline{(A + \bar{B} + C)(D + \bar{E})(\bar{F} + G)}} \tag{2.7-5}$$

$$= \overline{\overline{(A + B + C)} + \overline{(D + \bar{E})} + \overline{(\bar{F} + G)}} \tag{2.7-6}$$

$$= \overline{\bar{A}B\bar{C} + \bar{D}E + F\bar{G}} \tag{2.7-7}$$

which is precisely in the AND-OR-INVERT form. Next we note that because of the invert feature incorporated in the AOI gate, the gate can be used to provide complements of input variables if required. It is also readily verified that we can use an AOI gate as a NAND gate or as a NOR gate (Prob. 2.7-3) from which again we see that no other gate structure is needed to permit the realization of any function.

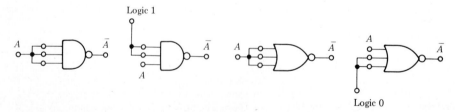

Figure 2.7-4 How the NAND gate and the NOR gate can be used as an inverter.

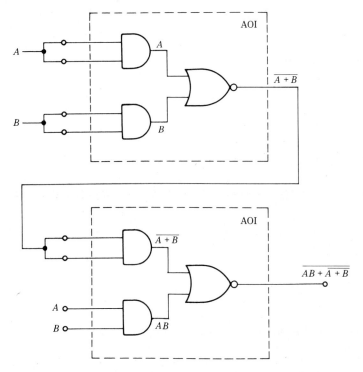

Figure 2.7-5 Two AND-OR-INVERT gates are used to generate the EXCLUSIVE-OR function.

Using AOI gates as inverters is hardly economical. With some ingenuity in algebraic manipulation we can devise a way to use the gates more effectively. As an example suppose that we have only the variables A and B and not their complements and want to generate the EXCLUSIVE-OR function $A \oplus B$. we can write

$$A \oplus B = \overline{AB} + \bar{A}\bar{B} \tag{2.7-8}$$

In this form we can generate $A \oplus B$ using three AOI gates, two of which would be used just to produce $\bar{A}$ and $\bar{B}$. Alternatively we can write

$$A \oplus B = \overline{AB + \bar{A}\bar{B}} = \overline{AB + \overline{A + B}} \tag{2.7-9}$$

In the last form the function can be realized using only two AOI gates, as shown in Fig. 2.7-5.

2.8 KARNAUGH MAPS

The Karnaugh map is an extremely useful device for the simplification and minimization of boolean algebraic expressions. In this and succeeding sections we shall discuss K maps and work examples with these maps to encourage the reader to develop some facility in their use.

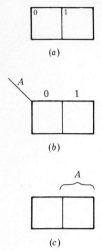

(a)

(b)

(c)

Figure 2.8-1 Three alternative schemes for identifying the boxes in a one-variable K map.

A K map is a geometrical figure which provides one region (box) for each row in a truth table. As we have noted, there is a one-to-one correspondence between truth-table rows and potential maxterms or minterms. We note as well that there is a one-to-one correspondence between K-map boxes and minterms and between such boxes and maxterms. Initially, we consider how the maps are constructed and the identification of boxes with truth-table rows, with minterms, and with maxterms, leaving for later the explanation of how the maps are used.

The K map for a single variable, say the variable A, is shown in Fig. 2.8-1. It consists simply of two adjacent boxes, corresponding to the fact that a truth table for a single variable has just two rows. Figure 2.8-1a to c shows three alternative ways in which the boxes are identified with the truth-table rows. In Fig. 2.8-1a the boxes have simply been numbered in the upper left-hand corner. The left-hand box corresponds to row 0, and the right-hand box corresponds to row 1. In Fig. 2.8-1b we have indicated the same information by noting that the left-hand box is the box corresponding to the truth-table row in which $A = 0$ and the right-hand box corresponds to the row in which $A = 1$. In Fig. 2.8-1c the understanding is that the box embraced by the bracket and labeled A is the box which corresponds to the truth-table row in which $A = 1$. In Fig. 2.8-2 we have drawn the one-variable K map and truth table side by side to show the correspondence again. In the truth table, the function $f(A)$ has been left blank to call attention to the fact that the form of the K map depends only on the

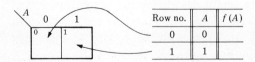

Row no.	A	$f(A)$
0	0	
1	1	

Figure 2.8-2 The correspondence between a one-variable truth table and the one-variable K map.

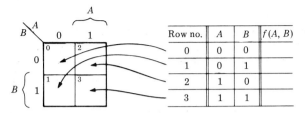

Figure 2.8-3 A two-variable truth table and its K map.

number of variables contemplated and not in any way on the boolean expression for which the map will be used.

A two-variable truth table and a two-variable K map are shown in Fig. 2.8-3. Note again the three alternative methods indicated to identify the boxes. Box 2 for, example, is not only labeled 2 but is also located at the intersection of $A = 1$ and $B = 0$, which are the entries in row 2 in the columns for A and B, respectively. Box 2 is also within the region of the A bracket and outside the region of the B bracket. An alternative two-variable K map as well as K maps for larger numbers of variables will be considered later. For the present, let us use the K map of Fig. 2.8-3 to replace a truth table.

A particular function is defined in the truth table of Fig. 2.8-4a. This same function is represented in the K map in Fig. 2.8-4b. Here we have simply entered in the boxes the 1s or 0s, as the case may be, from the corresponding row of the truth table. Since we understand that where an entry is not a 1 it is a 0 and vice versa, we can simply enter the 1s as in Fig. 2.8-4c or the 0s as in Fig. 2.8-4d. (Rather generally, in a truth table *both* 1s and 0s are entered while in a K map *either* 1s or 0s are entered. As we shall see, in reading a K map we shall want to concentrate on either the 1s or the 0s.)

As we can readily verify, the function defined in Fig. 2.8-4 is

$$f(A,B) = \bar{A}\bar{B} + AB = m_0 + m_3 \qquad (2.8\text{-}1)$$

$$= (A + \bar{B})(\bar{A} + B) = M_1 \cdot M_2 \qquad (2.8\text{-}2)$$

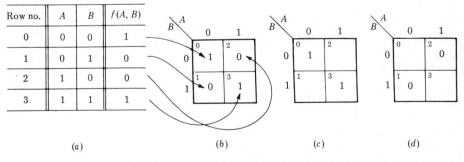

Figure 2.8-4 (*a*) A truth table defining a function. (*b*) Truth-table definition represented on a K map. (*c*) Only the 1s are entered on the map. (*d*) Only the 0s are entered on the map.

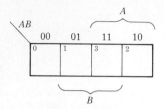

Figure 2.8-5 An alternative two-variable K map.

Thus we confirm that a function which is expressed as a sum of minterms m_0 and m_3 is represented by 1s in K-map boxes 0 and 3; i.e., box 0 is associated with m_0 and box 3 with m_3. Similarly, since the function is expressible also as the product of maxterms M_1 and M_2, we find 0s in boxes 1 and 2. Thus, if we were not given the function truth table explicitly but were given instead the minterms or maxterms, we could immediately represent the function on a K map.

A point especially to be noted in connection with entering minterms and maxterms on a K map is the following. A box in which some minterm, say m_i, is to be entered is the *same* box as the box in which maxterm M_i is to be entered. Thus if a function f has a maxterm $f = \bar{A} + B = M_2$ then a 0 is to be entered in box 2. If a (different) function g has a minterm $A\bar{B} = m_2$, then a 1 is to be entered in this *same* box.

An alternative two-variable K map is shown in Fig. 2.8-5. Note especially the ordering of the box numbers. The numbers proceed in the order 0, 1, 3, 2 rather than the natural order 0, 1, 2, 3. This pattern of ordering, as we shall see, appears as well in the K maps for larger number of variables. The purpose of this ordering will be discussed and explained below. The numbering across the top of the map, as is readily apparent, is consistent with the numbering in the boxes. In each case the left digit goes with the variable A and the right digit goes with the variable B. Observe that as we go across the top of the map from one box to the next, the two-digit numbers exhibit a change in just one or the other digit, never in both digits at the same time. This, as we shall see, is an essential feature of the ordering. Note, finally, that in the third scheme shown for identifying boxes the A bracket encompasses the boxes corresponding to $A = 1$ and the B bracket encompasses the boxes corresponding to $B = 1$.

The K map for three variables is shown in Fig. 2.8-6. Observe that, here

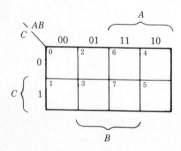

Figure 2.8-6 The K map for three variables.

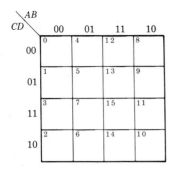

Figure 2.8-7 The K map for four variables.

again, in numbering columns we have followed the pattern of the alternative two-variable map of Fig. 2.8-5.

The K map for four variables is shown in Fig. 2.8-7. Here the ordering pattern of the map of Fig. 2.8-5 has been applied to the rows as well as the columns. In moving vertically boxes in the third row are numbered last, while in moving horizontally the third column is numbered last.

Karnaugh maps for larger numbers of variables can also be drawn. A five-variable map has $2^5 = 32$ boxes while a six-variable map has $2^6 = 64$ boxes. We shall defer drawing such maps until Sec. 2.12, and we shall turn our attention in the next section to the matter of how such maps are used to simplify logical expressions.

Before going on, however, we note (again) that there is a measure of arbitrariness in assigning variables to rows and columns of a K map and also to assigning of numerical significance to the logical variables. Thus in Fig. 2.8-7 the digit assigned to the variable A is taken to be numerically most significant, the digit assigned to B is next most significant, etc. Thus, minterm $A\bar{B}\bar{C}\bar{D}$ is assigned the number $1000 = 8$, and the minterm is m_8. We might have decided to have arranged matters otherwise. For example, if we chose to reverse the order of numerical significance, the K map would appear as in Fig. 2.8-8a. Or we

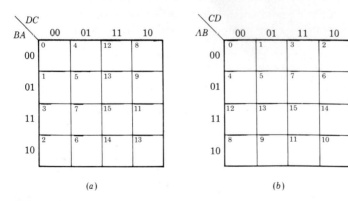

Figure 2.8-8 Showing that alternative assignments of numerical significances and association of variables with rows and columns are allowed.

might have preserved the numerical significances of Fig. 2.8-7 but decided to associate the variables A and B with the rows and C and D with the columns. In this case the K map would appear and the boxes would be numbered as in Fig. 2.8-8b. We are at liberty to make any assignment of numerical significances and any association of variables with rows and columns. What is required, of course, is that having adopted an assignment and association, we observe them consistently throughout.

2.9 SIMPLIFICATION OF LOGICAL FUNCTIONS WITH KARNAUGH MAPS

The essential feature of the K map is that adjoining boxes horizontally and vertically (but not diagonally) correspond to minterms or maxterms which differ in only a single variable. This single variable will appear complemented in one term and uncomplemented in the other. It is precisely to achieve this end that the boxes have been ordered and numbered in the way we have described. To see the benefit of this feature, consider, for example, minterms m_8 and m_{12}, which adjoin horizontally on the K map of Fig. 2.9-1. We have

$$m_8 \ (8 = 1000) = A\bar{B}\bar{C}\bar{D} \tag{2.9-1}$$

$$m_{12} \ (12 = 1100) = AB\bar{C}\bar{D} \tag{2.9-2}$$

These two minterms differ only in that the variable B appears complemented in one and uncomplemented in the other. They can be combined to yield

$$A\bar{B}\bar{C}\bar{D} + AB\bar{C}\bar{D} = A\bar{C}\bar{D}(\bar{B} + B) = A\bar{C}\bar{D} \tag{2.9-3}$$

Thus two terms, each involving four variables, have been replaced by a single term involving three variables. The variable which appeared complemented in one term and uncomplemented in the other has been eliminated. Now if the terms of Eq. (2.9-3) had appeared together with other terms in a logical function, we would eventually, by dint of comparing each term with every other, have noted that they might be combined. On the other hand, suppose that we had noted the presence of these two minterms by placing 1s in the appropriate

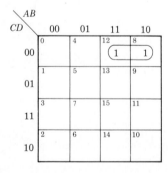

Figure 2.9-1 Minterms in adjacent boxes can be combined.

boxes of a K map, as shown in Fig. 2.9-1. Then we would have noted immediately that these minterms can be combined because the minterms correspond to *adjoining boxes*. The great merit of the K map is that it permits easy recognition through geometric visualization of combinations of minterms which can be combined into simpler expressions. The combining of minterms m_8 and m_{12} has been indicated on the K map of Fig. 2.9-1 by a line encircling the 1s in the adjacent boxes.

A general principle, then, which applies to a K map is that *any pair of adjoining minterms can be combined into a single term involving one variable fewer than do the minterms themselves*. This combined term is deduced by starting with either minterm and striking out the variable which appears complemented in one and uncomplemented in the other. Let us apply this rule to m_8 and m_{12}, which appear in Fig. 2.9-1. We note that in both these terms the variables A, C, and D are associated (by the numbering along the top and side of the map) with the *same* digits (A with 1 and C and D with 0). However, variable B is associated with 1 in minterm 12 and with 0 in minterm 8. Hence this variable is deleted. The two minterms combine into a single term in which A appears uncomplemented (since A is associated in *both* minterms with 1) and both C and D appear complemented (since these variables are associated in *both* minterms with 0). Thus

$$m_8 + m_{12} = A\bar{C}\bar{D} \qquad (2.9\text{-}4)$$

Observe that in reading the K map of Fig 2.9-1 we used the numbering along the top and side of the map. We did not explicitly use the minterm numbering in the individual boxes. When a logical function is given in terms of its minterms or equivalently its truth table, however, the minterm numbering in the boxes is very useful since it makes it easy to place the specified minterms on the map.

The four-variable map with minterms m_8 and m_{12} marked as in Fig. 2.9-1 is reproduced in Fig. 2.9-2. Here we have used the alternative scheme of identifying boxes. The two columns in which $A = 1$ are bracketed are marked A. We

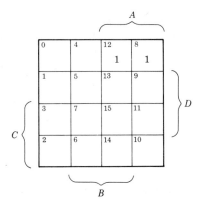

Figure 2.9-2 An alternative scheme for marking a K map.

have correspondingly bracketed and marked the two columns in which $B = 1$ and also the pairs of rows corresponding to $C = 1$ and $D = 1$.

Consider now how we would use the representation of Fig. 2.9-2 to read m_8 which appears in the map. We find that m_8 is *in* a column encompassed by the A bracket. Hence the A variable appears *uncomplemented*. We also find that m_8 is *outside* the columns encompassed by the B bracket. Hence the B variable appears *complemented*. Similarly m_8 is *outside* both the C and D bracketed rows; hence both C and D appear complemented. Altogether $m_8 = A\bar{B}\bar{C}\bar{D}$. In a similar way we would read $m_{12} = AB\bar{C}\bar{D}$.

When, now, it comes to reading the term corresponding to the *pair* m_8 and m_{12}, we proceed as follows. *Both* minterms are encompassed by A; hence A appears *uncomplemented*. *Neither* minterm is encompassed by C or by D; hence both C and D appear *complemented*. One minterm (m_{12}) is *in* the range encompassed by B while one minterm is *outside* the range of B. Hence variable B is deleted. Altogether $m_{12} + m_8 = A\bar{C}\bar{D}$.

2.10 ADDITIONAL LOGICAL ADJACENCIES

We have noted that minterms which are *geometrically* adjacent on a K map are also *logically* adjacent; i.e., the minterms differ in just a single variable. There are cases in which the boxes are not geometrically adjacent but are nonetheless logically adjacent. As can readily be verified, each box in the leftmost column is logically adjacent to the box in the rightmost column on the same row. Thus in Fig. 2.9-1 or 2.9-2 m_0 is adjacent to m_8, m_1 is adjacent to m_9, etc. Similarly, the boxes in the topmost row are adjacent to the boxes in the bottommost row, so that m_0 adjoins m_2, m_4 adjoins m_6, etc. We can visualize a geometrical as well as a logical adjacency between the left and right column by imagining the map wrapped around a vertical cylinder. We can visualize a geometrical as well as a logical adjacency between top and bottom rows by imagining the K map wrapped around a horizontal cylinder. Both left and right column adjacencies and top and bottom row adjacencies can be visualized simultaneously by imagining the K map wrapped around a doughnut.

Consider a K map with entries as in Fig. 2.10-1. As indicated by the circlings, we can combine the geometrically adjacent pairs with the result

$$m_8 + m_{12} = A\bar{C}\bar{D} \tag{2.10-1}$$

and
$$m_2 + m_3 = \bar{A}\bar{B}C \tag{2.10-2}$$

Next we can combine m_{10} with either m_8 or with m_2. Two alternative symbolisms to indicate a combining of m_{10} with m_2 are indicated in Fig. 2.10-1a and b. Using this combination of m_2 with m_{10}, we have

$$m_2 + m_{10} = \bar{B}C\bar{D} \tag{2.10-3}$$

In this case, the logical function defined in the K map is, from Eqs. (2.10-1) to (2.10-3),

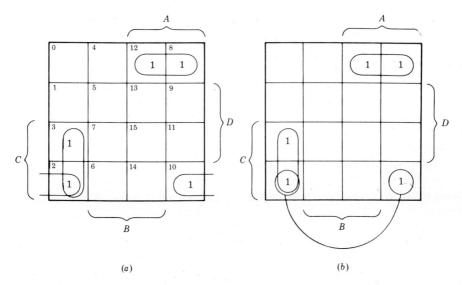

Figure 2.10-1 Alternative symbolism for indicating combinations of K-map boxes which are not geometrically adjacent.

$$f(A,B,C,D) = \Sigma m(2,3,8,10,12) = A\bar{C}D + \bar{A}\bar{B}C + \bar{B}C\bar{D} \quad (2.10\text{-}4)$$

as shown in Fig. 2.10-2. If we choose, we can combine minterm m_{10} not with m_2 but with m_8. In this case we have

$$m_8 + m_{10} = A\bar{B}\bar{D} \quad (2.10\text{-}5)$$

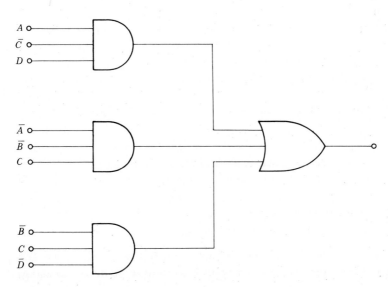

Figure 2.10-2 Implementation of the function of Eq. (2.10-4).

and from Eqs. (2.10-1), (2.10-2), and (2.10-5) we have

$$f(A,B,C,D) = \Sigma m(2,3,8,10,12) = A\bar{C}D + \bar{A}\bar{B}C + A\bar{B}\bar{D} \qquad (2.10\text{-}6)$$

Even though Eq. (2.10-6) appears to be different from Eq. (2.10-4), they are identical. If we derive truth tables for $f(A,B,C,D)$ using one equation and then the other, the tables will be identical. From the point of view of economy of hardware either result is equally acceptable. In both cases a single OR gate is required with a fan-in of 3, that is, with three inputs, and three AND gates are used, again each one with a fan-in of 3.

The following point needs a brief comment. In arriving at Eqs. (2.10-4) and (2.10-6) we have used a minterm twice in each case. In the first case, we combined m_2 with m_3 and then again combined m_2 with m_{10}. In the second case, we used m_8 twice. This repetitive use of a minterm is allowable since in using, say, m_2 twice we have simply taken advantage of the theorem of Eq. (1.15-5a), which in the present case yields

$$m_2 = \bar{A}\bar{B}C\bar{D} = \bar{A}\bar{B}C\bar{D} + \bar{A}\bar{B}C\bar{D} + \cdots \qquad (2.10\text{-}7)$$

2.11 LARGER GROUPINGS ON A K MAP

We have seen that two K-map boxes which adjoin can be combined, yielding a term from which one variable has been eliminated. In a similar way, whenever 2^n boxes adjoin, they can be combined to yield a single term from which n variables have been eliminated. Typical groups of four boxes are indicated in Fig. 2.11-1. In Fig. 2.11-1a the combinations $m_1 + m_5$ and $m_3 + m_7$ yield

$$m_1 + m_5 = \bar{A}\bar{C}D \qquad (2.11\text{-}1)$$

$$m_3 + m_7 = \bar{A}CD \qquad (2.11\text{-}2)$$

so that

$$(m_1 + m_5) + (m_3 + m_7) = \bar{A}\bar{C}D + \bar{A}CD = \bar{A}D(\bar{C} + C) = \bar{A}D \qquad (2.11\text{-}3)$$

The result would have been the same, of course, if the grouping had been made in the order $(m_1 + m_3) + (m_5 + m_7)$.

Reading the group $m_1 + m_3 + m_5 + m_7$ in a direct manner would proceed as follows. We note that all four are in boxes in columns in which $A = 0$. Hence this variable will remain in *complemented* form. In one column $B = 0$, and in one column $B = 1$. Hence the B variable is eliminated. Similarly we find that the C variable is eliminated and the D variable remains in uncomplemented form since in both rows $D = 1$.

Reading the remaining maps in Fig. 2.11-1, from Fig. 2.11-1c we have

$$f(A,B,C,D) = \Sigma m(1,5,9,13) = \bar{C}D \qquad (2.11\text{-}4)$$

since all four 1s fall in a row corresponding to $C = 0$ and $D = 1$. However the 1s are to be found in columns corresponding to $A = 0$ to $A = 1$ to $B = 0$ and to

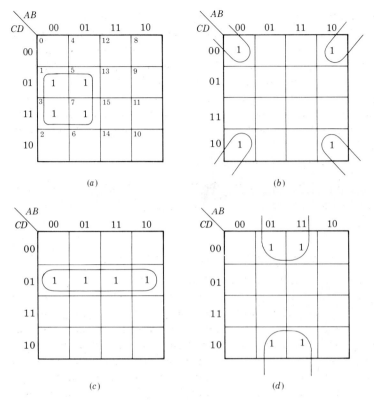

Figure 2.11-1 Representative adjacencies of four boxes.

$B = 1$. Reading Fig. 2.11-1b, we find, since the four corners are adjacent,

$$f(A,B,C,D) = \Sigma m(0,2,8,10) = \bar{B}\bar{D} \qquad (2.11\text{-}5)$$

Reading Fig. 2.11-1d, we have

$$f(A,B,C,D) = \Sigma m(4,6,12,14) = B\bar{D} \qquad (2.11\text{-}6)$$

Typical groups of eight boxes are shown in Fig. 2.11-2. In Fig. 2.11-2a we read $f = \bar{A}$ since the eight 1s lie all outside the range of the variable A but both inside and outside the ranges of all of the other variables. In Fig. 2.11-2b we read $f = \bar{D}$. In the four-variable case, sixteen 1s on a K map would mean that the function $f = 1$ independently of any variable. However, such groupings of sixteen are significant on a K map for five variables (Sec. 2.12) which has thirty-two boxes, etc.

For variety and completeness we now consider some cases in which the entries on the K map are 0s, representing maxterms, rather than 1s, representing minterms. The rule for grouping 0s is the same as for grouping 1s. The rule which determines whether or not a particular variable is eliminated remains the same in the two cases, but when a group of 0s is read, it leads to a *sum* rather

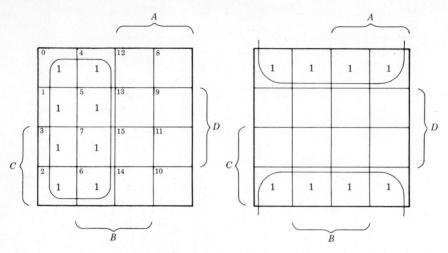

Figure 2.11-2 Representative adjacencies of eight boxes.

than a *product* of variables and the rule for determining whether or not a particular variable is to be complemented is reversed in the two cases. In Fig. 2.11-3*a* the group of two 0s is read

$$M_{11} \cdot M_{15} = \bar{A} + \bar{C} + \bar{D} \tag{2.11-7}$$

and the group of four 0s is read

$$M_0 \cdot M_1 \cdot M_4 \cdot M_5 = A + C \tag{2.11-8}$$

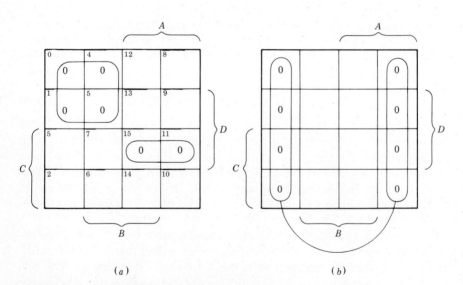

(a)　　　　　　　　　(b)

Figure 2.11-3 Representative adjacencies using 0s.

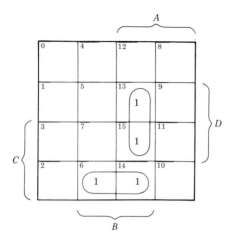

Figure 2.11-4 Minterm pairs which are physically but not logically adjacent and cannot be combined.

In Fig. 2.11-3b the group of eight 0s is read

$$M_0 \cdot M_1 \cdot M_2 \cdot M_3 \cdot M_8 \cdot M_9 \cdot M_{10} \cdot M_{11} = B \qquad (2.11\text{-}9)$$

Finally, we note the following points.

1. The number of K-map boxes which are to be read as a group must be a power of 2. That is, we may read $2^0 = 1, 2^1 = 2, 2^2 = 4, 2^3 = 8$, etc. We may not group three boxes, for example, even if they are all adjacent.
2. Suppose we have a situation as in Fig. 2.11-4. Here we have combined $m_6 + m_{14}$ and $m_{13} + m_{15}$. May we now also combine these groups of two into a single group of four? The answer is no in spite of the fact that these two groups appear to be adjacent; for one group was formed by a horizontal combination while the other group was formed by a vertical combination. Hence the variable (A) eliminated from $m_6 + m_{14} (= BC\bar{D})$ is different from the variable (C) eliminated from $m_{13} + m_{15} (= ABD)$. Hence no further combining is possible.

2.12 KARNAUGH MAPS FOR FIVE AND SIX VARIABLES

Suppose that in establishing a K map for five variables we follow the pattern which led us from the one-variable map to the four-variable map. We would then have a five-variable map, as in Fig. 2.12-1. Here we have added a variable and plotted two four-variable maps side by side. In numbering the rows and columns we have followed the reflected binary code (Sec. 1.28). This map preserves the features of the previous maps. Geometrically neighboring boxes continue to be adjoining, and, as before, the leftmost and rightmost columns continue to adjoin, as do the top and bottom rows. But now, as can be verified, boxes symmetrically located with respect to the vertical centerline

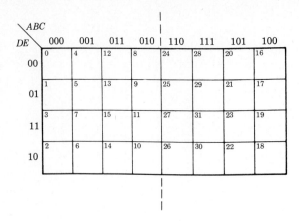

Figure 2.12-1 A possible five-variable K map.

(the dashed line in Fig. 2.12-1) also adjoin. For example m_7 adjoins m_{23}, m_{13} adjoins m_{29}, etc. Similarly, the previous adjacencies of the four-variable K map persist. Thus, m_1 and m_9 adjoin, as do m_2 and m_{10}, etc.

Since we need to take maximum possible advantage of the adjoining of minterms, the merit of the K map is precisely that it makes such adjoining minterms immediately apparent by visual inspection. Keeping these new adjoining boxes in the map of Fig. 2.12-1, it is entirely feasible to use this map as the five-variable K map. There is, however, an alternative arrangement which makes the visualization much easier. This alternative five-variable K map, the one which is rather generally used, is shown in Fig. 2.12-2 with both notations for identifying boxes. Here, all the adjacent terms previously established for the four-variable K map continue to apply both for the left-hand four-variable section corresponding to $A = 0$ and for the right-hand four-variable section corresponding to $A = 1$. In addition, however, each box in the section $A = 0$ is adjacent to the corresponding box in the section $A = 1$. For example, m_5 is adjacent to m_{21}, m_{15} adjacent to m_{31}, etc. These adjacent terms between the two sections suggest that in our mind's eye we place one section on top of the other. It is then easy to keep in mind that boxes vertically above and below each other are adjacent.

Following the same considerations which led to the five-variable map, a six-variable K map is drawn in Fig. 2.12-3. The usual adjacent terms apply within each four-variable subsection of the map. In addition there are adjacent terms horizontally and vertically between corresponding boxes in the subsection. For example, m_5 is adjacent to m_{21}; m_{63} is adjacent to m_{31} and m_{47}; etc.

The Karnaugh map has the merit of allowing visualization of adjacent terms. When the number of variables becomes large, however, say seven or more, the K map becomes so expansive that its value as an aid to recognizing adjacent terms becomes questionable. Hence, for the many-variable case, tabular procedures are preferred.

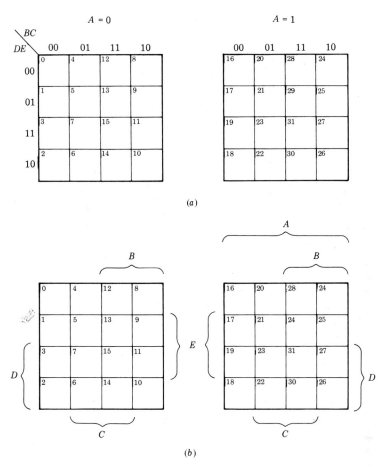

Figure 2.12-2 The more generally used five-variable K map. The two notations for identifying boxes are shown in (*a*) and (*b*).

2.13 USE OF KARNAUGH MAPS

When a logical function has been expressed in standard form in terms of its minterms, the K map can be used to simplify the function by applying the following principles:

1. The combination of boxes (minterms) which are selected must be such that each box is included at least once. As noted, however, a particular box may be involved in a number of different combinations.
2. The individual combinations should be selected to encompass as many boxes as possible so that all boxes will be included in as few different combinations as possible.

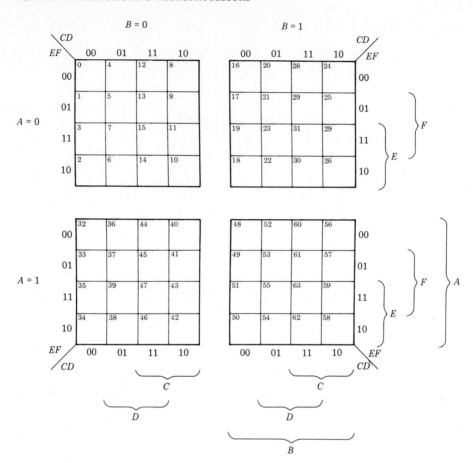

Figure 2.12-3 The K map for six variables.

The combinations are sometimes referred to as *products* and sometimes as *prime implicants*. (The reason for this terminology is presented in Prob. 2.13-1.) It may indeed turn out that it is not necessary to use all possible prime implicants to include every box at least once. In the example of Fig. 2.10-1 we saw just such a case. Here the prime implicants were $p_1 = m_2 + m_3$, $p_2 = m_8 + m_{12}$, $p_3 = m_2 + m_{10}$, and $p_4 = m_8 + m_{10}$, but the function in question could be expressed either as $f = p_1 + p_2 + p_3$ or as $f = p_1 + p_2 + p_4$. In either case we had no alternative but to use p_1 since otherwise m_3 would not be accounted for. For this reason p_1 is called an *essential* prime implicant. Similarly, p_2 is essential since, without p_2, m_{12} would not be accounted for. On the other hand, since we are at liberty to select or not to select p_3, this prime implicant is not essential. A similar comment applies to p_4.

When we have expressed a function as a sum of prime implicants, for each such implicant we shall require an AND gate. Further, the number of inputs to each such gate decreases as the number of boxes encompassed in the prime implicant increases. The economy of a gate structure is judged first of all by how few gates are involved. In different structures, with equal numbers of gates, economy is judged to be improved in the structure with the fewest total number of gate inputs.

Our preoccupation with finding prime implicants on a K map which encompass as many boxes as possible poses a potential hazard, illustrated in Fig. 2.13-1a, where we might be tempted to combine $m_5 + m_7 + m_{13} + m_{15}$ as noted by the dashed circle. If we were to do so, we would still find it necessary to add four additional prime implicants to take account of the four remaining 1s. Having done so, we would then find that all the boxes of the original combination of four have been accounted for and hence that this original combination is superfluous. The function is written out under the K map. A second, similar example is illustrated in Fig. 2.13-1b.

The following algorithm applied to a K map will lead to a minimal expression for a logical function and will avoid the hazard referred to above:

1. Encircle and accept as an essential prime implicant any box that cannot be combined with any other.
2. Identify the boxes that can be combined with a single other box in only one way. Encircle such two-box combinations. A box which can be combined into a grouping of two but can be so combined in more than one way is to be temporarily bypassed.
3. Identify the boxes that can be combined with three other boxes in only one way. If all four boxes so involved are not already covered in groupings of

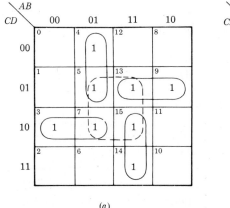

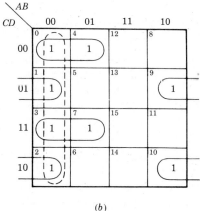

(a)   (b)

Figure 2.13-1 Two illustrations of a hazard associated with forming combinations on a K map:
(a) $f = (m_4 + m_5) + (m_3 + m_7) + (m_{14} + m_{15}) + (m_9 + m_{13})$
$\quad = \bar{A}B\bar{C} + \bar{A}CD + ABC + A\bar{C}D$
(b) $f = (m_0 + m_4) + (m_1 + m_9) + (m_3 + m_7) + (m_2 + m_{10})$
$\quad = \bar{A}\bar{C}\bar{D} + \bar{B}\bar{C}D + \bar{A}CD + \bar{B}C\bar{D}$

two, encircle these four boxes. Again, a box which can be encompassed in a group of four in more than one way is to be temporarily bypassed.
4. Repeat the preceding for groups of eight, etc.
5. After the above procedure, if there still remain some uncovered boxes, they can be combined with each other or with other already covered boxes in a rather arbitrary manner. Of course, we shall want to include these left-over boxes in as few groupings as possible.

This algorithm is illustrated in the following two examples. In the first example, the solution is completely determined by the algorithm. In the second example an easy exercise of judgment allows us to satisfy the requirements of step 5.

Example 2.13-1 A four-variable function is given as

$$f(A,B,C,D) = \Sigma\ m(1,3,5,6,9,11,12,13,15) \qquad (2.13-1)$$

Use a K map to minimize the function.

SOLUTION The K map for the function of Eq. (2.13-1) is drawn in Fig. 2.13-2a. We note that m_6 can be combined with no other box. Hence, we encircle it and accept it as an essential prime implicant. Next we note that m_0 and m_{12} can be combined in groups of two in only one way. We therefore encircle each of these groups of two, as in Fig. 2.13-2b. Other boxes which can combine in a group of two in more than one way are passed over. We then observe that m_3, m_5, and m_{15} can be incorporated into groups of four in only one way, and we note also that the groups so formed involve other boxes not all of which are incorporated in groups of two. Hence, we encircle these three groups of four as indicated in Fig. 2.13-2c. Finally, in Fig. 2.13-2d, all encirclements have been combined, and we observe that all boxes have been accounted for. Reading from this map, we find

$$f(A,B,C,D) = \bar{A}BC\bar{D} + \bar{A}\bar{B}\bar{C} + AB\bar{C} + \bar{C}D$$
$$+ \bar{B}D + AD \qquad (2.13-2)$$

Example 2.13-2 A four-variable function is given as

$$f(A,B,C,D) = \Sigma\ m(0,2,3,4,5,7,8,9,13,15) \qquad (2.13-3)$$

Use a K map to minimize the function.

SOLUTION The K map for the function of Eq. (2.13-3) is drawn in Fig. 2.13-3a. Applying steps 1 and 2 of the algorithm does not result in any selection of prime implicants. All four boxes m_5, m_7, m_{13}, and m_{15} satisfy the condition of step 3. Applying the procedure of step 3 to any one of them leads to the encirclement shown in Fig. 2.13-3b. Step 4 does not apply in the present case. We find that a number of boxes are not yet accounted for. As required by step 5, we combine them arbitrarily. It is rather obvious that the combinations indicated in Fig. 2.13-3c lead to the fewest additional

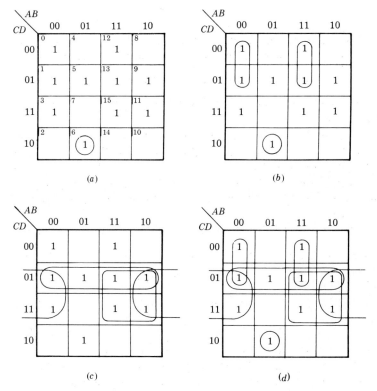

Figure 2.13-2 K map for Example 2.13-1.

prime implicants. The solution, read directly from Fig. 2.13-3c, is

$$f(A,B,C,D) = \bar{A}\bar{C}\bar{D} + \bar{A}\bar{B}C + A\bar{B}\bar{C} + BD \qquad (2.13\text{-}4)$$

For variety we now consider a problem in which a function is specified in terms of its 0s rather than its 1s, that is, in terms of its maxterms rather than its

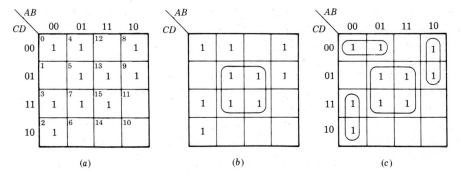

Figure 2.13-3 K map for Example 2.13-2.

minterms. In this case 0s rather than 1s are entered in the K map, and the solution appears in the form of a product of sums rather than a sum of products. The algorithm for combining minterms applies equally to maxterms, but with a change in terminology. Corresponding to the term prime implicant, defined as a product term in a sum representing a function, we have instead *prime implicate*, defined as a sum term in a product of sums.

Example 2.13-3 A four-variable function is given as

$$f(A,B,C,D) = \Pi M(0,3,4,5,6,7,11,13,14,15) \qquad (2.13\text{-}5)$$

Use a K map to minimize the function.

SOLUTION The K map is shown in Fig. 2.13-4. The algorithm leads uniquely to the groupings indicated. We then find directly from the map that

$$f(A,B,C,D) = (A + C + D)(\bar{C} + \bar{D})(\bar{B} + \bar{D})(\bar{B} + \bar{C}) \qquad (2.13\text{-}6)$$

The implementation of Eq. (2.13-6) using AND and OR gates is shown in Fig. 2.13-5. Observe that each term in Eq. (2.13-6) requires an OR gate and that all OR-gate outputs are combined in a single AND gate. Figure 2.13-5 is to be compared with Fig. 2.10-2, where to implement a sum-of-products function the order of the OR and AND gates is reversed.

Example 2.13-4 The minterms of a five-variable function have been entered on the K map of Fig. 2.13-6. Read the map.

SOLUTION Following the algorithm given above, the boxes with 1s have been combined as indicated. Readings of the combinations have been indicated on the map, and we find altogether

$$f(A,B,C,D,E) = A\bar{B}\bar{C}DE + ABCD + \bar{A}\bar{B}\bar{D} + B\bar{D}\bar{E} + C\bar{E} \qquad (2.13\text{-}7)$$

Example 2.13-5 Consider a K map as in Fig. 2.13-6, which was read in Ex-

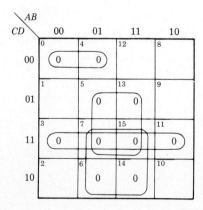

Figure 2.13-4 K map for Example 2.13-3.

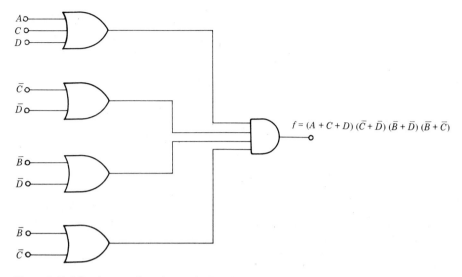

Figure 2.13-5 Implementation of gates in Eq. (2.13-6).

ample 2.13-4, but assume that the entries are not 1s but 0s, so that the map represents the function which is complementary to the function given in Eq. (2.13-7). Express this complementary function as a product of sums.

SOLUTION The grouping of 0s is the same as the grouping of 1s in the previous problem, but now a box *within* the range of A is associated with $\bar{A}$, rather than with A, etc. We therefore find

$$f(A,B,C,D,E) = (\bar{A} + B + C + \bar{D} + \bar{E})(\bar{A} + \bar{B} + \bar{C} + \bar{D})$$
$$(A + B + D)(\bar{B} + D + E)(\bar{C} + E) \qquad (2.13\text{-}8)$$

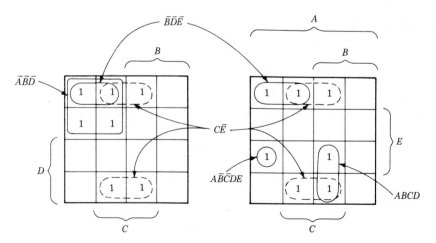

Figure 2.13-6 A five-variable K-map example.

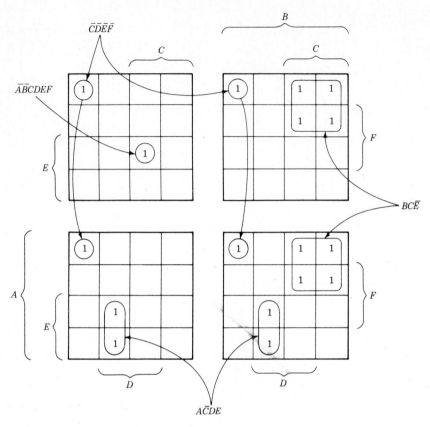

Figure 2.13-7 A six-variable K-map example.

Example 2.13-6 Read the K map of Fig. 2.13-7.

SOLUTION Boxes have been combined as indicated. The readings of the combinations have been indicated on the map, and we find altogether

$$f(A,B,C,D,E,F) = \bar{A}\bar{B}CDEF + \bar{C}\bar{D}\bar{E}\bar{F} + A\bar{C}DE + BC\bar{E} \quad (2.13\text{-}9)$$

2.14 MAPPING WHEN THE FUNCTION IS NOT EXPRESSED IN MINTERMS

Our discussion of mapping suggests that if a function is to be entered on a K map, the function must first be expressed as a sum of minterms (or a product of maxterms). In principle, such is the case. As a matter of practice, however, if the function is not so expressed, it is not necessary to expand the function algebraically into its minterms. Instead, the expansion into minterms can be ac-

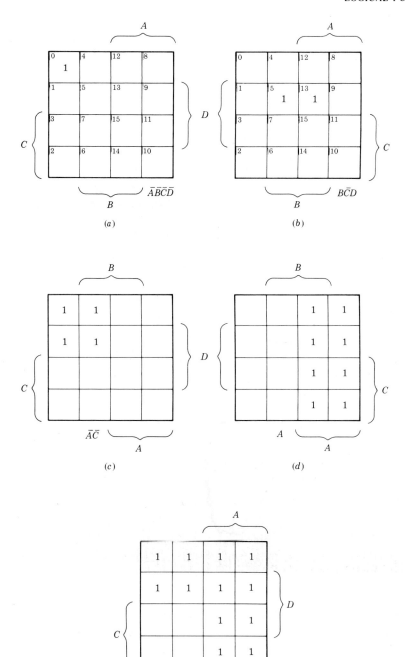

Figure 2.14-1 A logical function can be expanded into its minterms directly on a K map.

complished in the process of entering the terms of the function on the K map. To illustrate, consider that we propose to enter on a K map the function

$$f(A,B,C,D) = \bar{A}\bar{B}\bar{C}\bar{D} + B\bar{C}D + \bar{A}\bar{C} + A \qquad (2.14\text{-}1)$$

in which only the first term is a minterm. As in Fig. 2.14-1a, this first minterm can be entered directly on the K map. The second term $B\bar{C}D$ corresponds on the map to the boxes which lie inside the ranges of the variables B and D and outside the range of variable C *independently* of whether the box is inside or outside the range of variable A. Referring to Fig. 2.14-1b, we note that the range in which B and D overlap is the range encompassing boxes 5, 7, 13, and 15. Since we need also to be outside the range of C, we drop boxes 7 and 15 and are left with boxes 5 and 13. Since our term $B\bar{C}D$ is independent of A, we need make no further restrictions and the term is represented on the map in the manner shown. Similarly, as in Fig. 2.14-1c, the third term $\bar{A}\bar{C}$ is entered in all the boxes outside the range of A and C independently of B and D. Finally, as in Fig. 2.14-1d, the term A is entered every place in the range of A independently of all the other variables. The complete K map (Fig. 2.14-1e) results from combining the individual maps for the individual terms, and we find that

$$f(A,B,C,D) = A + \bar{C} \qquad (2.14\text{-}2)$$

We note in several instances, i.e., for m_0, m_5 and m_{13}, that 1s appear in the maps of more than just a single term. This situation causes no difficulty, for, as we have noted, a minterm added to itself still yields a single minterm.

2.15 INCOMPLETELY SPECIFIED FUNCTIONS

A logical function f is defined by specifying for each possible combination of variables whether the function has the value $f = 1$ or $f = 0$. Such a specification allows one to enter the minterms or maxterms on a K map immediately and thereafter to express the function in its simplest form.

Suppose that we undertake to write in simplest form a function f which is specified for some (but not all) possible combinations of the variables. In such a case a number of different functions are possible, all of which satisfy the specifications. They will differ from each other in the values assumed by the function for combinations of the variables which are not specified. The question then arises: How, from among the many allowable functions, can we arrive directly at the simplest function?

In practice, such incomplete specification arises in two ways. Sometimes we simply do not care what value is assumed by the function for certain combinations of variables. On other occasions, we may know that certain combinations of the variables will never occur. In this case, we may pretend that we do not care, since the net effect is the same.

To illustrate the procedure, using K maps, to simplify an incompletely specified function, consider that a function is defined by

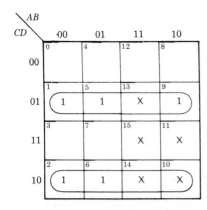

Figure 2.15-1 An incompletely specified function.

$$f(A,B,C,D) = \Sigma m(1,2,5,6,9) + d(10,11,12,13,14,15) \qquad (2.15\text{-}1)$$

In this equation the d stands for "don't care," so that our function has the value $f = 1$, corresponding to minterms $1,2,\ldots$, and is unspecified for combinations of variables corresponding to minterms $10,11,\ldots$. On the K map, as in Fig. 2.15-1, we locate 1s where specified, and where a don't care is indicated we locate a cross. The procedure thereafter is to interpret a cross as a 1 if so doing effects a simplification and to ignore it otherwise. If the crosses were all ignored, the map of Fig. 2.15-1 would yield

$$f = (m_1 + m_5) + (m_1 + m_9) + (m_2 + m_6) \qquad (2.15\text{-}2a)$$

$$= \bar{A}\bar{C}D + \bar{B}\bar{C}D + \bar{A}C\bar{D} \qquad (2.15\text{-}2b)$$

If we interpret as 1s the crosses in m_{10}, m_{13}, and m_{14}, we find that the function simplifies to

$$f = (m_1 + m_5 + m_9 + m_{13}) + (m_2 + m_6 + m_{10} + m_{14}) \qquad (2.15\text{-}3a)$$

$$= \bar{C}D + C\bar{D} \qquad (2.15\text{-}3b)$$

The remaining crosses in m_{11}, m_{12}, and m_{15} cannot serve either to reduce the number of terms in the function or to reduce the number of variables in a term. Hence, these crosses are simply ignored, i.e., judged to be 0s.

THREE

BASIC COMBINATIONAL CIRCUITS

3.1 INTRODUCTION

Digital systems are assembled from gates. The principal factor determining how fast a digital system can carry out its intended function is the speed at which its gates operate. The most important factor related to the speed of a gate is its propagation-delay time t_{pd}. It is the time required for a gate output to respond to a change in logic level at the gate input. Gates intended to operate rapidly, with times t_{pd} in the range from microseconds to nanoseconds (10^{-9} s), must employ electronic devices.

In an electronic digital system we find at any point in the circuitry that the voltage is at one value or another, representing one or the other of the two logic levels. Correspondingly, the electronic devices of the system are called upon either to conduct a substantial electric current or to conduct very little or no current. So long as the system is able to distinguish the two cases, i.e., large current and little or no current, the actual current is of no consequence. This situation is in marked contrast to the use of electronic devices in an analog system, where, in principle at least, every current change, no matter how small, has some significance. In short, in a digital system, an individual electronic device does *very little*. Therefore, in order to construct a digital system of some consequence, it is necessary to use many electronic components—thousands, hundred of thousands, and even millions.

Before about 1955, electronic devices available for construction of digital systems were semiconductor diodes and vacuum tubes. The diodes are relatively small, having dimensions in the range of tenths of inches, and they consume relatively little power. Vacuum tubes, on the other hand, are physically large, having dimensions in the range of inches, and consume relatively large amounts of power, typically in the range of some watts. Although to a large extent gates could be fabricated from diodes and resistors, it was also necessary to use vacuum tubes quite freely. As a result, digital systems of substantial capability were physically very large, used large amounts of power, and were quite expensive. The situation was materially improved by the advent of the transistor in the 1950s. A transistor, which is quite generally a one-to-one replacement for a vacuum tube, consumes much less power (tens of milliwatts), and like the semiconductor diode, an encapsulated individual transistor has physical dimensions in the range of tenths of inches.

Up to about 1965 only individually packaged semiconductor devices were commercially available, and engineers assembled gates and digital systems from these individual packages and from resistors. Semiconductor devices are fabricated by certain physical and chemical processes applied to and through the surface of a very pure wafer of silicon. The details of semiconductor fabrication are of no concern to us except to note that a typical semiconductor device has extensions, in the directions of the silicon wafer surface, which typically are in the range of some thousandths of an inch. In an individually packaged device most of the physical extension involves not the device itself but the encapsulation and the mechanical support required to provide for electrical connections. Hence, there began a series of technological developments (continuing to this day and with no end in sight) leading to a type of semiconductor device which is called an *integrated circuit* (IC). In an integrated circuit many transistors and diodes are fabricated on, i.e., integrated into, a single silicon wafer; integrated into the same structure are the resistors and even the interconnections required to fabricate a complete gate or many gates or even an elaborate digital system.

Commercially available IC *chips*, as they are called, are classified as small-scale integrated (SSI) chips, medium-scale integrated (MSI) chips, large-scale integrated (LSI) chips, and very-large-scale integrated (VLSI) devices. By one convention the designation SSI is applied when a chip has fewer than 12 logic gates, MSI for the range 13 to 99 gates, LSI for the range 100 to about 1000 gates, and VLSI beyond 1000 gates.

The origin of the concepts involved in digital systems is lost in antiquity. Doubtless primitive people could count, and the abacus, which can be used to compete favorably with a mechanical calculator, is at least 2500 years old. A simple digital mechanical calculator which could add and subtract was constructed in the 1600s. A mechanical device incorporating some of the concepts involved in modern-day computers was designed in the early 1800s. Mass-produced, and hence relatively inexpensive, mechanical desk calculators which could add, subtract, multiply, and divide were available in the 1930s. In the 1940s electronic circuits using vacuum tubes gave digital systems a speed not possible with mechanical devices, but these systems were physically large and consumed a great deal of power. In the 1950s transistors appeared, and integrated circuits began to evolve in the 1960s. In the early 1980s, the development of integrated circuitry has proceeded to the point where a small IC chip, dissipating about 1 W and easily held in the palm of the hand, can outperform systems available 30 years earlier which involved a room full of equipment and dissipated thousands of watts.

In this chapter we shall describe a number of SSI and MSI chips which provide a number of the basic circuits from which digital systems are assembled. We shall consider here only *combinational* circuits, i.e., circuits whose outputs depend only on the logic levels of present inputs and are not related to the past history of the circuit.

3.2 FAMILIES OF LOGIC CIRCUITS

There are a number of *families* of digital integrated logic circuits which are distinguished from each other by the type of semiconductor devices they incorporate and by how the semiconductor device (and resistors where used) are interconnected to form gates. The characteristics of the transistor types and the electrical features of the various families are described in detail in other texts.†
Here we comment on the matter very briefly to explain why, in the present chapter, where our interest is confined to SSI and MSI, we shall limit our discussion to a single family.

There are two types of transistors. One is the *metal-oxide-semiconductor* (MOS) transistor. This transistor can be fabricated so that the current flowing in it is carried by negative (n) electric charges (it is consequently called *n-channel* MOS) or by positive (p) charges (it is called *p-channel* MOS). The great merit of this family is that no resistors are required. Since the individual transistors occupy very little area on the silicon chip, they are eminently suitable for large-scale or very-large-scale integration. A MOS family uses either the n- or the p-channel MOS transistors. This family has rather inconvenient electrical characteristics for SSI and MSI and is not generally so used. It finds its principal application in LSI and VLSI. The second family uses both p- and n-channel devices on the same chip and is called *complementary-symmetry MOS* (CMOS). This CMOS family is used in LSI and, because it does not share some of the deficiencies of MOS, is also available in SSI and MSI. The family has the limitation of being relatively slow (long propagation delays) and is unable conveniently to supply current at its output to operate other chips (except other CMOS chips). Hence, again, CMOS SSI and MSI are not widely used in general applications.

The second transistor type is the *bipolar transistor*, at present fabricated in three families. One family is called *integrated-injection logic* (IIL). Like MOS and CMOS, it requires that no resistors be fabricated on the chip, and its circuit configuration is suitable for LSI. It is not presently available in SSI or in MSI.

A second bipolar transistor family is called *emitter-coupled logic* (ECL). It uses many transistors per gate, and even a two-input gate requires five transistors. It is the fastest family of logic, because it uses the faster bipolar (rather

---

†For example, H. Taub and D. L. Schilling: "Digital Integrated Electronics," McGraw-Hill, New York, 1977.

than the slower MOS) transistors and because it uses these bipolar transistors as efficiently as possible to make them respond with great speed. However, its very speed makes ECL a difficult family to use. The great speed with which transitions occur from one logic level to the other means that almost every length of wire used to interconnect chips must be treated as though it were a length of transmission line. ECL is available in SSI and MSI but is generally not a favorite except when its superior speed is really needed.

We come finally to the most widely used family by far when SSI and MSI chips are involved, *transistor-transistor logic* (TTL). The family was developed principally by the Texas Instrument Company but is now also available from other manufacturers. For the TTL family the Texas Instrument Company applies to all chips the general designation SN, standing for "semiconductor network." Other manufacturers use other designations such as DM (digital monolithic). There are two series, one assigned the identifying number 54 and the other the number 74. Series 54 is intended for applications, such as military, which make stringent demands. This series will operate in the range -55 to $125°C$. The series 74 is a lower-cost industrial version with an operating temperature range from 0 to $70°C$.

3.3 THE TTL SERIES

In semiconductor electronic circuits it is possible in a general way to improve the speed of operation (i.e., reduce the propagation delay and reduce the time required for transitions from one logic level to another) by sacrificing power. Since the higher power makes larger currents available, "stray" capacitors can be charged and discharged more rapidly. These stray capacitors are not deliberately incorporated into the circuitry but are an inevitable result of the physical extension and geometry of the circuitry. The availability of larger currents also makes it possible to turn transistors on and off more rapidly. When we use more power for the sake of speed, we often would like to know whether the speed increase is commensurate with the sacrifice in power. Accordingly, a useful figure of merit in this connection is the *speed-power product*, which is the product of the propagation delay and the power dissipation of a gate.

When standard bipolar transistors are operated in digital circuits and the transistor is turned on so that it is carrying current, the transistor generally finds itself operating in a manner which is characterized by the term *saturated*. It would take us far afield to explore this matter, and we mention it only to note that by virtue of this saturated operation it takes a relatively long time to turn the transistor off. Correspondingly, standard transistor digital circuits suffer a speed disadvantage. At some additional expense it is possible, however, to fabricate a type of transistor called a *Schottky transistor* which does not saturate and is therefore capable of operating at higher speeds.

Because of the trade-off possible between power and speed and because transistors can be fabricated as standard or as Schottky devices, TTL is avail-

Table 3.3-1 Typical performance characteristics of 54/74 family SSI

Series	Power and transistor type	Propagation delay time, ns	Power dissipation, mW	Speed-power product, pJ
54LS/74LS	Low-power, Schottky	9.5	2	19
54L/74L	Low-power, standard	33	1	33
54S/74S	Standard-power, Schottky	3	19	57
54/74	Standard-power, standard	10	10	100
54H/74H	High-power, standard	6	22	132

able in five series, listed with their characteristics in Table 3.3-1. It is apparent why the LS series is generally the most popular at present. Of course, if there are special constraints on allowable power, speed, or cost, other series would be the devices of choice.

Fan-Out

A source of a digital signal which is applied to a gate input must be able to establish at the input one voltage or another corresponding to the two logic levels. At each level the source must be able to satisfy the current requirements of the driven gate. Since the output of one gate is frequently the source of an input to another gate, it is necessary to know the drive capability of a gate; i.e., we need to know to how many gate inputs of driven gates we can connect the output of a driving gate. Manufacturers generally provide this information by specifying a gate *fan-out*. In TTL, provided each driver is driving gates of its same series, the fan-out is 10 for the standard and high-power series and 20 for the low-power series. When a driver is driving devices other than similar gates, we must refer to manufacturer's literature to determine input-current requirements and output-current availability to ensure that the burden on the driver is not excessive.

Noise Margin

Since the TTL family operates from a supply voltage of 5 V, all voltages in a TTL system are in the range between 0 and 5 V. When a driving gate is not burdened by being connected to other gate inputs, its low output voltage, corresponding to logic 0, may be as low as 0.1 V or even less for the 54/74 series. The high voltage, corresponding to logic 1, is about 3.4 V. When the output is low, the driving gate must allow current to flow back into itself from the driven gates. The driving gate is then described as *sinking* current from its load. At the high output level the driver supplies current to its load and is described as *sourcing* current. At the low voltage level current being sinked raises the output voltage, and at the high voltage level current being sourced lowers the output voltage. For the 54/74 series the manufacturer provides assurance that even when a gate is burdened by the maximum fan-out specified above, the low output voltage will not rise above 0.4 V and the high voltage will not drop below 2.4 V. The manufacturer also specifies that an input voltage of 0.8 V or lower will always be recognized by a driven gate as corresponding to a *low* (logic 0) voltage and an input voltage greater than 2.0 V will always be recognized as a *high* (logic 1) voltage. The two output voltages and input voltages are referred to by the symbols V_{OH}, V_{OL}, V_{IH} and V_{IL} and have, quite generally, the following definitions:

V_{OH}. The *minimum* output voltage a gate will provide when the output is at its *high* level

V_{OL}. The *maximum* output voltage which will be found when the output is at its *low* level

V_{IH}. The *minimum* voltage which can be applied to a gate input if the gate is to recognize that the input is *high*

V_{IL}. The *maximum* voltage which can be applied to a gate input if the gate is to recognize that the input is *low*

For the series 54/74 these voltages are as specified in Fig. 3.3-1 and lead to the (idealized) input-output voltage characteristic of a gate shown in Fig. 3.3-2. (The gate contemplated here is a NAND or a NOR gate with all inputs connected

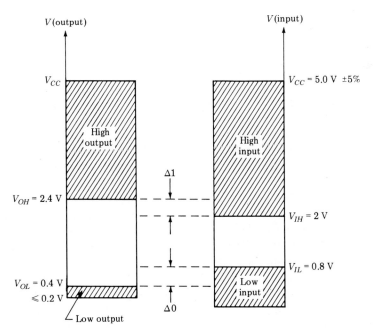

Figure 3.3-1 Voltage levels in TTL logic.

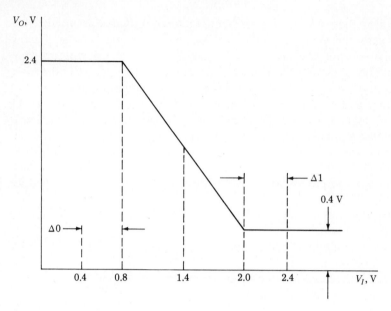

Figure 3.3-2 Idealized worst-case input-output plot of a TTL gate.

so that the gate acts simply as an inverter.) When the input voltage V_I is in the range 0 to 0.8 V or in the range greater than 2.0 V, the output V_O is constant at 2.4 V or at 0.4 V. In the range of V_I from 0.8 to 2.0 V, the output swings from its high level of 2.4 V to its low level of 0.4 V.

The relevance of these voltages can be seen from the following considerations. Suppose that a driving gate is at its low level at 0.4 V. The driven gate will recognize that its input is low because the input is less than 0.8 V, but in any real physical hardware implementation of a configuration of gates, spurious, random, unpredictable (noise) voltages may be superimposed on the connections which couple one part of the configuration with another. The margin for error at this low level is the difference $V_{IL} - V_{OL}$, represented by the symbol $\Delta 0$, as indicated in Fig. 3.3-1, and called the low-level *noise margin+* in the present case it has the value $\Delta 0 = 0.4$ V. The high-level noise margin $\Delta 1 = V_{OH} - V_{IH}$ also has the value 0.4 V. Thus if the noise voltage added to the 0.4 V input voltage should exceed 0.4 V, the corresponding output of the driven gate would be less than 2.4 V. Hence the margin for error at the output, originally $2.4 - 2.0 = 0.4$, will now be smaller. Let us assume that the noise pervades the entire system and that at every point the noise voltage is always in the direction to cause trouble. Then we can see that in a long cascade of gates we shall eventually arrive at a point where a logic 1 may be interpreted as a logic 0 or vice versa. Hence, altogether, the noise margins of a gate are important parameters and it is advantageous for them to be as large as possible.

It is useful to note that in specifying the parameters V_{OH}, etc., from which $\Delta 1$ and $\Delta 0$ are calculated, manufacturers are inclined to be extremely conservative. The noise margins of 0.4 V given above are more typically about 1.0 V or even larger.

In summary, a logic family or a series within a family is characterized by four parameters: (1) propagation delay, (2) power dissipation (from which two we can calculate the speed-power product), (3) fan-out, and (4) noise margins. The fan-out is often not an adequate parameter when we make interconnections between series and certainly not when we make interconnections between different families.

3.4 THE CMOS FAMILY

The CMOS (complementary-symmetry metal-oxide semiconductor) family uses a supply voltage which may range from 5 to 15 V. One rather distinctive feature of this family is that the input current required by a gate is insignificantly small, generally 1 pA or less. Since the available output current is of the order of at least 1 mA, to the extent that fan-out is determined only by available output current and required input current, the fan-out is astronomically large. Accordingly, the fan-out which designers will allow themselves is usually determined by considerations having to do with speed. Each additional gate to which a driving gate is fanned out increases the capacitative loading and correspondingly increases the propagation-delay time. The input capacitance of a gate lies in the range 5 to 10 pF, so that a fan-out of 5 will load a driving gate with 25 to 50 pF. When the load is 50 pF and operation is at a supply voltage of 5 V, propagation delays are in the range of 50 to 100 ns, appreciably longer than for TTL with comparable fan-out.

The noise margins of CMOS are about 1 V when a 5-V supply voltage is used, and the margins become larger with higher supply voltage.

A second distinctive feature of CMOS is that when a gate is holding its output fixed at one logic level, the power consumed is so insignificantly small that it is hardly an exaggeration to say that the power is absolutely zero. Power is consumed, however, when the gate is switching between logic levels. This power depends on the frequency of switching, on the capacitative loading, and on the supply voltage. For example, at a switching frequency of 10^5 Hz with a 50-pF capacitative load and a supply voltage of 5 V, the dissipated power is about 0.2 mW per gate, appreciably smaller than for TTL.

There are occasions when it is useful to have both CMOS and TTL in the same system. The less expensive and power-conserving CMOS is used where the speed of TTL is not required. When TTL is to drive CMOS, the TTL is able to supply adequate current to allow a fan-out to many CMOS gates, but even when both families use the same supply voltage (5 V), the output V_{OH} (TTL) is not high enough for the CMOS. The problem can be corrected by connecting a resistor between the 5-V supply and the output terminal of the TTL gate. When CMOS is to drive TTL, the voltage levels generated at the CMOS output are adequate for TTL, but the current furnished by CMOS may not be large enough. There are two CMOS families. In the 4000 family, the CMOS gates generally are not able to supply enough current, and special *buffers* must be interposed. The second CMOS series bearing the designation 54C/74C provides chips which are functional equivalents of many of the 54/74 TTL gates. These CMOS gates are typically about 50 percent faster than the 4000 series and are able to fan out to two low-power TTL gates.

3.5 THE ECL FAMILY

The ECL family of IC chips operates with a negative supply voltage of -5.2 V. The logic levels are therefore negative, being approximately -0.75 and -1.6 V. A fan-out as large as 25 is generally allowed. The noise margins are of the order of 0.3 V. As we have noted, the principal merit of ECL is its high speed. There are a number of series in this family. The most generally popular is the 10,000 series, which has the best speed-power product. Typically the gate propagation delay is about 2 ns, and the power dissipation is about 25 mW per gate. There is also an ECL II series with propagation delay of 4 ns and an ECL III series with propagation delay of 1 ns.

There are occasions when it is useful to use both TTL and ECL in the same system. To accommodate such cases, manufacturers make available *logic-level translators* which accept the positive voltage logic levels of TTL and translate them into the negative levels of ECL or vice versa.

3.6 PACKAGING

Integrated-circuit chips are generally, although not invariably, packaged in one of two main styles, shown in Fig. 3.6-1. The flat pack (Fig. 3.6-1a) is the more compact and is generally intended to be soldered permanently onto a printed circuit board. The dual-in-line (DIP) package (Fig. 3.6-1b) is somewhat more rugged and fits conveniently into a socket.

3.7 THE LOGIC-OPERATED SWITCH

In this text we deliberately avoid any discussion of the electronic circuitry used to implement our digital circuits physically. Digital systems are the subject of this text, not electronics. Yet an acquaintance with one very simple and elemental circuit using a transistor is very useful. Avoiding reference to it often requires so much circumlocution that is is worth examining the circuit even superficially.

A transistor is a semiconductor device with three terminals, the *emitter*, the *base*, and the *collector*. Consider the transistor used in the simple circuit of Fig. 3.7-1a. Here we connected a voltage called V_{cc} through a resistor R and across

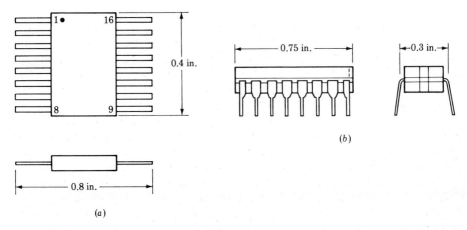

Figure 3.6-1 Appearance and approximate dimensions of 16-pin IC packages: (*a*) flat pack; (*b*) dual-in-line (DIP) package.

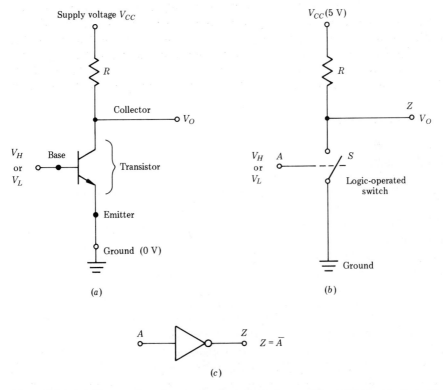

Figure 3.7-1 (*a*) The transistor does or does not conduct according as the input is V_H or V_L. (*b*) An equivalent circuit which uses a logic-operated switch. (*c*) The circuit in (*b*) performs the logic of inversion.

the collector and emitter terminals of the transistor. (The subscript on V_{CC} indicates that the terminal closest to the supply voltage is the collector.) The circuit is provided with electric power by a power-supply source; it may simply be a battery whose positive terminal is connected to the terminal marked V_{CC} and whose negative terminal is called *ground*. The ground is simply the point in the circuit with respect to which all voltages are measured. For simplicity, the battery is not actually shown in the figure. We expect to apply to the *base* of the transistor, i.e. between base and ground, one of two voltages V_H or V_L. V_H is an *input* voltage corresponding to the *high* voltage level, i.e., logic 1 in a positive-logic convention, and V_L corresponds to the low voltage (logic 0).

All we need to know about the circuit is that when the voltage applied to the base is V_L, the transistor does not conduct currrent, consequently there is no current in R, and the output voltage $V_O = V_{CC}$. When the input is V_H, the transistor conducts current and V_O goes (very nearly) to ground voltage (0 V). Thus to a good approximation the transistor circuit in Fig. 3.7-1a can be replaced by the circuit in Fig. 3.7-1b. There we have a *logic-operated switch*. When the voltage V_H is applied to the control terminal, the switch closes, and when the control terminal voltage is V_L, the switch opens. We easily see that the circuit can be used as an *inverter*. Suppose we plan to use the circuit with TTL voltage levels and correspondingly set $V_{CC} = 5$ V. If the input is at logic 0, S is open and $V_O = 5$ V, corresponding to logic 1, since any voltage above 2.4 V is logic 1. If the input is at logic 1 or higher, S is closed and $V_O = 0$ V, corresponding to logic 0, since any voltage less than 0.4 is logic 0. Thus the logic level at the output is always the complement of the level at the input, and the circuit can be represented as in Fig. 3.7-1c.

3.8 LOGIC-OPERATED SWITCH OR GATE; THE WIRED-AND CONNECTION

As can readily be verified, the two-switch circuit of Fig. 3.8-1a is a NOR gate with truth table as in Fig. 3.8-1b and logic symbol as in Fig. 3.8-1c. Only if the input logic levels A and B are both 0, so that both switches are open, will the output Z be at logic 1.

Next consider the circuit configuration in Fig. 3.8-2a. It consists of an AND gate followed by an inverter, as in Fig. 3.8-2b, and hence constitutes a NAND gate, as shown in Fig. 3.8-2c. The relevance of this configuration to our present discussion is that many TTL gates use precisely this arrangement.

Finally consider the circuit in Fig. 3.8-3, where we contemplate connecting the output (dashed connections) of two NAND gates as in Fig. 3.8-2. This dashed connection will combine the two logic-operated switches into a NOR gate, as in Fig. 3.8-1, and after connection the single output will be, using De Morgan's theorem,

$$Z = \overline{AB + CD} = \overline{(AB)} \cdot \overline{(CD)} \qquad (3.8\text{-}1)$$

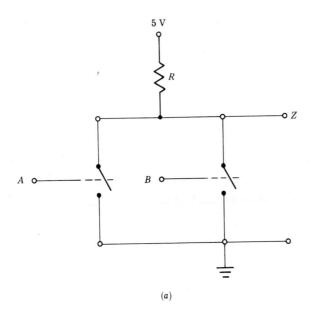

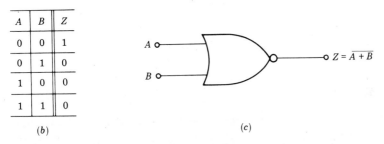

Figure 3.8-1 (*a*) Logic-controlled switches are used to make a NOR gate; (*b*) truth table; (*c*) symbol.

In the absence of the connection, the two individual outputs would be $\overline{AB}$ and $\overline{CD}$. Hence the simple operation of connecting the outputs with a wire has, in effect, added an AND gate. Such a connection (not always possible but effective with gates of the type shown in Fig. 3.8-2) is called the *wired*-AND connection and is represented by the symbolism in Fig. 3.8-4.

Figure 3.8-3 shows the wired-AND connection applied to NAND gates. However, it can readily be verified that the connection will produce a wired-AND effect no matter what logic was performed by the individual gates before connection. Thus we can use the connection with AND, OR, NOR gates, etc. All that is essential is that the logic-operated switch configuration be present at the gate outputs.

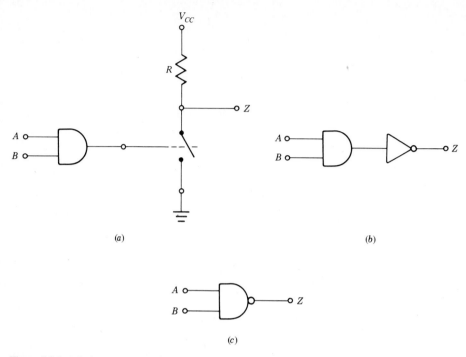

Figure 3.8-2 (*a*) An AND gate and a logic-controlled switch inverter are used to make a NAND gate. (*b*) An equivalent representation as an AND gate followed by an inverter. (*c*) Representation as a NAND gate.

Figure 3.8-3 also shows the wired-AND connection applied to two gates. It can readily be verified that the connection can equally well be applied to an arbitrary number of gates. The connection parallels the resistors R, and as more and more gates are paralleled, the equivalent resistance of the resistors so paralleled becomes progressively smaller. Consider, then, a many-gate case in which all logic-operated switches except one are open. Then the one closed switch (transistor) will have to carry the total current allowed through the small equivalent resistor. The transistor may overheat and burn out. To circumvent this difficulty manufacturers may omit the resistor entirely on the IC chip. Such a chip is described as having an *open collector*. After the chips are paralleled, the user provides a single resistor of appropriate resistance, *external* to the chip.

3.9 TOTEM-POLE OUTPUT

In one respect the logic-operated switch is an ideal configuration at the output of a TTL gate. We have already noted that when the gate output is low, the driving gate is called upon to sink current from the driven gate. When the out-

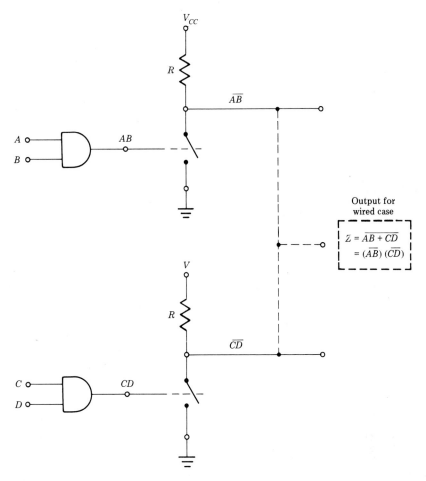

Figure 3.8-3 The output terminals of two NAND gates, as in Fig. 3.8-2, are wired together.

put is low, the switch is closed, as in Fig. 3.9-1*a*, and the current being sinked can flow easily to ground through the closed switch. (Actually, of course, the switch is a transistor, which does offer some opposition to current flow but very little compared with that offered by the resistor *R*.) This situation is fortunate

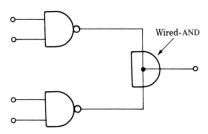

Figure 3.8-4 The symbol used to indicate a wired-AND connection.

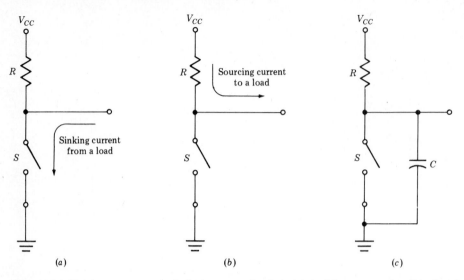

Figure 3.9-1 Used at a gate output, the logic-operated switch circuit sinks current when S is closed as in (a) and sources current when S is open as in (b). (c) When S is open, charging current for the capacitor C must be supplied through the resistor R.

because the current to be sinked is relatively large. When the switch is open, as in Fig. 3.9-1b, the driving gate sources current to its load. This current must flow through the resistor R and is therefore limited, but it turns out that the source current required is relatively small, so that the presence of the resistor causes no problem.

In a second respect, however, the logic-switch output arrangement is less than ideal. As indicated in Fig. 3.9-1c, there is always some capacitance bridged across the output of a gate. This capacitance is not deliberately introduced but is inevitably associated with the physical geometry of any electric circuit and increases with increase in fan-out. The capacitance slows the gate operation because as the output rises and falls in making transitions between logic levels, the capacitor must charge and discharge. The discharge is relatively fast because the capacitor discharges through the closed switch, but the charge is slow because the charging current must be supplied through the resistor while the switch is open. To speed the charging the resistor can be replaced by a second switch, leading to the configuration of Fig. 3.9-2 and called a *totem-pole output*. When A is low, S1 is open and S2 is closed so that Z is high. When A is high, the switches reverse and Z is low.

3.10 THE THREE-STATE OUTPUT

A useful modification of the totem-pole output is shown in Fig. 3.10-1. As long as the control terminal marked ENABLE is at logic 1, the circuit operates exactly like the circuit of Fig. 3.9-2 and the input logic variable A is complemented and

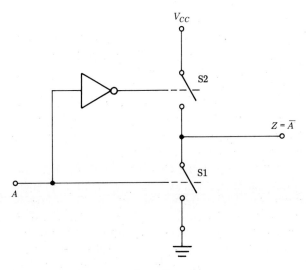

Figure 3.9-2 The totem-pole configuration.

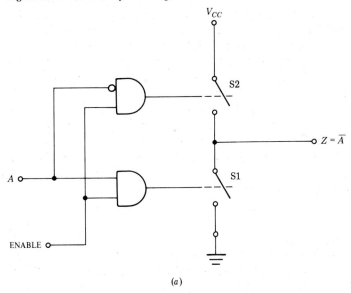

(a)

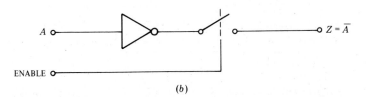

(b)

Figure 3.10-1 (a) Totem-pole output configuration with tristate feature. (b) Equivalent representation of a tristate output.

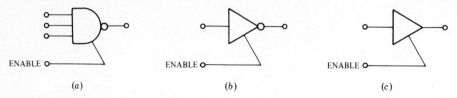

Figure 3.10-2 Symbolism to represent a tristate output on (*a*) a gate, (*b*) an inverter, and (*c*) a buffer.

the complement presented at the output. Thus the circuit is *enabled* to perform the function for which it is intended. However, as long as ENABLE is at logic 0, the outputs of both AND gates are at logic 0, switches S1 and S2 are open, and the circuit is *disabled*. Under these circumstances, the output line, which otherwise carries the logic variable $Z = \bar{A}$, is entirely *disconnected* from the circuit. The configuration is known as a *tristate* output, two of the states referring to the logic levels and the third state to the condition of disconnection. We shall have occasion below to see the merit of the tristate output. A tristate output on a gate in an inverter or a buffer is represented by the symbolism of Fig. 3.10-2*a*.

3.11 EXAMPLES OF IC GATES

As examples of commercially available IC gate chips we list in Table 3.11-1 a few representatives of TTL chips. The apostrophe before the device number stands for family and series. For example, the Texas Instrument

Table 3.11-1. Examples of TTL SSI gate chips

Device number	Description
′ 00	Quad 2-input NAND gate
′ 02	Quad 2-input NOR gate
′ 03	Quad 2-input NAND gate with open collector
′ 04	Hex inverter
′ 05	Hex inverter with open collector
′ 08	Quad 2-input AND gate
′ 09	Quad 2-input AND gate with open collector
′ 20	Dual 4-input NAND gate
′ 21	Dual 4-input AND gate
′ 27	Triple 3-input NOR gate
′ 30	8-input NAND gate
′ 32	Quad 2-input OR gate
′ 37	Quad 2-input NAND buffer
′ 38	Quad 2-input NAND buffer with open collector
′ 51	Dual AOI gate with 2 and 3 inputs
′126	Quad tristate buffer
′136	Quad 2-input EXCLUSIVE-OR gate

SN54LS/74LS02 becomes '02, etc. The terms "dual," "triple," "quad," and "hex" indicate respectively that the chip has two, three, four, or six identical but independent units fabricated on it.

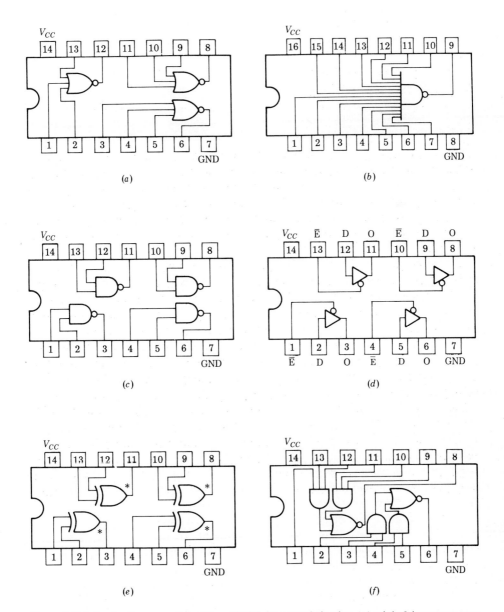

Figure 3.11-1 Logic diagrams of a number of TTL integrated circuits: (*a*) triple 3-input NOR gate ('27); (*b*) 13-input NAND gate ('133); (*c*) quad 2-input NAND gate ('00); (*d*) quad tristate inverter (buffer) with active-low ENABLE ('125); (*e*) quad EXCLUSIVE-OR gate ('136) (stars mark open-collector outputs); (*f*) dual, two-wide 2-input and 3-input AND-OR-INVERT gate.

Note that we have OR, NOR, AND, and NAND gates, some with open-collector outputs. The *buffers* are gates which are able to sink more current than regular gates and are used where larger than normal fan-out is required. The description of the '51 gate indicates that each AOI gate on the chip has two AND gates, one with two inputs and one with three inputs.

Diagrams indicating pin connections for a number of chips are shown in Fig. 3.11-1. Most SSI gate packages have 14 pins, but occasionally a 16-pin package is used. Two pins, V_{CC} and GND, are used to supply power. The fixed number of pins establishes a constraint on what can be included on the chip. To provide more inputs per gate the number of gates must be reduced.

3.12 CONTROL-TERMINAL SYMBOLS: MIXED LOGIC

Terminals on an IC chip can generally be classified as data terminals or control terminals. As a simple example, let us consider the situation in Fig. 3.12-1a. Here we have a NAND gate in which we choose to arrange for one of the input terminals to *control* the operation of the gate instead of accepting data. The control terminal is marked E (ENABLE). When the terminal E is at logic 1, the device operates straightforwardly as a three-input NAND gate; i.e., it is *enabled* to perform the function for which it is intended. When $E = 0$, however, the gate output is at logic 1 (of only incidental interest) and, most important, the gate output is entirely independent of, and unresponsive to, the inputs A, B, and C. That is, the gate has become *disabled* or *inhibited*. We have seen a similar example of a control terminal in the ENABLE terminal associated with the tristate output.

We have already noted that one and the same physical configuration of electronic components will perform one logic operation or another depending on the logic convention adopted. At present manufacturers invariably characterize their gates in terms of positive logic. The gate of Fig. 3.12-1a is enabled when the ENABLE terminal goes to logic 1. In positive logic, logic 1 is the HIGH (H) level. Hence it is at the HIGH voltage level that the ENABLE terminal is rendered *active*. That is, it is at the HIGH level that the function of the terminal, *as expressed by its name*, is carried out. Thus the ENABLE terminal in Fig. 3.12-1a is called an *active-high* ENABLE terminal. An alternative way in which the same idea is conveyed is by the statement "ENABLE is asserted high."

If it suits our whim or convenience, we can just as well refer to the control terminal in Fig. 3.12-1a as a DISABLE terminal. In this case, however, we should have an *active-low* terminal. Note that a terminal is active high or active low, or asserted high or low, depending on the name we assign to it.

We need a symbolism to indicate whether a control terminal is active high or active low. A widely used symbolism can be seen by comparing Fig. 3.12-1a and b. When a control terminal is active low, we indicate it by placing a bar, suggestive of a complementing bar, over the name assigned to the terminal. The symbolism is reasonable in the sense that a control level that disables is the

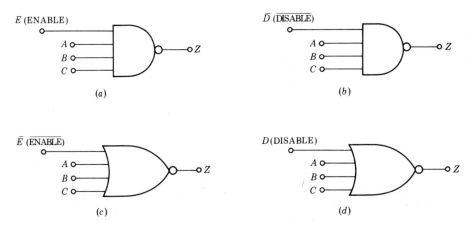

Figure 3.12-1 A gate input may be viewed as a *control* terminal.

complement of the level that enables. On the other hand, this feature of the symbolism would be preserved if we had used the symbols $\overline{\text{ENABLE}}$ and DIS-ABLE rather than the other way around. The fact that we do not use this alternative symbolism reflects an attitude on the part of logic designers subscribing to the sentiment that logic 0 is the quiet, passive, inactive state of a control logic level where no action is initiated while logic 1 is the active level. Hence in Fig. 3.12-1a the gate is enabled when ENABLE goes to logic 1. In Fig. 3.12-1b the job of the control terminal is to disable rather than to enable. Hence we pretend that someplace there is a virtual logic level DISABLE which goes to logic 1 when the gate is to be disabled and that it is the complement of this logic level, i.e., $\overline{\text{DISABLE}}$, which is actually applied to the control terminal.

The labeling on the control terminal of a NOR gate is shown in Fig. 3.12-1c and d. If named DISABLE, the control terminal is active high or asserted high, corresponding to logic 1 in positive logic. If named ENABLE, it is active low or asserted low and hence labeled $\overline{\text{ENABLE}}$.

In most cases, particularly when MSI and LSI chips are involved, it is not feasible or even useful to display all the individual gates of the package, and the chip is simply represented by a rectangular box symbol. Thus the box symbols for the gates of Fig. 3.12-1a and c appear as shown in Fig. 3.12-2a and b. We have used the mnemonic EN, which is rather universally understood to stand for ENABLE. Note that all the labels are placed inside the box. To indicate that a control terminal is active low, an inversion circle is added where the control line enters the box. If we had labeled the control terminal DIS (DISABLE), the inversion circle would appear in Fig. 3.12-2a instead of b. In any event, in both Fig. 3.12-2a and b the symbol EN appears uncomplemented. Hence we may assume that somewhere in the box there is a logic level which goes to logic 1 when the device is enabled. Generally whether or not such is actually the case is undeterminable and irrelevant. The point of the symbolism is precisely to allow a

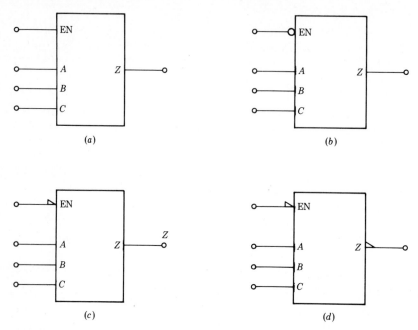

Figure 3.12-2 Box symbols for logic structures: (*a*) active-high enable input; (*b*) active-low enable input; (*c*) active-low enable input using newer symbolism; and (*d*) active-low enable and output.

description of the functioning of the device without inquiring into its internal structure.

Although the symbolism we have described is widely used in manufacturer's catalogs and literature, it has the less than happy feature that in the active-low case it suggests that somehow a logic inversion is involved. As can be seen in Fig. 3.12-1*c*, no such inversion occurs anywhere. Also in this active-low case, while we may pretend that somewhere there is a variable that goes to logic 1 to effect enabling, the fact is that the *real signal applied at the external terminal actually goes to logic 0.*

This feature, i.e., enabling at logic 0, will prevail so long as we use either positive logic or negative logic. For the *active* level can be *either high* or *low* although in either convention the *logic* levels are *always high or always low.* For this reason, in part, logic designers are beginning to adopt the convention of *mixed logic.* In this convention the *active* level of a logic variable, *whether high or low*, is taken to be logic 1. The symbol used in the mixed-logic convention to indicate an active-low terminal is a half arrowhead, as in Fig. 3.12-2*c*. Here we have a device which is enabled when the externally applied signal goes *low* to logic 1.

An inversion circle indicates that the logic levels on the two sides of the circle are the complements of one another. When we have logic 1 on one side we have logic 0 on the other, and vice versa. The situation is different with the half arrowhead. The logic levels on both sides are the *same*, both logic 1 or both logic 0. In Fig. 3.12-2*c* the gate is enabled when EN inside the box goes to logic 1. Correspondingly the gate is enabled when the externally applied signal also goes to logic 1. There is now agreement between the internal and external logic levels at which the chip is enabled and disabled. We can now preserve our prejudice that enabling (or whatever other action a control terminal is intended for) is accomplished at logic 1. We have no way of knowing from Fig. 3.12-2c anything about what goes inside the chip. We do not know what signal inside the chip goes to what voltage level to enable the chip. But the symbolism does tell us that, to enable the chip, the externally applied signal must go to the *low* voltage level, i.e., ENABLE is *asserted low*, the EN-ABLE terminal is *active low*, this low-voltage level being logic 1.

The mixed-logic convention offers no special advantage when our interest is in the theoretical aspects of logic-circuit design, but, as we shall see, it is very useful when we deal with real physical systems and devices characterized in terms of the activity of terminals which respond to real high or low voltages.

Finally, let us consider the possibility that the output Z, say, of the NAND gate of Fig. 3.12-1a is itself intended to be applied to a control input terminal of some other chip. Specifically, let us assume that the purpose of the NAND gate is to provide an activating control signal to the second chip when all three inputs A, B, and C are high. Then the output Z is a control signal, and it is at the level to provide activization when it is *low*. In this case the appropriate box symbol is as in Fig. 3-12-1d. Here again the half arrowhead at Z indicates that the signal here is *active low*. We note a second advantage of the arrowhead in that its direction indicates whether the terminal is an input or an output terminal. In general, then, at any terminal where an active-low input control signal is required or where such a signal is generated we append a half arrowhead symbol whose direction distinguishes input from output terminals.

At the outset of our present discussion of terminal symbols we drew a distinction between control and other terminals which we referred to as data terminals. Actually this distinction is quite artificial, and we can always view any input or output terminal of a gate or IC chip as having some intended function which it carries out on an individual basis or in concert with other terminals. Hence the comments which we have made about control terminals actually apply equally to all gate and IC chip terminals. It is generally useful and even quite necessary to provide each terminal with a functionally descriptive name and to indicate whether the terminal is active high or active low. In most cases the functional descriptions extend to many words, and it is customary to shorten them into brief mnemonics. The newer and more widely accepted symbol to indicate an active-low terminal is the half arrowhead. Still many writers continue to use the inversion circle.

3.13 CONTROL-SIGNAL SYMBOLS

When we have a chip with one or more control terminals, we must generate appropriate control signals for application to these control terminals. Since these control signals make transitions from one level to the other as time progresses, they are functions of time. We have used "function" on previous occasions in the sense that one logic variable may find itself at a logic level which is a function of the logic level of other variables. Here we use "function" to refer to the time dependence of a single logic variable.

A typical control function appears as in Fig. 3.13-1. Some control signals have a dependence on time which is perfectly predictable, e.g., the clock signals we shall describe in Chap. 4. Other signals do not have a predictable time dependence; e.g., the control signals generated in a calculator, which depend on what keys the user presses and when. In any event suppose that a chip needs to be enabled at certain times and under certain conditions. Suppose, further, that we do indeed generate a control signal which is at one logic level (tentatively not specified as high or low) precisely when the chip needs to be enabled and is at the other logic level at all other times. Then, quite reasonably, we may assign to the control signal the name ENABLE. More specifically, if the signal is HIGH when the chip needs enabling, the convention is to name the signal ENABLE (and if LOW to name it $\overline{\text{ENABLE}}$). If the enable *terminal* is active high, an EN-ABLE signal can be connected directly. If the enable terminal is active low, an $\overline{\text{ENABLE}}$ signal can be connected directly. Otherwise we shall have to interpose an inverter between signal source and terminal.

The ENABLE and $\overline{\text{ENABLE}}$ terminology has an inconvenient limitation. Suppose that in a digital-system logic-circuit diagram we see a line bearing a signal named $\overline{\text{ENABLE}}$ and also an active-low control terminal on a chip. Then we can presume that the signal is intended for application to the terminal. But suppose the terminal is not in evidence. Then we may not know whether $\overline{\text{ENABLE}}$ is the active-low enabling signal or the complement of an active-high enabling signal. Thus, if the signal in Fig. 3.13-1 were named $\overline{\text{ENABLE}}$, then, unless we were able to see the labeling on the controlled chip we would not be able to tell whether the chip is supposed to be enabled during the interval t_1 to t_2 or the interval t_2 to t_3.

To circumvent this disadvantage, the newer terminology substitutes

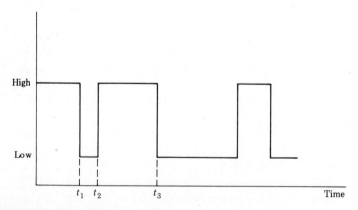

Figure 3.13-1 An arbitrary control signal.

ENABLE-H and ENABLE-L in place of ENABLE and $\overline{\text{ENABLE}}$. ENABLE-H is an active-high signal, and ENABLE-L is an active-low signal. If the signal in Fig. 3.13-1 is named, say, ENABLE-L, we shall know that it is intended to provide enabling during the interval t_1 to t_2. Of course, if the chip that requires the enabling has an active-high control terminal, the ENABLE-L signal will have to be inverted before application.

A signal named ENABLE would be appropriate for application to a device as represented in Fig. 3.12-2a, and $\overline{\text{ENABLE}}$ would be appropriate for a device represented as in b. Here the symbolism suggests that $\overline{\text{ENABLE}}$, whose active level is low, i.e., logic 0, is applied to an inverter and appears inside the device as ENABLE, which does the required enabling by going high to logic 1. When the mixed-logic convention is used, the terminology used to characterize the signals is ENABLE-H and ENABLE-L. The ENABLE-H signal is active and at logic 1 when it is high, and the ENABLE-L signal is active at logic 1 when it is low. If we have a signal ENABLE-H and the control terminal requiring the enabling signal is marked with a half arrowhead, an inverter will have to be interposed to invert voltage levels rather than to complement logic levels.

A signal ENABLE-H is a signal which disables when it is low; i.e., it is DISABLE-L. Since DISABLE $= \overline{\text{ENABLE}}$, we have

$$\text{ENABLE-H} = \overline{\text{ENABLE-L}} \qquad (3.13\text{-}1)$$

and

$$\overline{\text{ENABLE-H}} = \text{ENABLE-L} \qquad (3.13\text{-}2)$$

On the other hand, a signal which is at one level whenever enabling is required and at the other level at all other times, even if its level is always the *wrong level*, is nonetheless an enabling signal. For such a signal makes a precisely correct *distinction between the times* when enabling is or is not called for. Hence if we invert the signal ENABLE-H, we still have an ENABLE signal; but since the inverted signal is at the low level when it is supposed to be active, we have

$$\overline{\text{ENABLE-H}} = \text{ENABLE-L} \qquad (3.13\text{-}3)$$

and

$$\overline{\text{ENABLE-L}} = \text{ENABLE-H} \qquad (3.13\text{-}4)$$

Altogether we have

$$\text{ENABLE-H} = \overline{\text{ENABLE-L}} = \overline{\overline{\text{ENABLE-L}}} \qquad (3.13\text{-}5)$$

and

$$\text{ENABLE-L} = \overline{\text{ENABLE-H}} = \overline{\overline{\text{ENABLE-H}}} \qquad (3.13\text{-}6)$$

3.14 MIXED LOGIC APPLIED TO GATE STRUCTURES

In both positive and negative logic an AND gate generates an output at logic 1 only when all inputs are at logic 1, an OR gate when one or more inputs are at logic 1. In mixed logic, logic 1 is not associated with the HIGH or LOW voltage level but with *activity*. Hence, in mixed logic the AND and OR functions can be defined by the truth tables of Fig. 3.14-1a and b. Thus an AND gate generates an

A	B	Z
Inactive	Inactive	Inactive
Inactive	Active	Inactive
Active	Inactive	Inactive
Active	Active	Active

(a)

A	B	$\dot{Z}$
Inactive	Inactive	Inactive
Inactive	Active	Active
Active	Inactive	Active
Active	Active	Active

(b)

Fig. 3.14-1 Mixed-logic truth tables for (a) AND function $Z = AB$ and (b) OR function $Z = A + B$.

active level only when all inputs are at active levels. Of course, no matter what logic convention is used, all gate structures intended for some specified purpose must turn out to be equivalent. Still, depending on the logic convention used, the procedures for arriving at a required gate structure are somewhat different, as the following examples will show. Suppose we have available two control signals, both active-low, ALPHA-L and BETA-L, and we require an active-high signal GAMMA-H, which is active only when both ALPHA-L *and* BETA-L are active. Following the normal positive logic convention, we can prepare truth tables as in Fig. 3.14-2. In Fig. 3.14-2a a truth table is written out in terms of activities and specifies that GAMMA be active only when both ALPHA and BETA are both active. In Fig. 3.14-2b we have inserted 1s and 0s using the convention of positive logic. Thus, since ALPHA-L is active low, the inactive-high state is logic 1, etc. We read from Fig. 3.14-2b that the logic required is the logic provided by a NOR gate. Since we have used positive logic in making the entries in Fig. 3.14-2b, we need a positive-logic NOR gate such as one of the gates on the '02 chip.

Alternatively, with mixed logic, we proceed as follows. The requirement is for logic that provides an active output, logic 1, only for two active inputs, i.e., only when both inputs are also logic 1. This specification calls for an AND gate, as in Fig. 3.14-3a. Next we note that the inputs are active low. An active-low signal can be correctly effective only when applied to an active-low terminal. Hence, as in Fig. 3.14-3b we put half arrowheads on the inputs. The half ar-

ALPHA-L	BETA-L	GAMMA-H
Inactive	Inactive	Inactive
Inactive	Active	Inactive
Active	Inactive	Inactive
Active	Active	Active

(a)

ALPHA-L	BETA-L	GAMMA-H
1	1	0
1	0	0
0	1	0
0	0	1

(b)

Figure 3.14-2 (a) Truth table written in terms of the required activity levels of inputs and output. (b) The table with 1s and 0s replacing the activity levels assuming the convention of positive logic.

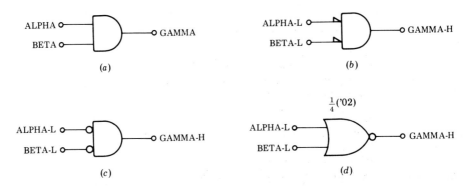

Figure 3.14-3 An example. Mixed logic development of a logic structure.

rowhead on a gate in a mixed-logic system is equivalent to an inversion circle in a positive-logic system. Hence we are led to the positive-logic structure in Fig. 3.14-3c. We need now to find among the commercially available IC gates an equivalent to the gate in Fig. 3.14-3c. Using De Morgan's theorem, we arrive again at the NOR gate as in Fig. 3.14-3d. The gate called for is one of the four NOR gates on the type '02 chip. Of course not all these steps are really required. If we had not intended this discussion to serve as an illustrative example, we could have started with Fig. 3.14-3b and gone directly to Fig. 3.14-3d.

As a second example consider that we have signals ALPHA-L, BETA-L, and GAMMA-H. We need to generate a signal DELTA-L. It is required that the DELTA signal be active whenever GAMMA is active *and* when either ALPHA *or* BETA is active. We again tentatively ignore the specifications concerning whether the signals are active high or active low. The italicized words *and* and *or* in the straightforward language statement of the specification call, of course, for an AND gate and an OR gate. We are therefore led directly to the configuration of Fig. 3.14-4a. Now taking account of the specified activity levels, we get the circuit in Fig. 3.14-4b. Applying De Morgan's theorem, we find that both gates are positive-logic NAND gates, and (see Fig. 3.11-1c) the structure uses two of the gates on the type '00 chip.

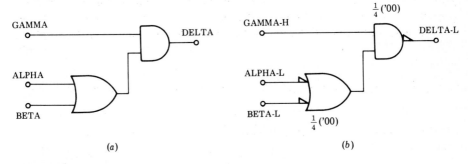

Figure 3.14-4 An example.

The mixed-logic procedure used in these examples to deduce a required gate structure has the following features:

1. It does not refer to logic levels 1 and 0 explicitly but to the matters of more immediate practical importance, i.e., the activity of signals and whether the signals are active high or active low.
2. An AND gate is viewed as a device which yields an active output when all inputs are active and an OR gate as one which yields an active output when one or more input is active.

Generally the initial gate structure displays only AND and OR gates (and sometimes EXCLUSIVE-OR gates; see Probs. 3.14-2 and 3.14-3). NAND gates and NOR gates appear when, as a second step, we take account of whether signals are active high or low and we seek an appropriate gate in a catalog where a positive-logic convention is used.

3.15 DECODERS

A number of gate structures involving multiple gates find such wide application that they are available as IC chips. These chips incorporate gates in such numbers that they are classed as medium-scale integration (MSI). In this section we shall discuss one such structure called a *decoder*; other widely used structures will be discussed in succeeding sections.

A decoder is shown in Fig. 3.15-1a; in its truth table (Fig. 3.15-1b) all the missing entries are 0s. The important characteristic of the decoder is that for each input A_1A_0 one and only one output is at logic 1. That is, at any time, one or another of the outputs (O_1, O_2, O_3, or O_4) is singled out from all the others. In the present case, this singled-out output can be distinguished in that it is at logic 1 when all the others are at logic 0. The decoder consists simply of AND gates. The inputs are applied to the gates directly or after logical inversion, as required. When $A_1 = A_0 = 0$, we have $O_0 = 1$, while $O_2 = O_3 = O_4 = 0$, etc. Each of the possible input combinations of A_1 and A_0 singles out one of the outputs. For simplicity of drawing, our decoder has only two inputs and four outputs. A decoder with n inputs would require 2^n gates and would provide 2^n outputs.

To appreciate why the arrangement of Fig. 3.15-1 is called a decoder consider the following. Suppose that we connect each AND-gate output to an individual electric circuit which causes a light bulb to turn on when the logic level at the gate output is logic 1. Suppose also that each bulb is used to illuminate a small card bearing numbers 0 to 3, which are invisible when the corresponding bulb is not lit. Then the net effect of the entire arrangement would be to make *explicit* what is presented only implicitly. Given the input logic levels, we can readily determine the number intended, but if we look instead at the output of the system, the number intended is explicitly singled out, i.e., the input information, given as a code word, has been decoded.

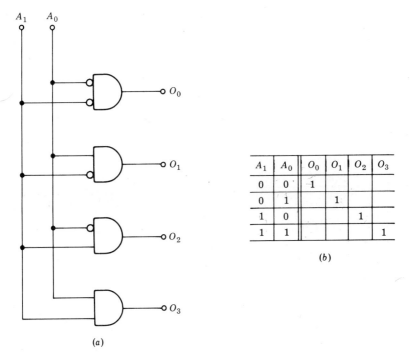

A_1	A_0	O_0	O_1	O_2	O_3
0	0	1			
0	1		1		
1	0			1	
1	1				1

(b)

(a)

Figure 3.15-1 A decoder: (a) gate structure; (b) truth table.

If it is appropriate, we need not provide the full complement of 2^n outputs. For example, say that the inputs are four lines being used to represent the decimal digits 0 to 9 in binary-coded decimal (BCD) form. Then only 10 lights are needed and the decoder need provide only 10 output lines, rather than the full possible number $2^4 = 16$. In this case, also, only 10 AND gates are required, and not all gates need have four inputs. Such is the case because there are don't-care conditions corresponding to the numbers 10 to 15, which will never be presented to the input. On the other hand, a decoder which is required to furnish m individually selectable outputs must have $2^n \geq m$.

The symbol A for the inputs (A_1, A_0) of the decoder was selected to suggest that these input bits collectively constitute an *address*; i.e., just as an address singles out one house from among many in a city, so the input *address* $A_1 A_0$ singles out one output line from among many. We shall have frequent occasion to refer to this concept of addressing.

The type '138 MSI chip decoder, shown in Fig. 3.15-2, is fabricated on a 16-pin package, and the encircled numbers are the pin numbers. This chip is a three-input, eight-output unit. Since it uses NAND gates rather than AND gates, the outputs are active low rather than active high, as in Fig. 3.15-1. Gate inputs which require no logical inversion pass through two inverters. The inverters are not actually required for logic purposes but provide buffering to reduce the burden the unit imposes on the source of the input address bits. Each gate has four

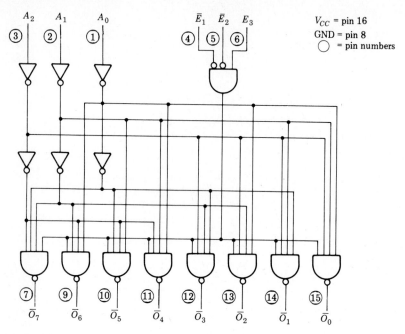

Figure 3.15-2 Logic diagram of the type '138 decoder.

inputs rather than the three required to accommodate the address bits. The extra inputs are all connected and provide an ENABLE control input. There are three ENABLE inputs, $\bar{E}_1$, $\bar{E}_2$, and E_3. We can use these inputs to provide an active-high or an active-low control or more generally arrange for the chip to be enabled only when three contributing signals have the proper logic levels simultaneously. The logic symbol for the device is shown in Fig. 3.15-3. Other decoders such as the type '155 dual 1-of-4 decoder are also available.

The newer functional symbol for the '138 decoder is shown in Fig. 3.15-4.

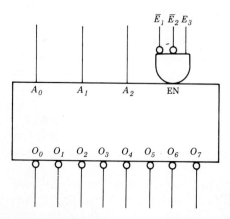

Figure 3.15-3 Logic symbol of the type '138 decoder.

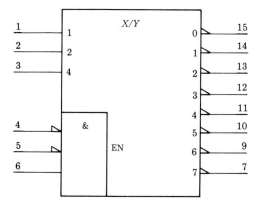

Figure 3.15-4 Newer symbolism for the type '138 decoder.

It incorporates a type of notation referred to as *dependency* notation. Input pins are on the left, output on the right. The numbers at the outward extremities of the input and output lines are again the pin numbers. The marking X/Y identifies the device as a decoder. The address inputs are pins 1, 2, and 3, which have, as indicated, the weights 1, 2, and 4. The sum of the weights of input pins activated determines the number of the output line which is activated. Thus if input lines 1 and 3 with weights 1 and 4, respectively, are activated, the output line 5 (1 + 4) identified as pin 10 is activated. The outputs, as indicated, are active low. The small rectangle labeled & and its associated inputs and marking EN indicate that input lines 4, 5, and 6 are combined in an AND gate to generate an enable control signal internally and that lines 4 and 5 are active low while line 6 is active high.

The type '139 is a dual two-input four-output line decoder in which the individual decoders are entirely independent of each other. Its newer symbol representation is shown in Fig. 3.15-5. The type '155 is also a dual two-input four-output decoder, but while each decoder has separate enable controls, there is a

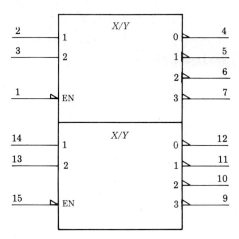

Figure 3.15-5 Symbol for the type '139 dual 2-line–to–4-line decoder. The units are independent of each other.

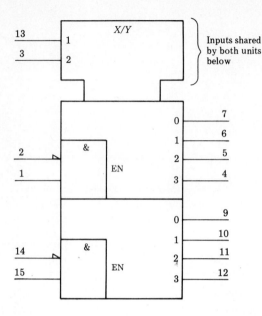

Figure 3.15-6 Symbol for the type '155 dual 2-line–to–4-line decoder. The symbolism indicates that the inputs are shared by both units.

single set of address lines which serves both decoders. The symbolism of Fig. 3.15-6 indicates this sharing of the address lines explicitly.

3.16 ENCODERS

An *encoder* performs a function which is inverse to the function performed by a decoder. An encoder is intended to operate with inputs which have the feature that, at any time, one is singled out to have a logic level different from all the others. (The encoder inputs are very often the outputs of a decoder.) To each singled-out input line a corresponding *code word*, with bits $A_0, A_1, \ldots$, appears on the output lines. Generally there need be no special relationship between the number of input lines and the number of output lines.

A possible truth table for an encoder is shown in Fig. 3.16-1a. Here we have assumed four input lines so that four output code words can be generated. We have assumed that the code words have 8 bits $A_0, A_1, \ldots, A_7$. The bits of the code words have been picked arbitrarily. We have arranged for each word to be different, although it is not required in principle that such be the case. A gate implementation of the encoder is shown in Fig. 3.16-1b. We note, for example, that $A_0 = 1$ whenever $I_3 = 1$ or $I_2 = 1$ or $I_0 = 1$. Hence the inputs to the OR gate which furnishes A_0 are I_3, I_2, and I_0. The appropriate inputs to the other gates are determined in a similar way.

Priority Encoder

Digital systems frequently include components intended to generate signals indicating that some action needs to be taken. For example, suppose that we out-

I_3	I_2	I_1	I_0	A_7	A_6	A_5	A_4	A_3	A_2	A_1	A_0
1				1	0	1	1	0	0	1	1
	1			1	1	0	1	0	1	0	1
		1		0	1	1	1	1	0	1	0
			1	1	1	0	0	1	1	0	1

(a)

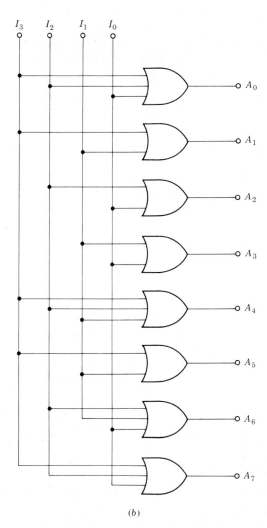

(b)

Figure 3.16-1 (a) A possible truth table for an encoder (0s to be understood in unfilled boxes); (b) a gate implementation of the truth table in (a).

fit a water tank with a switch mechanism in which the switch operates when the water level gets too high and there is danger of overflow. We can easily arrange for there to be a line which is normally at logic 0 but is changed to logic 1 when the switch operates. Then the change on the line from logic 0 to logic 1 is an indication that something needs to be done; i.e., it is a *request* for *service*. This same system may then very well have component parts which are intended to provide the needed response; i.e., they *service the request*. The service provided in the water-tank case might consist of closing an inlet valve, opening an outlet valve, etc. Frequently, in a digital system, there are a number of lines which indicate requests for service and correspondingly a number of system components which can provide service. The servicing component which is activated depends, of course, on the service-request line which presents the request for service. Quite generally each servicing component is distinguished from other such components by an address, i.e., a distinctive set of bits (an address code) through which the component is accessed through a decoder.

An encoder will normally be used to accept as inputs the service-request lines and provide as outputs the code of bits constituting the address of the component which will service the request. Since the encoder is intended to have only one input singled out at any one time, only one service request can be handled at one time. Such a situation is acceptable because generally the components which provide the service have elements in common and hence only one request can be serviced at a time.

Suppose, however, that two or more requests for service are generated at one time. Such a situation can be handled by assigning *priority* to each service-request line. If more than one request occurs simultaneously, the encoder output will address the servicing component corresponding to the request with highest priority. When that highest-priority request has been serviced, the corresponding service-request line will go back to logic 0 and the request of next highest priority can be serviced, etc.

The Fairchild type 9318 priority encoder (functionally the same as the Texas Instrument SN74148) is represented in the logic symbol of Fig. 3.16-2. Observe that all input, output, and control lines are active low. The device accepts eight inputs $\bar{I}_7, \bar{I}_6, \ldots, \bar{I}_0$ and provides three outputs $\bar{A}_2, \bar{A}_1$, and $\bar{A}_0$, which can generate $2^3 = 8$ addresses. $\overline{EI}$ is an enable input, and the purpose of the outputs $\overline{EO}$ and $\overline{GS}$ will be considered shortly.

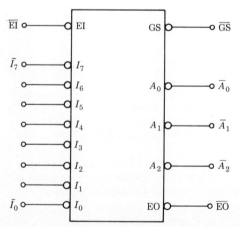

Figure 3.16-2 Logic symbol of the type 9318 priority encoder.

The logic of the encoder is shown in Fig. 3.16-3. The AND gates require multiple inputs. To avoid a complicated drawing we have represented the multiple inputs by a single line crossed by a slant with the number of inputs written alongside. Since all inputs are active low, the input I's are complemented, $\bar{I}_0, \bar{I}_1$, etc. Where an uncomplemented I or an uncomplemented EI appears, an inverter has been used, although again, for simplicity, it is not shown. The inputs furnished to each AND gate, whether supplied directly from the external world or after inversion on the chip, are listed at each gate.

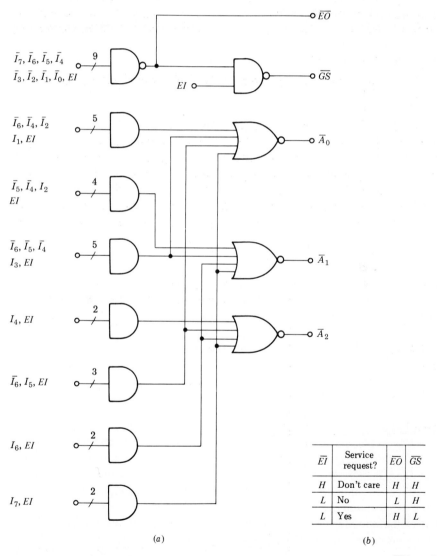

$\overline{EI}$	Service request?	$\overline{EO}$	$\overline{GS}$
H	Don't care	H	H
L	No	L	H
L	Yes	H	L

(a)   (b)

Figure 3.16-3 (a) Logic diagram of type 9318 priority encoder; (b) truth table for $\overline{EO}$ and $\overline{GS}$.

The encoder is enabled when the input enable $\overline{EI} = L$ (low) and the unit is disabled, when $\overline{EI} = H$ (high). When disabled, the encoder puts all outputs at H independently of the inputs. As can be verified (Prob. 3.16-2), the highest priority is assigned to $\bar{I}_7$ and the lowest to $\bar{I}_0$. When the encoder is enabled and when $\bar{I}_7 = L$, the output is $\bar{A}_2\bar{A}_1\bar{A}_0 = LLL = 7$ independently of the values of the other $\bar{I}$'s. When $\bar{I}_6 = L$, $\bar{A}_2\bar{A}_1\bar{A}_0 = LLH = 6$ provided that $\bar{I}_7$ is *not* L and independently of the remaining $\bar{I}$'s, and so on. Thus, when two or more input $\bar{I}$'s are simultaneously at L, the input with highest priority is encoded and the other inputs are ignored. When the output $\overline{EO}$ is $\overline{EO} = L$, the encoder thereby indicates that there is *no* service request; i.e., all the input $\bar{I}$'s are H. However, an output $\overline{EO} = H$ does not necessarily indicate that there is a service request because, as shown in Fig. 3.16-3b, we always have $\overline{EO} = H$ when $\overline{EI} = H$. Hence an additional output $\overline{GS}$ (group signal) is provided which is at L only when there is a service request.

In Fig. 3.16-4 we show how two 8-input encoders can be combined into a 16-input encoder. The following points can be verified (see Prob. 3.16-3).

1. When the $\overline{ENABLE}$ at the right is at H, the entire system is disabled and all outputs are at H.
2. When the system is enabled, the output address $\bar{A}_3\bar{A}_2\bar{A}_1\bar{A}_0$ indicates the highest-priority input line which is at L. $\bar{I}_{15}$ has highest priority, and if $\bar{I}_{15} = L$, then $\bar{A}_3\bar{A}_2\bar{A}_1\bar{A}_0 = LLLL = 15$ independently of what other inputs may be at L.
3. The scheme can be expanded. Three 8-input encoders can be combined into a 24-input encoder, etc.

In digital systems, designers often make available a line whose logic level is used to alert the system or system user to some situation of special interest or importance. This single-bit indication is called a *flag*, analogous to the flag raised or lowered by a signalman. Such a flag, the *priority flag*, has been incorporated into the system of Fig. 3.16-4. It is not essential to the present system but indicates whether there is a service request from any source.

3.17 CODE CONVERTERS

It often happens that information available in coded form must be translated into a different code. A logic circuit which accomplishes this translation is called a *code converter*. A code converter can be constructed by cascading a decoder and an encoder, as indicated in Fig. 3.17-1. A particular pattern of bits on the decoder input lines singles out a Z line. Corresponding to the Z line selected, a particular pattern of bits, i.e., a particular word, will appear at the output of the encoder. The maximum number of possible output words is 2^m, but the number of bits in the output word need bear no special relationship to the number of input lines to the decoder.

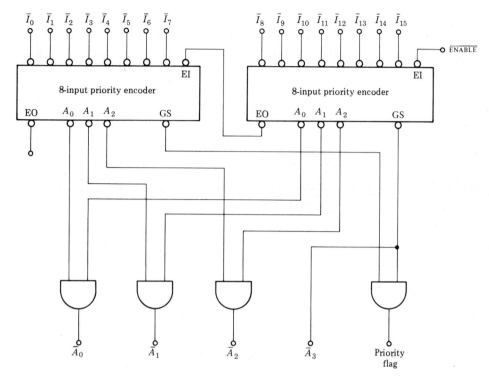

Figure 3.16-4 Two 8-input priority encoders used to make a 16-input encoder.

An interesting example of a code converter appears in connection with the digital display device represented in Fig. 3.17-2. This device, called a *seven-segment display*, has seven segments, labeled *a* to *g*, which can be individually illuminated. The illumination is provided by light-emitting diodes (LED). Segment *a* is turned on when input terminal *a* is raised to logic level 1; segment *b* is turned on when input terminal *b* is raised to logic 1; etc. (In other seven-segment displays the segments do not use LED and do not provide their own illumination. Instead an input logic 1 applied to an input terminal changes the man-

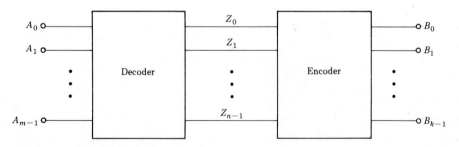

Figure 3.17-1 A code converter assembled by cascading a decoder and an encoder.

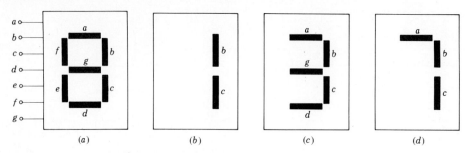

Figure 3.17-2 (*a*) A 7-segment display. In (*b*) to (*d*) the numbers 1, 3, and 7 are displayed.

ner in which the corresponding segment reflects or transmits light. Such displays are liquid-crystal displays, abbreviated LCDS.) The decimal digits can be made to appear in the display by appropriate selections of segments. Figure 3.17-2*b* to *d* shows the selection of segments which generate the numbers 1, 3, and 7, respectively.

Suppose, then, that the decimal digits are presented in BCD form and that we want to present the digits on a seven-segment display. Then we shall require a *code converter* which translates the incoming 4-bit BCD code into an appropriate output code word to illuminate the proper segments. For example, if the BCD input is $ABCD = 0011$, corresponding to decimal 3, we require the code-converter outputs (labeled to correspond to the seven-segment input as in Fig. 3.17-2*a*) to be $a = b = c = d = g = 1$ and $e = f = 0$. The details of the logic design of such a BCD–to–seven-segment code converter are left as a problem (Prob. 3.17-1).

It turns out, unhappily, that there is less than complete agreement concerning the terminology to be applied to code converters. For example, the BCD–to–seven-segment code converter we have just described, which is a rather standard commercially available IC component, is called a decoder by some manufacturers because the code converter joined to the seven-segment display takes BCD input and displays it *explicitly*. On this basis the combination of converter and display constitutes a *decoder* and by a somewhat dubious extension the term is applied to the code converter itself.

3.18 MULTIPLEXERS

A multiplexer performs the operation indicated in Fig. 3.18-1. Here we have a number of input lines, each with its own signal or logic level, and a single output line. The multiple-position switch is controllable, and depending then on where the control sets the switch, one or another of the input signal lines will be connected to the output line. A multiplexer, then, has a number of inputs and a single output and provides a means for selecting the single input which is to be transferred to the output.

A gate implementation of a multiplexer is shown in Fig. 3.18-2. Here four

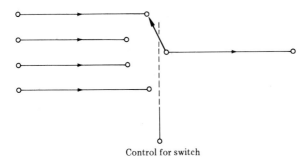

Figure 3.18-1 The function of a multiplexer.

Control for switch

inputs are provided ($I_0, \ldots, I_3$) requiring 2 bits S_1S_0 for selection, but of course the number of inputs is arbitrarily expandable at the cost of more AND gates and more address bits. The selection bits jointly determine which AND gate is enabled. Thus if $S_1 = S_0 = 0$, only gate G_0 will be enabled and I_0 will appear at the output of G_0. The outputs of all the other AND gates will be at logic 0; hence the output Z of the OR gate will also be $Z = I_0$. Selection bits $S_1S_0 = 01$, 10, and 11 will respectively transmit inputs I_1, I_2, and I_3.

Multiplexer as a Function Generator

A multiplexer can be used not only to select one of a number of lines but also to generate an arbitrary logical function of the *selection variables*. This

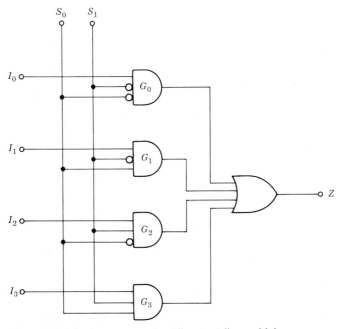

Figure 3.18-2 Logic structure of a 4-line–to–1-line multiplexer.

result might well be anticipated since we observe that a multiplexer consists of a two-level AND-OR structure and that inverters are provided for the selection lines.

Let us tentatively pretend that the input lines $I_0, \ldots, I_3$ are not present. Then (Fig. 3.18-2) the AND-gate selection-line inputs are precisely as required to generate all the minterms of the variables $S_1 S_0$. Thus, the gate G_0 generates $\bar{S}_1 \bar{S}_0$ (minterm m_0), the gate G_1 generates $\bar{S}_1 S_0$ (minterm m_1), etc. We may now view the inputs $I_0, \ldots, I_3$ as enabling inputs. If, say, $I_0 = 0$, then the output of G_0 is logic 0 independently of S_1 and S_0. But if $I_0 = 1$, the output of G_0 is $\bar{S}_0 \bar{S}_1$, and so on. Thus, the four AND gates enabled by the corresponding input $I_0, \ldots, I_3$ generate the four minterms of the selection variables, and the output of the multiplexer is the logical sum of the selected minterms. As we have already noted in Chap. 2, any function can be expressed as a sum of minterms.

For example, suppose we want to generate

$$Z = \bar{S}_1 + S_1 \bar{S}_0 \qquad (3.18\text{-}1)$$

We expand Z into minterms with the result

$$Z = \bar{S}_1(S_0 + \bar{S}_0) + S_1 \bar{S}_0 \qquad (3.18\text{-}2)$$

$$= \bar{S}_1 S_0 + \bar{S}_1 \bar{S}_0 + S_1 \bar{S}_0 \qquad (3.18\text{-}3)$$

$$= m_1 + m_0 + m_2 \qquad (3.18\text{-}4)$$

The minterm $m_1 = \bar{S}_1 S_0$ will indeed be generated if $I_1 = 1$, $m_0 = \bar{S}_1 \bar{S}_0$ will be generated if $I_0 = 1$, and, to generate $S_1 \bar{S}_0$ we need $I_2 = 1$. Hence, altogether, to generate the function of Eq. (3.18-1) we need but to arrange that $I_0 = I_1 = I_2 = 1$ and $I_3 = 0$.

The ability of a multiplexer to generate arbitrary functions can be extended to one more than the number of selection variables provided that the added variable, call it V, can be made available in complemented and uncomplemented form. Thus the multiplex of Fig. 3.18-2 can generate $Z = f(S_1, S_0, V)$. Again we start by expanding Z into its minterms. If, for example, we have the minterm $\bar{S}_1 \bar{S}_0 \bar{V}$, we generate it by applying $\bar{V}$ to the input I_0. To generate $\bar{S}_1 \bar{S}_0 V$, we apply V to input I_0. If we have both $\bar{S}_1 \bar{S}_0 \bar{V} + \bar{S}_1 \bar{S}_0 V = \bar{S}_1 \bar{S}_0 (\bar{V} + V) = \bar{S}_1 \bar{S}_0 (1)$, we set $I_0 = 1$ etc.

Example 3.18-1 Use the multiplexer of Fig. 3.18-2 to generate

$$Z = \bar{S}_1 \bar{S}_0 + \bar{S}_1 V + S_1 S_0 \bar{V} \qquad (3.18\text{-}5)$$

SOLUTION Expanding Z into its minterms, we find

$$Z = \bar{S}_1 \bar{S}_0 V + \bar{S}_1 \bar{S}_0 \bar{V} + \bar{S}_1 S_0 V + S_1 S_0 \bar{V} \qquad (3.18\text{-}6)$$

$$= \bar{S}_1 \bar{S}_0 (V + \bar{V}) + \bar{S}_1 S_0 V + S_1 S_0 \bar{V} \qquad (3.18\text{-}7)$$

$$= \bar{S}_1 \bar{S}_0 (1) + \bar{S}_1 S_0 V + S_1 S_0 \bar{V} \qquad (3.18\text{-}8)$$

Hence we require that $I_0 = 1$, $I_1 = V$, $I_3 = \bar{V}$, and since there is no term involving the product $S_1 \bar{S}_0$, we set $I_2 = 0$.

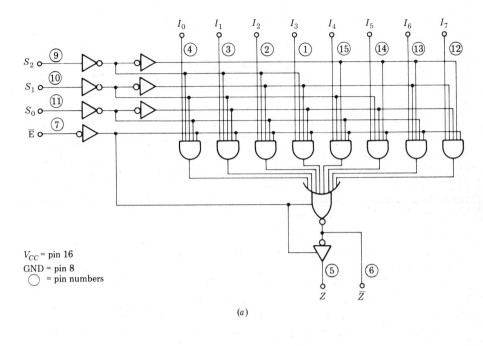

(a)

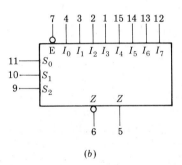

(b)

Figure 3.18-3 (*a*) Logic diagram and (*b*) logic symbol of the type '151 8-input multiplexer.

The type '151 is an eight-input multiplexer. Its logic diagram is shown in Fig. 3.18-3*a*, and its older (but at this writing more common) logic symbol in Fig. 3.18-3*b*. Note that it has an active-low ENABLE, it provides both active-high and active-low outputs, and the outputs have the tristate feature. The new symbol is shown in Fig. 3.18-4. The numbers outside the rectangle are pin numbers. The legend MUX stands for multiplexer. Pin 7, as we see, is an active-low ENABLE input. The triangles at the outputs (pins 5 and 6) indicate that these outputs are tristate. Pins 9, 10, and 11 are the selection inputs which have weights $2^0 = 1$, $2^1 = 2$, and $2^2 = 4$. The symbol $\frac{9}{7}$ indicates that these selection inputs, depending on which are active, i.e., high, can single out one or another of the signal inputs which are numbered from 0 to 7. The symbol G indicates that between the signal inputs and the selection inputs there is an AND *dependency*. It means, for example, that internally, on the chip, input 6 (pin 13) is

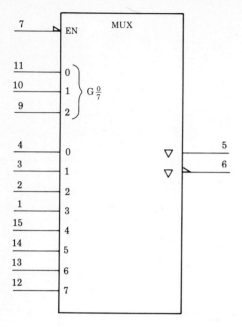

Figure 3.18-4 Newer symbol for the type '151 multiplexer.

applied to an AND gate which is enabled when pins 9 and 10 are high (active) and pin 11 is low (inactive) because under these circumstances the weight of the selection inputs is $2^2 + 2^1 = 6$.

The type '157 device is a quad 2-line–to–1-line multiplexer. It has a single ENABLE (active-low) input and a single selection input. These control inputs provide a common control for all four individual multiplexers on the chip. The newer symbol for the device is shown in Fig. 3.18-5.

3.19 MULTIPLEXING WITH OPEN-COLLECTOR AND TRISTATE OUTPUTS

Multiplexing, as we have seen, allows us to couple, one at a time, a number of different signal sources to a single line. Short of actually using a multiplexer, as described in the previous section, there are other ways of accomplishing the same purpose which are not different in principle but only in detail. Yet they are of practical importance.

Open Collector

Referring to the multiplexer circuit of Fig. 3.18-2, let us first note that if the OR gate were replaced by a NOR gate, the circuit would nonetheless continue to function as a multiplexer. We can readily undo the inversion occasioned by the NOR gate by adding an inverter in the Z line.

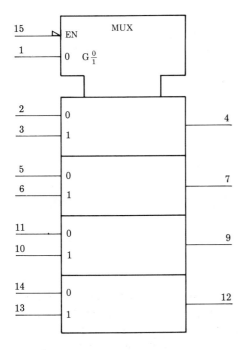

Figure 3.18-5 Symbol for type '157 quad 2-line–to–1-line multiplexer.

Next, let us consider, as in Fig. 3.19-1, that we have a number of identical IC chips whose circuitry, leading to an output terminal, is as shown. That is, the output is taken from a terminal of a logic-operated switch such as is described in Sec. 3.7 (see Fig. 3.7-1). Further, the switch is driven by an AND gate one input of which is an externally supplied ENABLE input. A second AND-gate input is a signal of some sort generated within the chip. The nature of this signal and the nature of the other externally applied inputs required to generate this signal are irrelevant. The chips are equipped with *open-collector* outputs, as described in Sec. 3.8. The outputs are paralleled, and the single common resistor needed to connect the collector terminals to the supply-voltage source is external to the chips.

We recall that the paralleled arrangement of logic-operated switches constitutes a NOR gate (see Fig. 3.8-1). Hence, altogether, the configuration of Fig. 3.19-1 consisting of an array of AND gates followed by the NOR gate constitutes a multiplexer by which we can transmit the signal of one chip or another to the output. Of course, we shall need to provide a decoder to assure that only one chip is enabled at one time. An additional decoder chip may not be required; for, as we have seen, many chips have multiple ENABLE inputs, as indicated in Figs. 3.15-2 and 3.15-3. In such a case we need only provide the selection inputs since the decoding is done right on the chip.

In summary, suppose we have IC chips equipped with open-collector outputs and that we need to multiplex outputs of these chips to a single line. Then we do not have to provide an additional multiplexer chip for the purpose but

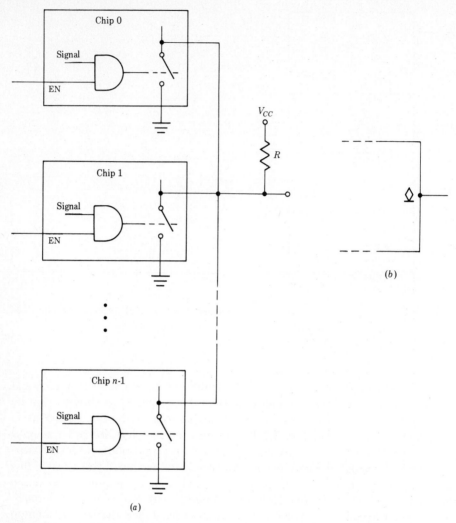

Figure 3.19-1 (*a*) Open-collector outputs can be multiplexed to a common line without the explicit addition of a multiplexer. (*b*) Symbol for an open-collector output.

need only connect all the outputs to that single line and provide a connection through a resistor to the supply voltage.

In the older symbolism there is no symbol to represent an open collector, and the user could learn of the availability of this feature only by reading the catalog description of the device. The open-collector representation in the newer symbolism is shown in Fig. 3.19-1*b*.

Tristate Output

Chips with tristate outputs can also be multiplexed without an explicit multiplexer. For with a tristate output, a chip whose output is disabled is actually

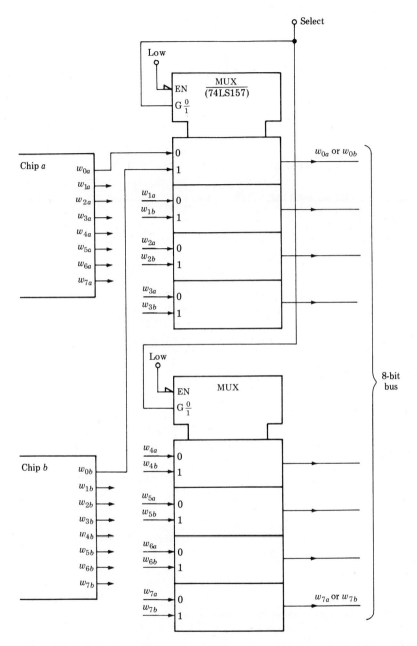

Figure 3.19-2 Two chips which generate 8-bit output words are multiplexed onto an 8-bit bus.

disconnected from the output line. Hence to arrange for multiplexing we need only connect all outputs to the single line and arrange for only one chip to be enabled at one time, either by using an external decoder or by using decoding features incorporated on the chip.

The principal reason for incorporating the tristate feature on a chip is precisely to allow multiplexing without using an explicit multiplexer. Much the same comment applies to the open-collector feature. Consider the situation shown in Fig. 3.19-2, where we have two chips which provide not a single output bit but an output consisting of an 8-bit *word*. The line or lines used in common by a number of signal sources is called a *bus*. In the present case, we need an 8-line bus instead of a single-line bus. Correspondingly we need eight two-input-line, one-output-line multiplexers. We have used for the purpose two quad type '157 chips shown in Fig. 3.18-5. If the chips a and b were equipped with tristate or open-collector output, the multiplexers would not be needed. Instead we would only have to connect outputs w_{0a} and w_{0b} directly to one line of the bus, w_{1a} and w_{1b} to the second line, and so on.

3.20 DEMULTIPLEXING

Suppose that we have a number of sources in which words are generated and a number of potential receivers, i.e., destinations, for these words. Suppose, further, that we want to be able to transmit a word from any source to any receiver. One way to accomplish this is to provide a separate bus (with lines equal in number to the number of bits per word) from every source to every

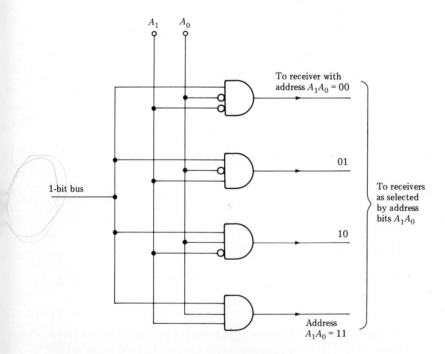

Figure 3.20-1 The logic structure of a demultiplexer.

receiver. An advantage of such an arrangement is that we would be able to transmit many words simultaneously. As a matter of practice it often turns out not to be feasible or convenient to provide such a multiple bus. Hence we resort to multiplexing, which allows us to use one bus for many different sources. We now clearly require, as well, a *demultiplexer*, i.e., a logic structure which will take a word *from* a bus and direct it *to* a selected receiver.

A 1-line–to–4-line demultiplexer is shown in Fig. 3.20-1. Note that the structure is a *decoder*, with the modification that each gate has an additional input to which the bus line is connected. Depending on the address provided by the address bits $A_1 A_0$, the input data will be directed to one destination or another.

The integrated circuit of Fig. 3.15-2, which we have characterized as a decoder, can also be used as a 1-line–to–8-line demultiplexer and, as a matter of fact, is described by the manufacturer as a decoder-demultiplexer. Note that the output of the gate with input pins 4, 5, and 6 (the ENABLE gate) provides one input of all the AND gates of the decoder. If then we set $\bar{E}_1 = \bar{E}_2 = $ LOW, the input E_3 is an appropriate input for a one-line bus.

FOUR

FLIP-FLOPS, REGISTERS, AND COUNTERS

4.1 INTRODUCTION

The circuit of Fig. 4.1-1, consisting of a pair of coupled inverters, is the basic structure of a most important and basic logic circuit, called a *static latch*. In Fig. 4.1-1*a* the structure is drawn in a circuit pattern which explicitly shows that the output of one inverter is connected to the input of the second and that the output of the second is connected to the input of the first. In Fig. 4.1-1*b* the circuit is drawn in a more generally convenient manner. We have labeled the two accessible terminals Q and $\bar{Q}$ in anticipation of the fact, which we shall verify, that the logic levels at these terminals are complementary to each other. In the following discussion we use the customary convention of positive logic in which H (the higher voltage level) represents logic 1 and L (the lower voltage level) represents logic 0.

Without any external intervention, the latch may persist indefinitely in one of two possible situations called *states*. Suppose we postulate that $Q = $ L; then the output of the bottom inverter is indeed $\bar{Q} = $ H. Hence the postulate $Q = $ L is entirely self-consistent, and if the latch is initially established in the $Q = $ L and $\bar{Q} = $ H state, it will remain in that state indefinitely. The second state of the latch, as is readily verified, is the one in which $Q = $ H and $\bar{Q} = $ L.

The essential and *new* element which the latch adds to the logic structures we have considered so far is that the latch can be used to establish and hold a logic level without any external intervention. In all the logic structures we examined earlier, the output of a gate depends on the gate inputs provided by some external source. In the absence of gate inputs, which we can, at least, imagine, we cannot unambiguously conceive of gate outputs.

Because of this independence of the latch from external inputs, a latch can

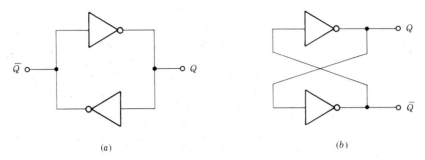

(a)   (b)

Figure 4.1-1 (*a*) Coupled inverters constituting the basic structure of the *latch*. (*b*) The circuit redrawn more conveniently.

be used to *store*, i.e., *register* or *remember* a logic bit. An array of *k* flip-flops can serve to *register* a *k*-bit word. Assume, for example, that we have the 8-bit word 11001010, which we want to store away and remember because we expect to need it later. We then arrange an array of eight latches. We would decide which terminal of each latch is to be the Q and which the $\bar{Q}$ and so label them. We would then establish the states of the latches as is shown in Fig. 4.1-2, in which there is a one-to-one correspondence of the latch states with the bits of our word to be remembered. The word has now been *written* into the *register* to remain there as long as we like. A *register* in this sense is the "writing paper" on which we can record any word we want to remember. Note, also, as appears in Fig. 4.1-2, that there is available at the $\bar{Q}$ terminals of the register a second word in which each bit is the complement of the bit of the word we have stored. We shall frequently find the availability of this second word convenient.

The two states of a latch are referred to as the *set* state and the *reset* state. The set state is the one in which the terminal we have elected to call Q is at $Q = H$ ($\bar{Q} = L$). The reset state is the one in which $Q = L$ ($\bar{Q} = H$). The reset state is frequently called the *clear* state. It is quite easy to put a latch in one

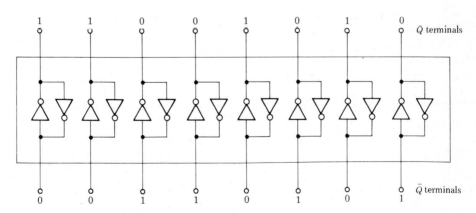

Figure 4.1-2 An array of latches serving as a register to store a word.

state or the other as we please. Suppose we want to put a latch in the set state. To accomplish this we need only connect the Q terminal temporarily to an external point which is at the high voltage level. This temporary connection drives Q high and $\bar{Q}$ low, and when the connection is removed, the latch will *remain* in the state with $Q = H$ and $\bar{Q} = L$. Correspondingly, a *temporary* connection of the Q terminal to an external point at the low voltage level will reset (or clear) the latch. The latch will remain in the reset state *permanently* if not further disturbed.

The static latch is one of a number of related logic circuits all of which are able to store a bit. Other related circuits we shall consider include the dynamic latch and the flip-flop.

4.2 A LATCH WITH NOR GATES

For greater convenience in manipulating the latch it is advantageous to replace the simple inverters with NOR gates or NAND gates. The extra input terminals of the gates provide *control* terminals and allow additional avenues of access to the latch.

The logic diagram and the logic symbol of a latch using NOR gates are shown in Fig. 4.2-1. The control terminals on the gates are labeled R and S for reasons that will appear shortly. If both R and S are $R = S = L$, the NOR gates are enabled and, so far as the other input of each gate is concerned, each gate is simply an inverter as required in a latch. Thus with $R = S = L$ the latch may be in either of its two possible states. The state in which it finds itself will depend on its past history. Thus when $R = S = L$, the latch is entirely uninfluenced by the R and S input terminals.

Suppose now that the R terminal becomes $R = H$; then the gate G1 becomes disabled and Q will become $Q = L$ while $\bar{Q}$ will become $\bar{Q} = H$. That is, the fact the R has become $R = H$ has reset the latch. It is for this reason that

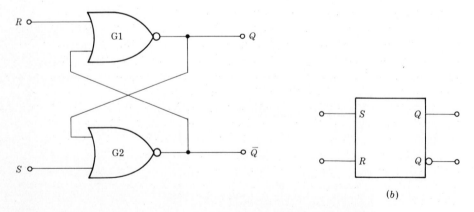

Figure 4.2-1 A latch using NOR gates: (a) logic diagram and (b) logic symbol.

the R terminal has been labeled R for *reset*. If the latch had been in the reset state originally, placing $R = H$ would have produced no state change. If the latch had been in the set state originally, placing $R = H$ would have caused a change from the set state to the reset state. Most important, in the reset state $\bar{Q}$, which is $\bar{Q} = H$ and is an input to gate G1, has now disabled G1 so that the gate can no longer respond to the logic level at R. Consequently, if we now restore R to $R = L$, the latch will *remain* in the reset state.

Altogether, we have the following result. With $R = S = L$, either state of the latch is possible. If R goes to $R = H$ permanently or temporarily, the latch will be reset. In a similar way, starting with $R = S = L$, if S (standing for *set*) goes to $S = H$ permanently or temporarily, the latch will go to the set state or remain in the set state if it is already in that state.

When the latch is intended to be left alone to remember a bit, it will have $S = R = L$. When we intend to store logic 0 in the latch, we arrange that $S = L$ while $R = H$, at least temporarily. To store logic 1 we shall arrange that $S = H$ while $R = L$. No useful purpose is served by arranging for both S and R to be $S = R = H$ simultaneously. As a matter of fact, there may well be a disadvantage in so doing; for suppose that starting with $S = R = H$, we now allow both S and R to become $S = R = L$ simultaneously. Then the resultant state of the latch will not be predictable. Absolute simultaneity is not possible, and if R should actually change first, we would pass first through the situation $S = H$, $R = L$. As a result the latch would go to the set state and remain in that state when S and R became $S = R = L$. Similarly, if S should change first, the latch would end up in the reset state. We note incidentally that with $S = R = H$ we would have $Q = \bar{Q} = L$ and the implication in Fig. 4.2-1 that the outputs are complementary would be incorrect.

The behavior of the latch is conveniently summarized by either of the truth tables of Fig. 4.2-2. The table in Fig. 4.2-2*a* requires no further explanation except to note that for reasons presented above the case $S = R = H$ is not used. In connection with the table in Fig. 4.2-2*b* we contemplate that the S and R inputs are changing in an arbitrary fashion. Thus there will be intervals when $S = R = L$, intervals when $S = L$, $R = H$, and invervals when $S = H$, $R = L$. Again, as noted, we exclude the case $S = R = H$. Let us then number the intervals in order $1, 2, \ldots, n, n + 1, \ldots$ as they occur in time. Then in an interval

S	R	Q	$\bar{Q}$
L	L	L or H	H or L
L	H	L	H
H	L	H	L
H	H	Not used	

(a)

S	R	Q_{n+1}	$\bar{Q}_{n+1}$
L	L	Q_n	$\bar{Q}_n$
L	H	L	H
H	L	H	L
H	H	Not used	

(b)

Figure 4.2-2 Truth tables for the SR NOR-gate latch.

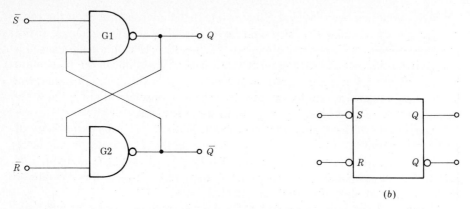

Figure 4.3-1 A latch using NAND gates: (a) logic diagram and (b) logic symbol.

$n + 1$ when $S = $ L and $R = $ H, we shall find $Q_{n+1} = $ L ($\bar{Q}_{n+1} = $ H) no matter what the logic levels of S and R were in the preceding time intervals. Similarly with $S = $ H and $R = $ L in the interval $n + 1$ we shall have $Q_{n+1} = $ H no matter what the previous history. However, if in the interval $n + 1$ we have $S = R = $ L, the state of the latch will be the same in that interval as it was in interval n.

4.3 A LATCH WITH NAND GATES

Anything that can be done with NOR gates can be done as well with NAND gates. The logic diagram and logic symbol of a latch using NAND gates is shown in Fig. 4.3-1. As before, we have arbitrarily labeled the upper of the output terminals as the Q terminal. In the present case it turns out that it is the lower control terminal that allows us to reset and the upper control terminal that allows us to set. This situation is the opposite of that in the NOR-gate flip-flop. Further, the control terminals are *active low* and are hence labeled $\bar{S}$ and $\bar{R}$ rather than S and R.

    The truth tables of the NAND-gate latch are given in Fig. 4.3-2 and are easily verified. When $\bar{S} = \bar{R} = $ H, both gates are enabled and either of the states is possible, the state being determined by the logic levels on $\bar{S}$ and $\bar{R}$ that

$\bar{S}$	$\bar{R}$	Q	$\bar{Q}$
L	L	Not used	
L	H	H	L
H	L	L	H
H	H	L or H	H or L

(a)

$\bar{S}$	$\bar{R}$	Q_{n+1}	$\bar{Q}_{n+1}$
L	L	Not used	
L	H	H	L
H	L	L	H
H	H	Q_n	$\bar{Q}_{n+1}$

(b)

Figure 4.3-2 Truth tables for the SR NAND-gate latch.

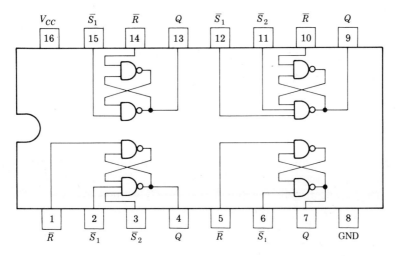

Figure 4.3-3 Logic diagram of the type '279 quad set-reset latch. Positive logic is assumed.

prevailed earlier. Starting with $\bar{S} = \bar{R} = $ H, if we change $\bar{R}$ from H to L, gate G2 will become disabled and $\bar{Q}$ will become (or remain) $\bar{Q} = $ H. Now both inputs of G1 are high and Q becomes (or remains) $Q = $ L. This output $Q = $ L of G1 is an input to G2 which is thereby disabled. Hence, if $\bar{R}$ should now return to $\bar{R} = $ H, it will produce no further change. Altogether, a change of $\bar{R}$ from high to low, even temporarily, will serve to reset the latch. In a similar way we can establish that a temporary change in $\bar{S}$ from high to low will set the latch.

The logic diagram (using positive logic) of the type '279 quad set-reset latch is shown in Fig. 4.3-3. Note that having 16 pins available on the package, the manufacturer has added extra $\bar{S}$ controls to two of the latches. Hence, without requiring extra chips, these two latches can be set by one or another of two control signals (or, of course, by both together). The control inputs are active low, and we might want to display this feature by the symbolism of mixed logic rather than by the bars over the S and R. In this case a single latch would be represented as in Fig. 4.3-4.

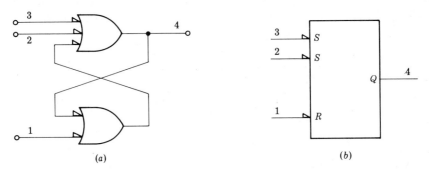

(a) (b)

Figure 4.3-4 (*a*) Logic diagram and (*b*) logic symbol of one latch of the type '279 using mixed logic.

4.4 THE CHATTERLESS SWITCH

As a simple yet useful application of a latch, consider the situation represented in Fig. 4.4-1. In Fig. 4.4-1*a* a switch is being used to make available a voltage $V_0 = 0$ or $V_0 = V$. These voltages may be the voltages corresponding to the logic levels in a digital system. If positive logic is being used, 0 V, represented in Fig. 4.4-1 as ground, would represent logic 0 while V volts would represent logic 1. The arrangement is intended to allow us manually to present one logic level or the other to the input of some digital system. Logic level 0 appears at V_0 when the switch is at position B, and logic level 1 appears when the switch is at A. If the resistor R were not present, the logic level of V_0 would be ambiguous when the moving arm of the switch was between contact positions. We have connected R to ground (0 V representing logic 0) so that V_0 is at 0 except when the switch makes contact at A. We could equally well have connected the resistor between the switch arm and V.

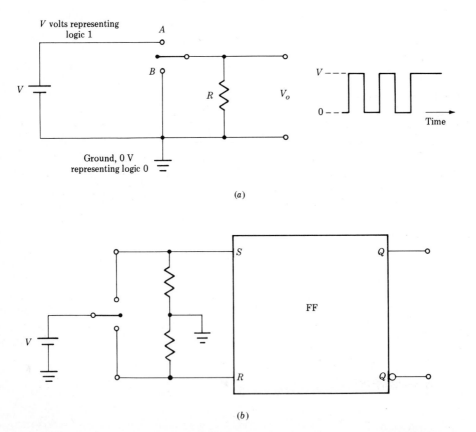

(a)

(b)

Figure 4.4-1 (*a*) A switch is used to establish one logic level or the other. (*b*) A latch is used to avoid the effect of chatter in the mechanical switch.

A common characteristic of a mechanical switch is that when the arm is thrown from one position to the other, it *bounces* or *chatters* several times before coming to rest in the new position of contact. Suppose that we throw the switch arm from position B to position A, intending V_0 to change from logic 0 to logic 1. Quite typically the switch arm will come in contact at A and bounce off several times. (The bounce is ordinarily not high enough to carry the arm back to contact with B.) As a result, as shown, the voltage V_0 will make several transitions rather than a single one between logic 0 and logic 1.

A *chatterless* switch is shown in Fig. 4.4-1*b*. A set-reset latch is employed. The S and R terminals have been connected to ground (logic 0) through resistors so that these terminals are at logic 0 except when connected to V (logic 1) by the switch. The switch can be thrown either way to establish logic 1 at either S or at R. If the switch is at R, then $Q = 0$; if it is at S, then $Q = 1$. Suppose, for example, we have the switch at R, so that $Q = 0$. Let us now throw the switch to S. Then at contact with S we shall have $Q = 1$. If the switch bounces off S (but not all the way back to R), we shall have $S = R = 0$. But with these inputs either state of the flip-flop is allowed, and the latch will simply remain at $Q = 1$, eliminating the effect of the bounce.

4.5 GATED LATCHES

The S and R latch inputs (or the $\bar{S}$ and $\bar{R}$ inputs) are often called data inputs since it is the information presented at these terminals which determines what is stored in the latch. It frequently turns out to be useful to provide a mechanism which will allow us to connect the latch to the data source or to isolate it. Such a latch is shown in Fig. 4.5-1*a*. When ENABLE $= 0$, the gates G1 and G2 are disabled, the latch is isolated from the data, $S' = R' = 1$ independently of S and R, and the state of the latch is as determined by past history. When EN-ABLE $= 1$, $S' = \bar{S}$ and $R' = \bar{R}$ and S and R become active-high set and reset inputs. The signal applied at the ENABLE input is called the *gate* or the *strobe*, and the circuit is called a *gated* or *strobed* latch or sometimes a *dynamic* latch. Correspondingly, the latch without isolation gates of Fig. 4.2-1 or 4.3-1 is called a static latch.

An important application of a gated latch is shown in Fig. 4.5-1*b*. Here we contemplate a line carrying data which are changing with time. This line may be one line of a multiple-line bus. At some time we would like to capture and hold the data D ($= 0$ or 1) on the line. To accomplish this we enable the latch. Since $S = D$ and $R = \bar{D}$, then, as can readily be verified from the truth table of the latch, we shall always have $Q = D$. Thus, so long as ENABLE is active, the latch output Q *will follow the data input D*. This feature of the operation is characterized by describing the latch as *transparent*. When we want to capture and hold the data, we disable the latch. The static part of the latch is left in the situation where either of its states is allowed and the state locked in will be determined by the value of D immediately before the dynamic latch was disabled. If indeed we had a multiple-line bus bearing a word, capturing the entire word would

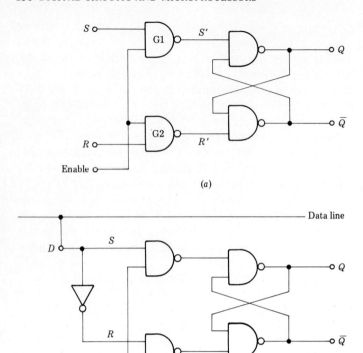

(a)

(b)

Figure 4.5-1 (a) A gated latch and (b) a type D gated latch.

require as many strobed latches as the word has bits and all such latches would be driven by the same ENABLE signal. A latch with a single D input, as in Fig. 4.5-1b, is called a type D latch.

Waveforms to illustrate the typical operation of a transparent latch are shown in Fig. 4.5-2. At time t_0 the latch is disabled because G (the enabling input to the isolation gates) is low. We assume arbitrarily that Q = L. From t_1 to

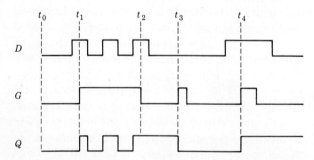

Figure 4.5-2 Waveforms to illustrate the operation of a transparent latch.

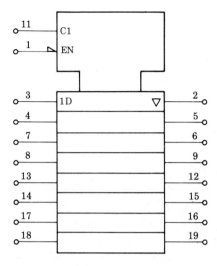

Figure 4.5-3 Symbol for the type '373 octal type D transparent latch.

t_2 the latch is enabled, and Q follows the input data D. At t_2 the latch is disabled, and the data $D = $ H are latched in. Other occasions of latching the data are shown at t_3 and t_4.

The type '373 chip is an octal type D transparent latch. Its logic symbol is given in Fig. 4.5-3. Each of the eight latches has a tristate output, and all are controlled by an active-low ENABLE input. The common ENABLE input signal for the isolation gates is here called C, which stands for clock. The reason for this terminology will be discussed in the next section. The 1 which appears in the symbol C1 indicates that this input *controls* inputs which have the same number 1. The 1 at the beginning of the label 1D indicates that the D input is *controlled* by the clock input.

4.6 CLOCKING

A universal characteristic of logic gates is that they introduce propagation delays in the logic signal transmitted through them. These delays may vary from sample to sample of a gate type of a single manufacturer and may even vary in a particular sample with aging, temperature, and other environmental changes. Logic signals passing through many gates may well suffer overall propagation delays which are hardly predictable and subject to considerable variability. Delays not properly taken into account may generate signals which go to logic levels other than those intended. Consider, for example, the situation represented in Fig. 4.6-1. The input A is initially $A = 0$ and goes to $A = 1$ at $t = t_0$. When $A = 0$, $B = 1$, and $C = 0$ so that $Z = 0$. When $A = 1$, we shall have $B = 0$ and $C = 1$, so that again we should have $Z = 0$. But suppose, as indicated in the waveform, that the delay through gate G1 is longer than the delay through gate G2. Then there will be an interval (equal to the difference in the delays) when both B and C will be $B = C = 1$, and for this interval we shall

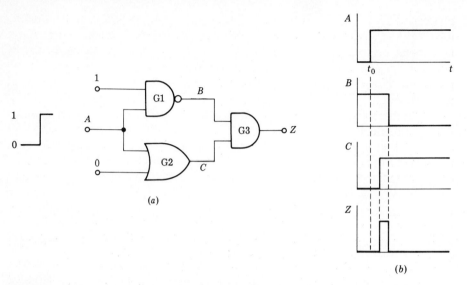

Figure 4.6-1 (*a*) A logic circuit that generates a hazard; and (*b*) waveforms.

have Z at the unintended level $Z = 1$. The excursions of logic signals to levels not intended, even if only briefly, are called *hazards*. In combinational circuits (circuits without memory) hazards are bad enough; but if they are brief enough, and if the devices which might respond to them are sluggish enough, they may be no cause for serious concern. Where they do cause a problem, sometimes simple procedures can be invoked to eliminate them (see Prob. 4.6-1). Suppose, however, that we have a system with memory, i.e., latches. As we have seen, even a brief incorrect level in the set or reset inputs will affect the state of the latch, and the correspondingly incorrect state of the latch may persist indefinitely.

It is therefore of great advantage to be able to arrange a latch in which the data terminal determines the eventual state of the latch but which has the feature that the exact moment of response to the data is determined by an auxiliary signal. It will then be possible to restrain the latch from responding until all logic levels which are to influence the latch have indeed established themselves at their final levels.

The gated latch of Fig. 4.5-1 provides (tentatively at least) precisely the restraining mechanism we require and serves as the basis for *synchronous* operation of digital circuits. In a synchronous system we apply at the ENABLE input a waveform which makes transitions back and forth from high to low, enabling and disabling the isolation gates G1 and G2. These gates are kept disabled so long as the input data (S and R or D) are not yet established at their proper final value, i.e., so long as the data are not *valid* and the gates are enabled when the data are valid.

In a digital system using such delayed registration of data in its storage devices, each cycle of the waveform applied at ENABLE advances the digital processing by one step. The rate at which processing proceeds is then determined by the rate at which these cycles occur, and hence the ENABLE waveform is appropriately called a *clocking* waveform. In most systems the clock cycles occur at a regular rate, like the ticking of a clock, and the term is even more appropriate. Since the entire system must operate in step, i.e., in synchronism, with the clock, a clocked system is called a *synchronous system*.

The time allocated to a clock cycle will depend on the speed (principally propagation delays) of the physical devices employed. Devices with long propagation delay will require a correspondingly longer clock cycle. It may be a matter of convenience to keep the latch isolated for as long as possible in each clock cycle, enabling the isolation gates only long enough to allow the latch to respond to the valid data. In this case the clock waveform would appear as a regular sequence of narrow pulses, and a cycle of the waveform could appropriately be called a *clock pulse*. However, it is useful to keep in mind that the clock need not consist of narrow pulse but may even be an entirely symmetrical waveform.

4.7 A LIMITATION OF THE LATCH AS A STORAGE ELEMENT

Two features are quite general in synchronous digital systems: (1) a common clocking waveform is used for all the storage elements in the system, and (2) the data inputs of the storage elements may be derived in part or even entirely from the outputs of other storage elements. When the clocked latches we have described are used as the storage elements, a serious difficulty arises.

To explore the matter in a simple example, we consider the situation represented in Fig. 4.7-1, where one latch receives its data from some external source but the second latch receives its data from the first latch. To be specific we consider that the latches are of the type shown in Fig. 4.5-1a, where the enabling transition of the clock, i.e., the transition which allows transfer of the input data to the latch, is the transition from logic 0 to logic 1 (low to high in positive logic). We assume that at $t = 0$, or shortly before the first enabling transition of the clock, both latches are in the reset condition ($Q_1 = Q_2 = 0$).

It is our intention that during the first clock cycle the first latch should go to the set state, $Q_1 = 1$, and that during the second clock cycle the second latch should also go to the set state. We might imagine (mistakenly, as we shall see) that such would indeed be the sequence that occurs. For at $t = 0$, $S_1 = 1$ and $R_1 = 0$ while $S_2 = Q_1 = 0$ and $R_2 = \bar{Q}_1 = 1$. Hence, as seen from the truth table of Fig. 4.2-2, the response of the latches to the first enabling transition of the clock waveform should be that the first latch sets but that the second latch remains reset. At the time of the next enabling transition of the clock at $t = t_1$ we shall have $S_2 = Q_1 = 1$ and $R_2 = \bar{Q}_1 = 0$. Hence, while the first latch should remain set, now the second latch should also go to the set state.

If our scheme really worked, we could add additional clocked latches to the cascade of two in Fig. 4.7-1 and we would have a circuit which, clock cycle by clock cycle, would shift data down the cascade. Such a cascade of storage ele-

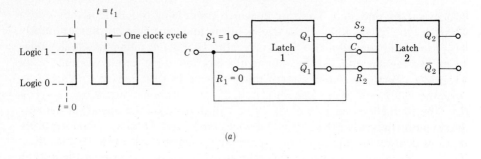

(a)

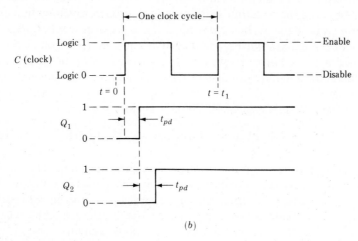

(b)

Figure 4.7-1 (a) A cascade of two latches and (b) response of cascade to clocking waveforms when $S_1 = 1$ and $R_1 = 0$.

ments, called a *shift register*, is a very useful and basic logic structure; it is discussed further in Sec. 4-17.

We can now see, as shown in the waveforms of Fig. 4.7-1b, that this anticipated sequence will not take place. Here we have drawn waveforms of the clock and of the logic levels at Q_1 and Q_2. In these waveforms we have taken account of the fact that there will be a propagation delay t_{pd} through a latch. Since $S_1 = 1$ and $R_1 = 0$, the first triggering transition induces a change in Q_1 from $Q_1 = 0$ to $Q_1 = 1$. This change appears in Q_1 at a time t_{pd} after the triggering transition. Initially Q_2 does not change since $S_2 = Q_1 = 0$ and $R_2 = \bar{Q}_1 = 1$. However, after the propagation delay through the first latch, S_2 becomes $S_2 = 1$ and R_2 becomes $R_2 = 0$. And now we note, most important, that, *even after Q_1 ($=S_2$) and $\bar{Q}_1$ ($=R_2$) have assumed their new values, the clock is still at $C = 1$, which is the level at which the second latch is coupled to its data terminals.* Accordingly, after an additional propagation delay, we find that Q_2 goes to $Q_2 = 1$. The overall result is that, after some delays, a single enabling transition of the clock has set both latches. (If there were additional latches in the cascade, they would also respond after each successive latch propagation delay so long as C remained at $C = 1$.) We did not intend this to be the response of the cascade. What we planned was for the first triggering transition to set the first latch and for the second triggering transition to set the second latch. More generally, for a longer cascade, setting of the latches should occur one at a time, clock cycle by clock cycle, in response to *successive* enabling transitions.

One way of relieving the difficulty is to arrange for the clock to stay at the enabling level for a very short time. In such a case the clock waveform in Fig. 4.7-1 would have the appearance of a train of positive pulses, the pulse duration being very short in comparison with the interval between pulses. In this case, if the clock-pulse duration were shorter than the propagation delay through a latch, the circuit would operate as required, for in such a situation we would have C returning to the disabling level $C = 0$ before the response of the first latch to the clock pulse became apparent at $Q_1 (=S_2)$ and $\bar{Q}_1 (=R_2)$. This solution however, requires the generation and transmission throughout a digital system of very narrow pulses. In many situations pulses narrow enough to avoid the timing difficulty described above may be too narrow to enable the latch long enough for reliable operation. Besides, transmitting very narrow pulses throughout a digital system is a matter beset with difficulties.

In summary, we find that the clocked latch has a deficiency in a synchronous system in which the latch data input is derived entirely or in part from the outputs of other latches. The difficulty is rather obviously related to the fact that the clock latch is transparent. Hence we run into trouble whenever in one clock cycle we try to *read* the data previously stored in the latch and to *write* new data into the latch. On the other hand, when we need a storage element into which we can write or from which we can read, but not both in one clock cycle, the latch is a perfectly serviceable device. In the next sections we shall consider circuits which have the feature lacking in the latch. These circuits are called *flip-flops*.

4.8 THE MASTER-SLAVE FLIP-FLOP

A type of clocked storage device which is not transparent is the master-slave flip-flop of Fig. 4.8-1. It consists of two individual latches of the type shown in Fig. 4.5-1. One latch is called the *master* and the other the *slave*. In addition there are data *input* gates 1A and 1B and a second set of *coupling* gates 3A and 3B, through which, when they are enabled, the data in the master latch can be transferred to the slave. The clocking waveforms applied to the input gates and to the coupling gates are complementary. When the clock waveform is at the level to enable the input gates, the input data at the S and R terminals are written into the master latch. However, when the input gates are enabled, the coupling gates are disabled, so that there is no transfer from master to slave. When the coupling gates are enabled, data are transferred from master to slave but since, at this time, the input gates are disabled, new data are not written into the master.

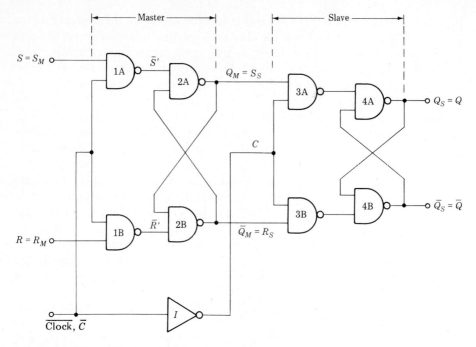

Figure 4.8-1 The master-slave flip-flop.

As the clock rises from the low to the high level to enable the input gates, the coupling gates must be disabled *before* the input gates allow transfer of data into the master latch, to prevent transfer of data to the output. Further, as the clock drops from high to low, the input gates must be disabled *before* the coupling gates are enabled. Accordingly the voltage levels at which the input gates and the coupling gates become enabled and disabled are adjusted so that the sequence of events is as represented in Fig. 4.8-2. Here a single clock cycle is shown, displaying finite rise and fall times so that different voltage levels are attained at different times.

If master-slave flip-flops are used in the arrangement of Fig. 4.7-1, the response of the flip-flops would be as shown in Fig. 4.8-3. At clock transition 1

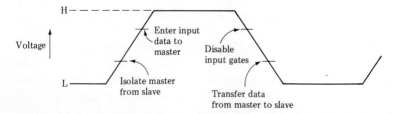

Figure 4.8-2 Sequence of events in a master-slave flip-flop during a clock cycle.

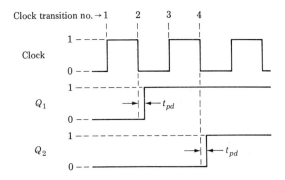

Figure 4.8-3 Response of the cascade of Fig. 4.7-1 when latches are replaced by master-slave flip-flops.

the new data ($S_1 = 1$, $R_1 = 0$) are written into the master latch of the first flip-flop, but no change occurs in the output Q_1. In response to clock edge 2 but *after a small delay* t_{pd}, the new data appear at the output Q_1. However, the same edge 2 *almost immediately* disables the input gates (1A and 1B in Fig. 4.8-1) of the second flip-flop, so that the second flip-flop makes no response at all to the change in Q_1. Hence, after one complete clock cycle, the new data have been written in the first flip-flop, but the state of the second flip-flop corresponds to the data ($Q_1 = S_2 = 0$, $\bar{Q}_1 = R_2 = 1$) held in the first flip-flop before the beginning of the clock cycle with edges 1 and 2. In the same way, the next clock cycle with edges 3 and 4 will transfer the input data ($S_1 = 1$, $R_1 = 0$) to the second flip-flop.

In other words, the master-slave flip-flop performs acceptably because the change at its output, if one is called for, occurs in response to a clock transition which *disables its input gates*. Hence the clock edge which updates the flip-flop output terminals to the data stored in the flip-flop blinds the flip-flop to the new data present at its input.

Note that the output response of the flip-flop, if any, occurs nominally at the negative-going edge, high to low, of the clocking waveform. The convention in this case, as appears in Fig. 4.8-1, is to label the clocking signal $\overline{\text{clock}}$, reserving the designation clock (without a bar) for the case where the response is to the positive-going transition.

The truth table for the SR master-slave flip-flop is identical to the truth table of the SR latch of Fig. 4.2-2. In the present case the symbols Q_n and Q_{n+1} are respectively the Q values in the nth and $(n + 1)$st clock intervals.

Direct Inputs

It is often a convenience, and at times even a necessity, to incorporate into a flip-flop a facility which will allow it to be set or reset by control signals which need not be synchronized with the clock. Such asynchronous inputs are also called *direct inputs*.

A master-slave flip-flop equipped with direct-set and direct-reset terminals is shown in Fig. 4.8-4. The terminals $\bar{R}_d$ are connected and are brought to a

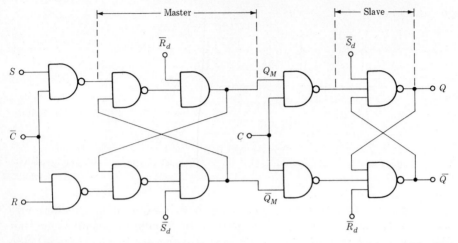

Figure 4.8-4 A master-slave flip-flop with direct (asynchronous) set and reset inputs. The direct inputs completely override the synchronous inputs.

single input pin, which constitutes the active-low direct-reset terminal. Similarly a common $\bar{S}_d$ input is an active-low control terminal. When $\bar{R}_d = 0$ and $\bar{S}_d = 1$, the flip-flop output Q will go to the reset state and the data inputs S and R and the presence of a clock waveform will have absolutely no effect on the output. Correspondingly $\bar{R}_d = 1$ and $\bar{S}_d = 0$ will set the flip-flop. The condition $\bar{S}_d = \bar{R}_d = 0$ is not to be used, and when $\bar{S}_d = R_d = 1$, the flip-flop is free to respond, in synchronism with the clock, to the data input S and R. The extra AND gates in the master latch, not present in Fig. 4.8-1, serve to restrain even a transient response to the clock input; i.e., the direct controls completely *override* the synchronous inputs (see Prob. 4.8-1). A circuit symbol for the flip-flop is shown in Fig. 4.8-5.

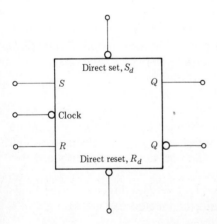

Figure 4.8-5 A logic symbol for the flip-flop of Fig. 4.8-4.

4.9 TIMING DIAGRAM FOR A FLIP-FLOP

Figure 4.9-1 is a typical timing diagram for the master-slave flip-flop of Fig. 4.8-1. A clock waveform is shown and (to clarify a point to be made below) has been drawn to appear as a sequence of positive pulses. Rather arbitrarily we have drawn waveforms for the logic levels at the set and reset data inputs. We assume that at the outset the flip-flop is in the reset state, and we have then drawn the output waveform (of the slave) at terminal Q, which results from the assumed R and S inputs. We keep in mind that when the clock is at logic 1, the data at S and R are transferred into the master while when the clock is at logic 0, the master is isolated from the input data but the state of the master is transferred to the slave.

The triggering edge of the clock waveform is the transition from logic 1 to logic 0. If we choose to describe the clock waveform as a sequence of positive pulses, we can say that the triggering edge is the trailing edge of the clock pulse. We note the synchronism between the clock waveform and the waveform of Q. Not every triggering edge of the clock produces a change in Q, but every change in Q occurs at the time of a triggering transition. Strictly speaking, the timing diagram should display a small propagation delay of the changes in the waveform of Q behind the triggering transition, but for simplicity we have chosen to ignore this delay in the figure.

Referring now to the timing diagram, we note the following. At the time of the triggering transition at the end of pulse 1, we have $S = 1$ and $R = 0$. Hence at that time, the flip-flop will go to the set state, $Q = 1$. Between the trailing edge of pulse 1 and the leading edge of pulse 2 there is an interval when both S and R are at logic 1. We have agreed normally to disallow any such occurrence, but since it occurs only for a time when the input gates of the flip-flop are disabled, it causes no difficulty in the present instance.

At the time of the beginning of pulse 2 and for an interval thereafter we find $S = 0$ and $R = 1$. As a result, the *master* flip-flop will reset at the time of the

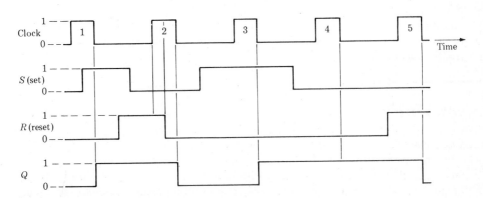

Figure 4.9-1 A timing diagram for the master-slave flip-flop of Fig. 4.8-1.

leading edge of pulse 2. Later, during the time of this clock pulse, we find that R returns to $R = 0$. However, this change in R will not affect the state of the master flip-flop, which will remain reset. At the time of the triggering edge of pulse 2, the reset state of the master will be transferred into the slave, as indicated in the figure in Q.

All through the time of pulse 3 we have $S = 1$ and $R = 0$. Hence at the triggering transition of pulse 3 we find that Q goes to $Q = 1$. During pulse 4 and at its triggering transition we find $S = R = 0$. Hence the triggering transition produces no change, and Q remains at $Q = 1$. Finally at the end of pulse 5, Q goes to $Q = 0$ since $S = 0$ and $R = 1$.

We add now a few comments concerning the clock waveform. We have referred to the clock waveform as a sequence of positive pulses and have noted that the triggering clock transition is the trailing edge of the pulse. If, however, we choose to do so, we can equally well view the clock waveform as a sequence of negative pulses. (In this case, to be sure, the interval between pulses would be shorter than the pulses themselves, but still the description is entirely reasonable.) If we do view the clock waveform as a sequence of negative pulses, we would be required to say that the triggering transition is the *leading* edge of the pulse. Suppose also that the clock waveform were to be used in connection with a master-slave flip-flop using NOR gates rather than NAND gates, as in Fig. 4.8-1. Then the triggering clock transition would be the transition from logic 0 to logic 1. In this case, if we viewed the clock waveform as positive pulses, the leading edge of the clock pulse would be the triggering transition, and if we viewed the clock waveform as negative pulses, the trailing edge would be the triggering transition. As often as not, in an actual physical situation, the clocking waveform is an entirely symmetrical square wave and does not have the appearance of either positive or negative pulses.

The point of these comments is that it lacks generality to refer to the triggering edge of the clock waveform as either the leading edge or the trailing edge, the positive-going edge or the negative-going edge. The essential point is that the response of the flip-flop is synchronized to the clock transition which carries the flip-flop from the condition where it is coupled to the input data terminals to the condition in which it is uncoupled. Still we need not be adamant about the matter; provided that we keep in mind what is essential, it may well be useful, convenient, and succinct to refer to clock pulses and their leading and trailing edges.

4.10 TWO-PHASE CLOCKING

Each master-slave flip-flop, as in Fig. 4.8-1, requires an inverter so that the clocking waveforms applied to master and slave will be complementary. In a large digital system requiring many flip-flops and hence many inverters, it may be advantageous to dispense with the individual inverters. Instead the inversion is done just once, and from this inverter two clocking complementary

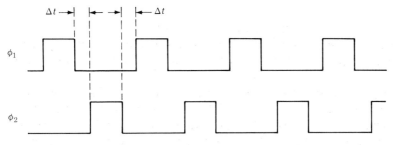

Figure 4.10-1 A two-phase clock waveform.

waveforms are bussed around to all the flip-flops, one for the master and one for the slave.

Referring again to Fig. 4.8-1, we have noted that there must never be a mechanism by which the data at the data terminals can be communicated directly to the slave flip-flop. If we generate clocking waveforms externally to the individual flip-flops, we can tailor them to our purpose and arrange for there to be no possibility of such direct communication. The two clocking waveforms generated with this consideration in mind generally have the form shown in Fig. 4.10-1 and are referred to as clock waveforms phase 1 (ϕ_1) and phase 2 (ϕ_2). Observe that with these clock waveforms gates 1A and 2A in Fig. 4.8-1 and gates 3A and 3B will never be enabled at the same time. Observe further in Fig. 4.10-1 that there is a safety margin Δt between the time one set of gates is disabled and the other set is enabled.

4.11 THE *JK* FLIP-FLOP

So far we have avoided setting both S and R at $S = R = 1$. For with such input data we would be trying both to set and reset at the same time and the end result would be ambiguous. We shall now modify the flip-flop to allow $S = R = 1$, and we shall find that the modified flip-flop has the property that, with $S = R = 1$, it toggles; i.e., it changes state with each successive triggering transition of the clock.

The modified flip-flop is shown in Fig. 4.11-1. The dashed rectangle represents the entire flip-flop except for the input gates, which are shown explicitly. The modification consists in providing additional input terminals at the input gates and making connections as shown from the outputs to the inputs. The data terminal previously called S is now called J, and the data terminal R is now K. In the absence of this modification the logic levels at S and R "steered" the clock waveform; i.e., depending on S and R, one or the other of the input gates 1A and 1B was enabled and the clock set or reset the flip-flop. The point of the modification is to arrange for this clock steering to be determined not by S and R alone but by the state of the flip-flop as well.

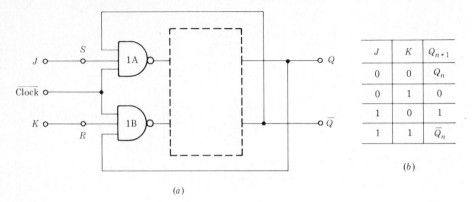

(a)

J	K	Q_{n+1}
0	0	Q_n
0	1	0
1	0	1
1	1	$\bar{Q}_n$

(b)

Figure 4.11-1 (a) The JK flip-flop and (b) truth table.

The operation of the JK flip-flop can be determined from the truth table in Fig. 4.11-1b. First let $J = K = 0$. Then both input gates are disabled, and the clock will not change the flip-flop state. Hence $Q_{n+1} = Q_n$.

Next, assume that $J = 0$ and $K = 1$ and that the flip-flop is in the reset state with $Q = 0$. Then gate 1A is disabled because $J = 0$, and 1B is disabled because $Q = 0$. Hence, the clock will not move the flip-flop out of the reset state. But suppose that although $J = 0$ and $K = 1$, as before, the flip-flop is in the set state instead, with $Q = 1$. Then the reset gate 1B is enabled, and the clock will cause a transfer of the flip-flop to the reset state with $Q = 0$. Similarly, with $J = 1$ and $K = 0$, the clock will set the flip-flop if it is not already in the set state.

Finally, let $J = K = 1$. Then which one of gates 1A and 2A is enabled depends entirely on Q_n and $\bar{Q}_n$, that is, on the state of the flip-flop. If $Q_n = 0$, then 1A is enabled. The clock will set the flip-flop to $Q_{n+1} = 1$. If $Q_n = 1$, the clock will reset the flip-flop to $Q_{n+1} = 0$. Thus, each cycle of the clock waveform will change the state of the flip-flop. The word *toggle* is used to describe this change of state induced by each clock cycle. Note that in the JK truth table $J = K = 1$ specifies $Q_{n+1} = \bar{Q}_n$. Note also that in the JK truth table, unlike the earlier SR truth tables, there is no combination of data inputs marked "not used."

The JK flip-flop is a circuit configuration in which the output of a flip-flop is connected to the input of a flip-flop. It happens in this case that input and output belong to the same flip-flop. Still we have noted that whenever such a connection is involved, we must not use a transparent latch. It is accordingly of interest to inquire what would happen if we made output-to-input connections as in Fig. 4.11-1 on the latch of Fig. 4.5-1. If the latch were reset, we would have $Q = 0$, $\bar{Q} = 1$; and with ENABLE high, gate G1 would be enabled and G2 disabled. The latch would then go to the set state. In the set state G1 would be disabled and G2 enabled. Hence the latch would go back to the reset state, and we start all over again. The result is that the latch would oscillate between states. Aside from the disadvantage associated with this oscillation, the fixed

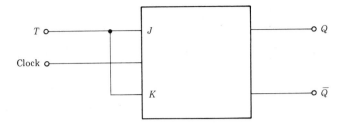

Figure 4.11-2 A toggle flip-flop.

state to which the latch would revert when ENABLE goes low would be unpredictable.

Toggle Flip-Flop

A flip-flop with a single control input which toggles when the control is active and remains unresponsive when the control is inactive is called a *toggle* flip-flop. As appears in Fig. 4.11-2, a toggle flip-flop can be constructed by connecting the J and K terminals of a JK flip-flop. The common terminal T is the control terminal. The flip-flop toggles when $T = 1$.

4.12 THE ONES-CATCHING PROPERTY OF THE MASTER-SLAVE FLIP-FLOP

The master-slave flip-flop, whether used as an SR device or as a JK device, has a disadvantage which can be serious. The difficulty is made clear by examining the waveform of Fig. 4.12-1. As we have noted, the master latch is connected to the data terminals when the clock is high and the output response, if one is to occur, takes place at the high-to-low clock transition at times t_1 and t_2. Through

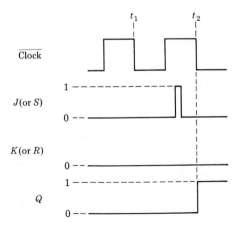

Figure 4.12-1 Waveforms to illustrate the 1s-catching property of the master-slave flip-flop.

the first clock cycle everything seems to be in order. We have $Q = 0$, and since also $J = K = 0$, there should be no change in Q at t_1 and such indeed is the case. However, in the second clock cycle, at time t_2, we again have $J = K = 0$, but we find that Q becomes $Q = 1$. The reason for this behavior is, as indicated, that when the clock was high, J was at $J = 1$ briefly. As a result the master latch became set. When J returns to $J = 0$, the master latch *remains set*. At time t_2 the bit stored in the master is transferred to the slave and hence Q becomes $Q = 1$. If it had been K that made the brief excursion to logic 1, then at t_2 the output would have responded by going to $Q = 0$ if not already at that level. If both J and K had gone briefly to logic 1, the flip-flop would have toggled, even if at the time of response t_2 we had $J = K = 0$.

Thus it appears that the response of the flip-flop is determined by which input was last at logic 1 (actually in the SR device, effectively in the JK device) while the input gates are enabled. This feature is referred to as the 1s-*catching property* of the flip-flop. (If our flip-flop had been assembled from NOR gates, we would have 0s-catching flip-flops.) This characteristic may sometimes be unacceptable because it makes the flip-flop more susceptible to hazards and brief spurious unpredictable disturbances (noise).

Typical of the JK master-slave flip-flops available in TTL small-scale integrated circuitry is the type '72. Its logic symbol and truth table are shown in Fig. 4.12-2. There are three J and three K data terminals, and the device responds to $J = J_1 \cdot J_2 \cdot J_3$ and $K = K_1 \cdot K_2 \cdot K_3$. The output changes in response to the negative-going edge of the clock waveform. Active-low asynchronous (direct) set and reset control inputs are provided. The type '73 is a dual unit providing, however, only single J and K inputs and only a direct reset for each flip-flop.

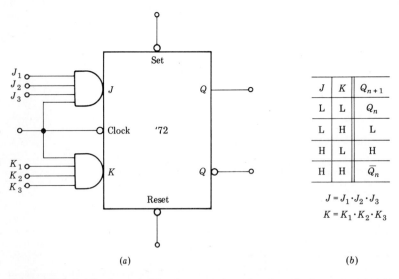

J	K	Q_{n+1}
L	L	Q_n
L	H	L
H	L	H
H	H	$\bar{Q}_n$

$$J = J_1 \cdot J_2 \cdot J_3$$
$$K = K_1 \cdot K_2 \cdot K_3$$

(a)   (b)

Figure 4.12-2 (*a*) Logic symbol for the type '72 master-slave flip-flop and (*b*) truth table in terms of voltage levels H and L.

4.13 AN EDGE-TRIGGERED *JK* FLIP-FLOP

The difficulty with the use of a latch in a synchronous system is often called the *race problem* for the following reason. Consider the case when the input data to a latch L_2 is the output of another latch L_1, as in Fig. 4.7-1. When the clock enables the input gates of both latches, L_2 responds to its input data but so also does L_1. Hence shortly after the input gates are enabled, the data applied to L_2 change. As we have already noted, one solution to the problem is to enable the latches with a clock pulse of very short duration, hoping to disable the gates before the input data can change. But in this case we run a *race* between the speed at which we can disable the gates and the speed at which the input data can change. We have seen how the master-slave flip-flop solves the race problem. It does so by arranging that the *output change of a flip-flop, if any, should be a response to the clock edge which disables the flip-flop from making any further response to input data*. The master-slave flip-flop solves the race problem but leaves us with the 1s-catching problem. The 1s-catching problem, in turn, is solved by designing an *edge-triggered* flip-flop. In such a flip-flop the output response is a response to the input data but only to the input data present *immediately before* the triggering transition of the clock waveform.

As we shall now verify, the flip-flop of Fig. 4.13-1 solves the race problem and also the 1s-catching problem and hence is an edge-triggered *JK* flip-flop. The triggering transition, as indicated, is the negative-going edge of the clock. The operation of the flip-flop uses to advantage the fact that there is a propagation delay through a gate.

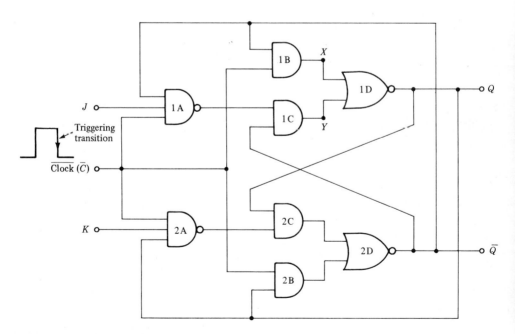

Figure 4.13-1 An edge-triggered *JK* flip-flop.

Let us consider that the flip-flop is reset, $Q = 0$, $\bar{Q} = 1$, and that $J = 1$ while $K = 0$, and let us follow the operation as the clock goes through a cycle from low to high and back from high to low. We anticipate, of course, that in response to the triggering transition the flip-flop will go to the set state.

Initially, as can readily be verified, terminal X is at logic 0 and terminal Y is at logic 1. When the clock rises, X goes to 1 and Y goes to 0. However in generating these changes the effect of the clock rise had to propagate through one gate (1B) to get to X but through two gates (1A and 1C) to get to Y. Hence the change at X occurs *before* the change at Y. The sequence of levels at the input of gate 1D is $XY = 01$ to 11 to 10. Since either X or Y is always 1, the net effect is that the output of gate 1D remains $Q = 0$ and there is no change in the state of the flip-flop. Now let the clock make its downward transition. Again X changes before Y, so that now the sequence is $XY = 10$ to 00 to 01. Since now there is a brief interval (about equal to the propagation delay t_{pd} through gate 1A) when $X = Y = 0$, the output Q will go to $Q = 1$ and the flip-flop will then go to the set state. Altogether the output response is a response to a clock transition which isolates the flip-flop from its input data source. Hence the race problem is solved.

Next, let us back up and consider that while the clock was still high, the input J went from $J = 1$ to $J = 0$. The only result of this change is that Y would go back to $Y = 1$ and stay at that level. Hence we see that even though there was an instruction to set, that is, $J = 1$, $K = 0$, if the instruction is changed at the last moment before the triggering transition, the flip-flop will respond to this updated instruction. Thus the flip-flop is an edge-triggered device and the 1s-catching difficulty is circumvented.

Typical of the edge-triggered flip-flop ICs which use the circuit of Fig. 4.13-1 is the type '112. This chip is a dual flip-flop, and the newer logic symbol for either of the units on the chip is shown in Fig. 4.13-2. The symbol C stands for clock. The half arrowhead on the input line indicates that the negative-going edge of the clock waveform is the triggering transition. The triangular marking at the clock line inside the box indicates that the flip-flop is *edge-triggered*. As is also indicated, the flip-flop has active-low direct-set and direct-reset control inputs. The 1 which appears last in the C1 label and first in 1J and 1K indicates that the clock exerts control over the J and K inputs. In general, a number which appears as the *last* symbol in a label indicates that the label

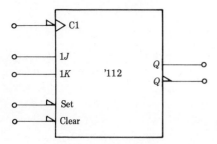

Figure 4.13-2 Logic symbol for the type '112 edge-triggered flip-flop.

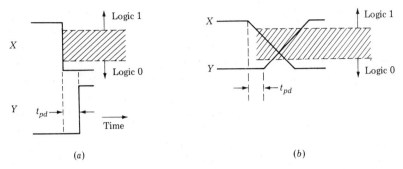

Figure 4.13-3 (*a*) Abrupt transitions in X and Y establish an interval when $X = Y = 0$. (*b*) Slow changes in X and Y do not establish such an interval.

identifies a *controlling* signal, while the same number appearing as the *first* symbol in a label identifies a signal whose effectiveness is *controlled*. Thus in Fig. 4.13-2 the symbolism indicates that the exact time when the JK inputs can be effective is controlled by the clock waveform.

We now discuss a potential difficulty that may develop with an edge-triggered flip-flop of the type in Fig. 4.13-1. As described, for proper operation there must be an interval when $X = Y = 0$ so that Q can become $Q = 1$. If the clock waveform transitions between logic levels are arbitrarily abrupt, the situation is as represented in Fig. 4.13-3*a*. At some time X drops abruptly from logic 1 to logic 0. It passes suddenly through a region of ambiguity (shaded) which is neither logic 1 for sure nor logic 0 for sure. At a time t_{pd} later Y similarly rises abruptly, and there is no ambiguity about the result that there is an interval when $X = Y = 0$ so that Q can become $Q = 1$. In Fig. 4.13-3*b* we have redrawn X and Y superimposed on each other and have taken into account the finite rise and fall times of these waveforms. Here we observe that there is no interval when it is unambiguously certain that $X = Y = 0$. The end result is that if we drive our flip-flop with a clock waveform which makes slow transitions between levels, the flip-flop may not operate properly.

4.14 THE TYPE *D* FLIP-FLOP

In Fig. 4.5-1 we indicated how an SR latch is modified into a type D latch. In a similar manner an SR flip-flop can be modified into a D flip-flop. Thus, if we start with the master-slave flip-flop of Fig. 4.8-1 and apply the data-line signal to S and its complement to R, as indicated in Fig. 4.14-1*a*, we have a type D flip-flop with logic symbol as in Fig. 4.14-1*b*. In response to the negative-going transition of the clock the logic level at the data input D will be written into the flip-flop and will appear at the output Q. It is especially to be noted that in the type D flip-flop of Fig. 4.14-1 the 1s-catching property of the master-slave flip-flop is *circumvented* because we never have $S = R = 0$.

As we shall consider in detail in succeeding chapters, in many digital sys-

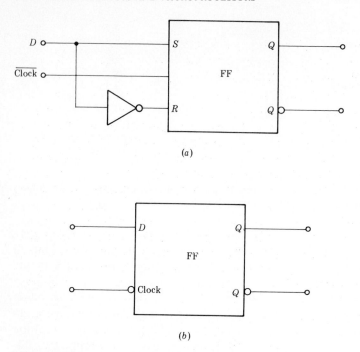

(a)

(b)

Figure 4.14-1 (*a*) An *SR* flip-flop modified into a type *D* flip-flop and (*b*) logic symbol.

tems the data presented to a flip-flop are presented in synchronism with the clock. Input data at any flip-flop input-data terminal change only once in the time of a clock cycle; i.e., they change once or not at all. Further, data changes, when they occur, are timed to happen shortly after the triggering transition of the clock. Occasions often arise when it is necessary to *delay* an input sequence of such synchronously presented bits by exactly one clock cycle. Since the *D* flip-flop can be used to accomplish this delay, there is a second reason for referring to this flip-flop by the designation type *D* (data, delay).

Waveforms illustrating this delay operation are shown in Fig. 4.14-2. We have made it appear as though the triggering edge of the clocking waveform occurred precisely where the data are changing. If such were the case, the response of the flip-flop would be ambiguous. As a matter of practice, the changes in data occur slightly *after* the triggering transition. The delay between triggering transition and the data change would be of the order of the propagation delay of a gate or of some other flip-flop. Such would be the delay encountered if the data themselves were taken from the output of another flip-flop driven by the same clocking waveform. There will also be a propagation delay (not indicated in the figure) between the output *Q* and the triggering edge of the clock waveform.

The type *D* flip-flop we have developed is eminently suitable for use in synchronous systems. It solves the race problem because it incorporates a master-slave arrangement. It solves the 1s-catching problem because it never allows

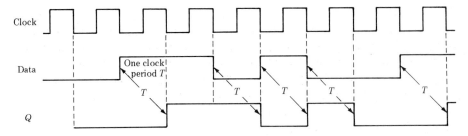

Figure 4.14-2 A type D flip-flop is used to delay a synchronous data input by one clock period.

$S = R = 0$. It is not affected by the rise or fall times of the clock waveform because its operation does not depend on propagation delays encountered by the clock waveform. In going to the type D, however, we have given up some of the versatility of the SR master-slave flip-flop with its two data terminals and the ease with which it can be modified into the even more versatile JK flip-flop. Now it turns out that if we are to be satisfied with a type D flip-flop, there is an alternative and somewhat more economical circuit available than our modified master-slave flip-flop.

This alternative type D flip-flop is shown in Fig. 4.14-3, and we now consider its operation. The output flip-flop that provides Q and $\bar{Q}$ consists of NAND gates 3A and 3B; gates 1A, 1B and 2A, 2B are two interconnected steering flip-flops. It can now readily be verified (Prob. 4.14-1) that the following statements are valid.

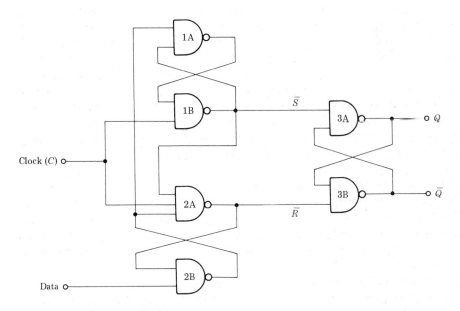

Figure 4.14-3 The type D flip-flop.

1. When $C = 0$, $\bar{S} = \bar{R} = 1$ independently of D. Hence gates 3A, 3B are enabled, and either state of the flip-flop is allowed. This result does not depend on the sequence by which we arrived at condition $C = 0$. With either state allowed, the output Q of the flip-flop therefore depends on the past history.

2. Starting with $D = 0$ and $C = 0$, let C become $C = 1$. Then $\bar{S}$ and $\bar{R}$ become $\bar{S} = 1$ and $\bar{R} = 0$, so that Q goes to $Q = 0$. If now while $C = 1$ there are any subsequent changes in D, $\bar{S}$ and $\bar{R}$ will remain unaltered, as will Q. When C returns to $C = 0$, $\bar{S}$ remains $S = 1$ and R becomes $\bar{R} = 1$, so that the output flip-flop remembers its previous input data and Q remains $Q = 0$.

3. Starting with $D = 1$ and $C = 0$, let C become $C = 1$. Then $\bar{S}$ and $\bar{R}$ become $\bar{S} = 0$ and $\bar{R} = 1$, so that Q goes to $Q = 1$. If now, while $C = 1$, there are any subsequent changes in D, $\bar{S}$ and $\bar{R}$ will remain unaltered, as will Q. When C returns to $C = 0$, $\bar{R}$ remains $\bar{R} = 1$ and S becomes $\bar{S} = 1$, so that the output flip-flop remembers its previous input data and Q remains at $Q = 1$.

In summary, then, when C makes a positive-going transition from $C = 0$ to $C = 1$, Q becomes $Q = 0$ if D was $D = 0$ and Q becomes $Q = 1$ if D was $D = 1$. Q can be changed in no other way. Changes in D when $C = 1$ do not affect Q. Hence, except for the fact that in the present case triggering takes place on the positive-going edge of the clock transition, the behavior is precisely the same as for the previous type D flip-flop. The flip-flop of Fig. 4.14-3 is edge-triggered, it makes no demands on clock-transition speed, and the output responds to a clock transition which also disables the flip-flop from responding to a change in input data.

Typical of the type D flip-flop IC chips available which use the circuit of Fig. 4.14-3 is the '74 dual D positive-edge-triggered flip-flop. This 14-pin device has two entirely independent flip-flops, each equipped (in addition to the input and output terminals shown in Fig. 4.14-3) with active-low direct-set and direct-reset inputs (See Prob. 4.14-2). The type '174 is a 16-pin hex D unit which makes available only the Q output of each flip-flop and which has a single common clock single direct-reset input common to all the flip-flops. The type '273 is a 20-pin octal unit whose logic symbol is given in Fig. 4.14-4. This '273 unit is also described as an 8-bit *nontransparent latch*.

At present, of all the available TTL IC flip-flop types available, the D as in Fig. 4.14-3 is the most favored. As noted, the D is not quite as versatile as the JK since the D does not immediately make responses corresponding to $J = K = 0$ and $J = K = 1$ available, i.e., remain in present state or toggle. The matter is readily remedied, however, with some additional logic. Thus to arrange for the flip-flop to remain in its present state we need only connect D to Q, and to make the flip-flop toggle we need only connect D to $\bar{Q}$. Altogether, then if we want to modify our D type to a JK type, we need only provide gates to generate $D = J\bar{Q} + \bar{K}Q$ (Prob. 4.14-3), as shown in Fig. 4.14-5.

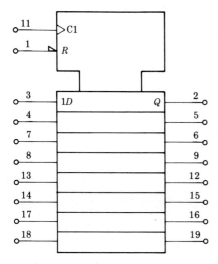

Figure 4.14-4 Logic symbol of the type '273 octal type D flip-flop.

4.15 SETUP, HOLD, AND PROPAGATION TIME

The timing of the response of a flip-flop to input data and clock waveform is often specified by manufacturers as shown in Fig. 4.15-1. The waveforms shown represent various transitions between logic levels. By way of acknowledgement of reality, the transitions are indicated as taking a finite time to rise or fall from one level to the other. Yet, even as displayed, the transitions are very much idealized. They are shown as rising or falling linearly with time. Actually the waveforms of transitions in digital systems may be rather complicated. In some cases, one or the other logic level may be approached asymptotically; in other cases, in the neighborhood of one level or another there may be some oscillation near the transition. And there will generally be some delay before a

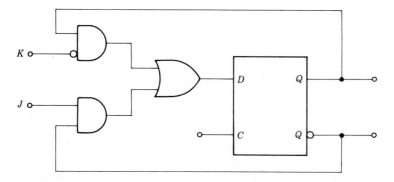

Figure 4.14-5 Logic added to convert a type D into a JK flip-flop.

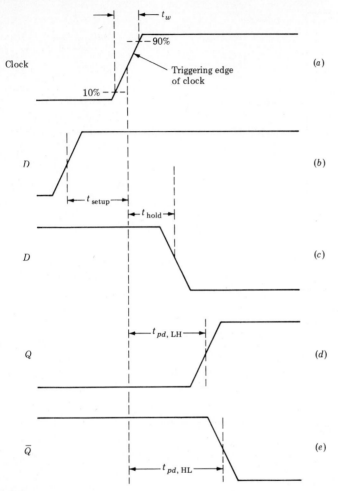

Figure 4.15-1 Timing diagrams used to define setup, hold, and propagation-delay times for a flip-flop.

waveform makes any but a rather small excursion in the direction it is headed. For these reasons, instead of trying to specify the time of transition from one level to the next, it is more convenient to specify the time for a transition to go from 10 to 90 percent of the total interval between levels. As indicated in the clock waveform transition in Fig. 4.15-1, the time is referred to as the transition width t_w.

The waveforms shown apply to a type D flip-flop, in which the triggering transition of the clock is assumed to be the positive-going transition from logic 0 to logic 1. This triggering transition is shown in Fig. 4.15-1a, and a transition in the input data D from logic 0 to logic 1 is shown in Fig. 4.15-1b. The relationship between the waveforms in Fig. 4.15-1a and b is intended to indicate that it is necessary for the transition in D to precede the clock-triggering transition by a time which is referred to as the *setup time* t_{setup}. If the flip-flop is to recognize and respond properly to the new data input D with certainty, the change in D must precede the clock edge by a time interval which is not less than t_{setup}. The waveform in Fig. 4.15-1c represents a transition of D from 1 back to 0. The relationship between the waveforms in Fig. 4.15-1a and c is intended to indicate that if the change in D is to be recognized without fail, the level $D = 1$ must be held for at least a time t_{hold} after the clock edge. Altogether, then, if the flip-flop is to respond to the change in D, the change must occur at least at time t_{setup} before the clock edge and must persist after the clock edge for at least a time t_{hold}. There are some cases in which data D may be released and allowed to return to its original level slightly in *advance* of the time of occurrence of the clock edge. This interval between release and clock edge is sometimes specified as a *release* time $t_{release}$ and sometimes specified as a *negative* hold time. Finally, we note that the times of occurrence of the various transitions are ordinarily taken to be the time when the transition is midway between the two logic levels.

The relationships between the clock edge and the waveform in Fig. 4.15-1d and e indicate that if the requirement with respect to setup and hold time are met, there will be a *propagation delay* t_{pd} between the clock edge and the response in Q and $\bar{Q}$ at the flip-flop output. The delay of the output which goes from the *low* to *high* level is $t_{pd,\mathrm{LH}}$, and the other delay is $t_{pd,\mathrm{HL}}$. Note that $t_{pd,\mathrm{LH}}$ and $t_{pd,\mathrm{HL}}$ need not be the same. As a matter of fact, we generally also find that the setup and hold time are somewhat different, depending on whether the data-input transition is positive or negative.

Manufacturers specify timing information in connection not only with the data input but also with the direct set and reset inputs if such are available. In any event, so that the information will be properly understood, the manufacturer will spell out in detail the circumstances under which the data were assembled. The transition widths of the applied clock edges and data input will be given, as well as the loads connected to the flip-flop outputs, these loads being tailored to represent the load seen by the flip-flop when fanned out to a reasonable number of gates. Often it is quite useful to forgo all the detailed timing information and have available some simple parameter which provides an indication of the speed with which the flip-flop can be operated. For this purpose, manufacturers specify a maximum (clock) frequency f_{max} at which the flip-flop can be operated. For a flip-flop which can be arranged to toggle, f_{max} is the maximum frequency at which the flip-flop can be made to toggle.

In the fast logic available, the setup, hold, and propagation times lie in the range from nanoseconds to tens of nanoseconds while maximum operating frequencies are in the range of 150 MHz.

4.16 REGISTER-TO-REGISTER TRANSFERS

We have already noted that a latch or a flip-flop can *store* or *remember*, i.e., *register*, a bit. An array of such latches or flip-flops is then a *register* into which we can *write* a word and from which we can *read* the word so stored when it suits our purpose. Registers, then, are the "writing paper" on which we write words required for future reference.

A very large part of the operations in a computer or other digital processor consists in nothing more than the transfer of words from one register to another. That such is the case is not surprising if we take note of the manipulations we perform even when doing a calculation or a data-handling chore (bookkeeping) using pencil and paper. For example, in a numerical calculation we may well have first to *transfer* to the paper on which we are performing our calculation the numbers which are *written* initially elsewhere, e.g., in mathematical table. We may then need to *transfer* several numbers to a single column so that we can add them, and then we may want to *transfer* the sum to some other location. It is not gross exaggeration to say that the manipulations performed in digital processes consist of a great deal of register-to-register transfers mixed with a little bit of arithmetic and logic operations.

Figure 4.16-1 shows two registers, register A (RA) and register B (RB) with provision for clearing RB and for transferring the contents of RA to RB. The registers consist each of 4-bit storage elements which are either clocked latches or flip-flop as appropriate. If we propose to read a word out of a register and also transfer a word into the same register during the same clock cycle, we shall need flip-flops. Otherwise, simple latches will be adequate. While 4-bit registers are indicated, the registers can be extended to any number. When the *clear* line is activated, all the latches or flip-flops of the registers are reset. This operation is written

$$0 \rightarrow RB$$

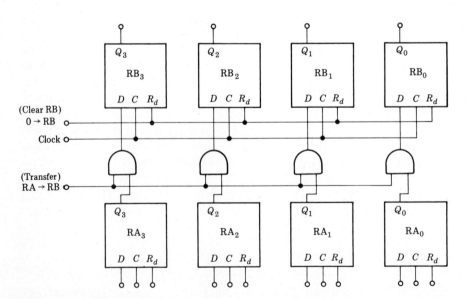

Figure 4.16-1 Registers are connected to allow transfer of contents of register A to register B.

When the *transfer* line is activated, on the first occasion thereafter when the clock goes to the active level as well, the word in RA will be transferred to RB. This operation is written

$$RA \rightarrow RB$$

[When we refer to a register and there is the possibility of an ambiguity about whether the register or its content is intended, parentheses are used, that is, (RA), to indicate the content. With such notation we would write (RA) → (RB) to indicate that the content of RA has become the content of RB as well.] The transfer operation is manifestly synchronous, depending as it does on the clock. As a matter of practice, it generally turns out as well that the *clear*-line signal is itself generated by a clock-driven circuit so that the clear operation is also synchronous. In the circuit of Fig. 4.16-1 it is not necessary to clear RB before transferring into it the word in RA. Clearing, if done, is done for its own sake. Also when a word is transferred, the contents of RA remain unaltered.

Figure 4.16-2 shows the use of a bus, with as many lines as there are bits in the registers, to permit transfers from any of three registers to any other register. It is apparent that the arrangement can be extended to an arbitrary number of registers. For simplicity we have omitted provision for clearing. Here we have assumed open-collector multiplexing as described in Sec. 3.19, the NAND gates being of the type shown in Fig. 3.19-1. Tristate buffers between registers and bus lines would serve as well. To effect a transfer from, say, register C to register A, that is, RC → RA, we would arrange that, in overlapping time intervals, the control signals RC → B (B stands for bus) and B → RA would both be activated.

4.17 SHIFT REGISTERS

A useful feature which can be incorporated into a register is the ability to perform the operation of shifting. A 4-bit shift register is shown in Fig. 4.17-1. In Fig. 4.17-1*a JK* flip-flops are used (*SR* flip-flops would serve as well), while in Fig. 4.17-1*b* type *D* flip-flops are used. The number of bits can be changed by adding or deleting flip-flops.

The array of flip-flops in the register constitutes a *synchronous system* since each flip-flop is driven by the same clocking waveform. The connection of each flip-flop to the preceding one on the left is such that at each triggering transition of the clock the state of the preceding flip-flop is transferred to the succeeding one. For example, if FF0 is in the reset state with $Q_0 = 0$, $\bar{Q}_0 = 1$, then $J_1 = 0$ and $K_1 = 1$. Hence no matter what the previous state of FF1, after the triggering transition we shall find FF1 in the reset state. Similarly if FF0 is in the set state, this set state will be transferred to FF1. Similar comments apply to the register in Fig. 4.17-1*b*. The state in which the first flip-flop finds itself after a triggering clock transition is determined by the logic level applied at *D* from an external source. The bit stored in the last flip-flop (FF3 in the present case) is lost; i.e., it has been shifted out of the register. It is especially to be

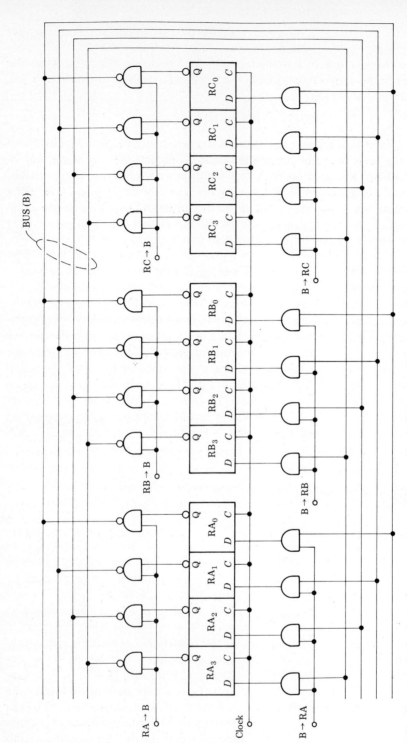

Figure 4.16-2 A common bus is used to transfer the contents of one of many registers to another of many registers.

162

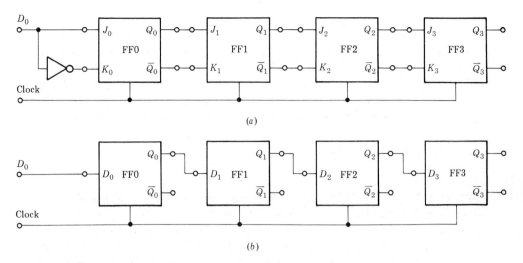

Figure 4.17-1 (*a*) A 4-bit register using *JK* flip-flops and (*b*) shift register using type *D* flip-flops.

noted that in the shift register, in each clock cycle, we read from, and write into, each bit-storage element. Hence flip-flops are required; latches are not acceptable.

As an example of the shift-register operation consider the waveforms of Fig. 4.17-2. Here in a 4-bit register we assume that initially the register is clear; i.e., all the flip-flops are in the reset state. The register may have been cleared by holding $D_0 = 0$ long enough to allow the occurrence of at least four clock edges. Alternatively the register may have been cleared by using the direct-reset terminals (not shown in Fig. 4.17-1). Now there is applied to the data input a sequence, in time, of input bits which are applied in *synchronism* with the clock. *Synchronous* operation means, on the one hand, that all flip-flops are driven by the same clocking waveform and, on the other, that input data are changed, if at all, once and only once per clock cycle. In the waveforms of Fig. 4.17-2 the input sequence is 11010, starting in the clock interval which ends at the time of clock edge 1. The fact that the input sequence 11010 begins with two successive 1s is evidenced in the waveform for D_0 by the fact that D_0 holds at the fixed level $D_0 = 1$ for *two* successive clock cycles.

We now observe that in successive clock cycles the input bit sequence is entered into, and shifted down, the register. The waveform for Q_0 is the input waveform D_0 delayed by one clock cycle, the waveform for Q_0 is delayed by two clock cycles, etc. Since we have specified the input sequence only over the course of five clock intervals, we are able to specify Q_0 only up to clock edge 6, Q_1 only up to clock edge 7, etc.

In Fig. 4.17-3 we have represented in an alternative tabular form the information presented in the waveforms of Fig. 4.17-2. The arrows indicate the transfers of bits from flip-flop to flip-flop. For convenience in visualizing data

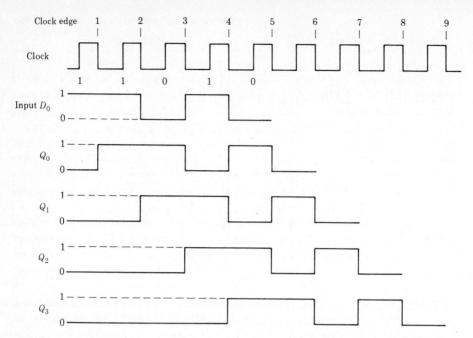

Figure 4.17-2 Waveforms, for the register of Fig. 4.17-1b, initially cleared, with input sequence 11010.

entering we have ordered the input bits on a time scale that runs backward from right to left.

4.18 ADDITIONAL FEATURES AND USES OF SHIFT REGISTERS

In this section we consider a number of interesting uses for shift registers involving generally some modification of the basic circuit of Fig. 4.17-1.

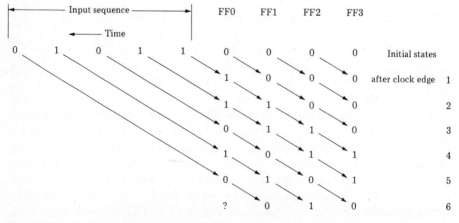

Figure 4.17-3 Tabular representation of shift-register response to input sequence 11010.

Serial and Parallel Data Formats

Digital data may be presented in either serial or parallel form. In a serial presentation, the individual bits of a word are carried on a single wire (plus a return) and are presented in a time sequence, one bit after another. In a parallel presentation all the bits of the word are presented simultaneously, using as many wires (plus a return) as there are bits. The serial format uses less hardware, but the parallel format saves time. For example, consider that a logic level must be held steady for 1 μs in order to be properly acknowledged. Then to transmit an 8-bit word in serial form would occupy 8 μs, while in a parallel format only 1 μs would be required.

In any event it is often necessary to change the form of presentation from serial to parallel and vice versa. A shift register can be used for this purpose. Suppose that word length of 8 bits is to be changed from serial to parallel form. To accomplish this, we use an 8-bit shift register and present the 8-bit serial word at the data input of the register, the individual bits being presented in synchronism with the clock. Then after eight clock cycles, and with the clock input disabled, the word will be registered in the register and all 8 bits will be simultaneously available, i.e., in parallel, at the eight flip-flop outputs.

To convert from parallel to serial form, we stop the clock and enter the individual bits, all available simultaneously, directly into the individual flip-flops. For this purpose we can use the data-input or the direct-input terminals of the flip-flops. After the word has so been placed in the register, we enable the clock line. Then, at the output of the last flip-flop and in synchronism with the clock there will appear in time sequence the individual bits of the word.

The shift register finds another application in connection with serial data. The register can be used to change the data rate (number of bits per unit time) by the simple expedient of changing the clock rate. Suppose, for example, serial data are being generated at a relatively slow rate, say by reading bits from a mechanically moving magnetic tape. And suppose the data have to be introduced synchronously to a digital system operating at a clock rate higher than the bit-generation rate at the tape. Then a block of data from the tape can be entered into a shift register using a clock rate appropriate to the tape rate. Thereafter the register is connected to the faster digital system and the clock rate is correspondingly increased to accommodate the faster system. The operation of data transfer having been completed, a second block of data is so processed, etc.

Shift-Right Shift-Left Register

The register of Fig. 4.17-1 shifts in one direction only. Because of the way we have arranged the interconnections the shifting is from left to right. There are times when it is useful to have a register which will shift in either direction. To reverse the shift direction we need only reverse the order of interconnections between flip-flops. Thus to shift right to left we need to connect the input of

FF2 to the output of FF3 and so on. A register which incorporates gates, as required, to reverse connections in response to a direction-control command input is called a shift-right shift-left register.

Register Rotation

We have already noted that the bit shifted out of the last flip-flop is lost and that it is necessary to supply an input bit to the first flip-flop from an external source. If we choose, however, we can connect the output of the last flip-flop to the data input of the first flip-flop. In this case we do not lose a bit and do not require an external input. Sometimes such a mode of operation is useful. Operations of this sort are referred to as *rotations* and are represented in Fig. 4.18-1. The arrows indicate the direction of data shift. In Fig. 4.18-1a we have a right rotation, and in Fig. 4.18-1b we have a left rotation.

An example of an integrated-circuit shift-register chip is the type '194, whose logic diagram is shown in Fig. 4.18-2. It is described by the manufacturer as a 4-bit bidirectional universal shift register. It has an active-low master reset ($\overline{MR}$) input which overrides all other inputs and clears all flip-flops. The flip-flops are of the SR type but are connected so that they operate as D flip-flops. Two selection inputs S_1 and S_0 determine how the device will operate. The inverters in the selection line together with each group of four AND gates A, B, C, and D constitute a 4-line–to–1-line demultiplexer which determines the source of the data input of each flip-flop. When gate A is enabled, each data input is the output of the flip-flop on the left or the input D_{SR}, that is, data to be shifted right, and shifting is to the right. When gate B is enabled, the input data are the logic levels presented at the *parallel-input* lines p_0, p_1, p_2, and p_3. When

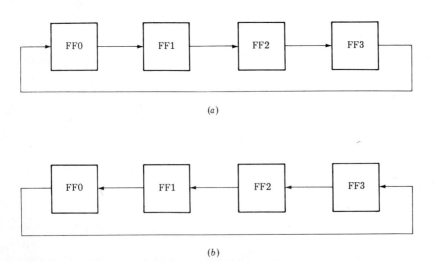

Figure 4.18-1 Rotation in a shift register: (*a*) right rotation and (*b*) left rotation.

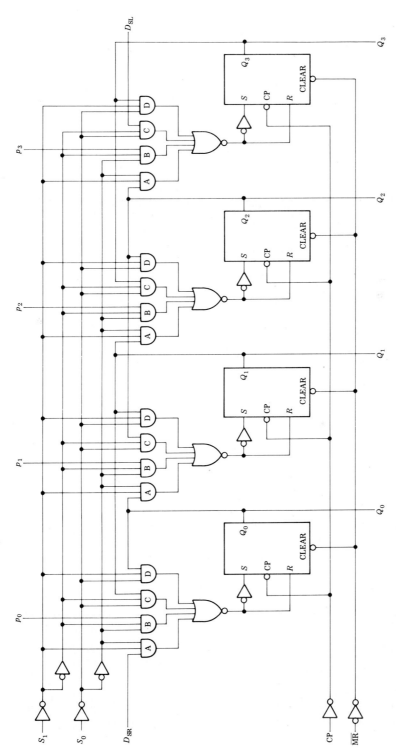

Figure 4.18-2 Logic diagram of the type '194 4-bit bidirectional universal shift register.

167

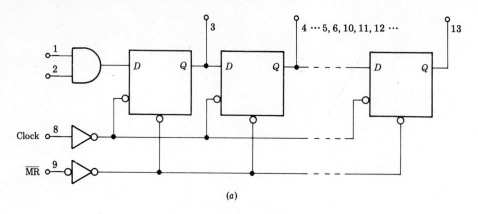

(a)

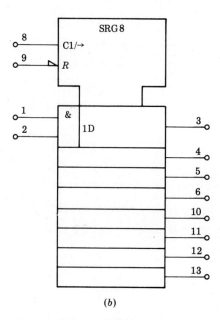

(b)

Figure 4.18-3 (a) Logic diagram of the type '164 8-bit serial-in parallel-out shift register and (b) logic symbol.

gate C is enabled, each data input comes from the right or the input D_{SL}, that is, data to be shifted left. Finally when gate D is enabled, the data input of each flip-flop is *its own* data output, so that each flip-flop simply reregisters its own present state. Under these circumstances, nothing changes, and the register is described as being in a *hold* condition.

There are also available a number of other IC shift-register chips, some with 8-bit length, some with 16-bit length. To show its newer logic symbol we present in Fig. 4.18-3a the logic diagram of the 8-bit serial-in parallel-out shift register type '164. Its logic symbol is shown in Fig. 4.18-3*b*. The notation SRG8 stands for shift register, 8-bits. The arrow pointing to the right indicates that the shift direction is down in Fig. 4.18-3*b* (to the right in Fig. 4.18-3*a*).

4.19 COUNTERS

We turn our attention now to another type of circuit configuration, which, like the registers considered above, consists for the most part of arrays of flip-flops.

A single flip-flop has two states. An array of n flip-flops has 2^n states. The state of an array of n flip-flops is specified by indicating which of the flip-flops are set and which are reset. A counter is an array of flip-flops which advances from state to state in response to an *event*. An event may be nothing more than a single cycle of a clock waveform. In any case, the counter then counts the number of events. The number of states through which a counter cycles before returning to a starting state is called the *modulo* (abbreviated mod) of the counter. A counter constructed with n flip-flops can have a modulo which is at most 2^n, but we can, if we choose, arrange for a counter not to cycle through all its possible states. In such a case the modulo will be less than 2^n.

4.20 THE RING COUNTER

The circuit of Fig. 4.20-1 is a mod-4 *ring counter*. We recognize that it is a shift register (using type D flip-flops, though other types would serve as well) connected to allow for the right rotation. At first, the *initiate* terminal is raised briefly to logic level 1, thereby setting FF0 and resetting all the other flip-flops. Thereafter the clock waveform is applied, and the counter will count clock cycles mod 4. Each successive clock triggering edge will advance the set state

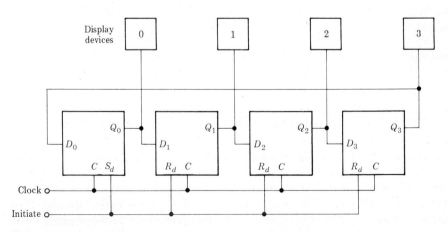

Figure 4.20-1 A mod-4 ring counter with a count-indication display.

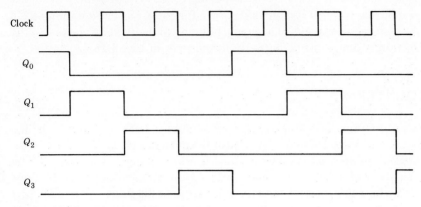

Figure 4.20-2 Waveforms of the mod-4 ring counter of Fig. 4.20-1.

by one flip-flop, and four successive clock cycles will return the counter to its initial state.

It is extremely simple to read the count registered in the ring counter. To determine the count we need only note which flip-flop is in the set state. For this purpose we have included four display devices. Each such device is connected to the Q output of a flip-flop. Imagine the devices to be electric light bulbs, which light up when the voltage corresponding to logic level 1 is applied to them. At logic level 0 they go out. Imagine, further, that in front of the bulbs we have placed translucent screens bearing the numbers 0, 1, 2, and 3, as indicated in the figure. Then as the counting progresses, we shall see the numerals illuminated in the order . . . 0, 1, 2, 3, 0, . . . , and we have a direct indication of the registered count.

Waveforms for the ring counter are shown in Fig. 4.20-2. Here are drawn the waveforms for the clock and for the Q outputs of the four flip-flops. We have started arbitrarily at a time when $Q_0=1$ and $Q_2=Q_3=Q_4=0$. These waveforms are very useful for the purpose of *sequencing*. Imagine that in a digital system there are a number of operations that need to be performed one after the other in time, i.e., sequenced. Imagine also that the individual operations can be accomplished by enabling a number of sets of gates. Then the waveforms of Fig. 4.20-2 would be ideal for such a sequential enabling function.

4.21 THE SWITCHTAIL COUNTER

The ring counter is elegantly simple but has the disadvantage of using flip-flops uneconomically. A ring counter with n flip-flops has a modulo of n, while n flip-flops would allow 2^n states. A modification of the ring counter which uses flip-flops more economically is the *switchtail counter* (also called the Johnson counter), shown in Fig. 4.21-1. Here the interconnection between flip-flops is as in Fig. 4.20-1 except that at the end of the cascade of flip-flops, i.e., at the

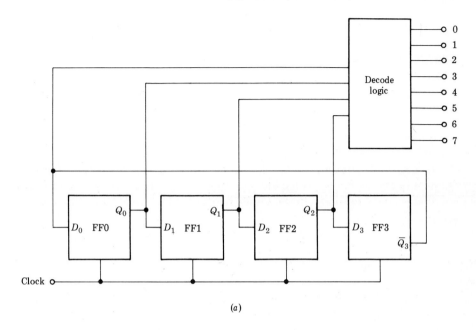

(a)

Count	Q_0	Q_1	Q_2	Q_3	Decode logic
0	0	0	0	0	$\bar{Q}_0\bar{Q}_3$
1	1	0	0	0	$Q_0\bar{Q}_1$
2	1	1	0	0	$Q_1\bar{Q}_2$
3	1	1	1	0	$Q_2\bar{Q}_3$
4	1	1	1	1	Q_0Q_3
5	0	1	1	1	$\bar{Q}_0Q_1$
6	0	0	1	1	$\bar{Q}_1Q_2$
7	0	0	0	1	$\bar{Q}_2Q_3$
0	0	0	0	0	$\bar{Q}_0\bar{Q}_3$

(b)

Figure 4.21-1 (a) A switchtail counter and (b) count sequence and decoding logic.

tail, the connection has been switched to $\bar{Q}_3$ rather than to Q_3. (Since the flip-flop array forms a ring, there is really no "end" to the cascade and the switch can be made between any two flip-flops.)

Assume that initially all the flip-flops of the counter have been cleared, so that $Q_0=Q_1=Q_2=Q_3=0$. Then the next clock-triggering edge will transfer 0s into FF1, FF2, and FF3, leaving them unaltered. However, because of the switch in connections at the output of FF3, FF0 will go to the set state. Hence the counter goes from $Q_0Q_1Q_2Q_3 = 0000$ to $Q_0Q_1Q_2Q_3 = 1000$. The sequence of states through which the counter gates is given in Fig. 4.21-1b. We observe that the counter cycles through eight states, i.e., twice the number of flip-flops, and then returns to its initial state. Thus with n flip-flops the ring counter has a modulo n while the switchtail counter has a modulo $2n$.

We need to provide for reading the count of the counter; i.e., as in the ring counter, we need as many individual outputs as there are count states. And we need to arrange that, at each count, one output is singled out by being at logic level 1 while all others are at logic 0 (or the other way around). That is, we need to provide a *decoder* for the counter (see Sec. 3.15). In Fig. 4.21-1*a* we have included a block which is to include the required array of combinational circuits, i.e., logic gates but no flip-flops, necessary for decoding. The logic equations relating the decode-logic block outputs to its inputs are given in the table of Fig. 4.21-1*b* (Prob. 4.21-1). Other features concerning ring and switchtail counters, such as self-starting features, are presented in Prob. 4.21-2.

4.22 OTHER SYNCHRONOUS COUNTERS

The ring and switchtail counters are synchronous counters since the clocking waveform (which also provides the events which are being counted) is applied simultaneously to all flip-flops. These counters suffer the limitation that they do not use flip-flops economically. In this respect the switchtail counter is a good improvement over the ring counter but, on the other hand, requires decoding, while the ring counter does not. We begin now to consider other synchronous counters using all or (if we choose) nearly all the available states. We call attention here to the synchronous operation principally to distinguish these counters from other counters which are not synchronous. We consider, first, counters which use all available states, that is, 2^n states in a counter with n flip-flops.

If we prepare a table in which the binary numbers are set down in order, we shall note that, at each count advance, the least significant bit, of numerical significance 2^0, *changes*. The next bit, of significance 2^1, *changes* at a count advance when the 2^0 bit is 1. The 2^2 bit *changes* when *both* the 2^0 and the 2^1 bit are 1. In general a bit changes whenever *all* the bits of lesser numerical significance are simultaneously 1. These observations lead rather obviously to the following scheme by which a counter can be arranged to follow the counting order exactly. For the least significant bit we use a flip-flop set to *toggle* in each clock cycle. For the next bit we arrange for a flip-flop to toggle whenever the first flip-flop is in the set state. In general, we shall arrange a sequence of flip-flops to register the individual bits, each flip-flop arranged to toggle when *all* the flip-flops corresponding to bits of lesser significance are simultaneously set.

The counter is shown in Fig. 4.22-1. If n flip-flops are used in the counter, the counter will have a modulo 2^n, a modulo equal to the number of states. The flip-flops used are JK and will toggle whenever $J=K=1$. By way of example, FF3 will toggle whenever $J_3=K_3=1$, and such will be the case when $Q_0=Q_1=Q_2=1$, as required. Of course, gate G1 serves no purpose and has been included only to make the figure look more orderly.

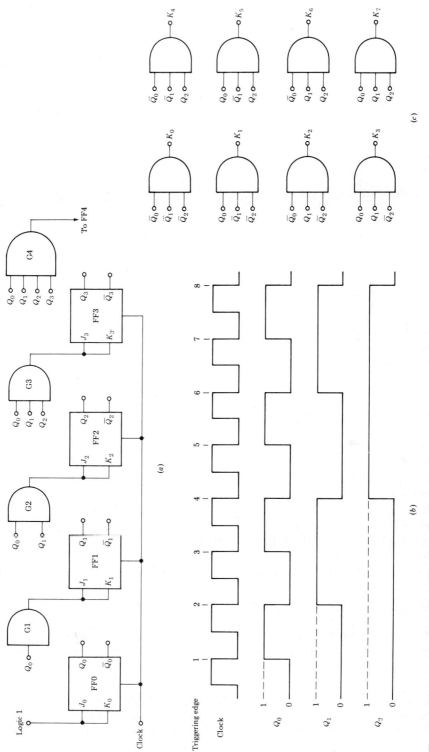

Figure 4.22-1 A synchronous mod-2^n counter which uses all available states: (a) the logic diagrams, (b) the waveforms, and (c) the decoding logic.

173

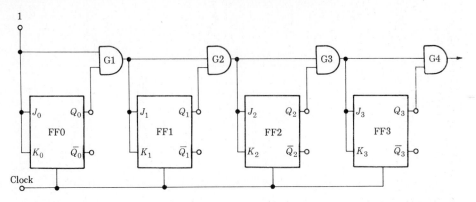

Figure 4.22-2 A synchronous mod-2^n counter in which the gate fan-in does not increase with n, the number of flip-flops.

The counter of Fig. 4.22-1 has the complication that the fan-in of the AND gates increases with increasing n and may easily become inconveniently large. An alternative scheme which avoids this feature is shown in Fig. 4.22-2. (Gate 1 is not actually required.) Again it is easily verified that the J and K terminals of a particular flip-flop will be at logic 0 and the flip-flop will not toggle except when *all* the preceding flip-flops are in the set condition, $Q_0 = Q_1 = Q_2 \cdots = 1$.

4.23 SYNCHRONOUS-COUNTER SPEED COMPARISONS

It is of interest to compare the speeds, i.e., the clock rates, at which we can operate the synchronous counters we have discussed. The fastest counters are the ring counters (simple or switchtail). Consider that a triggering edge of the clock has occurred in such a ring counter at time $t = 0$, in response to which the counter will advance its count. How long must we wait before allowing the occurrence of the next clock edge if we want to be certain that this succeeding edge will also be effective? In the ring counters only one flip-flop, say FF_k changes state at each triggering edge, this change taking place in response to the input data. This change has to be transmitted to the next flip-flop, FF_{k+1}. Hence we must first wait a time t_{pd} equal to the propagation delay of the flip-flop FF_k. Next we must allow the new input data to FF_{k+1}, that is, the output of FF_k, to remain steady for a time equal to the setup time t_{setup}, as discussed in Sec. 4.15. The hold time of the flip-flop is of no concern because the input data to a flip-flop changes only every n clock cycles. Altogether, the maximum allowable clock frequency is

$$f_{\max} = \frac{1}{t_{pd,\ \text{FF}} + t_{\text{setup}}} \qquad (4.23\text{-}1)$$

In the mod-2^n counter of Fig. 4.22-1 the situation is much the same except that we must take account as well of the propagation delay of the AND gates. We then have

$$f_{\text{max}} = \frac{1}{t_{pd,\,\text{FF}} + t_{pd,\,\text{gate}} + t_{\text{setup}}} \tag{4.23-2}$$

The situation is rather different in the counter of Fig. 4.22-2 because of the need to propagate logic levels through a cascade of AND gates. Consider that the counter is in the state $Q_0Q_1Q_2Q_3 = 0111$. At the next count we should have $Q_0Q_1Q_2Q_3 = 1111$. Then all the J's and K's of all the flip-flops will be at logic 1. Hence, at the next triggering clock edge all the flip-flops will toggle, and we shall have $Q_0Q_1Q_2Q_3 = 0000$, as required. But now return to the point when $Q_0Q_1Q_2Q_3 = 0111$. At this time, all the AND-gate outputs and all the J's and K's except at FF0 are at logic 0. When the clock edge sets Q_0, only after a propagation delays will the output of G1 become logic 1. Then there will be a second propagation delay before the output of G2 becomes 1, a third propagation delay before the output of G3 becomes 1, and so on. Thus, the change in level at Q_0 from $Q_0 = 0$ to $Q_0 = 1$ is propagated, domino fashion, through the AND gates. This sequential transmission through one logic structure after another, each transmission being accompanied by a delay, is referred to as a *ripple*; i.e., the change at Q_0 ripples through the AND gates. If the next clock edge occurs before the ripple is completed, not all J's and K's will be at logic 1. Some flip-flops will not toggle, and the count will be incorrect. A counter with n flip-flops needs $n - 2$ AND gates; hence we have in the present case

$$f_{\text{max}} = \frac{1}{t_{pd,\,\text{FF}} + (n - 2)t_{pd,\,\text{gate}} + t_{\text{setup}}} \tag{4.23-3}$$

The factor $n - 2$ appears here rather than $n - 1$ because, as we have noted, gate G1 in Fig. 4.22-2 is not really required.

4.24 SYNCHRONOUS COUNTERS OF ARBITRARY MODULO

The counters of Fig. 4.22-1 and 4.22-2 use flip-flops economically but have the limitation that their modulo is necessarily 2^n, n being the number of flip-flops. Often a counter must have an arbitrary modulo. For example, to count in the decade system, with which we generally feel most comfortable, we need counters with mod 10.

To construct a counter of arbitrary modulo, we start with a number of flip-flops adequate to provide a number of states equal to or larger than the modulo. Thus, suppose we wanted a counter of mod 5, 6, or 7. Two flip-flops would be inadequate because two flip-flops would provide only four states. However, three flip-flops would be sufficient since three flip-flops would provide $2^3 = 8$ states. Next, we make a decision (in many cases on an entirely arbitrary basis) about which of the possible states of the counter we shall bypass, and finally we decide (again perhaps arbitrarily) on the order in which the counter is to cycle

Table 4.24-1 The eight possible states for a set of three flip-flops

State	Q_2	Q_1	Q_0
S_0	0	0	0
S_1	0	0	1
S_2	0	1	0
S_3	0	1	1
S_4	1	0	0
S_5	1	0	1
S_6	1	1	0
S_7	1	1	1

through states that are not bypassed. Finally we use combinational logic to arrange the counter cycling to proceed from state to state as we require. To illustrate the procedure for such counter design, we shall undertake the design of a mod-5 counter.

The mod-5 counter requires three flip-flops. The possible states are listed in Table 4.24-1. Thus state S_0 is the state in which all the flip-flops are reset with $Q_2 = Q_1 = Q_0 = 0$, etc. Now let us arbitrarily decide that we shall use the last five states in Table 4.24-1 and that the counter is to sequence through the states in the order in which they appear in the table. That is, the sequencing is to be $S_3 \rightarrow S_4 \rightarrow S_5 \rightarrow S_6 \rightarrow S_7 \rightarrow S_3$, etc. Finally let us agree to use JK flip-flops (SR or D would serve as well).

What we require of our counter is spelled out in Tables 4.24-2 and 4.24-3. In Table 4.24-2 we indicate that if the counter is in state S_3, that is, in a "present state" S_3, then, at the next triggering edge of the clock waveform, the counter should find itself in "next state," which is S_4, and so on for the other entries in the table. A table like Table 4.24-2 is called a *state table*. In Table 4.24-3 we have repeated the state table but have also specified the individual

Table 4.24-2 State table for the mod-5 synchronous counter

Present state	Next state
S_3	S_4
S_4	S_5
S_5	S_6
S_6	S_7
S_7	S_3

Table 4.24-3 Transition table for the mod-5 synchronous counter

Present state			Next state		
Q_2^n	Q_1^n	Q_0^n	Q_2^{n+1}	Q_1^{n+1}	Q_0^{n+1}
0	1	1	1	0	0
1	0	0	1	0	1
1	0	1	1	1	0
1	1	0	1	1	1
1	1	1	0	1	1

states of the flip-flops corresponding to each counter state. The symbols Q_2^n etc., represent flip-flop states before and Q_2^{n+1}, etc., represent flip-flop states after the nth clock edge. Table 4.24-3 is called a *transition table*.

With the counter in any of the used states we shall need to provide, to each individual flip-flop, instructions concerning the state which it is next to assume at the triggering edge of the clock. We know how to provide such instructions. The rules are given by the truth table of Fig. 4.11-1b. For our present purpose, however, it is more convenient to have the truth-table information in an alternative form. The truth table of Fig. 4.11-1b tells us directly what the flip-flop will do, given the logic levels at J and K. We would prefer to have the same information available in the truth table in a form in which, given what the flip-flop must do, we are told directly what the logic level on J and K must be. Such an alternative truth table is given in Table 4.24-4. Thus, it indicates that if initially a flip-flop is in the reset condition and we want it to remain in the reset condition after the triggering clock edge, we must have $J = 0$ and it does not matter what the logic level is on K. From the original truth table of Fig. 4.11-1b we can easily verify that the entries in Table 4.24-4 are correct.

Tables 4.24-2 and 4.24-3 display the sequence of states through which the counter is to cycle. Table 4.24-4 tells us how to instruct the flip-flops. From these three tables we can deduce what the logic level on each J and K must be

Table 4.24-4 An alternative form for the truth table of a _JK_ flip-flop

$Q_n \rightarrow Q_{n+1}$		J	K
0	0	0	$\times$
0	1	1	$\times$
1	0	$\times$	1
1	1	$\times$	0

at each state of the counter. It is most convenient to enter these deduced results directly on Karnaugh maps for the J's and K's. There are three flip-flops and two data terminals, J and K, per flip-flop. Hence, there are six K maps in all, as shown in Fig. 4.24-1.

The K-map entries are arrived at in the following manner. Consider, say, that the counter is in the state S_3 with $Q_2Q_1Q_0 = 011$. Then we note from Tables 4.24-2 and 4.24-3 that the next counter state must be S_4 with $Q_2Q_1Q_0 = 100$. Thus Q_2 must go from $Q_2 = 0$ to $Q_2 = 1$. We now observe from Table 4.24-4 that to arrange for the flip-flop to go from $Q_2 = 0$ to $Q_2 = 1$ requires $J_2 = 1$ while K_2 may be $K_2 = \times$ (don't care). Hence in the K maps for J_2 and K_2 and in the boxes corresponding to $Q_2Q_1Q_0 = 011$ we put $J_2 = 1$ and $K_2 = \times$. The entries for the K maps of the other flip-flops are found in a similar manner.

This last detailed procedure ensures that the entries are the correct ones to make the counter go from state S_3 to state S_4. We now repeat the procedure for state S_4, and so on, keeping in mind that the next state after S_7 is the state S_3. Since states S_0, S_1, and S_2 will not occur, we enter don't-cares in all the K-map boxes corresponding to these states.

From the K maps we read

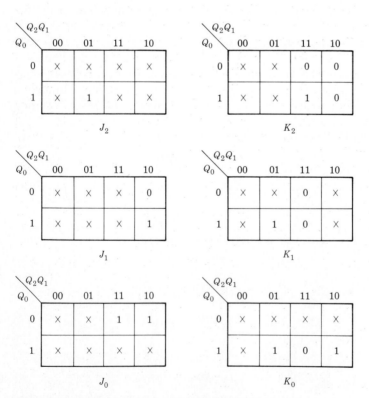

Figure 4.24-1 Karnaugh maps for the mod-5 counter.

$$J_2 = 1 \qquad K_2 = Q_1 Q_0$$
$$J_1 = Q_0 \qquad K_1 = \bar{Q}_2 \qquad (4.24\text{-}1)$$
$$J_0 = 1 \qquad K_0 = \bar{Q}_2 + \bar{Q}_1$$

In Fig. 4.24-2a we have drawn the circuit diagram of the counter by starting with three flip-flops and then interconnecting them as specified by the logic of Eqs. (4.24-1). We have added, as required, a common clock waveform for all the flip-flops. Waveforms for the counter are given in Fig. 4.24-2b. Here we have arbitrarily started in state S_3. Note that state S_7 is followed by state S_3 and that states S_0, S_1, and S_2 are never used.

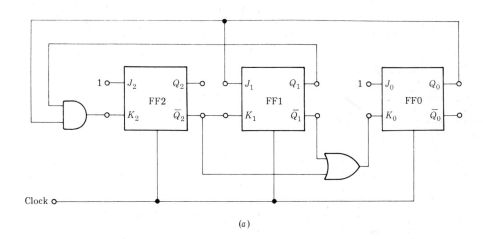

(a)

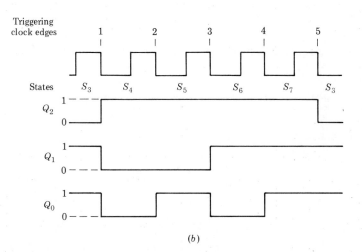

(b)

Figure 4.24-2 (a) Logic diagram of the mod-5 counter and (b) waveforms.

We have selected quite arbitrarily the states in the counter and the order in which the counter sequences from state to state. The question naturally arises whether the resultant counter might not have been simpler if we had used other states, if we had used a different order of sequencing, or if we had done both. That is, while the number of flip-flops is fixed, might we not have found it possible to use less logic, i.e., fewer gates, external to the flip-flops? The answer is yes. State selection and ordering does make a difference, but the matter is of no great consequence to us at present, and we shall consider the matter briefly in the problems of Chap. 7.

4.25 UP-DOWN SYNCHRONOUS COUNTER

There frequently arises a need for a counter whose direction of counting can be reversed so that the counter will, on command, count up or count down. Let us now examine how the mod-5 counter of the previous section can be modified to provide this reversibility feature. The counter will now require, in addition to the clock, an input whose logic level will specify the desired count direction. We shall call this added input M, the *mode* control. Let us agree that when $M = 1$, counting shall proceed in the up direction, $S_3 \to S_4 \to S_5 \ldots$, while when $M = 0$, counting proceeds in the down direction, $S_3 \to S_7 \to S_6 \ldots$.

The transition table for the up-down counter is given in Table 4.25-1. There are now two columns for the next state. The column for $M = 1$ is identical to the next-state columns of Table 4.24-3. The column headed $M = 0$ prescribes a reverse counting order. The procedure for completing the design is the same as the previous section except that four-variable K maps are now required. For now, the next state is determined not only by the variables Q_2^n, Q_1^n, and Q_0^n but by the additional variable M as well. The K maps for J_0 and K_0 are shown in Fig. 4.25-1. We read

$$J_0 = 1 \qquad K_0 = \bar{Q}_1 + \bar{M}Q_2 + M\bar{Q}_2 \qquad (4.25\text{-}1)$$

Generating and reading the K maps for $J_1, K_1, J_2,$ and K_2 is left as a student ex-

Table 4.25-1 Transition table for the up-down mod-5 counter

			Next state					
Present state			$M = 0$			$M = 1$		
Q_2^n	Q_1^n	Q_0^n	Q_2^{n+1}	Q_1^{n+1}	Q_0^{n+1}	Q_2^{n+1}	Q_1^{n+1}	Q_0^{n+1}
0	1	1	1	1	1	1	0	0
1	0	0	0	1	1	1	0	1
1	0	1	1	0	0	1	1	0
1	1	0	1	0	1	1	1	1
1	1	1	1	1	0	0	1	1

Q_0M

Q_2Q_1	00	01	11	10
00	×	×	×	×
01	×	×	×	×
11	1	1	×	×
10	1	1	×	×

$J_0 = 1$

Q_0M

Q_2Q_1	00	01	11	10
00	×	×	×	×
01	×	×	1	0
11	×	×	0	1
10	×	×	1	1

$K_0 = \bar{Q}_1 + \bar{M}Q_2 + M\bar{Q}_2$

Figure 4.25-1 The K maps for J_0 and K_0 for the up-down counter specified in the transition tables of Table 4.25-1.

ercise. The results, as can be verified, are

$$J_2 = 1 \qquad K_2 = Q_1Q_0M + \bar{Q}_1\bar{Q}_0\bar{M} \tag{4.25-2}$$

$$J_1 = \bar{Q}_0M + Q_0 \qquad K_1 = \bar{Q}_2M + Q_0\bar{M} \tag{4.25-3}$$

The circuit diagram of the counter is readily drawn (Prob. 4.25-1).

4.26 LOCKOUT

In the mod-5 counter of the previous section three states, S_0, S_1, and S_2, were not used. In a counter with a higher modulo the number of unused states may well be quite large. For example, a mod-33 counter would require six flip-flops ($2^5 = 32$, $2^6 = 64$), in which 31 states would be unused. It might happen, by chance, that the counter would find itself in such an unused state. For example, the counter might be driven to an unused state by a pulse of noise (an external spurious electrical intrusion) or might even settle initially into such a state when operating power is applied to it. In designing a counter, and in order to minimize the logic which must be added to the flip-flops, we have pretended that we don't care what happens when the counter is in an unused state. If the counter should go from an unused state to a used state either directly or after sequencing some unused state, we might not be seriously concerned; for once a used state is reached, the counter thereafter will sequence through its states in normal fashion. The time required for this return to a normal sequence might be considered a warm-up time or just an inevitable response to noise from which, in due course, a recovery is made. Yet the possibility exists that, having fallen into an unused state, the counter will cycle around a sequence of unused states on a permanent basis. Such a situation is called *lockout* and is, of course, to be avoided.

It is therefore necessary to check each unused state to make sure that no such state heads to lockout. Where lockout results we can remedy the situation by changing don't cares to do-cares, as required. Even if lockout does not occur, the counter starting with an unused state may sequence through many other unused states before finally reaching a used state. Here, too, we may well want to change some don't-cares to do-cares to hasten the process.

4.27 RIPPLE COUNTERS

The counters considered up to this point have all been synchronous counters. We consider now a type of counter which is asynchronous; i.e., the clocking waveform is not applied to all the flip-flops. Asynchronous counters have the advantage of possibly saving hardware; on the other hand, they have some speed limitations not shared by synchronous counters.

An asynchronous counter, called a *ripple* counter, is shown in Fig. 4.27-1 together with its waveform. The flip-flops must be set up to operate in the *toggle mode*. Thus, they may be JK flip-flops in which the J and K terminals are both fixed at the logic 1 level. Alternatively, they may be type D flip-flops in which the $\bar{Q}$ output terminal is connected to the D input terminal.

Note, in Fig. 4.27-1 that the external clock waveform, i.e., the clock waveform whose cycles are to be counted, is applied only to C_0, the clock input of the first flip-flop. All the other flip-flops derive the waveform applied to their

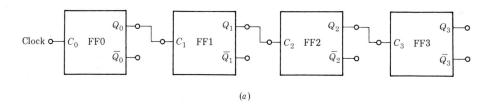

(a)

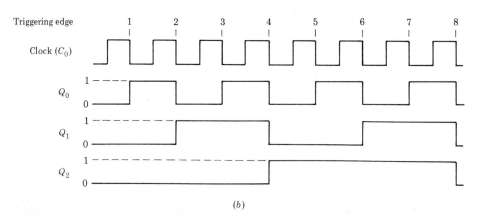

(b)

Figure 4.27-1 A ripple counter: (a) the logic diagram and (b) waveforms.

clock input terminals, C_1, C_2, C_3, etc., from the output terminals Q_0, Q_1, Q_2, etc., of the preceding flip-flop. For the effect of the external clock to make itself felt at a particular flip-flop, the influence of the clock must be propagated, i.e., ripple, through all the preceding flip-flops; hence the name.

In the waveforms of Fig. 4.27-1b we have assumed that the flip-flops respond, i.e., toggle, at the negative-going edge of the waveform applied at the clock input terminal. We have started at a point when all the flip-flops are in the reset state. For each flip-flop, other than FF0, the effective clock input is the Q output of the preceding flip-flop. Hence each such flip-flop toggles when the preceding flip-flop returns to the reset state. Observe that the waveforms of the ripple counter appear the same as the waveforms of the synchronous counter of Fig. 4.22-1. This result was to have been anticipated. In the synchronous counter, we established that a flip-flop toggles when and only when all preceding flip-flops are in the set state. The situation is the same in the present case: a particular flip-flop will toggle only when the preceding flip-flop is set and makes its transition from the set to the reset state. This preceding flip-flop, in turn, will make its 1-to-0 transition only when the flip-flop before it is doing the same thing, and so on. Finally we note that since the ripple sequences through states in the same manner as the synchronous counter, the decoder in Fig. 4.22-1c is suitable in the present ripple case as well.

There is actually a small difference between the waveforms of the synchronous counter and the ripple counter. This difference results from the flip-flop propagation delays, which, for simplicity, we have not taken into account in Figs. 4.22-1 and 4.27-1. The matter is made clear in Fig. 4.27-2, where in Fig. 4.27-2a we have redrawn the synchronous-counter waveform of Fig. 4.22-1 in

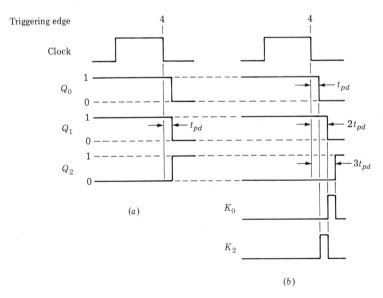

Figure 4.27-2 Waveforms in the neighborhood of clock-triggering edge 4: (a) the synchronous counter of Fig. 4.22-1 and (b) the ripple counter of Fig. 4.27-1.

the neighborhood of clock-triggering edge 4 and in Fig. 4.27-2b we have drawn the corresponding portion of the ripple counter waveforms of Fig. 4.27-1. Observe in Fig. 4.27-2a that there is a fixed delay, the propagation delay t_{pd} of a flip-flop, between the clock edge and the logic-level transition of any of the waveforms. In Fig. 4.27-2b, however, the delay becomes progressively larger, increasing by t_{pd} as we go from one flip-flop to the next.

This accumulation of propagation delays causes a difficulty in reading the count of the counter, as we can now see. Consider the output indications K_0 etc., of the decoder of Fig. 4.22-1c. Before clock edge 4 in Fig. 4.27-2a we have $Q_2Q_1Q_0 = 011$, and we shall have $K_3 = 1$ while all other K's are at logic 0, as required. At a time t_{pd} after clock edge 4 we shall have $Q_2Q_1Q_0 = 100$, and K_4 will become $K_4 = 1$ while all other K's will be 0. There is, of course, a delay t_{pd} before the count decoder registers the new count properly. This delay is ordinarily a matter of no serious concern. On the other hand, consider the situation in Fig. 4.27-2b. Again before clock edge 4 only $K_4 = 1$. Note, however, that there are now intervals when $K_0 = 1$ and when $K_2 = 1$. The decoder then is providing an incorrect indication, since, in the interval described we should have all K's except K_3 and K_4 held steady at logic 0.

As we have seen, ripple counters generate *decoding errors* which persist for some part of the interval of a clock cycle. To mask these errors, it is common to add to each gate of the decoder of Fig. 4.22-1 an additional input. These additional inputs are tied to a common terminal, and a *strobe pulse* is applied to this terminal. This strobe input is allowed to go to logic 1 only during the part of the clock cycle during which decoding errors are not present. While decoding errors are occurring, the strobe is at 0, all the decoder gates are disabled, and all the K's are at logic 0.

The time interval during which count-reading errors occur increases in proportion to the number of flip-flops in the cascade. A worst case occurs when all the flip-flops are in set state so that the counter is reading $11 \cdots 11$. At the next clocking edge the count should go to $00 \cdots 00$. However, only the first flip-flop responds directly to the input clock, and the transition from set to reset state has to ripple down the cascade of flip-flops. If there are n flip-flops, the ripple will not have completed itself until a time nt_{pd}. Suppose, now, that the period of the clocking waveform is smaller than nt_{pd}. Then before the count $00 \cdots 00$ has been registered in the counter, the first flip-flop, at least, will have been toggled back to the set state. Hence there never will be a time when the counter reads $00 \cdots 00$, and it will simply be impossible to read the counter correctly. Altogether then, when it is always necessary to be able to read the count, the ripple counter has a serious speed limitation in comparison with the synchronous counter of Fig. 4.22-1 or the ring counters.

The synchronous counter of Fig. 4.22-2, as we have seen, is also beset with a speed limitation resulting from the ripple of logic level which must go through the AND gates. However, we may well expect that the synchronous counter will be faster than the ripple counter because the delay through AND gates will be smaller than the propagation delay through flip-flops. We may note, as a point

Table 4.27-1 Count direction in a ripple counter

The clock input of each flip-flop is as given except for the first flip-flop, which is driven by an external waveform

Clock input connection	Clock edge direction for toggling	Count direction
Q	Negative-going	Up
Q	Positive-going	Down
$\bar{Q}$	Negative-going	Down
$\bar{Q}$	Positive-going	Up

of interest, that if the synchronous counter is driven faster than the ripple will allow, the counter will *count incorrectly*. If the ripple counter is driven faster than the ripple will allow, the counter will count correctly but we shall have *errors in count reading*.

Up-Down Ripple Counter

A ripple counter may use flip-flops which toggle on the negative-going edge or on the positive-going edge of the waveform applied to the clock input terminal. Also, we may connect each flip-flop clock input (except FF0) to the Q or to the $\bar{Q}$ output of the preceding flip-flop. Depending on the type of flip-flop, the counter will count up or down. In an up count the counter sequence is $Q_3Q_2Q_1Q_0 = 0000 \rightarrow 0001 \rightarrow 0010$, etc. In a down count the counter steps through its states in the reverse order, and the sequence is $Q_3Q_2Q_1Q_0 = 0000 \rightarrow 1111 \rightarrow 1110$, etc. It is left as an exercise (Prob. 4.27-1) to verify that the count direction is as given in Table 4.27-1. It is also left as an exercise (Prob. 4.27-2) to show how the circuit of Fig 4.27-1 can be modified into an up-down counter.

As with synchronous counters, asynchronous counters can also be constructed which have an arbitrary modulus. Some of the methods used are presented in Probs. 4.27-3 and 4.27-4.

4.28 INTEGRATED-CIRCUIT COUNTER CHIPS

There are a large number (about 20) of counter chips to be found in a TTL data catalog. All involve four flip-flops, and some of them are rather elaborate. The logic diagrams of three of the simpler ones are shown in Fig. 4.28-1. The type '93, shown in Fig. 4.28-1a is a ripple counter. The J and K terminals not indicated as having any connections are actually held at logic 1 by connections internal to the flip-flops. Hence all the flip-flops have $J = K = 1$ and are accordingly in the toggle mode. We observe that except for the active-high ANDed

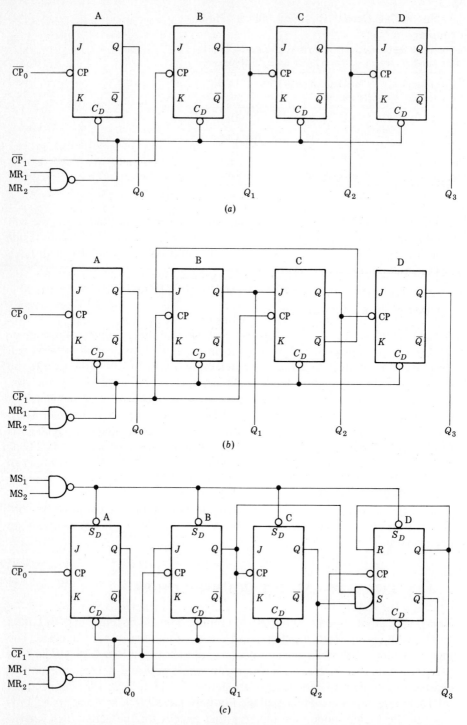

Figure 4.28-1 IC counters: (*a*) type '93 ripple counter; (*b*) type '92 divide-by-12 counter, and (*c*) type '90 decade counter.

master-reset controls MR_1 and MR_2, flip-flop A is isolated, while B, C, and D are interconnected in ripple-counter fashion. If we use flip-flop A alone, we have a mod-2 counter with clock pulse input $\overline{CP}_0$. If we use flip-flops B, C and D alone, we have a mod-8 counter with clock pulse input $\overline{CP}_1$. If we connect the Q output of flip-flop A to the line $\overline{CP}_1$, we have a mod-16 counter with clock input $\overline{CP}_0$. We can cascade type '93 chips simply by connecting the Q_3 output of one to the $\overline{CP}_0$ or $\overline{CP}_1$ input of the next.

In the type '92 counter of Fig. 4.28-1b, except again for the common master reset, flip-flop A is isolated from the others. Flip-flops B and C constitute a synchronous (common-clock) mod-3 counter which is connected in ripple fashion to flip-flop D. Hence the three together B, C, and D constitute a mod-6 $(= 3 \times 2)$ counter and all four together become a mod-12 $(= 2 \times 3 \times 2)$ counter. Altogether, then, we can use A alone with clock input $\overline{CP}_0$ as a mod-2 counter, B, C and D with $\overline{CP}_1$ clock input as a mod-6 counter, or all-four flip-flops, with input $\overline{CP}_0$ and Q_0 connected to $\overline{CP}_1$, as a mod-12 counter.

In the type '90 counter chip of Fig. 4.28-1c two active-high master resets and two active-high sets are provided. Again flip-flop A is isolated and constitutes a mod-2 counter with clock input $\overline{CP}_0$. The flip-flops B, C, and D, as can be verified (Prob. 4.28-1), are connected as a mod-5 counter with clock input $\overline{CP}_1$. If we connect Q_0 to $\overline{CP}_1$, we shall have a mod-10 $(= 2 \times 5)$ counter, i.e., a decade counter. With such a connection the clock would be applied at $\overline{CP}_0$. If we wish, we can connect Q_3 to $\overline{CP}_0$ instead and use $\overline{CP}_1$ as the clock input of a decade counter. In either case the modulus of the counter would be the same, but the waveforms generated would be different (Prob. 4.28-2).

Typical of the more elaborate counters which are available is the type '190. This device is an up-down decade counter with provision for presetting the counter asynchronously. It also makes available output signals which facilitate cascading counter chips in ripple or synchronous fashion.

FIVE

ARITHMETIC

In this chapter we shall describe how numbers, both positive and negative, are represented and manipulated in digital systems. We shall then consider how arithmetic operations are performed. The operation of addition will be emphasized, since all other arithmetic operations can be effected through the addition operation.

5.1 REPRESENTATION OF SIGNED NUMBERS

Numbers, like digital words generally, are stored, i.e., written in registers. When the set and reset states of the flip-flops in the registers are to be used to represent the *numerals* 1 and 0, it is most convenient and reasonable (though not absolutely necessary) to let the set state (logic level 1 at the Q output of flip-flop) represent the numeral 1 and to let the reset state represent the numeral 0. Thus if the state of a 4-bit register $A_3A_2A_1A_0 = 1101$ and the register is holding a number, the number is 1101 (base 2) = 13 (base 10). A representation of a 4-bit register is shown in Fig. 5.1-1a. The register has 16 positions and can be used to register a number from 0 to 15.

The register in Fig 5.1-1a is drawn in circular fashion to remind us that a register has a modulus. That is, it has a finite number of states and if it were to be cycled step by step through its states, it would eventually return to its starting point and then start all over. The register of Fig. 5.1-1 is described as a mod-16 register or a register with a four-place modulus. The pointer on the register is intended to indicate that the register can be used to keep a record of a

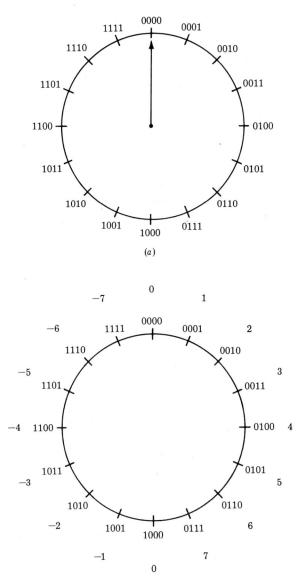

Figure 5.1-1 (*a*) A 4-bit mod-16 register. (*b*) The sign-magnitude method of assigning register positions to positive and negative numbers.

count or even to add and subtract. We could count by simply advancing the pointer by one position to register each additional count. To add 2 and 3 we would first "clear" the register, i.e., set it to 0000. Then we would advance the pointer by 2 positions and then 3 positions. The total advance would be 5 positions, and the pointer would correctly indicate 0101 (=5). To subtract 2 from 3 we would clear the register, advance it by 3 positions and then retard it by 2 positions. The final position would correctly indicate 0001 ($=1$). The end result of such an addition or subtraction would be correct provided that the result is a positive number in the range from 0 to 15. If the result is outside the range of the register, the result is correct only to within the modulus of the register. For example if we add 12 and 9 on a 4-bit register, the register will indicate $(12 + 9) - 16 = 5$ ($=0101$) and we write

$$12 + 9 = 21 = 5 \qquad \text{mod } 16 \qquad (5.1\text{-}1)$$

There are no plus signs or minus signs associated with a register, only register positions. How then shall we arrange to associate a sign with a number to indicate whether a number is positive or negative? We may, if we choose, simply assign positive and negative significance to the register positions in an arbitrary fashion. However, there are three schemes of special interest by which register positions can be associated with signed numbers. These schemes will now be examined.

A scheme which rather readily suggests itself is simply to single out one flip-flop in the register and to agree arbitrarily that the state of this specially reserved flip-flop is not to have a numerical significance but is to indicate the sign. We may agree (and this is the usual agreement) that when the sign flip-flop is reset (at logic 0) the sign is positive and when the flip-flop is set (at logic 1) the sign is negative. The 4-bit register of Fig. 5.1-1a with positions reassigned in this manner is shown in Fig. 5.1-1b. Let us refer to the leftmost of the 4 bits as the sign bit S, so that a register position previously referred to as $A_3A_2A_1A_0$ becomes now $SA_2A_1A_0$. Then $SA_2A_1A_0 = 0101 = +5$, while $SA_2A_1A_0 = 1101 = -5$. The scheme here is called the *sign-magnitude* representation of signed numbers. Observe that there are two zeros, $0000 = +0$ and $1000 = -0$. The remaining positions are divided evenly between positive and negative numbers so that the range of the register is from -7 to $+7$. We consider in the next sections alternative schemes of representation which are generally more useful.

5.2 THE TWOS-COMPLEMENT REPRESENTATION OF SIGNED NUMBERS

A modulus M having been specified, we can, with respect to that modulus and in the binary system of arithmetic, define the *twos complement* of a number N. $N^{(2)}$ is defined as

$$N^{(2)} = M - N \qquad \text{mod } M \qquad (5.2\text{-}1)$$

For example suppose we have a 4-bit modulus, so that the modulus is $M = 2^4 = 16 = 10000$. Let the number $N = 5$ (0101). Then the twos complement of $N = 5$ is $N^{(2)}(5)$ given by

$$N^{(2)}(5) = 2^4 - 5 = 10000 - 0101 = 1011 \qquad (5.2\text{-}2)$$

As further examples, the twos complements of $N = 0000, 0001, 0010$, and 0011 are evaluated by the subtractions

	10000	10000	10000	10000
$N =$	0000	0001	0010	0011
$N^{(2)} =$	10000	1111	1110	1101

In the first case the formal subtraction of 0 from 2^4 yields 10000, but as we note from Eq. (5.1-1), the result is to be written mod M and 10000 mod 16 = 0000; hence the result is 0000 and not 10000.

The evaluation of the twos complement of a number involves a succession, bit by bit, of subtractions from the binary number 10 (= 2 decimal). For example, in the subtraction above of 0001 we start by subtracting 1 from 10. That is, we seek the number which when added to 1 will bring the sum to 10. We are thus looking for the number which will *complement* the subtrahend in the sense that the subtrahend and difference complement each other to yield the sum 10. This first subtraction generates a borrow, which carries to the next more significant column, where again we then subtract 1 from 10 (=2). In general, in evaluating the complement of any number we find that after arriving at the first 1 in the subtrahend every subtraction is a subtraction from 10 (decimal 2). It is for this reason that the quantity $N^{(2)}$ is called the *twos complement* of N.

It is to be noted that the twos complement of a number *cannot be specified unambiguously unless a modulus is specified*. Thus, when the modulus is 16 (four binary places) the twos complement of 5 (101) is 1011. If the modulus were 32 (five binary places), the twos complement would be $100000 - 101 = 11011$.

There is a useful algorithm for calculating the twos complement of a number without the formal procedure of a subtraction:

1. Write the number using as many bits as is appropriate to the modulus, i.e., as many bits as in the register which is to register the number.
2. Starting from the bit of least numerical significance, leave unaltered the bits which are 0 up to the first 1 encountered. Also leave unaltered this first 1.
3. Complement all other bits.

By way of example, let us find the twos complement of the number +20 (decimal) assuming a seven-place modulus. Write the number as the 7-bit binary number 0010100. The 1 in the position of least significance remains unaltered as do the 0s to the right of that 1. Complementing all other bits we have 1101100.

In Fig. 5.2-1, we show the *twos-complement* schemes of assigning register positions to positive and negative numbers. Here we represent a negative number $-N$ by the twos complement (to within the modulus of the register) of N; that is, $-N$ is represented by $M - N$. Thus, in the present case of a 4-bit modulus the representation of -1 is $2^4 - 1 = 10000 - 0001 = 1111$, etc. Ob-

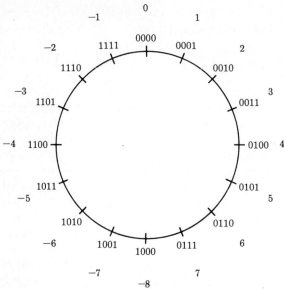

Figure 5.2-1 The twos-complement representation.

serve, that in this scheme there is just a single zero. Note also, as in the sign-magnitude scheme, that the leftmost bit serves to indicate sign. If this leftmost bit is 0, the number is positive; if the bit is 1, the number is negative.

The twos-complement register-position assignment scheme has the merit that as long as the result is within the range of the register we can add by advancing the register pointer and subtract by retarding the pointer. For example, suppose we want to find $4 - 6$. Then starting at zero, we advance the pointer 4 positions and then turn it back 6 positions. We may, if we choose, perform the operations in reverse order (retard first and then advance). In either event we wind up at 1110, which is the correct twos-complement representation of $-2\ (=4-6)$. Observe most particularly that if we had tried the same operation with the sign-magnitude operation, we would not have arrived at a correct result.

Next, it is to be observed that the twos complement register allows us to perform the operation of subtraction as an operation of *addition* of a negative number. Thus suppose we seek $N_1 - N_2$. We can write $N_1 - N_2 = N_1 + (-N_2)$. Since $-N_2$ is represented as $M - N_2$, we find that

$$N_1 - N_2 = N_1 + (-N_2) = N_1 + (M - N_2) \qquad (5.2\text{-}3)$$

That is, to *subtract* N_2 from N_1, we set the register pointer at N_1 and then *advance* (as in *adding*) the pointer by a number of places equal to the twos complement of N_2. An example will make clear why this process works. Consider again the subtraction $4 - 6$. Having set the pointer at 4, we need to retard the pointer by 6 positions. There are however 16 positions in our 4-bit register. Hence instead of *retarding* by 6 positions, we can arrive at the same place by advancing 10 positions since $10 + 6 = 16$, or, to put the matter another way, retarding by 6 positions is equivalent to advancing a number of positions equal to the twos complement of 6.

An example will make clear how numbers can be combined when the twos-complement register scheme is followed. Let us consider combining the decimal numbers 12 and 13. We shall calculate $12 + 13$, $12 - 13$, $-12 + 13$, and $-12 - 13$. Now 12 (decimal) = 1100 and 13 = 1101. A four-place register will encompass only the range -8 to $+7$. So let us try a five-place register. In a five-place register 12 = 01100 and 13 = 01101; $-12 = 10100$ and $-13 = 10011$, so that the five-place register has a range adequate for our numbers. But we must look ahead. We know that $12 + 13 = 25$ and $-12 - 13 = -25$. These numbers ($+25$ and -25) are outside the range of a five-place register. Hence we must use a six-place register whose range, as can be verified, extends from -32 to $+31$. The arithmetic now proceeds as follows

$$+12 = 001100 \qquad +13 = 001101$$

$$-12 = 110100 \qquad -13 = 110011$$

$+12 = 001100$	$+12 = 001100$	$-12 = 110100$	$-12 = 110100$
$+13 = \underline{001101}$	$-13 = \underline{110011}$	$+13 = \underline{001101}$	$-13 = \underline{110011}$
011001	111111	$(1)000001$	$(1)100111$

Note that in each of these four cases the operation performed is always addition. In the first case we get 011001, which we read directly as $+25$. In the second case, we recognize that the result is a negative number since the leftmost digit is a 1. Hence, having determined the magnitude of the result, we shall append a minus sign. The magnitude is determined by taking the twos complement of 111111, which we find to be 000001, or 1. Hence the result is -1. Observe that so long as a negative number is kept internal to a digital processor, it will retain its twos-complement form. That is, -1 will be registered as 111111. The operation of reading the sign and determining the magnitude will generally be called for only when we need a printout so that the result can be read by a human operator.

In the third and fourth additions above we note carries into the seventh position. Since these carries, which we have marked off by parentheses, are outside the range of modulus of our six-place registers, however, they will not register in our six-place registers and the numbers we shall read in the registers, in the twos cases, are 000001 and 100111, respectively.

5.3 THE ONES-COMPLEMENT REPRESENTATION OF SIGNED NUMBERS

Having established a modulus $M = 2^n$, the ones complement $N^{(1)}$ of a number N is defined as

$$N^{(1)} = (M - 1) - N \tag{5.3-1}$$

Thus, with a four-place modulus $M - 1 = 2^n - 1 = 1111$, and the ones comple-ments of $N = 0000,0001,0010$, and 0011 are calculated by the subtractions

	1111	1111	1111	1111
$N =$	0000	0001	0010	0011
$N^{(1)} =$	1111	1110	1101	1100

Observe that in every case the determination of the ones complement is achieved by a sequence of subtractions, digit by digit, from 1. Hence the termi-nology *ones complement*. The calculation of the ones complement is simpler than the calculation of the twos complement since in the present case borrow-ing carries from place to place are not generated. As a matter of fact, we hardly even need to perform a subtraction, for, as is easily recognized, the ones com-plement of a number can be generated simply by complementing every digit in the number, i.e., replacing 0s by 1s and 1s by 0s.

We may note in passing that an additional method of computing the twos complement of a number consists in first calculating the ones complement and then adding 1 to the result. For $N^{(2)} = M - N$ and $N^{(1)} = (M - 1) - N$ so that $N^{(2)} = N^{(1)} + 1$.

In Fig. 5.3-1 we show our four-place register in which a ones-complement scheme has been used to assign register positions to positive and negative numbers. In this register a number $-N$ is registered as $N^{(1)}$. Thus -1 becomes $1111 - 0001 = 1110, -2 = 1111 - 0010 = 1101$, etc. Note that again here, as in the two previous cases, all positive numbers have 0 as the leftmost digit and all negative numbers have 1. There are two zeros, this time side by side, with $0000 = +0$ and $1111 = -0$.

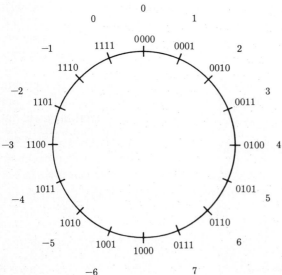

Figure 5.3-1 The ones-complement representation.

As in the twos-complement case, subtracting can be performed by advancing the register pointer. Thus, for example, to subtract 6, we advance the pointer 9 positions ($15 - 6 = 9$) rather than 10 positions ($16 - 6 = 10$) because in the present case the negative numbers have been shifted one place counterclockwise compared with the twos-complement register of Fig. 5.2-1.

A special situation develops when we advance the register so far that the pointer passes through 0000. In this case we shall know that an error of one count has occurred because we shall have passed through two zeros. We can alert ourselves to such a development by noting that a carry will have taken place into the digit position one place more significant than the most significant digit of the register. If we make some provision to note this carry, we can correct the result, when the carry so indicates, by adding 1 to our result.

As an example of the workings of our ones-complement register let us again combine the numbers 12 and 13. We have

$$+12 = 001100 \qquad +13 = 001101$$

$$-12 = 110011 \qquad -13 = 110010$$

$+12 = 001100$	$+12 = 001100$	$-12 = 110011$	$-12 = 110011$
$+13 = \underline{001101}$	$-13 = \underline{110010}$	$+13 = \underline{001101}$	$-13 = \underline{110010}$
011001	111110	1000000	1100101
		$\llcorner\!\longrightarrow 1$	$\llcorner\!\longrightarrow 1$
		000001	100110

In the first case we find the result $011001 = +25$. In the second case we recognize that the result is negative. To find the magnitude we take the ones complement, which is $000001 = 1$, so that the result is -1. In the third and fourth cases we find a carry into the seventh place. We are alerted to add 1, and having done so we ignore the carry.

5.4 ADDITION OF TWO BINARY NUMBERS

Suppose that we have two n-digit binary numbers $A = A_{n-1}A_{n-2}\ldots A_0$ and $B = B_{n-1}B_{n-2}\ldots B_0$ and seek the sum of the two numbers. The sum S will possibly have one more digit than the numbers being added, so that $S = S_n S_{n-1}\ldots S_0$. Each digit S_i of the sum is uniquely determined by the digits A_i and B_i of the numbers being added. Hence, for each S_i, we can prepare a truth table showing S_i for all possible combinations of A_i and B_i. This truth table could then be physically realized by a gate structure which need not involve more than two levels of gates. We would, of course, require as many gate structures as there are digits in the sum. Assume then that we have such a set of gate structures and that at time $t = 0$ the logic levels representing the numbers A and B are applied to the inputs of the gates. If the propagation delay of a gate is t_{pd}, the sum will be available at the gate outputs at a time $t = 2t_{pd}$.

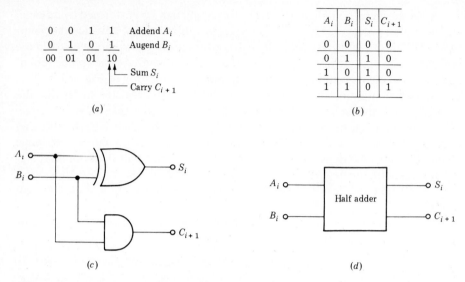

Figure 5.4-1 (*a*) Addition of two binary digits. (*b*) Truth table for sum and carry bits. (*c*) Gate realization of truth table. (*d*) Symbol for a half adder.

While the scheme for adding numbers is valid in principle, unhappily it turns out generally not to be feasible. For it is not at all unusual for our numbers A and B each to have 32 digits. In this case the number of columns on the input side of the truth table is 64, the number of rows in the truth table is $2^{64} \simeq 10^{19}$, and the number of gates involved in a physical realization is similarly of astronomical proportions. As a result, feasible schemes of addition generally depend on adding the digits column after column, much as a human calculator would operate.

In Fig. 5.4-1*a* we have added a single-digit augend digit A_i to a single-digit addend digit B_i. The addition generates a sum digit S_i in the same column and hence with the same numerical significance as A_i and B_i. The addition may also generate a carry digit C_{i+1}, which is of a numerical significance one order higher than the digits being added. As is easily verified, the truth table for the generation of the sum and carry bits is as given in Fig. 5.4-1*b*. The sum bit is generated by the EXCLUSIVE-OR operation, $S_i = A_i \oplus B_i$ while the carry bit is generated by the AND operation, $C_{i+1} = A_i B_i$. The gates are shown in Fig. 5.4-1*c*. Such a gate structure is called a *half-adder* and represented by the symbol in Fig. 5.4-1*d*.

The Full Adder

The column-by-column addition of two *n*-bit binary numbers is illustrated in Fig. 5.4-2. The least significant bits A_0 and B_0 are added first, generating a sum bit S_0 and a carry bit C_1. For this operation a half adder would be adequate. In

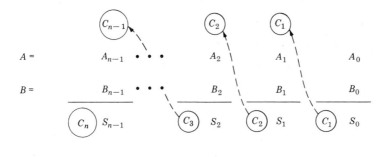

$$S = C_n S_{n-1} \cdots S_0$$

Figure 5.4-2 The addition of two n-digit numbers.

the next position, however, we have to combine 3 digits, the bits A_1 and B_1 and the carry bit C_1 from the previous column. Similar additions of 3 bits are required in the succeeding columns. The sum finally is $S = C_n S_{n-1} \ldots S_0$. The most significant bit in the sum is the carry into the nth column, and we have therefore chosen here for consistency to refer to it as C_n rather than S_n as in the previous section.

As in the addition of 2 digits, with 3 digits A_i, B_i, and the carry C_i there will be generated a sum S_i and a carry C_{i+1}. The truth tables for S_i and C_{i+1} are given in Fig. 5.4-3a. Karnaugh maps for S_i and C_{i+1} are given in Fig. 5.4-3b and two-level gate realizations are shown in Fig. 5.4-3c. An alternative gate structure which will produce the sum bit S_i consists of the cascade of two EXCLUSIVE-OR gates as in Fig. 5.4-3d. A set of gate structures which are adequate for the addition of 3 bits is called a *full adder*, represented by the symbol in Fig. 5.4-3e.

A full adder can also be assembled from two half adders and an OR gate, as shown in Fig. 5.4-4. The first half adder generates sum and carry bits S_i' and C_{i+1}' for A_i and B_i, and the second half adder combines the carry input C_i with S_i' to generate the sum output S_i and a carry C_{i+1}''. The final carry-out is $C_{i+1} = C_{i+1}' + C_{i+1}''$. While the figure suggests that A_i and B_i must be applied to the first half adder, actually the input to the first half adder may be any two of the three inputs C_i, A_i, and B_i. The third input is then introduced at the second half adder.

5.5 A SERIAL ADDER

In Fig. 5.5-1 we show how a single full adder can be used to add two n-bit numbers $A = A_{n-1}A_{n-2} \cdots A_0$ and $B = B_{n-1}B_{n-2} \cdots B_0$. Here the addition takes place *serially*, i.e., one column at a time in synchronism with the successive cycles of the clocking waveform.

Initially the addend and augend are each loaded into an n-bit shift register. An $(n+1)$-bit shift register is available to receive the sum. The registers shift to

Carry in C_i	Addend A_i	Augend B_i	Sum S_i	Carry out C_{i+1}
0	0	0	0	0
0	0	1	1	0
0	1	0	1	0
0	1	1	0	1
1	0	0	1	0
1	0	1	0	1
1	1	0	0	1
1	1	1	1	1

(a)

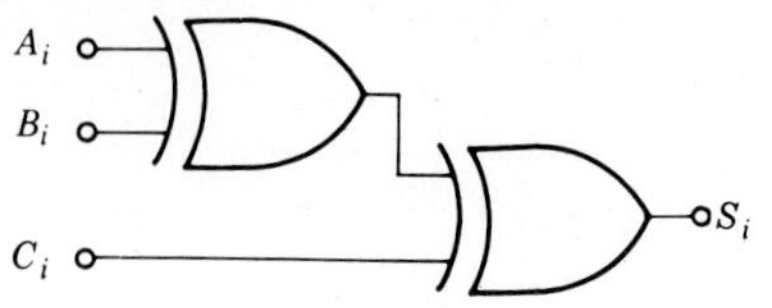

(d)

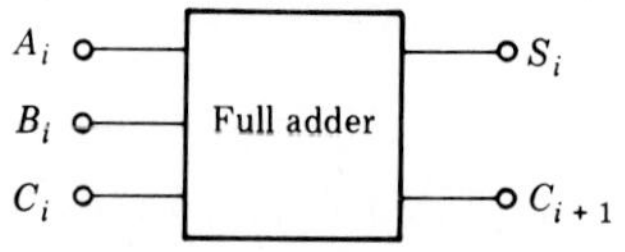

(e)

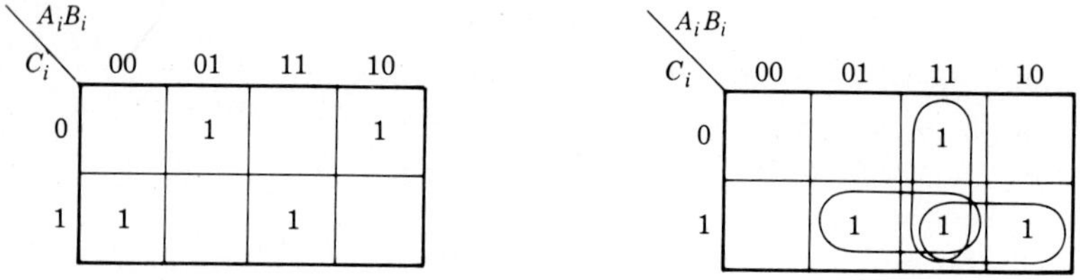

$S_i = \bar{A}_i B_i \bar{C}_i + A_i \bar{B}_i \bar{C}_i + \bar{A}_i \bar{B}_i C_i + A_i B_i C_i$

$C_{i+1} = A_i B_i + A_i C_i + B_i C_i$

(b)

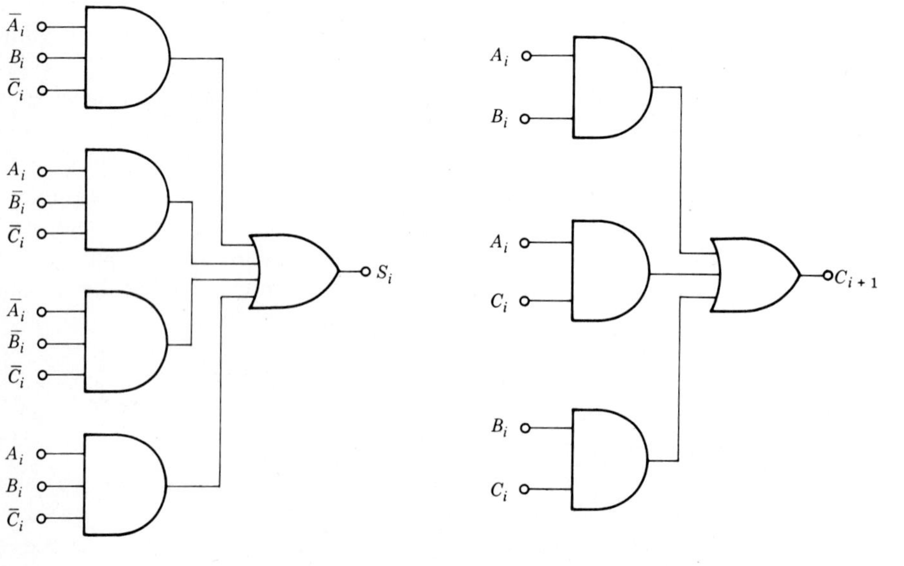

(c)

Figure 5.4-3 (a) Truth table for a full adder. (b) K maps. (c) Gate structures. (d) Alternative gate structure for the sum S_i. (e) Symbol for a full adder.

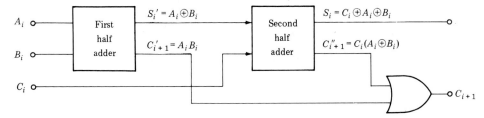

Figure 5.4-4 A full adder assembled from two half adders and an OR gate.

the right and the register loading is such that the least significant bits A_0 and B_0 are in the rightmost register positions. Initially, also, we assume that the type-D flip-flop is in the reset state so that $Q = C_i = 0$. The sum bits will be shifted into the register from the left, again 1 bit at a time. In the course of entering the sum, whatever bits may have been in the sum register will be shifted out and lost. Hence there is no need to clear the sum register at the outset of the addition sequence. The sum $S = C_n S_{n-1} S_{n-2} \cdots S_0$, indicated as being registered in the sum register, will be so registered at the completion of the addition and not at the outset.

Initially, then, before the first triggering edge of the clock waveform, the bits A_0 and B_0 will be present at the full-adder inputs A_i and B_i while the C_i input will be $C_i = 0$. At that time, too, the sum S_0 and C_0 generated by these bits will be present at the full-adder outputs S_i and C_{i+1} (we assume that the propagation delay time through the full adder, which is a combinational circuit, is

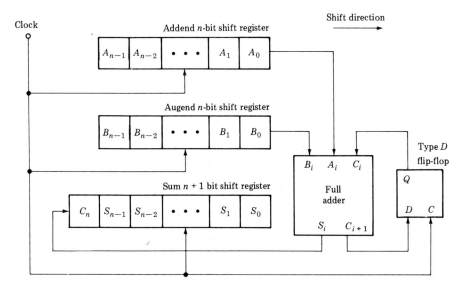

Figure 5.5-1 A serial adder.

small compared with the clock period). At the first triggering clock edge, a number of events will occur. The sum bit S_0 will register in the leftmost flip-flop of the sum register. The addend and augend registers will shift one position so that the bits of next higher order A_1 and B_1 will now be input to the full adder. The input C_1 to the type-D flip-flop will be transferred to its output so that C_1 will be present at the full adder input C_i. The purpose of the flip-flop is to provide precisely a one-clock-cycle delay so that the carry generated by adding a column will appear when required to be added to the bits of next higher order of significance.

After this first clock edge, the first sum bit has been registered, the inputs to the full adder are A_1, B_1, and C_1, and the full adder outputs are S_1 and C_2. The second clock edge moves S_0 one place to the right in the sum register and registers the newly calculated sum bit S_1 in the leftmost flip-flop of the sum register. This same second clock edge advances A_2 and B_2 to the full adder and also transfers C_2 to the C_i input. In this way, clock cycle by clock cycle, the sum bits are calculated, entered into the sum register from the left, and shifted down the register to make room for successively calculated bits. After n clock edges the A and B registers will be cleared; we shall have $A_i = B_i = 0$, and C_i will be the carry C_n generated by the addition $A_{n-1} + B_{n-1} + C_{n-1}$. The $(n + 1)$th clock edge will transfer this last bit into the sum register and the operation will be complete. At this moment the clock must be turned off.

5.6 PARALLEL ADDITION

The serial addition scheme of the previous section is economical of hardware but is relatively slow. A synchronously operating system is required, and an n-bit addition requires $n + 1$ clock cycles. A faster addition method in which all orders of the augend and addend are added in *parallel*, i.e., simultaneously, is shown in Fig. 5.6-1. The method uses more hardware since we require as many

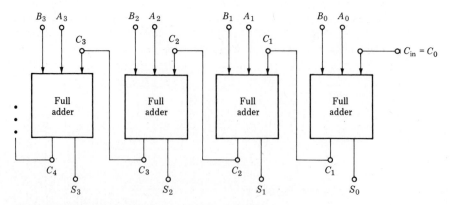

Figure 5.6-1 A parallel adder using an array of full adders.

full adders as there are bits in the numbers to be added. In principle, the first adder used to combine A_0 and B_0 could be a half adder. If a full adder is used, the input carry to this full adder is set to $C_{in} = C_0 = 0$. The first adder then combines A_0 and B_0 to yield a sum bit S_0 and a carry bit C_1. This carry bit is combined in the next full adder with the bits A_1 and B_1 to generate S_1 and C_2, and so on.

It is, of course, necessary that all the bits A_i and B_i be available at the same time to be applied to the inputs of the full adders. Hence it is to be understood in Fig. 5.6-1 that the numbers A and B are available in registers. These registers, which are not shown in the figure, are not required to be shift registers and are instead simply *storage registers*.

5.7 A SIMPLE ADDITION-SUBTRACTION CALCULATOR

The diagram of Fig. 5.7-1 shows a simple calculator with which we can combine, by addition or subtraction, a sequence of binary numbers. Numbers will be entered in a manner convenient to the human operator. As is the case with calculators generally, the operator will enter both the magnitude of the number and the indication whether the number entered is to be added or subtracted. The output indication, again for the sake of the human operator, will appear in sign-magnitude form. In the calculator itself numbers will appear in the ones-complement representation, and number manipulations will be carried out in a manner appropriate to that representation. The accumulated result of combining the input entries is kept in a storage register, appropriately named an *accumulator*. We assume that there is provision for clearing the register say by manipulating the direct-reset inputs of the register flip-flops. For simplicity, this feature has not been incorporated into the figure. The register has a clock line connected to all the flip-flop clock inputs. We assume that the type-D flip-flops respond to the transition of the clock from 1 to 0. We assume further that when switch SW (register) is open the clock inputs are held at logic 0 by some circuitry not shown. Hence a momentary closing of SW(register) connecting the clock line to logic 1, will raise the clock line from 0 to 1 and then let it fall back to 0 again. Thus, tapping SW(register) to make it close briefly will apply one clock cycle to the clock line. While, of course, the calculator may be expanded to accommodate an arbitrary number of bits, in the present case, to simplify the drawing, we have restricted the accumulator to 4 bits. Hence the range of the accumulated sum must be in the range $+7$ to -7. The bit in the most significant position is the sign bit.

In the 4-bit full adder there are four individual full adders. The input terminals $A_3A_2A_1A_0$ and $B_3B_2B_1B_0$ are shown, as are also the output terminals $S_3S_2S_1S_0$. Also shown are the carry input C_{in} to the first (lowest-order) full adder and the carry output C_4 from the last full adder. The other carry-outs and carry-ins which are connected (C_1 to C_2, C_2 to C_3, etc.) are not explicitly shown because we do not need access to these terminals. Notice particularly the connection of the output carry C_4 to the input carry C_{in}. This connection

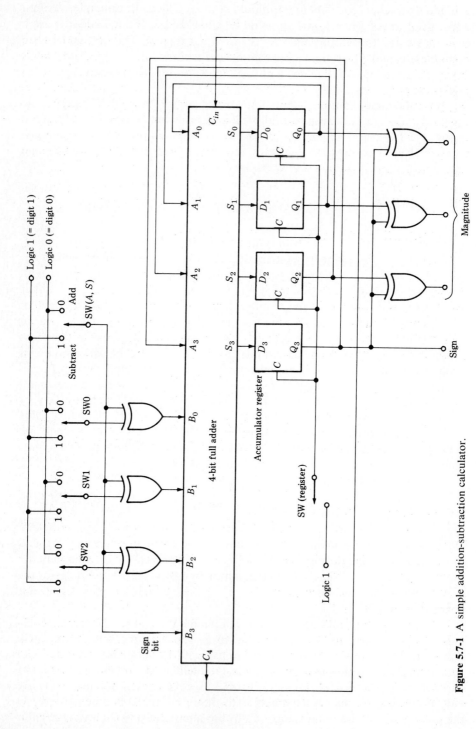

Figure 5.7-1 A simple addition-subtraction calculator.

will provide the correction required in ones-complement arithmetic whenever an overflow occurs into the bit position beyond the sign bit.

An input number is presented to the calculator by manipulating the switches SW2, SW1, and SW0. Thus 3 is presented by setting SW2, SW1, SW0 = 011. If this input number is to be added, SW(A, S) is set to the 0 (add) position. In this case the number presented to the adder is 0011, which in the ones complement representation is $+3$. If the number is to be subtracted, then SW(A, S) is set to 1 (subtract). In this case the sign bit becomes 1 and all the other input bits are complemented by the EXCLUSIVE-OR gates. The adder input is therefore $B_3B_2B_1B_0 = 1100$, which is -3. Assuming that the accumulator register is clear, the other adder input is $A_3A_2A_1A_0 = 0000$ and the sum output is $S_3S_2S_1S_0 = 1100 + 0000 = 1100$. Tapping SW(register) enters this sum in the accumulator. We can now enter a second number into the calculator by operating the input switches. This new number will again appear at $B_3B_2B_1B_0$, while the number already accumulated will appear at $A_3A_2A_1A_0$. Again, tapping SW(register) will add the new input to the sum already in the accumulator and will enter the new sum into the accumulator.

The Q_3 output of the leftmost flip-flop provides the output sign bit. If the number is positive, $Q_3 = 0$ and the magnitude of the number is to be read directly from the other flip-flops. If the number is negative, $Q_3 = 1$ and to get the magnitude of the accumulated result we need to complement the outputs of all the flip-flops. This complementing is again accomplished by EXCLUSIVE-OR gates when $Q_3 = 1$.

If we want the calculator to operate with the twos-complement representation, some changes must be made. The connection from C_4 to C_{in} must be removed. The carry input C_{in} must instead be connected to the switch SW(A, S). With the new connection, when SW(A, S) is set for subtraction, we shall have $C_{in} = 1$. The input $B_3B_2B_1B_0$ will still be the ones-complement representation of the input, but because of the 1 added by virtue of $C_{in} = 1$ the number entered into the full-adder array will be in the twos-complement representation. The number accumulated in the accumulator will then also be in the twos-complement representation. However, the simple scheme shown for converting to a sign magnitude output indication will not work in the twos-complement case.

5.8 SUBTRACTORS

Just as combinational circuits may be assembled to perform as half adders and full adders, so can we construct half subtractors and full subtractors. If A_i and B_i are bits of the *minuend* and the *subtrahend*, respectively, then the *difference* bit $D_i = A_i - B_i$ is specified by the truth table of Fig. 5.8-1a. If $A_i = 0$ and $B_i = 1$, it will be a *borrow* carry C_{i+1} to the column of next higher numerical significance. As is readily verified, the logic equations for D_i and C_{i+1} are

A_i	B_i	D_i	C_{i+1}
0	0	0	0
0	1	1	1
1	0	1	0
1	1	0	0

(a)

A_i	B_i	C_i	D_i	C_{i+1}
0	0	0	0	0
0	0	1	1	1
0	1	0	1	1
0	1	1	0	1
1	0	0	1	0
1	0	1	0	0
1	1	0	0	0
1	1	1	1	1

(b)

Figure 5.8-1 Truth table for (a) a half subtractor and (b) a full subtractor.

$$D_i = A_i \oplus B_i \qquad C_{i+1} = \bar{A}_i B_i \qquad (5.8\text{-}1)$$

A gate structure which generates D_i and C_{i+1} is called a *half subtractor.*

In subtracting multibit numbers we shall need to take account of a *borrow carry* C_i from a previous column. The truth table relating D_i and C_{i+1} to A_i, B_i and C_i appears in Fig. 5.8-1b. Gate structures which generate D_i and C_{i+1}, given in Fig. 5.8-1b, are called *full subtractors.* Full subtractors can be realized by combining two half-subtractors (and an OR gate) or by other combinational structures including the two-level gate structure. (See Prob. 5.8-1.)

A cascaded array of full subtractors entirely analogous to the array of full adders in Fig. 5.6-1 can be used to perform the operation of subtraction of one multibit number from another. In connection with our discussion of addition we have seen how the adder can be used to perform subtraction. To subtract B from A using an adder, we first form $-B$ and then add $A + (-B)$. In an entirely similar manner, a subtractor can be used to perform addition. There is no operation which can be performed using an adder which cannot be performed using a subtractor, and vice versa. Accordingly we confine our attention exclusively to one or the other. Since the choice generally is to favor the adder, we shall not discuss subtractors further.

5.9 FAST ADDERS

The parallel adder of Fig. 5.6-1 has a serious speed limitation which results from the fact that the carry has to propagate in sequence through one full adder after another; i.e., the carry has to ripple down the cascading stages. For example, consider that $C_{in} = 0$ and that at time $t = 0$ we apply $A_3 A_2 A_1 A_0 = 1111$ and $B_3 B_2 B_1 B_0 = 0001$. Then the result for the sum should be $C_4 S_3 S_2 S_1 S_0 = 10000$. Now initially at $t = 0$ $A_1 = 1$ and $B_1 = 0$ and $C_1 = 0$. Hence after a time equal to the propagation time of a full adder we shall have $S_1 = 1$ and $C_2 = 0$. However, some time after $t = 0$ we shall have $C_1 = 1$ (since $A_0 = B_0 = 1$) and as a result, after some additional propagation time we shall find that S_1 will change from $S_1 = 1$ to its correct value $S_1 = 0$ and the carry C_2 which was $C_2 = 0$ will change to $C_2 = 1$. That is, the outputs C_2 and S_1 will not establish themselves at a correct value until after a delay equal to the time for the first full adder to generate the carry out C_1 and for C_1 to propagate through the next full adder. In this same way there will be corresponding delays and C_4 will not be established at its correct value $C_4 = 1$ until the carry has propagated in sequence through each of the full adders. It is not unusual for adders to have as many as 32 or even 64 stages, in which case the delay may well become unacceptable.

Of course there will be cases in which the delay will not have to ripple very far; in this case, the delay before the adder provides the correct result may be minimal. For example, suppose that in an n-stage adder we have $A_{n-1}A_{n-2} \cdots A_1A_0 = 11 \ldots 10$ and $B_{n-1}B_{n-2} \ldots B_1B_0 = 00 \ldots 01$. Then the sum will be $C_nS_{n-1} S_{n-2} \cdots S_1S_0 = 01 \ldots 11$. In this case no carry will have been generated in any stage, and no ripple of carry will be required. However, we generally have no way of knowing beforehand what carries will need to be propagated over how many stages. Hence, in general, having applied inputs, we must wait for a time corresponding to the worst possible case before we can accept as correct the output indication of the adder.

We know, in principle, how to circumvent this difficulty associated with the ripple of the carry: we have only to arrange for *each* sum bit to be generated directly from *all* the input bits A_i and B_i. But, as we have noted, except for the case of very few bits, the amount of hardware required gets out of hand. Various compromises are possible, however, in which we allow ourselves to use more hardware than the minimum hardware associated with the ripple adder of Fig. 5.6-1. In return we are able to make a substantial reduction in the time which must be allowed for the addition process to be completed. Most successful schemes to increase adder speed use the principle of *look-ahead carry*. Here we look ahead, i.e., anticipate, when and where a carry may be generated, and added hardware is used to generate the carry more directly than by a carry ripple through all the previous stages. We now consider the most popular scheme at present for achieving this end.

5.10 THE LOOK-AHEAD CARRY ADDER

Considering again that A_i and B_i are the two input bits in the ith column of an addition of a multibit number, we define the quantities G_i and P_i as

$$G_i = A_iB_i \qquad (5.10\text{-}1)$$

$$P_i = A_i \oplus B_i \qquad (5.10\text{-}2)$$

in which G_i is called the *generate variable* and P_i is called the *propagate variable*. The terms are appropriate for the following reasons. If $G_i = 1$, it is because both A_i and B_i are $A_i = B_i = 1$. In this case there will be an output carry $C_{i+1} = 1$ quite independently of whether or not there is an input carry C_i. That is, the carry is *generated* by the values of the bits in the ith column. Similarly, if $P_i = 1$, it is because either $A_i = 1$ or $B_i = 1$ but *not both*; hence there will be an output carry C_{i+1} if and only if there is an input carry C_i. That is, an output carry is not generated in the column, but if there is an input carry, it will be *propagated* through the column.

It now turns out that all the sum and carry bits of the adder array of Fig. 5.6-1 can be expressed explicitly in terms of the input carry C_i and the variable G_i and P_i. We have, to start, that

$$S_i = A_i \oplus B_i \oplus C_i \qquad (5.10\text{-}3a)$$

$$= P_i \oplus C_i \qquad (5.10\text{-}3b)$$

We also have that

$$C_{i+1} = A_i B_i + A_i C_i + B_i C_i \qquad (5.10\text{-}4)$$

That is, $C_{i+1} = 1$ whenever any two or more of the inputs A_i, B_i, and C_i are 1. As can readily be verified, an alternative form in which C_{i+1} can be written is

$$C_{i+1} = A_i B_i + C_i (A_i \oplus B_i) \qquad (5.10\text{-}5)$$

This last expression for C_{i+1} is not as simple as the expression of Eq. (5.10-4), but it serves our present purpose since now we can rewrite Eq. (5.10-4) in the form

$$C_{i+1} = G_i + P_i C_i \qquad (5.10\text{-}6)$$

We now apply Eq. (5.10-6) to stage after stage and we find, as can be verified,

$$C_1 = G_0 + P_0 C_0 \qquad (5.10\text{-}7a)$$

$$C_2 = G_1 + P_1 C_1 = G_1 + P_1 G_0 + P_1 P_0 C_0 \qquad (5.10\text{-}7b)$$

$$C_3 = G_2 + P_2 C_2 = G_2 + P_2 G_1 + P_2 P_1 G_0 + P_2 P_1 P_0 C_0 \qquad (5.10\text{-}7c)$$

$$C_4 = G_3 + P_3 C_3 = G_3 + P_3 G_2 + P_3 P_2 G_1 + P_3 P_2 P_1 G_0 + \qquad (5.10\text{-}7d)$$
$$+ P_3 P_2 P_1 P_0 C_0$$

and so on. These equations, when put into words, are eminently reasonable. Consider the equation for C_4. It says that a carry will appear at the output of stage 3 if a carry is generated in that stage OR if a carry is generated in stage 2 AND if it is propagated through stage 3, OR, etc.

A multibit adder is now assembled in the following way. First we replace the full adder of Fig. 5.6-1 by units, as in Fig. 5.10-1. We shall refer to the units of Fig. 5.10-1 as *adder units* to distinguish them from the full adder of Fig. 5.6-1. These adder units have some features in common with the full adders. Both accept three inputs, the two input bits and the carry input from the previous column. Both provide the sum output. However, while the full adder provides the carry for the next stage, the present adder unit provides instead a propagation output P_i and a generation output G_i. The carry for the next stage is provided by an auxiliary structure. The assemblage of adder units and auxiliary structures to generate the carries constitutes a complete adding system. Such a system to accommodate an input carry C_0 and two 4-bit numbers is

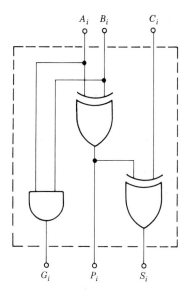

A_i B_i C_i

G_i P_i S_i

Figure 5.10-1 An adder unit which accepts A_i, B_i, and C_i and produces S_i, G_i, and P_i.

shown in Fig. 5.10-2. As is to be anticipated from Eq. (5.10-7) and, as can be seen in Fig. 5.10-2, the auxiliary circuits for generating the carry bit in each stage become progressively more complex as we advance from stage to stage.

In Fig. 5.10-2 we have added gates G1 and G2, which would not be required, if, continuing the pattern by which carries are produced, we simply wanted to produce the carry C_4. In such a case we would dispense with G1 and G2 and include instead the dashed connections. The modification has been made in order to make available two additional logic signals, *group progagate* $P(0-3)$ and *group generate* $G(0-3)$, whose purpose will be considered in the next section. For the present we shall simply note that

$$P(3-0) = P_3 P_2 P_1 P_0 \qquad (5.10\text{-}8)$$

while

$$G(3-0) = G_3 + P_3 G_2 + P_3 P_2 G_1 + P_3 P_2 P_1 G_0 \qquad (5.10\text{-}9)$$

If $P(3-0) = 1$, an input carry C_0 will be propagated through the entire group, while if $G(3-0) = 1$, there will be an output carry because there is a carry generated in one of the four stages which is propagated to the output. Note that $P(3-0)$ and $G(3-0)$ do not depend on any input carry except C_0 or on any of the carries generated within the unit. Hence these functions are in no way delayed by the rippling of the carry.

In the multibit adder of Fig. 5.6-1 the carry has to ripple from stage to stage. In the arrangement of Fig. 5.10-2, at each stage the carry bit C_{i+1} is generated using the input bits A_i and B_i directly as well as all the input bits in lower orders. Let us now compare the speed of the ripple-carry adder and the

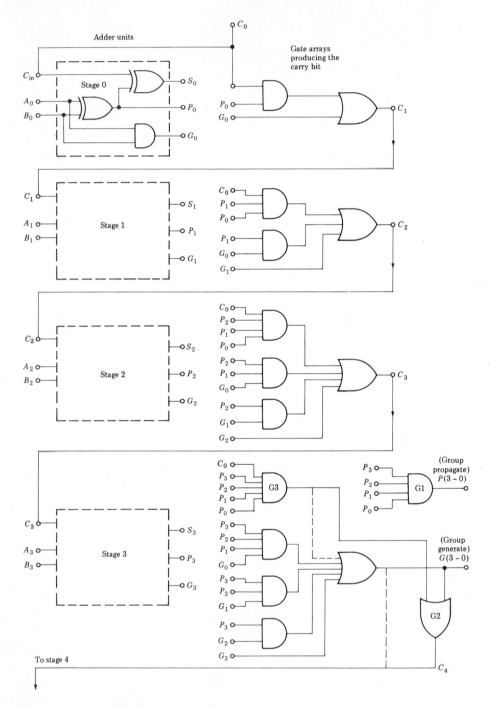

Figure 5.10-2 A multibit adder with look-ahead carry.

look-ahead adder. Consider first the ripple-carry adder. We note from Fig. 5.4-2 that (as is generally the case) the carry in each stage is generated in a two-level gate structure. If the propagation delay time of an average gate is called t_{pd}, in each stage the carry will appear at a time $2t_{pd}$ after the application of the input bits. Assume that the carry has to ripple through all stages of an n-bit adder, the situation in the worst possible case. Then, after applying the input bits we shall have to wait a time $2n(t_{pd})$ before we can confidently read the output of the adder.

Consider now the look-ahead adder. Let the input bits and the carry in C_0 be applied at $t = 0$. Keeping in mind that an EXCLUSIVE-OR gate is a two-level gate, we note that at $t = 2t_{pd}$ we shall have P_0 and G_0 and at $t = 4t_{pd}$ we shall have S_0. P_0 and G_0 as well as C_0 are applied to the first carry generator, which is also a two-level gate. Hence C_1 will be available at $t = 4t_{pd}$. Then C_1 and P_1 will be combined in stage 1. P_1 was available at the time $t = 2t_{pd}$. Hence to get the sum bit S_1 we have only to wait another $2t_{pd}$ for propagation through the second EXCLUSIVE-OR gate. Hence S_1 will be available at $t = 6t_{pd}$. We now note that just as C_1 was available at $t = 4t_{pd}$, C_2, C_3, etc., will be too. Hence the sum bits S_2, S_3, etc., will be available at $t = 6t_{pd}$. Thus after we get past the first stage there is no further delay in the generation of the sum bits. In an adder of few stages the difference in speed between the two types of adders may be small. For $n = 4$ we find that the delay is $8t_{pd}$ for the ripple adder and $6t_{pd}$ for the look-ahead adder. On the other hand, where many stages are employed, the difference is substantial.

We have represented that P_i should be given by $P_i = A_i \oplus B_i$. The assignment of this logical function to P_i is intuitively appealing and also, on this account, the adder unit of Fig. 5.10-1 has the simplifying feature that P_i is generated by the same structure as is used to generate S_i. Actually, P_i may equally well be given by $P_i = A_i + B_i$ and since an OR gate has a smaller propagation delay than does an EXCLUSIVE-OR gate, the use of the OR operation can increase the speed of operation. We can readily verify that P_i can be written as $P_i = A_i + B_i$ by preparing a K map for a function of the three variables A_i, B_i, and C_i and entering on that map the function C_{i+1} of Eq. (5.10-6), which is

$$C_{i+1} = G_i + P_iC_i = A_iB_i + (A_i \oplus B_i)C_i$$
$$= A_iB_i + A_i\bar{B}_iC_i + \bar{A}_iB_iC_i \qquad (5.10\text{-}10)$$

Reading the map in the manner to yield the simplest result, we find

$$C_{i+1} = A_iB_i + A_iC_i + B_iC_i = A_iB_i + (A_i + B_i)C_i \qquad (5.10\text{-}11)$$

The reason for the result is clearly that, if $A_i = B_i = 1$, a carry will be generated and transferred to the next stage in any event. Hence we *don't care* if the propagate mechanism also develops a carry in this case. That is, to the EXCLUSIVE-OR operation $A_i\bar{B}_i + \bar{A}_iB_i$ we can add a don't care term A_iB_i to get $A_i\bar{B}_i + \bar{A}_iB_i + A_iB_i = A_i + B_i$.

5.11 LOOK-AHEAD CARRY APPLIED TO GROUPS

It is readily apparent that if the scheme of Fig. 5.10-2 were applied to the addition of numbers with very many bits, the hardware involved would become unmanageable. Large computers frequently use 64-bit numbers. In this case the gate structure needed to generate just the last carry would itself involve 65 gates requiring up to 65 inputs. We are therefore prompted to inquire whether it might be useful to apply the principle of the look-ahead carry to small manageable groups of bits. Thus, suppose we divide the input bits into groups of 4, use the look-ahead carry scheme within each group of 4, and let the carry ripple from group to group. (The partitioning into groups of 4 is suggested since the commercial integrated-circuit chips available are generally designed to accommodate 4 bits.)

With these considerations in mind consider the arrangement of Fig. 5.11-1, which is an adder intended to accommodate 16 bits. Each rectangular block represents the complete assemblage of Fig. 5.10-2. Observe the convention by which we have reduced the number of lines which need to be drawn to represent inputs and outputs to the block. For example, the four inputs A_3, A_2, A_1, and A_0 are indicated by A_3-A_0. A single input-line arrow is then drawn. However, the dash drawn through the line and the accompanying number 4 make clear that the line actually represents four input lines. Within each block the look-ahead-carry principle is used, but in going from block to block we have a simple ripple of the carry. The outputs $P(3-0)$ and $G(3-0)$ in the first unit and the corresponding outputs in the succeeding units are not being used.

Now let us again assume that all input A_i and B_i as well as the input carry C_0 are applied at $t = 0$. Then how long shall we have to wait to be sure that the output indication of the adder $C_{16}S_{15}S_{14} \ldots S_1S_0$ is correct? Since we are not using the group propagation and generate outputs P and G, let us assume, in Fig. 5.10-2, that the connection by which the last carry C_4 is produced is as indicated by the dashed line. In this case the propagation delay through gate G2 is eliminated.

As we have seen, the carry-out C_4 of the first 4-bit unit in Fig. 5.10-2 will be available at $t = 4t_{pd}$ while the sum bits $S_3 - S_0$ will be available at $t = 6t_{pd}$. In the second 4-bit unit, the input carry C_4 is applied to $t = 4t_{pd}$; hence all its carries C_5, C_6, C_7, and C_8 will be available at $t = 6t_{pd}$ and the sum bits S_7-S_4 will be available at $t = 8t_{pd}$. Such is the case because the inputs A_7-A_4 and B_7-B_4 were applied at a time which is $4t_{pd}$ earlier than the time of application of C_4. During this time the propagation required through the adder units of the second group will already have taken place. Thus while the first 4-bit adder requires a waiting time of $6t_{pd}$, the second 4-bit adder adds an additional time $4t_{pd}$ to the time $4t_{pd}$ needed to generate C_4, for a total time $8t_{pd}$. Correspondingly, 12 bits are available after a time $4t_{pd} + 4t_{pd} + 4t_{pd} = 12t_{pd}$, and 16 sum bits and the last carry C_{16} are available after $16t_{pd}$. A 16-bit adder without look-ahead carry would require $32t_{pd}$. In general, if we use a single 4-bit adder, the time is $6t_{pd}$ versus $8t_{pd}$. However, if we use a cascade of more than one 4-bit adder, the look-ahead-carry

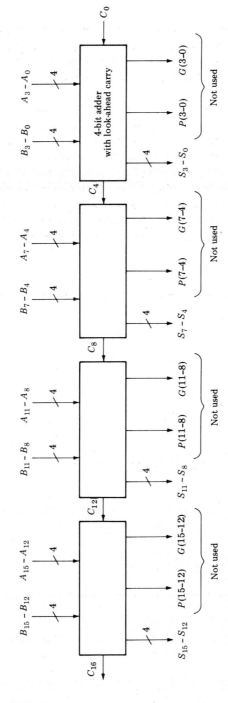

Figure 5.11-1 A cascade of four 4-bit adders with look-ahead carry. Each 4-bit adder with look-ahead carry is as given in Fig. 5.10-2. The cascade accommodates 16 bits.

211

adder makes its correct output available in half the time required by an adder without look-ahead.

The principle of a look-ahead carry can be incorporated in an adder to an even greater extent with a further speed improvement, as we shall see in the next section.

5.12 USE OF ADDITIONAL LOOK-AHEAD CARRY

To effect a further improvement in speed, manufacturers make available look-ahead-carry units (without adder units) for use in conjunction with cascades of 4-bit adders. Such a look-ahead-carry unit is intended for use with a cascade of four 4-bit adders, and its manner of connection to the cascade is shown in Fig. 5.12-1. The LAC unit accepts as inputs the carry in C_0 and the group-propagate and group-generate outputs of the first three 4-bit adder units and provides outputs

$$C_4^* = G(3-0) + P(3-0)C_0 \qquad (5.12\text{-}1a)$$

$$C_8^* = G(7-4) + P(7-4)G(3-0) + P(7-4)P(3-0)C_0 \qquad (5.12\text{-}1b)$$

$$\begin{aligned} C_{12}^* = G(11-8) + P(11-8)G(7-4) + \\ P(11-8)P(7-4)G(3-0) + P(11-8)P(7-4)P(3-0)C_0 \end{aligned} \qquad (5.12\text{-}1c)$$

These carry outputs replace the carries C_4, C_8, and C_{12} of Fig. 5.11-1. The LAC unit provides outputs (not used here) given by

$$P(15-0) = P(15-12)P(4-8)P(7-4)P(3-0) \qquad (5.12\text{-}2a)$$

and

$$\begin{aligned} G(15-0) = G(15-12) + P(15-12)G(11-8) + P(15-12)P(11-8)G(7-4) + \\ P(15-12)P(11-8)P(7-4)G(3-0) \end{aligned} \qquad (5.12\text{-}2b)$$

We observe that Eqs. (5.12-1a) to (5.12-1c) are identical in form to Eqs. (5.10-7a) to (5.10-7c) while Eqs. (5.12-2a) and (5.12-2b) are identical in form to Eqs. (5.10-8) and (5.10-9). Hence the gate structure of the LAC of Fig. 5.12-1 is identical to the carry-producing portion of Fig. 5.10-2 except that gates G2 and G3 are not used and, of course, the dashed connections are not made.

Assuming again that at $t = 0$ all inputs A_1 and B_1 and the input carry C_0 are applied, we ask, as before, how long we must wait before the correct sum is available. From Fig. 5.10-2 we see that the group P's and G's are available at $t = 4t_{pd}$. In Fig. 5.12-1 these group P's and G's must propagate through two more levels in the LAC unit to produce the carries C_4^*, C_8^*, and C_{12}^* so that these carries are available at $t = 6t_{pd}$. Finally, the sum bits are available after another interval of $2t_{pd}$, so that total waiting time is $8t_{pd}$. This last number is to be compared with $32t_{pd}$ in a ripple adder using no look-ahead carry at all.

We first saw how the look-ahead carry is implemented with 4 bits. Next we

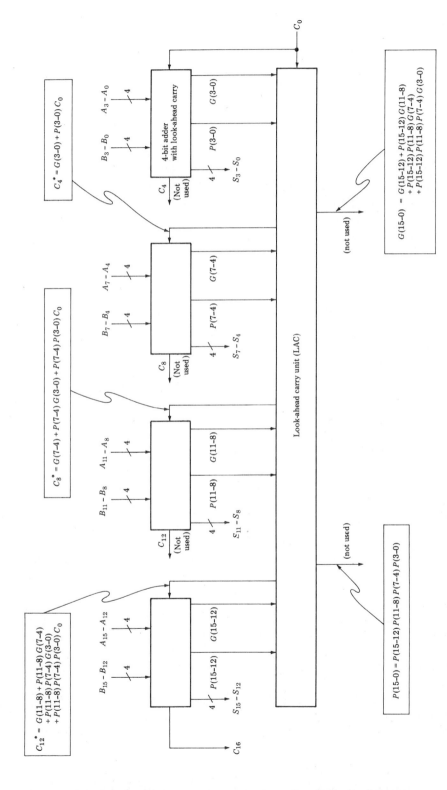

$C_4^* = G(3\text{-}0) + P(3\text{-}0)\,C_0$

$A_3 - A_0$

$B_3 - B_0$

4-bit adder
with look-ahead carry

$G(3\text{-}0)$

$P(3\text{-}0)$

$S_3 - S_0$

C_4
(Not
used)

C_0

$C_8^* = G(7\text{-}4) + P(7\text{-}4)\,G(3\text{-}0) + P(7\text{-}4)\,P(3\text{-}0)\,C_0$

$A_7 - A_4$

$B_7 - B_4$

$G(7\text{-}4)$

$P(7\text{-}4)$

$S_7 - S_4$

C_8
(Not
used)

$A_{11} - A_8$

$B_{11} - B_8$

$G(11\text{-}8)$

$P(11\text{-}8)$

$S_{11} - S_8$

C_{12}
(Not
used)

$C_{12}^* = G(11\text{-}8) + P(11\text{-}8)\,G(7\text{-}4)$
$\quad + P(11\text{-}8)\,P(7\text{-}4)\,G(3\text{-}0)$
$\quad + P(11\text{-}8)\,P(7\text{-}4)\,P(3\text{-}0)\,C_0$

$A_{15} - A_{12}$

$B_{15} - B_{12}$

$G(15\text{-}12)$

$P(15\text{-}12)$

$S_{15} - S_{12}$

C_{16}

Look-ahead carry unit (LAC)

(not used)

$G(15\text{-}0) = G(15\text{-}12) + P(15\text{-}12)\,G(11\text{-}8)$
$\qquad\quad + P(15\text{-}12)\,P(11\text{-}8)\,G(7\text{-}4)$
$\qquad\quad + P(15\text{-}12)\,P(11\text{-}8)\,P(7\text{-}4)\,G(3\text{-}0)$

(not used)

$P(15\text{-}0) = P(15\text{-}12)\,P(11\text{-}8)\,P(7\text{-}4)\,P(3\text{-}0)$

Figure 5.12-1 A look-ahead-carry (LAC) unit is added to the cascade of **Fig.** 5.11-1.

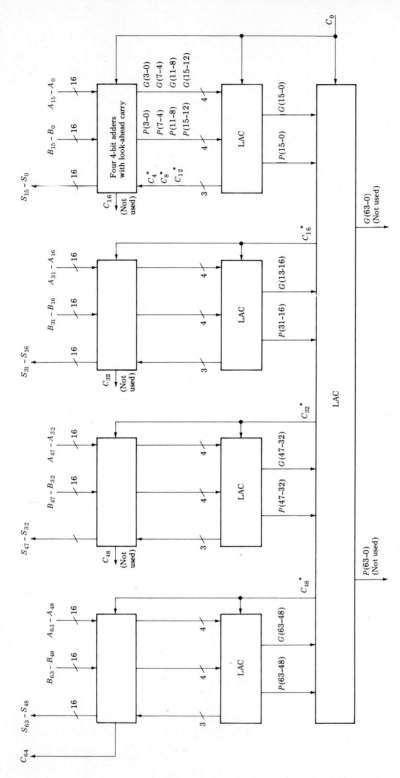

Figure 5.12-2 A total of five LAC units is used in a 64-bit adder.

saw how the principle is applied to 16 bits, or four groups of 4 bits. In a similar manner the implementation can be extended to 64 bits, or four groups of 16 bits. Each group of 16 bits is first treated as shown in Fig. 5.12-1. Then we add one more LAC unit identical to the LAC unit in Fig. 5.12-1. This new LAC unit accepts as inputs the input carry C_0 and the group P and G outputs of all the first level LACs. The new LAC then provides the carries C^*_{16}, C^*_{32}, and C^*_{48}. The details of the connections are shown in Fig. 5.12-2. It is left as an exercise to verify that the time required for an addition to be complete is $14t_{pd}$. This figure is to be compared with a time of $128t_{pd}$, which would be required for a 64-bit adder using no look-ahead carry.

5.13 THE ARITHMETIC LOGIC UNIT

An arithmetic logic unit (ALU) is a combinational device which accepts two n-bit input words $A = A_{n-1} \ldots A_0$ and $B = B_{n-1} \ldots B_0$. The inputs A and B may be numbers or may simply represent some arbitrary information in binary coded form. The ALU has a mode input M and a number of *function-selection* bits $S_0, S_1, \ldots$. The ALU generates an output *function* $F = F_{n-1}, \ldots F_0$, which is related to the inputs by logic or by arithmetic. The mode input M determines whether a logical function or an arithmetic function is to be generated. The function-selection bits determine what specific function is to be generated.

Like a multibit adder, an ALU can be assembled as a cascade of identical stages, as indicated in Fig. 5.13-1a. Here we have allowed two function-selection bits. A possible gate structure for one of the (identical) stages is shown in Fig. 5.13-1b. When an arithmetic operation is contemplated, say addition, we shall have to take account of the carry from stage to stage. In Fig. 5.13-1b a carry-in C_i and a carry-out C_{i+1} are provided for each stage. In Fig. 5.13-1a we have similarly provided a carry-in C_0 and a carry-out C_4 for the four-stage unit, anticipating that we may want to cascade this four-stage unit with others.

When a logical operation is called for, we set $M = 0$. As is to be seen in Fig. 5.13-1b, when $M = 0$ the input AND gate through which C_i is applied is disabled and the output function bit F_i is not influenced by the input carry. The output carry C_{i+1} may well depend on the selection bits and on A_i and B_i, but since C_{i+1} is not used when $M = 0$, the value of C_{i+1} is irrelevant. In any event, in the logic mode ($M = 0$) the function bit F_i depends on the selection bits and on A_i and B_i. The value of $A_{i-1}, A_{i-2}, \ldots, A_0$ and $B_{i-1}, B_{i-2}, \ldots, B_0$ have no influence on F_i. For each combination of S_0 and S_1 each F_i output of each stage depends only on the input bits A_i and B_i of that stage. For the relatively simple gate structure of Fig. 5.13-1b the response of the ALU in the logic mode is given in Table 5.13-1 (Prob. 5.13-1).

In the arithmetic mode $M = 1$, and the gate which accepts the carry is enabled. The response of the ALU when the input carry C_0 is set at $C_0 = 0$ is given in the central part of Table 5.13-1. In the first two cases, it turns out that the result is no different from the logical operation performed when $M = 0$. In

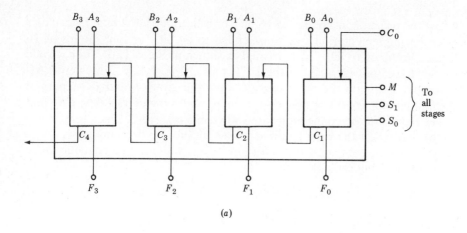

(a)

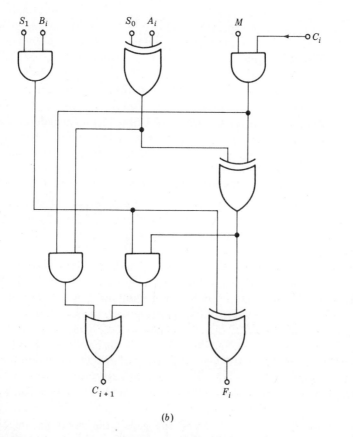

(b)

Figure 5.13-1 (a) An ALU assembled from a cascade of identical stages. (b) A possible gate structure for a stage.

Table 5.13-1 The functions generated by the logic structure of Fig. 5.13-1

		Logic function with $M = 0$	
S_i	S_0	Logical function F_i	Comment
0	0	$F_i = A_i$	Input A transferred to output
0	1	$F_i = \overline{A_i}$	Input A complemented & transferred
1	0	$F_i = A_i \oplus B_i$	EXCLUSIVE-OR
1	1	$F_i = \overline{A_i \oplus B_i}$	EXCLUSIVE-NOR

		Arithmetic functions with $M = 1$ and $C_0 = 0$	
S_1	S_0	Arithmetic function F	Comment
0	0	$F = A$	Input A transferred to output
0	1	$F = \overline{A}$	Ones complement of A
1	0	$F = A$ plus B	Sum of A and B
1	1	$F = \overline{A}$ plus B	Sum of B and ones complement of A

		Arithmetic functions with $M = 1$ and $C_0 = 1$	
0	0	$F = A$ plus 1	Increment A
0	1	$F = \overline{A}$ plus 1	Twos complement of A
1	0	$F = A$ plus B plus 1	Increment sum of A and B
1	1	$F = \overline{A}$ plus B plus 1	B minus A

the third case ($S_1 S_0 = 10$) the ALU generates the sum of A and B and, in the last case, the sum of B and the ones complement of A. We have used the word "plus" to indicate numerical addition to distinguish the operation from logical addition. In the last part of Table 5.13-1 we have tabulated the results when $C_0 = 1$. In the last case ($S_1 S_0 = 11$) B is added to the twos complement of A. Since this twos complement represents the negative of A, the resultant operation is a subtraction of A from B.

There is available a commercial arithmetic logic unit and a LAC generator which are designed to accommodate to each other. The functional diagrams of the units are shown in Fig. 5.13-2. The ALU accepts two 4-bit inputs. The input carry is here called C_n (corresponding to C_0 in Fig. 5.13-1), and the output carry, which is produced four stages later, is C_{n+4}. We note from the inversion circles at input and output that actually the inputs required are $\overline{A}_0$, $\overline{B}_0$, etc., and that the outputs provided are $\overline{F}_0$, etc. That is, inputs and outputs are *active low*,

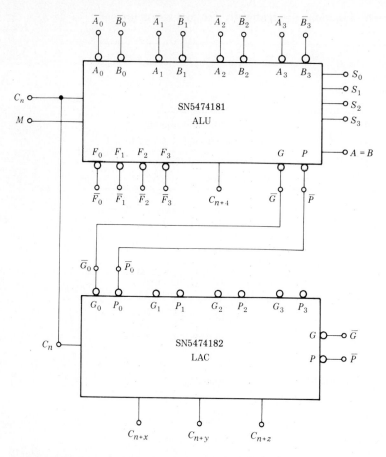

Figure 5.13-2 The terminal configuration of the commercially available ALU and LAC generator integrated-circuit chips. Interconnections are indicated.

the numeral 1 being represented by lower voltage and the numeral 0 being represented by the higher voltage. This feature need cause no inconvenience since inputs may well come from a register where both variable and complement are available and at the output we can readily provide an inversion as required. (The manufacturer points out that, if we prefer, we can use *active-high* inputs, in which case the unit will also provide active-high outputs. In this case, however, we must consider that the carry lines in and out indicate a carry at logic 0 rather than at logic 1. Also the logic or arithmetic function performed for some fixed set of selection bits is different in the active-high and in the active-low cases.)

The function generated by the ALU depends on the mode control M and on the logic levels at the selection input S_3, S_2, S_1, and S_0. These functions are listed in Table 5.13-2. Logic functions are generated when $M = 1$, and since there are four selection bits, 16 functions are available. It will be recalled (see

Table 5.13-2 The logic and arithmetic functions generated by the SN5474181 ALU

Selection input				$M = 1$ logic functions	$M = 0$ Arithmetic operations	
S_3	S_2	S_1	S_0		$C_n = 0$	$C_n = 1$
0	0	0	0	$F_i = \bar{A}_i$	$F = A$ minus 1	$F = A$
0	0	0	1	$F_i = \overline{A_i B_i}$	$F = AB$ minus 1	$F = AB$
0	0	1	0	$F_i = \overline{A_i} + B_i$	$F = A\bar{B}$ minus 1	$F = A\bar{B}$
0	0	1	1	$F_i = 1$	$F = $ minus 1†	$F = $ zero
0	1	0	0	$F_i = \overline{A_i + B_i}$	$F = A$ plus $(A + \bar{B})$	$F = A$ plus $(A + \bar{B})$ plus 1
0	1	0	1	$F_i = \bar{B}_i$	$F = AB$ plus $(A + \bar{B})$	$F = AB$ plus $(A + \bar{B})$ plus 1
0	1	1	0	$F_i = \overline{A_i \oplus B_i}$	$F = A$ minus B minus 1	$F = A$ minus B
0	1	1	1	$F_i = A_i + \bar{B}_i$	$F = A + \bar{B}$	$F = (A + \bar{B})$ plus 1
1	0	0	0	$F_i = \overline{A_i} B_i$	$F = A$ plus $(A + B)$	$F = A$ plus $(A + B)$ plus 1
1	0	0	1	$F_i = A_i \oplus B_i$	$F = A$ plus B	$F = A$ plus B plus 1
1	0	1	0	$F_i = B_i$	$F = A\bar{B}$ plus $(A + B)$	$F = A\bar{B}$ plus $(A + B)$ plus 1
1	0	1	1	$F_i = A_i + B_i$	$F = A + B$	$F = (A + B)$ plus 1
1	1	0	0	$F_i = 0$	$F = A + A$‡	$F = A$ plus A plus 1
1	1	0	1	$F_i = A_i \bar{B}_i$	$F = AB$ plus A	$F = AB$ plus A plus 1
1	1	1	0	$F_i = A_i B_i$	$F = A\bar{B}$ plus A	$F = A\bar{B}$ plus A plus 1
1	1	1	1	$F_i = A_i$	$F = A$	$F = A$ plus 1

†In twos-complement representation.
‡Each bit is shifted to the next more significant position.

Sec. 1.5) that there are precisely 16 functions of two logical variables, and it can be verified from the tabulation that every one of these functions does appear.

Arithmetic functions are generated when the carry facility of the ALU is enabled by setting $M = 0$. We are inclined to interpret the output word as a number when an arithmetic operation is performed and as a binary coded piece of information when a logic operation is performed. Yet it is of interest to note that some of the results of arithmetic operations are precisely the same as some of the logic operations. Still, when the results of operations are viewed as numbers, of course the presence of an input carry ($C_n = 1$) increases the magnitude of the number by unity.

A word is in order about the arithmetic entry under $S_3 S_2 S_1 S_0 = 0110$ with $C_n = 1$. Here we note that $F = A$ minus B. This subtraction is actually achieved by adding to A the ones complement of B (the number B with all bits complemented). If we want the result to be valid in the ones-complement representation we must use an end-around carry as in Fig. 5.7-1, or if we want a twos-complement representation, we must have $C_n (= C_0) = 1$, as specified in the tabulation.

When set in this manner for subtraction with $S_3S_2S_1S_0 = 0110$ and $C_n = 1$, if $A = B$, the result is $F_3F_2F_1F_0 = 0000$ and the output of the ALU is $\bar{F}_3\bar{F}_2\bar{F}_1\bar{F}_0 = 1111$. In the ALU an AND gate is provided whose inputs are $\bar{F}_3$, $\bar{F}_2, \bar{F}_1$, and $\bar{F}_0$ and whose output is the external terminal marked "$A = B$." Hence the ALU can be used a digital comparator which marks the equivalence $A = B$ by setting to 1 the "$A = B$" terminal. In this same subtraction mode of operation the ALU can also be used to indicate the relative magnitudes of the numbers A and B. For the active-low inputs and outputs specified in Fig. 5.13-2 (as can be verified, Prob. 5.13-2) the rules for determining relative magnitude are as follows:

C_n	C_{n+4}	Indication
L	L	$A \leq B$
L	H	$A > B$
H	L	$A < B$
H	H	$A \geq B$

The ALU chip has incorporated within itself the LAC feature already described. The logic structure of the ALU is shown in detail in Fig. B-1 of Appendix B. There we note that, as in Fig. 5.13-2, the unit provides group-carry $\bar{G}$ and group-propagate $\bar{P}$ outputs so that four ALU units can use one LAC generator to extend the LAC feature to 16 bits. The logic struction of the LAC unit is shown in Fig. B-2 of Appendix B. The details of the interconnections required for this purpose are given in Fig. 5.13-3. Here, for simplicity we have included only those terminals essential to show the interconnections. Finally, we note that the carry unit itself has group propagate and generate output terminals (not used here) to allow extension of the LAC beyond 16 bits.

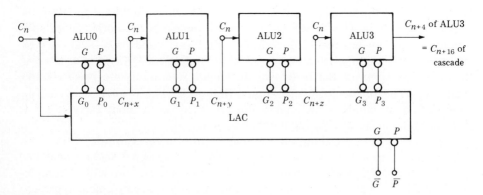

Figure 5.13-3 The interconnections required between the ALU and the LAC to accommodate 16 bits.

5.14 BCD ADDITION

In the BCD (binary-coded decimal) system of representing numbers, the binary digits are grouped into 4-bit nibbles, and each nibble represents a decimal digit. The BCD code has a disadvantage in that, of the 16 combinations of the 4 bits, only 10 are used. The binary representations for the decimal numbers 10 through 15 are excluded. On the other hand, the BCD code has an advantage which is sometimes very important. Consider, for example, the matter of converting from a straight binary number into its decimal equivalent and vice versa. To convert from binary into decimal we need to perform a computation in which, in the determination of *each* decimal digit, we need to take account of *every* binary digit. In the reverse conversion *each* binary digit, in general, depends on *every* decimal digit. As a result the hardware required to effect the conversions grows exponentially with the number of digits. In the BCD case, each decimal digit is associated with just 4 bits. Conversion hardware for $2N$ digits is only twice as extensive as for N digits.

Suppose now that we have a digital processor of some kind to which we present numerical data in decimal form and that after the processing (say some kind of computation) we want the results returned to us in decimal form. If the processing were rather formidable and much more involved than the decimal-to-binary and binary-to-decimal conversions, it would certainly be advantageous to make the conversions, but if the processing were rather simple, we might well want to avoid the conversions and do what processing is called for while the numerical data remain in BCD form. These considerations prompt us to look into the matter of addition of numbers in BCD code.

In Fig. 5.14-1*a* we add the numbers $3 + 4 = 7$, and the corresponding addition of BCD equivalents is straightforward. In Fig. 5.14-1*b* we add $7 + 5$ (selected to give a sum larger than 9). The result 1100 is correct as a binary representation but is not acceptable as a BCD representation. In BCD we want the result to be $12 = 00010010$. The difficulty arises, of course, because the *six* numbers 10 through 15 are excluded from BCD. But, as we shall see, the matter can be corrected by adding $6 = 0110$. The result then changes to the BCD representation of decimal 2, and, as required, a carry is generated, indicated by the encircled 1. In Fig. 5.14-1*c* we add $9 + 8$ and find the result $0001 = 1$. But

```
3 = 0 0 1 1        7 = 0 1 1 1              9 =   1 0 0 1
4 = 0 1 0 0        5 = 0 1 0 1              8 =   1 0 0 0
7 = 0 1 1 1       12 = 1 1 0 0 (not BCD)   17 = ①0 0 0 1 (not BCD)
                   6 = 0 1 1 0              6 =   0 1 1 0
                  ①0 0 1 0 (= 12 BCD)        ①0 1 1 1 (=17 BCD)

      (a)                (b)                      (c)
```

Figure 5.14-1 A procedure for adding BCD numbers.

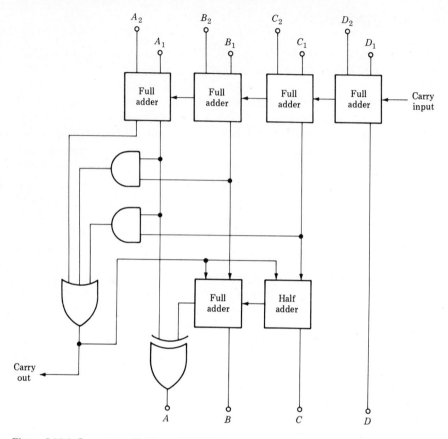

Figure 5.14-2 One stage of logic to add BCD numbers.

here too we are alerted to the fact that something is amiss because a carry (encircled 1) is generated. Again we find that the matter is corrected by adding $0110 = 6$. Altogether, then, we find that a procedure for adding BCD code numbers starts by adding the numbers as though they were straight binary numbers. If the result is not a BCD number, i.e., not 0 to 9, or if a carry is generated, then $0110 = 6$ is added to the number.

Hardware to effect addition of a decimal digit in BCD code including provision for a carry from the digit position of next lower order is shown in Fig. 5.14-2. The top row of four full adders adds the numbers $A_1B_1C_1D_1$ and $A_2B_2C_2D_2$. One or the other of the AND gates will find its output at logic 1 whenever the sum generated is in the range 10 to 15. The output of the OR gate will be at logic 1 whenever the sum is in the range 10 to 15 or whenever a carry is generated. Whenever the OR-gate output is a logic 1, the number $6 = 0110$ will be added as required (see Prob. 5.14-1).

5.15 MULTIPLICATION AND DIVISION

Multiplication and division are performed in the binary system in the same way as in the decimal system. An example of binary multiplication is shown in Fig. 5.15-1. The *multiplicand* is multiplied in turn by each one of the individual digits of the *multiplier*, each such multiplication forming a *partial* product. If the multiplier bit is 0, the partial product is 0. If the multiplier bit is 1, the partial product is the multiplicand itself. Hence the "multiplication table" which needs to be memorized to allow such multiplication is entirely trivial, and in the multiplication by a single multiplier bit no carries are generated. We start with the least significant bit and, as appears in Fig 5.15-1, successive partial products are shifted one position to the left. The product is then the sum of the partial products. In the general case the product can have a number of bits one greater than the sum of multiplicand and multiplier bits.

There are available a limited number of IC chips using combinational circuits which perform multiplication. For example the types '284 and '285 used together can accept two 4-bit input numbers and yield an 8-bit output product. More generally, however, where multiplication is called for, it is performed by a computing-type facility designed to follow an algorithm which effects the multiplication much in the manner of the example of Fig. 5.15-1. We shall give an example of such a multiplication in Sec. 10.17.

An example of division in the binary system is given in Fig. 5.15-2. As in the case with multiplication, binary division is easier then decimal division. In the example, since the divisor has three digits we inquire whether the divisor can "go into" the first three digits of the dividend. Finding that such is not the case, we use the first four digits of the dividend. Now we need not estimate (as in decimal arithemetic) what the quotient digit is. For since it is not 0 it must be 1. As is to be seen, the continuation of the division example follows precisely the steps of decimal arithmetic division. IC combinational chips to perform division are not generally available. Instead division is usually performed by some type of computing facility which carries out some appropriate algorithm.

```
      1 1 1 0     Multiplicand
        1 0 1     Multiplier
      -------
      1 1 1 0   }
    0 0 0 0     } Partial products
  1 1 1 0       }
-------------
1 0 0 0 1 1 0     Product = sum of partial products
```

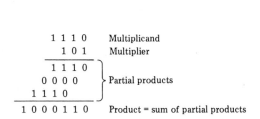

Figure 5.15-1 An example of multiplication in binary arithmetic.

```
          11101 ···
      ___________
101 | 10010011
      101
      ----
      1000
       101
      ----
        110
        101
       ----
         111
         101
        ----
          10
```

Figure 5.15-2 An example of division in binary arithmetic.

CHAPTER
SIX

MEMORY

We have seen that a flip-flop may serve to store, i.e., remember, a bit and that an array of flip-flops, i.e., a register, may remember a word. There are frequent occasions when the need arises to store words numbering into the hundreds, thousands, or even tens of thousands. Components which provide for such large storage are called *memories*. In some cases, individual bits in such memories are stored in flip-flops. In other cases, other storage mechanisms are used.

6.1 THE RANDOM-ACCESS MEMORY

We have noted that there are readily available, on a commercial basis, a wide range of logic gates. NAND gates, NOR gates, EXCLUSIVE-OR gates, etc., are available with varying numbers of inputs (fan-in) and with varying capacity to driving other gates (fan-out). They are furnished on integrated-circuit (IC) chips, and frequently there are many such gates on a single chip. Similarly, rather more complicated IC chips are available which provide complete multibit registers, counters, multibit arithmetic units, etc. Finally we may note here that there are also available commercially a wide range of IC packages which are *memory* devices; i.e., they make available, on an IC chip, facility for storing many words in a manner which allows us to keep track of the individual words and to recall individual words when and as we see fit.

The pin designations on an IC memory chip, as specified by the manufacturers, typically appear as in Fig. 6.1-1. The memory represented here has the capacity to store (memorize) 8 words, each word having 4 bits. The chip has eight individual registers $R_0, R_1, \ldots, R_7$, and each register consists of four flip-flops. The registers are identified by the logic levels on the terminals A_2, A_1, and

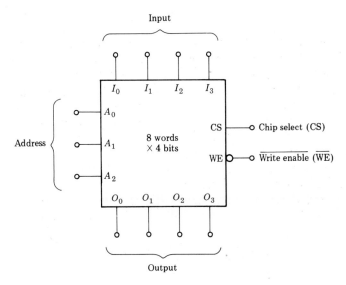

Figure 6.1-1 The pin designations on an 8-word, 4-bit/word IC memory chip.

A_0. These bits A_2, A_1, and A_0 are called the *address* bits, and the array of address bits is referred to as the *address*. When $A_2A_1A_0 = 000$, access is provided to register R_0. When $A_2A_1A_0 = 001$, access is provided to register R_1, and so on. Since there are 3 address bits, $2^3 = 8$ registers can be addressed. Each register, then, has an *address*, and a particular register is accessed by placing that register's address bits on the address terminals.

The 4 bits which are to be stored, i.e., *written*, into an addressed register are presented to the memory chip at the input terminals I_3, I_2, I_1, I_0. To write a word into a register, the register must be addressed, the word must be presented at the input, and *both* the $\overline{write\text{-}enable}$ ($\overline{\text{WE}}$) and the *chip-select* (CS) inputs must be enabled, i.e., rendered active. On the basis of the generally accepted convention (already discussed in Chap. 3), the diagram of Fig. 6.1-1 indicates that the external $\overline{\text{WE}}$ terminal is active low (active when $\overline{\text{WE}} = 0$ in a positive logic system) and CS is active high.

The process of *reading* the memory brings to the output terminals O_3, O_2, O_1, O_0 the word stored in the addressed register. To read the memory, we present the address, enable the CS input, and put the write enable input at $\overline{\text{WE}} = 1$. Thus $\overline{\text{WE}} = 0$ *writes* into the memory while $\overline{\text{WE}} = 1$ *reads* from the memory. For this reason, some manufacturers label the write-enable terminals as read/write ($R/\overline{W}$).

Both for reading and for writing the chip-select (CS) input must be enabled, i.e., active. If CS is not active, the chip is isolated from the external world. It is possible neither to write into the memory chip nor to read from it.

The total number of bits in the memory of Fig. 6.1-1 is $8 \times 4 = 32$. How the bits are arranged into words is described as the memory *organization*. The memory of Fig. 6.1-1 is described as an 8-word 4-bit/word memory.

Since we are able to *read* words from the memory and are able to *write* words into it, the memory we have described is reasonably called a *read-write* memory. Further, we are able to access any register in the memory we choose, i.e., at random, either to read out or write in a word. For this reason the memory is also characterized as a *random-access memory* (RAM).

6.2 STRUCTURE OF A SEMICONDUCTOR RAM

In principle, the logical structure of a semiconductor memory of the type we have been discussing is shown in Fig. 6.2-1. Here we have provided for 4 words of 2 bits each; i.e., the organization of the memory is 4×2. Our interest is in the logical structure of the memory and not in the details of its electronics. (The electronics is dealt with in other texts. See footnote on page 84.) Hence we have taken the liberty of incorporating some simplifications in comparison with a real physical memory. The arrangement uses the logic-controlled switch introduced in Sec 3.7. When the logic level on the control line (dashed line passing through the switch) is 1, the switch is closed and connection is made; when the control-line logic level is 0, the switch is open.

The bits are stored in the most elemental flip-flops, i.e., flip-flops which consist of cross-coupled inverters (see Sec. 4.1). The address bits A_1 and A_0 are applied to a decoder. When, for example, we have $A_1 = 1$ and $A_0 = 0$, the output of gate G_2 is at logic 1 while the outputs of all the other AND gates of the decoder are at logic 0. Hence only the flip-flops of the register for word 2 are accessed, since only the switches of these flip-flops are closed to make connection with the bit lines. That is, address input $A_1 A_0 = 10$ addresses word 2 and only word 2.

If *chip select* is at logic 0, the outputs of both gates G_0 and G_1 are at logic 0 and the bit lines are connected to neither the data input nor to the output terminals. If CS = 1 and $\overline{WE}$ = 0, the switches connecting I_1 and I_0 to the bit lines will be closed and the flip-flops will be found to assume states corresponding to the logic levels of the data inputs. If CS = 1 and WE = 1, the flip-flops will instead be connected to the output terminals so that the stored word can be read.

Commercial IC semiconductor memory chips presently available incorporate as many as 65,536 (2^{16}) bits. It is a tribute to the skill of IC designers and fabricators that such chips are available at prices reasonable enough to be used even by hobbyists. Because of the large number of active components which have to be fabricated on such large memory chips, we might wonder whether there might not be some advantage in removing the decoder portion of the chips and making available a separate decoder chip. There is a good practical reason why such is not the case. Consider, for example, a memory with $2^8 = 256$ words. If the decoder is on the memory chip, only 8 pin connections on the periphery of the chip are required for the address input. If the decoder were external to the memory chip, 256 pin connections would have to be provided. One of the constraints with which chip manufacturers must contend is the limited space around the chip periphery for pin connections.

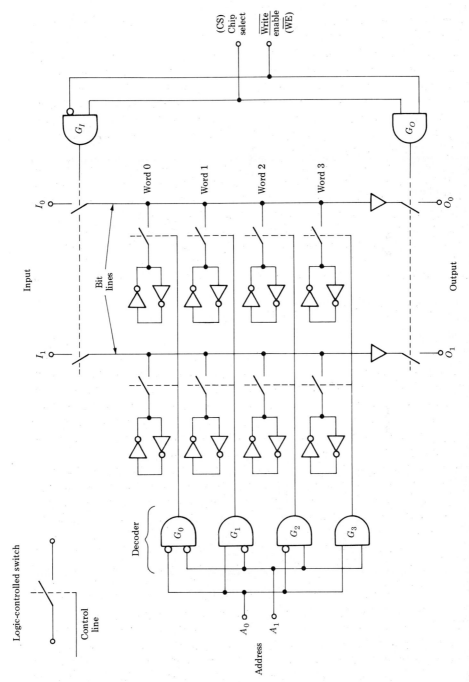

Figure 6.2-1 A structure for a 4-word 2-bit/word read-write RAM.

227

6.3 PARALLELING MEMORY CHIPS

There frequently arise cases in which the number of words available on a chip is not adequate or the number of bits per word is not adequate, or both. The matter can be remedied by paralleling chips.

Paralleling chips to increase the number of bits per word (but not the number of words) is illustrated in Fig. 6.3-1. Here we have paralleled two 8-word 4-bit/word chips to construct a memory in which the number of words remains at 8 but the number of bits has been increased from 4 to 8. The 3-bit input address is applied to the address pins of both memories. The CS terminals of the chips are joined, as are the $\overline{WE}$ terminals. *Chip-select* and *write-enable* inputs select and enable the chips simultaneously. Chip 1 accepts and stores 4 bits (0, 1, 2, 3), and chip 2 accepts and stores 4 bits more (4, 5, 6, 7). Of course, the paralleling can be extended to additional chips. Three 8-word 4-bit/word chips will yield an 8-word 12-bit/word memory, and so on. As chips are added, the address is applied simultaneously to the address input terminals of all chips. Similarly, all CS pins are connected together to become a single CS input, and the $\overline{WE}$ inputs are treated in the same way.

To provide maximum flexibility in the matter of bits per word, manufacturers make available memory chips with just a single bit per word. Thus we find, in manufacturers' catalogs, memories with organizations 256×1, 1024×1, 4096×1, etc. Having selected a chip with an adequate number of words, we then assemble an n-bit-per-word memory simply by paralleling n chips.

In Fig. 6.3-2 we show how two 8-word 4-bit/word chips can be paralleled to

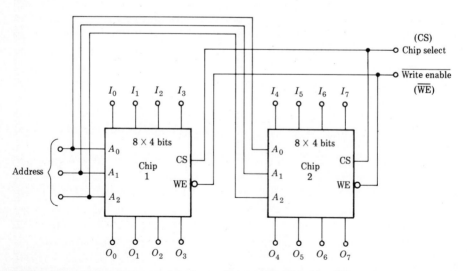

Figure 6.3-1 Two 8-word 4-bit/word memory chips are paralleled to make an 8-word 8-bit/word memory.

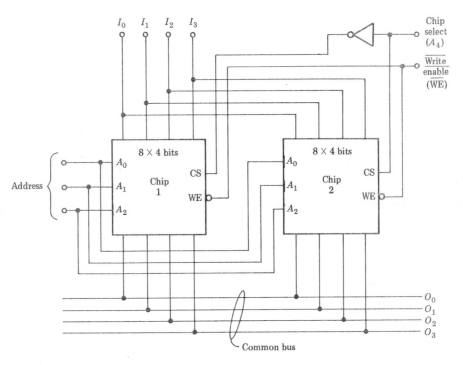

Figure 6.3-2 Paralleling memory chips to increase numbers of words keeping the number of bits per word fixed.

make a 16-word 4-bit/word memory. As before, the three address bits are applied to both chips, but instead of having a common CS input bit applied to the two chips, when the CS input on one chip is made active, the CS input on the other chip is inactive. The CS input of the memory system (the one on the input side of the inverter) is now an *additional address bit*, which we call A_4. When $A_4 = 1$, the chip addressed is chip 2, and when $A_4 = 0$, the chip addressed is chip 1. The chip-select address bit A_4 has selected one or the other of the chips; the address bits A_0, A_1, A_2 select the particular word location on the selected chip. The input data bits are applied in common to both chips, as is the $\overline{WE}$ input.

A special matter arises in the present case that does not arise when chips are paralleled to increase only the number of bits per word, as in Fig. 6.2-1. In the present case an output word is sometimes read from one chip and sometimes from the other. Presumably the word will have to be transmitted to the same destination independently of the chip from which the word originates. Hence the chip outputs will have to be applied to a common bus, and it is for this reason that such a bus is shown in Fig. 6.3-2. The matter of using a common bus for a number of input sources was discussed in Sec. 3.18 and succeeding sections under the general topic of *multiplexing*. There, we noted that one way

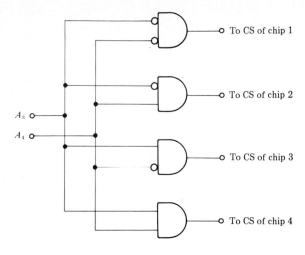

A_3 ○

A_4 ○

To CS of chip 1

To CS of chip 2

To CS of chip 3

To CS of chip 4

Figure 6.3-3 The address bits A_4 and A_5 drive a decoder which provides outputs to select one of four paralleled memory chips.

a number of sources could be arranged to share a common bus is to equip the sources with a tristate output. Note then, in Fig. 6.2-1 that we have so equipped our memory chips. A chip which is not selected has its bit lines disconnected from its output pins. The common bus can therefore carry the output logic levels of the selected chip without interference from the unselected chip. Not all commercial memory chips are equipped with tristate outputs. Instead some have outputs which are provided by gates which can be paralleled using the open-collector connection, described in Sec. 3.19.

The paralleling scheme of Fig. 6.3-2 can, of course, be extended to more chips. Suppose, for example, that we wanted to use the scheme to parallel four chips to make a 32-word 4-bit/word memory. We would then introduce a fifth address bit, A_5. Three address bits $A_0A_1A_2$ would, as before, be applied in common to the address input pins of the chips. The address bits A_4 and A_5 would be applied to a decoder, as shown in Fig. 6.3-3. The decoder outputs would then be used to activate the chip-select inputs of the four chips. In many cases, chip manufacturers include on the memory chip a multiple-input AND gate and arrange the output of this AND gate to be the CS input logic level for the chip. Where such gates are included, an external CS decoder is not necessary and chip-selection decoding can be done right on the chip itself. In a typical case a memory chip may have three chip-select inputs CS1, CS2, and CS3, and the chip is selected only when CS1 = CS2 = CS3 = 1. In such a case, as many as 8 (=2^3) can be paralleled without external decoding.

Common Input-Output Terminals

In order to reduce the number of pins around the periphery of a memory chip, manufacturers often use the same terminal pins for both memory input and memory output. In such cases the pins are referred to as input-output pins (I/O) or simply as data pins (D). A suitable arrangement is shown in Fig. 6.3-4. The

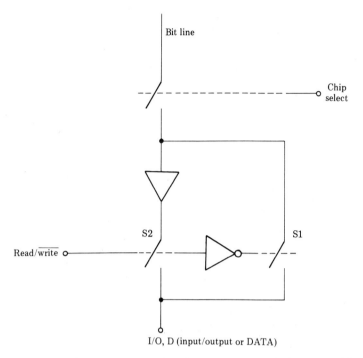

Figure 6.3-4 An arrangement which allows the same terminals to be used for both input and output.

switch in the bit line is closed when the chip select is at logic 1. When read/$\overline{\text{write}}$ is at logic 0, S1 is closed and we can write into the memory; when read/$\overline{\text{write}}$ is at logic 1, S2 is closed and we can read from the memory. To write into the memory we provide direct access to the bit line and assume that the source of the bit to be written is able to provide whatever voltage or current is required to set or reset the memory-bit flip-flop as required. When we are to read from the memory, we want to be sure that reading the state of a memory-bit flip-flop does not disturb the state of the flip-flop; i.e., the process of reading should leave the memory content unaltered. For this reason we have interposed a buffer between the bit line and the external I/O terminal.

6.4 ONE- AND TWO-DIMENSIONAL INTERNAL MEMORY ORGANIZATION

The external organization of decoder and switches in the memory of Fig. 6.2-1 is characterized as being one-dimensional or linear. There is generally an advantage to be found in an alternative two-dimensional arrangement. The distinction between the two is brought out in Figs. 6.4-1 and 6.4-2. In both cases we have assumed a 16-word 1-bit/word memory. In the first case there are 16

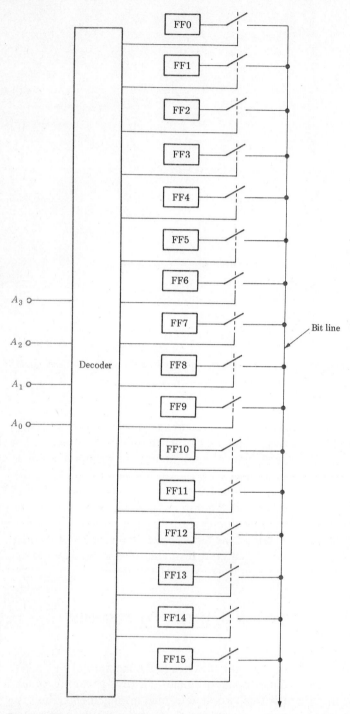

Figure 6.4-1 A 16 word 1-bit/word memory with a one-dimensional internal structure.

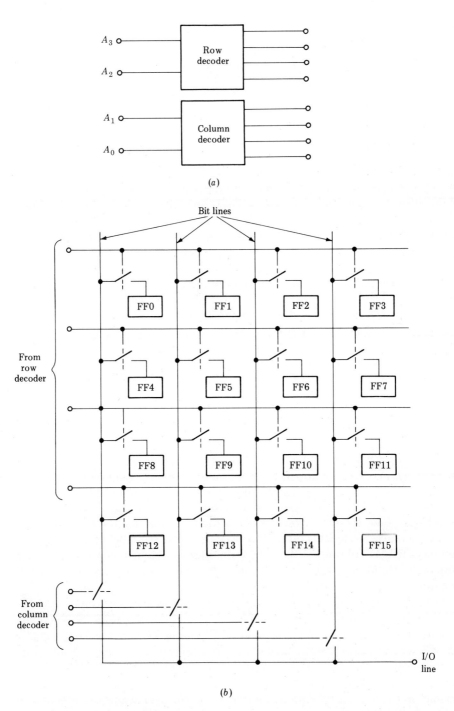

Figure 6.4-2 A 16-word 1-bit/word memory with a two-dimensional internal organization: (*a*) the two four-output decoder required; (*b*) the row-column two-dimensional arrangement of switches.

memory elements (flip-flops), 16 switches, and a decoder which has 4 input address bits and 16 outputs. The decoder has then 16 AND gates. In the second case, in Fig. 6.4-2, we use two decoders. Each decoder accepts 2 of the input address bits and has 4 outputs. Each decoder is composed of 4 AND gates, so that the total number of AND gates is 8. The eight decoder outputs by themselves are not able to do the complete job of decoding because there are 16 memory elements which must be singled out individually. The decoding is completed by the arrangement of switches. (It will be recalled, as pointed out in Sec. 1.7 and in Fig. 1.7-1, that a series arrangement of switches can be used to effect the AND operation.) As indicated, the output of one decoder, the *row decoder*, is applied to the lines which operate rows of switches, and the output of the other decoder, the *column decoder*, is applied to switches in the bit lines. At any input address $A_3A_2A_1A_0$ one row-decoder output and one column-decoder output are active. Accordingly one switch in a bit line closes, and all four switches in one of the rows close. The result is that a *single* memory element is connected to the input-output line. Thus the switching arrangement has completed the decoding left undone by the decoders.

The two-dimensional arrangement uses four more switches than the one-dimensional arrangement but uses eight fewer AND gates. The advantage becomes more apparent in larger memories. Consider, for example, a memory with 4096 ($=64^2$) words. The one-dimensional memory arrangement will require 4096 AND gates and 4096 switches. The two-dimensional arrangement will require only 64 + 64 ($=128$) AND gates and 4096 + 64 ($=4160$) switches.

6.5 THE READ-ONLY MEMORY

The memories discussed above are read-write memories. We can read from them or we may write into them. A *read-only memory* (ROM) is a memory from which we can read but into which we are not able to write. The contents of the memory are fixed and unalterable, having been established at the time of fabrication. Like the read-write memory, the read-only memory is a random-access memory. Hence it is rather inconsistent to use the label "random-access memory (RAM)" to refer to the read-write memory alone and not to the read-only memory. Many people have pointed out this inconsistency. Still the terminology has persisted and we shall use it.

There are also available ROM chips which allow the user rather than the manufacturer to establish the store of information in the memory. Such memories are called *programmable read-only memories* (PROM). Read-only memories are also available whose content of stored data can be changed. Such memories are called *erasable programmable read-only memories* (EPROM). These memories are still appropriately referred to as read-only memories since the erasing and rewriting operations cannot be performed while the memory is operating in a digital system. The memory must be removed from the system, and the memory modification may take some hours.

Memory location	Address			Data word			
	A_2	A_1	A_0	D_3	D_2	D_1	D_0
m_0	0	0	0	0	1	0	0
m_1	0	0	1	0	1	1	1
m_2	0	1	0	1	0	1	0
m_3	0	1	1	1	1	0	1
m_4	1	0	0	0	0	1	0
m_5	1	0	1	1	0	1	1
m_6	1	1	0	0	1	1	1
m_7	1	1	1	0	1	0	0

(a)

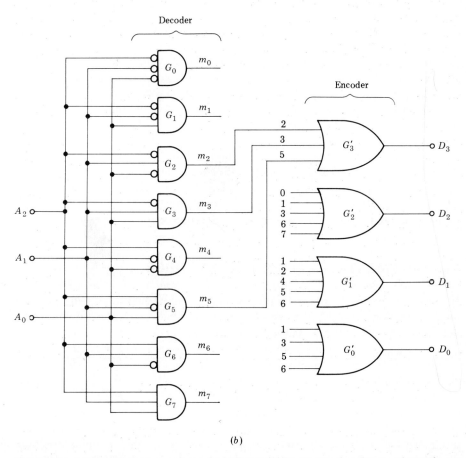

(b)

Figure 6.5-1 (a) Specification of an 8-word 4-bit/word ROM. (b) The decoder-encoder (code converter) which is a realization of the memory in (a).

In a ROM the bit stored at any location need not be changed. Hence the bits need not be stored in flip-flops, and the ROM can be assembled entirely with combinational circuits. A ROM is actually no more than a code converter and, like code converters generally, consists of a decoder and an encoder. As an example of a ROM let us consider how we can assemble a memory with an 8-word 4-bit/word organization. Specifically, let us consider that the content of the memory is given in the table of Fig. 6.5-1a. There are to be eight memory locations $m_0, \ldots, m_7$, which are to be addressed by three address bits A_2, A_1, A_0. The data word stored in memory location m_0 with address $A_2A_1A_0 = 000$ is $D_3D_2D_1D_0 = 0100$. The stored data words in the remaining locations are also given in the table.

The gate structure which constitutes the realization of the specified memory is shown in Fig. 6.5-1b. The array and AND gates $G_0, \ldots, G_7$ constitutes a decoder. Depending on the input address, one and only one AND-gate output $m_0, \ldots, m_7$ will be at logic 1 while all other output will be at logic 0. We have identified these AND-gate outputs with the memory locations on the basis, as we shall see, that the word stored in, say, memory location m_0 is determined by the OR-gate inputs to which m_0 is connected, etc. The array of OR gates $G'_0, \ldots, G'_3$ constitutes an encoder. To avoid the confusion which would result from displaying the profusion of connections from AND gates to OR gates, except in one case we have indicated the connections by numberings.

To verify that the connections are correct, refer to the table of Fig. 6.5-1a. There we note that $D_3 = 1$ when and only when $m_2 = 1$ or $m_3 = 1$ or $m_5 = 1$. Having connected gate G'_3 to m_2, m_3, and m_5, we shall have $D_3 = 1$ when and only when required. The other connections can be similarly verified. Alternatively the connections can be verified in the following manner. Consider, for example, that the input address in $A_2A_1A_0 = 011$. Here we require that $D_3D_2D_1D_0 = 1101$. We find that with this input address m_3 alone is $m_3 = 1$ and m_3 is connected to gates D_3, D_2, and D_0, as required.

6.6 IMPLEMENTATION OF A ROM ENCODER

It is of interest to consider, even superficially, something about the physical implementation of the ROM encoder since we shall thereafter be able to indicate how programmable ROMs are constructed.

A semiconductor diode, whose symbol is given in Fig. 6.6-1a, is a two-terminal device, the terminals being designated *anode* and *cathode*. When a voltage is impressed across the diode in the direction to make the anode positive with respect to the cathode (i.e., V in Fig. 6.6-1a is a positive number), a current I will flow through the diode in the direction indicated by the arrow. When, however, the applied voltage is reversed, no current will flow. The diode is a unilateral device and allows current flow in only a single direction.

The circuit of Fig. 6.6-1b involving two diodes and a resistor is a two-input OR gate. Here we consider that "ground," i.e., $0V$ is the voltage $V(0)$ corre-

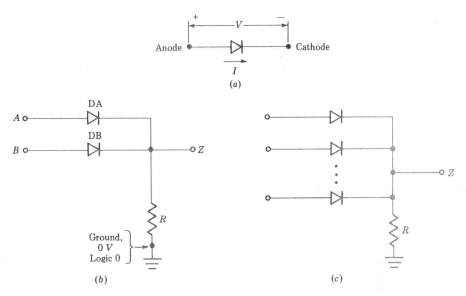

Figure 6.6-1 (*a*) Symbol for a diode. (*b*) An OR gate. (*c*) A multi-input OR gate.

sponding to logic 0 while some positive voltage, $V(1)$ corresponds to logic 1. If the voltages at A and B are both $V(0)$, that is, at logic 0, then neither diode will conduct and the output at Z will be at logic 0 also. If A is at $V(1)$ (logic 1) and B is at $V(0)$ (logic 0), then diode DA will conduct, diode DB will have across it a voltage in the reverse direction so that it will not conduct, and the output Z will be at logic 1. Similarly, if A is at $V(0)$ and B is at $V(1)$, DB will conduct and again Z will be at logic 1. If both A and B are at logic 1, then again Z will be at logic 1. Thus, altogether, as is required in an OR gate, the output will be at logic 1 if either or both inputs are at logic 1. To accommodate additional inputs to the OR gate we need but to add diodes in the manner shown in Fig. 6.6-1c. Most important, it is to be noted that what is essential in the present diode application is the diode's unilateral property. Other electronic devices, such as transistors, bipolar or MOS, which also have unilateral properties, may serve in place of the diodes.

The encoder of the ROM of Fig. 6.5-1 consists of an array of OR gates, and as we have just noted, an OR gate can be assembled with diodes and a resistor (Sec. 1.8). The OR-gate implementation of the encoder of the ROM of Fig. 6.5-1 is shown in Fig. 6.6-2. We see here a matrix of crossed decoder-generated address lines and output data lines. The three diodes connected to data line D_3 together with the resistor in that line constitute the three-diode OR gate shown as G'_3 in Fig. 6.5-1. Hence, as required, D_3 will be at logic 1 if m_2 or m_3 or m_5 is at logic 1. Similarly, we can verify that the other diodes are properly located. There are as many diodes in the encoder as there are 1s in the data-word columns of the table of Fig. 6.5-1a. In the circuit of Fig. 6.6-2, whenever a

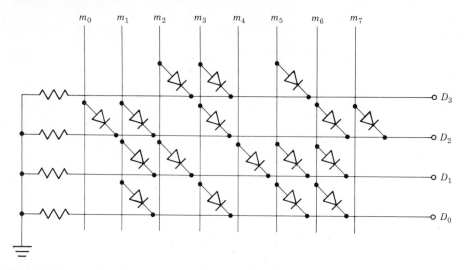

Figure 6.6-2 A physical implementation of the encoder portion of the ROM of Fig. 6.5-1 showing the diode connections between the address lines and the data lines.

1 appears in the table at the intersection of row m_j with column D_k, we locate a diode connecting address line m_j to data line D_k. In the RAM we need a flip-flop for each bit. In the ROM a diode or the absence of a diode establishes a bit permanently.

6.7 PROGRAMMABLE AND ERASABLE ROMS

A *programmable* ROM is one in which the chip manufacturer has included a connection at *every* intersection of the grid of address and data lines. (The connection consists of a diode, as in Fig. 6.6-2, or a transistor of some type.) In series with each connection the manufacturer includes a fusible link which can be melted, and thereby opened, by passing large enough current through it. We can single out an individual diode by proper input address and selection of data line. For example, suppose in the ROM of Figs. 6.5-1 and 6.6-2 we apply the address $A_2A_1A_0 = 010$. Then decoder output line m_2 will be at logic 1. Suppose now that we connect data line D_3 to a voltage source lower in voltage than the m_2 line. Then only the one diode (connecting m_2 to D_3) will conduct current. If we lower the voltage to which D_3 is connected, a point will be reached where the fuse in series with the diode will open and the connection between m_2 and D_3 will be broken. In this way we can systematically go through the intersections of a PROM, making disconnections as we please. A PROM may have many thousands of intersections, but commercial equipment is available that allows the programming to be done rather conveniently and in a reasonable time.

In *erasable programmable* ROMs the element used to make connections between decoder and data lines is not a diode but a MOS transistor. These devices provide connection or no connection according as there is an electric charge on the transistor *gate* or no charge. An individual transistor, one located at every intersection, can be singled out and its gate charged in a manner similar to that used for the diode PROM. The important and distinctive feature of these EPROMs is that exposure to strong ultraviolet radiation (for about 30 min) will allow the gate charges to leak off, thereby wiping the memory clean. Thereafter, a new store of information can be written into it.

6.8 VOLATILITY OF MEMORY

In addition to the terminals already described, physical IC memory chips have terminals which are used to deliver electric power to the chip. The power so delivered is used to operate the transistors in the chip. In both RAMs and ROMs these transistors are found in the input and output buffers and in the circuits which provide the switching mechanisms. In RAMs, as well, power is supplied to the flip-flops which store the individual bits. If power should be lost and then restored to a RAM, the new states of the flip-flops after power restoration will generally bear no useful relationship to the states before power loss. Thus, a temporary power loss will cause the loss of information in the memory. For this reason, a semiconductor RAM is described as being a *volatile memory*.

We have seen that in a ROM the stored information is determined by the location of diodes in the matrix of decoder and output lines. In some cases the diode connection is replaced by a transistor connection, which must then be powered like the other transistors. However, the important point is that stored bits are determined only by the location of a diode or transistor connection. Hence, in ROM, the store of information is permanent and *nonvolatile*, and the memory is restored unaltered when power is restored after a power loss.

When memory loss in a RAM due to power interruption must be avoided, it is necessary to establish a backup power system, generally a battery supply. Commercial components and systems are available which are designed to sense a falling supply voltage and to shift the RAM to the backup supply rapidly enough to avoid a memory loss.

6.9 SWITCHING TIMES OF MEMORIES

We have noted that logic gates require some time to respond to changes in input. The speed limitations of gates are generally expressed as *propagation delay times* between input changes and output responses. Occasionally, for very fast gates manufacturers also supply information on *rise-time* and *fall-time* response of output waveforms. For more complicated devices, more extensive information is supplied. For flip-flops, as we have seen (Sec. 4.15) manufacturers supply not only propagation times but also *setup times*, *holdtimes*, and *maximum toggle rates* Memories are rather more complicated devices. Memory chips are generally considered large-scale integrated (LSI) devices in comparison with medium-scale integrated (MSI) devices, such as counters and shift registers, and with small-scale (IC) devices such as simple logic gates.

The complication in specifying switching times in memories arises principally because of the large number of types of terminals: address terminals, input terminals, output terminals (these last two sometimes combined as data terminals), chip-enable terminals, and read-write terminals. Some manufacturers incorporate special features, which then require even more terminals. A typical glossary of timing-symbol definitions to be found in catalogs of memory components may contain more than 20 entries. The situation is not improved by the fact that different manufacturers often use widely different symbols. In the following we shall consider the most important and commonly used timing specifications.

A typical set of timing waveforms for a ROM is shown in Fig. 6.9-1. The input address is applied at $t = t_0$. There are a number of address terminals, and when an address is applied, some inputs will go from 0 to 1 and some from 1 to 0. Hence the address input is represented not by a waveform which makes an upward or a downward transition but by two waveforms changing in opposite directions and crossing at $t = t_0$. The data output also appears generally at a number of terminals (except in memories organized into 1-bit words), and so the data output is also represented as crossing waveforms. We see from the waveforms that if the address is applied at $t = t_0$, the addressed word appears at the output terminals of the memory with all bits correct, i.e., the output data becomes *valid*, only at time t_2 after an *access after address* time t_{AA}. Of course, no data output will appear until chip-select, (or more generally the multiple chip-select) inputs have been made active. The response time of the memory to the chip-select inputs is the *chip-enable* time $t_{CE} = t_2 - t_1$. The

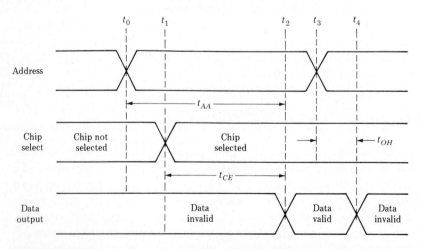

Figure 6.9-1 Memory timing waveforms illustrating the effect of an address change.

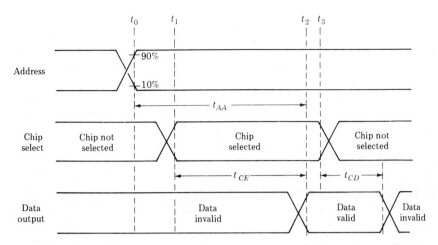

Figure 6.9-2 Memory timing waveforms illustrating the effect of a chip deselection.

waveforms are drawn in a manner which recognizes that $t_{CE} < t_{AA}$. The waveforms indicate that if the chip selects are activated at a time t_{CE} earlier than t_2, the delay of the activation $(t_1 - t_0)$ will not cause a further delay in the appearance of a valid output word. Some manufacturers specify not t_{CE} but the time $t_1 - t_0$, or the time by which chip-select activation can be delayed after application of the address without causing a further delay (beyond t_{AA}) in the appearance of valid output data.

The timing diagram of Fig. 6.9-1 indicates that the address is changed at $t = t_3$. The output data corresponding to the address applied at $t = t_0$ remain valid, however, until $t = t_4$. The interval of valid data beyond the time of address change is generally called t_{OH} (output hold). After $t = t_4$ the output data begin to change in response to the new address. At a time t_{AA} after t_3 the output data will again be valid and correspond to the address applied at $t = t_3$.

In the waveforms of Fig. 6.9-1 we have measured time from the occasions when the logic levels are at a midpoint between the logic levels 1 and 0. Some manufacturers prefer to take into account the rise and fall times of the waveforms. The times are then measured from the moments when the rising waveform has attained 90 percent of the logic 1 level and the falling level has fallen to within 10 percent of the logic 0 level. (We approximate very reasonably that the 90 and 10 percent points are reached simultaneously.) It is thus judged that a new address, new data, etc., are not valid until logic levels have completed about 90 percent of any required change. And if data are changing, the old data are no longer valid if a 10 percent change has occurred. With this point of view, we have drawn in Fig. 6.9-2 a timing diagram showing some of the same information in Fig. 6.9-1. In Fig. 6.9-2, however, we have considered that at $t = t_3$ and after valid data have appeared, the chip has been deselected instead of the address being changed. The delay in the chip response to the deselection of the chip is indicated as t_{CD} (chip disable). Where more than one chip is coupled to a common bus, it is important when transferring the bus from a first chip to a second that the first chip be deselected before the second is selected. To make it more convenient to arrange such timing, manufacturers generally arrange that t_{CD} be substantially shorter than t_{CE}.

The preceding discussion concerning timing deals only with ROMs. We now consider the matter of RAMs. When a RAM is being read, the timing considerations are nearly identical to those for ROMs. The *write-enable* terminal of the chip may be viewed as an additional *chip-enable* terminal. With this understanding the timing waveforms of Figs. 6.9-1 and 6.9-2 apply both to ROMs and to RAMs when the RAMs are being read.

When we propose to write data into a RAM, the *write-enable* input must be forced to the logic level corresponding to write. In order for this maneuver to be effective, however, some special timing considerations must be observed, as indicated in Fig. 6.9-3. Here, we contemplate that there is to be applied to the chip a write input pulse. We assume here, because it rather generally turns out to be the case, that the *write-enable* input is active low. For this pulse to be effective, it is necessary that before the occurrence of the leading edge of this write pulse the chip-select be made active and that both the address and the data input to be written be present at the chip terminals. That is, the chip select, the address, and the data must be *set up* in advance of the write pulse. The *setup* times are indicated in the timing diagram of Fig. 6.9-3*a*, and the definitions of the timing symbols are given in Fig. 6.9-3*b*. There is a limitation on the minimum width t_W of the write pulse. Finally, after the end of the write pulse the inputs must be held for a time so that the input data can be reliably established at their specified address. Hence there are *hold* times for chip select, for address, and for data. The waveforms of Fig. 6.9-3 have been drawn to allow easy indication of the various times. The figure makes it appear that the setup and hold times are longest for chip select, etc. Such is not necessarily the case. Frequently the setup times are very nearly all the same, as are the hold times; and both setup and hold times are rather small in comparison with the required minimum write pulse width.

Additional times are of interest in connection with a memory write operation. When $\overline{\text{WE}}$ is at logic 1, the memory is in the read mode and the output buffers of the memory are enabled while the input buffers are disabled. When $\overline{\text{WE}} = 0$, the memory is in the write mode and the situation of the input and output is reversed. The time required to switch from the read to the write mode is often called the *write delay* time, symbolized as t_{WD} (write delay) or t_{WS} (write setup). If the memory chip has a tristate output, the switch to the write mode sets the chip output in the high-impedance (high-Z) state and the time t_{WD} may then be represented by t_{ZWS}. The time required to effect the switch from the write mode back to the read mode is the *write-recovery* time t_{WR}.

The $\overline{\text{WE}}$ input on a chip enables *either* the input or the output connections of the memory. The chip-select input or inputs serve to enable or to disable *both* input and output connections. It is not generally essential but it is often a convenience to have available an input which will enable or disable the output connections alone. We shall always need to disable the output when the data

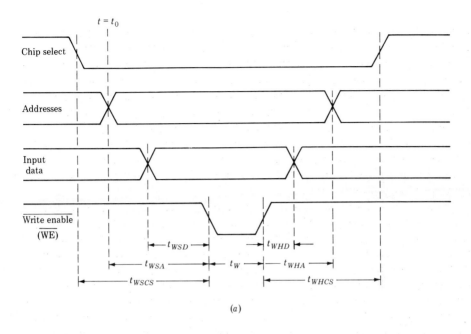

(a)

Symbol	Definition
t_{WSCS}	Write setup time for chip select
t_{WSA}	Write setup time for address
t_{WSD}	Write setup time for data
t_W	Width of write pulse
t_{WHD}	Write hold for data
t_{WHA}	Write hold for address
t_{WHCS}	Write hold for chip select
t_{WD}	Write disable delay time
t_{WR}	Write recovery delay time

(b)

Figure 6.9-3 (a) Timing waveforms associated with writing into a memory. (b) Definitions of timing symbols.

bus to which the output is connected is needed for another purpose. Many memory chips provide such a control input and label at either OD (output disable) or EO (enable output). This added input terminal is the basis for introducing additional timing parameters, the enable and disable times for the output buffers alone, for which there seems to be no generally accepted symbolism.

In Fig. 6.9-4 we have represented the logic of the control of a typical memory chip. We have provided here a $\overline{WE}$ input, two chip-select inputs CS and $\overline{CS}$, and an output-disable input $\overline{OD}$. We assume, as usual, that the control lines

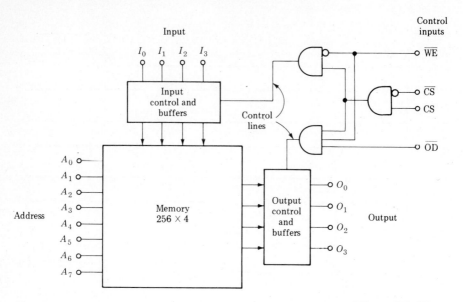

Figure 6.9-4 A typical commercial memory chip showing control inputs ($\overline{WE}$, CS, $\overline{CS}$, $\overline{OD}$), outputs, and address pins.

close switches at logic 1 and open them at logic 0. Hence, for example, when $\overline{OD} = 0$, the switches in the output circuit are open and the output is disabled as required.

Not all manufacturers specify timing characteristics of memory chips in the same way. And, as we have noted, the notation used may vary from manufacturer to manufacturer. Fortunately manufacturers are generally careful about providing a complete glossary of timing symbols.

There is a point of possible confusion in the way manufacturers specify values for timing characteristics. For example, we note that the Fairchild 93411 chip has a *typical* address access time $t_{AA} = 40$ ns while the maximum value of this parameter is 45 ns. In this specification we find no problem. Looking further, however, we find that the *typical* write pulse width is $t_W = 25$ ns while the *minimum value is specified* $t_W = 40$ ns. The interpretation of this apparent inconsistency is that the unit will typically operate properly if the user provides a write pulse width of 25 ns, but some units require t_W to be as long as 40 ns. Hence, the minimum pulse width that the user should provide is 40 ns. Rather generally when we find that a minimum specification is larger than a typical specification, the specification is to be read as a requirement that is imposed on the user.

The speed at which memory chips can be operated is easily estimated from the timing information already described. The minimum time for a read operation is approximately the access time t_{AA}. The minimum time for a write operation is about the sum of a setup time (the longest one), the write pulse width, and a hold time. In addition to specifying the usual timing information, some manufacturers specify the minimum recommended times which will allow reading or writing with reliability. These are the write-cycle time t_{WC} and the read-cycle time t_{RC}. These times are generally comparable, and when there is a difference, the read cycle is almost always the longer. The time t_{RC} for presently available units varies from about 50 to 1500 ns.

6.10 THE PROGRAMMABLE LOGIC ARRAY

A ROM is a combinational logic circuit. We apply inputs to the ROM, and the ROM provides one or more output bits, each being a logical function of the inputs. It is not surprising that such should be the case. For we have seen that a ROM consists of a first level of AND gates, which constitute the decoder, followed by a second level of OR gates, one for each output bit, which constitute the encoder. And we have seen that a two level AND-OR-gate structure will serve to generate the most general logical function of the inputs. Thus, in a ROM, if it suits our purpose, we may view the address bits simply as the inputs to a combinational circuit and the word readout as an array of bits each a separate function of all the input bits. In many cases, where rather complicated logic is required, a ROM may be rather substantially simpler hardware than a large collection of individual AND and OR gate chips.

Suppose now that we have in mind to build a ROM-type structure with the purpose of using it only for combinational logic and not as a memory. Suppose we wanted to be able to accommodate as many as 14 input bits and make available as many as 8 separate logical functions. If we build the device as a memory, it will be a formidable piece of hardware indeed, being a memory of 2^{14} by $2^3 = 2^{17}$ bits. If we are prepared to limit the complexity of the combinational logic to be performed, however, it turns out to be feasible to construct a ROM-type structure with a large number of inputs and outputs. Such combinational structures are called *logic arrays* and, as we would anticipate, have a structure not unlike ROMs. The logical functions generated by the logic arrays can be *programmed* during fabrication by selecting the sites at which connections are made in a crossed array of lines in a way similar to the programming of ROMs. For this reason the logic array is called a *programmed logic array* (PLA). If a manufacturer makes provision to allow programming by the user, the PLA is referred to as a FPLA, a field-programmable logic array.

A typical commercial PLA like the type 7575 does indeed accommodate 14 inputs and furnish 8 outputs. Its logic structure is shown in Fig. 6.10-1. The inputs $I_0, \ldots, I_{13}$ are applied to inverters to make available the complements $\bar{I}_0, \ldots, \bar{I}_{13}$ as well as the uncomplemented inputs. (The double inversion which provides the uncomplemented-variable lines performs no logic but serves to interpose buffering between the input pins and the rest of the chip.) The chip provides 96 AND gates. (If a 14-bit ROM were intended, the chip would require 2^{14} AND gates.) Each AND gate has a potential fan-in of 14. The AND-gate inputs

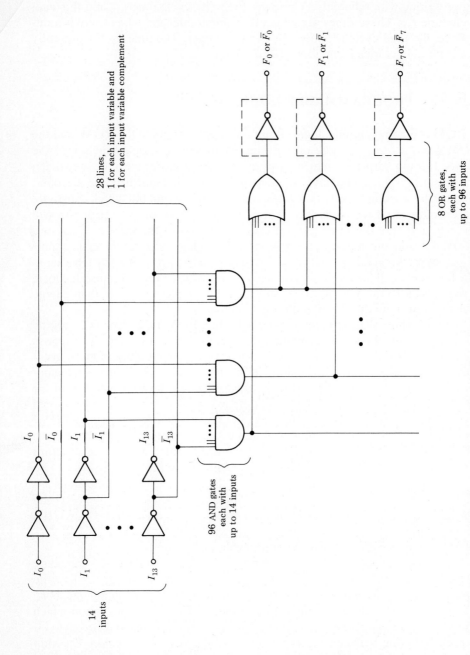

Figure 6.10-1 The logic-gate structure of a commercial (type '7575) programmable logic array.

are established during chip fabrication by the sites at which connections are made in the crossed array of I and $\bar{I}$ lines and input lines to the AND gates. If an AND gate has as inputs each of the I variables (either complemented or uncomplemented, but not both) the AND-gate output is a minterm. Otherwise the output is a sum of minterms. The OR gates each have a potential fan-in of 96, so that depending on the sites of connection, any or all of the AND-gate outputs can be applied to the OR-gate inputs. At the OR-gate outputs inverters are provided which can be bypassed if required, as shown by the dashed connection. We can therefore select at each output a function F or its complement $\bar{F}$.

Suppose we propose to use a PLA as in Fig. 6.10-1 to generate eight or fewer functions of the input variables. We can determine whether it is indeed possible to do so in the following way. We express each function as a sum of products, and we count the total number of different products in all the functions. A product that occurs more than once is counted only once. If the total number is 96 or less, the PLA is adequate for the job; otherwise not.

6.11 DYNAMIC RAMS

In the RAMs discussed above, individual stored bits are held in individual flip-flops. A second type of RAM is available in which the individual bits are stored not in flip-flops but in capacitors; i.e., a logic 1 bit is stored by placing a charge on a capacitor, and a logic 0 is recognized when there is no charge on the capacitor. The advantage of this capacitor-storage scheme is that a capacitor occupies much less space on an IC chip than a flip-flop. A capacitor-storage memory will have about 4 times the capacity of a flip-flop memory of comparable physical size.

A capacitor-storage memory has a serious inconvenience, however, in comparison with a flip-flop memory. A bit will remain stored in a flip-flop permanently for as long as the memory chip continues to be supplied with power, but a charged capacitor left isolated will inevitably lose its charge. (It is even possible, in the complexity of an IC chip, for leakage mechanisms to exist which place some charge on initially uncharged capacitors. But the more serious concern is leakage which will cause loss of charge.) Hence, to maintain the storage in a capacitor-storage memory, it is necessary to return periodically to each capacitor storage element while the stored bit is still unambiguously recognizable, and each such visited capacitor must be restored to the full charge value corresponding to the bit being stored. This operation of restoration of initial charge is described as a *refresh* operation. Typically, in available chips, each capacitor must be refreshed at intervals not in excess of 2 ms. Because of the constant refreshing activity which is required, capacitor-storage memories are called *dynamic* memories, in comparison with flip-flop memories, which are referred to as *static* memories.

The need for refreshing somewhat complicates the incorporation of a dynamic memory in a digital system. Where small memory capacity is required, about 64×10^3 bits or less, there is generally no advantage in using dynamic memories, but when large memory capacity is needed, about 128×10^3 or more, there is a cost advantage in using dynamic memories. In between these ranges the choice will be determined by a variety of factors related to the details of the overall digital system.

At the present writing the largest generally available static RAM has a capacity of 16 kilobits (actually $16,384 = 2^{14}$) while the largest dynamic RAM has a capacity of 64 kilobits (actually $65,536 = 2^{16}$). Static RAMs are available with word lengths of 8, 4, and 1 bit, while dynamic RAMs almost invariably have 1-bit word lengths.

6.12 DATA SENSING IN A DYNAMIC RAM

Leaving aside, for the present, the matter of refreshing, let us consider how a typical bit-storage capacitor is made accessible to the world outside the chip. The interface between an external data line D and a *bit-storage capacitor C_B* is illustrated in Fig. 6.12-1. The logic-controlled switches are implemented by transistors, generally MOS devices. As we shall see, the switches must be operated in a special time sequence. The generators needed to provide logic levels to control these switches are incorporated into the IC memory chip. Since our interest is in the logic of the memory and not in the details of the elec-

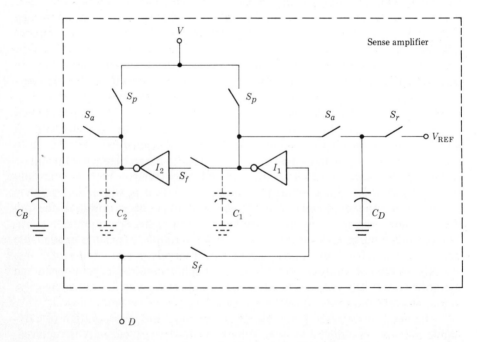

Figure 6.12-1 A sense amplifier used to read and refresh the bit stores on C_B.

tronics, we have again taken some liberties in the interest of simplification without distortion of principle. The circuitry interposed between C_B and D is called a *sense amplifier.*

When the two switches S_f are closed (they open and close together), the two inverters are connected so that they constitute a flip-flop. Then the output of one inverter is $V(1)$, the voltage value corresponding to logic 1, and the output of the other inverter is $V(0)$, the logic level corresponding to logic 0. These voltages $V(1)$ and $V(0)$ are also the voltages which are intended to be found ideally on C_B before any degradation due to leakage. The capacitors C_1 and C_2 are not components deliberately introduced in chip fabrication but are rather the inevitable and unavoidable stray capacitances present because of the length of the conductors connected to the inverter outputs.

We consider now how the *sense amplifier* is operated in order to sense the logic level on C_B and to bring the bit of information to the data terminal. Initially, all switches are open. The first operation to take place is that the two switches S_p close, bringing C_1 and C_2 to the same voltage. This equalization of voltages is undertaken so that the flip-flop (constituted when switches S_f close) will have no recollection of past history, i.e., no recollection of its previous state. Suppose, for example, that, with S_f closed the flip-flop had been in a state with the output of inverter I_1 at $V(1)$ and the output of I_2 at $V(0)$. Then when S_f opens the circuit, output voltages will be preserved for some time on the capacitors C_1 and C_2. If we were to close the switches S_f again very shortly after opening and without equalization, the flip-flop would revert to its original state. Even suppose that having opened S_f, we undertake, by operating other switches in the sense amplifier, to arrange that when S_f closes again, the flip-flop should find itself in the alternate state. Clearly the voltage difference preserved in C_1 and C_2 would prejudice the flip-flop in favor of returning to its original state and thereby make it more difficult to induce a change of state. We are interested in assuring a lack of bias in the flip-flop, because as we shall see, a sense amplifier is used to sense in rapid succession the bits stored in a large number of bit storage locations in the memory. In the first operation of equalization both C_1 and C_2 are *precharged* to the voltage V, and hence the operation is referred to as *precharging.* The value of the voltage V is determined by the details of the electronic circuitry by which the sense amplifier is implemented but is not relevant in the present discussion, where we are interested only in the logic of the operation.

The next operation consists in closing switch S_r so that the *dummy* capacitor C_D can charge to the reference voltage V_{REF}. The reference voltage $V_{RÈF}$ is selected nominally at a value $V_{REF} = [V(1) + V(0)]/2$ midway between $V(1)$ and $V(0)$. C_D having charged, S_r is reopened.

The third operation consists in opening switches S_p and then closing the switches S_a. And finally in the fourth and last operation we close the switches S_f. Suppose that the bit stored on C_B is logic 1. Then the voltage on C_B is $V(1)$ or somewhat less if there has been some loss of charge from C_B. We assume, however, that the charge loss has been limited and that the voltage on C_B, while it may be lower than $V(1)$, is comfortably higher than V_{REF}. Then after the closing of switches S_a the voltage at C_2 will be higher than the voltage at C_1. When the switches S_f close to form the flip-flop, the flip-flop will go to the state in which the output of I_2, the bit-storage capacitor, and the data output terminal will all go to the full voltage $V(1)$. The output current which the memory may be called upon to supply will be furnished by the inverter. It is important to note that in reading the bit on C_B we get an output voltage which is the *full* voltage $V(1)$ even if there has been some loss of charge before reading. Even more important, note that the process of reading the stored bit *restores the capacitor voltage to its full value V(1). That is, the process of reading the bit automatically refreshes the bit.*

6.13 FEATURES OF A DYNAMIC MEMORY

The organization of a 16-word 1-bit/word dynamic memory is indicated in Fig. 6.13-1. Note that the internal arrangement of the memory is two-dimensional. An active line from the row decoder closes all the switches in a row, thereby connecting each capacitor in a row to a bit line. An active line from the column decoder closes a switch in one bit line and activates the sense amplifier connected to that bit line. Altogether, then, the column and row decoders together single out a single capacitor and provide access to that 1-bit storage site for reading or writing.

In refreshing, it is not necessary to refresh the capacitors one at a time: all the capacitors in an entire row can be refreshed simultaneously. There is provision on the chip for activating all the sense amplifiers simultaneously and closing simultaneously all appropriate switches in the bit lines. Such simultaneous activation will refresh all the capacitors in the row selected by the row decoder. Consider, for example, a 4-kilobit 1-bit/word memory. Such a memory will have 64 rows and 64 columns of capacitors. Since each row must be refreshed every 2 ms, the allowable interval between the refreshing of one row and the refreshing of the next is $2000/64 = 31$ μs. Even if we allow 1 μs for a refreshing operation (a conservative estimate in a typical case), we then have the result that refreshing occupies only about 3 percent of operating time. Nonetheless, while refreshing is taking place, the memory is not available for other purposes, and the system in which the memory is incorporated must be made aware of the unavailability.

A 1-kilobit dynamic memory like the type 1103 is fabricated on an 18-pin chip. There are 10 address pins ($2^{10} = 1024$), a chip-enable pin, a read-write pin, input and output pins, a precharge input, and pins for power. A 4-kilobit memory like the type 2104 is fabricated on a 16-pin chip. Like the 1103, it has pins for power, a read-write pin, a chip-enable pin, and input and output pins. It has no precharge pin since the precharging operation is apparently taken care of automatically. Twelve address bits are required ($2^{12} = 4096$), yet there are only six address pins. The twelve required bits are put aboard the chip by multiplexing the bits through the address pins. Six row-address bits are presented to the chip, and by activating a pin called *row-address strobe* (RAS) these bits

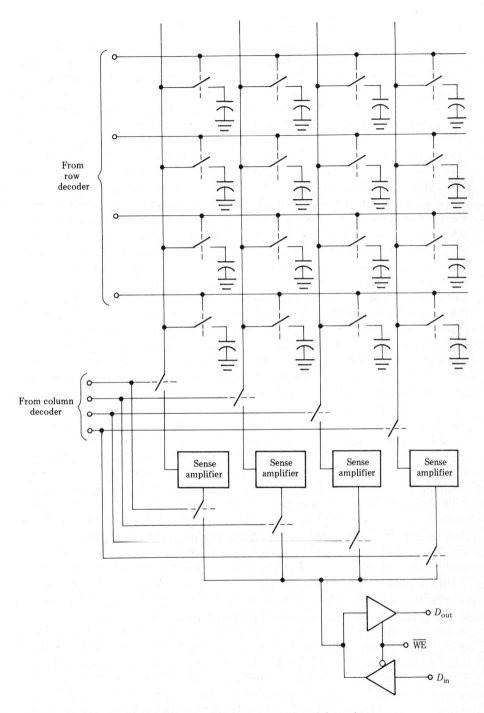

From
row
decoder

From column
decoder

Sense
amplifier

Sense
amplifier

Sense
amplifier

Sense
amplifier

D_{out}

$\overline{WE}$

D_{in}

Figure 6.13-1 The internal organization of a 16-word 1-bit/word dynamic memory.

are transferred to a 6-bit latch on the chip. Next the six column-address bits are presented to the input pins and are transferred to a second latch by activating the *column-address strobe* (CAS).

The comments of this section concerning refreshing and address multiplexing are intended to indicate that a dynamic memory is somewhat more difficult to use than a static memory. Manufacturers have available a number of dynamic-memory interface chips intended to assist in the use of dynamic memories.

6.14 SERIAL MEMORIES

The read-write memories and the read-only memories are random-access memories. The access time to a data word at any address is independent of the address of the word accessed immediately before. A different type of memory is the *serial memory*. Here data words stored become available for reading, or locations become available for writing in a serial manner that follows a predetermined sequential order. If we select an address at random, we shall find that the access time depends on the number of addresses interposed between the presently accessed location and the location to which access is desired. In an application in which serial memories are acceptable they offer the advantage of being more economical than random-access read-write memories.

A serial memory is shown in Fig. 6.14-1. There are n shift registers, and each shift register is a k-bit register. The memory has the organization $k \times n$, that is, k words of n bits each. To load the memory, input words are applied to the input bit lines $I_0, I_1, \ldots, I_{n-1}$ in synchronism with the clock. To allow such writing into the memory the $\overline{write\text{-}read}$ input will be at logic 1. An input word will appear at the output pins $O_0, O_1, \ldots, O_{n-1}$ after k clock cycles. In general, except for the delay as the input is shifted down the registers, the input words will appear at the output in the same sequence as they were read in. A memory of this type is called a first in-first out (FIFO) memory. When the memory has been filled, the data stored in the memory can be preserved by setting *write-read* to logic 0. The output bits will now be reintroduced to the register inputs, and the words will *recirculate*. The stored words will become available one after another in sequence and synchronously with the clock.

If the shift register uses static flip-flops, the flip-flops must be of a type suitable for use in synchronous systems. Such flip-flops were discussed in detail in Chap. 4 and include, among others, the master-slave flip-flop. Or, again, to use IC-chip real estate more economically, the flip-flops may be dynamic flip-flops, in which the storage of a bit is represented by a charge in a capacitor. A dynamic bit-storage element and inverter is shown in Fig. 6.14-2a. As usual, switches S_1 and S_2 are logic-operated switches which close when the control logic line is at logic 1 and open when the control-logic line is at logic 0. The latch is connected between the voltages $V(1)$ and $V(0)$, which are the voltages corresponding to logic 1 and logic 0, respectively. When S_2 is open, $\bar{Q}$ will become

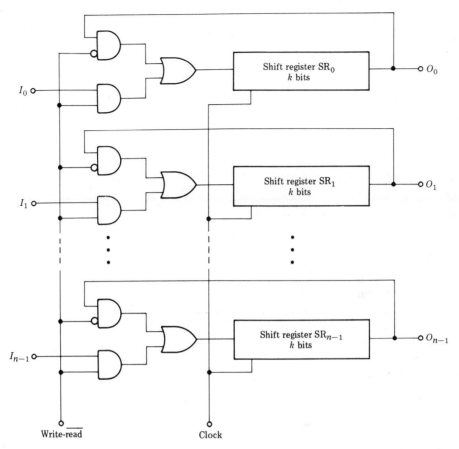

Figure 6.14-1 Shift registers used to construct a serial memory with k words and n bits/word.

$\bar{Q} = 1$, and when S_2 is closed, $\bar{Q}$ will become $\bar{Q} = 0$. An input data bit I is applied. A clocking waveform ϕ closes switch S_1 when $\phi = 1$, and the capacitor C charges to $V(1)$ or $V(0)$, depending on whether $I = 1$ or $I = 0$. Switch S_2 opens for $I = 0$ and closes for $I = 1$. In either event the complement $\bar{I} = \bar{Q}$ of the input appears on the output. While S_1 is open, the voltage across C will change. If, for example, C is at $V(1)$ the capacitor, which is charged, will lose charge and the voltage will decrease. There is a range of voltage over which switch S_2 will remain closed, but it will not remain closed indefinitely. If the capacitor C is left isolated for too long, it will eventually lose so much of its charge that S_2 will open and the stored bit will be lost.

Two dynamic bit-storage elements and inverters have been assembled into a dynamic flip-flop in Fig. 6.14-2b. Observe that there is required a clock composed of two separate waveforms ϕ_1 and ϕ_2. These clocking waveforms arrange that switches S_1 and S_2 are never closed at the same time. When $\phi_1 = 1$, the input I bit is stored on C_1 and $\bar{I}$ appears at node b. C_1 holds I while S_1 is open,

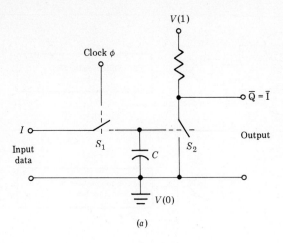

(a)

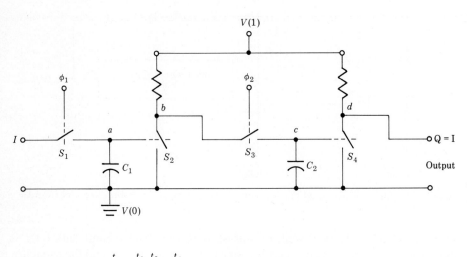

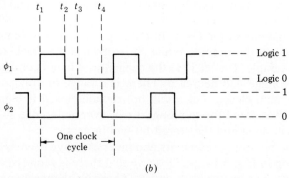

(b)

Figure 6.14-2 (a) A dynamic bit-storage element and inverter. (b) Two storage-inverter units are assembled in a dynamic flip-flop.

and when $\phi_2 = 1$, $\bar{I}$ is transferred to C_2 and the input bit $\bar{I}$ appears at the output terminals. The similarity between this dynamic flip-flop and the master-slave flip-flop assembled with static latches in Sec. 4.8 is quite apparent. Note especially that like the master-slave flip-flop, the present flip-flop has the following feature: the output change, if any is called for, occurs when S_1, is open, so that the flip-flop is not able to respond to a change in input. Such operation, as we have seen, is required to allow a flip-flop to operate successfully in a shift register or other synchronous system.

Typical of the commercially available dynamic shift registers which can be assembled into a serial memory is the Intel type 2405 1024-bit dynamic recirculating shift register. The logic incorporated on the chip, in addition to the register itself, is shown in Fig. 6.14-3. Like random-access memory chips, this chip has, in addition to data input and output terminals, two chip-select inputs $\overline{CS}_x$ and $\overline{CS}_y$. It also has a $W/\overline{R}$ terminal, which here means *write-recirculate* and corresponds to *write-read* in a random-access memory chip. The input clocking waveform is used to drive a clock generator on the chip which produces the two-phase clock waveform required by the dynamic flip-flops. At

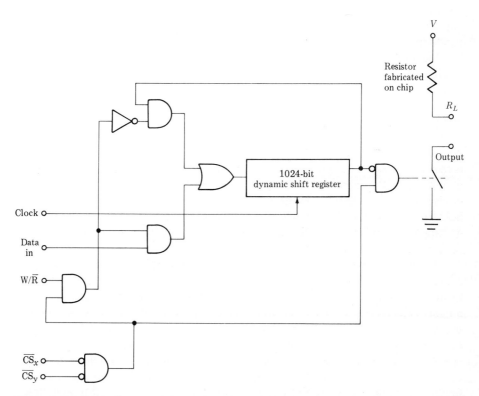

Figure 6.14-3 Logic diagram of the Intel type 2405 1024-bit dynamic recirculating shift-register serial memory.

the output, provision is made to allow the user to connect the terminal R_L to the terminal marked "output" and thereby to use the resistor and logic-controlled switch as an output buffer and inverter. Or the connection may be left unmade. In such case the chip has an *open-collector output*, which allows the use of the WIRED-AND connection (see Sec. 3.8).

The Intel type 2405 will operate at a maximum clock frequency 1 MHz. Because of the dynamic character of the memory, there is a minimum allowable clock frequency of about 1 kHz. This minimum clock speed is required to allow a shifting operation and hence a refreshing operation before a capacitor can lose so much charge that the stored logic level becomes ambiguous.

6.15 CHARGE-COUPLED DEVICES; SERIAL MEMORIES

The capacitors indicated in the dynamic latch and dynamic flip-flop of Fig. 6.14-2 and the capacitors indicated in the dynamic-memory cells of Figs. 6.12-1 and 6.13-1 are not capacitors in the conventional sense. We usually think of a capacitor as being composed of two conducting plates close together but electrically separated from each other by an insulator. A voltage difference impressed on the conductors establishes equal and opposite charges on the conductors.

The capacitors of dynamic memories and registers are different. They are fabricated on silicon chips by a technology which gives rise to devices called metal-oxide semiconductor (MOS) devices. A capacitor is formed by placing a conductor on the surface of the silicon semiconductor (the substrate), the conductor and substrate being separated by a thin insulator. If a voltage is applied to the conductor, there will form in the substrate, immediately under the conductor, a *depletion region*. All that we need to know about this depletion region is that it is a region in which charges can be held; i.e., if, say, a positive voltage is applied to the conductor, the depletion region forms, and if we somehow devise to inject negative charge into the depletion region, the charge will be held there. Thus the charges which in a conventional capacitor are held on conducting plates in an MOS device are held on a conductor and in the depletion region under the conductor.

The structure of a charge-coupled device (CCD) shift register and its mode of operation are shown in Fig. 6.15-1. Along the surfaces of the substrate are located, in close proximity, an array of conducting electrodes. An array of four adjacent electrodes driven by the four clock wave forms ϕ_1, ϕ_2, ϕ_3, and ϕ_4 shown in Fig. 6.15-1b provides the mechanism of a single dynamic flip-flop. Observe that clocks ϕ_1 and ϕ_3 are identical in waveform but displaced in time with respect to each other. A similar comment applies to clocks ϕ_2 and ϕ_4. The rather elaborate four-phase arrangement is required to give the flip-flop the operating features of a master-slave flip-flop to allow shift-register operation and to assure that data move in only one direction.

As can be seen in Fig. 6.15-1a and b, during the interval t_1 only ϕ_1 (of the four clocks) is at a positive voltage so that a depletion region forms only under

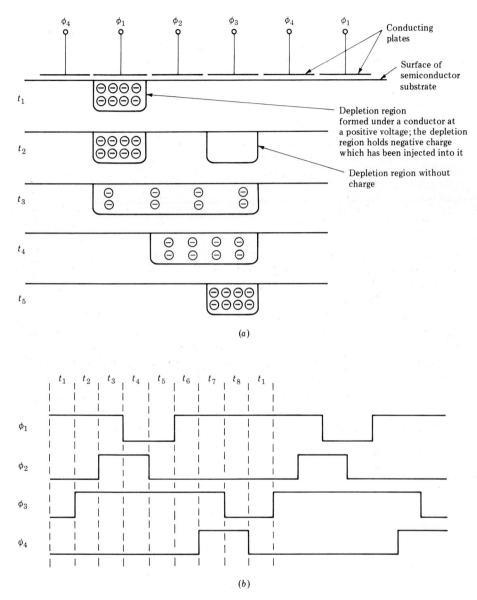

Figure 6.15-1 (*a*) The structure of a CCD shift register showing the charge distribution at various times identified in (*b*). (*b*) The waveforms of voltages applied to the metal electrodes.

ϕ_1. We assume that a logic 1 is stored when a negative charge is being held in the depletion region and a logic 0 is being held when the depletion region is empty. Since we have indicated charge in the depletion region under ϕ_1, we are assuming that logic 1 is being stored there. All the ϕ_1 electrodes are connected together (as are the ϕ_2 electrodes, etc.). Hence there are depletion regions (not shown) under these other ϕ_1 electrodes, and logic bits are being stored there in the form of charge or no charge. In the interval t_2 the depletion region under ϕ_1 persists while a new region is formed under ϕ_3. In the interval t_3 a region is formed under ϕ_2 as well, thereby generating a depletion region extending from ϕ_1 through ϕ_3. As a result the charge is now able to spread throughout the extended region. During the next two intervals t_4 and t_5 one and then another region is unformed, pushing the charge to the right, so that in interval t_5 the charge originally under ϕ_1 has been displaced laterally to a region under ϕ_3. Starting now in interval t_5, we can readily verify that in the succeeding intervals t_6, t_7, t_8, and finally back to t_1 the charge under ϕ_3 will be moved to ϕ_1. Hence altogether, after eight intervals, charge (or no charge) under a ϕ_1 electrode will have been moved to the next ϕ_1 electrode. Special arrangements (which we shall not consider here) must be made to inject charge into the first depletion region, as required, and to detect the presence or absence of charge at the last depletion region. This injection and detection will, of course, be done in synchronism and the clock waveform. Finally, it must be noted that there is some dissipation of charge as the charge transfers down the shift register. It is accordingly necessary to include provision for refreshing the charge at periodic intervals along the length of the structure. It turns out that the charge dissipation is so small that 100 or more flip-flops can be cascaded before refreshing is necessary.

The organization of the Intel type 2464 CCD serial memory is represented, with some simplification, in Fig. 6.15-2. The memory contains 256 recirculating shift registers, each having 256 bits. Accordingly, the memory capacity is $256 \times 256 = 65,536$ bits. The memory has a single data input and a single output line, so that the organization is $65,536 \times 1$. At each register shift, a new

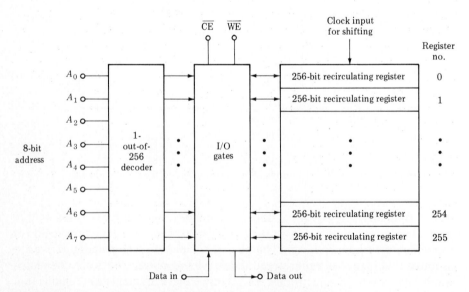

Figure 6.15-2 The organization of the Intel type 2464 CCD serial memory.

array of 256 bit positions, one from each shift register, is presented to the I/O gate circuitry. An 8-bit address input to the 1-out-of-256 decoder enables one path in or out, and 1 bit is read into or out of the memory. If the address input is fixed, then, as shifting progresses, the bit positions in one register will be presented serially for reading or writing. When the shifting is temporarily stopped or in the interval between shifts we can have access to a bit from each of the registers by changing the address. The 256 bits which can be accessed by changing address are available on a random-access basis. Of course, which such 256 bits are available depends on where the recirculating registers are stopped. The 256 bits in a single register are available only in a serial mode.

When the memory is being operated in a serial mode, the bit we want to access may be the bit presently available or the bit just passed. Hence access to a desired bit may take no shifts or may require 256 shifts. On the average the number of required shifts will be $256/2 = 128$ shifts. Since the Intel 2464 can be shifted at a 1-MHz rate, 128 shifts will require 128 μs. This access time in serial operation is called *latency* or *latency time* to distinguish it from the access time in nonserial memories, where delays are generally due to propagation delays in gates rather than the need to access bits in sequence.

6.16 MEMORY STACKS

The serial memories described in the preceding sections have the operating feature that the first word into the memory is the first word out (FIFO), but there frequently arises the need for a memory in which the last word in is the first word out (LIFO). Such a memory is shown in Fig. 6.16-1. Here again we use n shift registers, each with k bits, to provide a memory of k words each of n bits. The present memory differs from the memory of Fig. 6.14-1 in three respects:

1. The present memory does not provide for recirculation, there being no connection from the last flip-flop in the register back to the first.
2. Input data are written into, and read from, the same register stage. If we consider that a register stage consists of a type-D flip-flop, input bits are applied to the D (data) of the top flip-flops and a word is read out from the Q outputs of the same flip-flops.
3. The shift registers may be shifted in one direction or the other, depending on the logic level of the shift-direction input.

Let the write-enable input be at logic 1 and shift-direction control be set to shift downward. Let a sequence of words be presented at the input terminals I_0, $I_1, \ldots, I_{n-1}$ in synchronism with the clock. Then these words will be stored in successive locations in the shift-register memory. If, on the other hand, the shift-direction control is reversed, the words stored will appear at the output terminals $O_1, O_2, \ldots, O_{n-1}$, again in synchronism with the clock. The words will be read out in the order opposite that in which they were written, i.e., in a last-in first-out order.

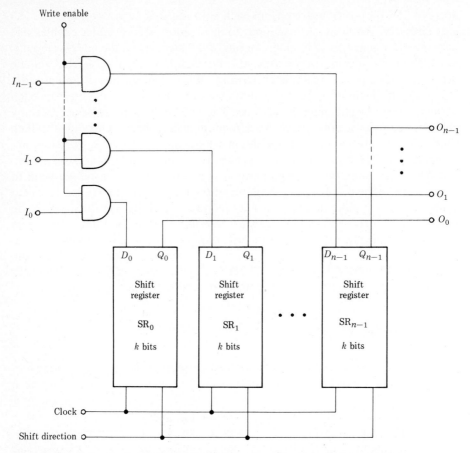

Figure 6.16-1 A last-in, first-out (LIFO) serial memory, often described as a stack.

The memory operation is rather reminiscent of an arrangement used to stack dishes in a restaurant, where dishes are loaded, one on top of the next, on a platform supported by a spring. When there are no dishes on the platform, the platform is flush with the counter. When a dish is placed on the counter, the weight of the dish causes the platform to sink. When successive dishes are stacked up, the platform sinks farther, leaving only the last dish accessible. Adding a dish *pushes* the stack of dishes down, while removing a dish allows the stack to *pop up*. These considerations explain why the serial memory of Fig. 6.16-1 is called a *stack*, the process of writing a word is called *pushing*, and reading a word is called *popping*. The terminology is quite appropriate. When a new word is to be written into the memory, all the words in the memory are *pushed* down one register stage to make room for the new word. When a word is read out of the memory, all the remaining words *pop up* by one stage.

An alternative way of constructing a last-in first-out memory is shown in Fig. 6.16-2. Here a random-access memory is coupled with a counter so that

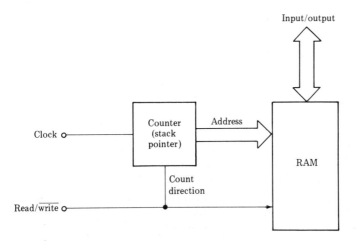

Figure 6.16-2 An alternative manner of constructing a stack.

the counter provides the address of the memory location being accessed. When the read-write control is at the write level, the counter is set to count, say, in the forward direction. With each clock cycle a new memory location is accessed. If words are presented to the memory input in synchronism with the clock, these words will be written in sequential locations in the memory. When read-write control goes to read, the counter direction reverses and words are read from the memory in the order opposite that in which they were written. In this memory of Fig. 6.16-2 push and pop are still used to indicate a write and a read operation, respectively, even though the terminology is not really descriptive here. In a LIFO memory, as in Fig. 6.16-2, the counter or other register which holds the address of the presently accessed memory location is referred to as the *stack pointer.*

6.17 BULK STORAGE

Semiconductor RAM chips, as we have seen, provide storage capacities in the range 64 kilobits. Increased capacities can, of course, be achieved by paralleling chips. Still, in a digital system of any sophistication, capacities in the range of many millions of bits may well be required. To attain and effectively use such large capacities with semiconductor chips, while not impossible, is generally quite inconvenient.

It turns out, however, that these large digital systems, i.e., computers, by one definition or another, do not generally require rapid access to all the information stored in memory. The term "rapid access" is used to indicate access times from tens of nanoseconds to tens of microseconds. Rather it is acceptable for the access time to the bulk of the memory storage to be from tens of milliseconds to tens of seconds and even many minutes. Data and information needed immediately are kept in short-access-time memory. As these data and information are used and are no longer needed, new information is transferred from the long-access-time memory into locations in the short-access time memory previously occupied by disposable data.

Commercially available media used to provide long-access-time bulk storage include magnetic tape on reels, magnetic-tape cassettes and cartridges, and magnetic disks. Each of these media provides a thin layer of magnetic material deposited on a supporting medium. Bits are stored by magnetizing small regions of the magnetizable medium in one direction for a logic 0 and in the other direction for a logic 1. The great merits of this bulk storage are that it brings down the cost per memory bit substantially and that it provides a non-volatile memory.

A length of magnetic tape and its read-write head are shown in Fig. 6.17-1. The relatively narrow tape shown moves in the direction of its length across the air gap of the magnetic circuit of the read-write head. To write into the tape we cause a current to flow in the coil in one direction or the other, thereby magnetizing the tape magnetic coating in one direction or another. As the tape moves across the head, bits are stored on the tape adjacent to each other along the tape length. To read the tape, we again cause the tape to move across the head. At each change in direction of tape magnetization, a voltage is induced in the head coil, the voltage polarity depending on the direction of change in magnetization. The mechanism of magnetic-disk storage is the same as tape storage. The difference is that in tape storage the magnetic coating is supported on a long very flexible plastic tape while in disk storage the supporting medium is a rather firm or only slightly flexible disk (called a *floppy disk*) whose geometry is like that of a phonograph record.

Magnetic Tape

At one extreme home computer hobbyists may well use for tape storage a good-quality audio tape cassette of the kind used to record music. At the other extreme are tapes intended for use with large computer installations and fur-

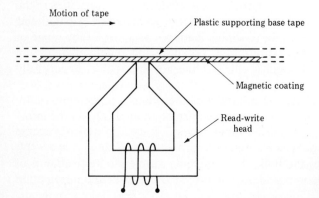

Figure 6.17-1 The tape and read-write head of a magnetic-tape bulk-storage facility.

nished in large reels. Typically a 10.5-in reel of such tape is 2400 ft long and $\frac{1}{2}$ in wide. It allows as many as 9 bits to be written side by side across the width of the track. Of course, to use such multitrack tapes we must provide as many read-write heads across the tape as there are tracks. Along the length of the tape bits can be written with a density of about 1600 bits/in. The total number of bits per track is 2400 ft $\times$ 12 in/ft $\times$ 1600 bits/in $\approx$ 46 million. And since we may well write a 9-bit word across the width of the tape, such a tape will hold $9 \times 46 = 414$ million bits.

A typical speed for a computer tape is 45 in/s. At this rate bits are read or written from each track at a rate 1600 bits/in $\times$ 45 in/s $= 72 \times 10^3$ bits/s. The worst-case latency time, assuming the tape is at one end while the required information is at the other end, is (2400 ft $\times$ 12 in)/(45 in/s) $\approx$ 10 min.

In order to write bits at the proper density and to ensure that the output at reading will be at normal level, reading and writing must be done only when the tape is moving at its proper speed. It is hardly likely that we shall want or be able to read or write an entire tape at one time, reading or writing instead relatively small portions from time to time. At each such reading or writing we shall have to accelerate and decelerate the tape. During these intervals when the tape is not running at proper speed we must avoid reading or writing. Thus we find that information is stored on the tape in conveniently sized blocks separated by interblock gaps used for acceleration and deceleration.

A large-computer tape-handling facility with provision for driving the tape, the necessary control mechanisms, and all the equipment for interfacing with a computer is a large and formidable piece of electromechanical machinery which may cost as much as a full-size automobile and be about one-third as large. In between this extreme and the simple audio-tape cassette, manufacturers provide a number of intermediate tape facilities, including special digital cassettes and digital cartridges.

Magnetic Disks

In magnetic-disk memories information is stored in concentric tracks on the phonographlike disk. While in a phonograph the track spirals from outer to inner rim, so that there is actually only one long track, in a magnetic disk, each track is a closed circle separate from the others. As in a tape memory, information is read and written by a read-write head. Because of the circular geometry of the disk, the disk can be kept rotating constantly even when neither reading nor writing is in process. The loss of time and storage space associated with acceleration and deceleration is thereby avoided. Bit density along a track may vary from 500 to 7000 bits/in. A typical rotational speed is 3600 r/min.

A wide range of disk memories is commercially available. Units are available with differing number of disks, and while some use disks with storage on only one side, others use both sides of the disks. The total number of recording surfaces may be as large as 24. When a single read-write head is used for each surface, the unit must have provision for moving the head from one track to another. The tracks on a surface are typically separated by about 10 mils and are 3.5 to 5 mils in width. The rapidly rotating disk carries along with it a thin layer of air caused by the viscous friction between air and disk. The head is shaped so that the moving air layer keeps the head separated from the disks by a distance measured in tens of microinches. This separation prevents wear on both the disk and the head. Other units have multiple read-write heads for each surface to reduce the time lost while heads are being moved about.

To access a particular part of disk surface it is necessary first to move a head to the proper track. The time required for this operation is called the *seek* time. Thereafter there is a *latency*-time delay until the required part of the track arrives at the head. The access time is the sum of the seek time and the latency time and is typically about 30 ms. The density of tracks on a disk is about 200 tracks/in, and the bit density per track is about 4000 bits/in. The storage capacity of a disk memory which has 20 surfaces is in the range of several hundred million bits.

The Floppy Disk

The magnetic-disk bulk memory has the great merit of enjoying, to some extent at least, the feature of being a random-access memory. In a tape memory, if we are at one end of the tape and need access to the other end, we must rewind the tape. In a disk memory, if we are at the outermost track, we can move the head directly to the innermost without pausing at the intermediate tracks, which may number many hundreds. Hence disk access times are measured in tens of milliseconds, while tape access times extend to minutes. Still, the disk drives we have described are sophisticated mechanical machines which have to be built to tight tolerances and are very expensive. (A 100-megaword unit may well cost the price of two automobiles.) The disks rotate at very high speed and must be rather rigid to maintain the small air gap between disk and head.

To meet the need for a less expensive disk memory there is available from many manufacturers a type of disk memory described as a *flexible-disk* storage system or more colloquially a *floppy-disk* system. In the floppy-disk system the disk and head make mechanical contact just like the tape and head in a tape system. Therefore the disk need not be particularly rigid and as a matter of fact can be thin enough to be slightly flexible. The floppy-disk rotational speed is 300 r/min, compared with 3600 r/min for the rigid disk. The number of tracks is 77, compared with 500 or more. Track density is 48 per inch, compared with 200 per inch. Total storage capacity of the floppy disk is about 30 million bits per surface in comparison with possibly 10 times that number for a rigid disk. Floppy-disk access time is in the range of hundreds of milliseconds, compared with tens of milliseconds for the rigid disk system.

To allow the disks to be handled conveniently and yet to protect them from dust, scratching, etc., they are permanently sealed in a plastic jacket called a *cartridge* so that the whole assembly resembles a phonograph record sealed in a jacket. The dimensions and features of the sealed package are shown in Fig. 6.17-2. There is an opening at the center of the cartridge to expose the hole that fits on the spindle. An elongated slot cut in the cartridge extends over the width

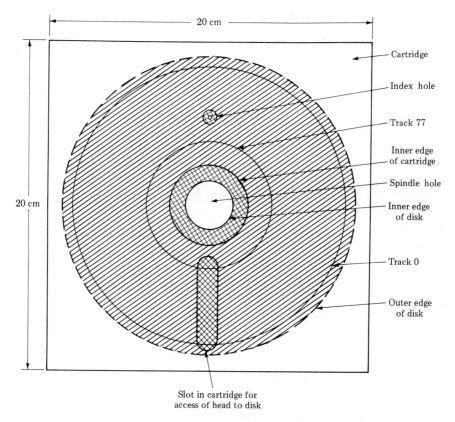

20 cm

20 cm

- Cartridge
- Index hole
- Track 77
- Inner edge of cartridge
- Spindle hole
- Inner edge of disk
- Track 0
- Outer edge of disk

Slot in cartridge for
access of head to disk

Figure 6.17-2 Geometry of a floppy disk in its cartridge. Disk is shaded. Single shading shows disk hidden by cartridge. Double shading shows disk exposed by openings in cartridge.

of the disk to allow access for the single head used with floppy disks. A small index in the disk and in the cartridge allows light to pass through when the disk is in a particular angular position, defined to mark the beginning of the track. The disk rotates in its cartridge. The inside of the cartridge is fabricated of material which minimizes friction between disk and cartridge and helps clean the disk.

6.18 SYMBOLISM

As we have noted, a new symbolism is being introduced to describe the functioning of IC chips. We consider here an example of this symbolism as applied to a memory chip.

The Texas Instrument type TMS 4016 is a 2048-word, 8-bit-per-word RAM. Its functional symbol is shown in Fig. 6.18-1a and further clarified by the table in Fig. 6.18-1b. The numbers in parentheses are pin numbers. In general, data input terminals are marked D and output terminals are marked Q. When a terminal serves as both input and output, it is marked DQ. When input

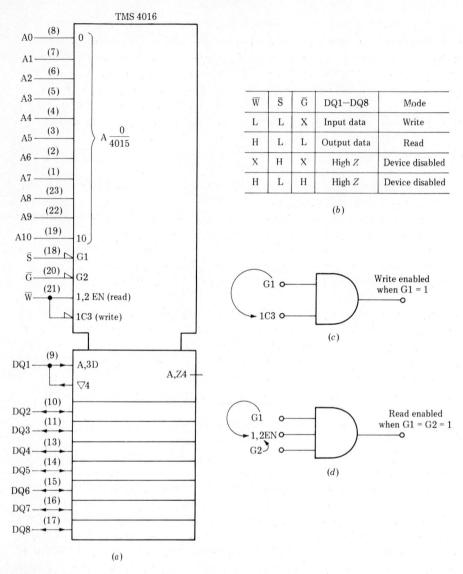

Figure 6.18-1 (a) Symbol for TMS 4016 RAM; (b) truth table; (c) and (d) explanations of AND-dependency symbolism.

and output are separate, the input lines are on the left and the output on the right. When, as in this case, input and output need to be combined, arrows are used to indicate data flow in both directions. The control section is on top, and underneath are eight boxes representing the eight controlled input-output lines. Since identical control is exercised over all eight lines, only one input-output-line box is marked with explanatory labels.

The bracket with the symbol alongside indicates that the 11 pins it encompasses establish the address and that address location numbers go from 0 to 4015. $\overline{S}$ is an active-low *chip-select* terminal, $\overline{G}$ is an active-low output-enable pin, and $\overline{W}$ is the *read-write* input. $\overline{W}$ is an active-low write control and also serves as an active-high read control. The operation of the device is spelled out in the table. When $\overline{W} = \overline{S} = L$, we write input data into the memory. The level of $\overline{G}$ does not matter because $\overline{G}$ affects only the output of data. When $\overline{W} = H$ and $\overline{S} = L$ and $\overline{G} = L$, the device will output data since $\overline{W}$ is at the read level, the chip is selected, and the output is enabled. The chip has a tristate output, when the chip is not selected ($\overline{S} = H$), the output is in its high-impedance (high-Z) state and hence disconnected from the input-output lines. Finally, when the output is disabled ($\overline{G} = H$), even if the chip is selected ($\overline{S} = L$), the device will again be disabled provided $\overline{W}$ is at the read level ($\overline{W} = H$). Now let us see how this same information is furnished by the symbolism in Fig. 6.18-1a.

Keep in mind that mixed logic is used. Thus when $\overline{S} = L$ the signal on pin 18 is active and hence at logic 1. Correspondingly, the internal signal G1 is also at logic 1. Whether this internal signal is high or low we need not inquire (fortunately, since we have no information about the structure internal to the chip). The internal symbols G (which are not related to the external symbol G on pin 20) indicate an AND *dependency*. That is, in effect the internal G signal is combined in an AND gate with other internal signals. The number after the G symbol identifies the other internal signal over which the G signal exerts control. The number which precedes an internal-signal label identifies the internal signals over which control is exerted. Thus the signal G1 exerts an AND control over the signal 1C3 in the manner indicated in Fig. 6.18-1c. If G1 is at logic 0, the AND gate is disabled and the signal 1C3 cannot be effective. As indicated in Fig. 6.18-1d, the 1,2EN control terminal cannot be effective unless both G1 and G2 are at logic 1.

The C in the label 1C3 stands for *control*. Since it is followed by the numeral 3, the signal 1C3, which is controlled by G1, in turn controls the effect on the chip of what happens at the terminal marked A,3D. This is the terminal which (when 1C3 = 1) accepts data (D) and allows their storage in the location specified by the address (A).

When the internal READ signal is active, the device puts out data, the data source being specified by the address (A). As noted, ordinarily an output line should appear at the right. In the present case, because there is a common input-output line, the output line must be transferred. The symbol Z stands for this transfer. Thus A,Z4 means that we take the data at address A and transfer them to the terminal marked 4. The triangle at this terminal indicates that the output is tristate.

We note a difference in the treatment of input and output labels quite independent of the need to transfer the output from right to left. The internal input line labeled A,3D identifies the source of its control. The output line does not. The reason for the distinction is that the data written into the device change the content of the memory but data read out do not.

SEVEN

SEQUENTIAL CIRCUITS

Logic circuits in which all gate inputs are furnished by external sources, there being no feedback, i.e., no connection from gate outputs back to gate inputs, are *combinational circuits*. In such circuits, the gate outputs are determined by the gate inputs. If, at time $t = t_0$, some of the gate inputs should change, then as a consequence some of the gate outputs may change. But the new gate outputs depend only on the gate inputs after $t = t_0$ and do not depend at all on what the gate inputs were before $t = t_0$. Such combinational circuits have no memory. The *outputs now* depend only on what the *inputs now* are, and the outputs do not depend on the earlier input values. Of course, when inputs change, there is a very brief interval when the outputs do not yet reflect input values before the change. But this brief interval is a result simply of the finite propagation delay through the gates. In principle, at least, gate propagation delays may be negligibly small.

Other circuits, which do involve feedback, exhibit the feature that the outputs depend not only on present inputs but also, to some extent, on the past history of the inputs. That is, the present outputs depend on the *sequence* of logic values at the input leading up to the present and not only on the present input values. Such logic circuits are called *sequential* logic circuits. The simple static latch is an example of a sequential circuit. So also are counters.

7.1 STATES

Each stage through which a sequential circuit advances is called a *state*. In each state the circuit stores a recollection of its past history so that it can know what to do next. One state is distinguished from another by its stored recollection. It would appear that, as time progresses, new items need to be added to the memory store and that, consequently, a limitless sequence of new and different states needs to develop. It turns out generally, however, that not all the past history is relevant, that not all the states through which the system progresses are different from one another, and that the total number of different states is quite limited. An example will serve to illustrate the matter.

Suppose that you are given the job of watching a row of five light bulbs numbered 1 through 5. These lights are normally off. One or another, but only one at a time, flashes on briefly from time to time. You are instructed that if light 1 flashes and then light 2 flashes and so on in the order of the numbering up through light 5, you are to wait briefly and then sound an alarm. You are instructed further that if the order of flashing does not follow the order of numbering, you should ignore the flashing until light 1 flashes. Thus, at the sequence 1, 2, 3, 4, 5 you sound the alarm. If you see a sequence 1, 2, 4, . . . , at the observation of the flashing of light 4 you can ignore whatever happens next because the required order has not been followed. You can continue to ignore the flashing until light 1 flashes again, since this flashing of light 1 may be the beginning of light flashes in the required order.

We can easily judge how many different and distinct states this system has by imagining that at the end of your tour of duty your replacement arrives and you need to tell him what is relevant for him to know. One message you might give him is that no lights have flashed, a second possible message is that light 1 has flashed, a third possible message is that you have seen the sequence 1 and then 2 and so on, up to the possible message that you have seen the sequence 1, 2, 3, 4, 5 and are about to sound the alarm. There is a total of six different messages that you might need to convey. Hence there are six remembrances and six different *states*.

The number of different sequences of flashes you might observe is actually limitless, but not all different sequences are different in a relevant manner. Suppose, for example, that you observed the sequence 3, 2, 4, 5, 1, 2, 5, 3, 1, 4, 2, 1, 2. All that you need to remember about this sequence is that the last two flashes were 1 and 2, and that is all you would have to report to your replacement. Thus, this sequence places the system in the same state as the simple sequence 1, 2 would. Again suppose you saw a sequence 1, 2, 3, 4, 2, 5, 3, 2, 1, 3. Then the system would be left in the same state as if no light had flashed.

We may choose to implement a sequential system with human beings, as in the example above, in which case we depend on human memory, but if we choose to implement a system with logic components, we shall use flip-flops as the memory. If the system has, say, six remembrance states, as in our example, we shall correspondingly need to have six flip-flop states. To have available six flip-flop states we would need three flip-flops. The flip-flops would then provide eight states, ranging from $Q_2Q_1Q_0 = 000$ to $Q_2Q_1Q_0 = 111$. Since we have eight flip-flop states and only six remembrance states, two of the flip-flop states would go unused.

7.2 COUNTERS AS SEQUENTIAL SYSTEMS

We shall assume initially that our sequential systems are synchronous; i.e., all flip-flops are driven by the same clocking waveform. Of course, it is to be understood that, as in all synchronous systems, the flip-flops used must be of the type that circumvents the race problem described in Chap. 4. Thus, for example, master-slave flip-flops would be suitable. Beginning in Sec. 7.11 we shall consider sequential systems which are not synchronous.

Let us return now to the synchronous counter already discussed in Chap. 4. Such counters are clearly sequential systems. To be sure, they are somewhat special in the sense that there is no input logic presented to the counter and the only waveform input is the clock, which serves only to provide synchronism in the operation of the flip-flops.

Let us consider, as an example, a mod-4 synchronous counter. Such a counter has four items to remember. If we wanted to read the count conveniently, we might arrange for the counter circuit to provide two outputs Z_1 and Z_0, which would read $Z_1Z_0 = 00, 01, 10, 11, 00$, etc., as the counter cycles from count to count. Without any reference to any detail of the circuitry of the counter we have described the operation of the counter in the diagram of Fig. 7.2-1. Here we have indicated four boxes representing the four remembrance states. Inside each box we have written out what it is that is to be remembered and have written as well the information concerning what outputs are to be furnished in each state. The arrows indicate the sequence the system is to follow. It is to go from the state with remembrance that the count is 0 to the state with remembrance that the count is 1 and so on. The diagram of Fig. 7.2-1 seems hardly to contribute anything to the discussion. Yet, as we shall see, particularly in more complicated systems, the design is often begun most effectively by the construction of just such a state diagram. When, as in Fig. 7.2-1a, the boxes representing the states bear the detailed description of the state, the diagram is generally referred to as a *flow diagram*.

Once we have pretty well grasped the performance required of a sequential system, we may find it more convenient to represent the system operation as in Fig. 7.2-1b. Here the circles represent the states, and we have arbitrarily labeled the states A, B, C, and D. (There is no particular significance to the fact that we have gone from rectangles to circles to represent states. It is simply standard practice resulting, no doubt, from the fact that, if there is a lot to write, rectangles are more convenient.) The representation of Fig. 7.2-1b is called a *state diagram*.

Since the counter has four states, we shall require two flip-flops, FF1 and FF0. The flip-flop outputs are Q_1 and Q_0, and the four available flip-flop states are $Q_1Q_0 = 00, 01, 10$, and 11. We now have to make an association between the remembrance states A, B, C, and D and the flip-flop states 00, 01, 10, and 11. That is, we have to make what is referred to as a *state assignment*. For example, we are initially at liberty to decide arbitrarily that remembrance state A is to be represented by flip-flop state $Q_1Q_0 = 00$, or by flip-flop state $Q_1Q_0 = 01$, and so on. Having selected a flip-flop state for remembrance state A, we then

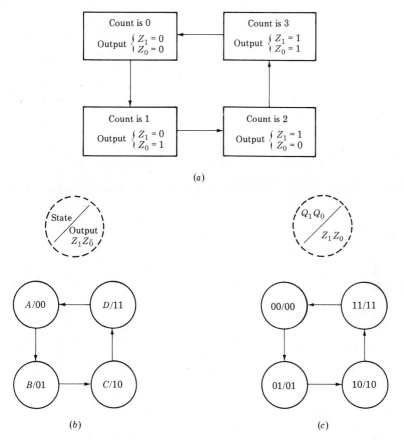

Figure 7.2-1 The state diagram for a mod-4 counter: (*a*) state described in words in a flow diagram, (*b*) state represented by a symbol in a state diagram, (*c*) state symbol replaced by a state assignment.

make a *state assignment* for state B from the three remaining flip-flop states, and so on to states C and D.

Rather generally, different state assignments in a sequential system lead to different logic circuits, some of which are better (simpler or more economical of components). We shall defer discussing the selection of state assignment, however. In the present simple case of the mod-4 synchronous counter it is apparent that an eminently reasonable state assignment is

Remembrance state	Flip-flop state
A	$Q_1 Q_0 = 00$
B	01
C	10
D	11

Present state	Present output $Z_1 Z_0$	Next state
A	00	B
B	01	C
C	10	D
D	11	A

(a)

Present state $Q_1^n Q_0^n$	Present output $Z_1 Z_0$	Next state $Q_1^{n+1} Q_0^{n+1}$
00	00	01
01	01	10
10	10	11
11	11	00

(b)

Figure 7.2-2 State tables giving in tabular form the same information as provided by the diagram of Fig. 7.2-1: (a) state table with symbolic representation of states; (b) transition table, i.e., a state table in which a state assignment has been made.

The advantage of this assignment is that the system outputs Z_1 and Z_0 can then be taken directly from the Q_1 and Q_0 flip-flop terminals. The flip-flop state diagram using this state assignment is given in Fig. 7.2-1c, where it is seen that $Q_1 = Z_1$ and $Q_0 = Z_0$. Hence no decoder will be required to generate the output logic levels Z_1 and Z_0. At each triggering edge of the clocking waveform the sequential system will advance from state to state in the direction indicated by the arrows.

The information in the state diagrams of Fig. 7.2-1b and c can be placed in tabular form, as shown in Fig. 7.2-2a and b. In these tables, as usual, the present state is the state in the nth clock interval; after the next clock triggering edge, in the $(n + 1)$th clock interval, the system in its next state. A state table as in Fig. 7.2-2b in which a state assignment has been made is called a *transition table*.

To proceed further in this design of the counter we must make a selection, again rather arbitrarily, of the type of flip-flop we propose to use, type D, RS, JK, toggle, etc. To be specific, let us assume that we shall use type D flip-flops. Then we find from Fig. 7.2-2b that when $Q_1 Q_0 = 00$, the next state is $Q_1 Q_0 = 01$. That is, Q_1 must remain at $Q_1 = 0$ while Q_0 must go to $Q_0 = 1$. We may be sure that such will indeed be the case if, in the present state, we arrange that the D input for Q_1 be $D_1 = 0$ while $D_0 = 1$. In a similar manner we can determine from Fig. 7.2-2b the present-state D values required in all present states. This information has been entered in the K maps of Fig. 7.2-3, from which we find that

$$D_1 = Q_1 \bar{Q}_0 + \bar{Q}_1 Q_0 \qquad (7.2\text{-}1a)$$

$$D_0 = \bar{Q}_0 \qquad (7.2\text{-}1b)$$

These equations are called the *excitation equations* for the flip-flops. They tell what the inputs, i.e., excitations, of the flip-flops must be to assure that the flip-flops *respond* as required at the triggering edge of the clock.

We can now use the excitation equations to draw the complete circuit of the mod-4 counter. The circuit is given in Fig. 7.2-4. We have redrawn the circuit in Fig. 7.2-5, where we have divided the circuit into two parts. One part

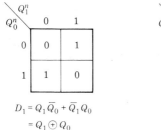

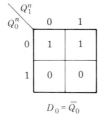

$$D_1 = Q_1\bar{Q}_0 + \bar{Q}_1 Q_0$$
$$= Q_1 \oplus Q_0$$

$$D_0 = \bar{Q}_0$$

Figure 7.2-3 K maps used to determine the excitation equation for the mod-4 counter using type D flip-flops.

consists of the flip-flops by themselves and is called *memory*, while the second part consists of gates and is called *logic*. The inverter in the logic box and the two inversion circles at the inputs to the AND gates are not essential. We could have avoided both inverter and inversion circles if we had chosen to use the $\bar{Q}_1$ output of FF1, as we did in Fig. 7.2-4. We have chosen not to do so in order to reduce the number of lines associated with the memory to the essential minimum.

In terms of the architecture of Fig. 7.2-5 we can describe the sequential operation of the system in the following terms. The relevant past history of the system, and the repository of the information which directs the next step of the system, is the memory, and the information in the memory is made available at the flip-flop outputs Q_1 and Q_0. These logic levels at Q_1 and Q_0 constitute the *present state* of the system. This present state is presented to *logic*, which generates, on the one hand, the output Z_1 and Z_0 appropriate to this state. (It is useful to keep in mind that the entire purpose of the system is precisely to generate this output.) On the other hand, the logic also generates logic levels which constitute the *next state* of the system. That is, on the basis of the presently available relevant record of past history, i.e., the present state, the logic generates and presents, to the D_1 and D_0 flip-flop inputs, logic levels which update

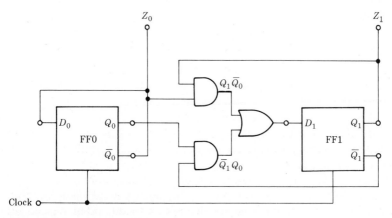

Figure 7.2-4 The logic diagram of the mod-4 counter.

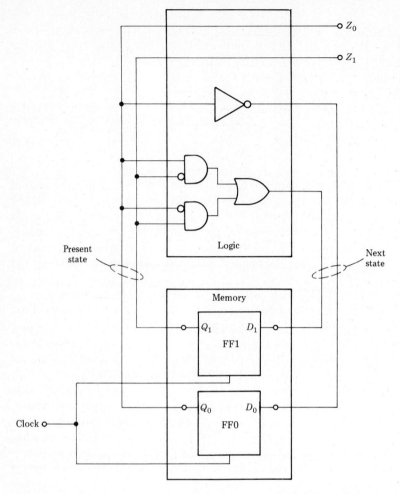

Figure 7.2-5 The logic diagram of Fig. 7.2-4 redrawn to divide it into a logic part and a memory part.

the memory. These input logic levels constitute the *next state*. At the triggering edge of the clock, the next-state inputs become the new present state, and the logic then is also able to generate a new updated next state.

It will be appreciated that our present discussion of the mod-4 synchronous counter is hardly intended simply for the purpose of arriving at a design for such a counter. We have already considered the design of such counters and even more complicated counters in Chap. 4. Instead our purpose is to establish a systemization for the design of sequential circuits, and our counter has served as an easy example which allowed us to be specific and to avoid vague generalizations. In any event, on the basis of our discussion to this point we can set down a procedure for design.

Step 1 We must think through the sequence of operations through which the system must progress. In this thinking-out process we must keep in mind what outputs we need the system to generate at each step in the sequence. We must also be perceptive enough to be able to distinguish between past history which is relevant and must be remembered and past history which is not relevant. In carrying out this process a *flow diagram* like that in Fig. 7.2-1*a* is an invaluable aid and often absolutely essential. In the mod-4 counter this thinking-through process was rather trivial, but in systems of some complexity the process may be the most difficult. Having decided what and how many states are required, we can then replace a flow diagram, as in Fig. 7.2-1*a*, by a simpler *remembrance-state diagram*, as in Fig. 7.2-1*b*.

Step 2 From the number of states we can determine the required number of flip-flops. A number n of flip-flops will be required if the number of states is in the range $2^{n-1} + 1$ to 2^n. A *state assignment* must be made associating each state of the state diagram with a flip-flop state. For the present we shall assume that any state assignment is as good as any other. If there are more flip-flop states than remembrance states, we shall simply not use some of the flip-flop states.

Step 3 Having made a state assignment, we can construct a transition table, as in Fig. 7.2-2*b*. Next we must decide what type of flip-flop we propose to use (type D, JK, etc.). Again we assume here that the choice is rather arbitrary and may well be determined by availability. Having selected a flip-flop type, we can now develop flip-flop data-input terminal-excitation logic equations from the state table. Flip-flops with two data terminals, like JK or RS flip-flops, will have twice as many excitation equations as the single-data-terminal flip-flops like the type D and the toggle flip-flops. However, rather generally, where the equations are more numerous, they will also be simpler. In any event, when the flip-flop excitation equations and the output-logic equations have been written, the circuit can be drawn.

7.3 AN UP-DOWN MOD-4 COUNTER

As an example of a slightly more complicated sequential circuit let us consider an up-down mod-4 synchronous counter. Like the up-down counter described in Sec. 4.25, this counter has an input-mode control terminal M. When the logic level applied to M is $M = 1$, the counter counts in the forward direction 0, 1, 2, 3, 1, 2, ... When $M = 0$, the counter counts in the reverse direction, 0, 3, 2, 1, 0, 3, ...

The flowchart for the up-down counter is shown in Fig. 7.3-1. As before, there are four rectangular boxes which describe the remembrance states and corresponding required outputs. There are also *decision diamonds*, which describe how the system responds to the logic level of the *input control M*. For example, if the system is in the state where the count is 1 and if $M = 1$, then at

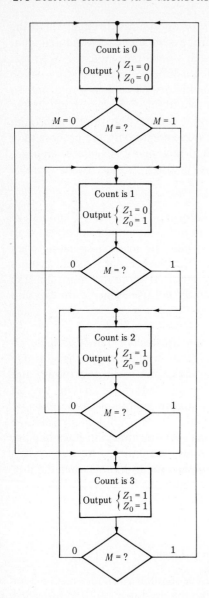

Figure 7.3-1 Flow diagram for a mod-4 up-down counter.

the next triggering clock edge the system goes to the count 2. If, however, $M = 0$, then, as indicated, the system goes to the state in which the count is zero. It is to be kept in mind that the system will spend the time of one clock cycle in each state and hence in each rectangular box. The system spends no time in the diamonds. The diamonds serve only to specify the direction the system takes.

The state diagram corresponding to the flowchart of Fig. 7.3-1 is shown in Fig. 7.3-2a. Again we have arbitrarily given the states the names A, B, C, and

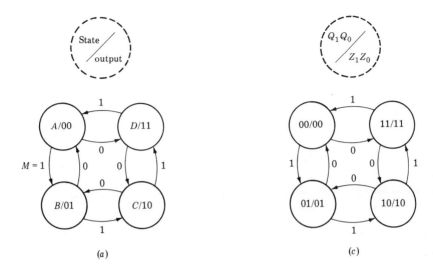

Present state	Present output $Z_1 Z_0$	Next state	
		$M = 0$	$M = 1$
A	00	D	B
B	01	A	C
C	10	B	D
D	11	C	A

(b)

Present state $Q_1^n Q_0^n$	Present output $Z_1 Z_0$	Next state $Q_1^{n+1} Q_0^{n+1}$	
		$M = 0$	$M = 1$
00	00	11	01
01	01	00	10
10	10	01	11
11	11	10	00

(d)

Figure 7.3-2 State diagrams and tables corresponding to the flow diagram of Fig. 7.3-1: (*a*), (*b*) states represented by symbols; (*c*), (*d*) state symbols replaced by state assignments.

D. In a state diagram we do not use decision diamonds, and a simpler expedient makes clear how the sequence from state to state is affected by the control input *M*. For example, the arrows and the labeling of the arrows make clear that when the system is in state *A* and $M = 1$, then at the next clock triggering edge the system will go forward to state *B*. On the other hand, if $M = 0$, the system will go backward to state *D*. The very same information which appears in the state diagram in Fig. 7.3-2*a* is repeated in tabular form in Fig. 7.3-2*b*. Note that now there are two next state columns, one for $M = 0$ and one for $M = 1$. Again we use the state assignment we used in the case of the unidirectional counter. This state assignment leads to the state diagram in Fig. 7.3-2*c* and the state table in Fig. 7.3-2*d*. This final state table in Fig. 7.3-2*d*, which includes the state assignment, allows us to deduce excitation equations for the flip-flops (again two in number), at least as soon as we have decided what type of flip-flop we propose to use. Let us again agree to use the type *D* flip-flop.

In the present case, the next state of the system depends not only on the

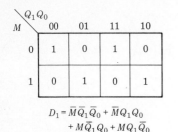
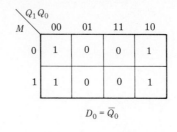

$$D_1 = \bar{M}\bar{Q}_1\bar{Q}_0 + \bar{M}Q_1Q_0$$
$$+ M\bar{Q}_1Q_0 + MQ_1\bar{Q}_0$$

$$D_0 = \bar{Q}_0$$

Figure 7.3-3 K maps used to determine the excitation equations for the mod-4 up-down counter.

present state, which is specified by the two variables Q_1 and Q_0, but also on the control input M. Hence the next state is determined by three variables Q_1, Q_0, and M. Correspondingly the two-variable K maps of Fig. 7.2-3 need to be replaced by the three-variable maps of Fig. 7.3-3. Let us see how a typical entry comes about. We note from the table of Fig. 7.3-2d that when the present state is $Q_1^n Q_0^n = 00$ and $M = 0$, the next required state is $Q_1^{n+1} Q_0^{n+1} = 11$. Therefore we require that $D_1 = 1$ and $D_0 = 1$ and hence in the K-map box $MQ_1Q_0 = 000$ for D_1 we enter 1 and also enter 1 in the corresponding box for D_0. The other entries are made as a result of similar considerations. (In the table we use the notation Q^n and Q^{n+1} since we explicitly want to distinguish present from next state. In the K maps the Q's represent the logic levels, at any time, at the flip-flop outputs. Hence in the K maps we use the symbols Q_1 and Q_0.)

We read from the K maps that

$$D_0 = \bar{Q}_0 \qquad (7.3\text{-}1a)$$

$$D_1 = \bar{M}\,\bar{Q}_1\bar{Q}_0 + \bar{M}\,Q_1Q_0 + M\bar{Q}_1Q_0 + MQ_1\bar{Q}_0 \qquad (7.3\text{-}1b)$$

and of course, since we arranged it so,

$$Z_0 = Q_0 \qquad (7.3\text{-}2a)$$

$$Z_1 = Q_1 \qquad (7.3\text{-}2b)$$

The circuit diagram is drawn in Fig. 7.3-4. Here again we have arranged the architecture into a logic block and a memory block. Comparing Fig. 7.3-4 with Fig. 7.2-4, we note that the present circuit is a bit more complicated than the earlier circuit, as would be anticipated. The essential point to note, however, is that the present circuit has an external input M which enters into the logic of the system, a feature not present in the earlier case.

7.4 A SEQUENCE DETECTOR

To extend our consideration of synchronous sequential systems further we consider in this section the design of a sequence detector. The architecture of

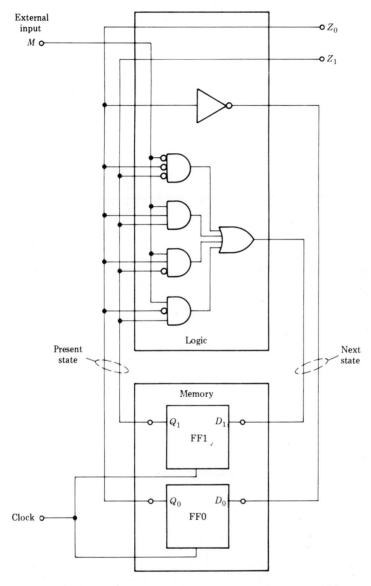

Figure 7.3-4 The logic diagram of the up-down counter drawn to exhibit a memory part and a logic part.

our system is to be as shown in Fig. 7.4-1. As before, the system consists of a logic block and a memory block. We do not know at the outset how many flip-flops will be required, but whatever the number, they are to be driven synchronously, i.e., all by the same clocking waveform. If the flip-flops are of type D, the number of lines n carrying the next state logic levels will be equal to the number of flip-flops. If JK flip-flops are used, logic inputs to the memory will

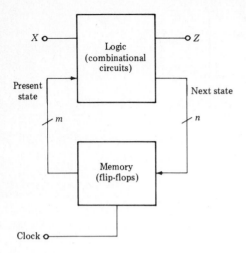

Figure 7.4-1 The architecture of a synchronous sequential system.

have to be provided for the J and for the K input of each flip-flop. In this case the number n will be twice the number of flip-flops. If the present-state outputs from the memory are taken only from the Q outputs, the number m of such lines will be equal to the number of flip-flops. If both Q and $\bar{Q}$ outputs are used, the number of lines may be as many as twice the number of flip-flops.

The system we propose to design has a single input X and a single output Z. Like the input variable M in the preceding section, the input X is to enter into the logic which determines the next state. We postulate at the outset that X is to be a *synchronous* input; i.e., changes in X are to occur synchronously with the clocking waveform. The notion of a synchronous input will be clearer after an examination of the situation represented in Fig. 7.4-2. Here we have drawn a clock waveform, and, assuming that the flip-flops respond to the negative-going edge of the clock, we have numbered the triggering edges. A representative X input waveform is also shown. In the clock interval which terminates at triggering edge 1 we have $X = 0$. Hence, returning to the system of Fig. 7.4-1, if it turns out that the system needs to remember the value of X in that interval, it will remember that $X = 0$ and this bit of information will be stored in the memory, i.e., make some change in the flip-flop state, at the time of clock triggering edge 1. Since, as we have seen, flip-flops have finite *hold* times (see Sec. 4.15), it will be necessary for the value $X = 0$ to persist, as indicated, slightly beyond the clock triggering edge.

In the clock cycle ending at edge 2 we have $X = 1$, and in the cycle ending at edge 3 we have $X = 0$. In the next *two* clock cycles X persists at $X = 1$; hence the input is read not as $X = 1$ but as $X = 11$. Thereafter the input X goes to $X = 0$ for three cycles and is read $X = 000$. Altogether for the time shown the input X is read $X = 010110001$. This reading results because the input is being timed against the clock, i.e., is being read and interpreted on a synchronous basis. If there were no clock against which X were to be timed, we would read X simply as $X = 010101$, taking no account of the time duration of the individual logic levels.

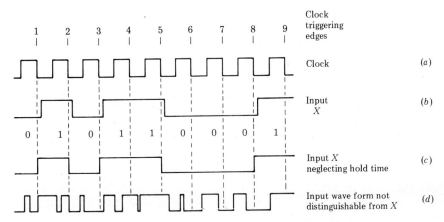

Figure 7.4-2 Waveforms to illustrate the idea of a synchronous input to a clocked sequential system.

Rather generally, when synchronous inputs are drawn on the same time scale as the clock waveform, the hold time is ignored and the input waveform is drawn as in Fig. 7.4-2c. In this case, clock transition and input X transition (if any) appear to occur at precisely the same time, and there might seem to be some ambiguity about the value of X at the clock triggering edge. But, as we have noted, what is intended is that the value of X to be read be the value of X immediately *before* the apparently coincident change.

Finally, let us assume for simplicity that the flip-flops are edge-triggered (see Sec. 4.13), and consider now that the input X appears as in Fig. 7.4-2d. We keep in mind that edge-triggered flip-flops respond only to the data input present immediately preceding the clock triggering edge. In this case, as can be verified, the system of Fig. 7.4-1 will not be able to distinguish the input waveform in Fig. 7.4-1d from the input waveform in Fig. 7.4-1c or b. This feature is again the result of the fact that the system reads the input on a synchronous basis against the standard of the clock.

Having disposed of these preliminaries concerning the meaning of a synchronous input, let us set ourselves a simple problem in the design of a sequential system involving one input and one output, as in Fig. 7.4-1. The problem is to design the system so that Z will be $Z = 1$ when and only when X has been $X = 1$ for *three or more* consecutive clock intervals. To make sure that there is no ambiguity in the specification of the problem we indicate in Fig. 7.4-3 a possible sequence of input bits and the resultant output. We shall assume, as we have been assuming all along, that the output logic level Z depends only on the state of the machine; i.e., the output is connected (through gates possibly) only to the outputs of the flip-flops. There is no direct connection between X and Z. Hence when the system is in a fixed state (as it is for an entire clock cycle), changes in X will not affect the output Z in any way. Of course, the value of X in one clock cycle may affect the state in the next cycle, and then Z may be affected by the change of state.

Clock cycle	1	2	3	4	5	6	7	8	9	10	11	12	13	14
$X =$	0	1	1	0	1	1	1	0	1	1	1	1	1	
$Z =$	?	0	0	0	0	0	0	1	0	0	0	1	1	1

Figure 7.4-3 A typical input sequence of value of X and the corresponding required output Z for the sequential system under design.

Referring now to Fig. 7.4-3, we consider that the clock cycle which we have labeled 1 is the first cycle available to our examination. (The machine may have been running for some time before we get to watch it.) In this first interval we are not able to indicate what is Z because the value of Z depends on the values of X in the three preceding intervals. In cycle 2, however, we can say that $Z = 0$ because we see that it is not possible for X to have been $X = 1$ in the three cycles preceding cycle 2. If X had been $X = 1$ in cycle 1, we would not have been able to determine Z in cycle 2. Proceeding along the sequence, we find that $Z = 1$ in cycle 8 because $X = 1$ in cycles 5, 6, and 7. Similarly $Z = 1$ in cycle 12 because $X = 1$ in cycles 9, 10, and 11. Also $X = 1$ in cycles 13 and 14 because in both cases X had been 1 for more than three preceding cycles. In cycle 14 $Z = 1$ quite independently of the value of X in that cycle.

Now let us turn to the design of the system. We noted earlier that in the general case, especially where the design is of some complexity, the starting point is a flowchart. In simpler cases, as in the present instance, we can start with the state diagram.

In beginning a state diagram it is necessary to start with a state, call it state A, defined in such manner that as the development of the state diagram unfolds, we shall never have to seek additional information about the sequence leading up to state A. In the present case, therefore, we define state A to be the state in which the system will find itself in a clock cycle if in the immediately preceding cycle X was $X = 0$. In this case, also, in this state A the output is $Z = 0$, as indicated in Fig. 7.4-4. Suppose, on the other hand, we had defined A as a state arrived at, say, in clock cycle k, after X was $X = 1$ in clock cycle $k - 1$. Then we should not know Z in cycle k, nor would we be able to continue to develop the state diagram. We would need to know the value of X in cycles k-2 and k-3.

The state A that we have selected as a starting point is suitable, but it is not the only suitable starting point. It would be acceptable to define state A as a state arrived at after three or more successive cycles in which $X = 1$.

In the cycle in which the system in is state A we shall have $X = 0$ or $X = 1$. If $X = 0$, need the system go to a different state? The answer is no. In state A the system must simply store the information that no immediately preceding cycles have occurred with $X = 1$. If then X should be $X = 0$, again the information which needs to be stored has not changed. Hence if the system is in state A, an $X = 0$ leaves the system in state A. This result is represented in Fig.

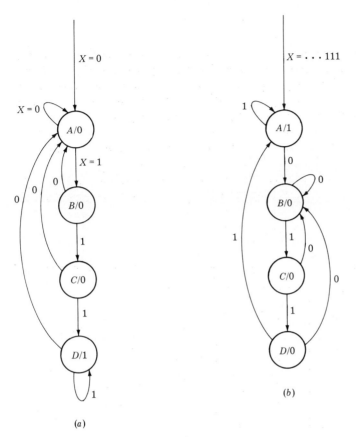

(a)

(b)

Figure 7.4-4 State diagram for the sequence detector. (a) $X = 0$ indicates that A is in the state in which the system will find itself in a clock cycle if X was $X = 0$ in the immediately preceding clock cycle. (b) $X = \ldots 111$ indicates that A is in the state in which the system will find itself if X was $X = 1$ in the immediately preceding three or more clock cycles.

7.4-4 by the arrow marked 0, which originates and also terminates on state A. If, when the system is in A an $X = 1$ should occur, then, of course, it needs to be remembered and so, as indicated, at $X = 1$, the system goes from state A to state B. In state B the output is again $Z = 0$ because only one $X = 1$ has occurred. Continuing, a second $X = 1$ takes the system from B to C, and a third $X = 1$ takes the system to state D, where $Z = 1$. Since the problem specification makes no distinction between three successive 1s and more than three successive 1s, the fourth and further successive 1s simply leave the system in state D. If at state B, C, or D an $X = 0$ should occur, the system need only remember that the sequence of consecutive 1s has been broken, and this is precisely the memory stored in state A.

Whenever, as at present, there is a single input variable X, each state in the state diagram must have two arrows leaving it, since one arrow corresponds to $X = 0$ and the other to $X = 1$. An arrow counts as leaving even if it returns to

Present state	Present output	Next state	
	Z	$X = 0$	$X = 1$
A	0	A	B
B	0	A	C
C	0	A	D
D	1	A	D

(a)

State	$Q_1 Q_0$
A	00
B	01
C	10
D	11

(b)

Present state $Q_1^n Q_0^n$	Present output Z	Next state $Q_1^{n+1} Q_0^{n+1}$	
		$X = 0$	$X = 1$
00	0	00	01
01	0	00	10
10	0	00	11
11	1	00	11

(c)

$Q^n \rightarrow Q^{n+1}$	J	K
$0 \rightarrow 0$	0	X
$0 \rightarrow 1$	1	X
$1 \rightarrow 0$	X	1
$1 \rightarrow 1$	X	0

(d)

$J_1 = XQ_0$

$K_1 = \overline{X}$

(e)

$J_0 = X$

$K_0 = \overline{X} + \overline{Q}_1 = \overline{XQ_1}$

$Z = Q_1 Q_0$

(f)

Figure 7.4-5 Completion of design of sequence detector: (a) state table, (b) arbitrary state assignment, (c) state table using state assignment, (d) truth table for JK flip-flops, (e) K maps for J's and K's of flip-flops, and (f) K map for output.

the same state. If there are two input variables, say X_1 and X_2, we have four possibilities $X_1X_2 = 00, 01, 10, 11$ and a state diagram would not be complete until we had indicated four arrows leaving each state.

In Fig. 7.4-4b we have drawn a state diagram starting with a state arrived at after X had been $X = 1$ for three or more successive cycles. It is left as a student exercise to verify that the diagram is valid. There are other valid starting points as well (see Prob. 7.4-1).

The remainder of the design is carried out in Fig. 7.4-5. In Fig. 7.4-5a we have translated the state diagram of Fig. 7.4-4a into a state table. In Fig. 7.4-5b we have made an arbitrary state assignment. In Fig. 7.4-5c the state diagram has been repeated using the state assignment in Fig. 7.4-5b. At this point we have decided, for the sake of variety to use JK flip-flops. In Fig. 7.4-5d we have set down the table (presented earlier; see Table 4.24-4) which specifies what logic levels are required for J and K for any required flip-flop transition. Next, in Fig. 7.4-5e we use K maps to deduce the excitation equations for J_1, K_1, J_0, and K_0, the four data inputs to the two flip-flops. Since the next state depends on the present state (Q_1 and Q_0) and also on the input X, a three-variable map is called for. As an example of how the K-map entries are made, consider say that $Q_1^n Q_0^n = 00$ while $X = 1$; then in the next state we must have $Q_1^{n+1} Q_0^{n+1} = 01$. Thus in Q_1 we need a *transition* $0 \rightarrow 0$, which requires that $J_1 = 0$ and $K_1 = X$, while in Q_0 we need the transition $0 \rightarrow 1$, which requires $J_0 = 1$ and $K_0 = 0$. The output Z depends only on the state Q_1Q_0, and hence Z is read from a two-variable K map. We find altogether that

$$J_1 = XQ_0 \qquad K_1 = \bar{X} \qquad\qquad (7.4\text{-}1a)$$

$$J_0 = X \qquad K_0 = \bar{X} + \bar{Q}_1 = \overline{XQ_1} \qquad\qquad (7.4\text{-}1b)$$

$$Z = Q_1Q_0 \qquad\qquad (7.4\text{-}1c)$$

The circuit is drawn in Fig. 7.4-6, which makes no attempt to display a separation into memory and logic.

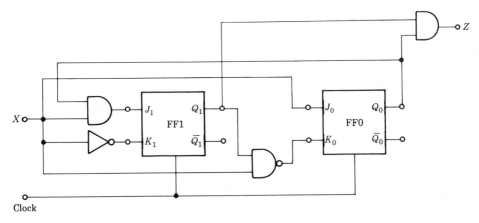

Figure 7.4-6 The logic circuit of the sequence detector.

7.5 MOORE AND MEALY CIRCUITS

In the examples of the previous sections we arranged for the outputs to be functions only of the state of the system. With such an arrangement, the value of an
input in clock cycle k cannot affect the output until, at the earliest, cycle $k + 1$.
Changes in input must first have an influence on the system state before they
can affect the output. It would then seem that some economies might be effected if we arranged for the outputs to be direct functions not only of the state
but also of the inputs. A circuit in which the outputs are functions of the state
only is called a *Moore circuit*. A circuit in which the outputs are functions of
both the state and the inputs is called a *Mealy circuit*. In Sec. 7.4 we designed
the sequence detector as a Moore circuit. In this section we shall repeat the
design as a Mealy circuit. The problem can now be restated in the following
manner: design a circuit that in clock interval k provides an output $Z = 1$ whenever, taking into account the value of X in interval k, there has been a sequence
of three or more successive values $X = 1$.

   The state diagram for the Mealy circuit is given in Fig. 7.5-1, which is to be
compared with the diagram of Fig. 7.4-4. In both cases, state A is a state arrived at after X has been $X = 0$, so that any sequence of input 1s has been interrupted and Z cannot be $Z = 1$ again until a run of at least three successive 1s
occurs. Note that in the Moore system the output Z is entered in the circle
which represents the state. Such an entry can be made because Z depends only
on the state. The symbolism in the Mealy system is different. Here starting in
state A, when $X = 1$, we go (as in the Moore case) to a new state B since, as we
realize, the system must remember that a first step toward a successful
sequence has occurred. The arrow leading from state A to state B has associated with it the notation 1/0. The entry to the left of the slant line stands for

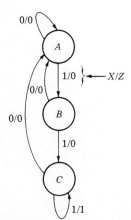

Figure 7.5-1 The state diagram for the sequence detector
designed as a Mealy circuit.

$X = 1$, and the entry to the right of the slant line stands for $Z = 0$. The total symbolism is to be read as follows: "Suppose that, in clock interval k, the system is in state A, and suppose that, in this same interval k, X has the value $X = 1$. Then, again, in this same interval k, we shall have $Z = 0$ and, after the next clock triggering edge, when we are in interval $k + 1$, the system will be in state B." If we ask now about the value of Z when, in interval $k + 1$, the system is in state B, we can have no answer until we specify the value of X in interval $k + 1$. We can, if we please, find the information by looking back at the diagram, where we note that in state B both $X = 0$ and $X = 1$ yield $Z = 0$.

The state C in Fig. 7.5-1 is a state in which it is remembered that there have been two successive 1s. Hence in the interval of that same state an $X = 1$ will be acknowledged as a third 1, and the output will be $Z = 1$. Observe now that the Mealy system has only three states while the Moore system has four states. Of course in both cases we shall require two flip-flops, but in the more general case it is clear that a reduction in the number of states may reduce the required number of flip-flops and the general complexity of the circuit.

The design of the Mealy sequence detector is carried out in Fig. 7.5-2. In Fig. 7.5-2a the information in the state diagram of Fig. 7.5-1 has been transferred to a state table. Note the difference between this table and the Moore table of Fig. 7.4-4a. In Fig. 7.5-2b an arbitrary state assignment has been made. Only three of the four flip-flop states have been used, and we have not used the flip-flop state $Q_1 Q_0 = 11$. In Fig. 7.5-2c we have entered the state assignment of Fig. 7.5-2b into the state table of Fig. 7.5-2a. Having decided again to use JK flip-flops, we have again set down in Fig. 7.5-2d the excitation requirements generally for JK flip-flops. K maps for J_1, K_1, J_0, and K_0 are given in Fig. 7.5-2c. A K map for Z appears in Fig. 7.5-2f, where a three-variable map is required because Z depends on X as well as the state $Q_1 Q_0$. The circuit diagram is drawn in Fig. 7.5-3; this time it is a logic-memory form. Note especially that Z is the output of a gate one of whose inputs is X.

We rather anticipate that a Mealy version of a sequential circuit will be more economical of physical components (hardware) than a Moore version. Such is generally (although not always) the case. In some situations, as in our sequence detector, the difference seems hardly significant. Still we might wonder whether there is any point to designing a system as a Moore circuit. The general opinion is yes. One reason is that the extra states of a Moore system and the independence of outputs from the input make it easier to follow the operation of a system as it steps through its states and hence makes troubleshooting much easier. A second reason is that in a Moore system the input need be read only at a time immediately before the occurrence of a clock triggering edge. Incorrect values of input at other times will not have an effect on the output. These incorrect input values may result either from some speed limitation of the input or from some spurious (noise) disturbance.

In Figs. 7.5-4 and 7.5-5 for the sake of completeness and to introduce some additional symbolism, we have drawn flowcharts for the Moore and for Mealy

Present state	Next state/Present output for Present input	
	$X = 0$	$X = 1$
A	A/0	B/0
B	A/0	C/0
C	A/0	C/1

(a)

State	$Q_1 Q_0$
A	00
B	01
C	10

(b)

PS $Q_1^n Q_0^n$	NS/Z	
	$X = 0$	$X = 1$
00	00/0	01/0
01	00/0	10/0
10	00/0	10/1

(c)

$Q^n \to Q^{n+1}$	J	K
$0 \to 0$	0	X
$0 \to 1$	1	X
$1 \to 0$	X	1
$1 \to 1$	X	0

(d)

X \ $Q_1 Q_0$	00	01	11	10
0	0	0	X	X
1	0	1	X	X

$J_1 = XQ_0$

X \ $Q_1 Q_0$	00	01	11	10
0	X	X	X	1
1	X	X	X	0

$K_1 = \overline{X}$

(e)

X \ $Q_1 Q_0$	00	01	11	10
0	0	X	X	0
1	1	X	X	0

$J_0 = X\overline{Q}_1$

X \ $Q_1 Q_0$	00	01	11	10
0	X	1	X	X
1	X	1	X	X

$K_0 = 1$

X \ $Q_1 Q_0$	00	01	11	10
0	0	0	X	0
1	0	0	X	1

$Z = XQ_1$

(f)

Figure 7.5-2 Completion of the design of a Mealy circuit sequence detector: (a) state table, (b) arbitrary state assignment, (c) state table using state assignment, (d) truth table for JK flip-flops, (e) K maps for J's and K's of flip-flops, and (f) K map for output.

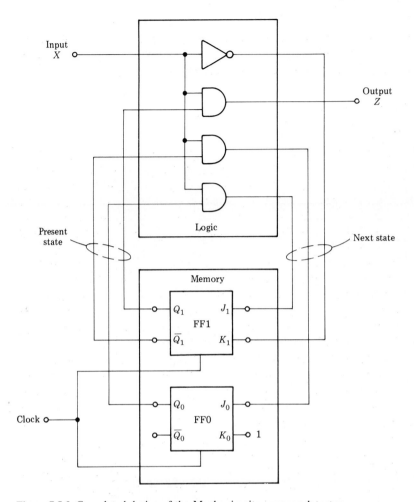

Figure 7.5-3 Completed design of the Mealy circuit sequence detector.

sequence detectors. In the diagram of Fig. 7.5-4 the only new symbols are the circles just above state A and state D. They have no special significance and are used as a matter of convenience when a number of arrows from a number of sources need to be directed to a single termination. In Fig. 7.5-5 the new oval boxes are used to specify outputs in a Mealy system. Thus, for example, we read that if the system is in state C and $X = 1$, then $Z = 1$ and the next state is again C. If $X = 0$, then $Z = 0$ and the next state is A.

Finally, we note again that the architecture of a sequential system is as shown in Fig. 7.5-6. The number of inputs may be zero (a simple counter) or n, the inputs being $X_0, X_1, \ldots, X_{n-1}$. The outputs are m in number, $Z_0, Z_1, \ldots, Z_{m-1}$. There must be at least one output, for if there are no outputs, the system does nothing. The logic box is a combinational circuit. It can be assembled from

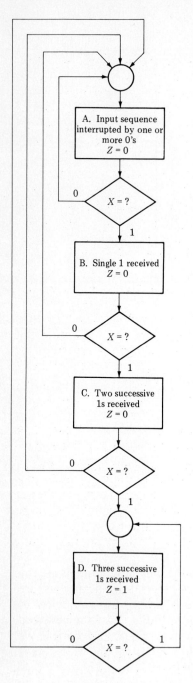

Figure 7.5-4 Flow diagram of the Moore circuit sequence detector.

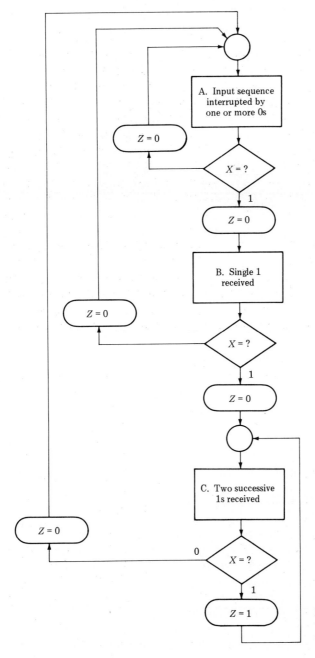

Figure 7.5-5 Flow diagram of the Mealy circuit sequence detector.

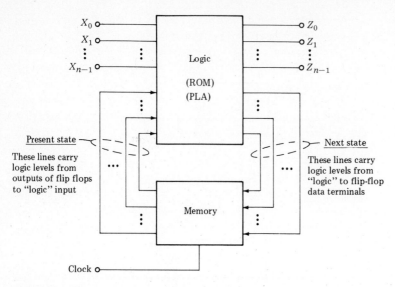

Figure 7.5-6 The architecture of a sequential circuit.

individual gates, or if it turns out to be economically feasible, the logic block may be a ROM or a PLA. The number of flip-flops must be adequate to provide all the required states.

   If there is no input line, the state table for the system will have just a single next-state column. One input will generate two next-state columns, and n inputs will generate 2^n next-state columns. When n is large, a completely detailed state table may be a frightful apparition; 6 inputs will generate 64 next-state columns.

7.6 ELIMINATION OF REDUNDANT STATES

As we have noted, the first step in the design of a sequential system is thinking through the remembrance states required. This process leads to a flowchart; in a simpler case we can bypass the flowchart and go directly to a state diagram. Suppose in thinking the matter through we fail, at one or more points, to recognize that a new state is required. In such a case, the system will simply not perform as required. If we find that the system does not work properly, there is no alternative to starting all over again, thinking the matter through more carefully. On the other hand, suppose that at various points in developing a flowchart or state table we mistakenly imagine that something new to remember has appeared and correspondingly add new states. In the latter case no harm has been done, for, as we shall see, simple procedures are available for eliminating these superfluous states.

   The important thing to keep in mind in dealing with redundant states is that a sequential system is built for the single purpose of providing a determined sequence of logic levels at its output or outputs in response to the applied sequence or sequences at its inputs. Thus, suppose we have two sequential systems. Suppose one has 4 flip-flops which are used to generate 16 states and suppose that, as it goes through its paces, it does indeed occupy, at one time or another, every one of its 16 states. Suppose the other system has only 2 flip-flops and only 4 states. Yet, suppose finally, that both systems provide the same output sequences for the same arbitrary input sequences. Then, so far as we are concerned, the two systems are identical and indistinguishable. To be sure, the 16-state system might have the *potentiality* for providing outputs which the 4-state system could not provide. Yet, again, until such time as we propose to take advantage of that potentiality the systems are indistinguishable. Hence, under such circumstances we would judge 12 of the 16 states of the 16-state system to be redundant. With these considerations in mind, let us now see how redundant states in a state table can be recognized.

Consider the situation represented in the state table of Fig. 7.6-1. Here we contemplate a Mealy system with a single input X and a single output Z. (Our comments will also apply for an arbitrary number of inputs and outputs and to a Moore system as well.) The entire state table has not been specified; instead we call attention to the fact that we find in the table two special states p and q. These states have the special feature that if the present state is p or if it is q, then no matter what the value of X, the output is the same and the next states are also the same. That is, we find two states p and q in the present-state column whose present output Z and next states are identical. Then it is intuitively clear that these states are indistinguishable and one or the other can be dispensed with. For if the present state is p or if it is q, the output is the same. Also if, say $X = 0$, then again in both cases the next state is r and the future of the system thereafter depends on the state r and not whether p or q preceded r.

An example of a state table from which redundant states can be eliminated is shown in Fig. 7.6-2a. Examining the rows of this table systematically, we find that states B and D have identical next-state and output entries. We therefore judge that state D is unnecessary because it is the same as state B,

PS	NS/Z $X = 0$	$X = 1$
⋮	⋮	⋮
p	$r/0$	$s/1$
⋮	⋮	⋮
q	$r/0$	$s/1$
⋮	⋮	⋮

Figure 7.6-1 A state table in which two states, p and q, have the same next states and outputs for all values of X.

PS	NS/Z	
	X = 0	X = 1
A	B/0	C/1
B	C/0	A/1
C	D/1	B/0
D	C/0	A/1
E	D/0	C/1

(a)

PS	NS/Z	
	X = 0	X = 1
A	B/0	C/1
B	C/0	A/1
C	B/1	B/0
E	B/0	C/1

(b)

PS	NS/Z	
	X = 0	X = 1
A	B/0	C/1
B	C/0	A/1
C	B/1	B/0

(c)

Figure 7.6-2 (a) A state table in which states B and D are the same. (b) The reduced state table after state D has been eliminated. (c) The state table reduced further by elimination of state E.

and we eliminate state D and its row. (Of course, we could have eliminated state B if we chose.) In the reduced state table Fig. 7.6-2b the state D has been eliminated wherever it appears and replaced by B. As a result of the fact that we have changed all D's to B's we now note in Fig. 7.6-2b that a new set of states A and E display their equivalence. We eliminate state E, and the new reduced state table appears in Fig. 7.6-2c. No further reductions are possible.

7.7 ELIMINATION OF REDUNDANT STATES BY PARTITIONING

In the previous section we saw that two states in a state table that have identical next states and outputs are actually identical states, so that one state can be eliminated. We shall now see that a state table may have redundant states even when the state table does not exhibit rows with identical next states and outputs.

To illustrate the point and to see how redundant states are discerned in a state table of the latter type we consider the state table in Fig. 7.7-1a. (Ignore, for the moment, the subscripts on the present-state entries.) An examination of the state table reveals no rows with identical next-state and output entries. Keeping in mind that the point of the sequential system is to provide *outputs* as required, we examine the *output entries* in the table. We note that the output entries are the same for all states except F. It is therefore clear that, regardless of whatever else we may determine, state F must be different from all the other states. For all the other states yield an output $Z = 0$ when $X = 0$ while state F yields $Z = 1$ when $X = 0$. To pursue this emphasis on outputs further let us tentatively take the attitude that since all the states except F have the same outputs, these states are really all the same state. On this basis we divide the states into two classes, or partitions, as indicated by the subscripts. All the states except F we put into partition 1 while state F we put into partition 2. This partition into classes is indicated by the subscripts on the states in the present-state (PS) column. Until we find the assumption untenable, we shall assume that all states in the same partition are actually the same state.

In Fig. 7.7-1b we have copied over the table in Fig. 7.7-1a except that we

PS	NS/Z	
	$X = 0$	$X = 1$
A_1	$B/0$	$C/0$
B_1	$D/0$	$E/0$
C_1	$G/0$	$E/0$
D_1	$H/0$	$F/0$
E_1	$G/0$	$A/0$
F_2	$G/1$	$A/0$
G_1	$D/0$	$C/0$
H_1	$H/0$	$A/0$

(a)

PS	NS	
	$X = 0$	$X = 1$
A_1	B_1	C_1
B_1	D_1	E_1
C_1	G_1	E_1
D_1	H_1	F_2
E_1	G_1	A_1
F_2	G_1	A_1
G_1	D_1	C_1
H_1	H_1	A_1

(b)

PS	NS	
	$X = 0$	$X = 1$
A_1	B_1	C_1
B_1	D_3	E_1
C_1	G_1	E_1
D_3	H_1	F_2
E_1	G_1	A_1
F_2	G_1	A_1
G_1	D_3	C_1
H_1	H_1	A_1

(c)

PS	NS	
	$X = 0$	$X = 1$
A_1	B_4	C_1
B_4	D_3	E_1
C_1	G_4	E_1
D_3	H_1	F_2
E_1	G_4	A_1
F_2	G_4	A_1
G_4	D_3	C_1
H_1	H_1	A_1

(d)

PS	NS	
	$X = 0$	$X = 1$
A_5	B_4	C_5
B_4	D_3	E_5
C_5	G_4	E_5
D_3	H_1	F_2
E_5	G_4	A_5
F_2	G_4	A_5
G_4	D_3	C_5
H_1	H_1	A_5

(e)

PS	NS/Z	
	$X = 0$	$X = 1$
a	$b/0$	$a/0$
b	$c/0$	$a/0$
c	$e/0$	$d/0$
d	$b/1$	$a/0$
e	$e/0$	$a/0$

(f)

$a = (A, C, E)$
$b = (B, G)$
$c = D$
$d = F$
$e = H$

(g)

Figure 7.7-1 (a) A state table. In the present-state column the states are partitioned according to output. (b) to (f) Stages in the reduction of the state tables. (g) The remaining states and their relationship to the initial states.

have indicated the class of states not only in the present-state column but in the next-state (NS) columns as well. We have not copied over the outputs because we no longer need them. The outputs as given in Fig. 7.7-1a have served to indicate an initial partition into two classes and, for our immediate purpose, can provide no further information. Now, examining the table in Fig. 7.7-1b we find that state D, initially placed in partition 1, actually cannot be the same state as the other states in partition 1. This can be seen from the fact that when $X = 1$, all other states in partition 1 go to states in the same partition (partition 1) while D goes to a state (F) in a different partition (partition 2). Suppose we start out with the system, on the one hand, in, say, state A and, on the other hand, in state D. Then, as can be verified from the table in Fig. 7.7-1a, if $X = 0$, in both cases we would have $Z = 0$. If, however, the next value of X were again $X = 0$, then in one case we should have $Z = 0$ and in the other case $Z = 1$. By an easy generalization of this observation we come to the following principle: *Two states whose next states in each next-state column are not in the same partitions must be different states.* Applying this principle to the table in Fig. 7.7-1*b*, we find that we can still persist in assuming that states A, B, C, E, G, and H are the same states and hence leave them all in partition 1. However, state D must be removed from that partition. We therefore put state D in partition 3. We have again copied the state table in Fig. 7.7-1*c* and have indicated throughout the table that state D is in partition 3.

Using the principle set forth above, we now find from the table in Fig. 7.7-1*c* that neither state B nor state G can remain in partition 1. Both these states go to states in each next-state column which are in the same partition. Hence while we must remove them from partition 1, we can place them both in the same partition, as indicated in the table in Fig. 7.7-1*d*. From Fig. 7.7-1*d*, in turn we find that states C and E must be removed from partition 1 but can remain in the same partition, i.e., partition 5. Finally in Fig. 7.7-1*e* we note that no further proliferation of partitions is required. All states that are in the same partition (A, C, and E in partition 5 and B and G in partition 4) have next-state entries in each column which are in the same partition.

When the partitioning is complete, all states still in the same partition are the same state. For example if we start with state A or C or E, and if we assume an entirely arbitrary sequence of input X's, then in every case the sequence of outputs will be the same. Hence, as indicated in the figure, since we have five partitions, there are only five states. Using lowercase letters to label these states, we have $a = (A, C, E)$, $b = (B, G)$, $c = D$, $d = F$, and $e = H$.

The final reduced five-state table in Fig. 7.7-1*f* is arrived at in the following manner. We enter state a in the present-state column. Next we look back at the original state table in Fig. 7.7-1*a*. No matter whether we look at the row for state A, C, or E, we find $Z = 0$ for $X = 0$ and $X = 1$; hence we make corresponding entries in the reduced table. If we look again at the row for A, we find that for $X = 0$ the next state is B, which is now included in state b. If we look at the row for C or E, we find that for $X = 0$ the next state is G, which is also included in state b. Hence in the reduced state table the next state for state a and for $X = 0$ is state b. The remainder of the reduced table is completed in the same manner. In this discussion we have made a point of showing that if state a is viewed as A or as C or as E, the result for the reduced table is the same. Actually it is not necessary to show that such is the case. For if A, C, and E are really the same state, the result is, of course, inevitable.

7.8 AN EXAMPLE

In this section we shall design another sequence detector to provide additional insight into the generation of a state diagram from a problem specification

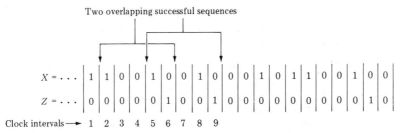

Figure 7.8-1 An input sequence and corresponding output sequence for a detector which looks for the sequence $X = 10010$ (overlapping permitted).

stated in words. Further, the example will give us an opportunity to apply the procedures available for eliminating redundant states.

Our sequence detector is to be a Mealy system and to have a single input X and a single output Z. In any clock interval in which $X = 0$ the output is to be $Z = 1$ provided that in the four preceding intervals the input was $X = 1001$. That is, a successful sequence leading to $Z = 1$ is $X = 10010$. To prevent uncertainty about what is intended, a possible input sequence and corresponding output have been specified in Fig. 7.8-1. The X values in clock intervals 2, 3, 4, 5, and 6 constitute a successful sequence, and consequently in interval 6 we have $Z = 1$. Observe that overlapping of successful sequences is allowed. Thus, the last 2 bits of the first successful sequence constitute the first 2 bits of a second successful sequence which immediately follows the first. Note also that if we had not specified X in clock interval 1, we should not have known whether the $X = 0$ in interval 3 constituted the end of a successful sequence and we should then not have known the value of Z in interval 3.

We shall bypass the flowchart and start with the state diagram. As noted earlier, we must define a first state by specifying enough of the history leading up to that state to avoid having to look back beyond that first state. There are many ways in which the first state can be defined in the present case. We shall take the first state to be the state arrived at after there has been a succession of two (or more) successive 1s. (Other possible first states are left for student consideration; see Prob. 7.8-1.) This first state is the state in which the system finds itself in clock interval 3 in Fig. 7.8-1. (Keep in mind that the state in any clock interval is not influenced by the input in that interval but only by the inputs in previous intervals.) In any event, this first state, state A in Fig. 7.8-2, is a state in which the first bit of a potentially successful sequence has been received and anything which happened earlier (before the two successive 1s) is irrelevant.

This first state A (arrived at after two successive intervals in which $X = 1$ and in which intervals Z will be $Z = 0$) is indicated in Fig. 7.8-2a. If now there should be a third $X = 1$, this third 1 will replace the second 1 as the first bit of a potentially successful sequence. In any event, no progress has been made toward a successful sequence. What the system must remember is the same as

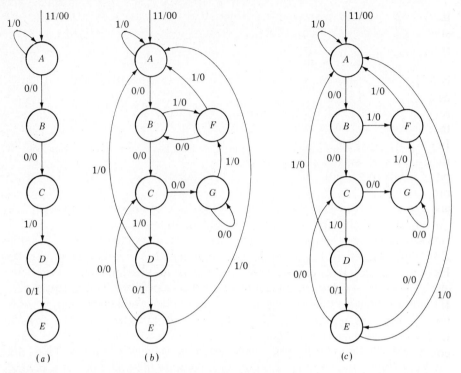

Figure 7.8-2 (*a*) An incomplete state table showing the development of a successful sequence. (*b*) A completed state diagram. (*c*) An alternative state diagram.

before. Hence, as indicated by the arrow that starts and terminates on state A, when $X = 1$, then $Z = 0$ and the "next" state is the state A itself. Now let us assume that the next four input bits are $X = 0010$; that is, a successful sequence appears. Then the occurrence of each new step must be remembered. Accordingly each new input generates a new state, as indicated in Fig. 7.8-2*a*. The last $X = 0$ generates an output $Z = 1$, and at the next clock triggering edge the system goes to state E.

The state diagram is completed in Fig. 7.8-2*b*. (Whether we develop the state diagram correctly or incorrectly, the diagram is not complete until two arrows leave each state.) If, when the system is in state B, we have $X = 1$, the sequence becomes invalid and we cannot go from B to C; so we introduce a new state F. For future reference we note here that F is a state arrived at after the sequence 1101 and hence is a state remembering that the first bit, i.e., the last 1, of a potentially successful sequence has been received. In F, suppose that the next input is $X = 0$. Then the sequence so far is 11010. All we need now to remember about the 11010 sequence is that the last two of its bits are potentially the first two bits of a successful sequence. But this remembrance is precisely the remembrance stored in B. Hence, as indicated, in F, an $X = 0$ yields $Z = 0$, the next state being state B again. If, in F, the next bit is $X = 1$, then the last 2 bits are successive 1s and the system goes to state A because state A has been precisely defined as the state of the system after two successive 1s.

In C, if the next input is $X = 0$, we have three successive 0s, the sequence is invalid, and we cannot go from C to D. We have therefore introduced the new state G. State G is a state which remembers that the sequence has been rendered invalid because there has been a sequence of more than two 0s and that no progress toward a successful sequence will be made until a 1 appears. In G, more 0s do not change what has to be remembered, so that $X = 0$ leaves the system in state G. On the other hand, in G, if $X = 1$, we again have the first bit of a potentially successful sequence. The state F is a state which remembers precisely that the first such bit has been received. Hence an $X = 1$ yields $Z = 0$ and takes the system from G back to F.

In D, an $X = 1$ means that two successive 1s have been received, and this is the recollection stored in A. Hence when $X = 1$, we go from D to A while $Z = 0$. Finally, let us keep in mind that overlapping of sequences is allowed. Hence, when we reach state E, not only have we completed a sequence but we already also have the first 2 bits 1 and 0 of a potentially successful new sequence. If in E we then get $X = 0$, we now have the sequence 100, that is, the first 3 bits toward a successful sequence. But this is precisely the sequence which led to C. Hence, on an $X = 0$ we go from E back to C. The state diagram is now complete.

In thinking through a state diagram, different people may arrive at apparently different but all equally correct diagrams. Of course, when all redundant states are eliminated, all valid diagrams must be identical, except of course, for the possibility that in different diagrams equivalent states have different names. To illustrate that different thinking may lead to apparently different diagrams we have drawn an alternative state diagram in Fig. 7.8-2c. There is only a single difference between the diagrams in Fig. 7.8-2b and c. In Fig. 7.8-2b when $X = 0$, we go from F to B, while in Fig. 7.8-2c when $X = 0$, we go from F to E. This change is allowed because B is a state at which it is remembered that the two immediately preceding bits are first a 1 and then a 0 while E is arrived at after the same immediately preceding history. And, given this history, nothing preceding it is relevant. (Of course, these considerations should make us suspect that B and E are identical states, although such redundancy is not easily apparent in either diagram.) It is now of interest to apply to the diagrams in Fig. 7.8-2b and c the procedures we have developed for eliminating redundant states.

The state table for the state diagram of Fig. 7.8-2b is presented in Fig. 7.8-3a. By inspection we see that state F is the same as state A. In Fig. 7.8-3b state F has been dropped and every state F entry has been replaced by state A. We now note in Fig. 7.8-3b that state E is the same as B; eliminating E, we have the five-state table in Fig. 7.8-3c. No further state reductions are possible by inspection. We can now try partitioning to see whether further reduction is possible. It is readily verified that it is not.

PS	NS/Z	
	X = 0	X = 1
A	B/0	A/0
B	C/0	F/0
C	G/0	D/0
D	E/1	A/0
E	C/0	A/0
~~F~~	~~B/0~~	~~A/0~~
G	G/0	F/0

(a)

PS	NS/Z	
	X = 0	X = 1
A	B/0	A/0
B	C/0	A/0
C	G/0	D/0
D	E/1	A/0
~~E~~	~~C/0~~	~~A/0~~
G	G/0	A/0

(b)

PS	NS/Z	
	X = 0	X = 1
A	B/0	A/0
B	C/0	A/0
C	G/0	D/0
D	B/1	A/0
G	G/0	A/0

(c)

Figure 7.8-3 (*a*) The state table corresponding to the state diagram in Fig. 7.8-2*b*. (*b*) A partially reduced state table. (*c*) The completely reduced state table.

In Fig. 7.8-4*a* we have set down the state table corresponding to the state diagram of Fig. 7.8-2*c*. Here it appears that no state reduction is possible by inspection. We therefore try the method of partitioning. The process is carried out step by step in the tables of Fig. 7.8-4. In Fig. 7.8-4*e* we finally find that no further partitioning is called for. Here too we find that *A* and *F* are still in the same partition as *B* and *E*. Dropping *E* and *F*, we arrive finally at the table in Fig. 7.8-4*f*, which is the same as the table in Fig. 7.8-3*c*.

We thus note that sometimes a state diagram or table will yield to reduction by inspection, and sometimes partitioning will be required. In a rather general case a table may yield some reduction by inspection and may yield further reduction by partitioning. Since inspection is simpler, it is always sensible to try inspection first and then to apply partitioning.

When a state table without redundant states has been generated, the remainder of the design follows the procedure specified earlier (see Fig. 7.5-2). In the present case since there are five states, we shall require three flip-flops. Since the next state depends on the present state (determined by the three flip-flops) and depends as well on the input *X*, the excitation inputs for the flip-flops will depend on four variables. If, as in Fig. 7.5-2, we elect to use *JK* flip-flops, we shall have to generate six K maps for the flip-flop excitations, i.e., one map for each *J* and one map for each *K* of each of the three flip-flops. We shall also have one K map for the output *Z*. Each of these K maps will involve four variables. When the maps have been filled in, we read the logic equations for all the *J*'s and *K*'s and for *Z*. Thereafter the circuit diagram can be drawn directly. Completion of these design procedures is left as a problem (Prob. 7.8-2).

7.9 STATE ASSIGNMENTS

Up to the present point we have been entirely arbitrary in our selection of state assignments. The question naturally arises whether some state assignments are better than others. The answer is yes. If we look again at Figs. 7.4-4 and 7.5-2,

PS	NS/Z	
	$X = 0$	$X = 1$
A	$B/0$	$A/0$
B	$C/0$	$F/0$
C	$G/0$	$D/0$
D	$E/1$	$A/0$
E	$C/0$	$A/0$
F	$E/0$	$A/0$
G	$G/0$	$F/0$

(a)

PS	NS	
	$X = 0$	$X = 1$
A_1	B_1	A_1
B_1	C_1	F_1
C_1	G_1	D_2
D_2	E_1	A_1
E_1	C_1	A_1
F_1	E_1	A_1
G_1	G_1	F_1

(b)

PS	NS	
	$X = 0$	$X = 1$
A_1	B_1	A_1
B_1	C_3	F_1
C_3	G_1	D_2
D_2	E_1	A_1
E_1	C_3	A_1
F_1	E_1	A_1
G_1	G_1	E_1

(c)

PS	NS	
	$X = 0$	$X = 1$
A_1	B_4	A_1
B_4	C_3	F_1
C_3	G_1	D_2
D_2	E_4	A_1
E_4	C_3	A_1
F_1	E_4	A_1
G_1	G_1	F_1

(d)

PS	NS	
	$X = 0$	$X = 1$
A_1	B_4	A_1
B_4	C_3	F_1
C_3	G_5	D_2
D_2	E_4	A_1
E_4	C_3	A_1
F_1	E_4	A_1
G_5	G_5	F_1

(e)

PS	NS/Z	
	$X = 0$	$X = 1$
A	$B/0$	$A/0$
B	$C/0$	$A/0$
C	$G/0$	$D/0$
D	$B/1$	$A/0$
G	$G/0$	$A/0$

(f)

Figure 7.8-4 (*a*) The state table corresponding to the state diagram of Fig. 7.8-2c. (*b*) to (*f*) Stages in the reduction of the state table by partitioning.

it is apparent that the state assignment we select will have a marked effect on where the 1s, 0s, and X's appear in the K maps for the flip-flop excitations and even in the map for Z. We should naturally like the 1s, 0s, and X's to fall into a pattern which yields the simplest possible logic expressions for the flip-flop input excitations. It turns out that there are no easily applicable rules which will yield a selection of the best state assignment. There are, however, a number of rules whose application will lead to a good state assignment—not necessarily the best but better generally than assignments selected at random. Some of these rules as well as verification that they are effective are considered in Probs. 7.9-3 and 7.9-4.

A word is in order about the number of possible different assignments. They are fewer than we might anticipate but also far more than we can contend with. For example, consider that we have four states A, B, C, and D and consequently use two flip-flops with outputs Q_1 and Q_0. One possible state assignment selects $A = Q_1Q_0 = 00$, etc., as in Fig. 7.2-2. But the assignment for A can be selected out of four possibilities, leaving three possibilities for B, two for C, and finally one for D. We might then expect the total number of assignments to be $4 \cdot 3 \cdot 2 \cdot 1 = 24$. However, interchanging the columns of 1s and 0s under Q_1 and Q_0 in effect simply interchanges the names of the flip-flops, so that Q_1

becomes Q_0 and vice versa. Also we can interchange 1s and 0s in either or both columns since such an interchange simply changes the labeling of the outputs of a flip-flop, the Q terminal being now called $\bar{Q}$ and vice versa. It is intuitively clear that such a name change or labeling change can have no effect on the complexity of a physical circuit. It then turns out that in the case of four states there are only three different possible state assignments, and in this case it is feasible to try them all; however, with five, six, seven, eight, and nine states etc., it turns out that the number of different assignments are, respectively, 140, 420, 840, and 10,810,800 etc.

7.10 ALTERNATIVE DESIGNS

In the preceding discussion our interest has been in the economy of a sequential-system design. We have sought to use the minimum number of flip-flops and the minimum possible number of additional logic gates. At present, when hardware is relatively so inexpensive, this philosophy of design is not necessarily the best, and it may even be advantageous to assemble a system on the basis of what appears intuitively natural and reasonable. Such a heuristic design procedure may be especially effective if it allows us to use easily available commercial components and generates a system in which the function of each component part stands out clearly.

As an example of such an intuitive design, based on our experience and sophistication with digital systems, let us return to the problem of the sequence detector introduced in Sec. 7.8. The detector was to respond to the sequence $X = 10010$. It naturally occurs to us that the problem here stems essentially from the fact that the input bits are presented to us one at a time rather than all at once. However, being wise in the ways of shift registers, we also realize that a shift register can be used to capture a time sequence of bits so that all the bits become available at one time. On this basis we are led rather naturally to "design" our sequence detector in the manner shown in Fig. 7.10-1. For now suppose that in a particular clock interval we have $X = 0$ and that in the four preceding clock intervals X has been 1001. Then in the particular clock interval we have $X = 0$, $Q_1 = 1$, $Q_2 = Q_3 = 0$, and $Q_4 = 1$. Then the output Z of the AND gate will be $Z = 1$, as required. To be sure, the system of Fig. 7.10-1 uses four flip-flops which allows 16 states while, as noted earlier, the system most economical of states requires only 5 states. Still when we consider that integrated-circuit chips are inexpensive and provide shift registers of four (and more) stages, the system of Fig. 7.10-1 may well be the design of choice.

As a second example of alternative designs, one based on our formalized procedure and one based on intuition and experience, consider the following sequence-detector problem. We want a detector which will provide an output $Z = 1$ whenever there has been a sequence of four successive 1s. We forbid overlapping and require each group of four clock intervals to be examined separately. A possible sequence X and its corresponding output Z are shown in

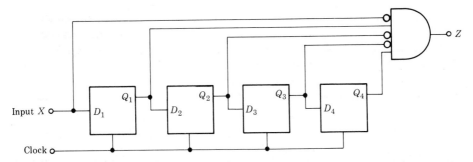

Figure 7.10-1 A heuristic design of the sequence detector that responds to the sequence $X = 10010$.

Fig. 7.10-2a. The state diagram for the sequential circuit is given in Fig. 7.10-2b. It is left as a student exercise to verify that the state diagram is valid and that it has no redundant states. State A is the state in which the system finds itself after it has just completed examination of a group of 4 bits and is the state in which it is prepared to receive the first bit of a new group of 4 bits. Starting in A, a sequence of four 1s takes the system to B, C, D, and back to A. The output $Z = 1$ when $X = 1$ and the system is in state D. If, starting in A, the

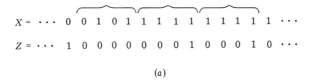

(a)

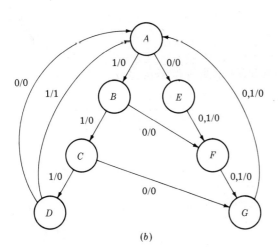

(b)

Figure 7.10-2 A sequence detector that responds to a sequence of four successive 1s with overlapping forbidden: (a) possible input sequence and the corresponding output, (b) state diagram of the detector.

received sequence of the next 4 bits is anything other than 1111, the states E, F, and G together with A simply idly count off the four intervals, leading the system back to A at the end, the level of Z holding at $Z = 0$ throughout. Since the state diagram exhibits seven states, three flip-flops are required. To complete the design it will be necessary to make a state assignment, select a flip-flop type, deduce the flip-flop excitation logic, and draw the circuit. These matters are left as student exercises.

Next let us consider how we might put together the system on the basis of what comes naturally. First, we shall of course use a shift register to make the 4 bits in the sequence available all at the same time, just as we did in the first example of this section. Next we need a means for separating the bits into independent groups of 4. For this purpose a mod-4 counter will be effective, the counter being used to count clock cycles. The circuit is shown in Fig. 7.10-3. Flip-flops FF1, FF2, and FF3 constitute the 3-bit shift register, while flip-flops FF4 and FF5 constitute a synchronous mod-4 counter. We have also made provision for resetting the system through the use of the direct reset R_d terminals of the flip-flops. After the reset switch has been closed briefly and then opened, the system is ready to receive a first bit, which will be accepted as the first of a group of 4. Hence at the opening of the reset switch the clock can be turned on and synchronously the input X applied. Note that the AND gate not only notes the coincidence of four 1s at X, Q_1, Q_2, and Q_3 but also serves as the decoder for the counter. This new design uses five flip-flops, which allow 32

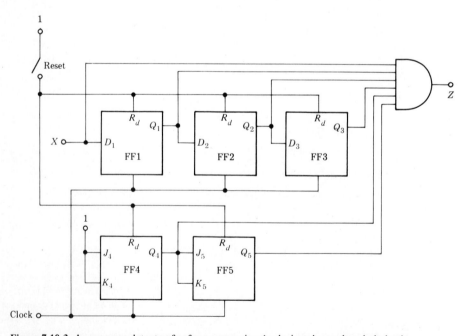

Figure 7.10-3 A sequence detector for four successive 1s designed on a heuristic basis.

states, and is to be compared with the first design, which needed only three flip-flops.

7.11 FUNDAMENTAL MODE SEQUENTIAL CIRCUITS

In Fig. 7.11-1a we present again the logic structure of a sequential circuit. If we please, we can reasonably take the attitude that the purpose of the flip-flop is to provide a *delay* between changes in the logic levels on the next-state line and the subsequent corresponding changes on the present-state lines. Changes on the input lines $X_0, X_1, \ldots, X_{n-1}$, if any, occur nominally at the time of a clock-triggering transition and the next-state lines $Y_p, Y_1, \ldots, Y_{k-1}$ respond immediately. However, the corresponding changes in the present-state lines $y_0, y_1, \ldots, y_{k-1}$ are *delayed* until the occurrence of the next triggering transition of the clock. These considerations suggest that the structure of Fig. 7.11-1b may equally well constitute a sequential circuit. Here the flip-flops have been replaced by elements which introduce a delay. The type of delay contemplated is the delay

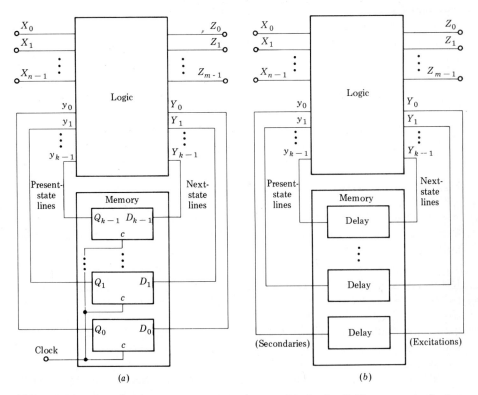

Figure 7.11-1 (*a*) The structure of a synchronous sequential circuit. (*b*) The structure of a fundamental-mode (asynchronous) sequential circuit.

which results when an electric signal is transmitted over a length of wire or through a logical gate or a cascade of gates. The essential difference between the delay provided in Fig. 7.11-1a and in b is that in the latter case the delay is determined entirely by the delay element itself and not by an external agency (the clock waveform). As a matter of practice it generally turns out that the delay elements in the circuitry of Fig. 7.11-1b are not elements deliberately introduced but are the propagation delays of the gates in the logic part of the system.

When the system in Fig. 7.11-1a is resting quiescently in one of its states, the inputs $y_0, y_1, \ldots, y_{k-1}$ may be different from the logic output $Y_0, Y_1, \ldots, Y_{k-1}$. In Fig. 7.11-1$b$ in such a quiescent condition, the logic inputs must be the same as the logic outputs. Still, in response to a change in an input line $X_0, x_1, \ldots, x_{n-1}$, the lines $Y_0, Y_1, \ldots, Y_{k-1}$ will change and at least for the time of the delay the Y's may be different from the y's. Since the Y's and the y's differ from each other only transiently and for an interval which is not externally controllable, there is a reluctance on the part of some to call them *next-state* and *present-state* variables. Instead the Y's are often called the *excitation* variables, and the y's are called *secondary* variables.

The sequential circuit in Fig. 7.11-1a which uses k flip-flops and has k state lines may have as many as 2^k distinct states. Correspondingly we expect that the circuit in Fig. 7.11-1b, which uses delay elements, will also have 2^k states.

As we have noted, sequential circuits which use clocked flip-flops are called *synchronous* systems. In contrast, circuits using delay elements are called *fundamental-mode* systems. Historically, fundamental-mode systems appeared before synchronous systems, but synchronous systems have many advantages: they are easier to design and offer freedom from concern about unpredictable and variable propagation delays. Fundamental-mode systems therefore have somewhat limited application at present.

7.12 AN ANALYSIS EXAMPLE

A simple example of a fundamental-mode circuit is shown in Fig. 7.12-1. We have drawn it in the pattern of Fig. 7.11-1b. It is easily recognized as a static latch, and we have labeled the terminals appropriately. The inputs X_0 and X_1 are the *reset* and *set* inputs, and the single output Z is the flip-flop Q terminal. In this present example there is a single state line Y connected to y, and it happens to be the same as the Z line. The delay in the line which provides *feedback* from logic output to logic input is not explicitly shown. As we have noted, this delay is actually provided by the propagation delays of the gates. Since the state is being determined by the logic level on a single line, we should expect the system to have two states.

The behavior of the circuit of Fig. 7.12-1 is described by the table of Fig. 7.12-2. Here we have provided a box corresponding to each of the eight possible combinations of the three logic input variables S, R, and y. In each box we

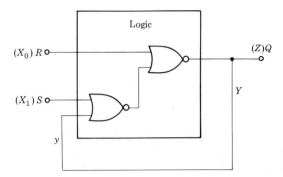

Figure 7.12-1 An example of a fundamental-mode circuit.

have entered the corresponding value of the output $Y (= Z)$. *When R and S are unchanging and the system is resting quiescently in one of its stable states, clearly we must have $Y = y$.* To indicate such stable states, the corresponding Y entry in the table has been encircled. Entries which are not encircled correspond to situations which can persist only transiently and are referred to as unstable states.

We observe, consistent with our expectation, that when $S = R = 0$, there are two stable states, one in which the *state variable* $y = 0$ and one in which $y = 1$. Suppose that we now change to $S = 0, R = 1$. Then, as indicated by the solid arrow, the system remains in the same stable state with $y = 0$. A further change to $S = 1, R = 1$ still leaves the system in state $y = 0$. Next let us change inputs from $S = R = 1$ to $S = 1, R = 0$. In spite of the way the diagram of Fig. 7.12-1 is drawn, consider that there is no propagation delay through the gates and that there is instead a delay element between Y and y. Then, as indicated in this table, with $S = 1, R = 0$, and $y = 0$ we shall have $Y = 1$. This situation will not persist. For after a delay the value $Y = 1$ will appear at y, and we shall have $y = 1$. We find, from the table, that $S = 1, R = 0$ and $y = Y = 1$ is a stable state. Thus altogether when we are in state $y = 0$ with $SR = 11$, a change to $SR = 10$ takes the system transiently through an unstable state, where $y = 0$ and $Y = 1$, and thence to a new stable state in which $y = 1$. This transition from initial stable state through a transient unstable state to a new stable state is indicated by the dashed arrow in Fig. 7.12-2. In a similar way, starting again at $SRy = 000$ if we should change S to $S = 1$, we should again pass through the unstable state at $SRy = 100$ and end up in the stable state at $SRy = 101$.

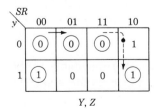

Y, Z

Figure 7.12-2 The transition table for the circuit of Fig. 7.12-1.

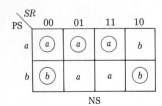

NS   **Figure 7.12-3** The state (flow) table for the circuit of Fig. 7.12-1.

Starting in the stable state at $SRy = 101$ a change to $SR = 00$ would leave up in the state $y = 1$. A change to $SR = 11$ or $SR = 01$ would take us back to the state $y = 0$.

The table of Fig. 7.12-2 is called a *transition* table; in it the states have been identified by the logic levels on the state lines. Somewhat more generally if we simply want to name states without making specific reference to logic levels, the table will appear as in Fig. 7.12-3. The states are here simply identified as states a and b, and this table can reasonably be called a *state* table. We see, of course, a correspondence between the present transition and state tables and the transition and state tables of synchronous systems. There is one restriction which applies in the asynchronous (fundamental-mode) case which does not occur in the synchronous case. In the asynchronous case, in each row there must be at least one NS (next state) entry which is the same as the PS (present state). Otherwise the state contemplated would not be a stable state. Also in the synchronous case, PS and NS refer to the states in one clock period and in the successive period. In the asynchronous case PS and NS refer to the logic levels on the y and Y lines. In the asynchronous case the table of Fig. 7.12-3 is often called a *flow table*.

7.13 A DESIGN EXAMPLE

When we analyzed a circuit in the synchronous case, we went from the circuit to a transition table, to a state table, and then to a state diagram. In the synthesis process, we reversed the order. Starting with a word description of the requirements, we reasoned out a state table and worked back to the circuit. A similar procedure is appropriate in the present asynchronous case, except that generally we can bypass the state diagram and start with the state table.

As a simple design example, we consider a circuit which is to have a single input X and two outputs Z_1 and Z_0. The circuit is to count, mod 4, the number of reversals of logic level on the input X. Thus, starting with $X = 0$ and $Z_1Z_0 = 00$, we require that as X goes through the sequence $X = 0 \rightarrow 1 \rightarrow 0 \rightarrow 1 \rightarrow 0$, etc., the output go through the sequence $Z_1Z_0 = 00 \rightarrow 01 \rightarrow 10 \rightarrow 11 \rightarrow 00$, etc.

We clearly require four stable states and are led rather inevitably to the state diagram of Fig. 7.13-1a. When $X = 0$, we are in a stable state a and the output is $Z_1Z_0 = 00$. When X changes from 0 to 1, we want to go to state b with

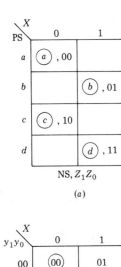

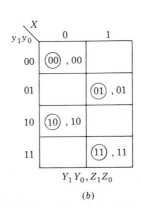

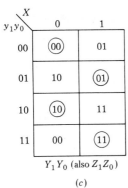

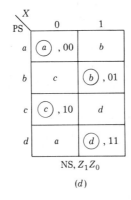

Figure 7-13-1 (*a*) The state diagram of the mod-4 counter. (*b*) A state assignment is made for the stable states of the counter. (*c*) Unstable states are given assignments to direct the circuit to the intended next state. (*d*) The flow table.

$Z_1Z_0 = 01$. From *b* we want to go to *c*, thence to *d*, and finally back to *a*. In Fig. 7.13-1*b* we have made a state assignment in accordance with which stable state *a* has the assignment $Y_1Y_0 = y_1y_0 = 00$, etc. The assignment has been selected to make $Y_1Y_0 = Z_1Z_0$ in every case so that the logic circuitry can be simplified.

Returning now to state *a*, we note that when we change *X* from 0 to 1, we go to a column in which there are *two* stable states. How shall we ensure that we end up in the correct state, that is, *b* and not *d*? A scheme which readily recommends itself is indicated in Fig. 7.13-1*c*. Here in the table location for $y_1y_0 = 00$ and $x = 1$ we have made the entry $Y_1Y_0 = 01$. Hence when the system is in state $y_1y_0 = 00$ (state *a*), a change in *X* from 0 to 1 causes an immediate change in Y_1 and Y_0 to $Y_1Y_0 = 01$. (Remember we assume the delay is in the feedback connections and not in the gates.) A short time later (the delay time) y_1y_0 assumes the same values as Y_1Y_0, and we have $Y_1Y_0 = y_1y_0 = 01$, which is precisely as required to settle the circuit in state *b*. If the entry in location $y_1y_0X = 001$ had been $Y_1Y_0 = 11$, then correspondingly we would have gone from state *a* to state *d*. In general, when we move to a column in which more than one stable state is available, we make appropriate entries in the locations corresponding to unstable states, to direct the system to the proper next stable ·

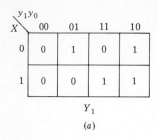

$$Y_1$$

(a)

$$Y_0$$

(b)

Figure 7.13-2 The K maps for Y_0 and Y_1 for the counter.

state. These directions, which are not included in the stable table of Fig. 7.13-1*a*, are included in the table in Fig. 7.13-1*d*.

In Fig. 7.13-1*d* we have not specified Z_1Z_0 in the table in locations with un-stable states. We (tentatively) take the attitude that since these states are very short-lived, the values of Z_1Z_0 are don't-cares.

We can now construct the logic diagram from the information in the table of Fig. 7.13-1*c*. From this table we may make entries in Karnaugh maps for Y_1 and Y_0 as in Fig. 7.13-2*a* and *b*. We read

$$Y_0 = X \tag{7.13-1a}$$

$$Y_1 = \bar{X}\bar{y}_1 y_0 + X y_1 + y_1 \bar{y}_0 \tag{7.13-1b}$$

and the circuit is drawn in Fig. 7.13-3.

7.14 RACES

In anticipating from the table of Fig. 7.13-1*c* that our asynchronous circuit will indeed operate as required, we have tacitly assumed that the delay Δ_0 between

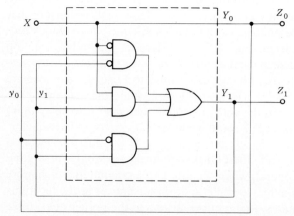

Figure 7.13-3 The circuit diagram of the mod-4 counter.

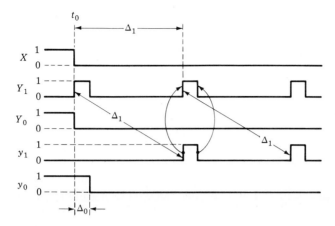

Figure 7.14-1 Waveforms for circuit of 7.13-3 for intended change from state b to c assuming $\Delta_1 > \Delta_0$

y_0 and Y_0 and the delay Δ_1 between y_1 and Y_1 are precisely the same. As a matter of practice it is not possible to make the two delays exactly equal and to maintain this equality indefinitely. We shall now see that the inequality of delays will cause the circuit to operate in a manner other than intended.

Let us assume that our system is in the stable state b ($Y_1Y_0 = y_1y_0 = 01$) and that we change X from 1 to 0, it being our intention that the system should now go to state $c(Y_1Y_0 = y_1y_0 = 10)$. The change in X will cause Y_1Y_0 to change *immediately* to $Y_1Y_0 = 10$. If the delays Δ_0 and Δ_1 are the same, then after a delay $\Delta_0 = \Delta_1$, y_1y_0 will become $y_1y_0 = 10$; but this last change in y_1y_0 will cause no further change in Y_1Y_0, and the system will indeed have been established in state c.

Next let us consider the same transition assuming that $\Delta_1 > \Delta_0$. Waveforms describing the sequence of events are shown in Fig. 7.14-1. The change in X from $X = 1$ to $X = 0$ takes place at $t = t_0$. Before $t = t_0$ the system is in state b with $Y_1Y_0 = y_1y_0 = 01$. At $t = t_0$, when X changes to $X = 0$, as required by the table of Fig. 7.13-1c, there is an immediate change in Y_1Y_0 to $Y_1Y_0 = 10$. After a time Δ_0, y_0 responds to Y_0 and changes to $y_0 = 0$. At this time ($t_1 = t_0 + \Delta_0$) we have $y_1y_0 = 00$. From the table we find that with $X = 0$ and $y_1y_0 = 00$, we must have $Y_1Y_0 = 00$. Hence, beginning at $t = t_1$ we have $Y_1Y_0 = y_1y_0 = 00$; that is, we are in state a and not in state c.

Eventually, after a time Δ_1, the changes in Y_1 will appear at y_1. As indicated by the curved arrows, these changes in y_1 will induce further changes in Y_1, which after a second delay Δ_1 will again appear in y_1, etc. Thus there will be an interval of duration Δ_0 when we shall indeed have $Y_1Y_0 = y_1y_0 = 10$; that is, the system will be in state c. Altogether, then, it appears that the system will oscillate between states a and c. Examining the circuit of Fig. 7.13-3, we observe that the delay Δ_0 is nominally zero. When X changes, y_0 can respond immediately, while the change, if any, in y_1 requires a signal to propagate through two levels of gates. Thus it appears that the waveforms of Fig. 7.14-1, after $t = t_0 + \Delta_0$, correspond to a situation in which the system is in state a $(Y_1Y_0 = y_1y_0 = 00)$ but disturbed at intervals Δ_1 by a very narrow pulse in the waveforms of Y_1 and y_1. This pulse of duration Δ_0 appears at Y_1, goes through the logic and the delay, and reappears at y_1, chasing itself around and around the feedback loop.

Actually the waveforms of Fig. 7.14-1 and the description above of a pulse chasing around the loop are unrealistic. In a real system, as a transition is propagated through gates, it suffers not only propagation delays but also a lengthening of its time of transition; the transition time becomes progressively longer with each propagation through a gate. Hence as our narrow pulse chases around the feedback loop and its rise and fall time become larger and larger in comparison with the duration of the pulse, the pulse will become washed out and disappear. Altogether, then, when we make our change in X from $X = 1$ to $X = 0$, expecting the system to go from b to c, there may be some brief flurry of activity, but the net result is that the system will go instead to a.

The difficulty we have just described results from the fact that the transition we sought to induce requires changes in two next state variables Y_1 and Y_0 and correspondingly two present state variables. Whenever a change is required in more than one such variable, the situation which results is termed a *race*. The changes in the Y's race each other through the delay elements and inevitably arrive at the y's at different times. Races are called *critical* or *noncritical*, depending on whether or not they affect the system operation adversely. The race we examined above was critical. It is left as a student exercise to verify that if we had assumed $\Delta_0 > \Delta_1$, the ensuing race would still be critical. Sometimes races are not critical. For example, suppose we undertake to make a transition to a stable state which is the only stable state in a particular column of the state table. If we move to that column, we must eventually end up in that single stable state. Sometimes races are critical or noncritical depending on the relative delays, and critical races can be eliminated by judicious tailoring of delays.

7.15 ELIMINATION OF CRITICAL RACES

In the design of an asynchronous circuit, when critical races develop, they must be eliminated. Sometimes this correction can be made simply by selecting a new state assignment. Such happens to be the case with our mod-4 counter of Sec. 7.13. A new state assignment, replacing the assignment given in Fig. 7.13-1, is given in Fig. 7.15-1. Here we have arranged that only a *single* state variable changes in every transition called for. Accordingly no races can develop. If we continue to use Y_1 and Y_0 as output terminals Z_1 and Z_0, the counter will count in Gray code. The Karnaugh maps for Y_1 and Y_0 are given in Fig. 7.15-2, and we read

$$Y_1 = \bar{X}y_0 + Xy_1 \tag{7.15-1a}$$

$$Y_0 = \bar{X}y_0 + X\bar{y}_1 \tag{7.15-1b}$$

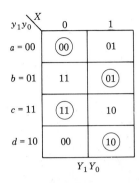

Figure 7.15-1 A transition table for the mod-4 counter in which the state assignment has been selected to avoid races.

More generally no state assignment is possible with which each state transition calls for just a change in a single variable. For such cases there are a number of remedies available, all depending on using more states than are actually called for. We illustrate one method by example.

In Fig. 7.15-3 we show a state table with four states. Ordinarily we would use two state variables. However, it is easily verified that, in this case, no state assignment will eliminate all races. Accordingly we shall use three state variables y_2, y_1, and y_0, thereby adding four redundant states. We now have eight states and with three state variables we can make a state assignment to each state. The original state a and its equivalent redundant state will be called a_1 and a_2. Similarly we have b_1 and b_2, c_1 and c_2, and d_1 and d_2. Of course, the system outputs, not specified in Fig. 7.15-3, are the same in state a_1 and a_2, etc., and the external world will never know whether the system is in state a_1 or in state a_2, etc.

The state assignment we shall now use for our eight states is given in Fig. 7.15-4. If we are in state a_1 we can go to b_1 or c_1 without generating a race, i.e., without changing more than one state variable, but we cannot go to d_1. If then we are in state a_1 and we need to go to a d state, we can go to state d_2, which externally is not distinguishable from d_1. If from d_2 we need to go to a b state, we cannot go to b_1 but can go to b_2. Altogether, as is easily verified, we can make any transition without generating a race. The expanded eight-state table is shown in Fig. 7.15-5. As an example of how we arrive at the entries consider the first row in Fig. 7.15-3. Here we find that if we are in state a and X_1X_0

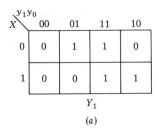

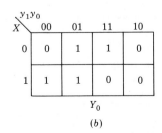

Figure 7.15-2 K maps for Y_1 and Y_0 for the race-free state assignment.

X_1X_0

PS	00	01	11	10
a	ⓐ	ⓐ	c	d
b	a	c	ⓑ	ⓑ
c	d	ⓒ	ⓒ	b
d	ⓓ	c	b	ⓓ

y_2y_1

y_0	00	01	11	10
0	a_1	b_1	c_2	d_2
1	c_1	d_1	a_2	b_2

Figure 7.15-3 A state table for which no assignment of four states will yield a race-free assignment.

Figure 7.15-4 The state assignment for the eight states used to avoid races.

becomes $X_1X_0 = 11$, we should go to state c. In the table of Fig. 7.15-4 we find we can go to c_1 but not c_2. Hence the c_1 entry in column $X_1X_0 = 11$. However, again from Fig. 7.15-4, we find that we cannot go from a_1 to d_1. Hence we go from a_1 to d_2, and correspondingly the entry under $X_1X_0 = 10$ in the table of Fig. 7.15-5 is d_2.

7.16 AN EXAMPLE

In the example of the mod-4 counter discussed above it was of course obvious that four stable states are required and the generation of the state table of Fig.

X_1X_0

	$y_2y_1y_0$	00	01	11	10
a_1	0 0 0	$ⓐ_1$	$ⓐ_1$	c_1	d_2
b_1	0 1 0	a_1	c_2	$ⓑ_1$	$ⓑ_1$
c_1	0 0 1	d_1	$ⓒ_1$	$ⓒ_1$	b_2
d_1	0 1 1	$ⓓ_1$	c_1	b_1	$ⓓ_1$
a_2	1 1 1	$ⓐ_2$	$ⓐ_2$	c_2	d_1
b_2	1 0 1	a_2	c_1	$ⓑ_2$	$ⓑ_2$
c_2	1 1 0	d_2	$ⓒ_2$	$ⓒ_2$	b_1
d_2	1 0 0	$ⓓ_2$	c_2	b_2	$ⓓ_2$

Figure 7.15-5 The four-state table of Fig. 7.15-3 expanded into a race-free eight-state table.

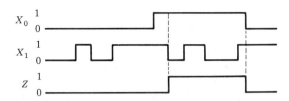

Figure 7.16-1 Waveforms illustrating the specified behavior of a fundamental-mode system.

7.13-1 was equally obvious. In the present section we shall consider a less simple example.

The problem is stated as follows. We require an asynchronous circuit with two inputs X_1 and X_0 and a single output Z. So long as $X_0 = 0$, the output Z is to be $Z = 0$ and is not to respond to changes in X_1. The first change in X_1 which occurs while $X_0 = 1$ is to cause Z to become $Z = 1$. Once Z has gone to $Z = 1$, Z should again be unresponsive to X_1 and Z should return to $Z = 0$ only when X_0 returns to $X_0 = 0$. We shall assume that X_1 and X_0 do not change at the same time and that changes in X_1 and X_0 are separated by an interval adequate to ensure that the system is stable before each change in either input variable. Waveforms for X_1, X_0, and Z in a typical case are shown in Fig. 7.16-1.

In thinking through the design of a synchronous circuit we found it useful to start with a state diagram which was then converted into a state table. In asynchronous circuits it generally turns out to be more convenient to bypass a state diagram and to start instead with a state table. In a state diagram, whether in a synchronous or an asynchronous case, there is a separate row for each state. Hence in reasoning through the operation of the circuit, each time we suspect that we have generated a new state, i.e., we think we have generated something new to be remembered, we must provide a new row. One way to help ensure that no essential states are missed is to provide a new state and a corresponding new row each time we change an input variable except when we are confident that a change returns us to a state already established. Such a procedure leads to a transition table with only one stable state per row, called a *primitive* transition table.

A primitive table for our problem is given in Fig. 7.16-2. As usual, a stable state is encircled. In every case an encircled stable state entered into the table is the same as the present state listed along the left side of the table. We have also entered the output Z for each stable state. Starting in a state a with $X_1X_0 = 00$, a change in X_0 takes us to a state b, the output Z remaining at $Z = 0$. In the box corresponding to PS a and $X_1X_0 = 01$ we have entered the unstable state b to assure that when we go from a in column $X_1X_0 = 00$ to column $X_1X_0 = 01$ we do indeed wind up in b rather than some other stable state which may appear in column $X_1X_0 = 01$. As we did in a previous case, we tentatively leave as a don't-care the output entry in the unstable state. Again, from a a change to $X_1X_0 = 10$ takes us to a stable state c. We have assumed that we shall not change X_1 and X_0 simultaneously. Hence in the row a and in column $X_1X_0 = 1$ we have left both the state and output as don't-cares. From b a fur-

X_1X_0 PS	00	01	11	10
a	ⓐ /0	b/–	–/–	c/–
b	a/–	ⓑ /0	d/–	–/–
c	a/–	–/–	e/–	ⓒ /0
d	–/–	f/–	ⓓ /1	c/–
e	–/–	f/–	ⓔ /0	c/–
f	a/–	ⓕ /1	d/–	–/–

NS/output, Z **Figure 7.16-2** A primitive flow table for a specified system.

ther change to $X_1X_0 = 11$ makes the output go to $Z = 1$, and so we provide an obviously required new state d with output $Z = 1$. On the other hand, starting from c, a change to $X_1X_0 = 1$ does not cause $Z = 1$ because the order of change of X_1 and X_0 is not as required. Hence such a change to $X_1X_0 = 1$ must take us to a state other than d. This new state is e, and the corresponding output is $Z = 0$. If from e we now change X_1 back to $X_1 = 0$, we have a change in X_1 when $X_0 = 1$ and we must go to a state for which again $Z = 1$. This state is f. The rest of the entries in the table are verifiable without difficulty.

7.17 ELIMINATION OF REDUNDANT STATES

We may anticipate that there will be redundant states in the table of Fig. 7.16-2. Unfortunately, the methods given earlier for eliminating such states are not suitable in the present case because of the don't-care entries. In a Karnaugh map where a don't-care is resolved into either a 0 or a 1 we can easily decide how to use the don't-cares to allow the optimal simplification. In a table where a don't-care may be resolved in as many ways as there are states, the matter is more complicated. We now present a new reduction procedure which is effective even when don't-cares are present. We shall develop the procedure by using the table of Fig. 7.16-2 as an illustration.

In Fig. 7.17-1a we have prepared a chart that allows us to compare each state with every *other* state. In the state table, when we compare row a with row b, we find that we are entirely at liberty to adjust the don't-cares so that states a and b can become the same single state. In each column either the entries are the same, or if there is an entry in a column of one row, the same column of the other row has a don't-care. In the chart we have indicated this *compatibility* by entering a check mark. The other check marks in the chart result from the same consideration applied to the appropriate rows.

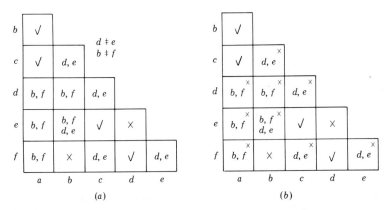

Figure 7.17-1 Implication charts used in a procedure to eliminate redundant states from the table of Fig. 7.16-2. (*a*) Information entered directly from primitive flow table. (*b*) Inequalities in *a* lead to further inequalities.

Next, consider rows b and c. We observe from column $X_1X_0 = 11$ that if we assume that states b and c are to be made equivalent, we would require state d to be equivalent to state e. That is, an assumption that $b = c$ *implies* that $d = e$. In the same way all other pairs of rows are examined to see what equivalents are implied by assumed equivalencies, and the results are entered in the *implication chart* of Fig. 7.17-1. Note that the assumed equivalence $b = e$ implies both that $b = f$ and that $d = e$. Finally we find that $b = f$ is *not* possible for the reason that in column $X_1X_0 = 01$ we find $Z = 0$ in one case and $Z = 1$ in the other. Likewise because of the difference in output $d \neq e$. These two inequalities ($b \neq f$ and $d \neq e$) are entered as crosses in the implication chart of Fig. 7.17-1*a*.

We next redraw the implication chart in Fig. 7.17-1*b*. Since we have the result from Fig. 7.17-1*a* that $d \neq e$ and $b \neq f$, we go through the chart in Fig. 7.17-1*b* putting crosses in the boxes that have entries d, e, or b, f, or both. In the present case we find that all boxes are crossed out except those with checks. (In a more general case, this second pass would generate new inequalities and additional passes would be required. The process is continued until no new inequalities are generated.)

We now find from the uncrossed boxes in Fig. 7.17-1*b* that the following pairs of states are compatible with each other:

$$(a, b), (a, c), (c, e) \text{ and } (d, f)$$

Note that what we have tabulated here is *compatibility* and not equivalence. If a were equivalent to b, $a = b$, and if $a = c$, we would also have $b = c$ which, as appears in Fig. 7.17-1*b*, is not the case. On the basis of these compatibilities we now explore what happens if we resolve don't-cares in such manner that $a = b$, $c = e$ and $d = f$; that is, we merge the compatible states (a, b) into a state α the compatible states (c, e) into a state β and compatible states (d, f) into state γ. These three states α, β, and γ include all the original states. We ignore the com-

X_1X_0 PS	00	01	11	10
α	$(\alpha)/0$	$(\alpha)/0$	$\gamma/-$	$\beta/-$
β	$\alpha/-$	$\gamma/0$	$(\beta)/0$	$(\beta)/0$
γ	$\alpha/-$	$(\gamma)/1$	$(\gamma)/1$	$\beta/-$

NS/output, Z

Figure 7.17-2 The reduced state table.

patible pair (a, c) first because assuming $a = c$ is inconsistent with assuming $a = b$. Also if we had used (a, c), (c, e), and (d, f), state b would not be accounted for.

Now let us construct a reduced state table from the original state table of Fig. 7.16-2. Clearly, when merging rows, whenever a specific entry and a don't-care are encountered in the same column, the specific entry must be listed. Also, in merging rows, when a stable and an unstable state are encountered, the entry must be listed as a stable state. For example in Fig. 7.16-2 consider merging rows a and b to form a row for the state α. Since we have decided that $a = b$, the unstable-state entry a in column $X_1X_0 = 00$ is now actually stable state a. Next consider again rows a and b but this time for column $X_1X_0 = 1$. Merging yields $d/-$. But state d is now one of the states merged into state γ. Hence the entry here is $\gamma/-$. Altogether the reduced state table is as shown in Fig. 7.17-2.

In this reduced state table (and in general) there is a special consideration which must be taken into account and which concerns the output Z. Consider the transition from state α to state β. In both initial and final states $Z = 0$. However, in the transition the system passes through unstable state β, where the output is left as a don't-care. It is therefore possible that in the transition Z may go from $Z = 0$, pass transiently through $Z = 1$, and settle at $Z = 0$. We should generally prefer to avoid the brief and unnecessary transition, and we can do so by replacing the don't-care by the Z logic level in the initial and final states. Hence it is appropriate in Fig. 7.17-2 to replace the $Z = $ don't-care by $Z = 0$ in row α column $X_1X_0 = 10$. When, on the other hand, there is to be a change in Z, we may well leave $Z = $ don't-care in the intermediate state. Whether this don't-

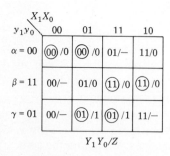

X_1X_0 y_1y_0	00	01	11	10
$\alpha = 00$	$(00)/0$	$(00)/0$	$01/-$	$11/0$
$\beta = 11$	$00/-$	$01/0$	$(11)/0$	$(11)/0$
$\gamma = 01$	$00/-$	$(01)/1$	$(01)/1$	$11/-$

Y_1Y_0/Z

Figure 7.17-3 The transition table corresponding to the state assignment $\alpha = 00$, $\beta = 11$, and $\gamma = 01$.

X_1X_0

y_1y_0	00	01	11	10
00				1
01				1
11			1	1
10	X	X	X	X

Y_1

X_1X_0

y_1y_0	00	01	11	10
00			1	1
01		1	1	1
11		1	1	1
10	X	X	X	X

Y_0

X_1X_0

y_1y_0	00	01	11	10
00			X	
01	X	1	1	X
11	X			
10	X	X	X	X

z

Figure 7.17-4 K maps for the state variables Y_1 and Y_0 and for the output Z.

care turns out to be a 1 or a 0 simply determines whether the change in Z occurs a bit earlier or a bit later.

In Fig. 7.17-3 we have selected a state assignment and constructed a corresponding transition table. We have changed Z in the one place as noted above, and we have avoided races by arranging for only a single variable to be involved in each state change. Karnaugh maps for Y_1, Y_0, and Z are given in Fig. 7.17-4. We read

$$Y_1 = X_1\bar{X}_0 + X_1y_1 \qquad (7.17\text{-}1a)$$

$$Y_0 = X_1 + X_0y_0 \qquad (7.17\text{-}1b)$$

$$Z = \bar{y}_1y_0 \qquad (7.17\text{-}1c)$$

This logic circuit is given in Fig. 7.17-5.

7.18 FURTHER EXAMPLE OF REDUNDANT-STATE ELIMINATION

In the previous section we described a procedure by which redundant states in the table of Fig. 7.16-2 can be eliminated. That example provided no opportu-

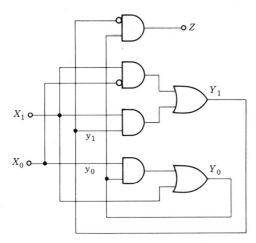

Figure 7.17-5 The circuit diagram.

nity of making all necessary comments in explaining the procedure for redundant states when don't-cares are involved. The matter is of interest because don't-cares may also occur in state tables in synchronous systems. We accordingly consider a second example.

Consider then the 10-state primitive flow table of Fig. 7.18-1a. The implication chart is given in Fig. 7.18-1b. Where there are only tautological implications we make no entry. (For example we find that the assumption that states 2 and 3 are the same implies only that state 2 is the same as 2 and state 3 is the same as 3; hence no entry is made. Similarly we find the assumption that states 8 and 9 are the same implies that 8 and 9 are the same.) Boxes with no entries are marked by checks. When we find states with different outputs in the same column, the corresponding implication chart box, i.e., the box at the intersection of the corresponding column and row, is crossed out. We have the information as noted in Fig. 7.18-1b that $1 \neq 10, 2 \neq 4, 2 \neq 6, 3 \neq 8$, and $3 \neq 9$. Accordingly we go through the chart crossing out all the boxes in which such paired states occur. This crossing-out process generates new inequalities. We need therefore to go through the chart again to cross out, in this second pass, the boxes whose entries include these new inequalities. For convenience, before making this second pass we have reproduced the chart in Fig. 7.18-1c eliminating all entries in crossed-out boxes.

We now look systematically through the chart of Fig. 7.18-1c starting, say, from the lower right-hand corner. The first box we note which still has an entry is the box at the intersection of states 8 and 9, and the entry is 4, 6. We look now to the box corresponding to states 4 and 6 and find that it is crossed out. Hence state 8 is not equivalent to state 9 and new crosses are then generated for the box at the intersection of states 8 and 9 and for all other boxes with entries 4 and 6. Similarly we have brought from Fig. 7.16-1b the information that $5 \neq 7$; so we add crosses as well in the boxes with the entry 5, 7.

If we had constructed a third chart we would find that only the boxes with entries 8, 9 were not crossed out. But we find that the box at the intersection of states 8 and 9 has been crossed out. Hence we cross out also the boxes with entries 8, 9. (We have not drawn a third chart but have crossed out these boxes in Fig. 7.16-1c.) Thus, by way of example, having found initially that $3 \neq 8$ because these states have different outputs for $X_1X_0 = 00$, we then determined that $4 \neq 6$; and because $4 \neq 6$ we find further that $8 \neq 9$.

We can now read from Fig. 7.16-1c which of the states are *not* incompatible with one another. (It turns out here that the only implication-chart boxes which are not crossed out are those which were originally checked. In a more expansive case, more generally, such will not be the case, and some of the boxes with entries will also remain uncrossed.) We find that we have the following pairs of compatible states, including state 6, which is compatible only with itself:

(5, 9)	(2, 10)	(1, 8)
(4, 8)	(2, 3)	(1, 5)
(4, 7)	(3, 10)	(6)

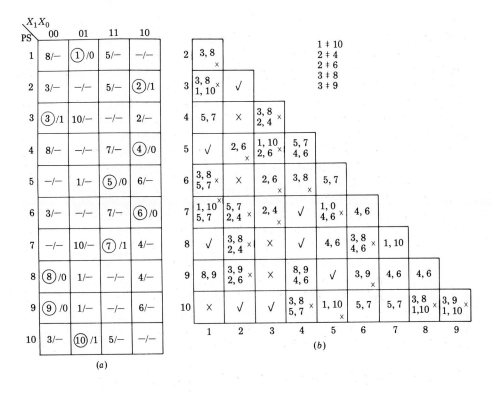

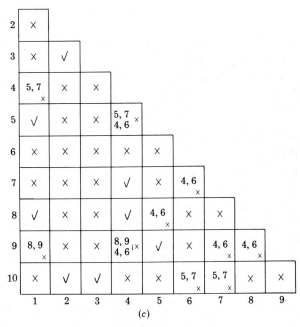

Figure 7.18-1 (*a*) An example of a primitive flow table. (*b*) Partial development of the implication chart. (*c*) Completion of development of the implication chart.

With a view toward reducing the number of states to a minimum we now under-take to form *maximal compatible class*. A compatible class is a group of states *each* of which is compatible with *each* of the others in the group. (Keep in mind that if *a* is compatible with *b* and *b* with *c*, it is not thereby implied that *a* is com-patible with *c*. Hence the formation of a compatible class requires that each prospective member of the class be checked for compatibility against every other member of the class.) A compatible class is *maximal* when it is not possi-ble to find any additional members of the class. We find in the present case the only maximal class which we can form with more than two members is the class (2, 3, 10); so that the maximal classes are

$$(2, 3, 10)$$

$$(5, 9) \qquad (1, 8)$$

$$(4, 8) \qquad (1, 5)$$

$$(4, 7) \qquad (6)$$

We propose now to use some of these compatible classes as states for a reduced state table. We must, of course, select enough classes to ensure that every state in the state table is included. We readily find that the minimum selection we can make which satisfies this requirement is the selection of five states which we label as follows:

$$a = (2, 3, 10)$$

$$b = (5, 9)$$

$$c = (4, 7) \qquad\qquad\qquad (7.18\text{-}1)$$

$$d = (1, 8)$$

$$e = (6)$$

We observe that if we had not combined the classes (2, 10), (2, 3), and (3, 10) into the single maximal compatible, we would have required six states.

Closure

The manner in which we have selected the states of a proposed reduced state table does not yet guarantee that the selection is acceptable. This is one more requirement which must be satisfied, called the *closure* condition.

Suppose, for example, that the present state of our system is $a = (2, 3, 10)$. When we want to know what the next state is for any column, we look to the original state table. We look to see the next state for state 2 or for state 3 or for state 10. The closure condition imposes the obvious requirement, for consis-tency, that in every case the next state in the original table must be in the same state in the reduced table. Thus suppose, referring to the state names in Eq. (7.18-1), we find that present states 2, 3, and 10 go to next states which are ei-

X_1X_0

PS	00	01	11	10
a	(a)/1	(a)/1	b/—	(a)/1
b	(b)/0	d/—	(b)/0	e/—
c	d/—	a/—	(c)/1	(c)/0
d	(d)/0	(d)/0	b/—	c/—
e	a/—	—/—	c/—	(e)/0

Figure 7.18-2 The reduced state table.

ther 5 or 9. Then present state a goes to next state b. But suppose states 2 and 3 go to 5 and 9, respectively, but state 10 goes to state 4. Then we shall be at a loss for a consistent next-state entry in the reduced table. The closure condition will have been violated, and our selection of reduced states is unacceptable.

Our intention in forming maximal classes of compatibles was to be able to include all the original states in a minimum number of reduced states. Because of the closure requirement, this preoccupation with maximizing classes sometimes defeats its purpose. It may turn out that there is an advantage in using compatible classes which are not maximal. An example of such a case is given in Prob. 7.18-1.

In the present case, we can easily verify that our selection of states for the reduced table satisfies the closure condition, and the reduced table is given in Fig. 7.18-2.

In summary, the procedure for eliminating redundant states from a state table which has don't-care entries is as follows:

1. We prepare an implication chart which makes provision for each pair of the states listed in the state diagram. On this chart we enter the implications of assuming that each member of a pair is equivalent to the other member. When states of a pair have different outputs, these states cannot be equivalent and we enter a cross in the corresponding box of the chart.
2. We next go through the chart, box by box, crossing out the boxes with state-pair entries already established as not equivalent; *i. e.*, we remove the inconsistencies. This process is continued, pass after pass through the chart being made until no further inconsistencies remain.
3. We list all remaining compatible states and assemble them into maximal compatible classes.
4. We tentatively adopt as candidates for the reduced state table as few as possible of these maximal compatible classes consistent with the condition that every original state be included at least once and that the closure restriction be satisfied.

5. By trial and error we check to see whether the number of reduced states can be reduced by using less than maximal classes to allow easier satisfaction of the closure restriction.

7.19 HAZARD AND ASYNCHRONOUS CIRCUITS

We have already noted in Sec. 4.6 that unequal propagation delays in gates can give rise to hazards. A hazard is a brief excursion to an unintended logic level. Consider, for example, the logic function defined by the K map of Fig. 7.19-1a. We combine minterms m_2 and m_6 into $B\bar{C}$ and minterms m_5 and m_7 into AC. In Fig. 7.19-1b gate p generates AC and gate q generates $B\bar{C}$. Suppose now that the inputs are $ABC = 111$, corresponding to m_7, and that we change C to $C = 0$ so that ABC becomes $ABC = 110$. This transition is indicated on the K map by an arrow. Initially we shall have p_0, the output of gate p, as $p_0 = 1$, and the output of q will be $q_0 = 0$, so that $Z = 1$. After the change in C we shall have $p_0 = 0$ and $q_0 = 1$, so that Z should remain $Z = 1$. However, if p_0 changes to 0 before q_0 changes to 1, for an interval we shall have $Z = 0$. Such a stituation, in which the output should remain at 1 but becomes 0 transiently, is called a *static hazard* in the 1s. Circuits with static hazards in the 0s are, of course, equally possible. In synchronous circuits, as we have seen, hazards need cause no problem, but in fundamental-mode circuits hazards may cause unintended state-to-state transitions. In such circuits it is therefore necessary to check for hazards (ei-

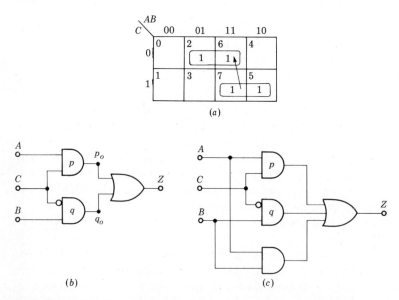

(a)

(b)   (c)

Figure 7.19-1 (*a*) A K map whose physical realization calls for two AND gates. (*b*) The physical realization. (*c*) A third gate is added to remove a hazard.

ther by analysis or by experiment) to determine whether they cause improper operation and if so, to take steps to suppress them.

As can be seen in Fig. 7.19-1a and b, the hazard is generated because the change in C represents a transfer out of the minterm pair $m_5 + m_7$ into the pair $m_2 + m_6$. Correspondingly the output $Z = 1$ depends first on the output p_o being $p_o = 1$ and then on the output q_o being 1. The remedy is to add a *redundant* minterm pair $m_6 + m_7 = AB$ and correspondingly a redundant gate which generates a logic 1 independently of the value of C. Such an added gate is shown in Fig. 7.19-1c, which is now free of the hazard. This scheme of adding a redundant gate can be used quite generally to remove static hazards.

In a second type of a hazard, termed a *dynamic hazard*, a change in an output is indeed intended, say the change $0 \rightarrow 1$. However, the circuit response is $0 \rightarrow 1 \rightarrow 0 \rightarrow 1$. That is, once the change has occurred, there is a brief return to the initial level before a final settling at the new level. Like static hazards, dynamic hazards may cause improper operation in asynchronous circuits. It turns out, fortunately, that if the logic structure of a fundamental-mode circuit is a two-level gate structure that generates sums of products, and if we have arranged to eliminate static hazards in the 1s, the structure will also be free of dynamic hazards.

An additional type of hazard that may be encountered in an asynchronous circuit is called an *essential hazard*. Consider a circuit with at least two feedback paths with state variables y_1 and y_0. It may happen that the generation and the feedback to provide y_1 are relatively so fast that y_1 changes before the circuitry generating y_0 has been able to respond completely to the change in input. Such a circumstance may again cause faulty operation. It is not correctable by adding redundant gates and requires instead adjustments of the delays.

EIGHT

CONTROLLERS

In Chap. 7 we introduced some important and useful ideas concerning sequential logic systems, i.e., systems with memory. To illustrate the design of sequential systems we used the example of the sequence detector. A type of sequential system which has a much wider range of applicability is the *controller*. Controllers are sequential systems providing appropriate logic levels at appropriate times to control a sequence of simple logic operations which, all together, carry out a complicated operation. We consider first how these simple logic operations can be accomplished.

8.1 REGISTER TRANSFERS

The elemental operations, logical or arithmetic, which can be performed on logical words are quite simple. A typical basic operation and the most important consists in simply transferring the contents of one register to a second register. A mechanism for such a transfer is shown in Fig. 8.1-1, where we have two registers, register A and register B. The registers are considered here to consist of an array of a number of static set-reset (RS) latches, as in Fig. 4.2-1. Only one latch of register A, the latch A_i, and one of register B, the latch B_i, is shown. The other latches are represented by the dots which appear on both sides of the latches. Two AND gates are interposed between the latches. These AND gates can be enabled by raising the *control terminal* marked "Move A to B" to logic level 1. At such enabling, S of B_i will assume the value Q of A_i, and R will assume the value $\bar{Q}$ of A_i. Latch B_i will therefore assume the state of A_i. When the "Move A to B" control terminal returns to logic level 0, both R and S will become 0 and the state of A_i will be latched into B_i. In short, putting the con-

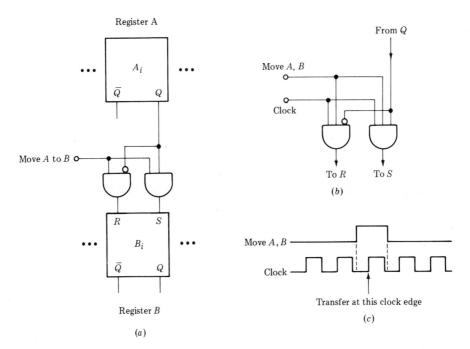

Figure 8.1-1 (*a*) Raising the control terminal "Move *A* to *B*" to logic 1 briefly moves the content of register *A* to register *B*. (*b*) A clock is added for synchronous operation. (*c*) Timing of the move operation.

trol terminal at its active level generates a *command* to which the circuit responds. The control terminal is accordingly often referred to as a *command terminal*. Note that in this process the word stored in register *A* will remain unaltered, but, of course, any word stored in register *B* before the transfer will be lost.

If, by way of example, register *A* and *B* are 16-bit registers, then 16 lines of connection are required as well as 16 pairs of AND gates. The inversion called for on the AND gate preceding the *R* input would be unnecessary if we had chosen to add a second line of connection from the $\bar{Q}$ output of A_i. We have chosen not to do so on the grounds that physically the implementation of an inversion is often simpler than adding a connection.

Most important, we note that to transfer the contents of register *A* to register *B* requires simply that we briefly enable an array of gates by changing the logic level of a control terminal. If we are dealing with a synchronous system (the usual case), we might well want the transfer to take place in synchronism with the clock. Such synchronous transfer can be effected by adding a clock input to the AND gates, as shown in Fig. 8.1-1*b*. Figure 8.1-1*c* shows a clock waveform and an enabling-level change at "Move *A* to *B*" which selects a particular clock cycle during which the transfer takes place.

Suppose that we have many registers and require the facility to effect a

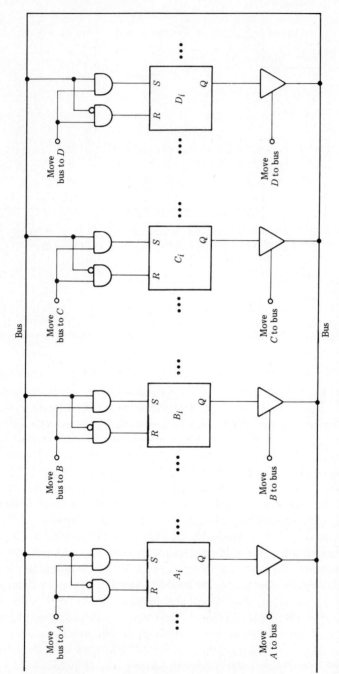

Figure 8.1-2 A number of registers share a common bus. By raising to logic 1 one input and one output control at a time, transfers between registers are accomplished.

transfer from any register to any other register. If we provided individual connections from each register to all others, the number of such connections might well get out of hand. In such a case we might well want to use a multiplexing scheme (see Sec. 3.19) in which a common bus is employed. Such a bus is shown in Fig. 8.1-2 and serves as an interconnection between many registers. Only four registers are indicated, and for each register only one static latch is shown. Correspondingly only one bus wire is shown. If the registers were, say, 16-bit registers, there would be 16 separate wires in the bus. Since all information must be transferred over a single bus, it is possible to make only one transfer at a time. If, for example, we wanted to make a transfer from A to C, we would raise to logic 1 the level at the control terminal "Move A to bus" and the state of register A would be placed on the bus. (In Fig. 8.1-2 we have used the tristate connection to couple the outputs of many registers to a single bus. Alternatively the *open-collector* connection of Sec. 3.19 might be used.) If now we also place at logic level 1 the terminal marked "Move bus to C," the transfer will be accomplished. But again the important point to note is that the transfer operation is achieved by enabling gates, in this case two sets of gates, by making available lines on which the logic level is changed to the enabling level.

8.2 OTHER OPERATIONS

Complementing

A second commonly required simple logic operation consists of complementing a word. Here we have in mind replacing a word in a register with a new word, each bit of the new word being the complement of the corresponding bit of the original word. Figure 8.2-1 shows the word originally in register A; the complement is to appear in register B. This transfer and complementing is accomplished by simply raising to logic 1 the "Complement" and "Move A to B" terminals. If a clock is employed, as indicated, "Complement" and "Move A to B" will have to be at logic 1 when the clock also rises to logic 1 and the transfer will take place synchronously with the clock edge. In Fig. 8.2-1a the register B may consist simply of an array of static latches.

Suppose, on the other hand, that we do not want to use a second register in which the complement is to appear. Rather we want to use only one register and we want the original word to be replaced by its complement. Then we propose to read from the register (to see what bit is in each flip-flop) and, in the same clock cycle, to write into the flip-flop, i.e., write into the flip-flop the complement of the bit just read. For this purpose we require that the flip-flops in the register be one of the special type (master-slave, etc., as discussed in Chap. 4) which allows such simultaneous reading and writing. In Fig. 8.2-1b we use JK flip-flops in the register. When the "Complement" line is at 1, the flip-flop will toggle at the clock triggering transition, thereby replacing each bit by its complement.

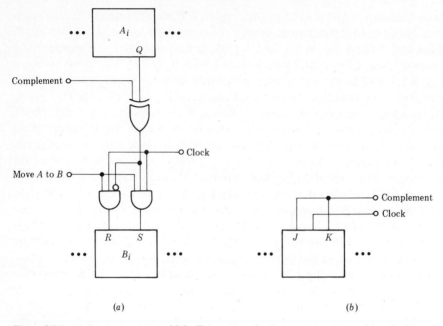

(a) (b)

Figure 8.2-1 (a) An arrangement which allows a transfer from register A to register B of the content of A (Complement = 0) or the bit by bit complement of A (Complement = 1). (b) An arrangement which allows complementing without transfer.

Shifting

Figure 8.2-2 shows an arrangement which allows a transfer from register A to register B. Depending on whether S_0, S_L, or S_R is at logic 1, the shift will be direct or will be accompanied by a shift in one direction or another. Three adjacent flip-flops of register A and three of register B are shown. Register B is here assumed to comprise type D flip-flops. There is a four-gate structure (three AND gates and an OR gate) associated with the D input of each flip-flop of the B register, but only one such structure is shown completely. If S_0 alone is $S_0 = 1$, the content of A_i will be transferred to B_i at the occurrence of the clock triggering edge. If S_L alone is $S_L = 1$, there will be a left shift and transfer. $S_R = 1$ will achieve a right shift and transfer. Of course, in a left shift we shall have to make special provision for the bit which is to be shifted into the rightmost flip-flop since this bit must be furnished by an external source. A similar comment applies to the bit to be shifted into the leftmost flip-flop in a right shift. In any event, and most important, we note again that the operation to be performed is accomplished by holding at logic 1, for one clock cycle, one or another of the control terminals S_0, S_L, or S_R.

Suppose we do not need the facility both to transfer and shift a word but only to shift it, keeping it in the same register. Then we should require nothing more than the shift-right–shift-left register already described in Sec. 4.18.

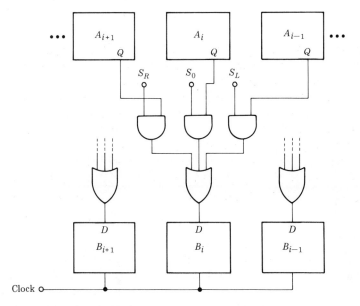

Figure 8.2-2 An arrangement which allows transfer from register A to register B without shifting $(S_R S_0 S_L = 010)$ with left shift $(S_R S_0 S_L = 001)$ or with right shift $S_R S_0 S_L = 100)$.

Incrementing and Decrementing

Often we must store a number in a register and incorporate in the register the facility to change the stored number by $+1$ or by -1. These operations are called *incrementing* and *decrementing*. A register that will respond to the *change-count* command, shown in Fig. 8.2-3, consists of an up-down counter (any type, ripple or synchronous) with the modification that the clock is not applied directly to the counter clock input. Instead an AND gate is added and the clock is passed through this added gate. The other AND-gate input is an enabling input called *increment*. If the change-count terminal is held at logic 1 for the direction of one clock cycle, the counter will increment or decrement its registration by 1, depending on the logic level of the mode control.

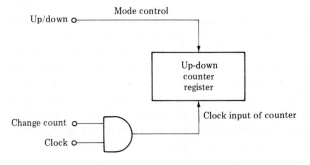

Figure 8.2-3 The counter register will increment or decrement its count depending on the logic level of the mode control if the "Change count" terminal is held at logic 1 for the duration of a clock cycle.

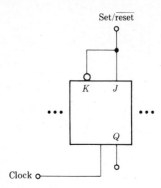

Figure 8.2-4 A JK flip-flop used as part of a register and provided with facility to be cleared or set.

Resetting and Setting

Suppose that we require the facility to clear a register (place Q of each flip-flop at $Q = 0$) or set a register (each $Q = 1$). An individual flip-flop of such a register is shown in Fig. 8.2-4. A JK flip-flop is being employed here. If the Set/$\overline{\text{reset}}$ input is at logic 1, then $J = 1$ and $K = 0$, so that at a clock triggering edge the flip-flop will set. If Set/$\overline{\text{reset}}$ if at logic 0, we shall have $J = 0$ and $K = 1$, so that the flip-flop will reset.

8.3 REGISTER RESPONSIVE TO MULTIPLE COMMANDS

We have seen that we can construct a register that will respond to one *command* or another. The command is conveyed by placing the logic level of some *control terminal* at the level which enables one gate or an array of gates. In a synchronous system which uses a clock the command will generally be carried out at the triggering edge of a clock waveform. Suppose that in some digital system we require the facility to command a number of operations. We may then choose to perform individual operations in separate registers or construct a register which is capable of responding to a number of different commands. The first alternative offers the advantage of flexibility; the second alternative may allow us to save some hardware.

As an example of a register which can respond to a number of commands, let us design a register which is able to respond to five commands. These five commands and the symbol to be associated with each command are listed in Table 8.3-1. Thus our register is to have five control terminals W, R, I, C, and Z. At any time only one of these terminals is to be held at logic 1 while all others are to be at logic 0. If, for example, we have $W = 1$, then at the triggering edge of the clock waveform the word on the bus should be entered into the register. The n flip-flops in the register are FF_0, FF_1, ..., FF_i, ..., FF_{n-1}. One line B_i of the n-line bus is shown, and the logic associated with just one flip-flop FF_i is shown in Fig. 8.3-1. We have here decided arbitrarily that JK flip-flops are to

Table 8.3-1 Commands to which register responds

Command	Symbol
1. Write the word on the bus into the register	W
2. Read the word in the register onto the bus	R
3. Increment the register	I
4. Complement the register	C
5. Clear the register so that all Q's are zero	Z

be used. In order to enter the logic on bus line B_i into FF_i at a clock triggering transition and when $W = 1$ we require that

$$J_i = B_i W \qquad \text{and} \qquad K_i = \bar{B}_i W \qquad (8.3\text{-}1)$$

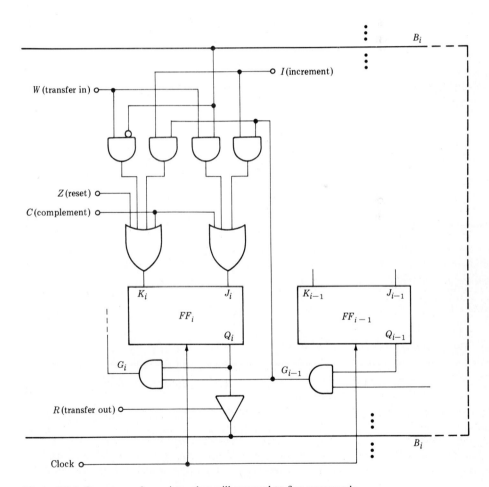

Figure 8.3-1 One stage of a register that will respond to five commands.

(We have used the symbol B_i both to represent the ith bus line and the logic level on the line.) To transfer the bit in FF_i onto the bus, i.e., to read the flip-flop onto the bus when $R = 1$, we require that

$$B_i = Q_i R \qquad (8.3\text{-}2)$$

Note that this transfer will take place as soon as $R = 1$ and the timing of the transfer does not depend on the clock. Of course, if the word so placed on the bus is to be placed in another register, this placement will occur at a clock triggering transition.

To increment the register at $I = 1$ we interconnect flip-flop stages the way we do in a counter. We have arbitrarily chosen to use a synchronous counter. Such a synchronous counter requires that the J and K inputs of each flip-flop be tied together and then connected to the outputs of the preceding flip-flops (see Fig. 4.22-2). We therefore require that for the ith flip-flop

$$J_i = K_i = G_{i-1} I \qquad (8.3\text{-}3)$$

Equation (8.3-3) applies to all flip-flops except the first flip-flop FF_0, which has no preceding stage. In this special case we require

$$J_0 = K_0 = 1 \cdot I \qquad (8.3\text{-}4)$$

To arrange that a flip-flop complement, i.e., toggle, when $C = 1$ we set

$$J_i = K_i = C \qquad (8.3\text{-}5)$$

Finally to make the flip-flop clear when $Z = 1$ but be unaffected by Z when $Z = 0$ we easily verify from the truth table of Fig. 4.11-1 that we require

$$K_i = Z \qquad J_i = 0 \qquad (8.3\text{-}6)$$

Altogether, keeping in mind that only one of the control variables W, R, I, C, and Z is at logic 1 at any time, we have from Eqs. (8.3-1) to (8.3-3), (8.3-5), and (8.3-6) that

$$J_i = B_i W + G_{i-1} I + C \qquad K_i = \bar{B}_i W + G_{i-1} I + C + Z \qquad (8.3\text{-}7)$$

and

$$B_i = Q_i R \qquad (8.3\text{-}8)$$

The first flip-flop FF_0 is special in that the terms $G_{i-1} I$ in Eq. (8.3-7) are replaced simply by the terms $1 \cdot I = I$, as indicated in Eq. (8.3-4).

In Fig. 8.3-1 the gates associated with FF_i called for by Eqs. (8.3-7) and (8.3-8) are shown. Of course a similar structure of gates (not shown) is required for each flip-flop in the register.

A block diagram of the register showing its connections to the bus is shown in Fig. 8.3-2. The five control command lines are indicated, as is the clock input.

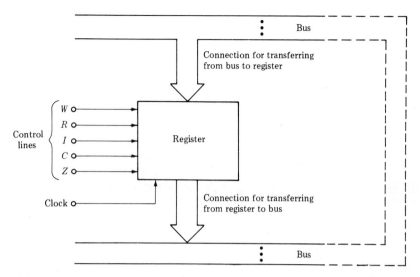

Figure 8.3-2 A functional representation of the register whose single stage is given in Fig. 8.3-1.

8.4 A SIMPLE CONTROLLER

We have seen that it is feasible in a straightforward manner to construct registers and combinational circuits which will allow us to perform simple arithmetical or logical operations on words and to store the result. Once an appropriate piece of hardware has been constructed, the operation is effected by the simple expedient of raising to logic 1 (or, if we please, lowering to logic 0) some control line which then serves to enable a gate or an array of gates. By this act of enabling, a *command* is given to which the piece of hardware then responds. The elemental operations whose hardware implementation we have examined include transferring to and from a bus, incrementing, complementing, and shifting. In a similar way we can build hardware to perform other elemental operations. Suppose, for example that an n-bit register holding the word $R_{n-1}, \ldots, R_i,$ $\ldots, R_0$ accepts an input word $A_{n-1}, \ldots, A_i, \ldots, A_0$ and then changes its registration to $R'_{n-1}, \ldots, R'_1, \ldots, R'_i,$ in which each new bit is $R'_i = R_i A_i$. Such a register performs the AND operation. Registers which respond to commands to perform other logical operations are equally possible. Thus we may have $R'_i = R_i + A$, $R'_i = R_i \oplus A_i$, etc. (see Probs. 8.2-1, 8.2-2).

If we need to perform a number of different arithmetic and logical operations on words, we may choose to construct a register which can be commanded to perform all the required operations. For example, we might design a register which allows transfers to and from a bus, complementing, incrementing, shifting, clearing, logical-ANDing, logical OR-ing, etc., or we might decide to use a number of registers, each individually allowing fewer operations but able between them to perform all the required operations. In the former case fewer register-to-register transfers will be required. In the latter case, the more numerous registers will individually be simpler, and the system may lend itself more easily to modification. (Such registers as we have been describing are called *working* registers, in contrast to *storage registers*, which serve only to store a word.) Alternatively we may decide to use registers for storage rather than for working by using combinational circuits which respond to commands, like the ALU described in Sec. 5.13. In any event, the beginning of the design of a digital system begins with a decision (at least on a tentative basis) of the component pieces of hardware to be used, what commands the components are to be capable of responding to, and how the components are to be interconnected. These features of the system are referred to as the *system architecture*. Once the architecture has been established, we can construct a *controller*, which will provide commands in the right sequence to the control lines of the components, as required, to cause the system to carry out its function.

Except in the very simplest cases, there is no design procedure that leads to the best architecture. Architectures are selected by designers on the basis of experience and simple good sense. Two designers may develop two individual systems of different architecture both of which perform the same function. It may be impossible to judge one design unambiguously superior to the other. One design may have merits in certain directions; the other may have advantages in other areas. The situation is roughly analogous to that which prevails in business (or in other human institutions). Consider, for example, a number of industrial companies which make widgets, all companies doing about the same annual gross business. They all need bookkeeping and accounting systems. The end result in each case must be the same. They must all keep records and make calculations so that they can collect their receivables, pay their payables, pay hourly workers for time worked, etc. But the grouping of functions into departments may well differ from company to company, and within a department the division of labor among the workers may also be different. In comparing two companies, it is most unlikely that there will be a precise one-to-one correspondence between departments or between the jobs of individual employees.

Let us now turn to the simple system whose architecture is given in Fig. 8.4-1. Here we have in mind a system for calculating the value of the arithmetic sum or difference of two n-bit binary numbers. Specifically we want to calculate the sums and difference $\alpha + \beta$, $\alpha - \beta$, $-\alpha + \beta$, and $-\alpha - \beta$ of the numbers in the α and β registers. The mechanism by which these numbers are entered into the α and β registers is not indicated in the figure. Let us assume that these numbers are entered asynchronously through the *direct-set* and *direct-reset* terminals of the individual flip-flops which constitute the register. If a flip-flop is to have a 0 entered into it, its *direct-reset* terminal is brought briefly to logic 1. If a 1 is to be entered, the *direct-set* is brought briefly to logic 1. When a number has been entered in this manner, all *direct* terminals are allowed to return to logic 0, so that the flip-flop can now respond to the clock triggering transition as called

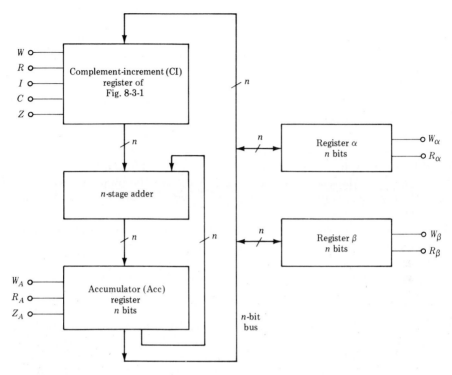

Figure 8.4-1 An architecture for combining arithmetically the content of the registers α and β.

for by the control terminals. The quantity $\pm\alpha\pm\beta$ is finally to wind up in the accumulator register and also in the α or in the β register.

All the registers and the adder accommodate n bits. The complement-increment (CI) register is connected to the adder, the adder is connected to the accumulator, and the accumulator is connected back to the adder, all by n-line connections. Since these n-bit connections are *dedicated*, i.e., each serves a single transfer function, they are not busses. There is also an n-bit bus to and from which we can transfer the contents of register α and register β. This two-way transfer feasibility is indicated by the bidirectional arrow. A common clocking waveform, not shown, is applied to all the registers. When $W_\alpha = 1$, at the clock triggering edge a word is transferred from the bus to register α; that is, a word is "written" into the register. When $R_\alpha = 1$, a word is "read" from the register onto the bus. Similar comments apply to the response of register β to W_β and R_β. When $W_A = 1$, the adder output will be registered in the accumulator, and when $R_A = 1$, the accumulator contents will be placed on the bus. The contents of the accumulator are permanently connected to the n-bit connection which returns to the adder. There is no control over that connection. The accumulator is cleared at the clock triggering transition if $Z_A = 1$.

Let us consider how the system of Fig. 8.4-1 can be directed to find $\alpha + \beta$ and to store the result in register α. A number of elemental operations, called *microoperations*, are needed, each requiring a clock cycle. The sequence is shown in Table 8.4-1.

Note that in this sequence of elemental operations both α and β were passed through CI. There is, of course, no need to do so, and the time of two clock cycles was thereby wasted. Still, on account of the architecture of our system we had no choice. If we had started with a more elaborate architecture which provided direct access to the adder, we would have been able to bypass the CI register. Note that there is no need to clear the CI register.

We shall now design a controller which will make the required logic levels available to sequence our machine through its steps. It is apparent that the controller is to be a sequential machine with six states, since six separate operations have to be performed. However, in the present case we encounter a situation which did not arise in Chap. 7 when we designed sequence detectors. In a sequence detector we were satisfied to allow the machine to run continuously since we considered that the input sequence was also continuous. In the present case we want to be able to stop the machine after the last step in the sequence. Otherwise the machine will continue around and around its sequence of operations. After one round the new registration in register α will be $\alpha' = \alpha + \beta$. After the next round we shall have $\alpha'' = \alpha' + \beta$, etc. And if we use a clock with a frequency commonly used in electronic digital systems (100 kHz or higher), we will not even have time to read the α register before it changes.

Therefore, to the six states corresponding to the six microoperations let us

Table 8.4-1

Clock cycle	Control lines to be set to logic 1	Comment
1	Z_A	Accumulator register cleared of any number that may have remained from a previous operation
2	R_α, W	Read α onto bus and write word on bus into CI register
3	R, W_A	Content of CI passed through adder (other adder input is zero) and registered in Acc
4	R_β, W	Content of β transferred to CI
5	R W_A	β added to Acc
6	R_A, W_α	Contents of Acc transferred to register α

add a seventh in which the controller will stop and *wait* when the sequence has been completed. This extra state will give us time to read the result of our computation and to put new numbers in the α and β registers. We then consider that to take the controller out of the waiting state, there is an input X to the controller from some external source. This input may be provided by a push-button switch. When the button is pushed, $X = 1$; otherwise $X = 0$. When $X = 0$, the controller, having started its sequence, will continue until it reaches the *wait* state. The next sequence will not begin until the button has been pushed so that X again becomes $X = 1$. As we now see, however, we have not solved our problem completely. Suppose that, having pushed the button, we fail to release it before the sequence has been completed. Then the controller may go through several cycles before it finally comes to reset in the *wait* state (at a clock rate of 100 kHz, the six-step sequence is completed in only 60 μs). Altogether, we are led to a controller described by the flowchart of Fig. 8.4-2*a*.

There are seven states which we have numbered from 0 to 6. The state number is given in the circle in the upper right-hand corner of the state boxes in Fig. 8.4-2*a*. In state 0, the wait state, all control inputs to the arithmetic unit of Fig. 8.4-1 are at logic 0. So long as $X = 0$ the controller remains in state 0. When the button is pushed and $X = 1$, the controller goes to state 1, where $Z_A = 1$, so that the accumulator register is cleared. The controller does not leave state 1 until the button has been released. At the release of the button the controller goes to state 2, where $R_\alpha = W = 1$, so that the content of the α register will shift to the CI register. After state 2 the progress to state 3 and the rest of the sequence proceeds independently of whether $X = 0$ or $X = 1$. The controller eventually ends up in state 0 and remains there until the button is pushed again. The state diagram is given in Fig. 8.4-2*b*.

8.5 IMPLEMENTATION OF CONTROLLER

Since the controller of the previous section has seven states, we require a sequential circuit of three flip-flops. We decide arbitrarily to use type D flip-flops. A transition table is given in Fig. 8.5-1*a*. In the first column, for identification of states, we have listed the states by their numbering in Fig. 8.4-2*a*. We have arbitrarily made the state assignment which is indicated in the second column. We have simply made, for each state, an assignment $Q_2 Q_1 Q_0$ which when read as a binary number is equal to the decimal identification number. The next states, for $X = 0$ and $X = 1$, are taken directly from the flowchart or state diagram of Fig. 8.4-2.

The controller is a Moore machine. The outputs are dependent entirely on the state of the controller, i.e., on the logic levels at Q_2, Q_1, and Q_0. The single input X has no direct influence on the outputs since X serves only to determine whether the controller sequences through its states or is held at rest. The outputs listed in the remaining columns can also be read directly from the flowchart.

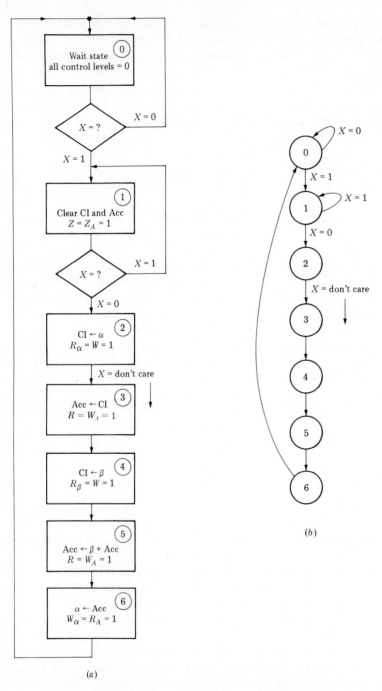

(a)

(b)

Figure 8.4-2 (a) The flow diagram of a controller which take the system of Fig. 8.4-1 through the microoperations required to add the contents of R_α and R_β and store the sum in R_α. (b) The state diagram.

Present state	Present state	Next state		Outputs								
	$Q_2Q_1Q_0$	$X=0$	$X=1$	Z	Z_A	R_α	W	R	W_A	R_β	W_α	R_A
0	000	000	001	0	0	0	0	0	0	0	0	0
1	001	010	001	1	1	0	0	0	0	0	0	0
2	010	011	011	0	0	1	1	0	0	0	0	0
3	011	100	100	0	0	0	0	1	1	0	0	0
4	100	101	101	0	0	0	1	0	0	1	0	0
5	101	110	110	0	0	0	0	1	1	0	0	0
6	110	000	000	0	0	0	0	0	0	0	1	1

(a)

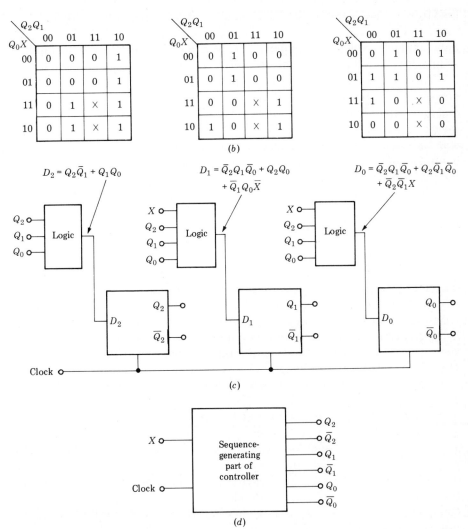

Figure 8.5-1 The design of the controller whose flow diagram and state table are given in Fig. 8.4-2: (a) transition table, (b) K maps for the flip-flop input excitations, (c) logic diagram for the sequence-generating part of the controller, and (d) symbol for logic system in (c).

In Fig. 8.5-1b we have constructed K maps for the excitations D_2, D_1, D_0 of the three flip-flops. The reading for each map is given directly under the map. In Fig. 8.5-1c we have drawn the circuit diagram of that part of the controller which determines the sequencing from state to state. (The part of the controller which generates the many required outputs is not shown.) The three gate structures which generate the three excitations D_2, D_1, and D_0 are not shown explicitly but are indicated by boxes labeled "logic." Inputs to the logic boxes are Q_2, Q_1, and Q_0 and the variable X. The logic-box outputs are expressed in the figure as boolean functions. Of course, if we choose, we can replace the three logic boxes using individual gates with a ROM. The inputs to the ROM, i.e., the address, would then be $Q_2Q_1Q_0$ and X and the outputs, i.e., the word read from the ROM, would be D_2, D_1, and D_0. Finally, the sequence-generating part of the controller (Fig. 8.5-1c) is represented as a block in Fig. 8.5-1d. The only terminals explicitly in evidence are the clock, the input X, and the flip-flop terminals required to implement the decoder which will generate the outputs.

The decoder for generating the outputs is given in Fig. 8.5-2. By way of example, we note from the table of Fig. 8.5-1a that Z and Z_A are at logic 1 when and only when $Q_2 = 0$, $Q_1 = 0$, and $Q_1 = 1$. Hence a single AND with inputs as indicated generates Z and Z_A. We note that R and W_A are at logic 1 when the state is $Q_2Q_1Q_0 = 011$ and also when $Q_2Q_1Q_0 = 101$. Hence here two AND gates and an OR gate are required as shown. The rest of the decoder is read in the same manner from Fig. 8.5-1a which, so far as the outputs are concerned, is a truth table showing the relationship of the outputs to Q_2, Q_1, and Q_0. Figures 8.5-1c and 8.5-2 together constitute the complete controller. When the controller is used in conjunction with the architecture shown in Fig. 8.4-1, we have a machine that will add two binary numbers.

Waveforms for the adding machine are shown in Fig. 8.5-3. We assume here that the flip-flops of the sequences respond to the negative-going edge of the clock waveform. The waveform for X represents the operation of the switch. At an arbitrary point in a clock cycle the switch is closed and X goes to logic 1. The switch remains closed for an undetermined number of clock cycles and then opens, again at an arbitrary point in the clock cycle. The waveforms shown are those at the output of the decoder and also the "waveform" of $\bar{Q}_2\bar{Q}_1\bar{Q}_0$. The latter is not actually generated anywhere in the system and has been included so that it will be apparent when the sequence is in the wait state. The waveforms start at a time when $X = 0$ (switch not pushed yet) and the system is in the wait state. At the time of the first negative-going clock transition after the switch has been pushed the system leave the wait state (state 0) and goes to the next state (state 1), in which next states Z and Z_A are 1. This state 1 persists until the time of the next negative clock transition after X goes back to $X = 0$. Aside from the enabling waveform Z and Z_A, all the other waveforms rise to the enabling level for a single clock cycle at a time. Some waveforms make this excursion to logic 1 just once as the sequences cycles through its states; others make it twice.

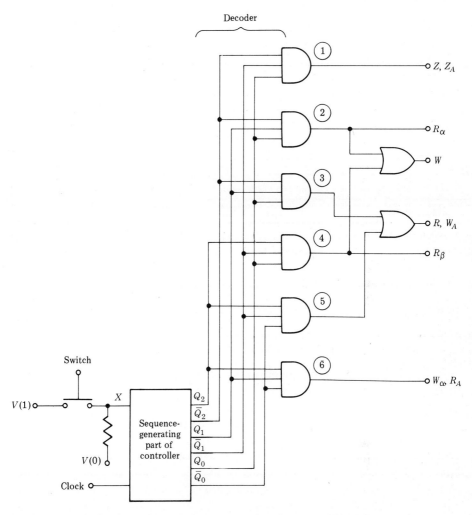

Figure 8.5-2 The decoder to be used with the sequence generator of Fig. 8.5-1.

8.6 THE SHIFT-REGISTER CONTROLLER

The controller of the previous sections is designed to require a minimum number of flip-flops. This design criterion of minimizing the number of states so that the number of flip-flops will be minimal was also observed in Chap. 7, where we designed sequence detectors. In Chap. 7 we noted, however, that there was an alternate design method using shift registers. The shift-register design uses more flip-flops but generally less logic, i.e., fewer gates to generate logical functions. And while, in the end, a shift-register design may not be as economical of hardware as a minimum-flip-flop design, the shift-register design

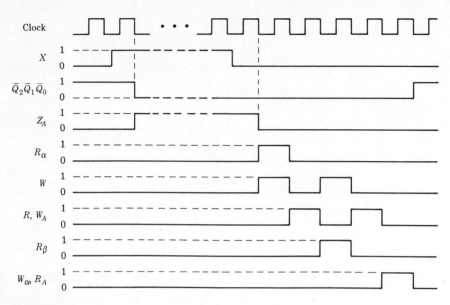

Figure 8.5-3 Waveforms of clock and of waveforms generated at the outputs of the decoder of Fig. 8.5-2.

has at least one great merit in being more orderly and systematized in the sense that we can easily determine precisely what each flip-flop does. Such is generally not the case in a minimal-state-number design.

These considerations prompt us to inquire into a shift-register design in the present case. We note first of all that while the controller designed in the preceding sections uses only three flip-flops, it uses a great deal of logic in the logic boxes of Fig. 8.5-1 and in the decoder of Fig. 8.5-2. Second, we note that the waveforms of Fig. 8.5-3 are reminiscent of the waveforms encountered generally in shift-register circuits. It is, in principle at least, rather obvious how to use a shift register to construct a sequence for our adding-machine controller. We have only to construct a six-stage shift-register ring counter and arrange that, at the outset, the first flip-flop will be set and all others reset. Then with each clock cycle the set condition ($Q = 1$) will move along the register and cycle by cycle we shall have available, in succession at the flip-flop outputs, the one-clock-cycle enabling waveforms we require. As a matter of fact, in a shift-register sequencer the problem of stopping the sequence to make a wait state available is easily solved. We need simply to avoid connecting the last flip-flop back to the first to complete the ring. Then, when the set condition is shifted out of the last flip-flop, the sequence automatically stops.

There is, however, one detail to be dealt with in the shift-register sequence which did not arise in the minimum state sequence. There we had no concern about the state in which the sequence might happen to find itself when power is applied to turn the system on. No matter what the initial state, the sequence, after a few clock cycles, will find itself in the wait state. In the shift-register sequence, on the other hand, we need a way of ensuring that at the outset one and only one shift register is in the set condition at any time and that the flip-flop so set is the first flip-flop in the chain of flip-flops. A circuit that will allow us to set up and start a shift-register sequence properly is shown in Fig. 8.6-1*a*. It involves a switch and uses the same clocking waveform as the sequencer.

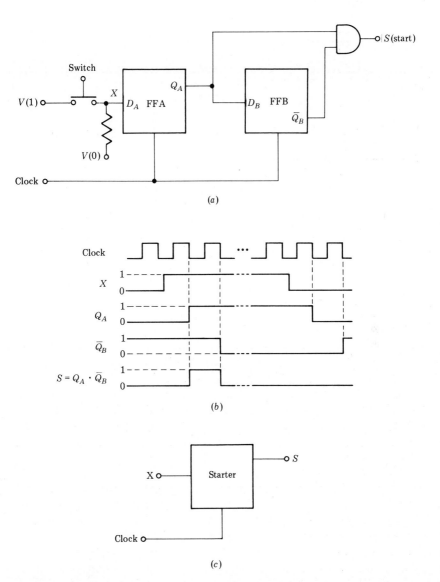

Figure 8.6-1 (*a*) A logic structure which, at the closing of the switch, generates a transition of *S* to logic level 1 which persists for one clock cycle. (*b*) Waveforms. (*c*) Symbol for starter.

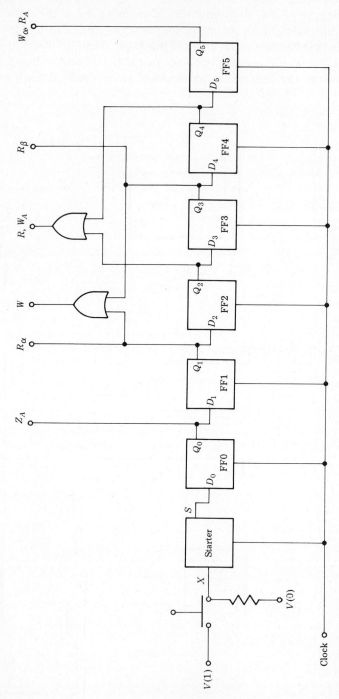

Figure 8.6-2 A shift register controller which can serve as a replacement for the "minimum-state" controller of Figs. 8.5-1 and 8.5-2.

346

Waveforms are given in Fig. 8.6-1b on the assumption that the type D flip-flops respond on the negative-going transition of the clock waveform. When the switch is open, $X = 0$ and $Q_A = 0$ while $\bar{Q}_B = 1$. At an arbitrary time in a clock cycle the switch is pressed and X becomes $X = 1$. At the next negative clock transition Q_A becomes $Q_A = 1$, and one clock cycle later $\bar{Q}_B$ becomes $\bar{Q}_B = 0$. For exactly one clock cycle $S = Q_A \cdot \bar{Q}_B = 1$. The later opening of the switch, no matter when, has no effect on S. Altogether, then, the closing and subsequent opening of the switch generate logic 1 at S for one cycle independently of how long the switch may remain closed. The circuit in Fig. 8.6-1a will be represented by the symbol in Fig. 8.6-1c.

The entire controller with this starter unit is shown in Fig. 8.6-2. When the switch is open, $X = 0$ and $S = 0$. After some clock cycles the entire shift register will have cleared and all outputs will be at logic 0. Closing the switch will set $S = 1$ for one clock cycle, and this set condition will propagate down the shift register. It is true enough that we use here many more flip-flops than in the minimal-state controller, and as a consequence there are many unused states; but observe how much less logic is used in the present case. Observe too that here there is a one-to-one correspondence between the flip-flop and the states through which the controller cycles. And finally observe how much simpler it would be to troubleshoot the present system.

8.7 CONDITIONAL RESPONSE OF CONTROLLERS

The controller of the preceding sections followed a fixed sequence of cycling through states, making available a fixed sequence of enabling logic levels to perform a fixed sequence of microoperation. In the more general case, we shall want a controller to follow different sequences under different circumstances. To direct the controller there will be available to the controller a number of inputs X_0, X_1, etc. In some cases an input, say X_0, will come from a source external both to the controller, and to the processer being controlled, and the logic level of X_0 will be determined by human intervention. For example, in our system above, the end result of the addition is, as a last step, transferred back to register R_α, but we might want to be able to choose whether the result will be transferred to R_α or R_β. And we might then arrange, say, that when we set $X_0 = 0$, the transfer is to R_α and when we set $X_0 = 1$, the transfer is to R_β. In other cases, an input, say X_1, may be determined by an outcome of the processing. For example, suppose that we want the end result transferred to R_α if the result turns out to be a positive number and transferred to R_β if the result turns out to be a negative number. Suppose further that negative numbers are represented in twos-complement form so that the sign bit is 0 or 1 as the number was positive or negative. Then the controller input X_1 would be the sign bit in the accumulator register, and we would want to arrange a transfer to R_α or R_β depending on whether X_1 was 0 or 1. These inputs X_0, X_1, etc., whether from an entirely external source or from a result of the processing, are precisely the inputs X_0, X_1, etc., in Fig. 7.5-6 which represented a generalized sequential circuit. Inputs generated by the processor are called *feedback inputs*.

In a minimum-state controller design, we always prepare a state table. In such a state table there is a next-state column corresponding to every possible combination of inputs. If there is one input there are two such columns, one for $X = 0$ and one for $X = 1$. If there are two inputs, there are four columns, three inputs eight columns, and so on. After the state table has been deduced, and after we have decided about the flip-flop type to be used and have made a state assignment, the remainder of the design leading to the controller is quite automatic. On the other hand, some comments are called for to clarify how the inputs X_0, X_1, etc., often called *conditional inputs* or *modifiers*, are handled in shift-register controllers.

Suppose, for example, that we do indeed want to be able to select whether R_α or R_β is to be the final repository of our result and that we provide for that purpose a control input *final register select* (FRS). Then we can see in Fig. 8.7-1 how this control input is made effective. All the controller of Fig. 8.6-5 remains unaltered except for the output of the last flip-flop in the chain since only the very last microoperation is affected. The last output is modified as shown by the addition of two AND gates. If FRS = 1, W_α will become $W_\alpha = 1$ during the last cycle of the sequence and the result will be written into R_α. If FRS = 0, R_β will be chosen.

Suppose, on the other hand, that we wanted to select register R_α or R_β not on the basis of the external input but on the basis of the sign of the result. Then in Fig. 8.7-1 we would replace FRS by the connection to the accumulator flip-flop which holds the sign bit. It is feasible to do so because, during the interval when the final transfer to R_α or R_β is to be made, the accumulator is not yet cleared and the sign bit is available.

Next consider a case in which there is a feedback input f to the controller, and suppose that it is required that the logic value of f during the kth clock cycle has to select the microoperation to be carried out during the $(k + 1)$th clock cycle. One way to achieve this end is to add a flip-flop (not part of the shift-regi-

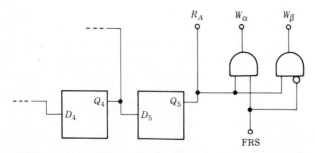

Figure 8.7-1 A modification of the controller of Fig. 8.6-2 which allows a controller response determined by the logic level of an input FRS (final register select).

To enable alternative microoperations

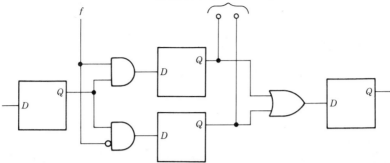

Figure 8.7-2 A shift-register controller which allows the logic level of a feedback input f established during one clock interval to control the microoperation performed during the next interval.

ster chain) in which we store the value of f so that it will be available when required. Then, as in Fig. 8.7-1, we would perform one microoperation or another in the $(k + 1)$th clock interval. A second possibility is to allow the controller to follow one of two alternative paths after interval k depending on the value of f. Such an arrangement, which provides alternate paths, is shown in Fig. 8.7-2. Here, if $f = 1$, the upper flip-flop is included in the shift-register chain while the bottom flip-flop is excluded. If $f = 0$, the bottom flip-flop is used and the upper flip-flop is excluded. Hence, depending on which flip-flop is used, one or the other of two alternative microoperations will be performed.

In Fig. 8.7-2 the paths are alternatives for the time of one clock cycle. After that one clock period the sequence returns to a single common path. In a more general case there may be more than two paths and the alternate paths may have different lengths. Such a situation is represented in Fig. 8.7-3, where four alternative paths are indicated, all of different length. The path is selected by the sequence-control inputs f_1 and f_2. Depending on the logic values of f_1 and f_2, one and only one of the lines C_0, C_1, C_2, or C_3 will be at logic 1 and the one corresponding sequence path will be selected.

Other manipulations which are easily incorporated into a shift-register sequence are indicated in Fig. 8.7-4. In Fig. 8.7-4a if $f = 1$, the sequence progresses from state $k - 1$ to k to $k + 1$ to $k + 2$. (We define here the state k to be the state when flip-flop k is in the set state.) When, however, $f = 0$, states k and $k + 1$ are bypassed and we advance from state $k - 1$ to state $k + 2$. In Fig. 8.7-4b when $f = 1$, the states k and $k + 1$ are not bypassed but are rendered ineffective. Whatever microoperations might have been performed when Q_k, and later Q_{k+1}, become logic 1 will not be performed. In both Fig. 8.7-4a and b the end result is the same in that the microoperations that would otherwise be performed in states k and $k + 1$ are actually not performed. The scheme in Fig. 8.7-4a has the potential merit of saving time because the sequence actually bypasses the states k and $k + 1$. If, however, as not infrequently turns out, the sequence must then wait for some operation being performed elsewhere to be

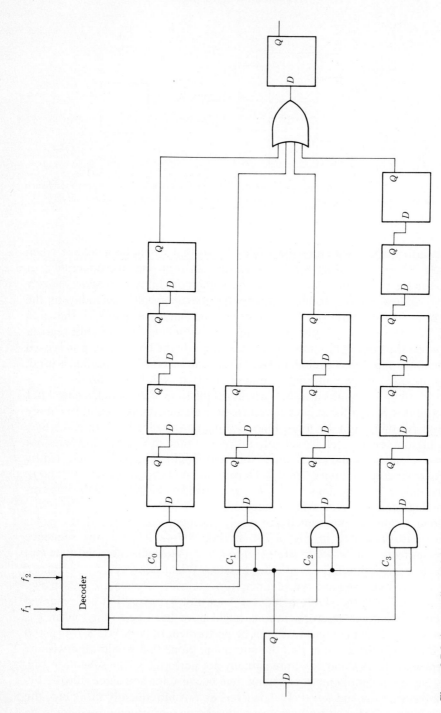

Figure 8.7-3 A controller which allows four different sequences of varying lengths depending on the inputs f_1 and f_2.

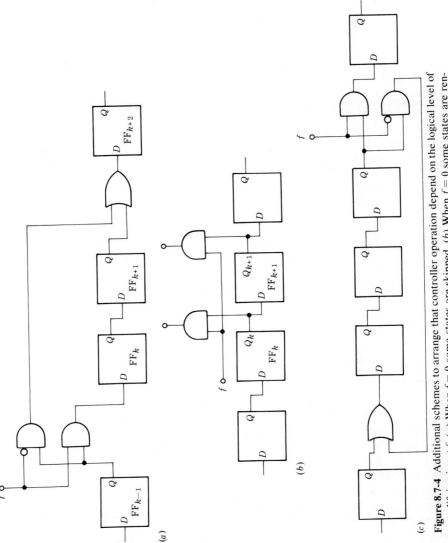

Figure 8.7-4 Additional schemes to arrange that controller operation depend on the logical level of a modifying input f. (a) When $f = 0$ some states are skipped. (b) When $f = 0$ some states are rendered ineffective. (c) When $f = 0$ some states are repeated.

351

completed, the schemes in Fig. 8.7-4a and b are comparable. Finally, it need hardly be said that the number of skipped states or microoperations is entirely adjustable.

Figure 8.7-4c indicates how we can arrange to make a sequence return to repeat some (or all) of its sequence, the repetition being performed as many times as we please. If $f = 1$, the sequence continues on its normal course. If $f = 0$, the sequence repeats a number of states and continues in this pattern of repetition until we again put f at $f = 1$.

8.8 SEQUENCE FOR SUBTRACTION

Let us return now to the machine of Fig. 8.4-1 used so far only to add the numbers in registers R_α and R_β. Suppose that we want to subtract rather than add to form and store $R_\alpha - R_\beta$. It is, as a matter of fact, with this point in mind that we incorporated into the machine the complement-increment (CI) register which actually serves no purpose in forming the sum. If we want to form $R_\alpha - R_\beta$, we have only to reverse the sign of the content of R_β, thereby forming $-R_\beta$, and then to add $R_\alpha + (-R_\beta)$. We assume, as before, that negative numbers are to be represented in twos-complement form. The twos complement is generated by complementing each individual bit of the number and then incrementing the number by 1. Hence, altogether to form $R_\alpha - R_\beta$ we first transfer R_α through CI to the accumulator register as before; we then transfer R_β into CI, where we then first *complement* and then *increment* before transferring from CI to the accumulator.

To accomplish the subtraction we need to modify the controller to provide for two additional microoperations which in turn call for two additional states. If we design a minimum-state controller, the state table will have two additional states. Since our original controller had seven states, the new controller will have nine states and four flip-flops will be required. In addition, we shall have to change the logic which takes the sequence through its paces, and we shall have to add logic to the decoder. If we design a shift-register controller, we shall have to add two flip-flops to the shift-register chain. The details of each of these designs is left as a student exercise.

Next suppose we want to form $-R_\alpha + R_\beta$. Then starting again with the original controller of Fig. 8.5-2 or Fig. 8.6-2, we would add two microoperations, this time to form the negative of the number in R_α. If we wanted $-R_\alpha - R_\beta$, we would have to add four microoperations.

We might well decide that four different controllers to perform the four operations $R_\alpha + R_\beta$, $R_\alpha - R_\beta$, $-R_\alpha + R_\beta$, and $-R_\alpha - R_\beta$ are really uncalled for. Instead we might design a single controller that could perform any of the four operations depending on the *instruction* we give to it. Such a controller is given in Fig. 8.8-1. For the purpose of holding the *instruction* we have added a 2-bit *instruction register*. We consider here that the instruction is placed in the instruction register by manual manipulation using switches, just as we register

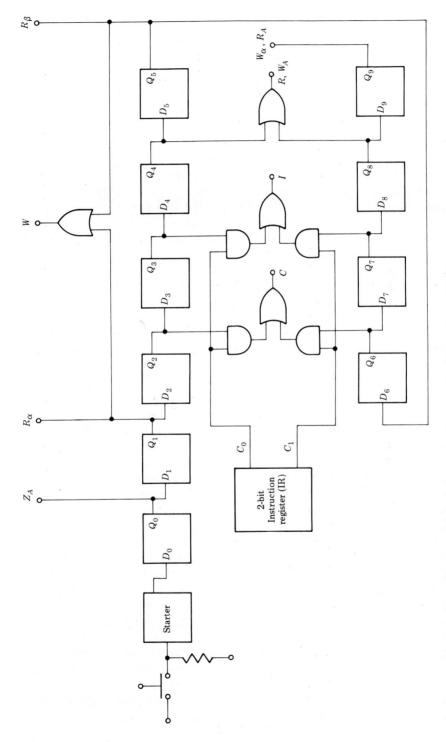

Figure 8.8-1 A shift-register controller to be used with the architecture of Fig. 8.4-1. The controller will place in register R_α one of the four quantities $\pm R_\alpha$ or $\pm R_\beta$ depending on the instruction in the instruction register.

| Instruction | | Total |
C_1	C_0	operation
0	0	$R_\alpha + R_\beta$
0	1	$-R_\alpha + R_\beta$
1	0	$R_\alpha - R_\beta$
1	1	$-R_\alpha - R_\beta$

Figure 8.8-2 The instruction code C_1C_0 for the four instructions of the controller of Fig. 8.8-1.

the numbers to be combined, i.e., the operands, in the registers R_α and R_β. To the original controller of Fig. 8.6-2 we have also added four additional states. In these states the numbers in the CI register will be complemented and incremented, as required, to change the sign of the operands. Complementing in the CI register is performed when terminal C in Fig. 8.8-1 (connected to C in Fig. 8.4-1) goes to logic 1. Incrementing is performed when terminal I goes to logic 1. When the instructions-bit lines are $C_0 = C_1 = 0$, all the AND gates in Fig. 8.8-1 are disabled, C and I are always at logic 0, and the net result is that the total operation performed is to generate the sum $R_\alpha + R_\beta$. The total operation for all the four possible instructions is given in Fig. 8.8-2.

8.9 A SIMPLE COMPUTER

The *controller* of Fig. 8.8-1 operating in conjunction with *storage registers* and *controllable registers* organized into the *architecture* of Fig. 8.4-1 will allow us to combine two numbers arithmetically by addition and subtraction. To use the machine we would put numbers in R_α and R_β, presumably manually by switches, since we have made no other provision. Then we would manually put an instruction into the instruction register (IR). Thereafter, everything proceeds automatically. We need only to push the start button and, after a while, we shall find our result in R_α.

Suppose, now, that we want to make our machine more elaborate. First, we want to be able to deal with more than just two numbers, or operands. Thus we may want to perform an addition of just two operands but we want to be able to select from a large number of operands. Or, having available a large number of operands, we may want to combine many operands. An obvious modification which is then called for is to replace the registers R_α and R_β with a large array of registers. Such a large array of registers is, of course, precisely a memory, as described in Chap. 6. If we want to be able to change operands easily, a RAM is called for.

In the controller of Fig. 8.8-1 a number of sequence steps deal with the operand stored in R_α, and a number of steps deal with the operand in R_β. It is apparent that following this pattern would lead to a very long sequence if many operands were involved. Each new operand adds steps to the sequence. We recognize, however, that each operand is actually subjected to the same microoperations. The operand is transferred from a storage register (or better, a location in memory) to the CI register and thence through the adder to the accumulator. If we need to change the sign of the operand, we complement and increment in the CI register. Otherwise the CI register does nothing. This sequence of microoperations is repeated over and over again for each operand. Hence it appears that actually we can manage with a controller which has a short sequence, a sequence which will process just one operand. However, with such a sequence controller, we would need some mechanism for adjusting the instruction to the controller, i.e., change operand sign or do not change sign, as each new operand is processed. One way to adjust the instruction is simply to stop the control sequence after it processes each operand and then manually change the instruction before allowing the sequence to process the next operand. But since we have a memory, we can store in the memory the information concerning how each operand is to be processed and the entire operation can be made quite automatic. With these considerations in mind we turn now to Fig. 8.9-1; it displays a system which will (with some manual intervention) allow us to combine arithmetically a large number of operands fairly automatically.

The system has a RAM memory. To be specific we assume a memory with 64 words, each word having 8 bits. A memory location is addressed by a 6-bit address ($2^6 = 64$). The memory has an enable input and a *read/write* input. When *enable* = 1, the memory is connected to the (8-bit) bus, and when *enable* = 0, the bus is isolated from the memory. When *enable* = 1, memory will read a word on to the bus or write a word into the memory, depending on whether *read/write* is 1 or 0. The memory location from which a word is read or into which a word is written is determined by the six address bits. The double-headed arrow connecting the memory to the bus indicates that information transfer between bus and memory is bidirectional.

In Fig. 8.9-2 we illustrate what typically might be contained in the memory serving our rather simple machine. In Fig. 8.9-2a we have written out in words and decimal numbers the content of some of the locations in the memory. In locations 0 to 6 we have written a *program* of instructions. At the other end of the memory we have stored some operands. If we can arrange for the machine to carry out the instructions given in the order listed, the machine will compute the quantity $-(49) + (-79) - (-52) + (121) + (82) = +127$, as can be seen by noting the contents of memory locations 59 to 63. The machine will then transfer this accumulated sum from the accumulator register to memory location 39 and then stop and wait for human intervention. As we shall see, there is a purpose in placing the instructions in successive locations in the memory. On the other hand, it is not important that the operands ($49, -79$, etc.) be located in successive locations. Neither is it important that we have placed the instructions at opposite ends of the memory. All that is required is that the instructions be placed (in successive locations) in one part of the memory and the operands be placed elsewhere. The order indicated in Fig. 8.9-2 is prompted principally by a proper respect for orderly bookkeeping. Memory locations not indicated

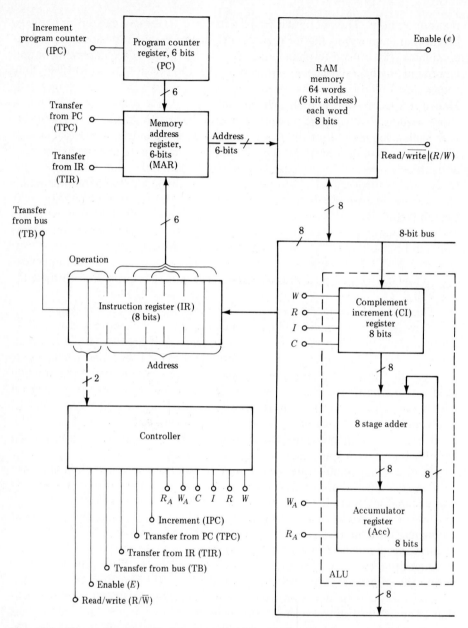

Figure 8.9-1 The architecture of a "computer" which will allow the arithmetic combination of a large number of operands.

Memory location		Memory location							Subtract from Acc	Memory location 59						
0	Subtract from Acc content of memory location 59	0	0	0	0	0	0		1	0	1	1	1	0	1	1
1	Add to Acc content of memory location 60	0	0	0	0	0	1		0	1	1	1	1	1	0	0
2	Subtract from Acc content of memory location 61	0	0	0	0	1	0		1	0	1	1	1	1	0	1
3	Add to Acc content of memory location 62	0	0	0	0	1	1		0	1	1	1	1	1	1	0
4	Add to Acc content of memory location 63	0	0	0	1	0	0		0	1	1	1	1	1	1	1
5	Transfer Acc content to memory location 39	0	0	0	1	0	1		1	1	1	0	0	1	1	1
6	Stop	0	0	0	1	1	0		0	0	X	X	X	X	X	X
⋮																
59	49	1	1	1	0	1	1		0	0	1	1	0	0	0	1
60	−79	1	1	1	1	0	0		1	0	1	1	0	0	1	1
61	−52	1	1	1	1	0	1		1	1	0	0	1	1	0	0
62	121	1	1	1	1	1	0		0	1	1	1	1	0	0	1
63	82	1	1	1	1	1	1		0	1	0	1	0	0	1	0

(a)   (c)

Code	Instruction
00	Stop
01	Add to Acc
10	Subtract from Acc
11	Transfer Acc content to

(b)

Figure 8.9-2 (a) A possible content of the memory in Fig. 8.9-1 written out to convey the intent of the memory content. (a) An instruction code. (c) The actual binary bit content the memory locations.

in the figure do of course have some content. (A cleared memory location with a content 00 . . . 00 has a content nonetheless.) But the content of these memory locations is not relevant to our present discussion. We propose to store our result in location 39 (not shown). The content of location 39 is not known and irrelevant. When the instruction is executed that writes the result into location 39, the previous content of that location will be lost.

We note that we have used four instructions: add, subtract, transfer, and stop. We arbitrarily use the 2-bit code of Fig. 8.9-2b to represent these instructions. In Fig. 8.9-2c we have rewritten the memory in binary form. In the memory locations which hold operands we have simply replaced decimal numbers by binary numbers. In memory locations holding instructions we have arbitrarily arranged for the two leftmost bits to represent the instruction and the remaining 6 bits to specify the location which holds the operand. This assignment of bit significance is expressly indicated for the first memory location. Memory locations 0 through 5 all hold instructions which call for an operation and refer to a specific memory location when the operand is stored. Memory location 6 calls for an operation, but since no operand is involved, we do not care about the six address bits.

Observe that the memory words are 8 bits long. If we propose to represent negative numbers in twos-complement form, the range of numbers we can accommodate extends from $+127$ to -128. We must then be careful to assure that as our machine accumulates the numbers we are combining, we never require the accumulated sum to extend outside the allowed range. The numbers entered into memory locations 59 through 63 have been selected arbitrarily except that we have observed this constraint about the range.

Returning to Fig. 8.9-1, we note that the section in the dashed box is the system of Fig. 8.4-1 without the registers R_α and R_β. (These registers have been replaced by the part of the memory which stores the operands.) This little system performs arithmetic (adding and incrementing) and logic (complementing) and is reasonably referred to as an arithmetic logic unit (ALU) although it differs in many respects from the ALU of Fig. 5.13-1. For simplicity we have left out the *clear* terminal Z_A, since the accumulator can be cleared using the instructions of Fig. 8.9-2b (Prob. 8.9-1).

Continuing our examination of Fig. 8.9-1, we note the presence of a program-counter (PC) register, instruction register (IR), a memory address register (MAR), and finally the controller which is to put our small computer through its paces and which we have yet to design. The detailed purpose of each register will be discussed shortly. For the present let us simply note the paths available for transfers of words (or parts of words) and the facilities that have been incorporated into each register. We note that there is an 8-bit bus to which the memory has a bidirectional connection. The ALU can accept a word from the bus on its input side and deliver a word to the bus from its output side. The instruction register can accept a word from the bus. The memory address register has two control inputs which can be used to transfer to the MAR the 6-bit word in the program counter or the rightmost 6 bits of the instruction register. The two leftmost bits of the instruction register are made available (not transferred) to the controller. Hence this 2-bit connection is indicated by a dashed rather than a solid line. The only operation which the program counter can perform is the increment operation. Finally, the controller has a control output line corresponding to each control input line of each register and of the memory. Whatever microoperations are performed will be performed whenever the corresponding control line goes to the enabling level. With the exception of the memory, all registers and the controller are clocked, and the actual moment at which a register accepts a transfer and increments it is the time of the triggering transition of the clock. The clock-waveform line, which is distributed throughout the system of Fig. 8.9-1, is not indicated on the drawing.

8.10 OPERATION OF THE COMPUTER

To see how our computer operates, let us consider that our memory is loaded as in Fig. 8.9-2c. We may imagine that to effect this loading the memory was temporarily disconnected from the system and that inputs (addresses, data, *enable*, *read/write*) were applied manually. Also we assume that at the outset the program counter (PC) and the accumulator register are cleared. (It does not matter whether the other registered are clear initially.) We shall now list in Table 8.10-1 and Table 8.10-2, clock cycle by clock cycle, the sequence of microoperations through which the controller must pace the system for the system to take note of the first instruction, carry out its intent and prepare to read the next instruction. When it is feasible to perform more than one microoperation during the course of one clock cycle, we shall take advantage

Table 8.10-1   Fetch cycle

Clock cycle	Symbolic description of operation	Control line to be enabled
1. Transfer content of program counter to memory address register	$PC \rightarrow MAR$	TPC
2. Transfer addressed instruction (in location 000000) to instruction register by (1) enabling memory to connect memory to bus, (2) setting $R/\bar{W}$ to 1 to read memory, and (3) transferring word on bus to instruction register;	$M \rightarrow IR$ ("M" represents addressed memory word)	$E, R/\bar{W}$, TB
increment program counter to prepare for calling forth the next instruction when response to first instruction has been completed	$PC + 1 \rightarrow PC$	IPC

of that feature in order to save time. It is especially to be noted that the only operations specified in the tabulation are those which will be affected by the fact that one or more control outputs of the controller go to the enabling level.

In the operations listed in Table 8.10-1 we have brought the first instructions from the memory into the instruction register. This part of the cycle of operations of the machine is called the *fetch cycle*. Now that the first instruction is available, the machine will proceed to respond to the instructions. The cycle of operations by which this response is carried out is called the *execute cycle*. These operations of the fetch cycle are, of course, carried out under the control of the controller, but the controller operation during the fetch cycle is independent of the two leftmost bits in the instruction register, which are available to the controller. As a matter of fact, since we did not clear the instruction register, we did not even know what these bits were. However, now that we have fetched this first instruction and registered it in the instruction register, the processing from this point will follow a course dependent on the instruction conveyed by the two *operation bits* of the instruction. Since the first instruction calls for *subtraction*, the *execution* of the instruction proceeds as shown in Table 8.10-2.

The machine has now carried out the first instructions. We shall arrange that, correspondingly, the controller we design will have completed its entire sequence and returned to its start. Hence the next operation to be performed is again to transfer the program counter to the memory address register. But, recall that we have incremented the program counter. As a consequence the instruction fetched will be the second instruction (in location 00001). The second instruction will be executed like the first except that since addition rather than subtraction is called for, the complement and increment operations will be bypassed. Thus we see that as the controller sequences, it fetches then executes, fetches then executes, etc. The fetching operation is always the same; the operations during execute depend, of course, on the instruction.

In putting together the simple system of Fig. 8.9-1 we made a number of

Table 8.10-2 Execute cycle

Clock cycle	Symbolic description of operation	Control line to be enabled
3. Transfer address part of register (6 right bits) to memory address register (address is 59)	IR (ADD) → MAR	TIR
4. Transfer addressed word from memory to bus and from bus to CI register	M → BUS BUS → CI	E, $R/\bar{W}$, W
5. Complement CI	$\overline{CI}$ → CI	C
6. Increment CI	CI+1 → CI	I
7. Register adder output into accumulator register	Adder → Acc	W_A

decisions (some of them quite arbitrary, some based on experience). These decisions concern the number and function of registers, the types of interconnections between registers and between registers and memory, the number of words in the memory, the number of bits per word, the number and type of operations which the ALU can perform, etc. These matters constitute the architecture and organization of the computer. Once an architecture and organization have been established, the job of designing the controller remains. (The controller for our machine is designed in the next section.)

There are, of course, many architectures and organizations which can be assumed by a piece of computing machinery. After many years of experimenting with a wide range of possibilities, computing machinery of the present time generally incorporates some common features, a number of which are to be seen in our simple computer and which we now point out.

First we note that the machine has a memory, in which we *store* at the outset all the instructions required to carry out a computation. For this reason the machine is called a *stored-program computer*. Since the machine is fully instructed, we should not have to interrupt it to provide further direction to its computation. The memory stores not only the instructions but the operands and the results of computation as well. Hence we shall have to make frequent references to the memory to read from it and to write into it. The addressed location is found in the *memory address register*, and it is not surprising that there is access to the MAR from a number of directions. In our case we can get to the MAR from the program counter and from the instruction register. (In more sophisticated computers additional direct and indirect means of access to the MAR are provided.)

Next we note that our machine has an arithmetic logic unit in which all arithmetic and logic operations are performed. The rest of the machine (aside from the controller) consists of nothing more than an array of registers. Even the memory is nothing but a collection of storage registers. And storage registers do not do anything. They just constitute the digital "writing paper" into which we write the digital words we need to keep for future reference. Our ALU is also rather simple. It complements, increments, and adds. More elaborate ALUs provide these functions and also perform logical operations (AND, OR, etc.), shift left or right, etc.

Observe that in manipulating the machine it is arranged that a number of matters be "understood." When an instruction has been carried out, it is "understood" *that the next instruction is in the next memory location. Hence the location of the next instruction need not be specified.* Again, when an addition is to be performed, the instruction specifies only one of the operands involved in the addition. It is "understood" that the other operand is in the accumulator register. Finally, the instruction gives no indication of where the result of the addition is to be stored. It is "understood" that the result is to be left in the accumulator. All these understandings effect a considerable economy in word length. Thanks to these understandings which have been incorporated into the machine, an instruction need only specify an operation and an address of an operand. Without these understandings an instruction would have to specify the operation, the source of the first operand, the source of the second operand, the place where the result is to be stored, and the source of the next instruction. Of course, such an elaborate instruction would require many more bits than the simpler instructions possible on account of the understandings.

8.11 DESIGN OF THE COMPUTER CONTROLLER

A design for the controller required in Fig. 8.9-1 is shown in Fig. 8.11-1. In this design, in order to achieve simplicity we display a deliberate and extreme disregard for economy of hardware. As usual, the *start element* and all the flip-flops are driven by a common clocking waveform (not explicitly shown). Closing the switch starts the shift-register sequence. As the output of each successive flip-flop rises in turn to logic 1, a microoperation is performed. We have stated in words what microoperations are performed at each step and have indicated in parentheses what control terminals must be made active for the microoperations to be performed. The first two steps in the sequence *fetch* the instruction and load it into the instruction register. This fetch part of the controller operation is the same regardless of the instruction fetched. After the fetch part of the sequence has been completed, the *execute* part begins. The operation to be executed is transmitted to the controller as a 2-bit operation code. In the controller these bits are applied to a decoder with four output lines. When the operation code is 10, subtraction is intended. The 10 decoder output line alone is at logic 1 and only the top AND gate is enabled. The shift-register sequence continues through the top row of flip-flops, arranging thereby to carry out the appropriate sequence for subtraction. An operation code 01 enables the second AND gate from the top. The resulting sequence is the same as for subtraction except that the *complement* and *increment* microoperations are bypassed. An operation code 11 calls for a transfer of the contents of the accumulator register back to memory. Two microoperations are required here. The first, as in the subtract and add operations, transfers the address from the instruction register to the memory address register. The second *writes* into the memory rather than reads from the memory, hence the inversion of logic level applied to the memory $R/\bar{W}$ control.

If the instruction is *subtract, add*, or *transfer*, the execute sequence, when completed, leads immediately back through the OR gate to the beginning of the fetch cycle. The next instruction is fetched, and a new execution begins, etc. If, on the other hand, the instruction is 00, which means *stop*, there is no return to the fetch cycle. The operation stops after the output of the bottom-most AND gate has been at logic 1 for a clock cycle. This "finished" output can be used, if we please, to indicate that the computer has completed its work and now requires further manual intervention.

The execute portion of the controller of Fig. 8.11-1 uses flip-flops rather more freely than necessary. An alternative execute portion shown in Fig.

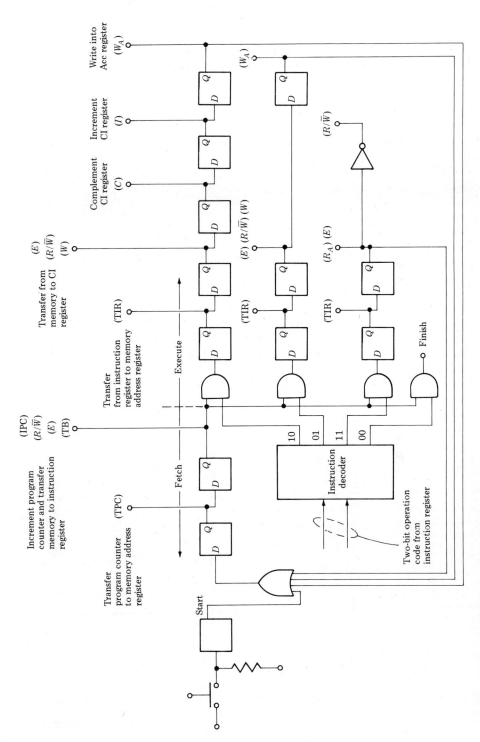

Figure 8.11-1 The controller of the "computer" of Fig. 8.9-1.

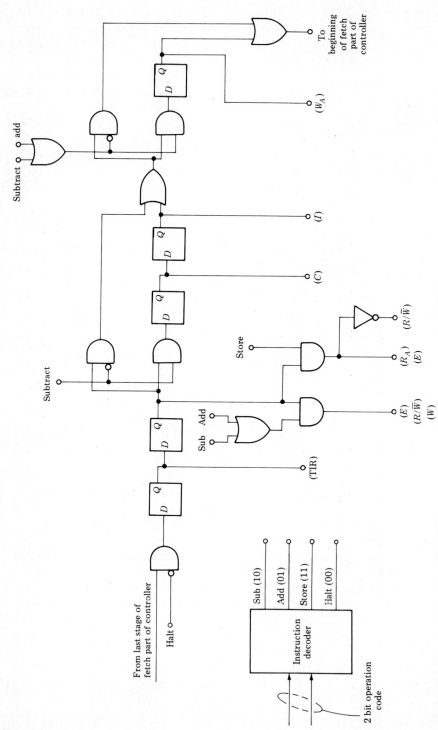

Figure 8.11-2 A controller alternative to the controller of Fig. 8.11-1 and one which uses fewer flip-flops but more gates.

8.11-2 is more economical in flip-flops albeit at the expense of requiring more gates. Five flip-flops are used, allowing for an execute sequence with as many as five microoperations. In every case except when the instruction is *halt*, the first sequence step calls for the TIR terminal to be raised to the active level. In the second step the *add* and the *subtract* instructions call for a common microoperation while the *store* instruction calls for an alternative microoperation. Unless the instruction is subtract, the third and fourth sequence steps are bypassed. If subtraction is called for, the third and fourth microoperations are *complement* and *increment*. Finally, again if *add* or *subtract* is called for, there is a common activation of the W_A input, as provided by the fifth step in the sequence. Otherwise this fifth step is bypassed.

8.12 INTERRUPTS

Once started, the controller of Fig. 8.11-1 chases around and around. It performs a fetch sequence then an execute sequence, goes back to a fetch sequence, etc., over and over until finally it encounters a halt instruction which stops it. The controller operates the rather simple-minded digital processor of Fig. 8.9-1, which is capable of doing not much more than adding and subtracting a column of numbers. Yet the mode of operation of this controller (fetch, execute, fetch, etc.) is of fundamental importance because controllers in the most sophisticated digital computers operate in this same mode.

It frequently happens that it is necessary to *interrupt* this repetitive fetch-execute cycling and to call upon the controller to generate a sequence of enabling command signals to carry out some special operation. The source requiring the special operation is described as *calling for an interrupt*, and the corresponding response of the controller is described as *answering a request for service*.

Figure 8.12-1 shows how the controller can be augmented to incorporate the ability to answer such a request for service. If the static latch is in the reset state with $\bar{Q} = 1$, the AND gate G_N for normal operation is enabled and the gate for an interrupt operation G_I will be disabled. After the start button has been pressed, a normal sequence will begin, first through the fetch portion of the controller, then through the execute portion of the controller, then back to fetch, and so on. Suppose that at some time a signal is received indicating that the service sequence is required. The signal calling for the interrupt need only be a brief excursion to logic 1 applied to the set input of the latch. When the latch sets ($Q = 1$, $\bar{Q} = 0$), G_I rather than G_N will be enabled. Suppose that the very first step of the fetch sequence has already started before the interrupt signal is received. Then the fetch sequence will continue and will be followed by the execute sequence. That is, the instruction which is in the process of being fetched and executed, will not be interrupted, but when the execution has been completed, since G_I is enabled and G_N not enabled, the sequencing will proceed through the auxiliary sequence generator for servicing the interrupt. As the

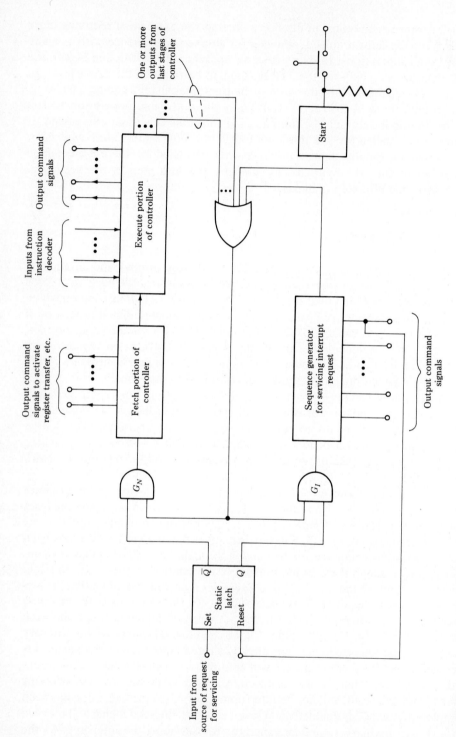

One or more outputs from last stages of controller

Output command signals

Inputs from instruction decoder

Execute portion of controller

Output command signals to activate register transfer, etc.

Fetch portion of controller

G_N

G_I

Sequence generator for servicing interrupt request

Output command signals

Start

Static latch

Set

Reset

$\overline{Q}$

Q

Input from source of request for servicing

Figure 8.12-1 A controller modification which allows response to an *interrupt* request.

sequence so proceeds, command signals will be generated to activate whatever microoperations are required. We have arranged that the last command signal, in addition to whatever microoperation it performs, will also reset the latch. With the latch reset the controller will go back to normal operation.

The latch in Fig. 8.12-1 is required to store the information that some source has made a request for an interrupt because it requires servicing. Such storage is required because the input-interrupt signal may be of brief duration and no response can be made by the controller until it has completed dealing with the instruction in the process of being carried out. One-bit "registers," like the latch, which do not record a word but serve to store some 1-bit piece of information to alert the controller to some situation, is called a *flag*. Thus the call for an interrupt *raises the interrupt flag*, and when the interrupt has been serviced, the flag is lowered.

Quite generally, a digital processor, whether it is a digital computer or even some processor of simplicity comparable to our machine of Fig. 8.9-1, does not stand alone. Inevitably it will operate in conjunction with some equipment which is external to the processor itself. In many cases this outside equipment serves as the means by which the processor can communicate with human beings. This outside equipment may consist, for example, of an electromechnical typewriter through which people can *input* data and instructions to the processor and through which the processor can *output* its results in a form which is conveniently understood by people. This external hardware is then referred to as input-output (I/O) equipment; almost every processor needs to incorporate an ability to control this input-output hardware in its controller. Frequently the interrupt facility of a controller is required precisely to assist in the handling of the I/O hardware.

A simple example of how an interrupt call can be serviced is indicated in Fig. 8.12-2. Here we contemplate that our add-subtract processor of Fig. 8.9-1 is combining a long list of numbers and the rate of processing (determined by the clock rate) is slow enough for us reasonably to have an interest, from time to time, in checking to see what the present total accumulation in the accumulator is. Further, at our request, we want to arrange for the accumulator registration be typed out on a typewriter. We assume the availability of an electromechanical typewriter which will respond, as we require, to logical activation of input lines.

In Fig. 8.12-2 we have reproduced, from Fig. 8.9-1, only the bus and the ALU and, of the ALU, only the accumulator. The rest of the processor is not relevant for our present purposes. To accomplish our purpose we press a start button, which we have provided to indicate to the processor that we want it to interrupt its normal operation and type out the latest accumulator registration. The accumulator is to transfer to the external register. Here the four less significant and the four more significant bits are separately decoded by two hex decoders. Each decoder provides 16 output lines, only 1 of each 16 being at logic 1, depending on the numerical significances of the input hex codes. We assume a typewriter with the 16 hex characters and assume as well that when the

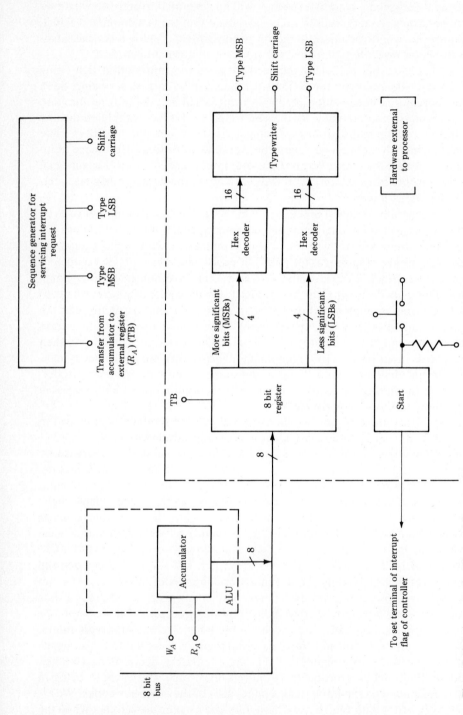

Figure 8.12-2 An example. The servicing of an interrupt that called for an output reading of the accumulator content.

terminal "Type MSB" is raised to logic 1, the typewriter will activate the key corresponding to the active line on the output of the MSB decoder. A corresponding input for the LSB typewriter input is assumed. And finally we assume an input which shifts the carriage one space so that each 2-digit hex number can be separated from others. As is also shown in the figure, to accomplish what is required, the sequence generator for servicing the interrupt request must have four command signals. Each time, then, we press the interrupt button, the processor will complete dealing with its present instruction and go to the service sequence to answer our request.

One difficulty is readily apparent in the scheme of Fig. 8.11-2. If we construct our sequence generator like the examples presented earlier, we shall have allowed only one clock interval for each operation (transferring, typing, and shifting). Transferring from accumulator to external register is easily accomplished in one clock interval, but, unless the clock rate is very slow, a clock interval will not be adequate for the required mechanical responses of the typewriter. One way to resolve difficulties due to slow response is to increase from one to many the number of flip-flops in a sequence generator between two points from which command signals are serviced. This method is, of course, wasteful of hardware. In any event, this problem of interfacing systems which do not operate at the same speed is a regularly recurring one, and in the next section we address ourselves to this matter.

8.13 HANDSHAKING

One method by which we can arrange communication between two systems which operate unsynchronously and often at unrelated and widely different speeds is called *handshaking*. Let us consider the matter specifically in connection with the transmission of data from a transmitting system to a receiving system.

In handshaking, the transmitter makes available to the receiver, in addition to the data to be transmitted, a line which conveys a logic signal called "*data valid*" (DAV). The receiver makes available to the transmitter a line which conveys a logic signal called *data accepted* (DAC). The arrangement is illustrated in Fig. 8.13-1. Presumably the transmitter will transmit word after word to the receiver over an n-bit data bus. When DAV = 1, it means that whatever processing and operations need to be performed to place a new word on the data bus have been completed and the word on the bus is settled and stable and ready to be read by the receiver; i.e., the word is *valid*. When DAV = 0, the word is not valid. A sequence of logic levels on DAV from 1 to 0 and back to 1 accompanies each change of word.

When DAC = 0, it means that the receiver is completely ready to receive the data word on the bus but will do so only if it finds that DAV = 1. If DAC = 1, the receiver will not accept the data; i.e., the receiver is, in effect, disconnected from the bus. Transmitter and receiver communicate over these

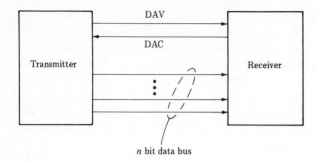

Figure 8.13-1 The operation of a transmitter and receiver of data are coordinated by the use of the *handshaking* lines DAV and DAC.

DAV and DAC lines. The receiver tells the transmitter when the data word has been accepted so that the transmitter can put the next word on the line. The transmitter tells the receiver when a new word has been stably established on the bus so that it can be read.

Suppose we start during an interval when $DAV = 1$ and $DAC = 0$, that is, a word is being transmitted and in the process of being accepted. Then we must assume that DAV does not become $DAV = 0$ until we have $DAC = 1$. Also, when, with $DAV = 1$ and $DAC = 0$ a word is accepted, a word must not be accepted again until DAV changes to $DAV = 0$ and then back again to $DAV = 1$. Otherwise the receiver will accept the same word twice. With such a system there will surely be intervals when the transmitter must *wait* for the receiver to complete some processing or when the receiver must *wait* for the transmitter. As a matter of fact, the precise point of the entire arrangement is to assure that the transmitter or receiver *will* wait when required. The sequence which the DAV and DAC lines go through as one word is transferred and preparations are made for transferring the next word shown in Table 8.13-1.

As an illustration of the use of DAV and DAC lines, consider the situation in Fig. 8.13-2, where we have two random-access memories of identical organization and it is our purpose to transfer the content of memory A (M_A) to memory B (M_B). Each word is to occupy the same address in B as it did when in A.

Table 8.13-1 Sequence of DAV and DAC logic levels as one word is transmitted and preparation made for the next word

Time interval	Transfer DAV	Receive DAC	Comment
1	1 valid	0 accepting	Word transferred
2	1 valid	1 not accepting	To make sure that data remain valid until after receiver disconnects
3	0 not valid	1 not accepting	Word being changed
4	0 not valid	0 accepting	No transfer because $DAV = 0$
5	1	0	New word transferred

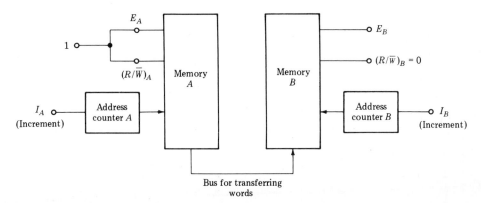

Figure 8.13-2 Two identical RAMs are connected to effect the transfer of the content of memory A to memory B.

We have permanently set the enable input E_A and the $(R/\overline{W})_A$ at $E_A = (R/\overline{W})_A = 1$ so that there is always a word output from M_A, the word being determined by a counter whose count constitutes the address of the selected word. In M_B we have set $(R/\overline{W})_B = 0$ so that M_B is permanently in the write mode and the operation of writing will occur when the enable terminal goes to $E_B = 1$.

If the entire system were to operate as a single synchronous system, i.e., driven by a single common clocking waveform, the design of a controller to effect the transfer from M_A to M_B would be quite elementary. As a matter of fact we would require only a single address counter which would provide a common address for both M_A and M_B. A two-state controller would do the job. In one state the controller would set $E_B = 1$ to read the word into M_B. In the second state the address counter would be incremented. The controller would then sequence through states write, increment, write, increment, etc. If the number of counter states is the same as the number of words in the memories, it does not matter what the initial address in the counter is. Also, if the controller continues to run after the job is completed, no harm will be done since we shall simply be writing the same words into the same places.

Next suppose that the two portions of the system A and B are to be driven by two separate independent and unrelated clocking waveforms Cl_A and Cl_B of frequencies f_A and f_B. It may be that $f_A > f_B$ or vice versa. It may even be that f_A and f_B change with time in a manner unrelated to each other. The two systems are connected *only* by the bus on which the word is transferred, and we shall interconnect the two separate controllers now required by DAC and DAV lines. We consider now the design of the two controllers.

The flow diagram for controller A is shown in Fig. 8.13-3a. We define the first state, $1A$, to be a state in which the address counter A is quiescent at a fixed address and the addressed word is on the bus. The word on the bus is the word we want to read; none of its bits are in the process of changing, so that the

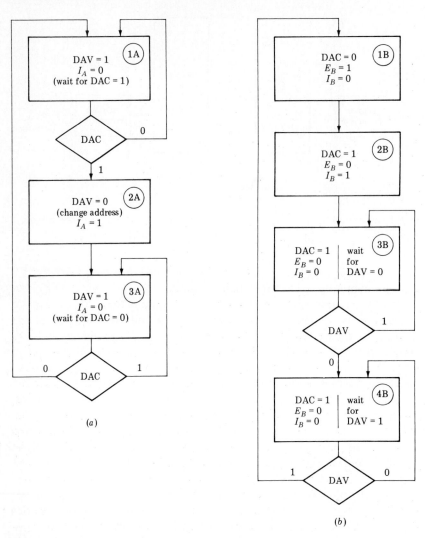

Figure 8.13-3 The flo ff chart for a controller to operate the system of Fig. 8.13-2 and to make available DAV and DAC signals.

word is valid and we have $DAV = 1$. This first state we also define to be one which is arrived at as a result of the fact that at the time of the triggering transition of Cl_A the line DAC from controller B to controller A was $DAC = 0$. This state then is the state during which a valid word is applied to an accepting receiver so that the word will be written into M_B. The actual writing requires only that the controller place E_B at logic 1 during this state.

So long as DAC remains $DAC = 0$ the transmitter must keep the same word on the bus and correspondingly keep $DAV = 1$. When DAC becomes $DAC = 1$, that is, the receiver has disconnected from the bus, the transmitter

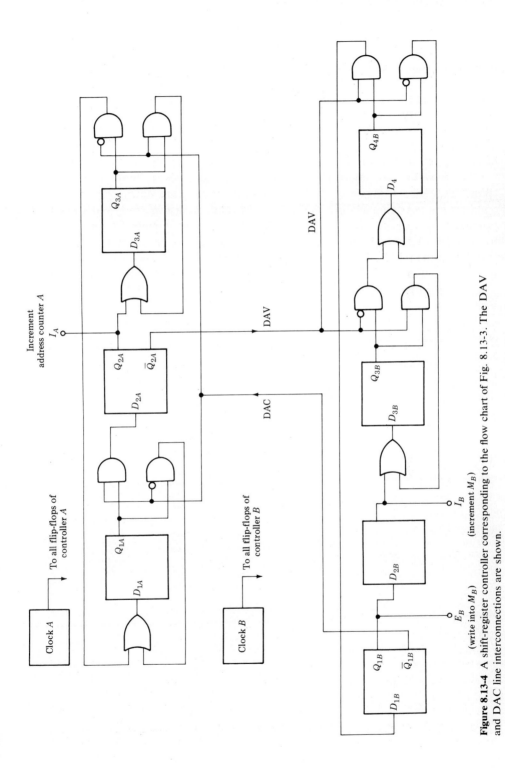

Figure 8.13-4 A shift-register controller corresponding to the flow chart of Fig. 8.13-3. The DAV and DAC line interconnections are shown.

controller may go to the next state, $2A$, where DAV will be DAV $= 0$ and the address counter A will be advanced. After the address has been changed, the transmitter again has a valid word on the bus and so the controller goes to a state, $3A$, in which again DAV $= 1$. In this state the controller waits until DAC again becomes DAC $= 0$, at which time the controller returns to its initial state. Note particularly that once an address increment has been' made, the next address change does not occur until DAC first becomes DAC $= 0$ and then becomes DAC $= 1$. In this way the controller makes certain that the receiver has accepted the transmitted word before a new word is placed on the bus.

The flowchart for controller B is shown in Fig. 8.13-3b. State $1B$ corresponds to state $1A$. When controllers A and B are in these states, the address counters are not being advanced, the data are valid, E_B is at $E_B = 1$, and a word transfer is in process. Note that controller A cannot leave state $1A$ until controller B has left state $1B$. Note further that the controller will not return to state $1B$ until first DAV has gone to DAV $= 0$ and then returned to DAV $= 1$. In this way it is assured that the next word transferred will be a new word.

A controller corresponding to the flowchart of Fig. 8.13-3 is shown in Fig. 8.13-4.

NINE

COMPUTERS

The system of Fig. 8.8-1 may, with some charity, be called a computer. Its essential merits are its simplicity and that it exhibits some important features that are found in more sophisticated computers, as well. On the other hand, our "computer" has the serious deficiency of not being able to do very much. In this chapter we shall consider some elaborations of computer design.

9.1 AN IMPROVED ARCHITECTURE

As we have noted, designing a computer or other digital processor generally begins with considering the architecture. Decisions have to be made about the type of component blocks to be used, i.e., numbers of registers, types of registers, operations which the registers and ALUs are to be able to perform, and, most important, what registers and components are to be interconnected so that data can be transferred. There is no design procedure by which a "best" architecture can be selected. Architectural structures are generally arrived at on the basis of the designer's experience and often by simply "improving" an existing design. An improvement of the system of Fig. 8.8-1 is shown in Fig. 9.1-1. As we may well expect generally, improvements, which allow a system to do more, lead to more complexity.

In our new machine, the memory, which is of course essential in a stored-program computer, is specified as a memory which will store 12-bit words. Actually, we shall not make any precise use of the word length, and the length is specified simply so that we can be more specific in the discussion which follows. Our machine will have a repertory of 16 instructions, for which we

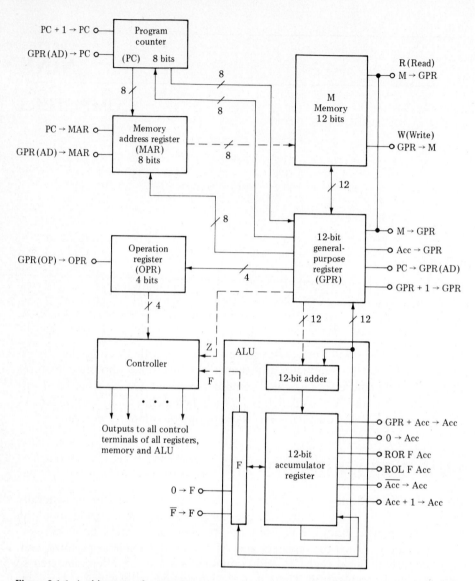

Figure 9.1-1 Architecture of a computer.

shall require 4 instruction bits. If we had remained with 8-bit words, we would have been reduced to a 4-bit address, allowing only a 16-word memory.

On previous occasions we have indicated that random-access memories are generally equipped with two control terminals and possibly others. One of these is an *enable* (E) terminal, and the other is a read/$\overline{write}$ (R/$\overline{W}$) terminal. The memory will allow a word to be written into it or read from it only if E = 1. To write we set R/$\overline{W}$ = 0, and to read we set R$\overline{W}$ = 1. In our present application it will be more convenient to have the memory equipped with two control terminals marked simply write (W) and read (R). When W = 1, the word present on the memory data terminals is written into the memory, and when R = 1, the word in memory is read out to the data terminals. When W = R = 0, neither reading nor writing will take place, and W = R = 1 is not allowed. We can readily add the required gating between the terminal W and R and the terminals E and R/$\overline{\text{W}}$ (Prob. 9.1-1). The gates are assumed to be incorporated in the memory of Fig. 9.1-1 and are not shown explicitly.

As before, we have a program counter (PC) and a memory address register (MAR). We do not have an instruction register, but now we do have a 12-bit general-purpose register (GPR) and an operation register (OPR), which is 4 bits long and will hold the operation part of the instruction. When an instruction (consisting of an operation part and an operand address part) is read from the memory, the instruction will first be read into the GPR. The operation part of the instruction will then be transferred to the OPR. The operand address part of the instruction will be transferred to the memory address register (MAR). When the GPR is just holding the 8-bit address, 4 bits of the GPR capacity will not be in use. On the other hand, the full capacity of the GPR will be used when the GPR is storing an operand rather than the address of an operand. The present arrangement affords us the convenience of being able to separate the operation part of an instruction from the operand address part. We shall then be able to perform some useful manipulations of the address part without involving the operation part.

As before, we have incorporated into the program counter the ability to be incremented. But now, in addition we have provided direct connection between the program counter and the general-purpose register so that the contents of either register can be transferred to the other. Even more, we have actually provided two separate paths, one from PC to GPR and one from GPR to PC, so that the contents of the registers can be interchanged during a single clock cycle. Of course, for this interchange to occur, the flip-flops of these two registers must be of the type from which we can read and into which we can write in the same clock cycle. As we have pointed out, master-slave flip-flops as well as a number of other types are suitable.

The general-purpose register is capable of four microoperations:

1. It can transfer to itself the addressed memory word. To effect this transfer we shall raise to logic 1 the GPR control terminal marked M $\rightarrow$ GPR and simultaneously set at logic 1 the READ terminal of the memory. The READ control terminal of the memory is used for no other purpose than allowing a memory word to be read into GPR; hence, as indicated, we are free to connect the READ terminal to the GPR terminal marked M $\rightarrow$ GPR.
2. It can transfer to itself the contents of the accumulator.
3. It can transfer to itself the 8 bits in the program counter, placing the bits, of course, in the eight register positions reserved for the address.
4. It can be incremented.

Our new arithmetic-logic unit is designed differently from the ALU of Fig. 8.9-1 and compared with that earlier design has an expanded repertory. The new ALU has only a single 12-bit register plus an extra 1-bit register F, that is, a flip-flop. The ALU, of course, has a substantial amount of logic, i.e., combinatorial circuitry, which is not shown. The ALU can perform eight microoperations:

1. It can add to its present registration the 12-bit number on the 12-bit line that comes from the memory buffer register.
2. It can clear the accumulator.
3. It can clear F.
4. It can complement F.
5. It can complement the accumulator.
6. It can increment the accumulator.
7. It can rotate right through F (ROR F, Acc).
8. It can rotate left through F (ROL F, Acc).

In the operation ROR F, Acc all bits in the accumulator are shifted one position to the right. The bit in the F flip-flop is shifted into the leftmost accumulator position, and the bit originally in the rightmost accumulator position is shifted into the F flip-flop. Hence if we view the accumulator and F flip-flop as a ring counter, the operation ROR, F Acc rotates the bits one position to the right. Correspondingly, ROL F, Acc rotates the bits one position to the left. The two operations are represented diagramatically in Fig. 9.1-2.

For simplicity, we assume here that each transfer path is reserved for a single transfer function; i.e., no buses have to be shared. Thus the 12 bits of the general-purpose register are always available to the ALU to accept or not as the ALU pleases, and the 12 bits of the accumulator register are always avail-

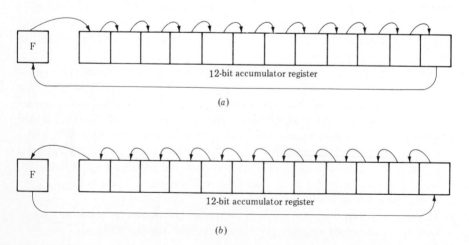

(a)

(b)

Figure 9.1-2 (a) The ROR F, Acc operation and, (b) the ROL F, Acc operation.

Table 9.1-1 System Components and Control Operations

Component	Control symbolism	Explanation
Memory	1. GPR → M	Write contents of GPR into addressed memory location
Program counter (PC)	2. PC + 1 → PC	Increment PC
	3. GPR(AD) → PC	Transfer address bits in general-purpose register to PC
Memory address register (MAR)	4. PC → MAR	Transfer from PC to MAR
	5. GPR(AD) → MAR	Transfer address bits in general-purpose register to MAR
Operation register (OPR)	6. GPR(OP) → OPR	Transfer operation bits in general-purpose register to OPR
General-purpose register (GPR)	7. M → GPR	Transfer addressed word to GPR
	8. Acc → GPR	Transfer contents of Acc to GPR
	9. PC → GPR(AD)	Transfer contents of program counter to address part of MAR
	10. GPR + 1 → GPR	Increment GPR
Arithmetic-logic unit (ALU)	11. GPR + Acc → Acc	Add number in GPR to number in Acc and leave sum in Acc
	12. 0 → Acc	Clear Acc
	13. ROR F, Acc	Rotate Acc to right through F
	14. ROL F, Acc	Rotate Acc to left through F
	15. 0 → F	Reset flip-flop F
	16. $\overline{F}$ → F	Complement flip-flop F
	17. $\overline{Acc}$ → Acc	Complement Acc
	18. Acc + 1 → Acc	Increment Acc

able to the general-purpose register. All paths over which word transfer will take place only in response to the activation of some control input are drawn as solid lines. The dashed path lines indicate transfer paths which require no such activation.

The controller will provide command signals to all the control terminals of the various registers and the memory; i.e., in appropriate clock cycles, as called for by the operation in the operation register, one or more control terminals will be raised to logic level 1. There are occasions, however, when the commands issued by the controller are required to depend on more than the operation part of the instruction. Instead, in the course of sequencing through the microoperations called for in the execution of a single instruction, the next microoperation in the sequence may depend on the results produced by the preceding microoperations. With this in mind we have made provision for two additional inputs to the controller. One of these comes from the GPR and is labeled Z. This line marked Z will be at logic 1 when (and only when) all 12 bits in the GPR are at zero. A further input F comes from the flag flip-flop associated with the accumulator register. We indicate these connections to make it reasonable when we say later that the controller follows one sequence or another depending on the logic level Z or on whether F is set or reset.

Table 9.1-1 lists all the components of our system, except for the controller, and all the symbols used to label the control terminals; for convenience, it states again, for each control terminal, the microoperation which is performed when the terminal is activated.

9.2 INSTRUCTIONS

As before, when the controller is started, it will run around and around, fetching an instruction, executing it, fetching another instruction, etc. Let us assume that we have manually set the program counter (PC) at the address of the first instruction. The sequence of microoperations followed in the present case to *fetch* an instruction is as follows:

Clock cycle	Microoperation	Explanation
1	PC → MAR	Transfer instruction location from program counter to memory address register
2	M → GPR PC + 1 → PC	Transfer addressed word to general-purpose register; increment program counter
3	GPR (OP) → OPR	Transfer operation part of instruction to operation register

When the sequence of fetch microoperations is complete, the operation part of the instruction has been transferred to the operation register. If there is an operand involved in the instruction, the address of this operand is left in the address part of the general-purpose register GPR (AD). Of course, not all instructions involve an operand; in such cases the contents of GPR (AD) at the end of the fetch sequence are of no particular relevance.

We shall now define a number of instructions for our computer. Of course, an instruction is feasible only if it can be effected by raising to the active level, in some sequence, the command terminals displayed in Fig. 9.1 1. If we keep our instructions simple and few, we shall keep the controller simple. In such cases, programs of instruction written to achieve some useful computational purpose will necessarily become longer. If we introduce complicated and numerous instructions, program writing becomes simpler but the controller become correspondingly more elaborate. We shall favor the alternative of few and simple instructions, the instructions being nonetheless representative of the instructions used in more sophisticated commercial components.

We introduce first a number of instructions which are quite elemental in the sense that each requires a single command terminal to be raised to the active level. Hence each can be executed in a single clock cycle and consists of a single microoperation. None of these involves a reference to the memory either for reading or writing, and hence none involves an address. We have:

Instruction (microoperation)	Explanation	Mnemonic
$0 \to$ Acc	Clear accumulator	CRA
$\overline{\text{Acc}} \to$ Acc	Complement accumulator	CTA
Acc $+ 1 \to$ Acc	Increment accumulator	ITA
$0 \to$ F	Clear flip-flop F	CRF
$\overline{\text{F}} \to$ F	Complement flip-flop F	CTF
PC $+ 1 \to$ PC	Skip next instruction if F is zero	SFZ
Rotate right	Rotate right through F and Acc	ROR
Rotate left	Rotate left through F and Acc	ROL

The SKIP instruction PC $+ 1 \to$ PC merits some comment. Suppose that this instruction is located at memory address K. During the *fetch* sequence of microoperations which reads this instruction out of the memory, the program counter PC is incremented so that PC is at $K + 1$. However, the execution of this instruction, like that of any instruction, causes an additional incrementing, so that after the execution we have PC $= K + 2$ and the instruction at memory address $K + 1$ is skipped over. We note further that this skip is conditional on the value of F. If F $= 0$, the skip microoperation PC $+ 1 \to$ PC is indeed executed. On the other hand, if at the time this skip operation is called forth it turns out that F $= 1$, then the instruction executes no operation at all. In setting up the architecture of Fig. 9.1-1 we intended this skip operation to be conditional on F. It was for this reason that F is one of the inputs to the controller. We shall see how this skip instruction in cooperation with a JUMP instruction (presented below) will allow our machine to select one course of action or another depending on the value of F.

We consider now additional instructions which require a *sequence* of microoperations for their execution.

ADD, address

Add to the present content of the accumulator the number (operand) located at the memory address which is specified as part of the instruction.

The fetch part of the cycle has transferred the operation part of this instruction to the operation register (OPR), and the operand address part of the instruction is left in the address part of the general-purpose register GPR (AD). The instruction is now executed by the following sequence of microoperations:

Clock cycle	Microoperation	Explanation
1	GPR(AD) → MAR	Transfer address of operand from GPR(AD) to MAR
2	M → GPR	Read from memory the word at the location whose address is in MAR
3	GPR + Acc → Acc	Add contents of GPR to contents of Acc, leaving sum in Acc

Frequently instead of adding to the accumulator an operand from memory we shall simply want to transfer such an operand to the accumulator. An instruction of this sort would be described as "load the accumulator" and might well have the mnemonic LDA. However, for the sake of economy we shall not introduce such an instruction. Instead, when we require such a "load" operation, we shall effect it by using, in sequence, the two instructions CRA (clear the accumulator) and ADD (add to accumulator).

The instruction ADD provides the address of the operand which is to be added to the accumulator. As we shall see, it is often of great convenience to have an instruction which, instead of providing the address of the operand, holds rather the address of a memory location which in turn holds the address of the operand. When an operand address is provided in this round-about manner, we say that the address is *indirect*. To indicate that an instruction involves an indirect address we shall append the symbol I to the instruction mnemonic. The difference between ADD (add to accumulator) and ADDI (add to accumulator, indirect) is made clear in Fig. 9.2-1. Here, to simplify we have written binary words in hexadecimal notation (see Sec. 1.13). In Fig. 9.2-1a we consider that memory location 03 contains the instruction ADD 37, which means that the accumulator is to have added to it the operand located in memory location 37. (The operation part of the instruction uses 4 bits, as do each of the numbers $3 = 0011$ and $7 = 0111$.) The operand is now found straightforwardly at memory location 37. In Fig. 9.2-1b, where indirect addressing is intended, we find at memory location 37 not the operand but the address of the operand. (Since location 37 contains

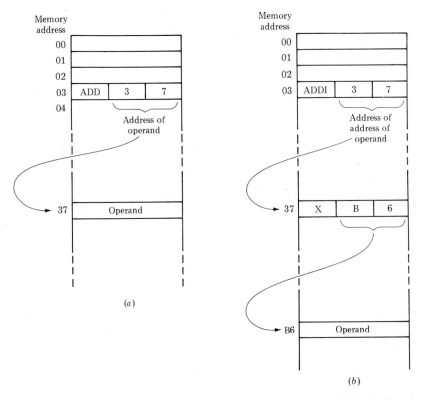

Figure 9.2-1 The difference between (*a*) a direct address instruction and (*b*) an indirect instruction.

only an address, only 8 of the 12 bits are relevant and the first 4 bits are don't-cares.) At location 37 we find that the operand is at memory location B6, and this is the operand which is added to the accumulator. The sequence of microoperations called for by the ADDI instruction is:

Clock cycle	Microoperation	Explanation
1	GPR(AD) → MAR	Transfer address from GPR to MAR
2	M → GPR	Transfer memory contents at addressed location to GPR (GPR will then have operand address)
3	GPR(AD) → MAR	Transfer operand address to MAR
4	M → GPR	Transfer addressed operand to GPR
5	GPR + Acc → Acc	Add contents of GPR to Acc

If we need to effect an indirect load of the accumulator, we can do so by the sequence of instructions CRA (clear accumulator) followed by ADDI.

The sequence of instructions CRA and ADD draws forth an operand from memory: i.e., they *read* the memory and transfer the word so read into the accumulator. The inverse instruction *writes* into the memory the contents of the accumulator. The mnemonic for this instruction is STA (store the accumulator). For this STA instruction we then have the following definition:

STA, address

Store the contents of the accumulator at a specified memory address.

The sequence of microoperations is:

Clock cycle	Microoperation	Explanation
1	GPR(AD) → MAR	Transfer address from GPR to MAR
2	Acc → GPR	Transfer Acc contents to GPR
3	GPR → M	Write GPR contents into memory at address held in MAR

We have noted that normally instructions are listed in memory in the order in which they are to be executed, and we access one instruction after another by incrementing the program counter. Yet, as we shall see, it is sometimes useful not to follow such a procedure but to jump to an instruction which is not in sequential order. The next several instructions provide just such an ability.

JMP, address

Jump to the instruction located at the memory location specified in the instruction.

To make clear the intent of his instruction, suppose that, as the controller fetches and executes instruction after instruction, it fetches the instruction JMP 29. Then the only execution which the controller performs is to transfer the address, that is, 29, not to the memory address register (MAR) but to the program counter (PC). The single microoperation called for is:

Clock cycle	Microoperation	Explanation
1	GPR(AD) → PC	Transfer address of next instruction from GPR to PC

Hence the *next* instruction which will be fetched is the instruction in memory location 29; and as long as no other jump instructions are encountered, the machine will next proceed in order to the instruction in memory location 30, 31, etc.

JMPI, address

Jump to instruction whose address is located at the memory address specified in the instruction.

This instruction is the *indirect* form of the JMP instruction given above. The address part of the JMPI instruction is the address of the memory location which holds the *address of the next* instruction. The microoperation sequence is:

Clock cycle	Microoperation	Explanation
1	$GPR(AD) \rightarrow MAR$	Transfer address to MAR
2	$M \rightarrow GPR(AD)$	Read address of next instruction from memory
3	$GPR(AD) \rightarrow PC$	Transfer address of next instruction from GPR to PC

Some explanation is in order before we present the next instruction. Suppose that we write a program (a list of instructions for the computer to carry out in order to accomplish some purpose) for our computer. Suppose, further, that we find that fairly often during the execution of the program a particular set of instructions recurs regularly. For example, the program might often call for the multiplication of two numbers. As we shall see, our machine will not be able to carry out such an instruction for multiplication directly. Instead, to effect a multiplication we shall have to arrange for the computer to go through a list of simpler instructions, i.e., a multiplication *routine*, to which it can respond. If we please, we can simply include this routine in our program each time a multiplication is required. There is, however, an alternative procedure which has obvious merit. Somewhere in memory we can store this routine just once. Then whenever multiplication is called for, we can jump to the stored routine, and when the multiplication routine has been completed, we can return to the place in our program from which we jumped.

This process of leaving the ordered sequence of instructions to go to a special routine is referred to as *calling a subroutine* or *jumping to a subroutine.* The end of a subroutine call must always be a *return* to the place in the program from which the jump was made.

Before jumping to a subroutine, we must *select a place in memory* where we propose to store the address to be restored to the program counter when the subroutine has been completed. This address of this *selected place* must be included in the instruction which calls up the subroutine. We must also include

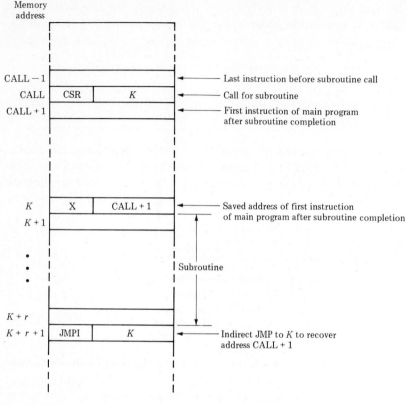

Figure 9.2-2 The manipulations involved in a subroutine call.

in the instruction the address in memory where the subroutine begins. Hence this CSR (call subroutine) instruction actually involves two addresses. However, since our CSR instruction, like all other instructions, can accommodate only one address, there must be some prior arrangement or understanding.

The means by which we propose to call a subroutine and then to return to the interrupted main program is shown in Fig. 9.2-2. The CSR instruction is in memory at the address CALL. The subroutine to which we are to jump is stored in r successive locations $K + 1$, $K + 2, \ldots, K + r$. As with the main program, we assume that the instructions in the subroutine are stored in successive memory locations in the order in which they are to be executed. We have exercised the forethought to arrange that the memory locations K and $K + r + 1$ shall be available for our purposes. Now to call the subroutine and then return from it we write into our program, at appropriate places, two instructions. The first instruction is the CSR instruction presently under discussion and having the definition:

CSR, address

Call subroutine. Store the return address to the main program, (i.e., the address CALL + 1) in the memory location specified in this instruction (i.e., address $= K$) and fetch the next from memory location $K + 1$.

The second instruction is written at memory location $K + r + 1$ and is the indirect jump instruction JMPI K which returns the program to the instruction at CALL + 1. The sequence of microoperations required to carry out the CSR instruction is detailed below.

Clock cycle	Microoperation	Explanation
1	GPR(AD) → MAR	Transfer to MAR the address where return address is to be stored; this storage address is K
2	GPR(AD) → PC PC → GPR(AD)	Interchange contents of PC and GPR(AD) [after interchange PC holds address K and GPR(AD) holds CALL + 1 since PC was incremented from CALL to CALL + 1 during fetch cycle]
3	GPR(AD) → M	Transfer GPR(AD) to memory [result is that address CALL + 1 will be written into memory location K]
4	PC + 1 → PC	Increment PC [PC will then hold address $K + 1$; next instruction will then be taken from location $K + 1$, which is first instruction of subroutine]

An explanation is again called for before describing the next instruction. There are occasions when a sequence of instructions must be followed over and over again a large number of times. Such a repetitive sequence is carried out by executing a *program loop*. The idea is that once the sequence has been completed, the next instruction encountered is a JUMP instruction which makes the program go back to the beginning of the sequence. The ISZ instruction is used to end this process of looping when it has been repeated the required number of times. Suppose that the looping needs to be done n times. Then the negative number $-n$ is stored in some appropriate location in the memory. At each looping the number $-n$ is read from memory, incremented, and returned to memory. When the looping has been performed n times, the number will have been incremented to zero. At this point the "next instruction," which is the instruction to jump back to the beginning of the loop, will be skipped and the program will advance out of the loop. The precise definition is:

ISZ, address

Increment and skip if zero. Read the number at the specified memory location, increment it, and return it to its original location. If, after the incrementing, the number is zero, skip the next instruction.

The microoperations required for this ISZ instruction are:

Clock cycle	Microoperations	Explanation
1	GPR(AD) → MAR	Transfer to MAR the location of the number to be incremented
2	M → GPR	Read number from memory
3	GPR + 1 → GPR	Increment number
4	GPR → M	Return number to memory
5	PC + 1 → PC (if GPR = 0)	Skip next instruction if GPR = 0

Note that to carry out this instruction, the controller needs to know when the registration in GPR is zero. But, as will be recalled, and as is indicated in Fig. 9.1-1, such information is made available over the line marked Z (zero). Note further that the program counter is incremented during the fetch cycle. Hence, if it is incremented again, as in clock cycle 5, PC will have been incremented twice and the jump instruction which returns the program to the beginning of the loop will be skipped.

9.3 SUMMARY OF INSTRUCTIONS

To allow an overall view of the computer we have postulated, we summarize here the entire repertory of instructions:

1. CRA clear accumulator
2. CTA complement accumulator
3. ITA increment accumulator
4. CRF clear flip-flop F
5. CTF complement flip-flop F
6. SFZ skip next instruction if F = 0
7. ROR rotate right
8. ROL rotate left
9. ADD add to accumulator
10. ADDI add indirect to accumulator
11. STA store in memory from accumulator
12. JMP jump
13. JMPI jump indirect

14. CSR call subroutine
15. ISZ increment and skip if $Z = 0$
16. HLT Halt

Note that, in addition to the instructions we have described we have added the essential instruction HALT.

The following sections give some examples displaying how our computer can be programmed to perform some useful functions.

9.4 ADDITION AND SUBTRACTION

In Fig. 9.4-1 we have made entries in memory as required to arrange for our computer to calculate the sum of three numbers and then store the sum in the memory. (All the numbers are expressed in hexadecimal code.) The first six memory locations 00 to 05 hold instructions. The leftmost 4 bits of an instruction define the operation. Since we have not established a code for the operations, we leave the operations written out in mnemonic form. The first four instructions have addresses. The HLT instruction has no address, so that the address part of this instruction has don't-cares entered. The operands which are to be added ($017 + 00B + 01C = 03E$) are stored in locations 06, 07, and 08. The sum is to be stored in location 09. The first instruction clears the accumulator and loads the accumulator with the contents of location 06. The second adds the contents of location 07, etc. We have stored the result in location 09. Suppose, however, that once the computation has been completed we no longer need the program or the operands. In that case, we could just as well have stored the result in any of the locations 00 to 08.

In the simple program of Fig. 9.4-1 we were able to see at the outset that we would require five locations 00 to 05 to write out the sequence of instruc-

Memory location				Explanation
00	CRA	×	×	Clear Acc
01	ADD	0	6	Add contents of 06 into Acc
02	ADD	0	7	Add contents of 07 to Acc
03	ADD	0	8	Add contents of 08 to Acc
04	STA	0	9	Store Acc contents at location 09
05	HLT	×	×	Halt
06	0	1	7	Operand at 06
07	0	0	B	Operand at 07
08	0	1	C	Operand at 08
09				← 03E will be stored here at program end

Figure 9.4-1 The memory content for a program to find the sum of three numbers.

tions. Hence we were able immediately to locate the first operand in location 06 and thereby write the first two instructions as CRA and ADD 06. In the more general case it will be much more convenient not to have to specify a precise numerical memory location for each operand until after the program has been completely written. It is more convenient to specify operand addresses in symbolic form, the symbols being eventually replaced by numbers when the program is complete. Such a procedure will also avoid having to change many numbers whenever a program step or operand is added or deleted.

The program of Fig. 9.4-1 is duplicated in Table 9.4-1 with the addresses in symbolic form. Since there is no need to make reference in the program to the locations of the first five entries in the program, no symbolic addresses have been assigned them. When the program is presented in the form of Table 9.4-1, eventually somebody (or something) will have to make a number of decisions. Thus, at what memory location is the program to start? In Fig. 9.4-1 we arbitrarily started the program at location 00, but of course it may suit our convenience to start elsewhere. Once the program's initial location has been decided, all succeeding instructions must follow in order in successive locations. However, there is no need for operands to follow immediately after the instructions, nor is it necessary for operands to be placed in successive locations.

Next let us use our computer to subtract one number from another, say 0B7 − 09C (hex). Our simpler machine of Fig. 8.9-1 had a subtraction instruction. Since our present machine has an organization and architecture which do not include such an instruction, we shall have to write a program. To effect a subtraction we must form the negative of the subtrahend. This sign change can be carried out in the accumulator by exercising the ability of the accumulator to complement and increment. We must load the subtrahend into the

Table 9.4-1 The Program of Fig. 9.4-1 Written Assigning Symbolic Addresses to Memory Locations to Which Reference Must Be Made

Symbolic location	Location content	Comment
	CRA	Clear Acc
	ADD W	Add contents of W into Acc
	ADD X	Add contents of X to Acc
	ADD Y	Add contents of Y to Acc
	STA Z	Store Acc contents at location Z
	HLT	Halt
W	017	Operand at W
X	00B	Operand at X
Y	01C	Operand at Y
Z	XXX	Storage location for result

Table 9.4-2 Program for Subtraction

Label	Contents	Comment
	CRA	Clear Acc
	ADD SUB	Add subtrahend into Acc
	CTA	Complement Acc
	ITA	Increment Acc
	ADD MIN	Add minuend to Acc
	STA DIF	Store at location labeled "DIF"
	HLT	Halt
SUB	09C	Subtrahend at location labeled "SUB"
MIN	0B7	Minuend at location labeled "MIN"
DIF	XXX	Location where difference will be stored (difference will be 0B7 − 09C = 01B)

accumulator first; for if the minuend were loaded first, the accumulator would no longer be available to change the sign. The program for the subtraction is given in Table 9.4-2. Here the terminology has been changed from "symbolic address" to the more customary term *label*.

Table 9.4-3 shows the program which calculates 0B7—09C—005. Here, since there are two subtrahends, the accumulator register must be used twice to change signs. When one sign change has been effected, the result must be stored in the memory to leave the accumulator available to change the sign of the second subtrahend.

9.5 USE OF JMP AND ISZ

As an example of the usefulness of the JMP and ISZ instructions and of the indirect feature, let us see how our machine can be used to form the sum of a large number (say 100) of addends. In any event, we shall have to put our 100 addends in memory. Thereafter we can write a program in which we simply include 100 successive ADD instructions, which differ from each other only in the operand address. A shorter and more elegant program is listed in Table 9.5-1.

The program provides a memory location (ANA) which holds the address of the next addend to be summed. After each addition this address is incremented. A second special memory counter location (CTR) is used to hold the count of the number of addends summed. The repetitive additions are programmed by providing for a looping over and over again until the job is done. The counter location holds the number −100 (decimal) = F9C (hex) at the outset. At each addition the counter is incremented until finally the counter reaches zero.

Table 9.4-3 Program for Subtraction Involving Two Subtrahends

Label	Contents	Comment
	CRA	Clear Acc
	ADD SUB(1)	Add to Acc contents of location "SUB(1)" (subtrahend 1)
	CTA	Complement Acc
	ITA	Increment Acc
	STA NSUB(1)	Store at location "NSUB(1)" (negative of subtrahend 1)
	CRA	Clear Acc
	ADD SUB(2)	Add subtrahend (2) to Acc
	CTA	Complement Acc
	ITA	Increment Acc
	ADD MIN	Add to Acc contents of location "MIN" (minuend)
	ADD NSUB(1)	Add contents of location "NSUB(1)"
	STA RES	Store at location "RES" (result)
	HLT	HALT
MIN	0B7	Minuend at location "MIN"
SUB(1)	09C	Subtrahend 1 at location "SUB(1)"
SUB(2)	005	Subtrahend 2 at location "SUB(2)"
NSUB(1)	XXX	Location for storage of negative of SUB(1)
RES	XXX	Location for storing result

Referring now to the program in Table 9.5-1, we find that after the accumulator has been cleared, the next instruction provides for an *indirect* addition. The memory location ANA holds not the addend but the address of the addend. At the outset, the address in ANA is the first addend address (FAD), and we note that at address FAD we do have the first addend. Having placed ADD(1) in the accumulator we now increment the address held in ANA. For this incrementing operation we have used an ISZ instruction. Although we do not anticipate that the entry in ANA will ever become zero, we find it convenient to use this instruction to increment even if by so doing we do not take advantage of the entire operation the instruction can perform. We next increment the number in the CTR location. As long as the CTR location has not yet reached zero, the next instruction is not skipped. This next instruction loops the program back to the ADDI instruction, as a result of which the next addend is added to the accumulator. Note that since it is necessary, at another point in the program, to refer back the ADDI instruction, it is necessary specifically to assign a label to its address. The program will loop 100 times until finally the contents of the counter location are zero. At this zero, the JMP instruction will be skipped, the result will be stored, and the computer will halt.

Table 9.5-1 A Program for Summing a Large Number of Addends

Label	Content	Comment
	CRA	Clear Acc
LOOP	ADDI ANA	Add to Acc the number whose address is at location "ANA" (address of next addend)
	ISZ ANA	Increment address of addend
	ISZ CTR	Increment number at location "CTR" and skip next instruction if increment makes the contents of CTR equal to 0
	JMP LOOP	JMP back to instruction labeled "LOOP"
	STA RES	Store result in location "RES"
	HLT	Halt
RES	XXX	Result to be stored here
ANA	FAD	This location holds address of next addend
CTR	F9C	This location holds count of number of additions to be done (Twos complement representation of -100)
FAD	ADD(1)	100 addends to be summed
	ADD(2)	
	.	
	.	
	.	
	ADD(100)	

9.6 PROGRAM FOR MULTIPLICATION

One way to program multiplication is simply to use a succession of additions. Thus to multiply 18 by 16 we add 18 to itself 16 times or 16 to itself 18 times. This rather inelegant scheme is not to be deprecated when used with quite small and slow computers. Even so well received a minicomputer as the DEC pdp-8 provides for no other method in its basic scheme of instructions. While this expedient is available to us also, we shall consider as well the method of multiplication which uses shifting and adding, the way multiplication is ordinarily done with pencil and paper (Fig. 5.15-1). We are able to use this method because we have incorporated in our machine provision for shifting the accumulator contents and because we have provided an input to the controller from flip-flop F, which is an extension of the accumulator.

The scheme is as follows. In the memory we provide locations for storing the multiplicand, the multiplier, and the sum of the partial products (multiplicand = MD, multiplier = MR, sum of partial products = SP). We transfer the multiplier to the accumulator register and circulate right, thereby shifting the least significant bit of the multiplier into the flag flip-flop F. The shifted multiplier is then returned to its location MR, so that we can use the accumulator to deal with the multiplicand. The multiplicand is then transferred to the accumulator. If $F = 1$, the contents of location SP (SP initially is a cleared memory location) are added to the multiplicand in the accumulator register and the accumulator content is then returned to location SP. We then return the multiplicand to the accumulator, rotate to the left, and return the shifted multiplicand to its storage location MD. If $F = 0$, addition of the multiplicand to the contents of SP is not done but the shift of the multiplicand is still performed. The right rotation of the multiplier is done so that we can check each bit of the multiplier and take one course or another according as the bit is 1 or 0. This check and consequent change in course of action can be made only by shifting the bit into the flip-flop F, since only this flip-flop in the ALU has a connection to the controller. The left shift of the multiplicand is done to multiply the multiplicand by successive factors of 2.

In our machine, since the numerical data have 12 bits, this process of adding partial products (whenever $F = 1$) and shifting must be done 12 times. We must therefore incorporate a *loop* into our program, and we must have a *counter* location in the memory which serves to count the numbers of times the loop is completed.

The program for multiplication is given in Table 9.6-1. We have assumed here that multiplicand and multiplier are such that the product can be contained in 12 bits. (At a maximum the product of two 12-bit numbers will extend to 24 bits.) The instructions in memory locations 1 and 2 clear the location SP, where the sum of partial products is to be stored. We have no direct means of clearing a memory location. Hence to clear SP we clear instead the accumulator register and then shift to SP the accumulator contents. Locations 3, 4, and 5 place the rightmost bit of the multiplier in the flag flip-flop F, shift the multiplier, and store it back into memory. Locations 6, 7, and 8 together determine the ensuing course of the program, depending on whether $F = 1$ or $F = 0$. Locations 9, 10, 11, and 12, which are part of the program if $F = 1$, add the multiplicand to the contents of location SP. Locations 14, 15, 16, and 17 shift the multiplicand and return it to its storage location. The clearing operation in line 13 is necessary to avoid shifting a 1 into the rightmost location of the accumulator when the multiplicand is shifted to multiply by 2. Location 18 increments the entry in the counter (CTR) location, and location 19 carries the program back to LOOP. The entry in CTR is FF4, which is the twos-complement hexadecimal representation of -12 (decimal).

9.7 PROGRAM ILLUSTRATING SUBROUTINE CALL

To illustrate a subroutine call, let us consider a program to compute the quantity $N_1 N_2 + N_3 N_4 + N_5 N_6 + \ldots$, the N's being unsigned positive numbers. Here there are repeated multiplications and additions. The program for addition is so simple that we may well write an addition program over and over again as frequently as it is called for. The multiplication program, on the other

Table 9.6-1 Program for Multiplication

Memory location	Label	Contents	Comment
1		CRA	Clear location where the sum of
2		STA SP	products SP, i.e., result of multiplication, will be stored
3	LOOP	ADD MR	Load contents of location MR into Acc
4		ROR	Rotate right to shift rightmost bit of multiplier into F
5		STA MR	Put shifted multiplier back into location MR
6		SFZ	Skip next instruction if F = 0
7		JMP 1	Jump to instruction at location labeled "1" (since F ≠ 0)
8		JMP 0	Jump to instruction at location labeled "0" (since F = 0)
9	1	CRA	Load contents of location MD into Acc
10		ADD MD	
11		ADD SP	Add contents of location SP to Acc
12		STA SP	Store Acc contents in location SP
13		CRF	Clear flip-flop F
14	0	CRA	Load contents of location MD into Acc
15		ADD MD	
16		ROL	Rotate left
17		STA MD	Put shifted multiplicand back into location MD
18		ISZ CTR	Increment counter
19		JMP LOOP	Counter not zero, jump back to instruction at "LOOP"
20		HLT	Halt
21	CTR	FF4	Hexadecimal representation of −12
22	MD	Multiplicand	Location to hold multiplicand
23	MR	Multiplier	Location to hold multiplier
24	SP	XXX	Location to hold result (cleared by first two instructions)

hand, is long enough to make it well worth while to install the mutiplication routine in a subroutine so that we can call it up repeatedly. The program in Table 9.7-1 calculates the quantity $N_1 N_2 + N_3 N_4$. The program is written so that if we want to add additional terms ($N_5 N_6$, etc.), we have but to enter the additional numbers and provide additional program steps to do the addition.

Memory locations 1 through 4 hold the data. Since we shall have to have

Table 9.7-1 Program in Which the Multiplication Program Appears as a Subroutine

Memory location	Label	Contents	Comment
1	A	N_1	Memory locations A, B, C, and D hold
2	B	N_2	numbers N_1, N_2, N_3, and N_4 to be combined
3	C	N_3	into $N_1 N_2 + N_3 N_4$
4	D	N_4	
5	T	FF4	Hexadecimal representation of -12
6		CRA	Puts N_1 in location "MD," reserved for
7		ADD A	multiplicand in multiplication subroutine
8		STA MD	
9		CRA	Puts N_2 in location "MR," reserved for
10		ADD B	multiplier in multiplication subroutine
11		STA MR	
12		CSR MULT	Calls subroutine at address "MULT"
13		CRA	Clears location "PR" to be used to
14		STA PR	store the partial result $N_1 N_2$
15		ADD SP	Stores partial result $N_1 N_2$ in
16		STA PR	location "PR"
17		CRA	Puts N_3 and N_4 in "MD" and "MR," where
18		ADD C	they are accessible to multiplication
19		STA MD	subroutine
20		CRA	
21		ADD B	
22		STA MR	
23		CSR MULT	Calls multiplication subroutine again
24		CRA	Loads Acc with $N_3 N_4$ from location "SP"
25		ADD SP	
26		ADD PR	Adds $N_1 N_2$ from location "PR" to form $N_1 N_2 + N_3 N_4$
27		HLT	Halts, leaving $N_1 N_2 + N_3 N_4$ in Acc
28	MULT		Holds (changeable) return address
29		CRA	Puts -12 in memory location labeled "CTR"
30		ADD T	
31		STA CTR	
32		CRA	Multiplication
33		STA SP	subroutine
34	LOOP	ADD MR	
35		ROR	
36		STA MR	

Table 9.7-1 Program in Which the Multiplication Program Appears as a Subroutine (*continued*)

Memory location	Label	Contents	Comment
37		SFZ	Multiplication
38		JMP 1	subroutine
39		JMP 0	continued
40	1	CRA	
41		ADD MD	
42		ADD SP	
43		STA SP	
44		CRF	
45	0	CRA	
46		ADD MD	
47		ROL	
48		STA MD	
49		ISZ CTR	
50		JMP LOOP	
51		JMP I MULT	Returns to main program
52	CTR		Labeled memory locations reserved for
53	MD		counter, multiplicand, multiplier, sum of
54	MR		partial products, and partial results
55	SP		
56	PR		

access to these numbers, their locations have been identified by labels. Location 5, labeled again for access, simply holds the number -12. It will be recalled that, in the multiplication routine, we start with the number -12 stored in a memory location labeled "CTR." When the multiplication is completed, this CTR will be cleared. Hence we need to have available the number -12 so that we can load it into CTR at the beginning of each new call on the multiplication subroutine. The instructions in locations 6 through 11 load the numbers N_1 and N_2 into those memory locations associated with the multiplication subroutine which are reserved for the multiplicand and multiplier.

Location 12 calls up the multiplication subroutine. The part of this subroutine between locations 32 and line 50 is identical to the program of Table 9.6-1. Location 28 holds the address of the memory location where the next instruction is to be found after the subroutine has been completed. There is no instruction in that memory location. This line is labeled ("MULT") since we shall have to read this address to get back to the main program. The first time the multiplication routine is called up, the address placed into this location (28) will be address 13. To look ahead, we may note that there is a second subroutine call in location 23. When the instruction of line 23 has been executed, it will cause the return address 24 (which is the new value of the return address) to be stored in line 28. The instruction in location 51 is a jump back to location "MULT" to pick up the return address, which takes us back to the main program. In the program of Table 9.6-1, where only a single multiplication was contemplated, the corresponding instruction (line 18 of Table 9.6-1) was HLT.

Once we have returned from the subroutine, the instructions in locations 13 through 16 clear a memory location labeled "PR" (partial results), where the product N_1N_2 is then stored. Locations 17 through 22 load N_3 and N_4 into the multiplication routine, and location 22 calls up the subroutine again. Locations 24 and 26 add N_1N_2 to N_2N_3 and put the sum back in location PR. Additional terms N_5N_6, etc., can be formed and added in the same way, and then finally a HLT instruction will have to be appended.

9.8 MICROPROGRAMMING

In Chap. 8 we considered a number of ways in which a controller can be designed. Now we consider an additional technique of accomplishing control, called *microprogramming*. As we shall see, a microprogram-controlled computer is, in a sense, a computer within a computer. For this reason we have delayed describing the method until we had some elementary experience with a computer-type structure.

We have seen that the microoperations performed by our computer are performed in response to signals applied to the control terminals of the registers, the ALU, and the memory. These signals so applied are called *command signals*. In any one clock interval one or more control inputs must be raised to logic level 1 by the applied command signals.

Referring now to our machine in Fig. 9.1-1, we can verify that there are 18 input control terminals which at one time or another will require a command to become active. Let us then imagine a read-only memory, as in Fig. 9.8-1, in which the words are 18 bits long so that we can make a one-to-one association between the bits of the word and the control input terminals. In Fig. 9.8-1 we have, on an entirely arbitrary basis, assigned bit 3 of the memory word to the control terminal which when activated accomplishes the microoperation GPR(AD) $\rightarrow$ MAR. Similarly we have assigned bit 7 to M $\rightarrow$ MBR and bit 11 to GPR + Acc $\rightarrow$ Acc. The bit-3 output of the ROM is connected to the control terminal in Fig. 9.8-1 marked GPR(AD) $\rightarrow$ MAR, and so on. Let us now see, by way of example, how we can arrange to use the ROM to carry out in proper sequence the microoperations necessary to execute an instruction.

We consider specifically the instruction ADDI, whose microoperations, five in number, are detailed on page 383. Let us then arrange for the ROM to have written into it, in five successive word locations, the sequence of words listed in Fig. 9.8-2. And finally let us assume that the address register of Fig. 9.8-1 is started at the address of the first word and then incremented through the remaining addresses in synchronism with the clock which drives the com-

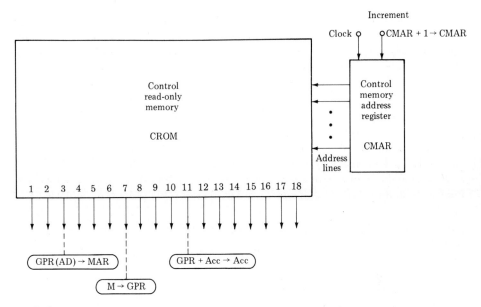

Figure 9.8-1 Words read in succession from a control ROM provide the sequential command signals required to control a processor.

puter of Fig. 9.1-1. During the first clock cycle only bit 3 is at logic 1, so that only the control terminal GPR(AD) → MAR is made active as required. In the second clock interval only bit 7 is at logic 1, so that the microoperation M → GPR is accomplished. In the third clock interval we again have GPR(AD) → MAR. In the fourth interval bit 7 is again at logic 1, so again the microoperation M → GPR will be executed. Finally in the fifth clock interval we shall have GPR + Acc → Acc. In this example, it turns out that in each clock cycle only one microoperation needs to be executed. Hence in each CROM word only 1 bit is at logic 1. When several microoperations need to be executed in the same clock cycle, a corresponding number of bits will be at logic 1.

Bit number

Word	1	2	3	4	5	6	7	8	9	10	11	12	13	14	15	16	17	18
1	0	0	1	0	0	0	0	0	0	0	0	0	0	0	0	0	0	0
2	0	0	0	0	0	0	1	0	0	0	0	0	0	0	0	0	0	0
3	0	0	1	0	0	0	0	0	0	0	0	0	0	0	0	0	0	0
4	0	0	0	0	0	0	1	0	0	0	0	0	0	0	0	0	0	0
5	0	0	0	0	0	0	0	0	0	0	1	0	0	0	0	0	0	0

Figure 9.8-2 The five successive microwords in the ROM of Figure 9.8-1 which provide the microinstructions to cause the execution of the microoperations required by the instruction ADDI.

Thus, altogether, by reading a succession of words, called *control words* or *microwords*, we carry out a sequence of *microoperations* stored in the read-only memory, and the end result is that we carry out an operation as required. The words in the ROM which identify the microperations are also called *microinstructions* (in contrast to the *instructions*, which are stored in the read-write RAM of the computer). To avoid ambiguity, the instructions of a machine may be called *macroinstructions* to distinguish them from the microinstructions stored in the control ROM. A computer whose controller operates as described here is called a *microprogrammed* computer. Note that such a computer has two memories: (1) like all computers, it has a RAM, which contains the instructions and data, and (2) in its controller it has a ROM, which contains the microinstruction used to execute the instructions. This second memory is generally referred to as the *control read-only memory* (CROM), and its address register is correspondingly called the *control memory address register* (CMAR).

9.9 MICROPROGRAM BRANCHING

The simple microprogramming scheme of the preceding section describes the principle of microprogramming but is not versatile enough to be of much use in a real situation. In this and the following sections we shall consider some elaborations.

In the arrangement of Fig. 9.8-1 we are able to read microinstructions only in the order in which they are written in the memory, but we should like to be able to branch or jump to an arbitrary location in the memory. An arrangement which allows such branching is shown in Fig. 9.9-1. Here we assume that there are N command bits to supply N inputs to the control terminals of the computer registers, and we assume that the number of microinstructions to be stored is such that an M-bit control memory address is required. We have then arranged for the number of bits in the ROM word to be $N + M + 1$. N bits are command bits, and M bits constitute the address to which a jump is to take place if indeed a jump is to occur. The extra bit is used to determine whether a jump is called for or not. This extra bit is the *load control bit*. If this bit is at logic 0, the *increment* input is at logic 1 and the address register will be incremented in each clock interval. If, however, the load control bit is at logic 1, incrementing will not occur. Instead we shall have logic 1 at the load-branch-address input terminal of the address register, and at the triggering edge of the clock the M-bit address to which we want to jump will be loaded into the address register. Of course, the address register of Fig. 9.9-1 is, in the matter of hardware implementation, more complicated than the register of Fig. 9.8-1. The first register must be able only to increment while the second register must be able to increment or to accept a parallel load.

In the control ROM of the microprogrammed controller of Fig. 9.9-1 we have provided enough bits per word for a word to contain an address as well as

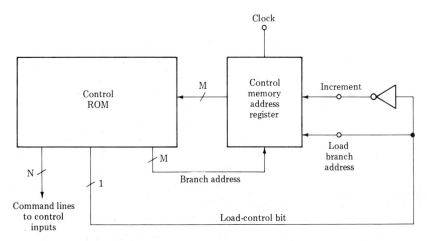

Figure 9.9-1 A modification of the arrangement of Fig. 9.8-1 which allows not only incrementing of the CROM address but also branching to an address specified by the preceding microword.

a microinstruction. This proliferation of bits is something which is generally avoided in establishing the word length of the RAM memory. There are two good reasons for this difference in inclination to extend word length: (1) RAMs are more expensive than ROMs of equal size, and (2) longer word length in the RAM, which holds instructions (rather than microinstructions) and data, would require correspondingly longer word length in nearly all the registers of the computer. Such is not the case when the ROM word length is increased. We therefore find generally that while designers add length to word size for instructions and data only after a deliberate decision to build a more expensive computer, bits are added to the control memory rather freely. At present microprogrammed control is coming to be regarded most favorably. It is the most systematized and orderly fashion of designing a controller, and the ROMs required in its hardware implementation are now inexpensive and readily available.

9.10 CONDITIONAL BRANCHING

We consider next the arrangement of Fig. 9.10-1. The *pipeline register* shown is not relevant to our present discussion and was included in the figure so that we can use the figure again in the discussion of the next section. For the present, then, we ignore the pipeline register and consider the dashed lines through this register simply to be continuations of the output lines of the control ROM.

The arrangement of Fig. 9.10-1 introduces additional flexibility into the controller. Here we have provided two load-control selection bits S_1 and S_0. The bits C_1 and C_2 are *status bits*, which are derived from some place in the com-

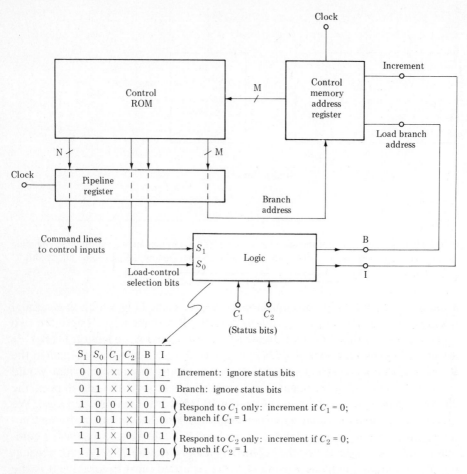

Figure 9.10-1 A further modification of a microprogrammed controller which allows the controller operation to be influenced by status bits.

puter and are intended to indicate whether or not some condition is satisfied. For example, the bit C_1 may be the controller input Z in Fig. 9.1-1. If C_1 (=Z) is $C_1 = 1$, the general-purpose register is cleared. If $C = 0$, this register is not cleared. Thus bit C_1 provides information about the status of the GPR. Similarly C_2 may provide status information about some other component of the computer. Thus, referring again to Fig. 9.1-1, C_2 may be F. Such status bits, when made available to the controller, allow the controller to follow one sequence or another depending on the logic level of the status bit.

The *logic* block in Fig. 9.10-1 is a combinational network whose truth table is as given (see Prob. 9.10-1); when $S_1 S_0 = 00$, the logic-block output I = 1 and the output B = 0. We assume that the control terminals of the control memory address register are active at logic 1. Hence when $S_1 S_0 = 00$, the register will increment. Similarly when $S_1 S_0 = 01$, the register will branch to the address specified by the address field of the microword whose instruction is being implemented. In both these cases the status bits are ignored. When $S_1 S_0 = 10$, the status bit C_1 determines whether incrementing or branching takes place, while when $S_1 S_0 = 11$, *status bit* C_2 determines whether incrementing or branching takes place. (Since I and B are always complementary to each other, we might have allowed just a single output line from the logic block and arranged the complementarity as in Fig. 9.9-1. We have not done so since at a later point we shall want to make some modifications permitting I and B to be at logic 0 simultaneously.)

9.11 PIPELINING

We shall see in this section how the addition of the *pipeline register* serves to increase the speed at which the microprogrammed controller can operate. Let us first consider, in the *absence* of the pipeline register, the time delays associated with the controller and the system it controls. Suppose, in the absence of the pipeline register, that a clock triggering transition occurs at time $t = t_0$. The time t_0 is the beginning time for the operation of establishing a new address in the control memory address register either by incrementing or by loading. How long must we now wait before we can allow the next triggering transition? First we must wait a time t_A to allow a valid address to be established at the output of the address register. (The address is valid after all M address-register output lines present the proper new bit to the ROM and no further changes are to occur.) Next we must wait the additional time t_M of the propagation delay through the control memory. After a time $t_A + t_M$ the addressed microinstruction will be validly established at the control memory output. We must now wait further for the controlled system to respond to the microinstructions, to complete its response, and to be ready for the next instruction. If we call the system response time t_R, the minimum allowable clock period is $t_A + t_M + t_R$. The longest of these component times is t_R, which must be long enough to accommodate the slowest microoperation, generally the operation of reading from, or writing into, a RAM.

The process of establishing a new ROM output microword *begins* at the moment of the occurrence of the clock triggering transition when the address register begins to increment or to load a branch address. It now occurs to us that we may be able to save time by *beginning* to establish a new microword before the controlled system has completed its response to the previous microword.

Let t_X be the propagation delay time of the logic box in Fig. 9.10-1, and let the clock period be $t_C = t_A + t_M + t_X$. At, say, $t = t_0$ a clock edge starts the address register in the process of incrementing and loading a branch address. At $t = t_0 + t_A + t_M$ a new microword is validly established at the ROM output, and at $t = t_0 + t_A + t_M + t_X = t_0 + t_C$ a valid load control bit has been supplied to the address register so that the next triggering clock edge can occur. With the clock period set at $t_C = t_A + t_M + t_X$ new valid microwords will appear at the ROM output in succession at the clock rate. Suppose now that the system response time t_R is less than the clock period. Then the controlled system will have adequate time to respond to each microinstruction. For example, suppose that the clock period is $t_C = t_A + t_M + t_X = 2 + 3 + 1 = 6 \, \mu s$ and that the system response time is $t_R = 4 \, \mu s$. New microinstructions will be presented to the controlled system every 6 μs, and the system will complete its response in 4 μs. Clocking edges at $t = 0, 6, 12 \, \mu s$ will generate valid microinstructions at $t = 6$, 12, 18 μs. The system will respond to the microinstruction which is presented at $t = 6$ during the interval from $t = 6$ to $t = 10$. The system then waits to receive its next microinstruction at $t = 12$ and makes its corresponding response from $t = 12$ to $t = 16$, and so on. The important point is that time is saved because the system makes its response to a microoperation *at the same time* that the next microoperation is making its way through the pipeline, i.e., through the combinational logic box, the address register, and the ROM. The clock period is 6 μs rather than 10 μs, as it would be if we waited for the system response to be complete before we started to generate a new microoperation.

The argument of the previous paragraph, which indicates how the clock rate can be increased, is actually *not valid*. It is assumed there that if, at $t = t_0$, a triggering transition occurs, a new ROM output microword will appear at $t_0 + t_A + t_M$, that in the intervening interval from t_0 to $t_0 + t_A + t_M$ *no change* will occur at the ROM output, and that during the interval the ROM output will hold the previous microword. Such is not the case. It is true that we need to wait a time $t_A + t_M$ to be sure that *all* changes in ROM output that are going to occur have indeed taken place. However, some changes may take place after a much shorter interval. Thus, while it may require 5 μs for a completely valid new ROM output to be established, some ROM outputs may change in as little as 0.1 μs. Since we must allow *no* changes in ROM output until the system has completed its response, we must wait for a completion of system response before we even *begin* the process of changing the address.

This difficulty is relieved by adding the *pipeline register* indicated in Fig. 9.10-1, as we shall now see. This register does not really constitute the pipeline since it is actually the propagation delays through the logic block, address register, and ROM which are analogous to a pipeline. The pipeline register serves rather as a "valve" at the end of the pipeline, allowing the pipeline to operate effectively. The pipeline register is driven by the same clock waveform which drives the address register. The clock transition which increments or loads the address register is the same transition which loads the pipeline register with the ROM output microword. The response of the controlled system can now begin at the instant when the pipeline register is loaded. *At this very same moment* we can begin to change the address in order to call forth the next microinstruction. While the controlled system is completing its response, the bits of the ROM output word may indeed be changing, but these changes cause no problem because the system is separated from the changing microinstruction because of the isolation provided by the pipeline register.

9.12 A MICROPROGRAMMED CONTROLLER

In the computer of Fig. 9.1-1 we included a controller to provide command enabling signals to all the component registers so that each register will perform one of its repertory of microoperations as is required. To illustrate the principle of microprogramming we shall now consider how the controller can be realized as a microprogrammed controller. The microprogrammed controller is shown in Fig. 9.12-1 and is patterned after the controller of Fig. 9.10-1. For simplicity we have omitted the feature of pipelining since pipelining does not affect the principle of operation, only its speed.

In the diagram of the complete computer system (Fig. 9.1-1) we note that the controller has inputs from the operation register (OPR), the general-purpose register (GPR), and the accumulator flag F. These two registers and the flag register are incorporated into Fig. 9.12-1. The condition-for-branching bit C_1 in Fig. 9.10-1 becomes the bit Z provided by the GPR. This bit supplies information concerning the *status* of the GPR. When the registration in the GPR is zero, $Z = 1$; otherwise $Z = 0$. Similarly the logic line F, replacing C_2, furnishes a *status* bit to the controller informing the controller whether the flag flip-flop F is set or reset. In the controller of Fig. 9.10-1 we made provision either to increment the control memory address register (CMAR) or to load into it the branch address. In the present case we have made provision, as well, to allow loading into the CMAR an address determined by the operation code registered in the operation register. (The actual address is determined by the OPR and the combinational mapping logic, as we shall see.) The command signal for loading this operation-register-determined address is marked "load routine." Note that the load-control-selection field now consists of 3 bits rather than 2 bits as in Fig. 9.10-1. We shall now describe how the microprogrammed controller operates.

The sequence of microoperations (written into the control ROM as a sequence of microwords), which carries out the necessary steps to fetch an instruction, is called the *fetch routine*. Similarly a sequence which causes the execution of an instruction is called an *execute routine*. At some location in the control ROM, say beginning at a location which we shall call ADDR(FETCH), we shall write the fetch routine. The controller will sequence through the fetch routine by incrementing the CMAR after each microoperation. At the end of the fetch routine, the operation called for by the fetched instruction will have been loaded into the operation register. Suppose, for example, that the instruction which has been fetched is the instruction ADDI. The routine for executing the ADDI instruction will be located in the control ROM beginning at a location ADDR(ADDI). It is therefore necessary, at the end of the fetch routine, for there to be a *branch* to the ADDI routine

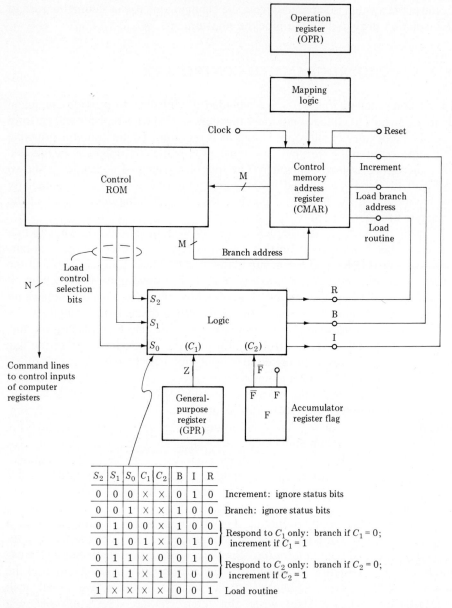

S_2	S_1	S_0	C_1	C_2	B	I	R	
0	0	0	×	×	0	1	0	Increment: ignore status bits
0	0	1	×	×	1	0	0	Branch: ignore status bits
0	1	0	0	×	1	0	0	Respond to C_1 only: branch if $C_1 = 0$;
0	1	0	1	×	0	1	0	increment if $C_1 = 1$
0	1	1	×	0	0	1	0	Respond to C_2 only: branch if $C_2 = 0$;
0	1	1	×	1	1	0	0	increment if $C_2 = 1$
1	×	×	×	×	0	0	1	Load routine

Figure 9.12-1 A further elaboration of the microprogrammed controller which makes provision for loading into the CMAR the starting CROM address for a routine.

which begins at ADDR(ADDI). This address ADDR(ADDI) is, of course, determined by the *operation code* in the operation register. It would be very convenient if we were able to arrange for the OP code for ADDI to be the same as the address ADDR(ADDI). If such were the case, a transfer to the ADDI routine could be accomplished by loading the OP code into the CMAR. Rather generally, however, it is not feasible to arrange this convenient feature, and therefore it is necessary to interpose between the operation register and the CMAR an appropriate combinational block which accepts the OP code as input and provides as output the instruction-routine starting address. This translation from OP code to starting address of a routine is called *mapping*, and in Fig. 9.12-1 is accomplished by the mapping-logic combinational block (which may possibly be a ROM). In any event it is now necessary to provide a facility not only for *incrementing* the CMAR and loading it with the *branch* address but also for loading it with the execution routine whose OP code is in the OPR. We have already incorporated just such a facility into the controller of Fig. 9.12-1.

The truth table for the logic block in Fig. 9.12-1 is a slight elaboration of the truth table in Fig. 9.10-1; this is allowed because we have provided an additional load control selection bit, S_2. So long as $S_2 = 0$, R $= 0$ and the remainder of the truth table in Fig. 9.12-1 is the same as given in Fig. 9.10-1. When $S_2 = 1$, R $= 1$ and the address of the instruction execution routine specified by the operation register will be loaded into the CMAR.

9.13 CONTROL ROM CONTENTS

Let us now consider what might be suitable contents of the control ROM of a microprogrammed controller for our simple computer of Fig. 9.1-1. These contents are shown in Fig. 9.13-1. The bits of the microwords fall into three classes, or fields. The *operation field* specifies the microoperation which is to be performed. The *address-selection field* specifies how the controller is to select the address in the control ROM where the next microoperation is to be found. When the address of the next microoperation is a part of the microword, this next address will be found in the *next address field*. When a next microinstruction is selected by incrementing the CMAR or by loading into that register an address determined by the operation register, the contents of the next address field will be irrelevant.

In control ROM locations ADDR(FETCH), ADDR(FETCH) + 1, and ADDR(FETCH) + 2, we find the microoperations which carry out the fetch routine (see page 380). After the first microoperation and also after the second, the address register is to be incremented; hence we find in these first two cases that the address field reads $S_2 S_1 S_0 = 000$. After the third microoperation in location ADDR(FETCH) + 2 has been carried out, the operation register (whose registration is decoded by the mapping logic) holds the CROM address of the beginning of the instruction routine which is to be executed. Hence in this case the load-routine input of the address register is to be activated, and correspondingly we find that $S_2 S_1 S_0 = 1 \times \times$.

For example, if the instruction so loaded into the address register were the instruction ADDI, we would next go through the sequence at ADDR(ADDI), ADDR(ADD) + 1, etc., which constitutes the routine for executing the ADDI instruction. When the instruction has been executed, we must return to the fetch routine. Hence the last microword of the ADDI routine has the

Memory location	Operation field	Address selection field			Next address field
		S_2	S_1	S_0	
ADDR(FETCH)	PC → MAR	0	0	0	
ADDR(FETCH) + 1	M → GPR; PC + 1 → PC	0	0	0	
ADDR(FETCH) + 2	GPR(OP) → OPR	1	X	X	
⋮					
ADDR(ADDI)	GPR(AD) → MAR	0	0	0	
ADDR(ADDI) + 1	M → GPR	0	0	0	
ADDR(ADDI) + 2	GPR(AD) → MAR	0	0	0	
ADDR(ADDI) + 3	M → GPR	0	0	0	
ADDR(ADDI) + 4	GPR + Acc → Acc	0	0	1	ADDR (FETCH)
⋮					
ADDR(ISZ)	GPR (AD) → MAR	0	0	0	
ADDR(ISZ) + 1	M → GPR	0	0	0	
ADDR(ISZ) + 2	GPR + 1 → GPR	0	0	0	
ADDR(ISZ) + 3	GPR → M	0	1	0	ADDR(FETCH)
ADDR(ISZ) + 4	PC + 1 → PC	0	0	1	ADDR(FETCH)
⋮					
ADDR(SFZ)	NOP	0	1	1	ADDR(FETCH)
ADDR(SFZ) + 1	PC + 1 → PC	0	0	1	ADDR(FETCH)

Figure 9.13-1 Partial contents of the CROM of Figure 9.12-1 if the controller is to be used with computer of Figure 9.1-1.

address-selection code $S_2S_1S_0 = 001$ (branch to address given in address field), and the address field holds the address ADDR(FETCH). Quite generally, in this same manner the last microword of every instruction execution routine will cause a branch back to ADDR(FETCH).

Next, let us consider the routine for ISZ (increment memory word and skip the next instruction if the incremented number has the value zero). This instruction is special because it involves the status bit Z (also called C_1). The routine for this instruction is written in Fig. 9.13-1, beginning at ROM location ADDR(ISZ) (see also page 388). The first 3 microwords have the address-selection field $S_2S_1S_0 = 000$ to call for incrementing of the CMAR. The GPR is incremented during the third microoperation. After this incrementing operation has been completed, we shall know whether the GPR is cleared, in which case Z = 1, or not cleared, in which case Z = 0. The fourth microoperation has the address-selection field 010, which indicates that the next microoperation address is to be determined by Z (C_1). If Z = 0, there will be a branch back to ADDR(FETCH), as indicated by the truth table of Fig. 9.12-1. If Z = 1, the CMAR will not be loaded with the branch address but will be incremented instead. If such incrementing occurs, the fifth microoperation PC + 1 → PC will be executed, and then there will be a branch to ADDR(FETCH).

Consider next the instruction SFZ (skip next macroinstruction if $\underline{F} = 0$). As can be seen in Fig. 9.12-1, we have used $\overline{F}$ as the status bit C_2, so that $C_2 = 1$ when F = 0. The microoperations required to execute SFZ are listed in Fig. 9.13-1, beginning at ADDR(SFZ). The first "microoperation" is actually no operation at all (NOP). It is achieved by arranging for all the command bits of the control ROM to be 0s. During the NOP interval the controller will have time to determine whether C_2 (=$\overline{F}$) is 0 or 1. The address-selection field in this microword is $S_2S_1S_0 = 011$, which, as the truth table of Fig. 9.12-1 shows, indicates that the controller is to respond to C_2. If $C_2 = 0$ (F = 1), there will be a branch to the address in the address field. The result will be that indeed no operation will have been performed and the controller will go back to the fetch routine. If, however, $C_2 = 1$, the CMAR will be incremented to ADDR(SFZ) + 1. At that location we find the microinstruction PC + 1 → PC, so that the program counter will be incremented and then the fetch routine will begin. The end result is that a macroinstruction will have been skipped over.

Other instructions can be written into the control memory following the same pattern as applied to the instructions in Fig. 9.13-1. The details are left as student exercises.

9.14 METHODS OF ADDRESSING

We have seen that rather generally (though not necessarily) an instruction consists of an operation portion and an address portion. The address portion may hold the address of an operand to be used in executing the instruction. On other occasions the address portion of the instruction may hold not the address of the operand but the address where the address of the operand is to be found. In the first case the address is described as a *direct address*; in the second case it is an *indirect address*. In computers, minicomputers, and microcomputers a wide range of addressing modes is employed, of which we consider a number in this section.

Direct. In *direct addressing*, as already noted, the instruction contains the address of the location in memory where the operand is to be found.

Indirect. In *indirect addressing*, again as noted, the instruction contains not the memory location where the operand is to be found but the address of the memory location where the address of the operand is to be found.

Relative. In *relative addressing* the address portion of the instruction contains a number N. The address, in memory, of the operand is found by adding the number N to the number in the program counter. For example, if the program counter (PC) holds the number 17, and if $N = 14$, the operand address is PC + $N = 17 + 14 = 31$. The number N may be positive, as in our example, or negative, so that the effective address PC + N may be higher or lower than the address in the program counter.

Indexed. In *indexed addressing*, as in relative addressing, the address portion of the instruction contains a number N, which may be positive or negative. However, in order to use indexed addressing the computer must be equipped with a special register (other than the program counter) used to allow indexed addressing and called, naturally enough, the *index register* (I). The address of the memory location where the operand is located is found by adding I + N. (In the simple computer of Fig. 9.1-1 we have no index register, and we have made no provision for indexed addressing.)

Register indirect. A computer that incorporates facility for *register indirect addressing* has a special register, often called a *pointer register* (P). This register P holds the address of the operand; i.e., it points to the memory location of the operand. An instruction which invokes register indirect addressing actually has no significant bits in its address portion. Instead the entire instruction is included in the bits assigned to the operation portion of the instruction. A typical instruction using register indirect addressing might specify "load the accumulator with the operand that is located in memory at the address given in register P."

Other common schemes for locating sources of operands or destinations of operands, described as *addressing modes*, include the following.

Immediate. In *immediate addressing* the address portion of the instruction contains not the address of an operand but the operand itself. Thus the instruction "load accumulator *direct* with 37" means load the accumulator with the content of memory location 37. On the other hand, "load accumulator *immediate* with 37" means load the accumulator with the number 37.

Inherent. Ordinarily an address that is part of an instruction refers to a location in memory. When an instruction indicates a source or a destination of some piece of data and no address is specifically in evidence because no reference is made to a memory location, the instruction is described as having an *inherent address*. For example, in the instruction "clear the accumulator" the "data" being moved are a word in which all bits are 0s and the "address" of the destination of these data is the accumulator register. Again, in the instruction "move the content of register R1 to register R2," R1 and R2 are the "addresses" from which a word is read and into which the word is written.

9.15 STACKS

In accessing information stored in memory we have already noted that, when possible, it is useful to have an understanding about the address of the next word to be written or read. Thus we found it very useful to store successive instructions in successive memory locations, which meant that we had to deal with the address of the next instruction only infrequently. Except when jump instructions are encountered, providing the address of the next instruction requires only that a counter, the program counter, be incremented.

In a similar manner it is very useful (when it is feasible to do so) to store data in a memory facility in such a way that new addresses can be established simply by incrementing (or decrementing) a counter. Such a memory facility is called a stack. We have already considered stacks in Sec. 6.16, where we noted the reason for the use of the name stack and why writing a word into a stack is called pushing and reading a word is called popping.

Any array of registers can be used as a stack. Usually, however, the storage facility used to implement a stack is a reserved section of a RAM. Such a section of a RAM together with the counter is indicated in Fig. 9.15-1. In programming we want to be able to remember what section of the RAM is being reserved for the stack. Accordingly, as in Fig. 9.15-1, we have assumed a memory of N-word capacity with location addresses extending from 0 to $N - 1$, and we have reserved for the stack the very end of the memory with addresses $N - 1$, $N - 2$, etc. The counter register which is incremented or decremented to go from one stack location to the next is called the *stack pointer* (SP). The terminology is appropriate since the stack pointer holds the address of, i.e., points to, the stack location being accessed for reading or writing.

The order in which data are pushed onto the stack is, first, data A in location $N - 1$, then data B in location $N - 2$, etc. The stack is shown in Fig. 9.15-1 after 4 words of data A, B, C, and D have been pushed onto it. In reading, i.e., popping, we first pop D, then C, and so on. One way we can implement the process of pushing a word onto the stack is the following:

1. Write the word into the memory location specified by the stack pointer.
2. Then decrement the stack pointer.

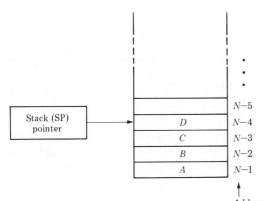

Figure 9.15-1 A section of a RAM is reserved for a stack. Stack addresses are provided by a stack pointer register (SP).

Having pushed a word onto the stack, suppose that we want to pop that same word. The procedure is as follows:

1. Increment the stack pointer.
2. Then read the word from the memory location specified by the stack pointer.

In the procedure above, pushing was done by first writing and then decrementing. There is no reason why we cannot change the procedure so that pushing is performed by first decrementing and then writing. If this reversed procedure is employed, of course the procedure for popping must also be reversed; i.e., we must first read and then increment. Suppose that using this reversed procedure we want to push into memory location $N - 1$. Then we must first set the stack pointer to N so that the decrement operation puts the stack pointer, i.e., the counter, at $N - 1$. If the stack-pointer counter has a modulus N, then setting the counter at N actually sets the counter at zero; that is, $00 \ldots 00$, decremented by 1 becomes $11 \ldots 11$.

The RAM of Fig. 9.15-1 is already part of our computer in Fig. 9.1-1. We have now added a stack pointer, but we need hardly belabor the point that this added stack pointer does not by itself make a stack available to a computer. To add such stack facility it is necessary to add to the repertory of instructions the controller of the system is able to carry out. There must be an instruction which will load into the stack pointer the address at which we propose to start the stack. There must be an instruction which loads the stack-pointer address into the memory address register. There must be an instruction which will push, i.e., increment, SP and write into memory and also an instruction which will pop, i.e., decrement, SP and read from memory. Some computers have instructions which will effect a number of push or pop operations in sequence, all in response to this single instruction.

It not infrequently happens that a program calls for subroutines that are nested within each other; i.e., a subroutine, say subroutine SRA, is called for. Within subroutine SRA it becomes necessary to call subroutine SRB. Before subroutine SRB has been completed, subroutine SRC must be called, and so on. We remember (Sec. 9.2) that, whenever a subroutine is called, we must save the address of the instruction to which we are to return after the subroutine has been completed. Thanks to its last-in-first-out feature, a stack makes an ideal arrangement for storing return address when subroutines are nested. As a last operation before leaving the main program for subroutine SRA we push the main-program return address ADDR(MAIN) onto the stack. Upon leaving subroutine SRA for subroutine SRB, we push the subroutine SRA return address ADDR(SRA) onto the stack, and so on. Hence return addresses are pushed onto the stack in the order ADDR(MAIN), ADDR(SRA), ADDR(SRB), etc. The last address pushed onto the stack is the first address required as the last subroutine is completed, and so on. Thus the process of finally returning to the main program is a matter of popping the stack to make available the addresses precisely in the order opposite to that in which they were pushed onto the stack.

We may well find that when a subroutine is called we need to save not only the return address to the main program but also the data in the accumulator, the status register, and other registers so that the main program can continue after the subroutine has been completed. The stack is also used effectively for this temporary data storage.

TEN

MICROPROCESSORS

10.1 INTRODUCTION

We use the term *large computer* to refer to computers whose physical dimensions extend from some relay racks of equipment to many rooms full of equipment and whose cost ranges from tens of thousands to hundreds of thousands of dollars. Minicomputers are smaller and less expensive, costing from thousands to tens of thousands of dollars and having physical dimensions ranging from the size of a bread box to the size of a relay rack. The large computers are used to solve a wide range of involved engineering or scientific problems or to handle and process large amounts of data. The minicomputers are often used in connection with some single dedicated purpose where the larger computer is neither necessary nor justifiable.

The large computers are manufactured by a relatively few companies such as IBM. Most engineers find that their only encounter with these large machines consists in having, from time to time, to write a program for the computer in some rather convenient programming language such as Fortran. Hence, important though the subject is, the design of large computers is something about which not every engineer need be extensively informed. A similar situation prevails in connection with minicomputers. Minicomputers are generally purchased as complete units from manufacturers, and the user's task is simply to learn how to program and use them.

On the other hand, a very large percentage of engineers will find it inevitably necessary to involve themselves in the design of small digital systems which incorporate some modest computational facility. Such small digital computers, i.e., *microcomputers*, find a very wide range of application. In a retail shop, a salesperson places an item on a scale and enters the price per pound on a small keyboard. A microcomputer, incorporated in the scale, calculates the product of the weight and price per pound and presents a digital display of the total price. In electronic test equipment such as oscilloscopes, digital voltmeters, frequency synthesizers, etc., microcomputers incorporated into the instruments provide many useful functions, e.g., selecting ranges, controlling displays, and recalibrating. Microcomputers are used in consumer items like sophisticated cameras and TV games. The automobile industry is using microcomputers to control fuel delivery and spark timing to assure best gas milage. Large vehicles, e.g., airplanes and trailer trucks, are equipped with computer-operated antiskid brakes. At airports and other transportation terminals, microcomputers are used in collecting fares, making change, issuing tickets, and confirming reservations. The future outlook for the range of application of microcomputers is nearly limitless.

As we have seen, a rudimentary computer consists of the following items: (1) a memory, (2) a control unit, (3) an arithmetic-logic unit (ALU), and (4) a number of registers. We have already noted in Chap. 6 that LSI memory chips have long been available. At the present writing memory chips with 64 kilobits are beginning to make their appearance. For some years there have also been available a number of LSI chips each containing the remaining components of the computer, i.e., the control unit, the ALU, and a number of registers. Such a chip is referred to as a *microprocessor* or as a *microprocessor unit* (MPU). Thus, a microprocessor chip and a memory chip together constitute a rudimentary computer.

The availability of the microprocessor and memory chip now makes it feasible to design rather sophisticated digital systems with quite inexpensive hardware which, in addition, occupies a small volume. For this reason, it is likely that anybody who is involved with the design of digital systems will need to know how to effect designs that incorporate microprocessors. The situation is different from that prevailing with large and medium computers, where most people need know little more than how they are programmed.

Microprocessors find application not only where some modest computational facility is required but also in the realization of digital systems generally. Suppose, for example, that we propose to build some sequential digital system whose implementation requires us to incorporate facility for counting, for shifting words, for incrementing, for combining words and numbers numerically and logically, etc. We might then build a system in which we provide a physical counter to count, physical shift registers to shift, adders to add and increment, and gate structures to perform the required logic. Such a system would be described as being implemented in *hardware*, the term "hardware" referring to the actual physical devices. Alternatively, we might take advantage of the fact that a microprocessor chip (in conjunction with one or more other chips, such as a memory) constitutes a digital processor which can be programmed to perform all the same operations of counting, shifting, incrementing, combining words logically and numerically, etc. Thus, we may well be inclined to replace the extensive hardware of the first method of implementation by the alternative scheme of using very much less hardware in a microprocessor system. However, the microprocessor system will have to be used in conjunction with a specially written program which will direct the microprocessor to carry out whatever algorithm is required to effect the digital processing. A program is often referred to as *software*. Hence, such a replacement of physical components with a program is described as *substituting software for hardware*.

In this chapter and the next we shall study the Intel 8080 microprocessor as a representative of microprocessors generally. We shall comment briefly, as well, on the Motorola 6800 microprocessor. At the present, these are among the most widely known and used microprocessor chips.

10.2 PROGRAMMER'S ARCHITECTURE OF A MICROPROCESSOR

We have already seen how to design the component parts of a microprocessor. We have seen how to design storage registers to store words and numbers. We have examined how the stored contents of such registers can be transferred from register to register using, if required, a single bus for all transfers. We have considered how to design processing registers, i.e., registers which not only store data but can also perform logical and numerical operations on their contents, shifting, incrementing, ANDing, or ORing with contents of other registers, etc. We have seen how to design an arithmetic-logic unit (ALU) to perform logic and arithmetic functions, if we so please, in a combinational circuit rather than in a processing register. Finally, we have studied how to design the control unit, the sequential system that advances a digital processor through a specified series of steps. All these components, together with the understanding we acquired as we studied them, are involved in the rather simple microcomputer, i.e., microprocessor plus memory, presented in Fig. 9.1-1.

It is to be noticed that in Fig. 9.1-1 there is a minimum of detail. The registers are simply represented as rectangles. Where a processing register is involved, no details indicate how gates are incorporated into the register to allow the processing called for. For example, the program counter has to be able to accept an input from the bus and has to be able to increment. We disposed of the matter by drawing a rectangle, labeling it "program counter," and providing two input terminals. One terminal is marked "PC + 1 → PC" (i.e., increment) and the second is marked "GPR(AD) → PC" (i.e., load address bits from the general-purpose register). Our attitude is that at the point where the matter was introduced into our discussion it was fair to say that "everybody knows" how to build such a register which will respond as required to an activation of one input terminal or the other. A similar situation applies to the controller. Here again we have simply indicated a rectangle with output command lines and a connection to the instruction registers. It is assumed that once we have more or less arbitrarily decided on the binary code word which is to be used to represent each instruction, "everybody knows" how to design a controller to provide the correct sequence of commands in response to each input instruction code. After all, we did design and present in Fig. 8.11-1 a controller which was able to respond to four instructions. The controller in Fig. 9.1-1 is not different in any manner that involves a principle. It is simply that the latter controller must respond to more instructions and provide more command outputs. In Sec. 9.12 we did, indeed, begin a design of the larger controller, but it was undertaken to illustrate the principle of microprogramming rather than because we had any special interest in the controller design. To illustrate our point further, let us recall that in Chap. 4 we considered how to design counters with modulo other than 2^n. We illustrated the procedure by designing a mod-3 counter, a mod-5 counter, and other counters of small modulo. We might, of course, have used as an example a counter of mod 137, but clearly no useful purpose would have been served. Our explanation (or excuse) for not providing detailed designs for the components in Fig. 9.1-1 is that the principles of design are known and that because of the relative complexity, i.e., more of same already encountered in smaller systems, such detailed design would be long drawn out, tedious, and unproductive.

All our apologies notwithstanding, we might nonetheless have devoted more attention to the design of larger processing registers and controllers if engineers were frequently called upon to design such components. In the course of such further analysis we might have come across shortcuts and alternative procedures with advantages in different situations, and we might have developed intuitive insight of the sort that not infrequently comes with familiarity and experience. But the fact is that the availability of microprocessor chips (and other supporting chips) generally obviates the need to design any elaborate controller or processor design. These days, when one has to assemble a moderately sophisticated digital system, generally the more fruitful approach is to avoid designing the requisite hardware and to implement the system with a microprocessor and software.

Turning now to the matter of microprocessor chips, we note that they are rather elaborate devices into which have been integrated as many as 5000 electronic components organized into hundreds or even thousands of gates. These gates are then organized into registers, controllers, etc. For example, we cannot help being impressed by the fact that the 6800 has incorporated into it the ability to execute 72 distinct instructions. Most of these instructions can be associated with more than one addressing mode. It then turns out that the total instructions number 197. The 8080 has a comparable instruction repertory. We may well imagine that the design of these and similar microprocessors occupied the attention of many persons for a long time.

We propose now to begin an examination of the architecture and use of our representative microprocessors. We might again be inclined to look into the details of the microprocessor circuitry down to the individual gates and flip-flops. Even if such detail were provided by the manufacturer (ordinarily not the case), such a course would not be productive. It might well be essential for a small and specialized group of engineers who professionally design microprocessors, but for engineers generally, interesting as the detailed study may be, the rewards would not be commensurate with the effort—even more so if it turned out, as it does, that a lack of a detailed study need not deter the user from making full and effective use of the device. In what follows we shall address ourselves to matters which engineers generally need to know about rather than to matters which fall into the province of the specialist.

In Fig. 10.2-1 we have drawn a "programmer's" diagram of the 8080 microprocessor; i.e., we have indicated only those components of the unit which will be referred to explicitly in writing a program. Of course, the 8080 has an ALU, and it has a control unit, but we have not indicated them. The microprocessor also has additional registers beyond those indicated, but these additional registers are "transparent" to the programmer. There are no instructions which make explicit reference to them and we have therefore chosen not to show them. Also shown in the figure is an external RAM, which will hold the data and instructions.

Turning now to the registers which are shown, we find that there is a program-counter register 16 bits long, as indicated by the number in parentheses. There is a stack-pointer register, which is also 16 bits long. Since the program counter and stack pointer are intended to hold memory addresses, we find, quite consistently, that the 8080 has a 16-bit address bus with lines labeled $A_{15}, A_{14} \ldots, A_0$ which are to be connected to the address input pins of the memory chip. The 16 lines of the address bus allow for a memory of as many as $2^{16} = 65,536$ words, but a less extensive memory may also be used. Since the 8080 is intended to be used with a memory in which the individual words are 8 bits long, we find that the other registers are correspondingly of the same 8-bit length. There is a bidirectional 8-bit bus with lines labeled $D_7, D_6, \ldots, D_0$, which carries data from microprocessor chip to the external memory and from the memory to the chip. The registers B and C, D and E, and H and L are general-purpose registers; they may be used individually or, as we shall see, paired so that B and C, D and E, or H and L can be used as a single 16-bit register. The accumulator register, like the accumulator of our earlier simpler processors, is special in that it can be used to provide some manipulation of the data it holds. Thus, the accumulator allows for shifting, incrementing, etc. It also generally holds one of the two operands involved in an arithmetic or logical operation and then holds the result of the operation.

The status register is unlike the other registers (it is called a register by sufferance and because we need some sort of a name for it). It consists of eight flip-flops, three of which are permanently in the set state and hence, in principle, serve no purpose. The other five flip-flops are *flag* flip-flops, whose states are noted on an individual basis and often bear no connection with each other.

The $\overline{\text{MEMW}}$ (MEMORY WRITE) line and the $\overline{\text{MEMR}}$ (MEMORY READ) lines from the MPU to the memory determine whether there is to be a transfer of information between MPU and memory and whether the memory is to be read or written into. When there is to be neither a reading nor a writing, both $\overline{\text{MEMW}}$ and $\overline{\text{MEMR}}$ are at logic 1. Under these conditions, the R/$\overline{\text{W}}$ memory input being at logic 1, the memory is activated to be read, but the OD (output-disable) input is at logic 1, the tristate *output* connections of the memory to the data

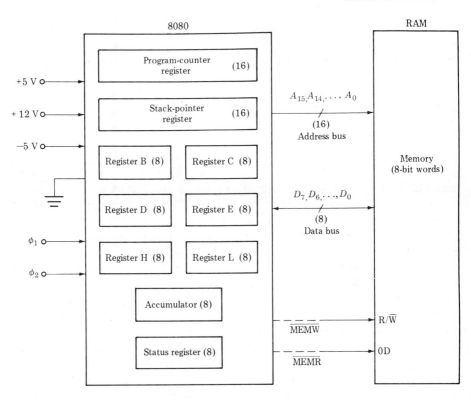

Figure 10.2-1 A programmer's view of the 8080 microprocessor.

bus are in the high-impedance state, and the memory is thereby actually disconnected from the data bus. If a writing operation is to occur, the $\overline{\text{MEMW}}$ is
brought to logic 0. The data bus is always connected to the input connections
of the memory, and even with $\overline{\text{MEMR}}$ at logic 1, a write operation will take
place when $\overline{\text{MEMW}}$ goes to logic 0. Of course, before a read or write operation
can be allowed, the MPU must establish a valid memory on the address bus.

In Fig. 10.2-1 we have made a point of using dashed lines for the parts of
the $\overline{\text{MEMW}}$ and $\overline{\text{MEMR}}$ lines which connect to the MPU. We intend thereby
to indicate that these lines do not actually originate in the MPU. As we shall
see later, they originate in an auxiliary unit, which in turn is controlled by signals from the MPU. However, the liberty we have taken here simplifies the
interconnections without violating any principle, and we shall set the matter
right later.

We have also indicated in Fig. 10.2-1 that the 8080 requires three supply
voltages, applied as indicated between the voltage input terminals and ground.
The unit also requires a clock input waveform. Actually the manufacturer
specifies that the clock input consist of two synchronous parts, ϕ_1 and ϕ_2. Some
details concerning the clock waveforms required are given in the next chapter.

The 8080A unit, somewhat faster than the 8080, will accept a clock frequency up to 2 MHz. Since the storage elements in the unit are of the dynamic type, which require periodic refreshing, there is also a minimum clock frequency of about 0.5 MHz.

We note further in Fig. 10.2-1 that we have shown 16 address lines, 8 data lines, 4 power-supply lines (including ground), and 2 clock lines, for a total of 30. Since the 8080 chip has 40 pins, 10 pins are at present unaccounted for. We shall pursue this matter in the next chapter.

10.3 ONE-, TWO-, AND THREE-BYTE INSTRUCTIONS IN THE 8080

In our simple-minded computer of Fig. 9.1-1 we arranged that each instruction stored in memory could be stored in the 12 bits of a single memory location. In the 8080, which is very much more sophisticated, there are only 8 bits in a memory location. We therefore find, not surprisingly, that many 8080 instructions need two memory locations or even three to store an instruction. Since 8 bits constitute a byte, we find accordingly that the 8080 has 1-, 2-, and 3-byte instructions.

An example of a 1-byte instruction is the instruction to INCREMENT THE ACCUMULATOR. The mnemonic for this instruction is INR A, and the binary code for it occupies one memory location. An example of a 2-byte instruction is the instruction ADD (to the accumulator) IMMEDIATE, or ADI data. The operation part of the instruction occupies 1 byte, and the data occupy the immediately succeeding byte. To be specific, we note that the manufacturer tells us that the instruction code for ADI is 11000110; suppose that the number to be added is decimal 15 = 00001111. Then the entire instruction would appear in two successive memory locations as indicated in Fig. 10.3-1. Finally, as an example of a 3-byte instruction we have the instruction LOAD THE ACCUMULATOR (with an operand from memory). This instruction must have included in it the 16-bit address of the operand. The mnemonic here is LDA. The operational part of the instruction requires 1 byte. The address requires 16 bits and hence uses 2 bytes. The manufacturer tells us that the code for this instruc-

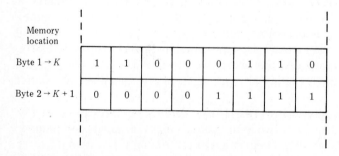

Figure 10.3-1 The 2-byte instruction "add (decimal) 15 to the contents of the accumulator."

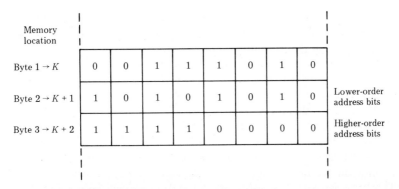

Figure 10.3-2 The 3-byte instruction "load accumulator with contents of memory location A_{15}, ..., A_0 = 1111 0000 1010 1010."

tion is 00111010. The address has eight *higher*-order bits $A_{15}, A_{14}, \ldots, A_8$ and eight *lower*-order bits $A_7, A_6, \ldots, A_0$. Suppose then that the address should be

$$A_{15}, A_{14}, \ldots, A_8; A_7 A_6, \ldots, A_0 = 11110000\ 10101010$$

Then the complete instruction would appear in three successive memory locations as shown in Fig. 10.3-2. Note that in the 8080 the lower-order address bits appear in byte 2 followed by the higher-order bits in byte 3. (In certain other MPUs the order is reversed, the higher-order bits before the lower-order ones.)

In our earlier, simpler computer each instruction occupied no more than one memory location. In that case, the controller would fetch an instruction, place the operational part in the instruction register and the address (if any) in an address register, and begin to execute the instruction immediately. In the present multibyte case, the first byte will tell the controller whether the instruction has more than 1 byte, and if so, the execution of the instruction will be deferred until all bytes have been fetched.

10.4 INSTRUCTIONS FOR DATA MOVEMENT

In this and succeeding sections we shall describe the instructions which constitute the repertory of the 8080. Here we consider the instructions which transfer the contents of a register to other registers or which effect a transfer of data between registers and memory.

The assembly-language mnemonic for such movement of data is MOV. The instruction which transfers the content of a register r2 to a register r1 is written

MOV r1, r2

It is important to keep in mind that this MOV instruction simply *copies* into r1 the contents of r2 and that the contents of r2 *remain unchanged.* Thus, after MOV r1, r2, r1 and r2 have the same contents, i.e., those present in r2 before the execution of the instruction. Of course, the previous contents of r1 are lost. The source registers may be any of the registers A, B, C, D, E, H, or L, and the destination registers may also be any of these same seven registers. For example MOV L, B will copy the contents of register B into register L. The 8080 will even accept as valid a MOV instruction in which source and destination are the same such as MOV C, C. Such an instruction will, of course, do nothing.

The MOV instruction can also be used to move data to or from the memory; however, since the memory is not a single register but may be as many as 2^{16} registers, it is first necessary to establish an address in memory from which data are to be read or into which data are to be written. This address is provided by the contents of the H and L registers. The H register holds the high address bits, i.e., the most significant bits $A_{15}, A_{14}, \ldots, A_8$, and the L register holds the low, i.e., the least significant bits. Thus, the instruction

MOV A, M; MOV M, A

moves to register A the contents of a memory location or to memory the contents of A, the selected memory location being established by the 16 bits in registers H and L. The instructions MOV H, M; MOV L, M; MOV M, H; MOV M, L are all allowed. The instruction MOV M, M turns out not to be useless but causes the microprocessor to halt.

A second type of MOVE instruction is the MOVE IMMEDIATE, 2-byte instruction with the mnemonic MVI. The word "immediate" means that the instruction furnishes the data itself rather than providing the address of a memory location where the data are to be found. Typically, if we wanted to place into memory an instruction which will move into register C the data 11001100, we would write into the memory, in two successive locations, the entries

MVI C

11001100

More generally we write the instruction

MVI r

$\langle B_2 \rangle$

in which r is the *destination* register of the data and $\langle B_2 \rangle$ stands for the second byte of the 2-byte instruction. The destination register may be any of the seven general-purpose registers A, B, C, D, E, H, or L. The instruction

MVI M

$\langle B_2 \rangle$

will move the byte B_2 into memory, the location in memory being given by the address held in the H, L register pair.

10.5 INSTRUCTIONS INVOLVING THE ACCUMULATOR DIRECTLY

Of all the general-purpose registers, the accumulator is the most versatile. It is therefore not surprising that there are a number of instructions concerned with moving data into the accumulator or from the accumulator to some other repository. Thus, we have the instruction LOAD ACCUMULATOR DIRECT. This is a 3-byte instruction and is written

LDA

$\langle B_2 \rangle$

$\langle B_3 \rangle$

in three successive memory locations. LDA is the operational part of the instruction, and B_2 and B_3 are respectively the low- and high-order memory address bytes. The instruction means that there is to be loaded into the accumulator the content of memory location $B_3 B_2$.

The reverse of the accumulator-load instruction is the STORE ACCUMULATOR DIRECT instruction, written

STA

$\langle B_2 \rangle$

$\langle B_3 \rangle$

This instruction transfers to memory location $B_3 B_2$ the contents of the accumulator. As usual, the contents of the accumulator remain unchanged.

The next two instructions are similar to the LDA and STA instructions, respectively, and involve the notion of a register pair. There are three such possible pairs, the pair B and C, the pair D and E, and the pair H and L. These pairs are invoked when we need, in effect, a 16-bit register to hold a memory address. We have already seen how H and L have been used as such a pair. In the pair B and C, B always holds the high-order address bits and C the low-order bits. Similarly, in the pair D and E, D holds the high-order bits and E the low-order bits. When the pair B and C is intended, we shall refer to the pair as simply register B; when D and E are intended, we shall refer to register D; and when H and L are intended, we shall refer to register H. It will be clear from the context whether a single register or a register pair is intended. If not clear, we shall specifically refer to *register pair* B, etc.

The instruction LOAD ACCUMULATOR INDIRECT

LDAX rp

loads the accumulator with the content of the memory location whose address is given by the register pair rp, but in this instruction rp must be either rp = B or rp = D. The pair rp = H is not allowed. The instruction reverse to LDAX rp is the instruction STORE ACCUMULATOR DIRECT

STAX rp

which stores the accumulator data in the memory locations specified in the register pair rp. Again rp = H is not allowed.

We may note that in the instructions LDAX rp and STAX rp there is no

Table 10.5-1 The 8080 Instructions Which Effect Transfers of Words from Register to Register and between Registers and Memory Locations

MOVE REGISTER — MOV r1, r2 — r2 → r1

Move contents of register r2 into register r1, leaving contents of register r2 unaltered

MOVE FROM MEMORY — MOV r, M — M[H, L] → r

Move to register r the contents of memory location whose address is held in register pair H

MOVE TO MEMORY — MOV M, r — r → M[H, L]

Move contents of register r to memory location whose address is held in register pair H

MOVE IMMEDIATE — MVI r, $\langle B_2 \rangle$ — $\langle B_2 \rangle$ → r

Move byte $\langle B_2 \rangle$ into the destination register r

MOVE TO MEMORY IMMEDIATE — MVI M, $\langle B_2 \rangle$ — $\langle B_2 \rangle$ → M[H, L]

Move byte $\langle B_2 \rangle$ into the memory location whose address is held in register pair H

LOAD REGISTER PAIR IMMEDIATE — LXI rp, $\langle B_2 \rangle \langle B_3 \rangle$ — $\langle B_2 \rangle$ → rp [low] / $\langle B_3 \rangle$ → rp [high]

Move byte $\langle B_2 \rangle$ into low-order part of register pair rp and move byte $\langle b_3 \rangle$ into high-order part of register pair rp

LOAD ACCUMULATOR DIRECT — LDA $\langle B_2 \rangle \langle B_3 \rangle$ — M[$\langle B_3 \rangle \langle B_2 \rangle$] → A

Move to Acc the contents of memory location whose address is given by $\langle B_3 \rangle$ (high-order address bits) and $\langle B_2 \rangle$ (low-order address bits)

STORE ACCUMULATOR DIRECT — STA $\langle B_2 \rangle \langle B_3 \rangle$ — A → M[$\langle B_3 \rangle \langle B_2 \rangle$]

Move contents of Acc to memory location whose address is given by $\langle B_3 \rangle$ (high-order address bits) and $\langle B_2 \rangle$ (low-order address bits)

need for rp = H; for if we want to load or store the accumulator and we want the memory address to be the pair H, L, we can use the instructions MOV A, M and MOV M, A.

The additional data-movement instructions in the 8080 repertory are tabulated in Table 10.5-1, along with those already discussed. The first column gives the descriptive name of the instruction. The second column gives the assembly-language mnemonic and indicates whether the instruction is a 1-, 2-, or 3-byte instruction. When an instruction requires a second byte $\langle B_2 \rangle$ or even a third byte $\langle B_3 \rangle$ as well, these bytes are written on the same line as the operational part of the instruction. It is understood, of course, that the 3 bytes occupy three

LOAD H AND L DIRECT	LHLD $\langle B_2 \rangle$ $\langle B_3 \rangle$	$M[\langle B_3 \rangle \langle B_2 \rangle] \rightarrow L$
		$M[\langle B_3 \rangle \langle B_2 \rangle + 1] \rightarrow H$

Move to register L the contents of memory location whose address is $\langle B_3 \rangle$ $\langle B_2 \rangle$. Move to register H contents of next memory location

STORE H AND L DIRECT	SHLD $\langle B_2 \rangle$ $\langle B_3 \rangle$	$L \rightarrow M[\langle B_3 \rangle \langle B_2 \rangle]$
		$H \rightarrow M[\langle B_3 \rangle \langle B_2 \rangle + 1]$

Move contents of register L to memory location whose address is $\langle B_3 \rangle$ $\langle B_2 \rangle$. Move contents of register H to next memory location

LOAD ACCUMULATOR INDIRECT	LDAX rp	$M[rp] \rightarrow A$
		$(rp \neq H)$

Move to Acc the contents of memory at address held in register pair rp; pair rp must not be pair H

STORE ACCUMULATOR INDIRECT	STAX rp	$A \rightarrow M[rp]$
		$(rp \neq H)$

Move contents of Acc to memory location whose address is given by register pair rp; pair rp must not be pair H

EXCHANGE H AND L WITH D AND E	XCHG	$H \leftrightarrow D$
		$L \leftrightarrow E$

Interchange contents of registers H and D and also contents of registers L and E

successive memory locations and should more properly appear one under the other. The actual microoperation or microoperations effected by the instruction are specified in the third column, where the symbol M stands for the memory, M[H, L] represents a memory location given by the content of the register pair H, and M[$\langle B_3 \rangle \langle B_2 \rangle$] is a memory location specified by the address $B_3 B_2$. We have also spelled out in words precisely what each instruction does.

It is hardly to be recommended that the reader undertake to memorize this list of instructions now. Readers who eventually find themselves making extensive use of the 8080 will inevitably become more and more familiar with these and the other 8080 instructions, yet to be considered. In that event, users will eventually find themselves quite comfortable with the instructions, much as we find ourselves at ease with any new language or complicated procedure to which we apply ourselves diligently. But even to the more casual user we suggest that it is worth the effort to develop some familiarity with these and other instructions on the grounds that the instructions are quite characteristic of the instructions to be encountered rather generally in other microprocessors. Time devoted to becoming familiar with one microprocessor is very helpful no matter what microprocessor is finally chosen.

10.6 ARITHMETIC INSTRUCTIONS

We consider now a second type of 8080 instruction, referred to as *arithmetic instructions*. One purpose of these instructions is to add and subtract the contents of registers or to add and subtract the contents of registers and memory locations. When an addition or subtraction is involved, we must specify the source of each of the operands and the place where the result is to be stored. Hence, such an operation, involving three memory addresses or register identifications, might well require an uneconomically large number of bytes. To circumvent this difficulty, it is general practice in microprocessors (and other small computing facilities) to have it understood that *one of the operands is to be found in the accumulator and that the result is to be placed in the accumulator*. We have already met this idea in Chap. 9, and we find, as well, that this arrangement is almost always employed in the 8080. A second purpose of the arithmetic instructions is to increment or decrement registers or the content of memory locations.

When the CPU responds to instructions which call for an arithmetic operation (addition, subtraction, increment, and decrement), the CPU, of course, uses its arithmetic logic unit (ALU). The ALU is also used for logical operations. When the ALU is involved, it frequently happens that after the ALU operation the sequence of instructions to be followed depends on the result at the ALU output. For this reason, the 8080 provides a number of flags, five in all, which together constitute the status register of Fig. 10.2-1. These flags monitor the ALU output, and each serves to store an ALU output bit which may be needed for further development of the program. Four of these flags are listed in Table 10.6-1 together with their significance. The Z flag stores a record of whether or not the result is zero. The S flag records whether the most significant bit is 0 or 1. If the ALU output is a number, and if we are using the twos-complement representation for negative numbers, the S (sign) flag records whether the number is positive or negative. The CY flag records whether there is a carry or a borrow out of the highest-order bit, as might occur in an addition or subtraction operation. The parity flag P records whether the parity of the result is odd or even. This flag is not as generally useful as the Z, S, and CY flags but has a function in certain applications when the microprocessor is used as a component in a data transmission system. The function of the fifth flag will be described later.

In any event, when the execution of an arithmetic operation has been completed, the status register will immediately reflect the status of the result at the *output of the ALU*. Thus, for example, if a number is added to the contents of the accumulator, then by the time the result is settled in the accumulator, the status register will already know whether there was a carry, whether the result is positive or negative or zero, and what the parity of the result is. It is important to note, however, that not all instructions involving the ALU affect all the flags. If a particular flag is not affected by an instruction, that flag is left in the state it was at the end of the execution of the previous instruction. In examining the instructions to be considered below, we shall sometimes find that some of the flags affected can hardly serve a useful purpose. We may reasonably assume that this feature was allowed simply because it simplified the controller design. After all, we can always ignore a flag if we choose to do so.

If we were restricted to using 8-bit numbers to accommodate to 1-byte-sized memory words and registers, we would not be able to do precision arithmetic, but the difficulty is easy to circumvent. For example, if we want to work with 16-bit numbers, we can simply split the 16 bits into 2 bytes and hold the 16-bit number in two memory locations. Suppose then that we want to add two 16-bit numbers N_1 and N_2. N_1 has the 8 *more*-significant bits $N_1(M)$ and the 8 *less*-significant bits $N_1(L)$. Similarly, N_2 is composed of the parts $N_2(M)$ and

Table 10.6-1 Four of the 8080 Flags

Flag name	Symbol	Meaning of registration	
Zero	Z	$=\begin{cases}0\\1\end{cases}$	result is not zero result is zero
Sign	S	$=\begin{cases}0\\1\end{cases}$	result is positive result is negative
Carry	CY	$=\begin{cases}0\\1\end{cases}$	no carry or borrow occurred a carry or borrow did occur
Parity	P	$=\begin{cases}0\\1\end{cases}$	result has odd parity result has even parity

$N_2(L)$. These numbers can now be added as follows. First, we use an instruction which adds $N_1(L) + N_2(L)$. We arrange that this addition shall leave in the *carry* flag flip-flop a record of whether, in this addition, there is a carry out of the most significant bit. Next, we use an instruction which forms the sum $N_1(M) + N_2(M) + content of the carry flag$. As a result of these two additions we shall indeed have formed the sum $N_1 + N_2$. Suppose, further, that the instruction which carries out the instruction "add two 8-bit numbers and add to this sum the content of the carry flag" leaves in the carry flag a record of whether this addition, in turn, generates a carry out of the most significant bit position. Then we shall be able to extend the precision of our arithmetic

Table 10.6-2 The Arithmetic Instructions of the 8080*

ADD REGISTER	ADD r	$A + r \rightarrow A$

Add number in register r to number in Acc and leave sum in Acc

ADD IMMEDIATE	ADI $\langle B_2 \rangle$	$A + \langle B_2 \rangle \rightarrow A$

Add number B_2, which is second byte of instruction, to Acc and leave sum in Acc

ADD MEMORY	ADD M	$A + M[H, L] \rightarrow A$

Add number in memory, at address given by H and L registers, to number in Acc and leave sum in Acc

ADD REGISTER WITH CARRY	ADC r	$A + r + CY \rightarrow A$

Add to Acc the number in register r and add also number in carry flag and leave sum in Acc

ADD IMMEDIATE WITH CARRY	ACI $\langle B_2 \rangle$	$A + \langle B_2 \rangle + CY \rightarrow A$

Add to Acc the number B_2, which is second byte of instruction, and add also number in carry flag and leave sum in Acc

ADD MEMORY WITH CARRY	ADC M	$A + M[H, L] + CY \rightarrow A$

Add to Acc the number in memory whose address is in H and L registers and add also number in carry flag and leave sum in Acc

SUBTRACT REGISTER	SUB r	$A - r \rightarrow A$

Subtract number in register r from number in Acc and leave difference in Acc

SUBTRACT IMMEDIATE	SUI $\langle B_2 \rangle$	$A - \langle B_2 \rangle \rightarrow A$

Subtract number B_2, which is second byte of instruction, from number in Acc and leave difference in Acc

All these arithmetic instructions (except **DAD rp**) affect *all* the five flags.

limitlessly. For we shall be able to add 3-byte (24-bit) numbers, 4-byte (32-bit) numbers, etc.

Similar considerations apply to the process of subtraction. We shall require an instruction which subtracts, i.e., forms $N_1 - N_2$, and an instruction which forms $N_1 - N_2 - $ *content of the carry flag.* Altogether then we are not surprised to find in the repertory of 8080 instructions the instructions "add," "add with carry," "subtract," and "subtract with borrow." With these comments we are ready to look at some of the arithmetic instructions.

The addition and subtraction instructions are listed in Table 10.6-2. The first three provide for addition *without* carry and differ from each other in the

---

| SUBTRACT MEMORY | SUB M | $A - M[H, L] \rightarrow A$ |

Subtract from Acc the number in memory whose address is in H and L registers and leave difference in Acc

| SUBTRACT REGISTER WITH BORROW | SBB r | $A - r - CY \rightarrow A$ |

Subtract from Acc the number in register r and subtract also number in carry flag and leave result in Acc

| SUBTRACT IMMEDIATE WITH BORROW | SBI $\langle B_2 \rangle$ | $A - \langle B_2 \rangle - CY \rightarrow A$ |

Subtract from Acc the number B_2, which is second byte of instruction, and subtract also number in carry flag and leave result in Acc

| SUBTRACT MEMORY WITH BORROW | SBB M | $A - M[H, L] - CY \rightarrow A$ |

Subtract from Acc the number in memory whose address is in H and L registers and also subtract number in carry flag and leave result in Acc

| DECIMAL ADJUST ACCUMULATOR | DAA | |

Contents of Acc are modified as would be required if contents were result of adding two BCD numbers. The procedure is (1) If value of less significant 4 bits in Acc is greater than 9, or if AC flag is set, 6 is added to these less significant bits. (2) If, after step 1 is complete, value of more significant bits is greater than 9, or if CY flag is set, 6 is added to these more significant bits

| ADD REGISTER PAIR rp TO REGISTER PAIR H AND L | DAD rp | $rp + H, L \rightarrow H, L$ |

16-bit number in register pair rp is added to number in register pair H, L and sum is left in H and L. *Only* flag affected is CY. If there is a carry out of this 16-bit addition, CY is set; otherwise CY is reset

source of the addend which is to be added to the augend in the accumulator. In the first case, the addend is found in one of the general-purpose registers. In the second case, the operand is included in the (2-byte) instruction. In the third case, the addend is in memory. Observe, as in the case with the MOVE instructions, that there is no single instruction which allows us to specify the address of a memory location and to add the memory contents to the accumulator. To carry out such an operation we must first use an instruction such as LOAD REGISTER PAIR IMMEDIATE to establish the memory address in the register pair H and L. The next three instructions are identical to the first three instructions except that they add in the carry bit if any. The next six instructions are identical to the first six except that subtraction is called for instead of addition and a borrow bit is subtracted rather than a carry bit added. The last two instructions in Table 10.6-2 are included because they are also instructions involving arithmetic, but they are somewhat special and are discussed below.

We consider now the next-to-last (and rather special) instruction in Table 10.6-2. It will be recalled that in Sec. 5.13 we suggested that it might sometimes be reasonable to do arithmetic using BCD numbers. We considered there one way in which addition of BCD might be effected and also presented the hardware to perform the addition. The 8080 allows such BCD addition through the use of the DECIMAL ADJUST ACCUMULATOR instruction with mnemonic DAA. Applying the principle that there is a merit in substituting software for hardware, the 8080 carries out a little program in response to the DAA instruction. We have not specified the microoperations involved but have written out in words precisely what the instruction does. It is necessary, however, to add one small piece of hardware in the form of an additional flag flip-flop, called the *auxiliary carry flag* AC. When two 8-bit numbers are added in straightforward binary addition, the AC flag is set when there is a carry out of the fourth bit, just as the CY flag is set if there is a carry out of the eighth bit.

Suppose now that we have a two-decimal-digit number N_1 (such as might be represented in 8 binary bits) and a second two-decimal-digit number N_2. To add these numbers in the 8080 we first add N_1 and N_2 as though they were straightforward binary numbers. Next, we invoke the DAA instruction. This instruction examines the four less significant bits of the result and the state of the AC flag. If this 4-bit number is greater than 9, or if AC is set, 6 is added to these bits. Next, the four more significant bits are examined. This second part of the procedure must wait until after the addition (if any) of 6 to the less significant bits, since this addition will generate a carry if no carry was already generated. Again, if the more significant bits have a value greater than 9, or if a carry is generated (the carry here will set the CY flag), 6 is added to these bits. As can be verified (see discussion in Sec. 5.13), this DAA procedure will yield the BCD sum correctly. Just as in straightforward binary addition, so here, we can use the CY to allow increased precision by extending the addition process to 4 decimal digits, or 6 digits, etc. An assembly-language program for adding N_1 and N_2, both BCD numbers is as follows:

Label	Contents	Comment
	SUB A	Subtract A from A to clear Acc
	ADI $\langle N_1 \rangle$	Add the number N_1 to Acc
	ADI $\langle N_2 \rangle$	Add number N_2 to Acc
	DAA	Decimal adjust Acc

We previously identified four flag flip-flops in the status register and indicated that there was also a fifth one. The AC flag is the fifth one. Altogether, then, the five flags in the status register are Z (zero), S (sign), P (parity), CY (carry), and AC (auxiliary carry). *All* the instructions in Table 10.6-2, except one (DAD rp), affect *all* five flags.

Finally, we note the last instruction involving addition, which is different from the others in that it does not involve the accumulator. This DAD rp instruction processes 16 bits (2 bytes) at a time and affects *only* the CY flag.

10.7 SOME EXAMPLES

Let us consider now some simple assembly-language program examples using the instructions presented so far. These instructions serve to move data from register to register and from memory to register and vice versa and to perform addition and subtraction. The following program adds two 1-byte numbers N_1 and N_2:

Label	Contents	Comment
SUM	MVI A $\langle N_1 \rangle$	Load number N_1 into Acc
	MVI B $\langle N_2 \rangle$	Load number N_2 into register B
	ADD B	Add contents of B to contents of Acc and leave sum in Acc

In this program we have made an entry SUM in the label field not because one is required but to serve as a reminder that, in general, a program has such a field. If the sum $N_1 + N_2$ is 11 111 111 (= 377 octal = 255 decimal) or less, the carry flag CY will not be set. If the sum is larger than 377, CY will be set.

The following program adds two 2-byte numbers $N_1 + N_2$. N_1 is a 2-byte number with more significant byte $N_1(M)$ and less significant byte $N_1(L)$. Similarly, $N_2 = N_2(M)N_2(L)$.

Label	Contents	Comment
SUM	LXI B $\langle N_1(L)\rangle$ $\langle N_1(M)\rangle$	Load register *pair* B, i.e., B and C, with 2-byte number $N_1(M)N_1(L)$
	LXI D $\langle N_2(L)\rangle$ $\langle N_2(M)\rangle$	Load register *pair* D, i.e., D and E, with 2-byte number $N_2(M)N_2(L)$
	MOV A, E	Move to Acc contents of E, which holds byte $N_2(L)$
	ADD C	Add to Acc contents of C, which holds byte $N_1(L)$
	MOV L, A	Move sum $N_2(L) + N_1(L)$ to register L in order to make Acc available for adding $N_2(M) + N_2(M)$
	MOV A, D	Move to Acc contents, of D, which holds byte $N_2(M)$
	ADC B	Add to Acc contents of B, which holds byte $N_1(M)$; add also *carry bit*, if any, generated when sum $N_2(L) + N_1(L)$ was formed
	MOV H, A	Move sum $N_2(M) + N_1(L) + CY$ from Acc to register H so that entire result is now in register pair H, L

10.8 INCREMENT-DECREMENT INSTRUCTIONS

The 8080 has six instructions which allow incrementing and decrementing registers, register pairs, and the contents of a memory location whose address is in the register pair H, L. These instructions are listed in Table 10.8-1. As indicated, in four of the cases the flags Z, S, P, AC (but not CY) are affected, and in two of the cases none of the flags is affected. The registers which can be incremented or decremented include the accumulator and any of the other general-purpose registers B, C, D, E, H, and L. Any of the register pairs B and C, or D and E or H and L can be incremented or decremented.

10.9 LOGIC INSTRUCTIONS

The instructions available in the 8080 that involve logical operations are listed in Table 10.9-1. The operations are three in number and include AND, OR, and EXCLUSIVE-OR. To avoid confusion between logical and arithmetic operations we have used the symbols $\wedge$ and $\vee$ to represent AND and OR. As with the addition and subtraction instructions, one operand is always to be found in the ac-

Table 10.8-1 Increment and Decrement Instructions of the 8080

INCREMENT REGISTER	INR r	r + 1→ r
Increment contents of register r; all flags affected *except* CY		
DECREMENT REGISTER	DCR r	r − 1 → r
Decrement contents of register r; all flags affected *except* CY		
INCREMENT REGISTER PAIR	INX rp	rp + 1 → rp
Increment contents of pair rp; *no* flags affected		
DECREMENT REGISTER PAIR	DCX rp	rp − 1 → rp
Decrement contents of register pair rp; *no* flags affected		
INCREMENT MEMORY	INR M	M[H, L] + 1 → M[H, L]
Increment contents of memory location whose address is in register pair H, L; all flags affected *except* CY		
DECREMENT MEMORY	DCR M	M[H, L] − 1 → M[H, L]
Decrement contents of memory location whose address is in register pair H, L; all flags affected *except* CY		

cumulator, and the result is placed in the accumulator. There are three allowed sources for the second operand, a general-purpose register, a location in memory, or the instruction itself, i.e., in an immediate instruction where the operand is the second byte of the instruction. There are, accordingly, $3 \times 3 = 9$ logical instructions.

These logical operations are performed on a bit-by-bit basis. Carrying out a logical operation between 2 bytes involves eight separate operations, each involving 1 bit from each of the 2 bytes. An example is given in Fig. 10.9-1. Here

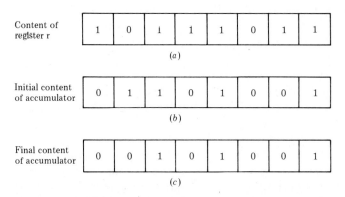

Figure 10.9-1 Initial contents of (*a*) a general-purpose register and (*b*) the accumulator. (*c*) The contents of the accumulator after the execution of the instruction ANA r.

Table 10.9-1 The Logic Instructions of the 8080

AND REGISTER ANA r $A \wedge r \to A$

Contents of register ANDed with contents of Acc and result placed in Acc; CY flag cleared

AND MEMORY ANA M $A \wedge M[H, L] \to A$

Contents of memory location whose address is in register pair H, L are ANDed with Acc and result placed in Acc; CY flag cleared

AND IMMEDIATE ANI $\langle B_2 \rangle$ $A \wedge \langle B_2 \rangle \to A$

Second byte, B_2, of instruction ANDed with Acc and result placed in Acc; CY and AC flags cleared

OR REGISTER ORA r $A \vee r \to A$

Contents of register ORed with contents of Acc and result placed in Acc; CY and AC flags cleared

OR MEMORY ORA M $A \vee M[H, L] \to A$
Contents of memory location whose address is in register pair H, L are ORed with contents of Acc and result placed in Acc; CY and AC flags cleared

OR IMMEDIATE ORI $\langle B_2 \rangle$ $A \vee \langle B_2 \rangle \to A$

Second byte, B_2, of the instruction ORed with contents of Acc and result placed in Acc; CY and AC flags cleared

EXCLUSIVE-OR REGISTER XRA r $A \oplus r \to A$

Contents of register r EXCLUSIVE-ORed with contents of Acc and result placed in Acc; CY and AC flags cleared

EXCLUSIVE-OR MEMORY XRA M $A \oplus M[H, L] \to A$

Contents of memory location whose address is in register pair, H, L are EXCLUSIVE-ORed with contents of Acc and result is placed in Acc; CY and AC flags cleared

EXCLUSIVE-OR IMMEDIATE XRA $\langle B_2 \rangle$ $A \oplus \langle B_2 \rangle \to A$

Second byte, B_2, of instruction EXCLUSIVE-ORed with contents of Acc and result placed in Acc; CY and AC flags cleared

the content of the accumulator and of a register r is specified, and also shown is the result that will appear in the accumulator after the instruction ANA r (AND register) is carried out.

All the logical instructions affect *all* the flags. Thus, as always, the Z, S and P flags will record whether the ALU output is zero, whether the most significant bit is 1 or 0, and whether the parity is odd or even. Since a logical operation involves no carry from bit position to bit position, we would imagine that any registration recorded in the AC and CY flags would be irrelevant. Such is indeed the case, but we need to keep in mind that the ALU has incorporated in it, in every bit position, logic to generate a carry, as will be called for when the input bits are interpreted as numbers. When a logic operation is called for, the carries so generated will not be transferred to the next higher bit position. Still the carry generated in the fourth bit position and in the eighth bit position are available at the ALU output and will be duly recorded in the AC and CY flags unless some specific alternative response is provided by the controller. In the 8080, as Table 10.9-1 shows, in all but two cases the AC and CY flags are cleared. With the two ANA instructions only the CY flag is cleared. It may well be that when a logical operation is executed, we have no interest in the flags. Still, at each point in the development of a program, we need to be precisely alert to the state of the flags because of their effect on the way the program unfolds.

10.10 THE COMPARISON INSTRUCTIONS

There are three instructions which allow us to compare the numerical values of the number $N(\text{Acc})$ registered in the accumulator, on the one hand, with a second number $N(r, M, I)$ in a register or in memory or immediately available, i.e., given as part of the instruction. If $N(\text{Acc}) = N(r, M, I)$, the equality will set Z to $Z = 1$; and if $N(\text{Acc}) \neq N(r, M, I)$, then Z will remain or be reset to $Z = 0$. If $N(\text{Acc}) < N(r, M, I)$, the CY flag will be set to $CY = 1$. If $N(\text{Acc}) > N(r, M, I)$, the CY flag will be left undisturbed. We can therefore deduce that $N(\text{Acc}) > N(r, M, I)$ if we find $CY = 0$ and if we have had the foresight to clear CY before using the comparison instruction. The comparison instructions are described in Table 10.10-1.

Table 10.10-1 Comparison Instructions of the 8080

COMPARE REGISTER   CMP r   A − r

Contents of register r and of Acc applied to ALU input. ALU instructed to perform subtraction A − r. Result of this subtraction is *not* registered in Acc or any other register. All flags are affected in normal fashion. If A = r, then A − r = 0 and this result will be recorded in Z flag and we shall have Z = 1. If A < r, we shall have Z = 0 and, further, the subtraction A − r will generate a *borrow* out of most significant bit position and we shall have CY = 1

COMPARE MEMORY   CMP M   A − M[H, L]

Operation performed is same as in CMP r except that comparison is made not with contents of general-purpose register but with contents of memory location whose address is held in H, L register pair

COMPARE IMMEDIATE   CPI ⟨B_2⟩   A − ⟨B_2⟩

A 2-byte instruction; in this case comparison is made with ⟨B_2⟩, the second byte of the instruction

Table 10.11-1 The Rotate Instructions

ROTATE LEFT	RLC	$A_n \to A_{n+1}$ $(n \neq 7)$; $A_7 \to A_0$; $A_7 \to CY$

Each bit in Acc register except most significant bit, A_7, is shifted one bit position to left. Bit A_7 is transferred to A_0 position and also to CY flag. No other flags are affected

ROTATE RIGHT	RRC	$A_n \to A_{n-1}$ $(n \neq 0)$; $A_0 \to A_7$; $A_0 \to CY$

Each bit in Acc register except least significant bit, A_0, is shifted one bit position to right. Bit A_0 is transferred to A_7 position and also to CY flag. No other flags are affected

ROTATE LEFT THROUGH CARRY	RAL	$A_n \to A_{n+1}$ $(n \neq 7)$; $A_7 \to CY$; $CY \to A_0$

Each bit in Acc register except most significant bit, A_7, is shifted one bit position to left. Bit A_7 is transferred to CY, and contents of CY are transferred to A_0. No other flags are affected

ROTATE RIGHT THROUGH CARRY	RAR	$A_n \to A_{n-1}$ $(n \neq 0)$; $A_0 \to CY$; $CY \to A_7$

Each bit in Acc register except least significant bit, A_0, is shifted one bit position to right. Bit A_0 is transferred to CY, and contents of CY are transferred to A_7. No other flags are affected

10.11 THE ROTATE INSTRUCTIONS

There are four instructions which cause the accumulator to operate like a shift register. Two of the instructions perform a right shift, and two perform a left shift. The CY flag of the status register is involved in all four instructions, but no other flags are affected. The details of these instructions are spelled out in Table 10.11-1 and in Fig. 10.11-1.

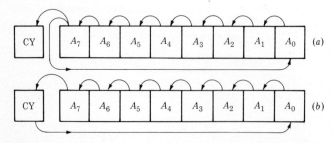

Figure 10.11-1 The instructions (*a*) "rotate left" and (*b*) "rotate left through carry."

10.12 THE COMPLEMENT AND SET INSTRUCTIONS

There are two COMPLEMENT instructions and one SET instruction, as listed in Table 10.12-1. They allow us to complement the accumulator, complement the carry flag, and set the carry flag. If we want to reset the carry flag, we can do so by using the "AND register" instruction, which performs the AND operation between a register and the accumulator. We select as the register specified in that instruction the accumulator itself. The result is that the accumulator is ANDed with itself, leaving the accumulator content unchanged. However, as we note, the instruction does clear the CY flag.

Table 10.12-1 The Complement and Set Instructions

COMPLEMENT ACCUMULATOR	CMA	$\overline{A} \rightarrow A$
Each bit of Acc replaced by its complement; no flags affected		
COMPLEMENT CARRY	CMC	$\overline{CY} \rightarrow CY$
Bit in CY flag replaced by its complement; no other flags affected		
SET CARRY	STC	$1 \rightarrow CY$
Carry flag set to 1; no other flags affected		

10.13 AN EXAMPLE

As an example of a simple program using some of the data-transfer and logical instructions of the 8080, consider the following. Suppose that we hold in memory a two-digital-decimal number, the numbers having been made available in the form of ASCII code characters with even parity. If the number is 59, we have $5 = 00110101$ and $9 = 00111001$ and the number occupies two memory locations M_1 and M_2. Each memory location has two 4-bit parts $M_1[H]$, $M_1[L]$ and $M_2[H]$, $M_2[L]$. In each of the ASCII code numbers only the right-most 4 bits have numerical significance. These 4 bits represent the number in BCD code. The other 4 bits serve to establish parity and to distinguish the numbers from the other character symbols. Suppose now that we want to put together the two 4-bit BCD codes into a single byte. (We might well want to effect such a consolidation to save a memory location and in anticipation of performing an arithmetic operation with the number.)

This process of deleting bits which no longer serve a purpose and consolidating useful bits into a single byte is called *packing*. The program which follows accomplishes the packing and returns the packed byte to a memory location M_3.

Label	Contents	Comment
	LDA $\langle M_1[L]\rangle$ $\langle M_1[H]\rangle$	Load Acc with contents of memory location M_1
	ANI $\langle 00001111\rangle$	AND Acc with 00001111, thereby arranging that all 4 left bits become 0s and all 4 right bits remain unchanged (this process of clearing locations which hold irrelevant bits is called *masking*)
	RLC RLC RLC RLC	Rotate left 4 times so that BCD bits are in the four left bit positions and four right bit positions are all 0s
	MOV B, A	Move Acc contents to register B so that Acc is available to process second character
	LDA $\langle M_2[L]\rangle$ $\langle M_2[H]\rangle$	Load Acc with second ASCII character from location M_2
	ANI $\langle 00001111\rangle$	Mask four left bit positions
	ORA B	OR contents of register B with Acc; the two BCD numbers are now packed into a single byte
	STA $\langle M_3[L]\rangle$ $\langle M_3[H]\rangle$	Store contents of Acc in memory location M_3

10.14 THE JUMP INSTRUCTIONS

In spite of the large number of instructions which we have already introduced we find that the computations and data manipulations of the 8080 are still severely limited. The versatility of programming possibilities is greatly enhanced by the two JUMP instructions incorporated into the 8080's repertory. Both are 3-byte instructions. One jump instruction is unconditional, which, as usual, we describe as follows:

JUMP   JMP $\langle B_2\rangle$ $\langle B_3\rangle$ $\langle B_3\rangle$ $\langle B_2\rangle \rightarrow$ PC

Transfer to program counter the address $\langle B_3\rangle$ $\langle B_2\rangle$ given in second and third bytes of instruction.

The net effect of this instruction is that after the jump has been executed the next instruction to be executed is the instruction at address $\langle B_3\langle\rangle B_2\rangle$.

The second jump is a *conditional* jump instruction, the jump occurring if and only if the specified condition is satisfied. The conditions referred to are the conditions of the four flags Z, S, P, and CY. The AC flag is not involved in these conditional jump instructions. There are four flags, each flag has two states, and there is a conditional jump instruction associated with each state of each individual flag. Hence the jump instruction actually expands into the eight instructions which are listed in Table 10.14.1 on page 440.

The jump instructions do not affect any of the flags. Depending on the flag states, a conditional jump may or may not take place, but in any event after the jump instructions have been executed, the flag states are the same as before.

As a simple example which involves a conditional jump instruction, consider the following program. Here we assume that we have two unsigned numbers N_1 and N_2 in two successive memory locations K and $K + 1$ and that we want to transfer to memory location $K + 2$ the larger of the two numbers.

Label	Contents	Comment
	LXIH $\langle K[L] \rangle$ $\langle K[H] \rangle$	Load register pair H with address K of number N_1
	MOV A, M	Move to Acc the contents of memory whose address is in register pair H
	INX H	Increment contents of register pair H (register pair H now holds address $K + 1$ of number N_2)
	CMP M	Subtract from Acc the contents of memory location in register pair H and set CY and Z flags appropriately. If $N_1 = N_2$, then Z = 1, if $N_1 < N_2$ CY = 1. Acc contents not altered. If CY = 0, then $N_1 \geq N_2$
	JNC $\langle END[L] \rangle$ $\langle END[H] \rangle$	If CY = 0, then $N_1 \geq N_2$ and number already in Acc is number to be stored in memory location $K + 2$. In this case, jump to instruction in memory location labeled "END." If CY = 1, we need to move N_2 into Acc, a transfer carried out by next instruction
	MOV A, M	Move to Acc the contents of memory whose address is in register pair H
END	INX H	Increment contents of register pair H (register pair now holds address $K + 2$)
	MOV M, A	Store Acc contents in memory location whose address is in register pair H

Table 10.14-1 The Conditional Jump Instructions

JUMP IF ZERO FLAG IS RESET (result is not zero)	JNZ$\langle B_2\rangle$ $\langle B_3\rangle$	If Z = 0, $\langle B_3\rangle\langle B_2\rangle \to$ PC
JUMP IF ZERO FLAG IS SET (result is zero)	JZ $\langle B_2\rangle$ $\langle B_3\rangle$	If Z = 1, $\langle B_3\rangle\langle B_2\rangle \to$ PC
JUMP IF SIGN FLAG IS RESET (sign is positive)	JP $\langle B_2\rangle\langle B_3\rangle$	If S = 0, $\langle B_3\rangle\langle B_2\rangle \to$ PC
JUMP IF SIGN FLAG IS SET (sign is minus)	JM $\langle B_2\rangle\langle B_3\rangle$	If S = 1, $\langle B_3\rangle\langle B_2\rangle \to$ PC
JUMP IF PARITY FLAG IS RESET (parity is odd)	JPO $\langle B_2\rangle\langle B_3\rangle$	If P = 0, $\langle B_3\rangle\langle B_2\rangle \to$ PC
JUMP IF PARITY FLAG IS SET (parity is even)	JPE $\langle B_2\rangle\langle B_3\rangle$	If P = 1, $\langle B_3\rangle\langle B_2\rangle \to$ PC
JUMP IF CARRY FLAG IS RESET (no carry or borrow)	JNC $\langle B_2\rangle\langle B_3\rangle$	If CY = 0, $\langle B_3\rangle\langle B_2\rangle \to$ PC
JUMP IF CARRY FLAG IS SET (a carry or borrow is indicated)	JC $\langle B_2\rangle\langle B_3\rangle$	If CY = 1, $\langle B_3\rangle\langle B_2\rangle \to$ PC

In the program on page 439, we might have called forth memory contents by using the LDA instruction. The 3-byte instruction LDA $\langle K[L]\rangle$ $\langle K[H]\rangle$ would accomplish the same purpose as the first 4 bytes of the program as written. On the other hand, the indirect addressing scheme, where the memory address is in register pair H, allows the convenience of accessing successive locations, as required in the present case, by simply using the 1-byte INX H instruction. Note also that because the address was in register pair H we could use the CMP M instruction, thereby making possible a comparison with the contents of a memory location without calling the contents out into one of the general-purpose registers.

10.15 THE CALL AND RETURN INSTRUCTIONS

We have already noted in Sec 9.7 the advantage of being able to call up a subroutine. When a subroutine is called, it is necessary to save the address in the main program to which the computer is to return after the subroutine program has been completed. In the scheme of Sec. 9.7 we reserved a memory location immediately preceding the subroutine program to save this return address. In the 8080 and in microprocessors generally an alternative and more convenient scheme is used to save the return address. A stack is used for this purpose.

As noted in Sec. 6.16, a stack is a random-access memory (or a specially set-aside portion of a larger memory) which operates on a last-in first-out (LIFO) basis. The address of the stack location being referenced is held in a counter. In the 8080 (and other microprocessors) this address counter is called the *stack pointer*, and the stack is a set-aside portion of the same random access memory which is providing storage facility for the microprocessor. This memory, if the full memory capacity is being used, has a capacity of 2^{16} words. The *top* of the memory is considered the memory with location 0000 (hex), and the *bottom* of the memory has address FFFF (hex). Suppose, then, that the main program is stored at the top of the memory, say starting at 0000. We might then very reasonably use the bottom of the memory for the stack since we need to ensure that the stack does not encroach on sections of the memory reserved for other purposes.

In organizing the control operations which manipulate the stack it can be arranged so that as additional words are stored in the stack, the stack grows either in the downward direction or in the upward direction. Suppose we choose growth in the downward direction. Then we must take account of the fact that after the stack pointer reaches FFFF, its next registration will be 0000. Thus, as the stack grows, we are concerned lest the stack encroach on the main memory stored beginning at the top of the memory. Such a difficulty may arise even though memory space between the bottom of the main memory store and the top of the stack is available. If we try to avoid this difficulty by starting the stack well above FFFF, we may find wasted memory at the bottom of the stack since when we start to write a program it is often difficult to judge how many stack locations will be required. For these reasons, in the 8080, as in other microprocessors, the stack is designed to grow from the bottom toward the top. Then if we start the stack at FFFF, we need only be concerned about whether the stack, growing up, meets the other stored items which are growing down. If we still run into trouble, it is because we simply have not provided enough memory capacity and not because we failed to use memory wisely.

Having decided that the stack is to grow upward, we still have a choice of how the stack is to operate. On the one hand, we can arrange it so that when a new word is to be placed on the stack, it is stored in the location addressed by the stack pointer, *after* which the stack pointer decrements. In such a case, when we want to retrieve the top word of the stack, we must *first* increment the stack pointer and then read. On the other hand, we can arrange it so that in placing a new word on the stack we *first* decrement and then store. In this case, in retrieving a word we first read and then increment. In the 8080 this second alternative is used. Therefore if we want to store a word at location FFFF, we must first set the stack pointer at 0000. With these preliminary remarks we can now consider the 8080 CALL instructions.

The CALL instruction is a 3-byte instruction in which the second and third bytes specify the address of the beginning of the subroutine being called. The execution of this CALL instruction accomplishes the following operations: (1) It stores on top of the stack the address of the instruction immediately following the CALL instruction. This instruction is the main program instruction to which the computer should return after the subroutine has been completed. (2) It transfers to the program counter (PC) the address of the first instruction in the subroutine being called. Since addresses are 16 bits long, two memory locations are required to store the main-program return address. Hence after the address storage is complete, the stack pointer has a registration which is 2 rather than 1 less than its registration before the CALL instruction. Altogether the CALL instruction is described as follows:

CALL SUBROUTINE	CALL $\langle B_2 \rangle$ $\langle B_3 \rangle$	$PC[high] \rightarrow SP - 1$
		$PC[low] \rightarrow SP - 2$
		$SP - 2 \rightarrow SP$
		$\langle B_3 \rangle$ $\langle B_2 \rangle \rightarrow PC$

Here, SP represents the registration of the stack pointer just before the CALL instruction is executed. The symbol PC[high] represents the high-order bits of the address of the instruction immediately following the CALL instruction. Similarly PC[low] are the low-order bits of this same instruction.

Like the JUMP instruction, the CALL instruction is available both unconditionally and conditionally, the conditions examined again being the states of four of the five flags. The mnemonics for these conditional CALL instructions are as follows:

CNZ   Call if zero flag is reset (Z = 0, result is not zero)
CZ   Call if zero flag is set (Z = 1, result is zero)
CP   Call if sign flag is reset (S = 0, sign is positive)
CM   Call if sign flag is set (S = 1, sign is minus)
CPO   Call if parity flag is reset (P = 0, parity is odd)
CPE   Call if parity flag is set (P = 1, parity is even)
CNC   Call if carry flag is reset (CY = 0, no carry or borrow)
CC   Call if carry flag is set (CY = 1, carry or borrow indicated)

When we have called up a subroutine and the subroutine has been completed, there must be a return to the main program. For this reason there are available a RETURN instruction and a conditional RETURN instruction. The RETURN instruction puts back into the program counter the address stored in the stack. The RETURN instruction is a 1-byte instruction and has the following description:

RETURN	RET	$SP \rightarrow PC[low]$
		$SP + 1 \rightarrow PC[high]$
		$SP + 2 \rightarrow SP$

The conditional RETURN instructions have mnemonics RNZ, RZ, etc., as in the JUMP and CALL instructions.

Before we can use the CALL instruction, we must load an address into the stack pointer in order to establish the memory location from which the stack will grow. For this purpose we can use the instruction LXI ("load register pair immediate") since the stack pointer is one of the register pairs with which the

LXI instruction may be used. Alternatively we can establish the stack pointer starting address by loading the H, L register pair first and then transferring the contents of this pair to the stack pointer. For this purpose, there is available the following instruction:

MOVE REGISTER PAIR H TO SP	SPHL	H, L → SP

It often happens that when a subroutine has been called, it requires the services of a second subroutine, which requires the services of a third subroutine, and so on. Such a situation is described as *nesting* subroutines. In these circumstances the stack works very effectively. As each subroutine and sub-subroutine is called, return addresses are piled on the stack, and as returns from the sub-subroutine and subroutine are to be effected, the return addresses must be retrieved exactly in the order opposite that in which they were stored. Precisely this last-in first-out feature is an essential characteristic of the stack.

As an example of the use of the CALL and RETURN instructions, consider that we shall have frequent occasion to convert a number in the range from 00 (hex) to 0F (hex) (0000 to 1111 binary) to ASCII code. If the need for conversion is frequent enough, we should like to be able to call on a conversion subroutine instead of having to rewrite the conversion program each time it is needed. It is left as a student exercise (Prob. 10.15-1) to verify (1) that if the number is in the range 00 to 09 the conversion is effected simply by adding 0011 0000 (30 hex) and (2) that if the number is 10 (decimal) or larger the conversion is effected by adding 0011 0111 = (0011 0000 + 0000 0111).

In the program that follows we call forth the contents of a memory location $M[H, L]$ and, knowing it to be a number in the range 0 to 15 (decimal), make a conversion to the ASCII representation and then return the number to its original memory location. We include an instruction which initializes the stack-pointer registration so that the stack will start in memory location FFFF.

Label	Contents	Comment
	LXI SP 00 (hex) 00 (hex)	Load stack pointer with registration 0000 (hex). A decrement in SP will start stack at FFFF
	LDA M [L] M [H]	Load Acc with data in memory location $M[H, L]$
	CALL $\langle B_2 \rangle$ (ASC) $\langle B_3 \rangle$	Call subroutine that begins at memory address $B_3 B_2$ (subroutine is at address labeled ASC)
	STA M [L] M [H] . . .	Store Acc contents back at memory location $M[H, L]$

Label	Contents	Comment
ASC	CPI 10 (decimal)	Compare Acc with 10 (decimal). If Acc is less than 10, we have CY = 1. (If CY = 0, then A ≥ 10 and we must add 0011 0000 and also 0000 0111
	JC ⟨B_2⟩ (LTN) ⟨B_3⟩	If CY = 1, jump to instruction LTN (less than ten)
	ADI 0000 0111	Add immediate second byte (because A ≥ 10)
LTN	ADI 0011 0000	Add immediate second byte (needed in every case)
	RET	Return to main program (STA, above)

10.16 THE PUSH AND POP INSTRUCTIONS

Suppose that when we call up a subroutine there are data in the accumulator, the flags, and the general-purpose registers which we shall need when the subroutine is completed. It is easy to imagine a subroutine program which might use the registers in such a way that the needed data would not be preserved. In such a case before calling the subroutine we would have to store the needed data in some place from which they could be retrieved. Better still, we might arrange this process of storing to be incorporated as part of the subroutine at the beginning of the subroutine. Correspondingly, the last instructions of the subroutine would restore to each register the data present before the subroutine was called up. In principle, we might store the data anywhere in the random-access memory, but in practice it is much more convenient to store those data on the stack. The stack portion of memory is restricted to last-in, first-out operation, but in the present case this LIFO feature is no inconvenience at all.

As we have noted, the operation of writing data onto the top of a stack is called a *push operation,* and the process of reading data from the top of a stack is called a *pop operation*. The 8080 has two PUSH and two POP instructions. Data which are pushed are pushed in the form of a 16-bit word. Thus the pushed data are a 2-byte word, stored in two memory locations; hence two stack-pointer decrements are required so that SP can point to the two successive memory locations in which the data are to be stored. We may note parenthetically that the CALL instruction involves an implied *push* operation and that there, too, the pushed data were a 16-bit word, i.e., the contents of the program counter. One PUSH instruction is used to push onto the stack the contents of register pair B (B and C) or D (D and E) or H (H and L), as follows:

PUSH REGISTER PAIR	PUSH rp	rp[H] $\to$ SP $-$ 1
		rp[L] $\to$ SP $-$ 2
		SP $-$ 2 $\to$ SP

Before execution of the instruction, if the stack-pointer registration is SP, the high-order bits of the register pair are placed at SP $-$ 1 and the low-order bits at SP $-$ 2; when the execution is complete, the new stack-pointer registration is SP $-$ 2. The pushed register pair cannot be the stack pointer itself.

Correspondingly there is a POP instruction which is precisely inverse to this PUSH instruction:

POP REGISTER PAIR	POP rp	SP $\to$ rp[L]
		SP $+$ 1 $\to$ rp[H]
		SP $+$ 2 $\to$ SP

Before the execution of the instruction, if the stack-pointer registration is SP, the contents of memory location SP are transferred to the low-order register of register pair rp, the contents of location SP $+$ 1 are transferred to the high-order register of the pair, and when the execution is complete, the new stack-pointer registration is SP $+$ 2. The popped word cannot be transferred to the stack pointer itself.

There is a second PUSH instruction. It pushes onto the stack the accumulator contents and a second byte, called the *processor status word* (PSW). Five of the bits of the PSW are the contents of the five flags Z, S, P, CY, and AC; the other three are dummy bits and serve no purpose except to supplement the five flag bits so that an 8-bit word is formed. Corresponding to this PUSH instruction is a POP instruction which performs precisely the inverse operation:

PUSH PROCESSOR STATUS WORD	PUSH PSW	A $\to$ SP $-$ 1
		PSW $\to$ SP $-$ 2
		SP $-$ 2 $\to$ SP
POP PROCESSOR STATUS WORD	POP PSW	SP $+$ 1 $\to$ A
		SP $+$ 2 $\to$ PSW
		SP $\to$ SP $+$ 2

There is one additional instruction involving the stack:

EXCHANGE STACK TOP WITH H AND L	XTHL	L $\leftrightarrow$ M[SP]
		H $\leftrightarrow$ M[SP $+$ 1]

The contents of the L register are exchanged with the contents of the memory location whose address is specified by the contents of the SP register. The contents of the H register are exchanged with the contents of the memory location whose address is 1 more than the contents of the SP register. While this instruction is being executed, the registration of the stack pointer remains unaltered.

As an example of the use of the stack and some of the stack instructions we consider now multiple-precision addition. Suppose we have in memory two 32-bit numbers N_1 and N_2 and we want to add these numbers and store the sum in memory. Each of the numbers will have 4 bytes and will occupy four memory locations. The sum will also have to occupy four memory locations, and if there is a carry out of the thirty-second bit position, we shall leave this carry in the carry flag. In order to avoid a profusion of symbols to represent locations of N_1, N_2, and the sum we shall use real numbers. Thus using hexadecimal numbers throughout, let us assume that N_1 is stored in memory locations 0041, 0042, 0043, and 0044; that N_2 is in locations 0051, 0052, 0053, and 0054; and that the sum is to be stored at locations 0061, 0062, 0063, and 0064. In all cases we assume that the lowest-order bits are stored in the lowest-numbered location, and so on, the highest-order bits being in the highest-numbered memory location.

Of course, we can call forth the individual bytes of N_1 and of N_2 and store the bytes of $N_1 + N_2$ by using the 3-byte instructions LDA $\langle B_2 \rangle \langle B_3 \rangle$ (load Acc from memory location $B_3 B_2$) and STA $\langle B_2 \rangle \langle B_3 \rangle$ (store Acc in memory location $B_3 B_2$). However, since successive locations are used for N_1, N_2, and $N_1 + N_2$ it would be of advantage to be able to load registers with starting addresses and then get successive addresses by using the 1-byte increment instruction. We can use the three register pairs H, D, and B for this purpose; however we also need a register to keep count of the number of bytes we have added so that we can stop when we have added the 4 bytes. Since all register pairs are committed, and since the accumulator is needed to perform the addition, we may look to the use of the stack. The following program is written as a main program, which loads the starting information into the registers, and a subroutine, which actually performs the multiple-precision addition. The stack is used initially simply because a subroutine is called up and again to free the register pair B. The program also illustrates the use of the XTHL instructions to make an extra register pair available in the stack.

Label	Contents	Comment
	LXI H 41 00	Load register pair H with starting address of N_1
	LXI D 51 00	Load register pair D with starting address of N_2
	LXI B 61 00	Load register pair B with starting address of $N_1 + N_2$
	MVI A 04	Set Acc at 4, corresponding to 4 bytes to be added

Label	Contents	Comment
	LXI SP 70 00	Initialize SP in anticipation of a CALL instruction (any place is acceptable provided there is no overlapping)
	CALL MPADD . . .	3-byte instruction which calls up multiple-precision add subroutine (MPADD)
MPADD	PUSH B	Push contents of register pair B to stack to make register available to hold Acc contents
	MOV B, A	Move Acc contents to register B
	ANA A	AND Acc with itself in order to clear CY
ADD W	LDAX D	Load the accumulator with number in memory location whose address is in register pair D
	ADC M	Add to number in the Acc number in memory location whose address is in H, L pair. Add also contents of CY flag
	XTHL	Interchange stack top contents with contents of register pair H, L. This instruction places starting address for sum $N_1 + N_2$ in pair H, L. This address, originally in register pair B, was last data pushed onto stack in execution of PUSH B instruction above
	MOV M, A	Move contents of Acc to memory location whose address is in H, L pair
	INX H	Increment register pair H, L to arrange that when next set of bytes of N_1 and N_2 is added, sum will be stored in next-higher-numbered memory location
	XTHL	Again interchange stack top contents with contents of register pair H, L in order to put starting address of N_1 back into pair H, L
	INX D	Increment address location in pair D
	INX H	Increment address location in pair H
	DCR B	Decrement register B

At this point all address locations for N_1, N_2, and $N_1 + N_2$ have been incremented, and the count of the number of bytes to be processed has been decremented. Now we need only loop through the additions until the number of bytes to be processed has been decremented to zero. The program continues:

	JNZ ADD W	If registration in register B is not zero, jump back to instruction whose address label is ADD W (add word); if B = 0, go on to next instruction

At this point the subroutine has been completed, and we should like to use the RET (RETURN) instruction to get back to the main program. The address at which the main program is to begin again was stored on the stack by the CALL instruction. The RET instruction will put the address at the top of the stack back into the program counter. We therefore need to keep in mind that after the CALL instruction we used the PUSH B instruction. We must hence first use a POP B instruction to get the return address back to the top of the stack. The subroutine is accordingly completed as follows:

POP B	Pop the stack back to register B to get main-program return address back to top of stack
RET	Return to main program

10.17 AN EXAMPLE: MULTIPLICATION

In this section we consider the arithmetical operation of multiplication, both because of its fundamental importance and because it is an interesting yet simple programming example.

Multiplication with binary numbers is entirely straightforward and is performed exactly as in decimal arithmetic (see Fig. 10.17-1). The multiplicand is multiplied in turn by each of the bits of the multiplier. Thus multiplication is easier than in the decimal system, since the result of this multiplication is zero or the multiplicand itself, according to whether the multiplier bit is 0 or 1. To take account of the increase in numerical significance of successive multiplier bits as we go to the left there is a corresponding left shift of successive partial products. The product is then formed by adding all the partial products. When the multiplication is carried out by pencil and paper, it is indeed best, as in Fig. 10.17-1, to form all the partial products first and then add; for in this way we need perform only one operation of adding. When, on the other hand, the multiplication is done by microprocessor, it is better to add each partial product as soon as it is formed, thus avoiding the need for registers to hold the partial products until we are ready to add them.

In the procedure of Fig. 10.17-1 we start by using the rightmost least significant multiplier bit, then the next more significant bit, etc. Once a partial product has been written down, we never need to erase it in order to shift it to a new

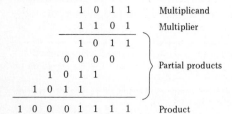

Figure 10.17-1 The "normal" manner of carrying out a multiplication.

```
 1  0  1  1        1  0  1  1        1  0  1  1        1  0  1  1
(1) 1  0  1        1 (1) 0  1        1  1 (0) 1        1  1  0 (1)
 1  0  1  1        1  0  1  1     1  0  0  0  0  1   1  0  0  0  0  1  0
                   1  0  1  1        0  0  0  0                  1  0  1  1
             1  0  0  0  0  1   1  0  0  0  0  1  0   1  0  0  0  1  1  1  1
```

      (a)   *(b)*   *(c)*   *(d)*

Figure 10.17-2 How the microprocessor program carries out a multiplication.

position. In writing our microprocessor multiplication program, however, it turns out to be more convenient to arrange the procedure otherwise. We start with the leftmost most significant bit and shift partial products and sums of partial products after they have been formed. The procedure is shown step by step in Fig. 10.17-2, where we have done the same multiplication as in Fig. 10.17-1.

In Fig. 10.17-2a we have formed the partial product using the leftmost multiplier bit (circled). In Fig. 10.17-2b we have copied over the result in Fig. 10.17-2a except that we have shifted it one place to the left. Here, too, we have formed the next partial product and added. The result in Fig. 10.17-2b is copied over in Fig. 10.17-2c, except that we have shifted again. Finally, proceeding in the same manner, we show the final result in Fig. 10.17-2d.

We shall now assume that in memory location 0040 (hex) we have a 1-byte multiplicand and in memory location 0041 we have a 1-byte multiplier. The program which follows will form the product and store the result in memory. Since the product of two 8-digit numbers may extend to as many as 16 digits, we shall store the result in memory locations 0042 and 0043.

Label	Contents	Comment
	LXI H 40 00	Load register pair H, L with 0040, which is address of multiplicand
	MOV E, M	Move multiplicand from memory to register E
	MVI D 00	Clear register D, which is other half of register pair D, E (reason will appear below)
	INX H	Increment register pair H, L to memory location of multiplier
	MOV A, M	Move multiplicand from memory to Acc
	LXI H 00 00	Clear register pair H, L. So far H, L has been used to hold addresses. We now begin to use it to hold partial products as they are formed, to shift and to add
	MVI B 08	Load register B with number 8. There are 8 multiplier bits and by decrementing register B we shall know when we have used all the bits and multiplication is complete

Label	Contents	Comment
MULT	DAD H	Add contents of register pair H, L to themselves. This addition multiplies contents by a factor of 2. This multiplication is then equivalent to a *left shift* (first performance of this operation has no net effect since register pair starts out cleared)
	RAL	Rotate Acc left through carry, putting most significant multiplier bit in CY flag
	JNC CHANGE COUNT	3-byte instruction calling for jump to instruction whose address label is CHCNT, but jump is conditional and will occur if there is no carry, i.e., if CY = 0. Otherwise next instruction is executed
	DAD D	Add contents of register pair D, E to register pair H, L. Register E holds multiplicand (earlier we cleared register D)
CHCNT	DCR B	Decrement register B
	JNZ MULT	3-byte instruction calling for jump to instruction whose address label is MULT, but jump is conditional and will occur only if contents of register B are not zero. If registration of B is zero, multiplication is complete and result can be stored as provided by following instruction
	SHLD 42 00	Store contents of register pair H, L in memory location 42

A summary of the 8080 instructions is given in Appendix C. Included in the listing are a number of instructions which will be discussed in Chap. 11.

10.18 THE TYPE 6800 MICROPROCESSOR

It is surely apparent by now that it is a major undertaking to become familiar enough with a particular microprocessor to use it effectively. In this chapter we have simply described most of the 8080 instructions and given a few examples of program writing. Much remains to be said. It will be recalled that there are still 10 pins on the 8080 chip whose function we have not yet described. We shall pursue the matter further in Chap. 11. Although it is not feasible here to discuss other microprocessor chips with comparable completeness, there are a good number of different microprocessors commercially available. They have a great similarity, and yet they have interesting and important differences. To provide some small idea of the similarities and differences we briefly consider some of the features of the type 6800 microprocessor chip.

Figure 10.18-1 shows a programmer's view of the 6800 connected to a peripheral RAM. Like the 8080, the 6800 is a 40-pin device; 16 of the pins provide an address bus, and there is an 8-bit data bus. There is a single read-write ($R/\overline{W}$) output line. There are two input lines which accept clocking waveforms ϕ_1 and ϕ_2. The unit is powered by a single 5-V source, which uses

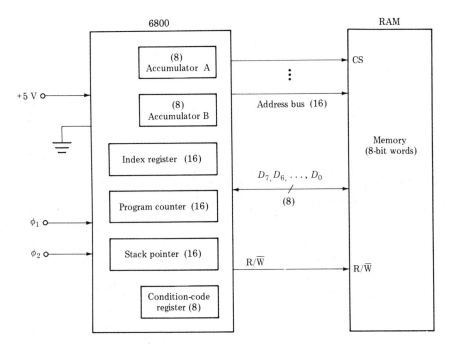

Figure 10.18-1 A programmer's view of the 6800 microprocessor.

one pin, and there are two ground pins. Of the 40 pins 2 are not used. Altogether we have accounted for 32 pins. The other 8 pins are used much like the 10 pins in the 8080 we have not yet considered. We defer this matter until the next chapter.

In the 8080 the peripheral memory was controlled by two lines, $\overline{\text{MEMR}}$ and $\overline{\text{MEMW}}$, through which we could arrange to read into memory, write from memory, or, when required, free the data bus from the memory so that the bus could be used for some other purpose. In the 6800 there is only a single memory control line $\text{R}/\overline{\text{W}}$, which determines whether there is a reading or writing operation. To free the bus from the memory chip it is necessary to use a chip select (CS) as one address input line of the chip. When the address line to CS is at logic 0 (or logic 1 when there is a $\overline{\text{CS}}$ input), the bus will be free.

The 6800 has two 8-bit accumulators A and B, instead of one accumulator as in the 8080. The accumulators serve the same general function as in the 8080. In operations involving the ALU, whether arithmetical or logical, the accumulators initially hold one of the operands and finally hold the result of the operation. The 6800 accumulators respond to shift and rotate instructions similar to those of the 8080. The accumulator also responds to an instruction (mnemonic ABA) which adds the content of the accumulators, leaves the sum in accumulator A, and leaves the initial content of B unaltered. The availability of the two rather versatile accumulator registers is an advantage in the 6800, which, taken with other features, serves to compensate for the lack of the general purpose register pairs B, C and D, E in the 8080. Like the 8080, the 6800 has a 16-bit program counter and a 16-bit stack pointer.

10.19 TYPE 6800 ADDRESSING MODES

In the 8080 when it is necessary to access a memory location for storing or retrieving some data, there are generally two ways of incorporating the address of the memory location into instructions: (1) the address is included directly in the instruction; e.g., the three-byte instruction LDA $\langle B_2 \rangle$ $\langle B_3 \rangle$ loads into the accumulator the data in the memory location whose address is $B_3 B_2$; (2) the address of the memory location is found in the register pair H, L; e.g., the 1-byte instruction MOV A, M moves to the accumulator the content of the memory location whose address is found in register pair H, L. In the 6800 some additional memory-addressing modes have been incorporated.

The first addressing mode available in the 6800 is called *direct addressing*. In this mode, the memory address is made a part of the instruction, but the assumption is made that the higher-order byte of the memory address is 00 (hex). Hence since the instruction need only specify the lower-order address byte, such an instruction with direct addressing is a 2- rather than a 3-byte instruction. A limitation of the direct addressing mode is that only the part of the memory from address 0000 (hex) to 00FF is accessible. Like the 8080, the 6800 also uses instructions in which 3 bytes are used, so that the full address can be made part of the instruction. In the 6800 this mode of addressing is given the name *extended* to distinguish it from direct addressing.

The 6800 also incorporates a facility for *indexed addressing*, which is not directly available in the 8080. This mode of addressing uses the 16-bit *index register*, which is the third 16-bit register in Fig. 10.18-1. An instruction using indexed addressing is a 2-byte instruction. The memory location addressed is then calculated by adding the second byte of the instruction to the contents of the index register. For example, in the assembly-language mnemonic LDA B N, X the X indicates that indexed addressing is intended. The instruction means that accumulator B is to be loaded from the memory location calculated by adding the 1-byte number N to the contents of the index register. If the contents of the index register were, say, 2615 (hex) and $N = 32$ (hex), the memory location accessed would be $2615 + 32 = 2647$. Indexed addressing is useful in that it allows us to extend the advantage of direct addressing, i.e., 2- rather than 3-byte instructions, to any portion of the memory. First we set the index register to an address A_I in whose neighborhood we need access. Thereafter a 2-byte instruction will yield access to all locations from A_I to $A_I + FF$ (hex).

10.20 THE 6800 CONDITION CODE REGISTER

The condition code register of the 6800 is comparable to the status register of the 8080. As in the 8080 and as shown in Fig. 10.20-1, the condition code regis-

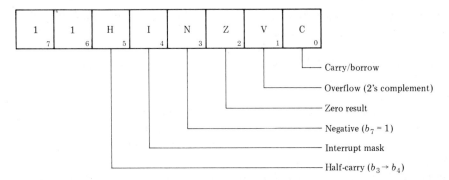

Figure 10.20-1 The condition code register of the 6800.

ter is an 8-bit register. Two of the flip-flops in the register, 6 and 7, are permanently in the set state and serve only to fill out the register to 8 bits. Bit 4 is the interrupt mask bit which we shall not discuss here. The C bit (carry/borrow) is the same as the CY bit of the 8080. The Z bit (zero) is the same as the 8080 Z bit. The N bit (negative) is set when the highest-order bit b_7 at the ALU output is $b_7 = 1$ and is the same as the S bit (sign) in the 8080. The H bit (half carry) is the same as the auxiliary carry bit AC in the 8080 and indicates a carry from b_3 to b_4. The 6800 has no parity bit, but it does however have a V bit (overflow). This overflow bit—particularly its distinction from the carry bit—merits comment.

If we use a 1-byte register to hold a number without reference to sign, the number $b_7 b_6, \ldots, b_0$ has the range 0 to 255 (decimal). If we add the numbers in two registers and the sum exceeds 255, there will be a carry out of the most significant bit. This carry will set the CY flag in the 8080 (or the C flag in the 6800), and, as we have seen, the carry output indication will allow us to do multibyte addition.

Suppose, now, that we propose to use our register to hold positive and negative numbers in accordance with the twos-complement representation. Then let us write the number as $s b_6 b_5, \ldots, b_0$, in which the bit b_7 has become the sign bit and b_6 is now most significant numerical bit. The range of number representation now extends from $+127$ to -128. If we add the numbers in two registers and the numbers added are of *different* sign, the sum will be within the range of the register. If we add numbers of like sign and the sum is less positive than $+127$ or less negative than -128, again everything is in order. But if we add numbers of like sign and the sum is outside the range $+127$ to -128, the result will be in error. For example

$$
\begin{array}{ll}
+98 = 01100010 & -98 = 10011110 \\
+54 = \underline{00110110} & -54 = \underline{11001010} \\
+152 \neq 10011000 \,(= -104) & -152 \neq 01101000 \,(= +104)
\end{array}
$$

Of course, short of using longer registers, there is nothing we can do about the matter. But we should certainly find it useful to be alerted to the fact that an error has occurred. Note that a carry cannot be used as an error indication. In the example above, the result is in error in both cases. There is no carry in the first case, but there is in the second.

It is now left as a student exercise (Prob. 10.20-1) to verify that the following scheme provides an indication that an error, i.e., an overflow error outside the register range, has occurred. Generate a logical variable C_n which is $C_n = 1$ when there is a carry out of the highest-order numerical bit (b_6) position and $C_n = 0$ otherwise. Generate a logical variable C_s which is $C_s = 1$ if there is a carry out of the sign-bit position and $C_s = 0$ otherwise. Generate the variable V given by

$$V = C_n \oplus C_s \tag{10.20-1}$$

If $V = 1$, there is an overflow error. The V flag in the condition code register of the 6800 is determined precisely in this manner.

ELEVEN

INPUT-OUTPUT OPERATIONS

Up to the present point we have studiously avoided any consideration of communication between the microprocessor unit and the world outside the chip (with the single exception of the transfer of information back and forth between the microprocessor and memory). Yet we hardly need belabor the point that such communication is of fundamental importance. If the microprocessor chip with its memory is to be used simply to perform a computation or data manipulation, at a minimum we need a mechanism for introducing data and instructions at the outset and reading out the result when the computation or manipulation has been completed. More generally the microcomputer system may well be intended not only to compute and manipulate data but also to control the operations of some external process. In such a case the microcomputer system may have to accept new data at unpredictable occasions during the very time some computation or manipulation is in process, and the system may also be required to provide output control signals at equally unpredictable times. The matter is further complicated by the fact that the external hardware with which communication is required (called the *peripherals*) may well comprise devices that are not able to operate in synchronism with the microprocessor clocking waveform or at speeds comparable to that of the microprocessor. These peripherals may consist of mechanical push buttons and switches, typewriter keys, magnetic tape devices, etc. In this chapter we shall discuss such communication between microcomputer and peripherals. The subject is generally called *input-output* (I/O) communication.

11.1 THE GENERATION OF I/O CONTROL SIGNALS IN THE 8080

In order to understand how the 8080 makes control signals needed for I/O communication available, it is necessary to describe briefly some details of the internal operation of the microprocessor chip.

As we have already noted, the timing of the 8080 is established by two clocking waveforms ϕ_1 and ϕ_2, which must be supplied to the MPU from an external source. These clocking waveforms are shown in Fig. 11.1-1a and b. The *cycle time* t_{cy} (the period) of the two waveforms is the same. In the 8080, t_{cy} at minimum is about 0.5 μs, corresponding to a frequency of 2 MHz, and at a maximum about 2.0 μs, corresponding to a frequency of 0.5 MHz. The duty cycles of the waveforms, i.e., relative times spent at the higher and lower voltage levels, are not strictly specified except that typically $t_{\phi_1} = \frac{2}{9}t_{cy}$ and $t_{\phi_2} = \frac{5}{9}t_{cy}$. The times at which ϕ_1 and ϕ_2 dwell at the upper voltage level do not overlap. The rise of ϕ_2 is delayed some 80 ns or more after the rise in ϕ_1. These clocking waveforms drive the MPU controller, and the controller advances from state to state in synchronism with these clocking waveforms. Accordingly the time t_{cy} is called the *state time*, as indicated. For as we have noted, a controller, and hence the machinery it controls, advances from one state to the next at each clock cycle.

The entire sequence of states through which the controller runs in processing an instruction is called an *instruction cycle*. Included in the instruction cycle are the states associated with fetching the instruction and the states associated with executing the instruction. Consider, for example, the instruction ADD r, which adds the number in register r to the number in the accumulator. The instruction requires a single communication with a device external to the

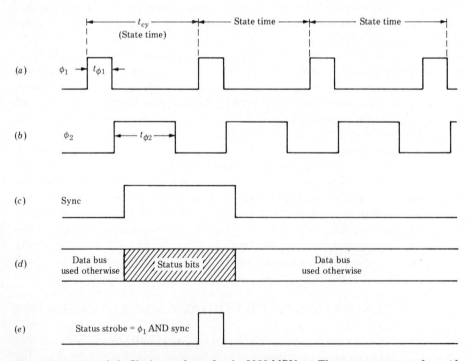

Figure 11.1-1 (a) and (b) Clock waveforms for the 8080 MPU. (c) The sync output waveform. (d) Timing of status bits on data lines. (e) Timing of the status strobe.

MPU. The external device is the memory, and the communication is for the purpose of fetching the single-byte instructions. It turns out that three states are used for the extraction of the instruction from the memory, and one additional state serves to accomplish the addition. These four states, which together effect a communication with the external device (the memory) and then process the data communicated, are jointly called a *machine cycle*. Thus the ADD r instruction is carried out in one machine cycle consisting of four states. Quite generally, then, each sequence of states associated with effecting a communication with an external device and then processing the transferred data is a machine cycle, and an instruction cycle is made up of one or more machine cycles. There must be at least one machine cycle because every instruction requires a fetch operation, which in turn requires a machine cycle. At most, an instruction cycle may consist of five machine cycles. An example of such a five-machine-cycle instruction is the instruction SHLD, which stores the content of the register pair H, L in two successive memory locations. The instruction is a 3-byte instruction; hence fetching these 3 bytes requires three machine cycles; then two additional machine cycles are required, one to store the contents of register L and one to store the contents of H.

During the first state of each machine cycle, the 8080 chip makes available to the world outside itself information concerning the operation which it is in the process of performing. This information is used to control and direct the activity of the peripheral devices, whether they are memory chips or other components. The manner of this control is shown in Figs. 11.1-1 and 11.1-2.

One of the output terminals of the 8080 to which we have not yet made reference is the *sync* (synchronization) output terminal. At this terminal the 8080 generates the waveform shown in Fig. 11.1-1c. This waveform is normally at logic zero except that beginning in the *first* state of each machine cycle it rises for one state time to logic 1. The rise in the sync waveform is timed to occur at a short delay time after the leading edge of the ϕ_2 clock waveform, and the fall in sync occurs at a comparable delay after the next rise in ϕ_2. (The delay is less than 120 ns.) Now ordinarily the eight data lines D_0 through D_7 in Fig. 11.1-2 are used to transfer data from or to the CPU chip. However, for the duration of the sync interval the data lines are used for a different purpose. During this interval the CPU puts on these eight data lines 8 bits which are called *status bits* since they serve to tell the outside world about the status of affairs inside the chip, i.e., what operation the CPU is intending to perform.

The status bits (or some of them) may well be required during the entire machine cycle. Yet, of course, the data lines will be needed during the same machine cycle to transfer data back and forth between CPU and memory and between CPU and peripherals. Hence we need to hold onto the status bits while freeing the data lines. As can be seen in Fig. 11.1-1d, the status bits are placed on the data lines only for the time during which *sync* = 1. At all other times the data lines are available for other purposes. To keep the status bits available even after *sync* returns to logic 0, we use a latch, as indicated in Fig. 11.1-2. The pulse which operates the latch, thereby catching and holding the status bits, is called the *status strobe* (STSTB); it is generated by ANDing the

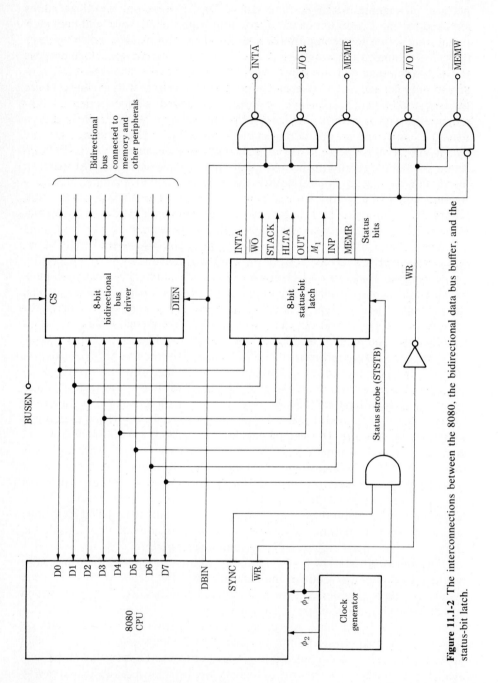

Figure 11.1-2 The interconnections between the 8080, the bidirectional data bus buffer, and the status-bit latch.

sync waveform and the clock waveform ϕ_1. As can be seen in Fig. 11.1-1e, this status strobe becomes active comfortably after the time when the status bits are first put on the data lines. Hence there is plenty of time for the status bits to become validly established. And the status strobe becomes inactive comfortably in advance of the time when the data lines are to be used for other purposes.

We consider now how the status bits available at the output of the status latch are combined with other signals from the 8080 to generate signals to be used to control communication between the 8080 and memory and between the 8080 and other peripherals. First we take note in Fig. 11.1-2 of two additional control signals furnished by the 8080. One is the output signal $\overline{\text{WR}}$ ($\overline{\text{WRITE}}$). When this (active-low) signal is at logic 0, it indicates that the CPU has placed data on the data lines and that the data are stable. Hence if we have a memory chip connected to the data lines and we set at the appropriate levels the control terminals of the memory chip ($R/\overline{W}$ and OD, output disable), the data will be *written* into the memory. The second control output signal is DBIN (data bus in). When DBIN = 1, the CPU chip indicates that the data bus is in the input mode; i.e., the CPU chip is processing the transfer of data (say from memory) into one of the registers internal to the 8080 chip. Correspondingly, when DBIN = 0, the transfer of data is in the other direction, i.e., out of the CPU.

We now refer back to Fig. 10.2-1, where we showed control signals $\overline{\text{MEMR}}$ and $\overline{\text{MEMW}}$ connected respectively to the OD and $R/\overline{W}$ input terminals of a memory chip. It can now be verified (Prob. 11.1-1) that if we complement DBIN to make available $\overline{\text{DBIN}}$, then $\overline{\text{DBIN}}$ can serve as the signal $\overline{\text{MEMR}}$ which is applied to the OD memory input and $\overline{\text{WR}}$ can serve as the signal $\overline{\text{MEMW}}$ applied to the $R/\overline{W}$ memory input. However we shall see in the next section that in the 8080 the designers chose not to use $\overline{\text{DBIN}}$ and $\overline{\text{WR}}$ directly to provide $\overline{\text{MEMR}}$ and $\overline{\text{MEMW}}$. In the next section we shall also continue our discussion of Fig. 11.1-2.

11.2 ISOLATED AND MEMORY-MAPPED INPUT-OUTPUT

As we have noted, data need to be communicated between CPU and memory and between CPU and other peripheral devices. These other peripheral devices may be treated as simply additional memory chips. Such treatment is indicated in Fig. 11.2-1, where the CPU is in communication with a memory chip and two other peripherals. The address lines are connected to the address inputs of the memory. One address code is reserved to single out each peripheral. When a peripheral is addressed, the output of its decoder will be at logic 1 and peripheral will be enabled. Then we can transfer data to or from the peripheral, depending on the logic levels of $\overline{\text{MEMR}}$ and $\overline{\text{MEMW}}$. (Again we have indicated, as seen in Fig. 11.1-2, that $\overline{\text{MEMR}}$ and $\overline{\text{MEMW}}$ are not furnished directly by the CPU.) Having used two addresses for the two peripherals in Fig. 11.2-1, we still have available $2^{16} - 2$ addresses for memory loca-

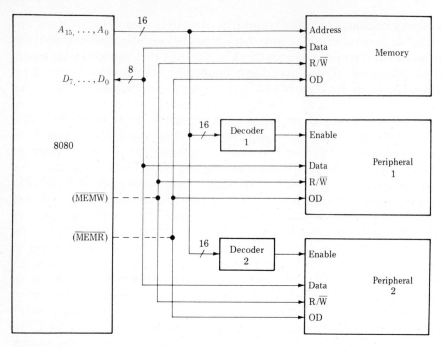

Figure 11.2-1 Memory-mapped input-output in which peripherals are treated as extensions of the memory.

tions. The decoding for the memory is done right on the memory chip. Quite frequently, as noted in the figure, a decoder entirely separate from the peripheral will be required for each peripheral. Since the decoders must accommodate 16 bits, they may be expensive and we may prefer to avoid them. As a means of eliminating the decoders consider the following arrangement. Let us assume that the memory chip is equipped with two $\overline{CS}$ ($\overline{CHIP\ SELECT}$) inputs so that when either of these inputs is at logic 1, the memory is not selected. (These $\overline{CS}$ inputs are not shown in Fig. 11.2-1.) Let us connect one address line, say A_{15} directly to the ENABLE input of peripheral 1 and to one memory $\overline{CS}$ input and say A_{14} directly to the ENABLE input of peripheral 2 and to the other $\overline{CS}$ input. Let us use the other 14 address lines $A_{13}, \ldots, A_0$ for memory addressing. Then we can dispense with the decoders. When $A_{15} = 1$, or when $A_{14} = 1$, we shall address respectively peripheral 1 or 2. When $A_{15} = A_{14} = 0$, the address refers to a memory location. Of course, we shall have reduced the number of addressable memory locations from $2^{16} - 2$ to 2^{14}. If the addressing capacity is still adequate, we may find that this scheme for eliminating decoders is quite acceptable.

The peripheral devices to which data are "shipped" or from which data are received are generally referred to as *ports*. The scheme we have just described to transfer data between any port and the CPU, treating any port in the manner of a memory, is called *memory-mapped input-output*. It is an entirely feasible scheme that can be used with the 8080. It makes available, for the purpose of communication between ports and CPU, all the instructions which move data between memory and the CPU. Memory-mapped I/O has the disadvantage, however, of infringing somewhat on the number of addresses available for memory addressing. It has a further disadvantage: Since a memory or port address must be provided, a 16-bit address must be included in, or implied by, the instruction. In some cases, such as LDA (load accumulator direct) the address is included in the 3-byte instruction. In other cases, such as MOV A, M (move to accumulator from memory), the instruction itself involves only 1 byte, but the address is in the H register pair and at some point program steps were required to load the address into the H register pair. It must not be imagined that these disadvantages are very serious. A number of microprocessors, e.g., the 6800, provide no other method of input-output. Still the designers of the 8080 decided it would be simpler and more convenient to make available an additional I/O scheme that would isolate the access to memory from the access to other ports. They have therefore included facility for this *isolated* I/O on the chip.

To see how isolated I/O operates, refer to Fig. 11.1-2. Note that one of the status bits held by the latch is named OUT. Its full name is OUTPUT WRITE, to distinguish it as an enable write operation into an *output port* and not a memory write, which would write into memory. When we examine the details provided by the manufacturer about the working of the 8080, we find that OUT is at logic level 1 when and only when the instruction about to be executed is a write operation into a port other than memory, using isolated I/O. We now also observe that when OUT = 1, the terminal marked $\overline{\text{I/O W}}$ (input-output write) has the logic value $\overline{\text{I/O W}} = \overline{\text{WR}}$, while the terminal $\overline{\text{MEMW}}$ is held fixed at logic 1. When OUT = 0, then $\overline{\text{I/O W}} = 1$ and $\overline{\text{MEMW}} = \overline{\text{WR}}$. Thus we have two separate terminals to use for writing: $\overline{\text{MEMW}}$, which becomes active when we want to write into memory, and $\overline{\text{I/O W}}$, which becomes active when we want to write into some peripheral other than memory.

All the instructions introduced so far which are concerned with communication between CPU and peripherals provide only for communication with memory. To allow use of the isolated I/O to transfer data out of the CPU the 8080 provides a special 2-byte instruction:

OUT
$\langle B_2 \rangle$

The second byte $\langle B_2 \rangle$ is the address of the port involved. This 8-bit address appears on the eight less significant address lines $A_7, \ldots, A_0$ and is *duplicated* on the eight more significant address lines $A_{15}, \ldots, A_8$. Since the address has only 8 bits, only 256 ports can be addressed, but it is rather difficult to imagine a situation where that number would not be more than adequate. When the OUT $\langle B_2 \rangle$ instruction is executed, the data placed on the data bus are the contents of

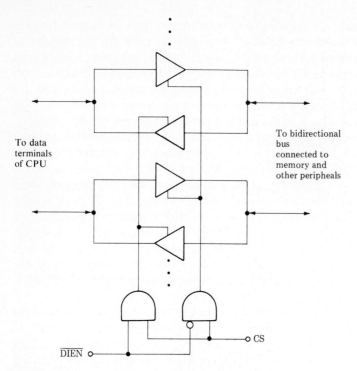

To data
terminals
of CPU

To bidirectional
bus
connected to
memory and
other peripheals

DIEN

CS

Figure 11.2-2 Logic diagram of a bidirectional bus driver.

the accumulator. Thus the OUT $\langle B_2 \rangle$ instruction is rather limited in comparison with the instruction available for use with memory-mapped I/O. In memory-mapped I/O we can involve any register, not only the accumulator.

Referring again to Fig. 11.1-2, we observe that it includes an 8-bit bidirectional bus driver. The bus driver consists of eight pairs of buffer amplifiers. Two such pairs are shown in Fig. 11.2-2. When CS (chip select) is at CS = 0, all amplifiers are inoperative, i.e., the outputs go to the high-impedance state as in tristate outputs, and the bus connected to memory and other ports is entirely isolated from the CPU. When CS = 1, either the top or bottom amplifier of each pair becomes operative. When CS = 1 and $\overline{\text{DIEN}}$ (data in to bus enable) is $\overline{\text{DIEN}}$ = 0, the top amplifier alone of each pair is rendered operative to establish a transmission path for data from the CPU to bus. When $\overline{\text{DIEN}}$ = 1, the bottom amplifier becomes operative, allowing transmission from the bus to the CPU. The buffers perform no logic on the data they transmit. The amplification provided, if any, is not generally significant. Instead each buffer amplifier operates on relatively little input current and is able to provide relatively much more output current. Hence interposing the buffer between bus and CPU assures that the CPU will not impose an excessive load on an input port and vice versa. In Fig. 11.1-2 we note that an input signal BUSEN (bus enable) has been applied to the CS input of the bus driver. This BUSEN signal is not furnished by the CPU and, when available, is normally supplied from some other place in the microprocessor system, maybe even by a manually operated switch. In any event, when BUSEN = 0, the bus is freed from the CPU and can then be used for communication between peripherals without involving the CPU. One such type of communication involves direct data transfer between memory and some other peripheral, a type of transfer referred to as DMA (direct memory acess).

We can now summarize our discussion of the OUT $\langle B_2 \rangle$ instruction in the following way. During this instruction's execution we must have BUSEN = 1. Also DBIN = $\overline{\text{DIEN}}$ = 0, so that the bus driver is set for data transfer out from the CPU to the bus. Early in the time allocated to the execution of the instruction the data and port address are put on the data and address lines and the OUT status bit is established at logic 1. After the address bits have become stably established, i.e., valid, the $\overline{\text{WR}}$ output of the CPU becomes active ($\overline{\text{WR}}$ = 0) and the output $\overline{\text{I/O W}}$ goes to logic 0, thereby writing the accumulator content into the output port. The total time required to fetch and execute the OUT $\langle B_2 \rangle$ instruction is the time of 10 states (10 × 0.5 μs = 5 μs at a clock rate of 2 MHz). The $\overline{\text{WR}}$ signal is active only during the very last state.

Referring again to Fig. 11.1-2, we note that the status latch also provides an output MEMR. This output is at logic 1 whenever a memory read operation is to be effected. During such a read operation DBIN will also be at logic 1, so that we shall have $\overline{\text{MEMR}}$ = 0, thereby providing a read signal to memory. When MEMR = 1, we have INP (input) at logic 0. The CPU provides an instruction

IN
$\langle B_2 \rangle$

and when this instruction is being executed, and only then, the status latch output INP (input) goes to logic 1 while MEMR remains at logic 0. During this instruction DBIN also goes to logic 1, so that the signal $\overline{\text{I/O R}}$ becomes $\overline{\text{I/O R}}$ = 1, thus providing a signal to read from isolated I/O.

In summary, then, the interconnections indicated in Fig. 11.1-2 provide signals $\overline{\text{MEMR}}$ and $\overline{\text{MEMW}}$ which become active respectively when a read or write operation from *memory* is to occur. Such will be the case whenever a fetch operation is being carried out or any instruction is being executed which requires access to memory. But when we want to access any port other than memory, the instructions which can be used are OUT $\langle B_2 \rangle$ or IN $\langle B_2 \rangle$. These two instructions activate outputs $\overline{\text{I/O W}}$ and $\overline{\text{I/O R}}$, respectively, and allow writing to, or reading from, isolated I/O.

A matter concerning the timing of the $\overline{\text{I/O W}}$ and the $\overline{\text{I/O R}}$ outputs is clarified in Fig. 11.2-3. These output control signals are active only during the last of the 10 states over which the OUT and IN instructions extend. When the clock frequency is 2 MHz, a state lasts for 0.5 μs and correspondingly, as appears in the figure, the $\overline{\text{I/O W}}$ or $\overline{\text{I/O R}}$ pulse used to control peripherals also lasts 0.5

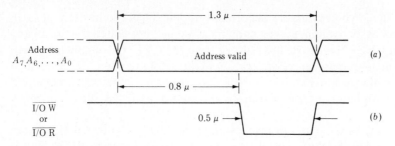

Figure 11.2-3 The timing of $\overline{I/OW}$ or $\overline{I/OR}$ signal relative to the interval during which a valid address is available at the address bus.

μs. However, a valid address is established on the address lines $A_7, A_0, \ldots, A_0$ (and duplicated on $A_{15}, A_{14}, \ldots, A_8$) about 0.8 μs before the control pulse becomes active. In this way we allow time for the address bits to propagate through decoders where required and, for the peripheral addressed, properly to acknowledge what is being singled out.

We shall have occasion later to consider the INTA and $\overline{\text{INTA}}$ signals, which appear in Fig. 11.1-2. That still leaves four signals $\overline{\text{WO}}$, STACK, HLTA, and M_1. These signals are not ordinarily used in simple microprocessor systems, but they serve a useful purpose in testing a system to determine whether it is working properly and they find application when dynamic memories are employed. We shall not consider them further except to note the following details. $\overline{\text{WO}} = 0$ indicates that either a memory *write* or isolated I/O *output* operation is in process. STACK $= 1$ indicates that the address bus holds the stack address as provided by the stack pointer. HLTA $= 1$ when the CPU is acknowledging that it has halted operation in response to an instruction to do so. Finally, M_1 provides a signal to indicate that the CPU is in the fetch cycle for the first byte of an instruction.

11.3 USE OF IN AND OUT INSTRUCTIONS

Suppose that, at some point in a program, a numerical result is generated which is of immediate interest to the human operator, who would then like to have the result made available. To be specific let us assume that the result is a 2-digit decimal number represented in the CPU as two BCD numbers combined into 1 byte. Then, by using the OUT $\langle B_2 \rangle$ instruction in conjunction with the additional hardware shown in Fig. 11.3-1 the result can be made available in a visual display. First the byte holding the result would be moved to the accumulator of the CPU if it was not already located in that register. Next we would invoke the OUT $\langle B_2 \rangle$ instruction. The address byte $\langle B_2 \rangle$, available on either low or high address lines, would be arranged to be the address that would bring to logic 1 the output of the address decoder. After the address and data had been

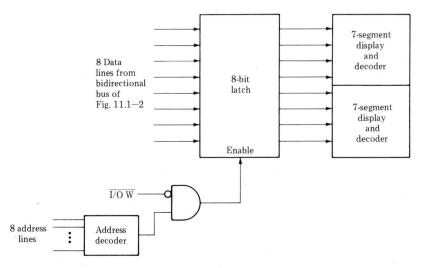

Figure 11.3-1 Hardware required to allow the use of OUT instruction to display the contents of accumulator.

validly established, the OUT instruction would cause the $\overline{\text{I/O W}}$ line to become active, i.e., go to logic 0, and the output of the AND gate would then enable the 8-bit latch briefly and then return the latch to the disabled condition. During the brief enabling period, the data of interest would be latched into the latch, and the CPU would thereafter be free to go about its further business. The human observer would now be free to read the data at leisure on the two seven-segment displays (see Sec. 3.17). We assume that the display hardware incorporates the decoders required to convert the BCD number, each encoded into four binary bits, into voltages appropriate to light up the proper segments of the displays. At any point in a program where we want the visible output data to be updated we need only include the OUT $\langle B_2 \rangle$ instruction.

Of course, in Fig. 11.3-1 a separate address decoder is not absolutely needed. The AND gate can do the address decoding if we add additional inputs to it to accommodate as many address lines as we find it necessary to use. If, for example, only eight ports were being used, we could arrange that in each port address all bits were 0 except one (00000001, 00000010, etc.) and a single address line would be adequate.

In Fig. 11.3-2 we contemplate the inverse process of reading data from some port into the CPU accumulator. Here the byte of data is established by eight mechanical switches. When a switch is open, the data line is at logic 1, and when the switch is closed, the data line is at logic 0. In the previous case we were concerned with catching the data in the brief interval when they were available in the accumulator. In the present case the data are available for as long as we like, but we do not want to use the data bus any longer than necessary. Hence we use an 8-bit tristate unidirectional buffer which is enabled by

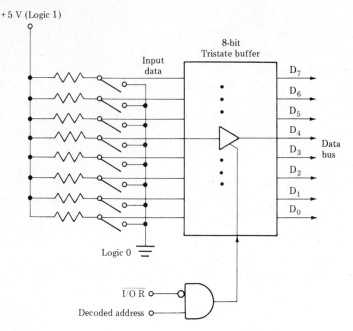

+ 5 V (Logic 1)

Figure 11.3-2 Hardware required to allow use of IN instruction to transfer data (set up by switches) into the accumulator.

a port address and the signal $\overline{I/O\ R}$. When the IN $\langle B_2 \rangle$ instruction is executed, during the brief (one-clock-cycle) period when $\overline{I/O\ R} = 0$, the input data will be connected to the bus but otherwise the bus will be released for other purposes.

11.4 AN UNENCODED KEYBOARD

In this section we consider an example that is instructive in a number of ways. It will illustrate input and output connections, the use of the IN and OUT instructions, and the substitution of software for hardware.

We contemplate a 64-key keyboard which is to be used to enter data into a microprocessor system. We specifically assume that, in response to the operation of a key, an identification of the key which has been depressed is to be entered into the accumulator of the CPU. Thereafter, as we please, we can transfer the data elsewhere, say to memory, so that the accumulator will be available to receive more data. We identify the keys by the numbers 1 through 64 and consider that only one key is depressed at a time. We require that when a key is operated, the number of that key shall appear in the accumulator. We have numbered the keys beginning with 1 rather than with 0 so that 0 in the accumulator can serve as an indication that no key has been depressed.

We might arrange for each key to generate logic 1 or 0 on a line, according to whether it is open or closed. These 64 lines would then be applied to the inputs of OR gates, i.e., an encoder (see Sec. 3.16), to generate the binary code representing the number of the operated key. Thereafter we would only need to use the IN instruction to transfer the encoded key number into the accumulator. We prefer to dispense with the hardware of an encoder here, however, and instead to generate the key identification number by writing an appropriate program.

The arrangement we propose is shown in Fig. 11.4-1. We have here a matrix of eight horizontal and eight vertical wires. The wires are not connected,

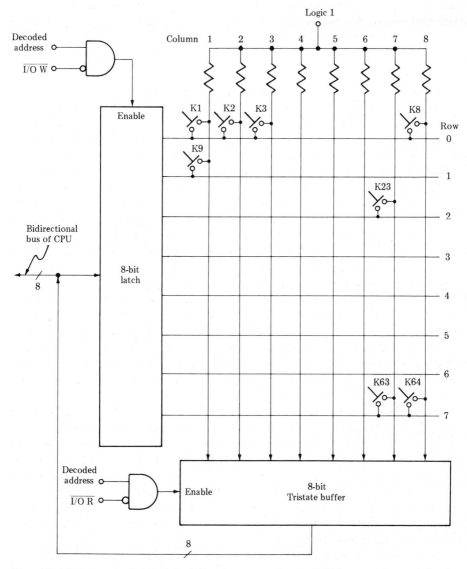

Figure 11.4-1 An unencoded keyboard, showing connections to CPU buses and control signals.

but, as indicated, a connection between a horizontal and vertical wire can be made by closing a switch K1, K2, etc. There are 64 switches K1 through K64, one at each intersection (not all the switches are shown). The horizontal wires are driven by the 8-bit latch which receives the registration of the accumulator in response to the OUT $\langle B_2 \rangle$ instruction, $\langle B_2 \rangle$ being the latch address. The data held on the eight vertical wires will be transferred to the accumulator in response to the instruction IN $\langle B_2 \rangle$, where $\langle B_2 \rangle$ is the tristate buffer address. When all the switches are open, all these vertical lines will be at logic 1, as is to be noted from the connections to a logic 1 voltage source. Suppose, however, that one of the horizontal lines, say the line of row 2, is at logic 0, and suppose that switch K23, connecting row 2 to column 7, is closed. Then because of the resistors in the column lines, the line of column 7 will go to logic 0. In short, if only one row line goes to logic 0 and only one switch is closed, only one column line will go to logic 0 and these two lines at logic 0 identify the operated switch. As a matter of fact, the way the column and row lines have been numbered in Fig. 11.4-1 means that the closed switch has the number $N = (8 \times$ row number) + column number.

We consider now a program for accomplishing our purpose. First we undertake to determine whether any key has been depressed; if not, we leave the accumulator cleared.

Label	Contents	Comment
WAIT	MVI, A 0000 0000	Move number zero immediately into Acc
	OUT $\langle$LATCH$\rangle$	Output 0000 0000 to latch and to all row lines
	IN $\langle$BUFFER$\rangle$	Input registration of column lines to Acc
	CPI 1111 1111	Compare Acc to pattern 1111 1111; if no key depressed, we have $Z = 1$
	JZ $\langle$WAIT$\rangle$	If $Z = 1$, no key depressed, wait, i.e., go back to instruction labeled "WAIT"

If a key has been depressed, we shall have $Z = 0$, the JZ instruction will do nothing, and the the program continues. The program operates as follows:

Label	Contents	Comment
	MVI B 0000 0001	We tentatively assume that key 1 is closed and correspondingly enter its number in register B
	MVI C 1111 1110	In register C we establish a pattern of bits which, when transferred to Acc and outputted to latch, will bring to logic 0 first row in Fig. 11.4-1 marked "0"

Label	Contents	Comment
ROW	MOV A, C OUT ⟨LATCH⟩	Move scanning pattern to Acc and output it to latch
	RLC	Rotate left. Scanning pattern in Acc is changed to 1111 1101 in anticipation that closed key might not be found in row 0. This operation does not change scanning pattern already outputted to latch
	MOV C, A	Move modified scanning pattern back to register C because Acc is needed for other purposes
	IN ⟨BUFFER⟩	Input to Acc the data on column lines
	CPI 1111 1111	Compare Acc to pattern 1111 1111. If no key is depressed *in row being tested*, we have $Z = 1$.
	JNZ ⟨ ⟩ [COL]† ⟨ ⟩	If $Z = 0$, key has been depressed. Jump to place in program labeled "COL," which will identify column of depressed key. If $Z = 1$, no key has been depressed in row being tested. In this case continue with next instruction

	MOV A, B
	ADI
	⟨decimal 8⟩
	MOV B, A
		Since no key is depressed in row just tested, add 8 to register B. Register B now holds the number of key in next row and in column 1

	JMP ⟨ ⟩ [ROW] ⟨ ⟩	Jump back to place in program labeled "ROW." Next row will then be tested because of modification of scanning pattern already made
COL	RAR JNC ⟨ ⟩ [END] ⟨ ⟩	Rotate right through carry. If bit moved into carry flag is 0, we have found depressed key. In this case (CY = 0) we are finished
	INR B JUMP ⟨ ⟩ [COL] ⟨ ⟩	If rotation does not move a 0 into carry, key in column tested is not depressed. Increment key-number register and go back to test next column
END	HLT	

†The entry in brackets gives the label corresponding to the address in the unspecified bytes above and below.

In Fig. 11.4-1 it is worth noting that when data are output from the CPU to the latch, $\overline{\text{I/OW}}$ will be active but $\overline{\text{I/OR}}$ will be inactive. Hence the tristate buffer will be in its high-impedance state, and the connection of the buffer to the bidirectional bus will not interfere with transmission from CPU to latch. Correspondingly, when the buffer data are to be inputted to the CPU, the latch will be disabled.

11.5 CONTROL OF PERIPHERAL DEVICES

We have seen how the signals $\overline{\text{I/O R}}$ and $\overline{\text{I/O W}}$ can be used to read data into or out of the accumulator. These signals can also be used to allow the microprocessor to exercise a measure of control over peripheral devices even when reading or writing is not involved. Thus, suppose that a microcomputer system includes a tape recorder and that we want to be able to include in a program an instruction capable of starting or stopping the recorder. The hardware shown in Fig. 11.5-1 together with the instructions IN $\langle B_2 \rangle$ and OUT $\langle B_2 \rangle$ will allow such control. Thus, suppose we include in a program the instruction OUT $\langle B_2 \rangle$, where $\langle B_2 \rangle$ is the address to which the decoder in Fig. 11.5-1 is intended to respond. Then during the course of the execution of this instruction there will appear at the SET input of the latch a positive pulse (corresponding to the negative pulse in Fig. 11.2-3b) which will set the latch. Correspondingly an instruction IN $\langle B_2 \rangle$ will reset the latch. In turn, the state of the latch can be used to open or close electromechanical switches which can start or stop a motor, enage or release a clutch, etc. Since, as we have seen, there are as many as 256 addresses available, we can control a whole host of devices to start and stop motion, to open and close valves, to cause typewriter keys to strike, etc. All we need do is arrange that, as required, our program include IN and OUT instructions appropriately addressed to the latches provided to respond to these instructions.

11.6 TIMING LOOPS

Suppose that we want to transmit alphanumeric characters to an electromechanical typewriter. Each key of the typewriter might be outfitted with the hardware of Fig. 11.5-1. To type a character we might use an OUT $\langle B_2 \rangle$ in-

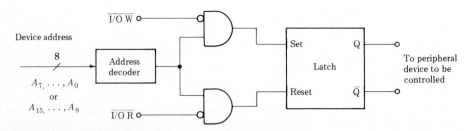

Figure 11.5-1 The $\overline{\text{I/OW}}$ and $\overline{\text{I/OR}}$ signals are used to set and reset an addressed latch. The latch, in turn, can be used to control an arbitrary peripheral device.

struction, the byte $\langle B_2 \rangle$ holding the address of the key to be hit. (If the typewriter responds to ASCII code, the address bytes are simply the ASCII codes for the characters to be printed.) The OUT $\langle B_2 \rangle$ instruction sets the latch, the latch energizes an electromagnet, and the electromagnet pulls down the typewriter key. We must now keep the electromagnet energized long enough for the relatively slow mechanical key to complete its response. Thereafter we can use a second instruction IN $\langle B_2 \rangle$ to reset the latch and release the key. It may well be necessary to keep the latch set for many tens of milliseconds, a time which is very long compared with the duration of a clock cycle and with the time required to fetch and execute an instruction. (Clock cycle time for the 8080 is in the range from 0.5 to 2.0 μs, and even the most complicated instruction requires only 18 clock cycles.) Hence we must interpose a program between the OUT instruction and the IN instruction whose sole purpose is to allow the passage of time. Such *time-delay programs* are used so frequently in microprocessors with associated peripheral equipment that they generally appear as subroutines. Thus a typical program calling for the operation of a typewriting key would be:

Label	Contents	Comment
	OUT $\langle B_2 \rangle$	Set latch to depress address key
	CALL $\langle\ \ \rangle$ [TIMING] $\langle\ \ \rangle$	Call unconditionally the subroutine which begins at address labeled "TIMING"
RELEASE	IN $\langle B_2 \rangle$	Reset latch to release key

In a timing routine we start by loading a number into a register. We then decrement the register. The decrementing instruction is followed by a conditional jump instruction. If after decrementing the register is not at zero, we jump back to the decrementing instruction, i.e., we loop back, but when the register reads zero, we leave the loop and advance to the next instruction, which is an unconditional RETURN to the main program, i.e., to "RELEASE." The time delay is determined by the number initially placed in the register and the clock rate. If the time delay afforded by a single register is not long enough, we can use two registers. The second register is decremented by 1 each time the first register goes through the entire decrementation cycle from its initial registration to zero. Thus the total number of decrementing operations required to clear both registers depends on the product (not the sum) of the two registrations. Only when both registers are clear do we terminate the subroutine looping. A flowchart for a timing subroutine is shown in Fig. 11.6-1. Here we assume that the registers involved are the registers D and E. The subroutine program is as follows:

Label	Contents	Comment
TIMING	MVI E $\langle N_E \rangle$	Move number N_E into register E
LOAD	MVI D $\langle N_D \rangle$	Move number N_D into register D
WAIT	DCR D	Decrement register D
	JNZ $\langle \quad \rangle$ [WAIT] $\langle \quad \rangle$	If register D is not zero, jump back to decrement instruction at address "WAIT." Otherwise continue to next instruction
	DCR E	Decrement register E
	JNZ $\langle \quad \rangle$ [LOAD] $\langle \quad \rangle$	If register E is not zero, jump back to instruction at address "LOAD" to put N_D back into register D
	RET	Return unconditionally to main program

Manufacturers provide information on the number of clock cycles required to execute an instruction. For the 8080 this information is given in App. C. The time for one clock cycle is the reciprocal of the clock frequency. From the main program above, which calls for a TIMING subroutine, from the subroutine itself, and from the timing parameters N_E and N_D, we can count up the number of clock cycles between the pulses which set and reset the latch in Fig. 11.5-1. Knowing the time for a clock cycle, we can then determine the total timing interval established. The details of the computation are left as a student exercise (Prob. 11.6-1). It may happen that, when the timing subroutine is needed, the registers D and E are holding needed data. Then, at the beginning of the subroutine, we shall have to push these register contents on to the stack and pop them just before the return.

11.7 INTERRUPTS

As we have already noted, a microprocessor chip and its associated memory operates in conjunction with external peripheral equipment, keyboards, display devices, components which require control signals, etc. From time to time one peripheral or another will require the microprocessor to provide it with some servicing. For example, a key will be depressed on a keyboard, and it will be necessary for the microprocessor to transfer the key indication to its accumulator and then possibly to some storage location in memory. For the microprocessor to be able to service the peripheral, the microprocessor must suspend any other program routine it may be pursuing. One way to arrange the matter is to provide for the microprocessor to suspend its operations periodically and determine whether there is a signal from the peripheral to indicate that it needs

Enter from main program

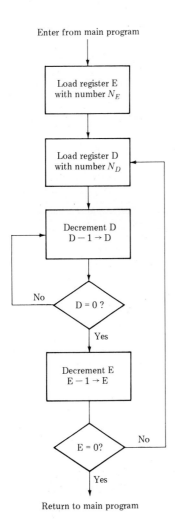

Return to main program

Figure 11.6-1 Flowchart for a timing subroutine.

servicing. If this happens to be the case, the microprocessor jumps to a program subroutine which provides the servicing. When the servicing has been completed, the microprocessor returns to the interrupted program. This straightforward scheme of servicing a peripheral is entirely feasible but has two disadvantages: (1) the peripheral which requires servicing simply has to wait until the microprocessor makes one of its periodic inquiries; (2) if when the inquiries are made no servicing is needed, the time used in making the inquiries has simply been wasted.

To avoid these disadvantages the 8080 (like other microprocessors) provides an alternative scheme for responding to requirements for servicing. The 8080 has an input pin labeled "INT" (interrupt request). When this pin is brought to logic 1 even briefly (for at least a time comparable to the clock period), the microprocessor completes the execution of the instruction on which it is engaged and then begins to respond to the call for service. Hence the response of the microprocessor is nominally immediate, and no time is wasted in unnecessary inquiries.

If there were only a single potential source of a servicing request, the servicing subroutine could be started at some single and predetermined location. The appearance of a signal at the INT input could then be interpreted by the microprocessor as a CALL instruction for the subroutine at that predetermined location. But since generally there will be a number of potential sources of interrupt requests, we require a means of identifying the source of the request and arranging for the subroutine called up to be the one appropriate to the source. In short, there must be many starting points for servicing subroutines and a means of getting to the right one.

The 8080 provides eight predetermined addresses at which a service subroutine can start. It is most convenient to specify these locations in the octal system. The high-order bits of these starting addresses are in every case 000. The low-order bits are 000, 010, 020, 030, 040, 050, 060, and 070. In decimal notation this low-order numbering is 0, 8, 16, 24, 32, 40, 48, and 56, or 8 times the next to least significant octal digit. Nominally, then, one service subroutine has available the low-order address range 000 to 007, the next 010 to 017, etc. If the seven address locations available for one subroutine are not adequate, we can use a JUMP instruction to carry the subroutine program to some other available location in memory where the subroutine can be continued.

When the 8080 receives an interrupt pulse, the microprocessor completes the execution of the instruction being executed. It then arranges (with the cooperation of auxiliary hardware, as we shall see) for the very next instruction loaded into the instruction register to be an instruction which calls up a subroutine beginning at one of the eight starting addresses. We have previously not indicated the binary code for individual instructions except on a few occasions above when we wanted to give examples of 1-, 2- and 3-byte instructions, but it is appropriate here to look at the form of the binary code which calls up a subroutine in response to an interrupt. The binary code is

7	6	5	4	3	2	1	0
1	1	N_5	N_4	N_3	1	1	1

The three binary digits $N_5 N_4 N_3$ determine the subroutine starting address from the eight such possible addresses in accordance with the rule that the address is 8 times the numerical significance of the number $N_5 N_4 N_3$. Thus if $N_5 N_4 N_3 = 110$ (= 6), the starting address is 000 060 (octal) and the actual address is

15	14	13	12	11	10	9	8	7	6	5	4	3	2	1	0
0	0	0	0	0	0	0	0	0	0	1	1	0	0	0	0

To see precisely how the 8080 responds to an interrupt in a specific case, let us consider the situation represented in Fig. 11.7-1. Here we contemplate a keyboard with the features that when a key is pressed, the key code is regis-

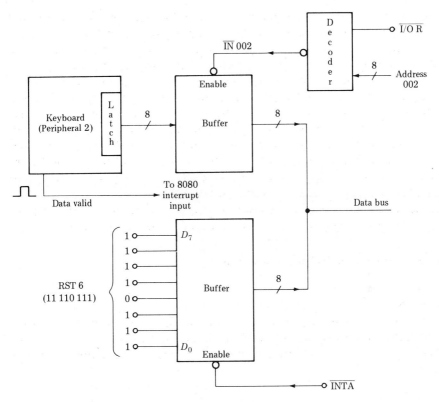

Figure 11.7-1 The hardware associated with a system to allow the CPU to respond to an interrupt request.

tered in its latch and thereafter a *data-valid* pulse is made available. (Keyboards of this type are available commercially.) When a key is pressed, we want the microprocessor to accept the data provided by the key operation and then, presumably, process the data in some manner. There are other peripherals aside from the keyboard, and we have arbitrarily assigned to the keyboard the identification *peripheral 2*. The subroutine which services the keyboard starts at memory location 060 (octal). Correspondingly we have connected the eight inputs of the lower buffer to logic levels to form the instruction code 11 110 111 (= 367 octal), the "6" determining that the total starting address is 000 060 (octal). Now when the microprocessor receives the data-valid pulse on its INT input terminal, the 8080 system set up in Fig. 11.1-2 makes available a negative pulse signal $\overline{\text{INTA}}$ (interrupt acknowledge). The buffer is then enabled, and the instruction code 11 110 111 is placed on the microprocessor data bus and transferred into the microprocessor. The transfer is special, however, in that the code is not transferred into the accumulator or other general-purpose register but into the *instruction register*. Hence, the end result is that the instruction register now holds the instruction that calls up the required subroutine. Of course, as always, when the microprocessor branches to a subroutine, it must first save in the stack the return address to the main program. This sequence of events which is initiated by an interrupt request is called the RESTART instruction; its mnemonic is RST n, where n represents $N_5N_4N_3$. More formally we have:

RESTART   RST n $PC[high] \rightarrow SP - 1$
$PC[low] \rightarrow SP - 2$
$SP - 2 \rightarrow SP$

$00000000\ 00N_5N_4N_3000 \rightarrow PC$

The high-order 8 bits of the next instruction address are moved to the memory location whose address is 1 less than the registration of SP. The low-order bits are moved to the location 2 less than the registration of SP. SP is decremented twice. The next instruction to be fetched and executed is the instruction at $00000000\ 00N_5N_4N_3000$.

11.8 INTERRUPT ENABLE AND DISABLE

We can easily imagine situations in which, at least for a time, we do not want a microprocessor system to respond to an interrupt. For example, if the system is controlling some process which must be completed at some fixed time, it may not be possible to allow time for responding to requests for servicing. To accommodate to this requirement, the 8080 chip has an *interrupt flip-flop*, i.e., an *interrupt flag*. When this flag is in the set state, the microprocessor will accept and respond to an interrupt call, but when the flag is reset, the microprocessor will not respond to the interrupt. The state of this flag is indicated at the 8080 output terminal labeled "INTE" (interrupt enable). The 8080 indicates that its interrupt facility is in the enabled condition by setting INTE high. To provide control over the interrupt mechanism of the chip two instructions are provided:

ENABLE INTERRUPT   EI
Enable the interrupt mechanism of the microprocessor chip following the execution of the *next* instruction

DISABLE INTERRUPT   DI
Disable the interrupt mechanism of the microprocessor chip following the execution of *this* instruction

---

Note that the DI instruction, like all other instructions, calls for an immediate response while the EI instruction calls for the microprocessor to carry out first the *next* following instruction in the program after EI and only then to do what is commanded by the EI instruction. The need for this special feature will be explained shortly. When we arrive at a point in a program where we want to disallow interrupts, we use DI. The microprocessor will then fail to respond to an interrupt until we countermand the instruction by using EI.

A typical microcomputer may well involve more than just a single peripheral. We shall examine later the mechanism by which the 8080 identifies the peripheral requiring service and decides on the order in which service requests are to be processed. Only one interrupt can be handled at any one time. For the present we note that frequently, although not necessarily always, when one interrupt request is being serviced we prefer that it not be interrupted in turn in response to a second interrupt request. The 8080 takes care of this matter automatically. Immediately on receiving an interrupt request, it resets the interrupt flag. Since the flag does not automatically set at the end of the service routine, it is necessary at the end of every service routine specifically to include an EI instruction. If such a second interrupt is received while the first request is being serviced, the 8080 will record this second request and undertake its servicing after the interrupt has been set by EI. Only one such unserviced interrupt request is remembered.

As in every subroutine program, the *last* instruction is the RET (RETURN) instruction which gets back to the main program. The EI instruction should then be the *next-to-last* instruction. Since there is a one-instruction delay in the execution of EI, the interrupt mechanism does not become enabled until after the RET instruction has been executed. The need for this delay can be seen from the following example. Suppose that there is an extended period during which new interrupt requests are made before servicing of the previous request has been completed. The microprocessor goes from interrupt routine to interrupt routine without ever getting back to the main program. And suppose that each new service routine begins immediately after the EI instruction and before the RET instruction. Each service subroutine starts by pushing a return address and possibly other data onto the stack. The RET instruction pops the data from the stack, but if the RET is not executed, the memory capacity may well be overtaxed.

An interrupt request is a special type of call instruction. As is generally the case with call instructions in which we leave a main program, we want to save the contents of the accumulator, the flag register, and the other registers; when the service routine is complete, we shall need to restore these registers. The pattern of instruction types encountered in connection with a service routine thus appears as in Fig. 11.8-1. Since the memory space allocated to an RST n instruction comprises only eight memory locations, it may not be possible to fit a program as in Fig. 11.8-1 into the available space. Accordingly, a common procedure is to use just the first three of the memory locations corresponding to RST n for the instruction JUMP $\langle B_2 \rangle \langle B_3 \rangle$, the jump carrying the program to a memory location where adequate space is available. If, on the other hand, we do not propose to use all of the eight available RST n instructions to call up separate interrupt subroutines, we can allow a program starting at the address corresponding to RST n to encroach into RST $n + 1$, etc.

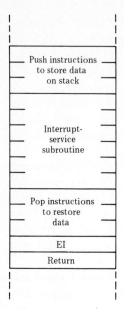

Figure 11.8-1 A typical service subroutine.

11.9 POLLED INTERRUPT

The arrangement of Fig. 11.7-1 is appropriate hardware when there is only one possible source of an interrupt request. We consider now one appropriate hardware arrangement and its corresponding software when there are a number of peripherals to be serviced.

The hardware external to the 8080 system of Fig. 11.1-2 is shown in Fig. 11.9-1. Here we indicate three peripherals, but the system can be expanded to accommodate more. When a peripheral requires service, it generates a pulse which is applied to the SET input of a latch. The latches, one for each peripheral, will now remember the requests and continue to alert the microprocessor that service is required until the microprocessor takes the required action. These latches are then appropriately referred to as *flags*—more specifically *external flags*, since they are external to the microprocessor. As we shall see, when an interrupt request is serviced, its flag will be lowered; i.e., the latch will be reset.

The outputs of the flags are combined in an OR gate which then provides an indication to the INT input of the 8080 that some one (or more) of the peripherals requires service. As we shall see, from the software we have yet to write, the subsequent response of the 8080 is as follows. First it reads into itself the status of all the flags. It then looks at each flag bit in turn. This process of inquiring of each peripheral in turn to find out whether service is required is called *polling*. After providing the service required or determining that no service is required, the microprocessor moves on to the next peripheral.

The microprocessor has to exert some control over the external hardware.

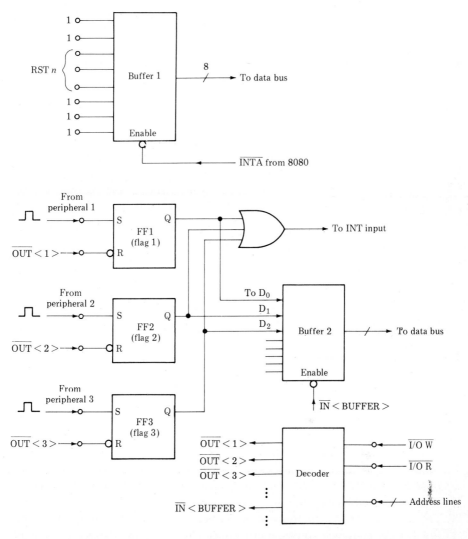

Figure 11.9-1 Hardware associated with a system to allow the CPU to respond to service requests from a number of sources. The instruction RST n calls up the polling subroutine.

At proper times it must transfer to itself the status of the flags and clear each flag in turn as the polling progresses. For this purpose, as before, we shall use in IN $\langle B_2 \rangle$ and OUT $\langle B_2 \rangle$ instructions, where B_2 is the address of peripheral to be controlled. As noted earlier, control pulses are generated on lines as required by combining in a decoder the address and the $\overline{\text{I/O W}}$ and $\overline{\text{I/O R}}$ outputs of the system of Fig. 11.1-2. We need three individual addressed pulses for clearing the flags. They are generated in response to the OUT $\langle B_2 \rangle$ instruction and are called OUT $\langle 1 \rangle$, OUT $\langle 2 \rangle$, and OUT $\langle 3 \rangle$. A single IN $\langle$BUFFER$\rangle$

control pulse is used to enable the buffer and read the status of the flags into the accumulator.

The total service subroutine for the case represented in Fig. 11.9-1 has four parts. One subroutine takes care of the polling, and three additional service subroutines provide the three services called for by the three potential sources of an interrupt request. The polling subroutine is as follows:

Label	Contents	Comment
POLL	IN ⟨BUFFER 2⟩	Input to Acc status of flags by enabling BUFFER 2
	RAR	Rotate Acc right so that first bit D_0 will appear in carry flag, where it can be tested
	JC ⟨ ⟩ [SUBROUTINE 1] ⟨ ⟩	If carry = 1, jump to subroutine which services first peripheral. Address of subroutine is in second and third byte of this instruction. If carry = 0, continue with next instruction
	RAR	Rotate Acc again to test D_1
	JC ⟨ ⟩ [SUBROUTINE 2] ⟨ ⟩	If carry = 1, jump to subroutine which services second peripheral
	RAR	Rotate Acc again to test D_2
	JC ⟨ ⟩ [SUBROUTINE 3] ⟨ ⟩	If carry = 1, jump to subroutine which services third peripheral

If the first peripheral requires service, the first JC instruction in the polling routine above will cause a jump to the service subroutine for the first peripheral. In that service subroutine the first instruction should be $\overline{\text{OUT}}$ ⟨1⟩ to the FLAG 1. The next-to-last instruction will be EI, and the last instruction will be RETURN. The program will consequently go back to the main program at the point where it was interrupted. If now the second or third peripheral or both require service, no instructions of the main program will be fetched; instead the program will jump back to the polling program once more. In the polling program the first instructions will again read in the status of the flags and again test FLAG 1. Since FLAG 1 has been cleared, however, there will be no jump to the service routine for the first peripheral, and instead the polling routine will move ahead to test FLAG 2. In this way all flags will eventually be tested and all services will be provided. Note that even after service has been provided to the first peripheral, the polling routine will again check FLAG 1 before it checks FLAG 2. When the last service program called for has been completed, all the flags will have been cleared and the microprocessor will go back to the main program.

The order in which the flags are tested establishes a relative priority among the peripherals, first tested having the highest priority, and so on. As a matter of practice, the order of priority assigned to peripherals should depend not only on relative importance but also on the time consumed by the corresponding service routine. Thus if servicing a less important peripheral requires 1 ms when a more important peripheral requires several seconds, the lesser peripheral may well be assigned a higher priority.

In the polling scheme described above, when a peripheral of low priority initiates a request for service (even if it is the only peripheral requesting service), it must wait until all other peripherals of higher priority have been polled. This feature may not always be acceptable. An alternative scheme which circumvents the polling routine is indicated in Fig. 11.9-2. Here a priority encoder (see Sec. 3.16) is used. The flag bits which in Fig. 11.9-1 are joined in an OR gate are here applied to the inputs of the priority encoder. Input 7 has highest priority and input 0 lowest. The 3-bit output of the encoder is the binary representation of the decimal number by which the inputs are identified. This encoder output provides the 3 bits of the instruction RST n ($n = N_5 N_4 N_3$). If any peripheral needs service, the encoder output GS provides an interrupt request to the processor. The INTA response from the processor then "jams" into the instruction register one of the restart instructions RST 7, RST 6, etc. (Actually, for a reason noted in Sec. 11.10, the instruction RST 0 is not generally used.) There is no polling. The processor goes directly to the service subroutine required to respond immediately to the peripheral of highest priority.

11.10 OTHER I/O COMMUNICATION

We consider now additional pins on the 8080 through which the microprocessor communicates with the outside world. We look first at the input pin called READY and the output pin called WAIT.

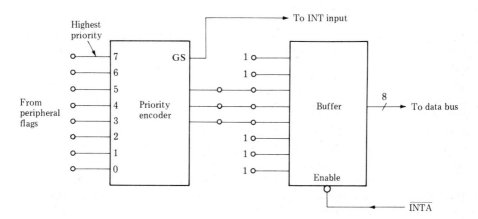

Figure 11.9-2 A priority encoder allows service to be furnished to the peripheral of highest priority requiring service without polling.

We have already noted that in fetching and executing an instruction the microprocessor goes through a number of machine cycles and that in negotiating each machine cycle the processor goes through a number of states. The processor goes from state to state in step with the clock. We have also noted that in the first state of every machine cycle (called T_1) the processor places on the address bus the address of a memory location or an I/O device and makes status information on the data bus available. We now note, further, that when the processor enters the second state T_2 of a machine cycle, it actually does not advance the processing but simply examines the READY input. If the READY input is high, the processor advances to the third state T_3 and to states T_4 and T_5 as well, if such additional states are called for, to continue the processing. In state T_2 if the processor finds that READY is low, however, it does not go to state T_3 but to a WAIT state T_w, where the processor remains idle, doing nothing, waiting for the READY input to go high. The processor can remain in the WAIT state indefinitely, its time in that state extending over an integral number of clock cycles. When READY does go high, the processor leaves state T_w to go to state T_3 and then continues the processing. When the processor goes to the WAIT state, it alerts the outside world to that condition by raising the output WAIT pin to the high level. In summary, the timing is as follows. If at the beginning of state T_2 the processor finds READY low, it enters the WAIT state and at the beginning of the WAIT state raises the WAIT pin to high. Thus there is an interval of a clock cycle between the time the processor recognizes that a WAIT is called for and the time when it acknowledges to the outside world that it is indeed waiting.

The READY input allows the processor to accommodate to relatively slow peripherals, including even certain types of memories which respond very slowly. Such peripherals can be equipped with a handshaking type of output which is applied to the READY input. This output of the peripheral will be designed to stay low until adequate time has elapsed for the peripheral to respond to the processor properly.

As an example of the use of the READY and WAIT terminals of the 8080 we consider the circuit shown in Fig. 11.10-1. The purpose of this arrangement is to allow *single-step operation* of the microprocessor, in which the processor sits idly in the wait state until the pushbutton S is depressed. It then advances through the remaining state T_3 (and possibly T_4 and T_5) of the machine cycle, returns to go through T_1 and T_2 of the next machine cycle, and finally comes to RESET again in the WAIT state T_w. At each push of the button the processor completes one machine cycle, starts on the next cycle, and then stops. Single stepping allows us (with the aid of additional hardware) to monitor what is on the address bus and on the data bus in each machine cycle. This mode of operation is invaluable in debugging a program.

In Fig. 11.10-1, FF2 is, in principle, not essential to the operation, but the 8080 has certain timing requirements such as setup and hold times which the READY input signal must meet. The manufacturer specifies that quite generally these specifications can be met by applying the READY signal not directly to the

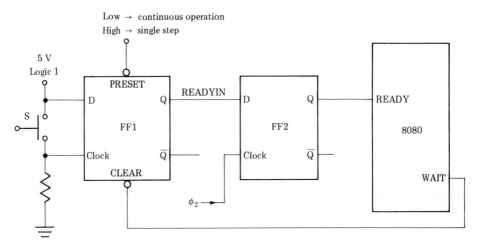

Figure 11.10-1 An arrangement to allow single-step operation.

READY input but in the manner shown. Here, a READYIN (ready input) is applied to a type-D edge-triggered flip-flop using ϕ_2 as the clocking waveform. At each positive-going edge of ϕ_2 READYIN is transferred to READY, and the level so clocked in is held at least for one clock cycle. The manufacturer explains why FF2 is not incorporated right into the 8080 chip by noting that timing requirements make it necessary for the function of FF2 to be performed by fast bipolar devices rather than by the slower MOS devices fabricated into the 8080 chip. In any event, having made these comments to avoid misrepresenting the 8080 chip, we shall ignore FF2 in our subsequent discussion and pretend that READYIN is connected directly to READY.

The flip-flop FF1 is positive-going edge-triggered type-D flip-flop with active-low PRESET and CLEAR inputs (such as the type 7474). When PRESET and CLEAR are high, these asynchronous inputs have no effect on the flip-flop, and at each positive-going clock edge the level at D is transferred to Q. The asynchronous inputs override the clocked input. When PRESET is high and CLEAR is low, Q goes low and $\overline{Q}$ goes high. When PRESET is low and CLEAR is high, Q goes high and $\overline{Q}$ goes low. The characteristic of the type 7474 is that when both PRESET and CLEAR are low, both Q and $\overline{Q}$ go high.

Consider, first, that we put PRESET low. Then READY is high, indicating that there is no need for WAIT. The WAIT output will be low, and so also will CLEAR. Both Q and $\overline{Q}$ are high. The microprocessor will operate continuously, never stopping in the WAIT state. Now let us put PRESET high, so that READY goes low. The processor will continue cycling through its states until it gets to state T_2. There it will sense a call for a WAIT and will consequently go to state T_w. At the beginning of state T_w WAIT will go high, acknowledging that the processor is waiting. We now have both PRESET and CLEAR high; i.e., both are at the inactive level. However, since PRESET went high first, the effect of the low level at

CLEAR will persist and READY will remain low. The processor will remain in the WAIT state indefinitely. Now, let the switch S be depressed. READY goes high, and the processor leaves the WAIT state and enters state T_3. At the beginning of state T_3 the WAIT output goes low and READY goes back to low. However, once the processor has been released from the WAIT state, it will continue through the machine cycle until it gets back to the WAIT state. In the WAIT state the WAIT output is again high, so that the processor can once again respond to the switch S.

We consider next the pins HOLD and HOLDA (hold acknowledge). HOLD is an input pin, and when it is put high the processor suspends its operation. The processor also releases the address bus and the data bus. That is, the address pins and data pins of the processor are put in the high-impedance state (see Sec. 3.10), so that in effect the processor is disconnected from address and data buses. This disconnection allows external devices to gain control of the buses. One example of the usefulness of such a HOLD facility is to be seen in connection with *direct memory access* (DMA). There are occasions when large amounts of data need to be written into, or read from, memory, the source or destination of the data being some external device. It will clearly save time to transfer the data directly between device and memory instead of through the processor. For this purpose the buses must be available, and since the processor cannot use the buses, the processor must suspend its operation. The processor acknowledges that it is holding by raising to the high level its HOLDA output.

The processor examines the HOLD input in each machine cycle during state T_2, the same state in which the READY input is examined. If HOLD is found to be high, the processor sets an internal flip-flop flag but then goes ahead to finish the machine cycle (not necessarily the instruction). It then goes into a *hold mode* (not the WAIT state), but the processor releases the buses at the point in the machine cycle when it no longer requires them. Thus, in states T_4 and T_5 operations are performed which are entirely internal to the processor, and the buses are made available even while the processor is going through T_4 and T_5 if it turns out that these states are used in the machine cycle.

The final pin on the 8080 is the RESET input. When the RESET input is raised high and held at that level for at least three clock cycles, a number of things happen: (1) the program counter (PC) will be reset to zero; (2) the interrupt facility will be disabled, in recognition of which the INTE output will go low; and (3) if the processor happens to be in the hold mode, it will leave that mode, and correspondingly the HOLDA output will go low. However, the contents of the flags, the accumulator, the stack pointer, and other registers will not be affected. When the RESET input is allowed to return low, the processor starts operation immediately, beginning with the instruction at memory location zero. Since the memory location zero is involved in the RESET operation, this memory location is not ordinarily available in connection with an interrupt subroutine.

The RESET input must inevitably be used when power is applied to the processor. For when power is first applied, the registrations that will appear in the various registers are entirely unpredictable, being determined by random factors. If, using RESET, we start the processor at memory location zero, we can arrange for the first instructions to clear registers, reset flags, and initialize the stack pointer. In this way the program to be run will not encounter inappropriate and unintended status flag indications, register contents, etc.

If we want the system not to start as soon as RESET returns low but to wait for an explicit start-up signal, we can arrange it in the following way. Immediately after the instructions which clear the register of inappropriate random data we use the instruction EI to enable the interrupt facility and then the instruction HLT to stop the processor. Now when we want to start running the program, we introduce from an external source an interrupt and jam the starting address of the program into the processor.

ASCII CODE (hexadecimal with most significant bit zero)

ASCII Code	Character	ASCII Code	Character	ASCII Code	Character
00	NUL	14	DC4	28	(
01	SOH	15	NAK	29	)
02	STX	16	SYN	2A	*
03	ETX	17	ETB	2B	+
04	EOT	18	CAN	2C	,
05	ENQ	19	EM	2D	-
06	ACK	1A	SUB	2E	.
07	BEL	1B	ESC	2F	/
08	BS	1C	FS	30	0
09	HT	1D	GS	31	1
0A	LF	1E	RS	32	2
0B	VT	1F	US	33	3
0C	FF	20	SP	34	4
0D	CR	21	!	35	5
0E	SO	22	"	36	6
0F	SI	23	#	37	7
10	DLE	24	$	38	8
11	DC1 (X-ON)	25	%	39	9
12	DC2 (TAPE)	26	&	3A	:
13	DC3 (X-OFF)	27	'	3B	;

ASCII Code	Character	ASCII Code	Character	ASCII Code	Character
3C	<	53	S	6A	j
3D	=	54	T	6B	k
3E	>	55	U	6C	l
3F	?	56	V	6D	m
40	@	57	W	6E	n
41	A	58	X	6F	o
42	B	59	Y	70	p
43	C	5A	Z	71	q
44	D	5B	[	72	r
45	E	5C	\	73	s
46	F	5D	]	74	t
47	G	5E	$\wedge(\uparrow)$	75	u
48	H	5F	$-(\leftarrow)$	76	v
49	I	60	'	77	w
4A	J	61	a	78	x
4B	K	62	b	79	y
4C	L	63	c	7A	z
4D	M	64	d	7B	{
4E	N	65	e	7C	|
4F	O	66	f	7D	} (ALT MODE)
50	P	67	g	7E	–
51	Q	68	h	7F	DEL (RUB OUT)
52	R	69	i		

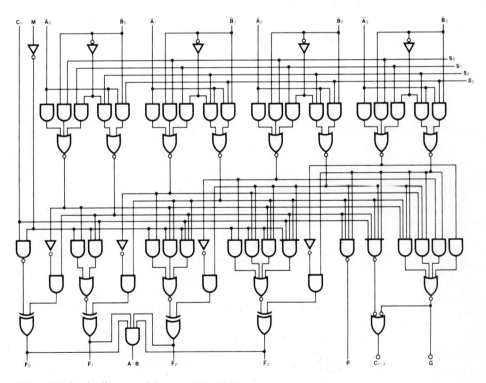

Figure B.1 Logic diagram of the type 181 ALU.

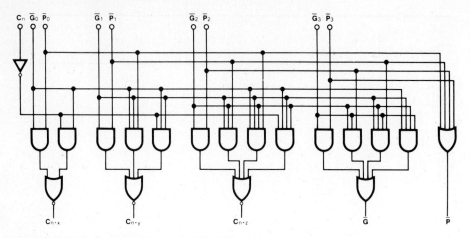

Figure B.2 Logic diagram of the type 182 LAC unit.

C

8080 INSTRUCTION SET

Where two numbers of clock cycles are given, the smaller number is required if the condition is not met and the larger number is required if the condition is met.

Mnemonic	Description	Clock cycles
MOV r1, r2	Move register to register	5
MOV M, r	Move register to memory	7
MOV r,M	Move memory to register	7
HLT	Halt	7
MVI r	Move immediate register	7
MVI M	Move immediate memory	10
INR r	Increment register	5
DCR r	Decrement register	5
INR M	Increment memory	10
DCR M	Decrement memory	10
ADD r	Add register to A	4
ADC r	Add register to A with carry	4
SUB r	Subtract register from A	4
SBB r	Subtract register from A with borrow	4
ANA r	AND register with A	4
XRA r	EXCLUSIVE-OR register with A	4
ORA r	OR register with A	4
CMP r	Compare register with A	4
ADD M	Add memory to A	7
ADC M	Add memory to A with carry	7
SUB M	Subtract memory from A	7
SBB M	Subtract memory from A with borrow	7
ANA M	AND memory with A	7
XRA M	EXCLUSIVE-OR memory with A	7
ORA M	OR memory with A	7
CMP M	Compare memory with A	7

Mnemonic	Description	Clock cycles
ADI	Add immediate to A	7
ACI	Add immediate to A with carry	7
SUI	Subtract immediate from A	7
SBI	Subtract immediate from A with borrow	7
ANI	AND immediate with A	7
XRI	EXCLUSIVE-OR immediate with A	7
ORI	OR immediate with A	7
CPI	Compare immediate with A	7
RLC	Rotate A left	4
RRC	Rotate A right	4
RAL	Rotate A left through carry	4
RAR	Rotate A right through carry	4
JMP	Jump unconditional	10
JC	Jump on carry	10
JNC	Jump on no carry	10
JZ	Jump on zero	10
JNZ	Jump on no zero	10
JP	Jump on positive	10
JM	Jump on minus	10
JPE	Jump on parity even	10
JPO	Jump on parity odd	10
CALL	Call unconditional	17
CC	Call on carry	11/17
CNC	Call on no carry	11/17
CZ	Call on zero	11/17
CNZ	Call on no zero	11/17
CP	Call on positive	11/17
CM	Call on minus	11/17
CPE	Call on parity even	11/17
CPO	Call on parity odd	11/17
RET	Return	10
RC	Return on carry	5/11
RNC	Return on no carry	5/11
RZ	Return on zero	5/11
RNZ	Return on no zero	5/11
RP	Return on positive	5/11
RM	Return on minus	5/11
RPE	Return on parity even	5/11
RPO	Return on parity odd	5/11
RST	Restart	11
IN	Input	10
OUT	Output	10
LXI B	Load immediate register pair B and C	10
LXI D	Load immediate register pair D and E	10
LXI H	Load immediate register pair H and L	10
LXI SP	Load immediate stack pointer	10
PUSH B	Push register pair B and C on stack	11
PUSH D	Push register pair D and E on stack	11
PUSH H	Push register pair H and L on stack	11
PUSH PSW	Push A and flags on stack	11
POP B	Pop register pair B and C off stack	10
POP D	Pop register pair D and E off stack	10
POP H	Pop register pair H and L off stack	10

Mnemonic	Description	Clock cycles
POP PSW	Pop A and flags off stack	10
STA	Store A direct	13
LDA	Load A direct	13
XCHG	Exchange D and E, H and L registers	4
XTHL	Exchange top of stack, H and L	18
SPHL	H and L to stack pointer	5
PCHL	H and L to program counter	5
DAD B	Add B and C to H and L	10
DAD D	Add D and E to H and L	10
DAD H	Add H and L to H and L	10
DAD SP	Add stack pointer to H and L	10
STAX B	Store A indirect	7
STAX D	Store A indirect	7
LDAX B	Load A indirect	7
LDAX D	Load A indirect	7
INX B	Increment B and C registers	5
INX D	Increment D and E registers	5
INX H	Increment H and L registers	5
INX SP	Increment stack pointer	5
DCX B	Decrement B and C	5
DCX D	Decrement D and E	5
DCX H	Decrement H and L	5
DCX SP	Decrement stack pointer	5
CMA	Complement A	4
STC	Set carry	4
CMC	Complement carry	4
DAA	Decimal adjust A	4
SHLD	Store H and L direct	16
LHLD	Load H and L direct	16
EI	Enable interrupt	4
DI	Disable interrupt	4
NOP	No operation	4

PROBLEMS

Chapter 1

1.6-1 Prove that the OR function is both commutative and associative.

1.7-1 An airplane crew consists of two pilots and one engineer. Arrange a circuit of switches which are operated when a crew member leaves her seat and generates a warning when the engineer leaves her post or when both pilots leave their posts.

1.7-2 We have represented Fig. 1.7-1 as an example of a logical system which performs the AND operation and represented Fig. 1.7-2 as an example of the OR operation. Suppose now that we reverse the definitions of all the variables A, B and Z; that is, A is true when the switch is open, etc. Verify that in this case Fig. 1.7-1 becomes an OR circuit and Fig. 1.7-2 becomes an AND circuit.

1.8-1 Assume that logic 0 is represented by the voltage 0 V (ground) and logic 1 is represented by 5 V.

 (*a*) Show then that the diode circuit of Fig. P1.8-1*a* is an OR gate and the circuit of Fig. P1.8-1*b* is an AND gate. (Assume that the diodes are ideal in every respect.)

 (*b*) Now replace the positive logic of (*a*) by negative logic so that logic 1 and 0 are represented respectively by 0 and 5 V. Show that now the OR gate has become an AND gate and vice versa.

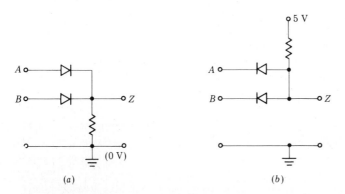

(*a*) (*b*)

1.11-1 Find the equivalents in the decimal system of the following binary numbers: (*a*) 11001, (*b*) 10101, (*c*) 0.01101, (*d*) 10011.1011.

1.12-1 Convert to the binary system the following decimal numbers: (*a*) 29, (*b*) 137, (*c*) 259, (*d*) 163.

1.12-2 Convert to the binary system the following decimal numbers: (*a*) 17.74, (*b*) 27.159, (*c*) 11.111, (*d*) 9.99.

1.12-3 The procedure for converting a decimal number to a binary number consists, as described in Sec. 1.12, of a succession of divisions by 2 (i.e., by the radix of the binary system). Similarly the conversion of a decimal number to a number in a system with radix R consists of a succession of divisions by the radix R.

 (*a*) Convert the decimal number 119 to a base 7 system.

 (*b*) Convert decimal 57 to a base 3 system.

 (*c*) Convert decimal 99 to a base 5 system.

1.12-4 (*a*) Convert the decimal number 0.69 to a base 3 number.

(*b*) Convert the decimal number 79.46 to a base 4 number.

1.13-1 (*a*) Convert the octal numbers 765 and 627 to base 2.

(*b*) Convert the hexadecimal numbers BEEF and CAB7 to base 2.

(*c*) Convert the decimal numbers 987 and 526 to numbers with a hexadecimal base.

(*d*) Convert the binary number 101101101.10101101 to octal and to hexadecimal base numbers.

1.14-1 Prepare truth tables for the functions:

(*a*) $f(A, B, C) = A(B + \bar{C})(\bar{B} + C)$

(*b*) $f(A, B, C, D) = A[\bar{B} + \bar{C}(\bar{B} + D)]$

1.15-1 Verify, by trying all possible cases, that all of the theorems in Eqs. (1.15-2) to (1.15-5) are valid.

1.15-2 Use a three-variable truth table to verify the theorem of Eq. (1.15-11*a*).

1.15-3 By algebraic manipulation, and using the other available theorems, prove the theorems of Eqs. (1.15-11*a*) and (1.15-11*b*).

1.16-1 Verify that $\overline{\bar{A}B + A\bar{B}} = AB + \bar{A}\bar{B}$.

1.16-2 Prove that if we complement a logical expression and then replace each variable by its complement, we shall have formed the dual of the expression.

1.16-3 Find the complements of the following expressions:

(*a*) $(X + Y\bar{Z})(\bar{X} + \bar{W}V)$

(*b*) $A[B + \bar{C}(D + \bar{E})]$

(*c*) $A + B(\bar{C} + D\bar{E})$

1.17-1 Draw a Venn diagram for four variables. Start with a three-variable diagram and add a fourth closed contour which divides the map into 16 regions which fall into a one-to-one correspondence with the rows of a four-variable truth table.

1.17-2 Use a Venn diagram to prove that the following equations are valid:

(*a*) $A\bar{C} + \bar{A}B + \bar{B}C = A\bar{B} + B\bar{C} + \bar{A}C$

(*b*) $\bar{A} + \bar{B} = \bar{A}B + A\bar{B} + \bar{A}\bar{B} = \overline{AB}$

1.19-1 Prove that the EXCLUSIVE-OR operation is commutative and associative.

1.19-2 We have n logic variables $A_0, A_1 \ldots A_{n-1}$. At any time some of these are at logic 1 some at logic 0. We need a gate structure by which we can determine whether the number of variables at logic 1 is odd or even. Explain how EXCLUSIVE-OR gates can be used for this purpose.

1.20-1 Prove that neither the NAND operation nor the NOR operation is associative.

1.22-1 Verify that $f_2 = \overline{A \supset B} = A\bar{B}$ and that $f_4 = \overline{B \supset A} = \bar{A}B$.

1.25-1 By algebraic manipulation, using the theorems of boolean algebra, verify the following equations:

(*a*) $(A + \bar{B} + AB)(A + \bar{B})\bar{A}B = 0$

(*b*) $(A + \bar{B} + A\bar{B})(AB + \bar{A}C + BC) = AB + \bar{A}\bar{B}C$

(*c*) $(AB + C + D)(C + \bar{D})(C + \bar{D} + E) = AB\bar{D} + C$

(*d*) $\bar{A}B(\bar{D} + D\bar{C}) + (A + D\bar{A}C)B = B$

1.25-2 Simplify the following expressions:

(*a*) $(A + B)(\bar{A} + C) + (\bar{A} + \bar{B} + \bar{A}BC)(A + \bar{A}B)(\bar{A} + B)$

(*b*) $A\bar{B}\bar{C} + AD + CD + AC\bar{D} + \bar{A}B + B\bar{D} + \bar{A}D + AB$

1.25-3 A *majority* gate structure provides an output at logic level 1 when a majority of the inputs are at logic 1. For the case of three inputs A, B, and C write a logic expression for a variable Z which is $Z = 1$ whenever a majority of the inputs are 1. Simplify the expression and draw the gate structure using AND and OR gates.

1.25-4 Simplify the following expressions:
(a) $A + \bar{A}B + (\overline{A + B})C + (\overline{A + B + C})D$
(b) $A\bar{B} + AC + BCD + \bar{D}$
(c) $\bar{A} + \bar{A}\bar{B} + BC\bar{D} + B\bar{D}$
(d) $A\bar{B}C + (\bar{B} + \bar{C})(\bar{B} + \bar{D}) + \overline{A + C + D}$

1.25-5 (a) There are three wall switches a, b, and c. Let the variable $A = 1$ represent the condition that switch a is in the UP position, $A = 0$ that it is in the DOWN position. Similarly variables B and C are associated with switches b and c. Write an expression for a variable Z which can be made $Z = 1$ or $Z = 0$ by operating each switch individually independently of the position of the other switches. Assuming that the switches can be used to provide logic inputs to gates, draw the gate structure by which Z can be realized.

(b) Keeping in mind that switches in series and in parallel can perform the AND and OR operations as in Figs. 1.7-1 and 1.7-2, draw the circuit of an arrangement which will allow a light to be turned ON or OFF by any one of three switches. (The switches may be multiblade switches whose blades are ganged.)

1.26-1 A technician in a chemical laboratory has four chemicals A, B, C, and D each of which he may keep in one or another of two storage bins. He finds it convenient, from time to time, to move one or more chemicals from one bin to the other. The nature of the chemicals is such that it is dangerous to keep B and C together unless A is in the same bin. Also, unless A is in the bin, it is dangerous to keep C and D together. Write an expression for a logical variable Z which will have the value $Z = 1$ for every dangerous storage arrangement.

1.27-1 For the gate circuit of Fig. P1.27-1 write the function $f(A, B, C, D)$ and simplify.

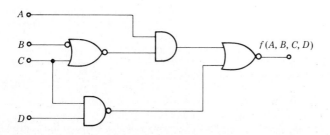

1.28-1 (a) An algorithm for converting from a binary to the reflected code of Sec. 1.28 is the following:
1. The leftmost reflected digit is the leftmost (most significant) binary digit.
2. The next reflected digit is the sum, mod 2, of the first two binary digits etc. (Modulo-2 addition, sometimes called EXCLUSIVE-OR addition, has the rules $0 + 0 = 0$, $0 + 1 = 1$, $1 + 0 = 1$, $1 + 1 = 0$.)

For example,

Binary	1100	1100	1100	1100
Reflected	1	10	1 0 1	1 0 1 0

Verify that the algorithm works.

(*b*) The algorithm for the reverse conversion is indicated in the following example:

Reflected 1010 1 0 1 0 1 0 1 0 1 0 1 0

Binary 1 1 1 1 1 1 0 1 1 0 0 0

Explain why the algorithm works.

1.30-1 In a received 4-bit word one of the bits is a parity bit used to establish even parity. Show how EXCLUSIVE-NOR gates can be used to determine whether the parity has been preserved.

Chapter 2

2.1-1 Rewrite the following expressions in the form of a standard sum of products:

(*a*) $f(A, B, C, D) = (A\bar{B} + \bar{A}B)(C + \bar{C}D)$

(*b*) $f(X, Y, Z) = (\bar{X} + \bar{Y})(\bar{X}\bar{Y} + Z)$

(*c*) $f(A, B, C, D) = \overline{(\bar{A}BC + D)(B + \overline{CD})}$

(*d*) $f(A, B, C) = (\bar{A} + \bar{B})(A + \bar{A}B)(\bar{A} + \bar{B} + \bar{A}BC)$

(*e*) $f(A, B, C) = A \oplus \bar{B} \oplus C$

2.2-1 Rewrite the following expressions in the form of a standard product of sums:

(*a*) $f(A, B, C) = A\bar{B} + \bar{B}C$

(*b*) $f(A, B, C, D) = \overline{(A + B + C)(B + C + \bar{D})}$

(*c*) $f(X, Y, Z) = (X + \bar{Y})\bar{X}Y + Z$

(*d*) $f(A, B, C) = (A \oplus B)C + \bar{A}(B \oplus C)$

(*e*) $f(A, B, C, D) = \overline{AB} + \overline{BC} + \overline{CD}$

2.4-1 Express the following functions as a sum of minterms:

(*a*) $f(A, B, C) = A + \bar{B} + C$

(*b*) $f(A, B, C) = (A + \bar{B})(B + \bar{C})$

(*c*) $f(A, B, C, D) = AB + BC\bar{D} + \bar{A}C\bar{D}$

(*d*) $f(A, B, C, D) = A(\bar{B} + C\bar{D}) + \bar{A}BC$

2.4-2 Express the following functions as a product of maxterms:

(*a*) $f(A, B, C, D) = (\bar{A} + C)D + \bar{B}D$

(*b*) $f(X, Y, Z) = \overline{(XY + Z)}(Y + XZ)$

(*c*) $f(A, B, C, D) = A\bar{B}C\bar{D}$

(*d*) $f(A, B, C, D) = A\bar{B}C + AB\bar{D}$

2.5-1 For each of the following functions: (1) prepare a truth table, (2) express the function as a sum of minterms, (3) express the function as a product of maxterms, (4) express the complement of the function in terms of minterms and in terms of maxterms.

(*a*) $f(A, B, C) = A(B + \bar{C})$

(*b*) $f(A, B, C) = (\bar{A} + B)(A + B + \bar{C})(\bar{A} + C)$

(*c*) $f(A, B, C, D) = (A + \bar{B})(C + \bar{D})(\bar{A} + \bar{C})$

(*d*) $f(A, B, C, D, E) = \bar{A}E + BCD$

2.6-1 For the following expressions draw a gate structure which generates the function directly in the form in which it is written. Then replace the direct gate structure (1) with a two level AND-OR structure and (2) with a two level OR-AND structure.

(*a*) $f(A, B, C) = [\bar{A}(B + \bar{C}) + A]\bar{B} + C$

(*b*) $f(A, B, C, D) = [(A\bar{B} + C)D + \bar{A}\bar{C}]BD + \bar{A}BC\bar{D}$

2.7-1 (*a*) Draw a two-level gate structure, using only NAND gates, which generates the function $f(A, B) = A \oplus B$.

(*b*) Repeat using NOR gates only.

2.7-2 (*a*) Draw a NAND-NAND gate structure for $f(A, B, C, D) = A + \bar{B} + C\bar{D}$.

(*b*) Repeat using a NOR-NOR gate structure.

2.7-3 Show that an AOI gate structure can be used as a NAND gate and that it can also be used as a NOR gate.

2.7-4 For each of the functions given in Prob. 2.5-1 draw a generating gate structure (*a*) using only NAND gates and (*b*) using only NOR gates.

2.7-5 Draw the NAND-NAND gate structure and also the NOR-NOR structure for the functions:

(*a*) $f(A, B, C) = \Sigma(0, 1, 3, 7)$

(*b*) $f(A, B, C, D) = \Pi(1, 5, 6, 8, 11, 13)$

2.7-6 Generate the following functions using an AOI gate:

(*a*) $f(X, Y, Z) = XY + \bar{X}\bar{Y}Z$

(*b*) $f(A, B, C, D) = \Sigma(2, 3, 5, 7, 9, 14)$

(*c*) $f(A, B, C, D) = \Pi(2, 3, 4, 7, 10, 11, 15)$

2.13-1 (*a*) Verify that the function of $f(A, B, C) = \Sigma(1, 3, 5)$ can be written in the form $f(A, B, C) = \bar{A}\bar{B}C + A\bar{B}C + \bar{A}C + \bar{B}C$.

(*b*) Each one of the product terms is called an *implicant* of the function f in the sense that if the product term has the value 1, it is thereby implied that $f = 1$ as well. A *prime implicant* is an implicant from which no variable can be deleted without causing the remainder of the product term to lose its property of being an implicant. Find the prime and nonprime implicants of $f(A, B, C)$.

2.13-2 Use a K map to find the simplest expressions for the following functions:

(*a*) $f(A, B, C) = \Sigma(0, 2, 3)$

(*b*) $f(A, B, C) = \Sigma(1, 2, 4, 6, 7)$

(*c*) $f(A, B, C) = \Sigma(0, 1, 2, 3)$

(*d*) $f(A, B, C) = \Sigma(0, 2, 4, 6)$

(*e*) $f(A, B, C) = \Sigma(0, 3, 5, 6)$

2.13-3 Repeat Prob. 2.13-2 but let the numbers specified as minterm numbers be maxterm numbers instead.

2.13-4 Use a K map to find the simplest expression for the following functions:

(*a*) $f(A, B, C, D) = \Pi(0, 5, 7, 13, 14, 15)$

(*b*) $f(A, B, C, D) = \Pi(1, 4, 6, 8, 11, 13, 14)$

(*c*) $f(A, B, C, D) = \Pi(1, 2, 4, 5, 7, 8, 10, 11, 13, 14)$

(*d*) $f(A, B, C, D) = \Pi(0, 5, 7, 8, 9, 10, 11, 13)$

2.13-5 Repeat Prob 2.13-4 but let the numbers specified as maxterm numbers be minterm numbers instead.

2.13-6 Use a K map to find the simplest expression for the following functions:

(*a*) $f(A, B, C, D, E) = \Sigma(0, 4, 8, 12, 16, 20, 24, 28)$

(*b*) $f(A, B, C, D, E) = \Sigma(0, 2, 5, 8, 13, 15, 18, 21, 24, 29, 31)$

(*c*) $f(A, B, C, D, E) = \Sigma(3, 4, 6, 9, 11, 13, 15, 18, 25, 26, 27, 29, 31)$

(*d*) $f(A, B, C, D, E) = \Sigma(1, 5, 8, 10, 12, 13, 14, 15, 17, 21, 24, 26, 31)$

2.13-7 Repeat Prob. 2.13-6 but let the numbers specified as minterm numbers be maxterm numbers instead.

2.13-8 Use a K map to find the simplest expression for the following functions:

(*a*) $f(A, B, C, D, |E, F) = \Pi(2, 3, 6, 7, 10, 14, 18, 19, 22, 23, 27, 37, 42, 43, 45, 46)$

(*b*) $f(A, |B, C, D, |E, F) = \Pi(6, 9, 13, 18, 19, 25, 27, 29, 41, 45, 57, 61)$

(*c*) $f(A, B, C, D, E, F) = \Pi(4, 5, 6, 7, 8, 18, 20, 23, 25, 26, 27, 28, 37, 38, 42, 44, 49, 51, 58, 59, 60, 63)$

2.13-9 Repeat Prob. 2.13-8 but let the numbers specified as maxterm numbers be minterm numbers instead.

2.14-1 Use a K map to simplify the following functions:

(a) $f(A, B, C, D) = \bar{A}\bar{B}C + AD + B\bar{D} + C\bar{D} + A\bar{C} + \bar{A}\bar{B}$

(b) $f(A, B, C, D) = (A + B + \bar{C})(\bar{B} + \bar{D})(\bar{A} + C)(B + C)$

(c) $f(A, B, C, D, E) = A + BC + \bar{C}D\bar{E}$

(d) $f(A, B, C, D, E) = (A + B)(B + C)(C + \bar{D})(D + \bar{E})$

2.15-1 Use a K map to simplify the following expressions:

(a) $f(A, B, C, D) = \Sigma m(0, 1, 4, 5, 9, 11, 14, 15) + d(10, 13)$

(b) $f(A, B, C, D) = \Sigma m(0, 13, 14, 15) + d(1, 2, 3, 9, 10, 11)$

(c) $f(A, B, C, D) = \Sigma m(0, 6, 9, 10, 13) + d(1, 3, 8)$

(d) $f(A, B, C, D) = \Sigma m(1, 4, 7, 10, 13) + d(5, 14, 15)$

(e) $f(A, B, C, D, E) = \Sigma m(1, 4, 6, 10, 20, 22, 24, 26) + d(0, 11, 16, 17)$

2.15-2 A logic circuit has five inputs and a single output. Four of the inputs A, B, C, D represent a decimal digit in *BCD*. The fifth input is a control input. When the control is at logic 0, the output is at logic 0 when the decimal number is even and is at logic 1 when the decimal number is odd. When the control is at logic 1, the output is 0 except when the input is a multiple of 3. Design the circuit.

2.15-3 A logic circuit accepts as inputs two 2-bit numbers $A = A_1A_0$ and $B = B_1B_0$ and provides a 4-bit output $P = P_3P_2P_1P_0$ which is the numerical product of A and B. Design the circuit.

Chapter 3

3.3-1 TTL gates with characteristics as in Fig. 3.3-2 are individually connected to operate as inverters and then are connected in a cascade, the output of the first inverter connected to the input of the second, etc. The input of the first is initially held at 2.4 V. Suppose that from some noise source a spurious voltage of magnitude 0.5 V is added at each gate junction, the polarity of the noise at every junction being in the wrong direction. How many gates can we allow in the cascade before the output of a gate finds itself closer to the wrong logic level than to the correct level?

3.3-2 In the circuit of Fig. P3.3-2 an abrupt downward voltage transition from logic 1 to logic 0 occurs at the input at time $t = 0$. On a common time scale make plots of the voltage transitions at points X, Y, and Z and at the output. Ignore the rise and fall response times of the gates.

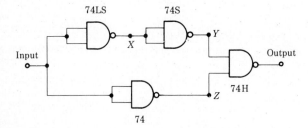

3.8-1 Two logic operated switch circuits are shown in Fig. P3.8-1. In each case find the logical relationship between Z and A and B.

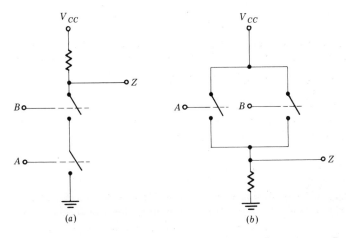

(a)   (b)

3.11-1 We have available the variables A, $\bar{A}$, B, $\bar{B}$, C, and D ($\bar{C}$ and $\bar{D}$ are not available). Show how we can generate the function

$$Z = (\bar{A} + \bar{B})\,(\bar{C} + \bar{D})\,(A + \bar{C})\,(B + \bar{D})$$

using only a single type of the IC packages listed in Table 3.11-1.

3.11-2 Use a single one of the IC packages listed in Table 3.11-1 to generate simultaneously the function $Z = (\bar{A} + B + C)\,(D + E)$ and $(A + \bar{B} + D)\,(C + \bar{E})$. All the variables and their complements are available.

3.11-3 Using two IC packages in the list of Table 3.11-1, construct a circuit which can be used to determine whether or not a group of 3 bits has odd parity.

3.14-1 In the style of *mixed* logic we describe gates as being either OR gates or AND gates (references to NOR gates or NAND gates are avoided), and we specify as well whether the input terminals accommodate active-high or active-low signals and also the active level of the output generated. Accordingly, what is the description in *positive* logic of gates described in *mixed* logic as:

    (*a*) An OR gate with active-low inputs and output
    (*b*) An AND gate with active low-inputs and output
    (*c*) An OR gate with active-high inputs and active-low output
    (*d*) An AND gate with active-high inputs and active-low outputs
    (*e*) An OR gate with active-low inputs and active-high output
    (*f*) An AND gate with active-low inputs and active-high output.

3.14-2 An EXCLUSIVE-OR is described in *mixed* logic as a device which accepts two inputs, say X and Y, and provides an output which is active when X or Y but not both are active.

    (*a*) Draw the mixed-logic symbol for a gate which accepts X low and Y low and generates Z high.

    (*b*) Draw the symbol for a gate which accepts X low and Y high and generates Z low.

    (*c*) Show that the gates specified in (*a*) and (*b*) are physically the same gate as one which accepts both inputs active high and generates an active-high output.

3.14-3 We require a logic-gate structure with four inputs, A, B, C, and D, to generate an output Z which is active if one or the other but *not* both of the following conditions are satisfied: (1) both inputs A and B are active; (2) either C or D or both are active.

(*a*) Assume A and B are available active high, C and D are available active low, and Z is to be active low.

(*b*) Assume all inputs and the output are active high.

In both cases show how the structures can be physically realized using commercially available gates as in Table 3.11-1.

3.14-4 Inputs A low, B high, C low, and D high are provided. Draw gate structures using the gates available in Table 3.11-1 which will provide outputs Z high given by:

(*a*) $Z = (A + D)(\bar{B} + C)$

(*b*) $Z = A\bar{B}\bar{C} + BD$

(*c*) Repeat (*a*) and (*b*) if the requirement is that Z be active low.

3.14-5 Inputs A low, B high, C low, and D high are provided. Draw gate structures using the gates available in Table 3.11-1 which will provide outputs Z low given by:

(*a*) $Z = (\overline{A + B + C})(\bar{B} + D)$

(*b*) $Z = (A + \bar{B} + C)(C \oplus D)$

(*c*) $Z = A + B + C + D$

3.14-6 We have a box containing a light which lights up in response to an activation of its active-low input terminal. The light is controlled by the following signals: (1) turn on light (TOL-H), (2) inhibit (IN-L), (3) there is an emergency (EMERG-L), (4) the time is not right (TNR-H). The light is to go on when so instructed provided the time is right and the instruction is not countermanded by the inhibit signal. If, however, there is an emergency, the light is to go on independently of any other instructions. Draw a mixed-logic diagram of the logic structure required to implement the system and show its physical realization in terms of positive-logic gates.

3.15-1 Show how two type '138 decoders (Fig. 3.15-2) can be combined to construct a decoder with 4 input address lines and 16 output lines.

3.15-2 Show how to use nine type '138 decoders as in Fig. 3.15-2 to construct a decoder with 6 input address lines and 64 output lines.

3.15-3 Draw the gate structure of a decoder which accepts the 4-bit BCD representation of the decimal digits and has 10 output lines, one of which is singled out corresponding to each digit.

3.15-4 In Fig. 3.15-4 what input pins must be brought to what voltage level (H or L) in order to bring pin 10 to a low level?

3.16-1 An encoder has eight input lines $I_0, ..., I_7$ and generates a 3-bit output word. The output word is the reflected-code representation of the decimal number of the input line which is rendered active. Show the gate structure of the encoder.

3.16-2 Verify that the priority encoder of Fig. 3.16-3*a* does operate as described in the text. Also verify the entries in the table of Fig. 3.16-3*b*.

3.16-3 Verify the description given in the text in Sec. 3.16 concerning the operation of a cascade of type 9318 priority encoders.

3.16-4 Draw the logic diagram of a priority encoder which has four inputs $I_0, ..., I_3$ and two outputs A_1 and A_0. I_3 is to have priority over I_2, etc. Provide an enable input, an enable output, and a group-signal output. Arrange for all inputs and outputs to be active high.

3.17-1 Design a code converter which accepts as input the BCD representation of a decimal digit and provides as outputs appropriate lines to light up the proper segments of a 7-segment display to present the input decimal number.

3.18-1 Show how two multiplexers of the type shown in Figs. 3.18-3 and 3.18-4 can be combined (with other simple gates) to construct a 1-out-of-16 multiplexer.

3.18-2 Show how nine multiplexers of the type shown in Figs. 3.18-3 and 3.18-4 can be combined (with other simple gates) to construct a 1-out-of-64 multiplexer.

3.18-3 In the multiplexer described by the logic symbol of Fig. 3.18-4 we want to make available at the output the complement of the logic level at pin 14. What inputs are required for this purpose, and where shall the output be taken?

3.18-4 Use the multiplexer of Fig. 3.18-2 to generate $Z = S_1 + S_0$.

3.18-5 Use the multiplexer of Fig. 3.18-2 to generate $Z = S_1 S_0 + S_0 V + \bar{S}_1 \bar{S}_0 \bar{V}$.

3.18-6 We have seen that the multiplexer of Fig. 3.18-2 will generate directly any function of S_1 and S_0 and any function of $S_1 S_0$ and V if V is available in complemented and uncomplemented form. It may well be good economy of IC packages to use the multiplexer for added variables even at the expense of having to provide additional gates. Thus use the multiplexer, and other gates as required, to generate $Z = S_1 \bar{S}_0 + S_0 W + VW + S_0 \bar{W}$.

  Hint: Consider the possibility that the I inputs can be not only 1, 0, V, or $\bar{V}$ but can also be some logical function of V and W.

3.18-7 (*a*) Use an eight-input multiplexer to generate the function $Z = \Sigma m(0, 3, 5, 6, 9, 10, 12, 15)$

  (*b*) Draw a structure using only NAND gates which generates the same function.

  (*c*) Assume that the NAND gates are available in dual four-input IC packages. Compare the number of packages required in the two methods of implementation.

Chapter 4

4.3-1 Consider a cross-coupled gate configuration as in Fig. 4.2-1 except that OR gates are used.

  (*a*) Show that when the data input terminals enable both gates, the two output terminals can both remain permanently at logic 0 or both at logic 1 and hence that the circuit constitutes a latch, i.e., a device with two stable states.

  (*b*) Show that by manipulation of the data terminals it is possible to induce a transition in one direction but not in the other.

  (*c*) Repeat parts (*a*) and (*b*) for AND gates.

  (*d*) If one gate is an AND gate and the other is an OR gate, show that the resulting circuit is a latch and that it is possible to induce transitions in either direction.

4.5-1 (*a*) In the gated latch circuit of Fig. 4.5-1 add an additional input terminal to each of the gates which are cross-coupled, i.e., to the gates which are directly connected to Q and $\bar{Q}$. Show that these added terminals are active-low $\overline{direct\text{-}set}$ and $\overline{direct\text{-}reset}$ inputs $\bar{S}_d$ and $\bar{R}_d$ which can be used to provide a means of setting or resetting the latch before the enabling input becomes active.

  (*b*) Now consider, say in Fig. 4.5-1*b*, that $\bar{S}_d = 1$ and $\bar{R}_d = 0$, so that the direct inputs are adjusted to reset the latch. Suppose also, however, that $D = 1$ and that EN-ABLE is made active. There is now a conflict between the direct input instruction and the gated input. Show that, after ENABLE is rendered inactive, the final state of the latch will be determined by the direct inputs but that while ENABLE is asserted, the gated input has an effect.

  (*c*) Show how the circuit can be modified to provide direct inputs which *completely override* the effect of the gated input.

4.6-1 In Fig. 4.6-1 consider, in the more general case, that the input to the top input terminal is a signal B and to the bottom terminal is a signal C. Add an additional gate which generates $\bar{B} + C$ and applies this signal to the gate G_3. Show that in this case the logic relationship between Z and A, B and C is not changed but that the hazard shown in Fig. 4.6-1b is eliminated. (The matter of hazard elimination is considered further in Sec. 7-19).

4.8-1 Show that the direct set and reset controls of the master-slave flip-flop of Fig. 4.8-4 completely override the synchronous inputs.

4.13-1 (a) Show that the circuit of Fig. P4.13-1 is an edge-triggered flip-flop depending for its operation on the propagation delay of the input NOR gates. (b) Show that the flip-flop is suitable for use in a synchronous system in that the output responds to the clock transition which disables the NOR gates.

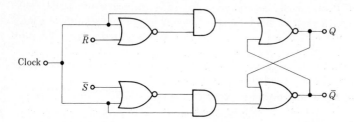

4.13-2 The flip-flop circuit of Fig. P4.13-2 is used in emitter-coupled logic (ECL).

(a) Show that it is an edge-triggered flip-flop suitable for use in a synchronous system in that the output responds to the clock transition which disables the input gates.

(b) Show that the circuit has the limitation characteristics of flip-flops which depend on propagation delay, i.e., dependence on the speed of transition of the clock waveform. Specifically, show that the flip-flop may not operate properly if the transition time of the clock waveform is very long in comparison with the time constant rC.

(c) Show that feedback connections from outputs to input gates can transform the flip-flop to a $\bar{J}\,\bar{K}$ flip-flop.

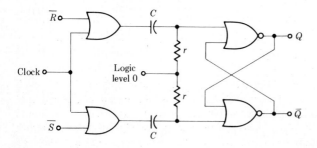

4.13-3 The flip-flop in Fig. P4.13-3 is used in transistor-transistor logic (TTL). (Reverse-biased junction diodes are used as physical implementations of the rC combinations represented in the circuit.)

(a) Describe the operation of the circuit and show that it is suitable for use in a synchronous system in that the output responds to the clock transition which disables the input gates.

(b) Take into account the fact that the capacitor cannot charge instantaneously and that, when charged, the capacitor will discharge through r. Discuss qualitatively the corresponding timing considerations which must be taken into account in connection with both the data input and the clock waveform.

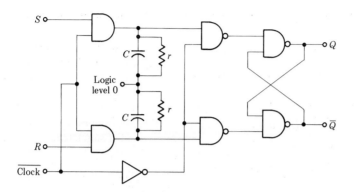

4.14-1 Verify all the statements made in Sec. 4.14 concerning the operation of the type D flip-flop of Fig. 4.14-3.

4.14-2 Suppose that all the NAND gates of Fig. 4.14-3 are replaced by NOR gates. For this case rewrite the description of the operation of the flip-flop.

4.14-3 Without adding gates, modify the type D flip-flop of Fig. 4.14-3 so that it is equipped with active-low direct-set and direct-reset input terminals which completely override the synchronous input.

4.14-4 Verify that the circuit of Fig. 4.14-5 operates as is required of a JK flip-flop.

4.16-1 (*a*) We have available two *n*-bit registers A and B in which the individual bit storage elements are simple SR static latches. We have a transfer-enable signal RA $\rightarrow$ RB. Show the structure by which we can, on command, transfer the content of RA to RB.

(*b*) Suppose that we have instead two signals; one ($0 \rightarrow$ RA) can be used to clear RA, and the second is the transfer signal RA $\rightarrow$ RB. Show how the hardware needed to effect the transfer can be simplified if we are prepared to accept a two-step transfer operation.

4.17-1 In the 4-bit shift register of Fig. 4.17-1 assume that initially $Q_0 = Q_1 = 0$, $Q_2 = Q_3 = 1$. Draw the waveform of each flip-flop output if the input sequence 10101 is applied at D_0 synchronously with the clock.

4.18-1 Draw the logic diagram of a 3-stage shift-left shift-right register using type D flip-flops. The register is to have terminals D_{SR} (data input for shift right), D_{SL} (data input for shift left), M (mode control to determine shift direction) and, of course, a clock terminal.

4.20-1 (*a*) Consider a 4-bit ring counter as in Fig. 4.20-1 in which the count sequence is $Q_0Q_1Q_2Q_3 = 1000 \rightarrow 0100 \rightarrow 0010 \rightarrow 0001 \rightarrow 1000$, etc. Show that if by accident due to some spurious noise disturbance the counter finds itself in any other than these four allowed states, the counter will sequence through disallowed states, never returning to the intended sequence.

(*b*) Next consider that the counter is modified in that D_0 is no longer connected to Q_3; instead we add a gate to arrange that $D_0 = \bar{Q}_0\bar{Q}_1\bar{Q}_2$. Show that in this case the counter will be self-correcting, so that no matter in which state the counter starts, it will eventually settle into the intended sequence.

(c) Modify the correcting circuit if the intended sequence is one in which a single 0 rather than a 1 is to rotate around the counter.

4.21-1 Design a decoder for a 5-bit switch-tail counter which will give an explicit indication of the count.

4.21-2 (a) Consider the 4-bit switch-tail ring counter of Fig. 4.21-1 whose count sequence is given. Suppose that by accident when power is first applied or because of a noise disturbance the counter finds itself in a state not in the intended sequence. Show then that the counter will continue to sequence through unintended states, never settling into the intended sequence.

(b) Modify the counter by replacing FF_0 by a JK flip-flop. The input to J_0 is to be $J_0 = \bar{Q}_2 \bar{Q}_3$ and $K_0 = Q_3$. Show that now the counter will be self-correcting so that no matter what its initial state, it will eventually settle into the intended sequence.

4.21-3 The switch-tail counter sequences through an even number of states equal to $2N$, N being the number of flip-flops. Consider a counter with $N = 3$ with FF_0, FF_1, and FF_2 in which FF_0 is a JK flip-flop. Construct a counter in which $\bar{Q}_0$ is connected to D_1 and Q_1 to D_2 and in which $J_0 = Q_2$ and $K_0 = \bar{Q}_1$. Show that this counter will sequence through an odd number of states (five).

4.24-1 Design a synchronous mod-3 counter using JK flip-flops. Arrange that the counter sequence through the states $Q_1 Q_0 = 00 \rightarrow 11 \rightarrow 10 \rightarrow 00$, etc.

4.24-2 Design a synchronous mod-5 counter which follows the sequence which is given in Table 4.24-2 using:

(a) SR flip-flops

(b) Type D flip-flops

(c) Toggle flip-flops

4.24-3 Verify the K maps of Fig. 4.24-2 and verify the map reading in Eq. (4.24-1).

4.24-4 Design a synchronous mod-5 counter which sequences through the states $S_0 \rightarrow S_2 \rightarrow S_4 \rightarrow S_6 \rightarrow S_7 \rightarrow S_0$, etc., the states being defined in Table 4.24-1 using (a) JK flip-flops and (b) type D flip-flops. Check to make certain that lockout does not occur.

4.24-5 Design a synchronous mod-7 counter which sequences in order through all the states of Table 4.24-1 as listed except state S_3. Arrange that if the counter accidentally finds itself in S_3, it will go to state S_0 as the next state. Use only toggle flip-flops.

4.24-6 (a) Design a synchronous mod-6 counter that sequences in order through the first six states of Table 4.24-1. Use type D flip-flops.

(b) Design a mod-3 counter which sequences through the first three states of Table 4.24-1. Construct a mod-6 counter by cascading the mod-3 counter with a mod-2 counter. That is, the mod-2 counter is to change state each time the mod-3 counter completes its sequence.

(c) Draw the waveforms for both designs of the mod-6 counter.

(d) In each case design a count decoder.

4.24-7 Refer to the timing waveforms of a mod-8 synchronous counter as given in Fig. 4.22-1b. The decoder is given in Fig. 4.22-1c. Let the clock period be T. Assume that the propagation delay of a flip-flop is $t_{pd} = 0.1T$ when a flip-flop goes from set to reset state and is $t_{pd} = 0.2T$ when a flip-flop goes from reset to set state. Redraw the waveforms taking into account these propagation delays. On the same time scale draw the waveforms of the decoder outputs $K_0, \ldots, K_7$. Show that transient decoding errors occur because of the unequal propagation delays.

4.25-1 Draw the logic diagram of the counter whose logic is given by Eqs. (4.25-1) to (4.25-3).

4.25-2 Design a mod-8 up-down synchronous counter.

4.25-3 Design a mod-7 up-down synchronous counter which sequences in order through all the states in Table 4.24-1 except state S_0.

4.25-4 Design an up-down synchronous decade counter.

4.27-1 Verify the entries in Table 4.27-1.

4.27-2 (*a*) Show that the ripple counter of Fig. 4.27-1 can be converted into an up-down counter with a mode (direction) control M by replacing the direct connection $C_{k+1} = Q_k$ by a gate structure which arranges that $C_{k+1} = MQ_k + \bar{M} \bar{Q}_k$. Draw the logic circuit of a mod-8 counter.

(*b*) Show that the design in part (*a*) has the undesirable feature that there are occasions when the count will be changed simply by the operation of changing the count direction even when the clock is quiescent. Show how the design may be modified to circumvent this difficulty.

4.27-3 (*a*) A mod-10 (decade) ripple counter is shown in Fig. P4.27-3. In FF_0 and FF_3 the active-low direct-reset terminals are kept permanently inactive by being set at a voltage corresponding to logic 1. The flip-flops toggle on the negative-going edge of the waveform applied to the clock input. Draw 10 cycles of an input clock waveform and on the same time scale draw the waveforms of Q_0, Q_1, Q_2, and Q_3. Start in the state $Q_0Q_1Q_2Q_3 = 0000$. Show that after the ninth clock triggering transition we have $Q_0Q_1Q_2Q_3 = 1001 (= 9)$. Show that the immediately following positive-going edge of the clock takes the counter to $Q_0Q_1Q_2Q_3 = 1111$ (during the state, the count decoder will have to be disabled) and that the next negative-going clock edge returns the counter to the initial state.

(*b*) Generalize the idea of the design of part (a). Draw logic diagrams of mod-12, mod-14, mod-19, and mod-27 counters.

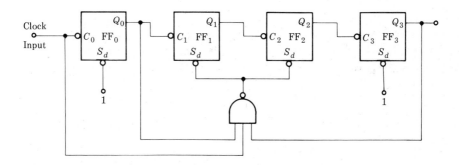

4.27-4 The flip-flops in the ripple counter of Fig. P4.27-4 are $\bar{J}\bar{K}$ flip-flops with active-low data terminals. They respond to the positive going edge of the waveforms applied at the clock input. They have the further characteristic that when the clock is high, a positive-going transition at the external $\bar{J}$ terminal will set the flip-flop and at the $\bar{K}$ terminal will reset the flip-flop. (These flip-flops are actually the flip-flops presented in Prob.

4.13-2 modified into $\bar{J}\bar{K}$ flip-flops.) In Fig. P4.27-4 all $\bar{J}$ and $\bar{K}$ terminals not indicated are held at logic 0. In the last flip-flop, the clock is held high.

(a) Show that if we ignore the connection to $\bar{J}_0$, the first N flip-flops constitute an up-counting ripple counter of modulo 2^N.

(b) Show that by virtue of the addition of the last flip-flop and the feedback to $\bar{J}_0$ the counter has a modulo $2^N + 1$ (not 2^{N+1}).

(c) Using the principle illustrated and using flip-flops only (no gates), construct a mod-3 and a mod-5 counter.

(d) Construct a mod-7 counter, a mod-11 counter and a mod-25 counter.

Hint: $7 = 2(2 + 1) + 1$; $11 = 2(2^2 + 1) + 1$; $25 = 2^3(2^1 + 1) + 1$.

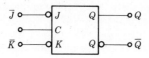

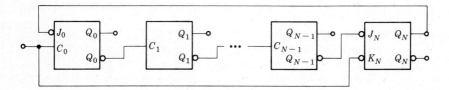

4.27-5 Ripple-type counters of arbitrary modulo can be constructed by adding gates to a counter array of flip-flops in a manner to cause the counter to bypass some states. There is no special design procedure, and some ingenuity is required. An example is given in Fig. P4.27-5. All J and K terminals not explicitly displayed are at logic 1.

(a) Draw waveforms for the counter and verify that it has a modulo of 5.

(b) Using the pattern suggested by the counter shown, draw the logic diagram of a mod-9 counter.

(c) Try your hand at a mod-7 counter.

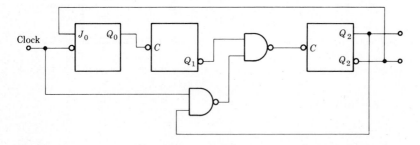

4.28-1 Verify that the flip-flops B, C, and D in Fig. 4.28-1c are connected as a mod-5 counter.

4.28-2 Draw the waveforms for the decade counter of Fig. 4.28-1c for the following two cases:

(a) The external clock is applied at $\overline{CP}_0$.

(b) The external clock is applied at $\overline{CP}_1$.

Chapter 5

5.1-1 Perform the following additions and subtractions of binary system numbers:

(a) $1101 + 110$ (e) $1000 - 111$

(b) $101011 + 101010$ (f) $10100 - 1111$

(c) $1111 + 1$ (g) $10001 - 1110$

(d) $111 + 11$ (h) $10101 - 1010$

5.2-1 In order to accommodate numbers which range over very many orders of magnitude, computers store binary numbers in a floating-point representation, the number N being represented as $N = F2^E$. F is a fraction whose most significant bit is 1, and E is an exponent of the base 2. Two registers are used, one for F and one for E. Thus $F = S_F F_{-1} F_{-2} \ldots$ and $E = S_F E_k E_{k-1} \ldots$, where S_F and S_E are sign bits. Assuming that negative numbers, whether fractional parts or exponents, are specified in twos-complement representation, write out the register contents for the following numbers, assuming that F is an 8-place register and E is a 4-place register:

(a) $+110.101$ (c) $+.00001101$

(b) -110.101 (d) $-.00001101$

5.2-2 Find the twos-complement representation in the binary system of the following decimal numbers:

(a) $+17$ (c) $+32$

(b) -17 (d) -32

In each case use the smallest allowable register.

5.2-3 Using the twos-complement representation, perform the following additions and subtractions and express the result in sign-magnitude form:

(a) $A + B$ (c) $-A + B$

(b) $A - B$ (d) $-A - B$

where the magnitude of A is 110101 and of B is 110011.

5.2-4 In the decimal system we form the *tens* complement of a number in a manner which corresponds to the *twos* complement in the binary system. Thus in a two-position decimal register with registration positions $00, 01, \ldots, 98, 99$, the tens complement of 37 is $100 - 37 = 63$.

(a) Draw a two-position decimal register and indicate on it the numerical significance in sign and magnitude of the register positions.

(b) What is the largest positive number represented?

(c) What is the largest-magnitude negative number?

(d) In a register with an arbitrary number of positions how can we tell from the leftmost digit whether the register position represents a positive or negative number?

(e) Using only the operation of addition and representing negative numbers in tens-complement form, calculate $46 + 39$, $46 - 39$, $-46 + 39$ and $-46 - 39$.

5.2-5 Without formally using the operation of subtraction determine the twos complement of:

(a) 110111 (c) 1010100

(b) 00001 (d) 1100101

5.2-6 Suppose that we combine two numbers, each within the range of a register used in twos-complement representation, the result, however, being outside the register range. Show that we can detect that an error has resulted by checking whether there is a carry out of the most significant register position and whether there is a carry out of the next to most significant position. Show that if one or the other carry is generated, but not both, the register range has been exceeded.

5.3-1 Find the ones-complement representation in an eight-place register of the following decimal numbers:

(a) +8   (c) +21
(b) −8   (d) −21

5.3-2 Using the ones-complement representation, perform the following additions and subtractions and express the result in sign-magnitude form:

(a) $A + B$ (c) $-A + B$
(b) $A - B$ (d) $-A - B$

where the magnitude of A is 111001 and of B is 101101.

5.3-3 In the decimal system we form the *nines* complement of a number in a manner which corresponds to the ones complement in the binary system. Thus in a two-position decimal register with registration positions 00, 01, . . . , 98, 99, the ones complement of 37 is $99 - 37 = 62$. Repeat for this nines-complement case all the parts of Prob. 5.2-4 which applied to the tens-complement case.

5.4-1 The full adder of Fig. 5.4-3 requires nine gates.

Show that if C_{i+1} is available, S_1 can be generated as

$$S_i = \bar{C}_{i+1}(A_i + B_i + C_i) + A_iB_iC_i$$

and that the full adder can in this way be realized in eight gates. Is this saving of a gate necessarily an advantage? Compare the number of gate levels through which a signal must pass.

5.4-2 (a) Verify that

$$X \oplus Y = \overline{\overline{XY} X \ \overline{XY} Y}$$

and that

$$XY + XZ + YZ = \overline{\overline{XY} (X \oplus Y) Z}$$

(b) Use the results of part (a) to show that a full adder can be constructed from six NAND gates with two inputs each. How would the propagation delay of this arrangement compare with the structure of Fig. 5.4-3?

5.4-3 Derive the logic equations for a full adder which accommodates two 2-bit input numbers plus a carry-in bit. The unit accepts as inputs $A_{i+1}A_i$ and $B_{i+1}B_i$ and C_i and generates outputs $S_{i+1}S_i$ and C_{i+2}.

5.4-4 Design a combinational logic circuit which accepts as inputs a 3-bit number and generates an output which is the square of the input.

5.4-5 A *comparator* is a digital circuit which accepts two input numbers A and B and provides three outputs. The first, second, or third output is active depending on whether $A = B$ or $A > B$ or $A < B$. Design a combinational comparator which accommodates two 3-bit numbers.

5.5-1 The serial adder of Fig. 5.5-1 has the numbers 01101 and 00111 stored in the two 5-bit addend and augend registers, respectively. Make timing charts of the operation of the adder through the interval of six clock cycles. Start by drawing the clock waveform and underneath, on the same time scale, draw the waveforms of the full-adder output and of the type D flip-flop output.

5.6-1 In the parallel adder of Fig. 5.6-1 assume that the sum and carry bits are generated by the gate structures of Fig. 5.4-3c. Ignore the delay associated with generating the complements of variables such as are called for in the circuit for generating S_i and assume that the delay of each gate is the same. Assume a 4-bit adder, $C_0 = 0$, and that just before time $t = 0$, $A = B = 0$, so that the output sum and carry bits are also 0. At $t = 0$ we apply $A = 1111$ and $B = 0001$. Show the sequence of changes through which the output $C_4 S_3 S_2 S_1 S_0$ will go starting from 00000 and ending at 10000.

5.7-1 In the calculator of Fig. 5.7-1 the registration in the accumulator register is -4. The input switches are set to subtract 5. What are the values of C_4, S_3, S_2, S_1, and S_0? When the SW (register) switch is tapped, what will be the subsequent output indication of the calculator?

5.7-2 (a) Consider that a sequence of numbers has been added and subtracted to the accumulator of Fig. 5.7-1. Assume that the final accumulation is within the range of the accumulator but that during the sequence of operations there has occurred an overflow outside the range of the accumulator. Show that, nonetheless, the final result will be correct. Show that this result continues to apply if the twos-complement representation is used.

(b) Step by step form the accumulation $-5 - 6 + 4$ and show that the end result is -7 even though combining the first two numbers gives the result -11, which is outside the range of the accumulator.

5.8-1 (a) Show that a full subtractor can be assembled from two half subtractors and an OR gate.

(b) Draw the two-level gate structures for the generation of D_i and C_{i+1} as called for by the truth table of Fig. 5.8-1.

5.8-2 Show that a full adder can be converted into a full subtractor by the use of a single inverter.

5.10-1 Verify that Eq. (5.10-4) can be rewritten in the form given in Eq. (5.10-5).

5.10-2 Verify the expression given in Eq. (5.10-7) for the carry bits.

5.10-3 Consider that in the look-ahead carry adder of Fig. 5.10-2 the variable P_i is generated by an OR gate with delay t_{pd} rather than by an EXCLUSIVE-OR gate. Find the total delay of the adder.

5.10-4 In a TTL data book, look up the type '83A 4-bit binary full adder with fast carry. Examine the logic diagram and verify that the sum bits are generated by using two EXCLUSIVE-OR gates as in Fig. 5.10-2 but that P_i is generated as $P_i = A_i + B_i$.

5.12-1 In Fig. 5.12-1 all the bits A_i and B_i as well as C_0 are applied at $t = 0$. How long must we wait before we can be sure that the sum is correctly available?

5.13-1 Verify the entries in Table 5.13-1 for the simple ALU unit of Fig. 5.13-1.

5.13-2 In Sec. 5.13 a table is given which lists the relative magnitudes of the two ALU inputs A and B in terms of the applied carry input C_n and the observed carry output C_{n+4}. Verify the entries in the table.

5.14-1 For the circuit of Fig. 5.14-2 show that whenever the sum generated by the top row of full adders is in the range 10 to 15, an output carry will be generated and that $6 = 0110$ will be added to the sum.

5.14-2 Design a combinational circuit that accepts a 4-bit binary number and generates the corresponding (two-digit) decimal number in BCD representation.

5.14-3 Convert the decimal numbers 267 and 134 to BCD and carry out the addition of the numbers.

5.15-1 Perform the following multiplications and divisions:

(a) 1101×101 (c) $1001101 \div 101$

(b) 1001×1111 (d) $110011 \div 1111$

Chapter 6

6.1-1 A RAM memory chip stores words 4 bits in length. It has separate input and output terminals, a CS and a $\overline{WE}$ control, and two pins used to supply power. The memory is packaged as a 24-pin chip, all the pins being used. What is the organization of the memory?

6.3-1 Using the memory chips of Fig. 6.1-1, draw a diagram to show how they can be organized into an 8-word 16-bit/word memory.

6.3-2 Using the memory chips of Fig. 6.1-1, draw a diagram to show how they can be organized into a 32-word 4-bit/word memory.

6.4-1 A RAM chip is organized as a 16,384-word 1-bit/word memory. Compare the number of switches and gates required to access each bit for one- and two-dimensional internal organization.

6.5-1 The content of a 4-word 8-bit/word ROM is specified in the table. Draw the corresponding logic structure of the decoder and encoder.

Address		Data word							
A_1	A_0	D_7	D_6	D_5	D_4	D_3	D_2	D_1	D_0
0	0	0	1	1	0	0	1	1	0
0	1	1	0	1	0	1	0	1	0
1	0	1	1	1	0	0	0	1	1
1	1	0	0	1	1	1	0	0	1

6.5-2 We have a 2,048-word 4-bit/word ROM which has 11 address inputs. We require an 8,192-word 1-bit/word ROM with 13 address inputs. Draw a diagram to show how the required conversion can be accomplished by combining the ROM with a multiplexer.

6.6-1 Draw the diode and resistor structure of the encoder portion of the ROM whose content is specified in Prob. 6.5-1.

6.9-1 A ROM chip has timing parameters $t_{AA} = 250$ ns, $t_{CE} = 150$ ns, and $t_{OH} = 100$ ns.

(a) A valid address is applied at time $t = 0$, the chip select is made active at $t = 50$ ns, and a new address is presented at $t = 300$ ns. What is the time range over which valid data are available corresponding to the first address?

(b) Repeat part (a) for a chip select made active at $t = 200$ ns.

6.10-1 (a) We want the PLA of Fig. 6.10-1 to be field-programmable. Each AND gate is to have access to any of the input I's or its complement and each OR gate to have access to any AND-gate output; we are to be free to select active high or low outputs. How many fusible links would have to be incorporated into the FPLA?

(b) How many links would be required in a PROM with the same number of inputs and outputs as the FPLA of part (a)?

6.10-2 A ROM is to be used to generate four functions F_0, F_1, F_2, and F_3 of four input variables I_0, I_1, I_2, and I_3.

$$F_0 = I_0 + I_1 + I_2 + I_3 \qquad F_1 = I_0 I_1 I_2 I_3.$$
$$F_2 = I_0 \oplus I_1 \oplus I_2 \oplus I_3 \qquad F_3 = (I_0 + I_1)(I_2 + I_3)$$

Design the ROM and draw its logic circuit, i.e., the AND- and OR-gate structure. Draw a second circuit in which the encoder portion displays the individual diodes.

6.10-3 A combinational circuit is to be constructed that will accept a 3-bit input number and generate an output which is the square of the input. Make a truth table for the squarer. Show that the squarer can be implemented using no other hardware than a ROM which has a 3-bit address and a 4-bit output word.

6.10-4 A combinational circuit is to be designed that will generate the numerical product of two 2-bit input numbers A_1A_0 and B_1B_0. The input bits are to be active high, the outputs to be active low. Design the circuit following the pattern of a PLA. Express the outputs as sums of products and draw the diagram of the required gate structure.

6.14-1 Refer to Fig. 6.14-2a. Show that if the position of the switch S_2 and its resistor are interchanged, the circuit will provide an output I rather than $\bar{I}$. Using this result, modify Fig. 6.14-2b so that it provides the output $\bar{Q}$ as well as Q. Show now that if the output is connected to the input, the flip-flop will toggle.

6.15-1 Suppose that in a CCD shift-register serial memory using a cascade of 100 stages the total loss of charge from beginning to end should not exceed 5 percent. What is the required charge efficiency, i.e., the fraction of the charge in one bit position which is transferred to the next position?

Chapter 7

7.3-1 A synchronous sequential system is to remain in a state A until a mechanical switch is closed for a brief time. At the closing, the system is to go to state B. At a second brief closing of the switch the system is to advance to state C, and so on. In practice the clock period will be very much shorter than the interval when the switch is closed. Draw a flowchart for the system.

7.3-2 In the four-state flow charge of Fig. P7.3-2 the state assignments are given in the upper right-hand corner above each state rectangle. Type D flip-flops are to be used. There are three input variables X_0, X_1, and X_2. When the system is in state A and $X_0 = 1$, the next state is B independently of X_1 and X_2, etc.

    (*a*) Make a state table.
    (*b*) Make a transition table.
    (*c*) Find the excitation equations of the flip-flops.
    (*d*) Draw the circuit in a manner which separates the logic from the memory.

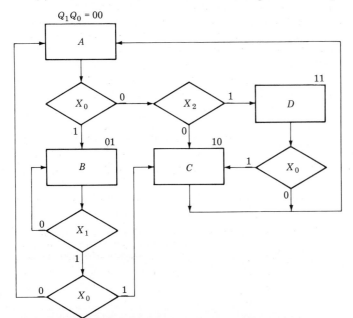

7.4-1 (*a*) At a traffic intersection of two streets, one running north and south (NS) and the other running east and west (EW) traffic lights are installed providing for red, yellow, and green indications. Make a flowchart showing the sequence of states through which the lights should go. Assume that the system is driven by a clock whose period is 5 s. Traffic in each direction is to be allowed for 20 s and the yellow light transition is to be allowed for 5 s.

(*b*) Assume that we want NS traffic to be uninterrupted except when there is a car at the intersection wanting to go EW. A sensor is installed to indicate waiting EW cars. Modify the flowchart.

(*c*) Assume that separate sensors are installed, one to indicate a westbound car and one to indicate an eastbound car. Modify the flowchart.

(*d*) Assume that at the intersection there is a button that can be operated by a pedestrian. Pressing the button makes all lights go red for 5 s at the end of the current time allocated for traffic so that pedestrians can cross in any direction. Modify the flowchart.

7.4-2 A machine is to be built which is to guide a novice player in the game of dice. The game is played with the following rules. Player wins if first throw is 7 or 11 and game is over. Otherwise player continues throwing until number of first throw recurs, giving a win, or until 7 or 11 appears, giving a loss. The machine operates as follows. The player starts by pressing button marked NEW GAME in response to which sign lights up saying FIRST THROW. Having thrown, the player sets switches to represent the number and then presses the button marked REGISTER, thereby transferring the number to a register for storage. If the number is 7 or 11, sign lights up reading YOU WIN and remains lit until NEW GAME is started. If not 7 or 11, sign lights up saying THROW AGAIN. The player again sets switches to indicate number and again presses a REGISTER to let the machine know that the input has been updated. Play continues until a win or lose outcome. On a loss, a sign lights up reading YOU LOSE. Draw a flow diagram for this dice machine.

7.4-3 Figure P7.4-3 shows an incomplete four-state flowchart in which the state assignments are as indicated. The input X is *asynchronous*; $X = 0$ except when a mechanical switch is closed by a human operator, making $X = 1$. Take account of the *setup* time of flip-flops and its variability from one flip-flop to another. Show that if the switch is closed at an unpropitious time, the system may go from A to either C or D rather than to B. Suggest a remedy.

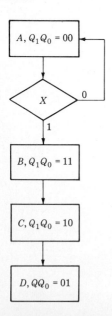

7.4-4 In a synchronous system it is assumed that the active edge of the clocking waveform arrives at each flip-flop at the same time. A time difference, if it should occur, is called a *clock skew*.

(a) Discuss qualitatively the difficulties clock skew can cause.

(b) Consider a mod-2 ring counter with two flip-flops FFA and FFB. Let there be a skew τ betwen the flip-flop clock waveforms. For each of the states of the counter describe the circuit behavior as τ increases from $\tau = 0$

7.5-1 A four-state synchronous system with states A, B, C, and D has four inputs X_0, X_1, X_2, and X_3 and one output Z. From A the system goes to B. From B it goes to C if $X_0 = 0$. While in B, if $X_0 = X_1 = 1$, the output is $Z = 1$, this being the only condition for which an output is specified. If $X_0 = 1$ and $X_1 = 0$, the circuit stays in state B. If $X_0 = X_1 = 1$ and also $X_2 = 0$, the state transition is from B to D, but if $X_0 = X_1 = 1$ and $X_2 = 1$, the circuit remains in B. From C we go to C if $X_0 X_3 = 11$, to A if $X_0 X_3 = 01$ or 10, and to D if $X_0 X_3 = 00$. A always follows D. Draw the flowchart.

7.5-2 Develop a state diagram for a Moore circuit that yields an output $Z = 1$ during one clock cycle provided there have been three 1s on the input X line during *exactly* the three preceding clock intervals. If there were 1s during four or more cycles, the output is $Z = 0$.

7.5-3 Repeat Prob. 7.5-2 except as a Mealy circuit, i.e., the determination whether there have been exactly three 1s is to be made during the time of occurrence of the third 1.

7.5-4 Develop a state table for a Mealy synchronous circuit with a single input X and a single output Z. The circuit makes $Z = 1$ whenever *exactly* one pair of identical bits has been input provided that the pair was preceded by exactly a pair and provided also that the bits in the successive pair are different. For example,

X	0	0	0	1	1	0	0	1	1	1	0	0	1	1
Z	?	?	0	0	0	0	1	0	1	0	0	0	0	1

7.5-5 (a) Develop a state table for a Mealy synchronous circuit with two inputs X_0 and X_1 and a single output Z. Z becomes $Z = 1$ in the interval when $X_0 = X_1$ provided the inputs have also been equal in the immediately preceding interval. Once $Z = 1$ it holds this value so long as X_0 and X_1 continue to be equal.

(b) Repeat part (a) for a Moore circuit.

7.7-1 Eliminate the redundant states, if any, from the following state tables. Make reduced state tables.

Present	Next state/Z	
state	$X = 0$	$X = 1$
A	$A/0$	$D/0$
B	$E/0$	$C/0$
C	$D/1$	$A/0$
D	$F/1$	$A/1$
E	$E/0$	$D/0$
F	$E/0$	$C/1$

(a)

Present	Next state/Z	
state	$X = 0$	$X = 1$
A	$B/0$	$C/1$
B	$A/1$	$E/0$
C	$F/1$	$C/0$
D	$D/0$	$C/1$
E	$A/1$	$B/0$
F	$B/0$	$D/1$

(b)

7.7-2 Eliminate the redundant states, if any, from the following state tables. Make reduced state tables.

Present state	Next state/Z		Present state	Next state/Z	
	$X = 0$	$X = 1$		$X = 0$	$X = 1$
A	E/0	D/0	A	A/0	B/0
B	A/1	F/0	B	H/1	C/0
C	C/0	A/1	C	E/0	B/0
D	B/0	A/0	D	C/1	D/0
E	D/1	C/0	E	C/1	E/0
F	C/0	D/1	F	F/1	G/1
G	H/1	G/1	G	B/0	F/0
H	C/1	B/1	H	H/1	C/0
	(a)			(b)	

7.7-3 Eliminate the redundant states, if any, from the following state table and make a reduced state table.

Present state	Next State/Z $X_1X_0 =$			
	00	01	10	11
A	D/0	D/0	F/0	A/0
B	C/1	D/0	E/1	F/0
C	C/1	D/0	E/1	A/0
D	D/0	B/0	A/0	F/0
E	C/1	F/0	E/1	A/0
F	D/0	D/0	A/0	F/0
G	G/0	G/0	A/0	A/0
H	B/1	D/0	E/1	A/0

7.7-4 Find a minimal state table equivalent to the state table given.

Present state	Next State/Z		Present state	Next state/Z	
	$X = 0$	$X = 1$		$X = 0$	$X = 1$
A	B/0	C/0	G	J/0	L/0
B	D/0	E/0	H	H/0	A/0
C	F/0	G/0	I	J/1	A/0
D	H/0	I/0	J	D/0	A/0
E	J/0	K/0	K	B/0	A/0
F	D/0	L/0	L	B/0	A/0

7.8-1 Referring to the state diagram of Fig. 7.8-2, propose alternative definitions which can be used for the initial state A.

7.8-2 Starting with the reduced state table of Fig. 7.8-4f, find the flip-flop excitation equations if JK flip-flops are to be used to implement the circuit. Draw the logic diagram of the sequence detector. Use the state assignments $Q_2Q_1Q_0 = 000, 001, 010, 011$, and 101 for the states A, B, C, D, and G respectively.

7.8-3 A four-state sequential circuit is characterized by the state table given. Using the state assignment given, find the excitation equations for the flip-flops and draw the logic diagram for (a) type D flip-flops, (b) JK flip-flops, and (c) toggle flip-flops.

Present state	Next state/Z		State	Q_1Q_0
	$X = 0$	$X = 1$	A	00
A	$D/1$	$C/0$	B	01
B	$A/0$	$C/0$	C	11
C	$B/0$	$C/0$	D	10
D	$D/0$	$C/0$		

7.8-4 For the state table and state assignment given find the flip-flop excitation equations and draw the logic circuit.

Present state	Next state/Z		State	Q_2	Q_1	Q_0
	$X = 0$	$X = 1$	A	0	0	0
A	$E/0$	$A/1$	B	0	0	1
B	$A/0$	$C/1$	C	1	1	1
C	$D/1$	$C/0$	D	1	0	0
D	$B/1$	$E/1$	E	1	0	1
E	$C/0$	$F/0$	F	0	1	1
F	$B/0$	$D/0$				

7.9-1 (a) Make an arbitrary state assignment for a four-state sequential circuit involving two flip-flops with outputs Q_1Q_0. Determine the number of ways in which the assignment can be changed by interchanging columns under Q_1 and Q_0 or by interchanging 0s and 1s in one or both columns or by making both types of interchanges. Show that there are eight such effectively equivalent assignments and that hence there are only three essentially different possible assignments. Find these three assignments.

(b) A sequential system has S states and uses F flip-flops with $2^{F-1} < S \leqslant 2^F$. Show that the number N of essentially different state assignments is

$$N = \frac{(2^F - 1)\,!}{(2^F - S)\,!\,F\,!}$$

7.9-2 The three essentially different state assignments for a four-state synchronous system are given. A four-state table is also given. For each one of the possible state assignments find the logic diagrams of the circuits which implement the state diagram. Use type D flip-flops. Does one state assignment yield a more economical circuit than the other two?

State	Q_1Q_0				Present state	Next State/Z	
	1	2	3			$X = 0$	$X = 1$
A	00	00	00		A	$D/0$	$B/0$
B	01	11	10		B	$C/1$	$D/1$
C	11	01	01		C	$A/0$	$B/0$
D	10	10	11		D	$A/0$	$C/0$

7.9-3 Entries are indicated in two rows of a state table in Table P7.9-3a. Since there are two inputs X_1 and X_0, there are four next-state columns. The rows are special in that, for each present state, the next-state entries are the same. The outputs (not indicated) are not the same, so that $A \neq B$. Assume that there are eight states in the table so that three flip-flops are required. Type D flip-flops with inputs D_2, D_1, and D_0 are to be used.

(a) Using the state assignment given in Table 7.9-3b for the four states A, B, C, and D, to the extent possible from the limited information given, fill in the K maps from which we can read the excitations required for D_2, D_1, and D_0.

(b) Repeat part (a) but use the state assignment given in Table P7.9-3c. In this second assignment we have arranged for the assignments given to the pair of states A and B and given to the pair of states C and D to be different in only a *single* bit. Such assignments are referred to as being *logically adjacent*. In part (a), the assignments are not logically adjacent.

(c) From the results of part (a) and (b) formulate a rule concerning state assignments to be made when two present states have the same next-state entries in every column. If some but not all of the next-state entries are the same, is the rule still useful?

Table P7.9-3

Present state	Next State $X_1X_0 =$			
	00	01	11	10
•	•	•	•	•
A	C	C	C	C
•	•	•	•	•
B	D	D	D	D
•	•	•	•	•

(a)

State	Q_2	Q_1	Q_0
A	0	0	0
B	1	0	1
C	0	1	1
D	1	0	0

(b)

State	Q_2	Q_1	Q_0
A	0	0	0
B	0	0	1
C	0	1	1
D	1	1	1

(c)

(d) In the state table of P7.9-3a assume that in column $X_1X_0 = 01$ and $X_1X_0 = 10$ the states C and D have been interchanged. Show that even in this case the assignment in P7.9-3c is better than the assignment of P7.9-3b.

7.9-4 Entries are indicated in two rows of an eight-state state table in Table P7.9-4a. There are two inputs X_1 and X_0, and so there are four next-state columns. Type D flip-flops are to be used. Two possible state assignments are given in Table P. 7.9-4b and c.

Table P7.9-4

Present state	Next state $X_1X_0 =$			
	00	01	11	10
•	•	•	•	•
A	C	D	E	F
•	•	•	•	•
B	C	D	E	F
•	•	•	•	•

(a)

State	Q_2	Q_1	Q_0
A	0	0	0
B	0	0	1
C	0	1	0
D	0	1	1
E	1	1	1
F	1	1	0

(b)

State	Q_2	Q_1	Q_0
A	0	0	0
B	1	0	1
C	1	0	0
D	1	1	1
E	0	0	1
F	0	1	0

(c)

(a) In Table P7.9-4b the assignments are *logically adjacent* (see Prob. 7.9-3) for the pairs A and B, C and D, D and E, E and F, and C and F. Using this assignment, to the extent possible from the limited information given, fill in the K maps from which we can read the excitations required for the flip-flop inputs D_2, D_1, and D_0.

(b) Repeat part (a) for the assignment of Table P7.9-4c. In this case the pairs referred to in part (a) do not have adjacent assignments.

(c) From the comparison of the results of parts (a) and (b) formulate a rule concerning assignments to be made to next states in a row of a state table.

7.12-1 Make a transition table for the fundamental-mode circuit of Fig. P7.12-1.

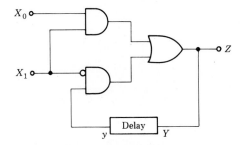

(a) Show that the circuit has two stable states for $X_1X_0 = 00$ and also for $X_1X_0 = 01$.

(b) If the circuit is in the stable state $Z = 0$ with $X_1X_0 = 00$, what must be done to put it in the state $Z = 1$ with $X_1X_0 = 00$?

7.12-2 Make a transition table for the fundamental-mode circuit of Fig. P7.12-2.

(a) Show that the circuit has one stable state for $X = 0$ and one stable state for $X = 1$.

(b) Assume, as indicated in the figure, that the delays are external to the gates and are located in the feedback connections. The delays are equal at a value Δ. The circuit is in the stable state with $X = 0$, and at time $t = 0$, X makes a transition to $X = 1$. Draw waveforms of y_1, y_0, Y_1, Y_0, and Z showing the sequence of changes which takes the circuit to the other stable state.

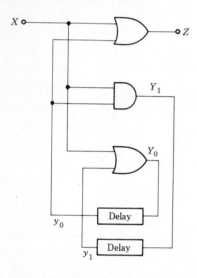

7.13-1 A fundamental-mode circuit has two inputs X_1 and X_0 and an output Z. When $X_1X_0 = 00$, the circuit has two stable states, one with $Z = 0$ and one with $Z = 1$. If the circuit is in the state with $Z = 0$, a change to $X_1X_0 = 01$ and a return to $X_1X_0 = 00$ will cause a state change. Similarly a change to $X_1X_0 = 10$ and a return to $X_1X_0 = 00$ will cause a reverse change in the state. On the basis of this word description of the required circuit performance, make a transition table. Make an arbitrary state assigment and draw the circuit. Verify that the circuit is a NOR-gate latch.

7.15-1 Find a state assignment free of critical races for the flow table of Fig. P7.15-1.

PS \ X_1X_0	00	01	11	10
a	d/0	b/0	d/1	$\textcircled{a}$/1
b	d/1	$\textcircled{b}$/1	$\textcircled{b}$/0	a/0
c	d/0	$\textcircled{c}$/0	b/0	$\textcircled{c}$/0
d	$\textcircled{d}$/0	c/0	$\textcircled{d}$/1	c/1

NS, Z

7.15-2 Refer to the stable table of Fig. P7.15-2. Show that if two state variables are used, there is no state assignment which completely avoids critical races.

PS \ X_1X_0	00	01	11	10
a	ⓐ	b	d	ⓐ
b	a	ⓑ	ⓑ	d
c	ⓒ	ⓒ	b	a
d	c	b	ⓓ	ⓓ

NS

7.15-3 Find a state assignment for the state table of Fig. P7.15-2 which is entirely free of critical races.

7.17-1 In the state table given it would seem eminently reasonable to assign values to the don't-cares to make $A = B$ and $E = F$.

Present state	Next state/Z $X = 0$	$X = 1$
A	$B/-$	$E/0$
B	$B/1$	$E/-$
C	$F/0$	$C/0$
D	$B/1$	$A/1$
E	$D/0$	$C/-$
F	$D/-$	$C/1$

(a) Show that such an assignment leads to a reduced state table with four states.

(b) Next make an assignment whose merit is not obvious; i.e., in states A and E replace the don't-cares by 0 and in B and F replace the don't-cares by 1. Show that now the reduced state table has only two states.

7.17-2 Eliminate redundant states if any and make reduced state tables for the following tables which have don't-care entries.

Present state	Next state/Z $X = 0$	$X = 1$
A	$-/0$	$B/0$
B	$A/1$	$D/-$
C	$D/-$	$E/1$
D	$-/0$	$B/-$
E	$C/0$	$E/1$

Present state	Next state/Z X_1X_0 00	01	11	10
A	$A/0$	$E/1$	$A/0$	$C/-$
B	$B/0$	$C/0$	$C/-$	$C/-$
C	$C/0$	$B/-$	$A/1$	$C/-$
D	$D/0$	$E/-$	$E/0$	$A/-$
E	$E/0$	$B/-$	$A/-$	$D/-$

7.18-1 (a) Find the maximal compatibles for the following state table.

Present state	Next state/Z	
	$X = 0$	$X = 1$
A	C/1	D/ –
B	C/ –	C/ –
C	B/0	D/ –
D	A/0	E/ –
E	B/ –	E/ –

(b) Show that if the maximal compatibles are used as states, the reduced state table has three states.

(c) Show that by using other than maximal compatibles in every case it is possible to reduce the state table to two states.

7.18-2 The reduced flow table in Fig. P7.18-2 describes an asynchronous system. Make a state assignment which avoids critical races and draw the logic circuit.

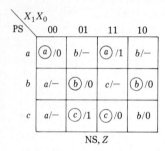

NS, Z

7.18-3 The primitive flow table in Fig. P.7.18-3 describes an asynchronous system. Make a reduced state table and draw the logic circuit.

X_1X_0 PS	00	01	11	10
a	d/–	–/–	e/–	(a)/1
b	d/–	(b)/1	e/–	–/–
c	d/–	–/–	e/–	(c)/0
d	(d)/0	b /1	e/–	a/–
e	–/–	b/–	(e)/0	c/0

NS, Z

7.18-4 A fundamental-mode circuit has inputs X_1 and X_0 and a single output Z. When $X_1X_0 = 00$, $Z = 0$. To make $Z = 1$ we must first have $X_0 = 1$ while $X_1 = 0$ and next change X_1 to 1. To return Z to $Z = 0$ we must return to $X_1X_0 = 00$, the order of return being of no consequence.

(*a*) Make a primitive flow table.
(*b*) Eliminate redundant states if any.
(*c*) Make a state assignment which avoids critical races.
(*d*) Draw the logic circuit.

Chapter 8

8.1-1 Suppose that we find it acceptable to accomplish a register-to-register transfer in two steps; i.e., first we clear B, and then we load B with the content of A. Show that in this case we can use less hardware than in Fig. 8.1-1. Draw the logic diagram and waveforms for such an asynchronous transfer.

8.2-1 (*a*) A register with individual stages A_i is to be coupled to a bus whose lines bear the bits B_i. The components of register A are SR static latches. Draw the logic diagram of a circuit associated with one stage of the register which will allow us to command the transfer into the register stage of the bit which results when A_i is ANDed with B_i; that is, $A_i B_i \rightarrow A_i$. Repeat for (*b*) $A_i + B_i \rightarrow A_i$, (*c*) $A_i \oplus B_i \rightarrow A_i$, and (*d*) $A_i \oplus \bar{B}_i \rightarrow A_i$.

8.2-2 Repeat Prob. 8.2-1 for JK flip-flops and synchronous operation.

8.2-3 A register A consists of type D flip-flops. For each of the following cases individually draw the logic structure associated with one stage A_i of the register which will allow us to command the modification of the register content in the manner indicated: (*a*) $0 \rightarrow A_i$, (*b*) $1 \rightarrow A_i$, (*c*) $\bar{A}_i \rightarrow A_i$.

8.3-1 Draw the logic diagram of a 3-bit register using JK flip-flops which has associated logic providing two control terminals called ADD and INCREMENT. When activated, INCREMENT causes the registration to be augmented by 1, and ADD adds the register content to the number on a bus and leaves the sum in the register.

8.3-2 Draw the logic diagram of a 3-bit register using type D flip-flops with three control terminals called ROTATE LEFT, ROTATE RIGHT, and COMPLEMENT. ROTATE RIGHT moves each bit one position to the right, the rightmost bit transferring to the leftmost flip-flop. ROTATE LEFT causes the reverse shifting. COMPLEMENT replaces each bit by its complement.

8.3-3 Draw the logic diagram of a 3-bit register using JK flip-flops which has associated logic providing control terminals DECREMENT, COMPLEMENT, SET, and RESET. DECREMENT reduces the registration by 1, COMPLEMENT replaces each bit by its complement, and SET and RESET respectively set and reset each bit.

8.3-4 Draw the logic diagram of a 3-bit register using JK flip-flops which has associated logic providing control terminals ADD and SUBTRACT. When activated, ADD adds the number on a bus to the number in the register. SUBTRACT subtracts the number on the bus from the number in the register. In both cases the result is left in the register.

8.4-1 Construct a flow diagram for a controller to direct the operation of the system of Fig. 8.4-1. The controller is to have a starting switch represented by the variable X and is to have a second conditional input Y. When $Y = 1$, the operation to be performed is the calculation of $\alpha - \beta$, and when $Y = 0$, it is $\beta - \alpha$. The result is to be stored in register β.

8.4-2 We require a circuit which in response to the closing of a mechanical switch generates a positive pulse. The pulse is synchronous with a clock and lasts for a single clock cycle. The switch must be opened and closed again to generate a second pulse.

(*a*) Construct a flowchart for a Moore machine which will generate the pulse. Keep in mind that the switch may close at an arbitrary time in the clock cycle.

(*b*) Complete the design and draw the logic circuit using type D flip-flops. Try all possible state assignments to see whether there is a best one.

(c) If the switch signal is applied to a type D flip-flop, the flip-flop output will provide a synchronous, albeit delayed, transition in response to the switch operation. Assuming that such a synchronous transition is available, construct a flowchart for a Mealy machine which will accomplish the same function as the Moore circuit. Design and draw the logic circuit.

8.4-3 An adding-subtracting machine is to be constructed according to the following specifications. Numbers, in binary representation, are to be entered by setting an array of two-position switches. The number entered is to be added or subtracted from the contents of an accumulator register according to whether an ADD button or a SUBTRACT button is depressed. Twos-complement representation is to be used in the accumulator register.

(a) Establish an architecture for the system.

(b) Construct a flow diagram.

(c) Design the controller for the system using a minimum number of states and draw the logic circuit.

8.4-4 A two-digit decimal number is stored in two 4-bit registers in BCD form. Register M holds the more significant digit, register L the less significant digit. The numbers are to be transferred so that they appear side by side in an 8-bit register R. Available for effecting the transfer is a 4-bit bus accessible to M and L but only to the four rightmost positions of register R. The transfer operation is to occur in response to the operation of a switch.

(a) Establish an architecture for the system specifying the control terminals on each register.

(b) Construct a flow diagram.

(c) Design the controller for the system using a minimum of states and draw the logic circuit.

8.4-5 An electronic combination lock has a reset push button X_0 and three operate buttons, X_1, X_2, and X_3. The lock will open only if the operate buttons are pushed in the right order. If the order is wrong, the reset button must be pushed to allow a new attempt. Construct a flow diagram, design the circuit, and draw its logic diagram.

8.5-1 Design a ROM code converter to replace the three logic boxes in Fig. 8.5-1 that generate the excitations for the flip-flops.

8.5-2 Verify that the decoder of Fig. 8.5-2 generates control output signals at the times when they are needed.

8.5-3 Deduce the excitation equations required in the design of Fig. 8.5-1 if JK flip-flops are substituted for the type D.

8.6-1 Make a flowchart and a state table for the controller whose logic diagram is given in Fig. P8.6-1.

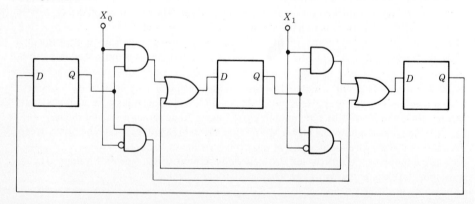

8.6-2 Suppose that a flow diagram calls for a "wait" state; i.e., the controller is to stop and implement no further microoperation until it receives a READY signal from some source. Show how such a wait state can be incorporated into a shift-register controller. Show the logic for both type D and JK flip-flops.

8.7-1 A flow diagram of a sequential system is shown in Fig. P8.7-1. There are four states A, B, C, and D and five conditional variables X_0 to X_4, which determine the order of sequencing. Design a shift-register controller for the system.

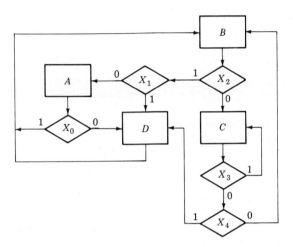

8.7-2 Design a shift-register controller which implements the state table given

PS	NS/Z	
	$X = 0$	$X = 1$
A	D/1	B/0
B	D/0	B/0
C	E/0	A/0
D	C/0	B/0
E	E/0	B/0

8.8-1 (*a*) Design a shift-register controller to be used with the architecture of Fig. 8.4-1 which forms the quantity $R_\alpha - 2R_\beta$ and leaves the result in the accumulator.

(*b*) Repeat for the result $2(R_\alpha - R_\beta)$.

8.8-2 Design a shift-register controller to be used with the architecture of Fig. 8.4-1. The system is to form the sum of the absolute values of the contents of R_α and R_β and is to leave the result in the accumulator. (Note that the controller will have to have the sign bits of the numbers in the registers as controlling inputs.)

8.8-3 Design a shift-register controller to be used with the architecture of Fig. 8.4-1. If the content of either (or both) R_α and R_β is negative, the controller clears the accumulator but does nothing else. If both are positive, the system determines which of the contents is larger and leaves that larger number in the accumulator. (See the note in Prob. 8.8-2.)

8.9-1 (*a*) In the architecture of Fig. 8.9-1 we have not provided a control terminal to clear the accumulator. Show that this clearing operation can be performed using only the instructions listed in Fig. 8.9-2*b*.

(*b*) There is normally no need to clear the CI register. Show, however, that if we please, we can clear it using again only the instructions listed.

8.9-2 The numbers $N_1 = 106$, $N_2 = 16$, $N_3 = -85$, $N_4 = 45$, and $N_5 = 36$ are stored in memory locations 50 to 54 of the memory of Fig. 8.9-1. Write a program in the manner of Fig. 8.9-2*c* which forms $3(N_1 - 2N_2 + N_3 + N_4 - N_5)$ and stores the result in memory location 49.

8.11-1 Suppose we modify the structure of Fig. 8.9-1 as follows: (1) we reserve 3 bits for instructions so that we can have more than four instructions, and (2) we equip the accumulator with an output terminal X_0, which indicates when the accumulator registration is zero. This accumulator output is one of the input variables to the controller.

(*a*) Modify the controller so that it will respond to the instruction "stop if the accumulator is clear."

(*b*) Modify the controller so that it will respond to the instruction "fetch the next instruction not from the memory location in the program counter but from a memory location whose address is specified in this instruction."

8.13-1 (*a*) Make state tables for the controllers whose flowcharts are given in Fig. 8.13-3.

(*b*) Using *JK* flip-flops, redesign the handshake controllers so that they use a minimum number of flip-flops.

Chapter 9

9.1-1 A RAM has control terminals *enable* (E) and $\overline{read\text{-}write}$ (R/$\overline{\text{W}}$). We prefer to operate the memory by activating either a *read* (R) terminal or a *write* (W) terminal. Design the logic required to be interposed between the R and W terminals and the terminals of the memory.

9.1-2 Design a typical stage of the accumulator register of Fig. 9.1-1.

9.1-3 Design typical stages of the GPR register and of the PC register. Remember that these registers must be able to interchange contents during one clock cycle.

9.1-4 Suppose, in the architecture of Fig. 9.1-1, we use a memory that has a capacity of 65,536 words, each 22 bits long.

(*a*) What is the number of instructions that can be incorporated into the computer?

(*b*) How many bits in the registers PC, MAR, OPR, and GPR?

9.2-1 In memory location 17 there is the instruction "add to the accumulator the operand whose address is to be found in location 31." This operand has the value −27, and the number already in the accumulator is +42. Assume that the code for the instruction is 10. (All preceding numbers are decimal.) Beginning at the time of the completion of the previous instruction, specify, to the extent possible, the content, in binary notation, of each register in Fig. 9.1-1 after each clock cycle until the execution of the instruction is complete.

9.2-2 Using the architecture and microoperations of Fig. 9.1-1, write the sequence of microoperations which would execute the instruction:

(*a*) that called for replacing the positive number *N* in some location by the number 4*N*.

(b) that called for replacing the number N by $-N$.

9.2-3 An *arithmetic* shift of a register content is a shift left to multiply by 2 or a shift right to divide by 2. When the content is a positive number, the digit 0 must be shifted into the vacated leftmost or rightmost end position.

(a) Assume that a register holds a negative number in ones-complement representation. Show that in this case, in an arithmetic shift, 1s must be shifted into the vacated end positions for shifts in either direction.

(b) Assume that a register holds a negative number in twos-complement representation. Show that in this case 0s must be shifted into the rightmost vacated end position for a left shift and 1s must be shifted into the leftmost vacated end position for a right shift.

(c) Using the architecture and microinstructions of Fig. 9.1-1, write the sequence of microoperations that will execute the instruction calling for replacing the content N of the accumulator by the number $4N$. Assume that N is known to be negative and is given in twos-complement representation.

(d) Repeat part (c) if the content N is to be replaced by $N/4$.

9.5-1 Write an assembly-language program that will replace a number N stored in memory by the number $4N$. It is not known whether the number is positive or negative. If negative, it is given in twos-complement representation. (Refer to Prob. 9.2-3.)

9.5-2 Write an assembly-language program that will complement each bit of the content of memory location 30 (hex) and place the result in location 31.

9.5-3 Write an assembly-language program that will shift the content of memory location 30 (hex) one position to the left. A 1 is to be moved into the vacated rightmost position and the result is to be placed in location 31.

9.5-4 Write an assembly-language program that will set to 0 the four most significant bits of the content of memory location 30 (hex) and move the result to location 31.

9.5-5 Write an assembly-language program which divides the content of memory location 30 (hex) into two 6-bit sections and stores them in memory locations 31 and 32. The six most significant bits of location 30 are to go to the least significant bit positions of location 31 while the six least significant bits of location 30 go to the least significant bit positions of location 32. The most significant bit positions of locations 31 and 32 are to be cleared.

9.5-6 Memory locations 30 and 31 (hex) hold two positive numbers. Write an assembly-language program that will write the larger of the two numbers in memory location 32.

9.5-7 Memory locations 50 through 70 (hex) hold entries some of which are positive numbers and some negative. Write an assembly-language program that will write into memory location 71 the number expressing how many of these entries are negative.

9.7-1 Memory locations 50 through 53 (hex) hold the positive numbers N_1, N_2, N_3, and N_4. Write an assembly-language program that forms the product $N_1 N_2 N_3 N_4$ and leaves the result in location 54.

9.7-2 Memory locations 50 through 70 (hex) hold positive numbers. Using the program of Prob. 9.5-6, write a program employing a subroutine that will write the largest of these numbers in memory location 71.

9.8-1 Assign to the outputs of the CROM of Fig. 9.8-1 the operations specified by the correspondingly numbered microoperations in Table 9.1-1. With this assignment write out the content of the CROM (as in Fig. 9.8-2) which will execute the instructions(a) JMPI, (b) CSR, (c) ISZ.

9.8-2 The machine of Fig. 9.1-1 does not have a *subtract* instruction. Write out the content of the CROM of Fig. 9.8-2 which will provide an instruction that subtracts from the accumulator the content of a memory location and leaves the result in the accumulator. Use the assignment indicated in Prob. 9.8-1.

9.8-3 The CROM of Fig. 9.8-1 has 18 outputs corresponding to the 18 microoperations listed in Table 9.1-1. Recommend an alternative arrangement that would allow the use of a CROM with fewer bits per word (albeit at the expense of additional logic). What is the minimum acceptable numbers of bits per word?

9.9-1 Design the control memory address register of Fig. 9.9-1 which can be incremented or loaded. Assume that $M = 4$.

9.10-1 Draw the gate structure of the logic box of Fig. 9.10-1.

9.12-1 Draw the gate structure of the logic box of Fig. 9.12-1.

9.15-1 A section of a RAM is to be used as a stack. Design the hardware to be associated with the RAM so that when one command terminal is made active, a stack-pointer register will be incremented and then a word on a bus will be written into the memory. There is also to be a second command terminal, which, when activated, will read the word back onto the bus and then decrement the stack pointer.

Chapter 10

10.12-1 (*a*) From among the 8080 instructions find two 1-byte instructions either of which can be used individually to clear the accumulator.

(*b*) Find a 2-byte instruction which will clear the accumulator.

10.12-2 Write a program that complements each bit of the word in memory location 0040 and places the result in location 0041.

10.12-3 Write a program to add the contents of memory locations 0040 and 0041 and place the sum in location 0042.

10.12-4 Write a program to shift the content of memory location 0040 1 bit to the left, the result being returned to location 0041. The rightmost bit position is to be left cleared.

10.12-5 Write a program that places the least significant 4 bits of the contents of memory location 0040 in memory location 0041. The four most significant bit positions are to be left cleared.

10.12-6 Write a program to clear memory locations 0040 and 0041.

10.12-7 Write a program that divides the content of memory locations 0040 into two 4-bit portions and stores them in memory locations 0041 and 0042. The four most significant bits of location 0040 are to go to the four least significant bit positions of location 0041. The four least significant bits of location 0040 are to go to the four least significant bit positions of location 0042. The four most significant bit positions of locations 0041 and 0042 are to be cleared.

10.12-8 Write a program which loads the same number N into registers B, C, D, and E. Write it in a manner which requires the fewest number of bytes.

10.12-9 Write a program which subtracts the content of register E from the content of register B and saves the result in the D register.

10.12-10 Write a program which subtracts the content of register *pair* B from the content of register *pair* D and saves the result in register *pair* D

10.12-11 Write a program that transfers the contents of memory locations 0041, 0042,

0043, and 0044 to memory locations 0051, 0052, 0053, and 0054, respectively, and leaves the original locations cleared.

10.12-12 Memory location 0040 holds number N_0, and location 0041 holds number N_1. Write a program that will transfer to location 0042 (*a*) the larger of the two numbers and (*b*) the smaller of the two numbers.

10.12-13 Memory locations 0060 through 0067 contain a table of squares of the numbers 0 through 7, respectively, i.e., location 006x holds the number x^2 for x from 0 to 7. Memory location 0040 holds a number x between 0 and 7. Write a program which uses the table of squares to place x^2 in memory location 0041.

10.12-14 Write a program which replaces the number in memory location 0040 by its negative. Negative numbers are expressed in twos-complement representation.

10.12-15 Memory locations 0040 and 0041 hold a 16-bit number, the most significant bits being in location 0041. Write a program that will place the twos complement of the number in locations 0042 and 0043, the most significant bits to be placed in location 0043.

10.14-1 There is a series of numbers stored in successive memory locations beginning in location 0042. The length of the series is given by the number registered in memory location 0041. Write a program that will add the series of numbers and store the sum in location 0040. Assume that as the sum is formed no carries are generated and that the sum can be contained in 8 bits.

10.14-2 Repeat Prob. 10.14-1 assuming instead that a 16-bit number is required to hold the sum.

10.14-3 There is a series of numbers stored in successive memory locations beginning in location 0042. The length of the series is given by the number registered in memory location 0041. Write a program that will determine how many of the numbers in the series are negative and will store this number in memory location 0040.

10.14-4 There is a series of numbers stored in successive memory locations beginning in memory location 0042. The length of the series is given by the number in location 0041. Write a program that will determine which of the series is the largest and will store that number in location 0040. Assume that the numbers are all unsigned 8-bit numbers.

10.14-5 Write a program which shifts to the left the number in memory location 0040 as many times as is necessary to move the most significant 1 of the number into the most significant bit position. Store the result in memory location 0041, and store in location 0042 the number of shifts required. If the number in location 0040 is zero, locations 0041 and 0042 are to be cleared. (If we agree that the binary point of the number is to be located after the leftmost bit, the process here changes the number to scientific notation, that is 0.0010110 becomes 1.0110000×2^{-3}.)

10.14-6 A series of ASCII characters (Appendix A) is stored in successive memory locations starting in location 0041. The end of the series is marked by the carriage return character CR (hex 00). Write a program which determines the number of characters in the series (excluding the CR character) and writes the number in location 0040.

10.14-7 A series of ASCII characters (Appendix A) is stored in successive memory locations starting in location 0041. The length of the series is given by the number stored in location 0040. The ASCII characters have seven significant bits, the leftmost bit in every case being 0. Write a program in which the leftmost bit is changed to 1 as required in each case to give the characters *even parity*. The modified characters are to remain in their original locations.

10.14-8 A series of ASCII characters (Appendix A) is stored in successive memory locations starting in location 0042. The length of the series is given in location 0041. A second series of identical length starts in location 0062. Write a program that clears location 0040 if the two series are the same and sets all the bit positions if the series do not match.

10.14-9 Write a program to add two multiple-byte numbers. The number of bytes involved is in memory location 0030. The numbers themselves begin in memory locations 0041 and 0061, respectively. Least significant bytes are given first. The sum is to replace the number starting in location 0041.

10.14-10 There is a list of entries in successive memory locations beginning in location 0041 and extending to location $0041 + K$. The number K is stored in location 0040. There is also an entry in location 0030. Write a program which checks to determine whether the entry in location 0030 is one of the entries in the list. If this entry is present, the program does nothing. If the entry is not present, the program adds it to the list in location $0040 + K + 1$ and changes the number in location 0040 to $K + 1$.

10.15-1 An 8-bit register has its four most significant bits all 0s and the remaining bits are used to represent the hexadecimal digits 0 to F. Verify, from Appendix A, that to convert the registration to an ASCII character we add 30 (hex) if the digit is 9 or less and add 37 (hex) if the digit is greater than 10.

10.20-1 Verify that an overflow error has occurred if and only if V given by Eq. (10.20-1) is $V = 1$.

Chapter 11

11.1-1 Refer to Figs. 10.2-1 and 11.1-2. Show that the signal $\overline{\text{DBIN}}$ can serve as the signal $\overline{\text{MEMR}}$ and that $\overline{\text{WR}}$ can serve as $\overline{\text{MEMW}}$.

11.3-1 (*a*) There is available externally to the microprocessor a switch and buffer arrangement as in Fig. 11.3-2. All switches are permanently open except possibly one, say D_3. We wish to clear memory location 0040 (hex) if that switch is closed. If the switch is open, the memory location is to set to 0001 (hex). Write an appropriate program.

(*b*) Consider the special cases where the switch is in lines D_0, D_6, or D_7. Show how the instructions RAL, RAR, ORA A or ADD A can be used to make one or another flag provide the required information about whether the switch is open or closed.

11.3-2 There is available externally to the microprocessor a switch and buffer arrangement as in Fig. 11.3-2. All the switches are permanently open except possibly one. Write a program that will clear memory location 0040 (hex) and then register in that location the number of times that the one switch has closed. When the switch is examined and found closed, the closed condition is not to add to the count unless there has been an open interval between closures. Assume that the switch has been debounced.

11.3-3 At one point in the execution of a program, the microcomputer is to be instructed to examine the situation of one of the switches in Fig. 11.3-2 and to stop executing further instructions unless it finds the switch closed. Write the program steps required to effect such a wait.

11.3-4 At one point in the execution of a program, the microcomputer is to be instructed to examine one of the switches in Fig. 11.3-2 and not to proceed with further instruction execution until it sees the switch *change* from open to closed or vice versa. Write the program steps required to effect such a wait.

11.3-5 In the arrangement of Fig. 11.3-2, assume that only one switch is closed at any particular time. In changing switches we open the initially closed switch before closing a new switch so that there are intervals when no switch is closed. Write a program which will determine whether a switch is closed and store the number of that switch (0 through 7) in the B register of the microprocessor.

11.3-6 The switches of Fig. 11.3-2 are operated as described in Prob. 11.3-5. Write a program which takes note of which switch is closed, waits until a new switch is closed, and records the number of the new switch in memory location 0040 (hex).

11.3-7 Memory location 0040 (hex) holds a two-decimal-digit number in BCD code. Write a program that will present the number on the display of Fig. 11.3-1 provided the two digits are not equal. If the digits are equal, the display is to read 00.

11.3-8 Write a program that will determine which one switch is closed in Fig. 11.3-2 and will present the switch number (0 to 7) on one of the seven-segment displays of Fig. 11.3-1.

11.3-9 Write a program which continuously monitors one of the switches in Fig. 11.3-2 and complements each bit position in memory location 0040 (hex) at each new closing.

11.3-10 In addition to the switch in Fig. 11.3-2 there is available another switch labeled LOAD. Show the hardware and write a program which continuously monitors the LOAD switch. When the LOAD switch is found closed, the input data in Fig. 11.3-2 are transferred to memory location 0040 (hex).

11.6-1 Write a subroutine which generates a delay equal to 1 ms times the number registered in the accumulator. Assume that the 8080 is operating with a 2-MHz clock. Use the timing information given in App. C. Ignore the time used by the CALL and RETURN instructions.

11.6-2 Using the hardware of Fig. 11.5-1, write a program that will generate at the Q output of the latch a positive pulse whose duration is 10^3 clock cycles.

11.6-3 Use the hardware of Fig. 11.3-1. Write a program that will present sequentially on one of the seven-segment displays the numbers 0 through 9. Assume that the CPU operates on a 2-MHz clock. Provide timing displays so that the displayed number changes every second.

11.6-4 Write a program that will debounce a mechanical switch. When there is a change in switch position, the CPU waits a reasonable time and examines the switch position again to see whether it is in the same new position.

11.6-5 Using appropriate hardware auxiliary to the CPU, write a program that will generate a square-wave waveform. Consider both a symmetrical and an unsymmetrical waveform.

11.7-1 Refer to Fig. 11.7-1. Write a program which will cause the CPU to wait for an interrupt signal from the keyboard and will then place the data from the keyboard in a memory location.

11.9-1 Refer to Fig. 11.9-1. Write a program which, in response to an INT input, polls the peripherals and services them in order. Locate the service subroutines at arbitrary locations labelled INT 1, INT 2, and INT 3. Before responding to the interrupt request, the register pairs B, D, and H and the PSW register are to be saved.

11.9-2 Figure P11.9-2 shows a "daisy chain" scheme for assigning priority to interrupt requests from peripherals. Explain the operation. Which peripheral has the highest priority?

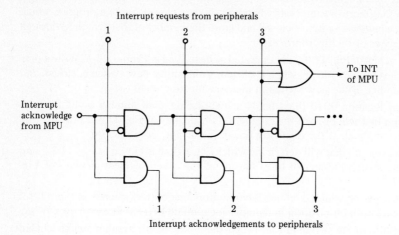

Interrupt requests from peripherals

To INT of MPU

Interrupt acknowledge from MPU

Interrupt acknowledgements to peripherals

INDEX

INDEX